HOMELESSNESS

HOMELESSNESS: A SOURCEBOOK

Rick Fantasia
and
Maurice Isserman

Facts On File®

AN INFOBASE HOLDINGS COMPANY

Homelessness: A Sourcebook

Copyright © 1994 by Rick Fantasia and Maurice Isserman

Facts On File, Inc.
460 Park Avenue South
New York NY 10016

Library of Congress Cataloging-in-Publication Data
Fantasia, Rick.
    Homelessness: a Sourcebook / Rick Fantasia and Maurice Isserman.
      p. cm.
      ISBN 0-8160-2571-1
      1. Homelessness—United States—Encyclopedias. 2. Homeless persons—
United States—Encyclopedias. I. Isserman, Maurice. II. Title. III. Series.
HV4505.F36   1993
362.5′0973—dc20   92-37762

Printed in the United States of America

Text Graphics by Marc Greene

BP VC 10 9 8 7 6 5 4 3 2 1

This book is printed on acid-free paper.

"I am aware that many object to the severity of my language; but is there no cause for severity? I will be harsh as truth, and as uncompromising as justice."
—*William Lloyd Garrison*
The Liberator, January 1, 1831 (first issue)

This book is dedicated to the memory of two gentle men, who could also be as harsh as truth, and as uncompromising as justice: Michael Harrington and Mitch Snyder.

CONTENTS

ACKNOWLEDGMENTS

The authors gratefully acknowledge the assistance of Shelley Abend, Elaine Bernard, Joel Blau, Peter Dreier, Eric Hirsch, Phil Kasinitz, James Wright, the National Coalition for the Homeless, and the reference librarians at Smith College and Hamilton College.

AUTHORS' NOTE

Statistics regarding the problem of homelessness are notoriously vague, fragmentary, and disputed. Throughout this book, we have attempted to make use of the most reliable and recent statistics available. Where significantly different estimates exist, we have tried to indicate the range of opinion. Sources on which we have relied heavily, such as the U.S. Conference of Mayors annual report on hunger and homelessness, vary from year to year in the kinds of data offered, and the locales covered. Readers should thus bear in mind that the apparent scientific precision of statistical analysis is often misleading; the statistics on homelessness that follow can best be understood as indications of the general dimensions of the problem.

HOMELESSNESS AND
AMERICAN SOCIETY

In June 1990 the *New York Times* ran an article by reporter John Tierney on the troubled life and death of a homeless man named Brian Lockhart. Lockhart, a 42-year-old Vietnam veteran and an African American, was a familiar and well-liked figure in Greenwich Village, where he could usually be found sitting on a milk crate by a subway stop at the corner of 12th Street and Seventh Avenue. Although Lockhart was a panhandler, those who regularly passed by him on his milk crate did not seem to mind it when he asked for their help. Whenever he could, he liked to do them small favors as well. After nagging one man for several weeks the previous winter for going outside without a warm hat, Lockhart bought and presented him with a woolen cap. He often had a small notebook open on his lap, where he wrote poems with such titles as "Walking Alone," "Winter Chill" and "Lonely Man." At night he slept in the subways. He joked that he had New York City's most expensive alarm clock: "It takes six transit cops to wake me up."

The day Lockhart died of cardiac arrest, the news spread quickly through the neighborhood. Someone made a sign and put it on the corner where he liked to sit. Others left bouquets of flowers. As Tierney reported, "Neighbors, merchants and commuters stopped throughout the day to reminisce about his smile, his easy wit, his kindness to all, his small gifts to some of his countless friends."

But there was a darker side to the life of this friendly streetcorner poet. Uptown in Harlem, where a more formal memorial service was held, family members and acquaintances spoke of a man who had been a drug dealer and petty thief. Lockhart had even stolen the rent money from his pregnant wife, and then abandoned her and their newborn child. Lockhart's son, who was 19 when his father died, told the reporter from the *New York Times:* "I appreciate the people from downtown being so nice to him, and coming up to the service. But don't romanticize him."

Lockhart's life suggests some of the complexities of that much-used and often poorly understood abstraction "homelessness." Viewed through one prism, Lockhart elicits our sympathies, even our admiration. "He was an easy guy to respect," recalled one of his Greenwich Village neighbors. "Despite the fact that he was homeless, he was able to make the people he spoke to feel like he cared about them." This vision of Lockhart harkens back to a traditional view of "the hobo" in American life, the plucky wanderer celebrated in fiction and folk song, living at the margins of society and suffering hardships as a result, but still good-spirited, resourceful and decent. Viewed through another prism, Lockhart's life merges into the more contemporary and threatening image of the "underclass," that predatory world of street criminals, addiction and violence that has engulfed the inner cities of the United States in recent decades. "He always had his little tramps and his drugs," a Harlem acquaintance recalled of Brian Lockhart. "He would go clean every now and then

1

. . . but it never lasted." This grimmer, competing vision of the homeless elicits contempt rather than sympathy and fear rather than admiration.

Lockhart himself, in an essay he was asked to write for a college newspaper about homelessness, drew on both the image of the homeless as victims of society and that of the homeless as parasites on society. Imagine, he asked the students, that "your family and friends have all turned their back on you and it is the middle of November." Yet he also wrote of the homeless as people whose condition was, in the final analysis, their own fault: "Somewhere something in their life snapped and went to hopelessness, failure, and self-destruction."

The story of Brian Lockhart raises a range of troubling questions: about his own life and about our society. We might ask how it could happen that a person apparently as generous, talented and intelligent as Brian Lockhart could ever be reduced to begging on the street and sleeping in the subway? Was Lockhart's life confirmation of President Ronald Reagan's view, expressed in 1986, that: "What we have found in this country, and we're more aware of it now, is one problem that we've had, even in the best of times, and this is the people who are sleeping on the grates, the homeless who are homeless, you might say, by choice." Or were other forces at work that drove Lockhart to the desperate life he "chose" to live? In his particular case, for example, we might want to ask what effect fighting in a distant, unpopular and brutal war had on his ability to steer a more conventional and responsible course through life. In high school Lockhart had been a model student. He returned from Vietnam with a drug addiction and persistent mental disorders.

Lockhart's story also raises some difficult questions to consider about those of us who *read* his story, those of us, that is, who are fortunate enough not to be homeless ourselves. Did our sympathies for Lockhart change as we learned more about his life? Would our empathy and concern have been less pronounced if he had *not* been a Vietnam veteran? Or *not* been portrayed as a very warm, nonthreatening character? Or would we have retained more sympathy if he had *not* abandoned a wife and a child? And who, ultimately, was to "blame" for his situation? Was it his own fault for being a drug addict? Or was it the experience of the Vietnam war that caused a model student to become mentally shaken and physically addicted? Or is the question of "blame" even relevant? Should anyone have to sleep in the street, regardless of his personal character and life decisions?

There are hundreds of thousands, perhaps millions of "Brian Lockharts" all over America these days. One of the extraordinary aspects of the homeless problem is how rapidly it has spread across the country into many different kinds of communities. A *New York Times* poll taken in 1990 revealed that 54 percent of Americans report that they see homeless people in their neighborhoods or on their way to work; in New York City that percentage jumped to 82 percent. We seem to have grown, if not accepting, at least accustomed to the presence of what sociologist Joel Blau, in a recent insightful book on homelessness, has aptly called the "visible poor." In 1962 the social critic Michael Harrington wrote a book called *The Other America* in which he argued that Americans were deceiving themselves if they believed they lived in an affluent society, because a large proportion of Americans were living in poverty. The poor were the "other" Americans, because they lived in communities that were separate from and thus "invisible" to their better-off fellow citizens. By the 1980s the poor were no longer invisible. By then the homeless had become—and remain—an inescapable presence in contemporary America because they share our public space, on streetcorners, in parks, subways and train stations, and libraries. We see these people every day, and inevitably we make assumptions about their lives. These assumptions harden into stereotypes, and these stereotypes may prevent us from understanding the true causes and possible solutions to the problem of homelessness.

Brian Lockhart lived in a city, and we tend to think of homelessness as an urban problem, but there are also many homeless people living in small towns and rural communities in the United States today. He was black, and many of the homeless are drawn from the nation's minorities, but there are also many white homeless people in the United States today. He was a drug addict, and many of the homeless are substance abusers, but many are not. (And some acquired their addictions to drugs or alcohol only *after* they were reduced to life on the streets.) He was an adult male, and men are the most visible portion of the homeless population, but there are also many women and children homeless in the United States today.

No single homeless individual is representative of the entire homeless population. But by talking about an individual, we hope to suggest that all homeless people, whatever their personal characteristics and shortcomings, do share a common humanity with their more fortunate fellow citizens. In a mass society, where face-to-face interactions have been supplanted by the powerful images offered up by the media, it has become all too easy to place labels on individuals and think that, as a result, we understand all that we need to know about them. Suffering in the mass becomes abstract and difficult to empathize with. Individual suffering is somehow more readily comprehensible, and suggests at least the possibility of common bonds. Homeless people are not a separate order or breed, distinct from ordinary people. In the pages that follow, we will have much to say that can be expressed only by the use of statistics, and we will employ (as sparingly as possible) the language of social policy analysis. But numbers and jargon should not obscure human realities. "Homelessness" is an abstract category that we impose on the lives of millions of disparate individuals, people with their own dreams as well as their own shortcomings. As an analytic tool, the category of "homelessness" is useful only to the extent that it helps to illustrate some of the common problems (and the sources of those problems) that afflict those people we choose to label "the homeless."

POVERTY AND HOMELESSNESS IN THE AMERICAN IMAGINATION: THE HISTORICAL DIMENSIONS

Let us begin by considering other historical periods in which some Americans found themselves living without shelter. From the earliest settlements of the American colonies, treatment of the poor tended to mirror the Elizabethan poor laws in England, which categorized and divided the poor into "neighbors" or "strangers." Communities were obligated to assist those who were permanent residents and deport impoverished "strangers" to their place of origin. Thus "outdoor relief," as it was called, consisted of the provision of money, firewood, food and provisions to longtime village residents in need, while a needy newcomer or stranger passing through town could expect little more than rough escort to the village limits and expulsion. As historian Michael Katz argued in his book *In the Shadow of the Poorhouse* (1986), the strict value distinctions drawn between "neighbors" and "strangers" in the provision of charity reflected the stability of early preindustrial communities. As agriculture gave way to industry in the early 19th century, migration in search of employment became more common. In an increasingly mobile society, just who was and who was not a member of a particular community became more difficult for the authorities to determine.

Industrial workers in the 19th century were subjected to the insecurity of a factory system whose periodic contractions produced frightening bouts of unemployment as well as rising costs for poor relief. Critics of poor relief charged that the able-bodied poor were receiving aid along with those who were incapable of work. The old distinction drawn between "neighbors" and "strangers" gave way to new categories. A main object of poor law reform was an attempt to distinguish the "undeserving" able-bodied poor from the "deserving" disabled poor in an effort to remove the former from the public relief rolls. Partly this was accomplished by the transformation of descriptive or administrative distinctions (such as "the poor" and "paupers") into moral categories, categories into which all of the poor were placed in the public mind. Thus, poverty was viewed not as a result of social or economic misfortune, but as the willful product of sinfulness, laziness and immorality, a characterization that might stigmatize and discourage those who would seek relief. The distinctions drawn between the deserving and the undeserving poor served the dual purpose of increasing the supply of cheap labor for industry while providing public authorities with a justification for limiting public funds for poor relief.

By the mid-19th century, "poorhouses" had been established in almost every rural county and urban neighborhood. They were the institutional embodiment of the moral distinction that by then was commonly drawn between the "worthy poor" and the "unworthy poor." The poorhouse was designed to minimize the expense of pauperism to local communities, while physically separating the poor from the rest of the community in order to deter others from requesting public assistance. Often built in outlying areas, the poorhouse (or "the almshouse" or the "country farm") maintained strict sets of rules and regulations designed to "rehabilitate" those whose poverty was believed to be the result of their own sloth and vice. The inmates of poorhouses were required to labor in workshops where, according to historian David Rothman, "the threat of punishment, decreased rations, and solitary confinement hung over those who did not fulfill their assignments" (1987). Any transgression, such as attempting to leave the institution, or entertaining visitors or wasting or pilfering food, was treated harshly by the overseers of the poorhouse. Those who established and ran the poorhouses essentially viewed poverty as a crime. The poor were considered criminals, who, through a process of strict moral and behavioral control, might be "rehabilitated."

Poorhouses did not prove the cure for homelessness. A larger economic and social transformation brushed aside the puny attempts of public authorities to deter the wandering of the unemployed. The appearance of large numbers of "tramps" after the Civil War terrified wealthy middle-class Americans. Hundreds of thousands of men wandered (or tramped) from town to town seeking employment, public relief or a handout. Most of the tramps were young, unmarried men, who, because of the social disruption of the war years, large-scale immigration from Europe and the economic depression of 1873, had chosen or had been forced to take up a life on the road. Some, such as Professor Francis Wayland of Yale University, claimed to see in the appearance of the tramps the harbinger of a collapse of civilized society into bloody anarchy. Speaking at a charity conference in Boston in 1877, he described the tramp as "a lazy, shiftless, incorrigible, cowardly, utterly depraved savage . . . Having no moral sense, he knows no gradations in crime . . . He has only one aim— to be supported in idleness." But according to the account of one tramp, there was little ease or comfort available in this life of "idleness." As an unemployed mechanic wrote in a letter to the *National Labor Tribune:*

Twelve months ago, left penniless by misfortune, I started from New York in search of employment. . . . During this year I have traversed seventeen states and obtained in that time six weeks' work. I have faced srarvation; been months at a time without a bed, when the thermometer was 30 degrees below zero. Last winter I slept in the woods, and while honestly seeking employment I have been two and three days without food. When, in God's name, I asked for something to keep body and soul together, I have been repulsed as a "tramp and vagabond."

Though scorned for their alleged unwillingness to work, tramps actually played a vital economic role as a mobile reserve labor force in late 19th-century America. Many were skilled artisans, such as carpenters, while the unskilled provided labor for seasonal industries such as agriculture and extractive industries such as lumbering and mining. The social reformer Henry George understood the link between changing social and economic conditions, the growing rift between the experience of the rich and the poor: "The 'tramp,' " he wrote in 1879, "comes with the locomotive, and almshouses and prisons and are as surely the marks of 'material progress' as are costly dwellings, rich warehouses, and magnificent churches."

When prosperity temporarily returned to the American economy at the end of the 1870s, some of these wandering men found permanent jobs and homes; but hundreds of thousands of others remained migratory laborers. Neighborhoods sprang up in many cities, such as New York City's Bowery District, that were devoted to housing and servicing these men, communities characterized by flophouses, saloons, pawnshops, cheap restaurants, used clothing stores and religious missions. By the 1930s these areas had become known collectively as "skid row"—the name deriving from the 19th-century waterfront district of Seattle, where timber was "skidded" along greased log roads until it reached the water where it could be floated to sawmills.

In the 20th century skid rows shrank in size and changed in character. Increasing mechanization in agriculture and extractive industries reduced the demand for migratory labor. (The remaining demand in agriculture was satisfied by a workforce that was largely minority, often foreign born, and thus largely "invisible" to the general population.) By the early decades of the 20th century, skid rows came to be associated in the public mind with a more or less permanent "home guard" of alcoholics and other "derelicts," overwhemingly white, male and aging—and considered by many to be responsible for their own poverty.

Those assumptions were challenged by the onset of the Great Depression. The stock market crash of 1929 ushered in the worst economic downturn in American history and a renewed wave of homelessness. Millions of Americans lost their jobs and homes as a result. In 1933, 12 million workers were unemployed in the United States, one-quarter of the U.S. workforce, while millions of others clung to part-time work or work with greatly reduced wages.

The connections between the rise in unemployment and the rise in homelessness were difficult to miss. In testimony provided before a U.S. Senate committee in 1933, a detective for a railroad company reported that back in 1929 the railroads counted a total 13,875 "trespassers" on their property (those walking along the rails, sleeping in boxcars, etc.). By 1931 that number had increased to 186,028, a jump of well over 1000 percent. A 1932 survey by the Children's Bureau of the Department of Labor of emergency relief efforts in 60 cities revealed that various agencies, mostly private charities, were sheltering almost 400,000 homeless persons. Those who were unable to find places in agency shelters, and those who had given up hitchhiking or riding the rails in search of work, built shacks made of any materials at hand in the numerous "shantytowns" (or "Hoovervilles," named for President Herbert Hoover) hastily constructed in cities across the nation. Families of migrant laborers often lived in their cars, trucks, tents and makeshift shacks near the fields where they worked or hoped to find work.

Entering the White House in the midst of the Great Depression, President Franklin Delano Roosevelt secured passage of an array of social legislation that represented a substantial shift in official policies toward the poor. Traditional policies, as we have seen, had hinged on the notion that poverty and homelessness were a matter of individual morality. During the Great Depression these guidelines were largely discarded and replaced by programs that recognized the social and economic nature of poverty in an industrial society.

In his 1932 speech accepting the Democratic nomination for president, Roosevelt pledged a "new deal for the American people." Roosevelt's "New Deal" administration established an array of social programs intended to counter the effects of the Depression. These included government programs that created jobs, provided emergency relief, built large and small-scale public works projects, introduced modern social security and unemployment insurance systems and secured legal rights for workers to organize unions.

Two pieces of New Deal legislation were directly concerned with solving the nation's housing crisis. The 1934 National Housing Act established the Federal Housing Administration (FHA) to insure loans by banks and other private lending institutions for housing construction and improvements. FHA regulations reduced the size of down payments and lengthened the repayment time for mortgages. By 1939 the FHA had insured 400,000 housing units, nearly a quarter of the units financed since the passage of the National Housing Act. By providing creditors with insurance against default, the act made it possible for Americans of relatively modest means to afford to buy a house.

FHA insurance was one of the factors contributing to the enormous expansion of homeownership over the next half century, which increased from under 48 percent of American households in 1930 to 65 percent 50 years later. FHA policies had other, not entirely intended, social consequences. Reflecting President Roosevelt's own antipathy to urban life, FHA policies favored construction of suburban single-family homes rather than urban apartment dwelllings and until 1948 deliberately and unapologetically fostered racially segregated neighborhoods. FHA policies thus contributed to the postwar flight of the white middle classes from the cities and the continued neglect of the urban housing stock. The National Housing Act of 1934 also established the Federal Savings and Loan Insurance Corporation (FSLIC) to insure mortgages offered by federally chartered savings and loan associations.

The National Housing Act of 1937, also known as the Wagner-Steagall Act, established the United States Housing Authority (USHA) as an agency of the Department of the Interior. The USHA extended low-interest federal loans to local agencies for slum clearance and public housing projects. It also provided rent subsidies for low-income renters. By 1940 the Wagner-Steagall Act had provided funding for 334 public housing projects, amounting to over 118,000 housing units. The establishment of the USHA in peacetime represented the first ongoing federal commitment to the construction of public housing.

The Great Depression made a lasting impression on those who lived through it. It also supplied American historical memory with some of its most vivid images of hopelessness and despair, in the photographs of migrant farmworkers in California taken by Dorothea Lange and other photographers from the New Deal's Farm Security Agency and in works of fiction, such as John Steinbeck's *The Grapes of Wrath*.

The New Deal did not end the Great Depression, but it alleviated its worst aspects. In the year after World War II the federal government remained committed to an active intervention in the economy (often through defense spending) and to social welfare spending. Federal policies did not succeed in eliminating poverty (as a new generation of reformers, such as Michael Harrington in his book *The Other America*, would point out in the 1960s), but they did prevent the kind of widespread homelessness that had been a problem in the 1930s. By the 1950s the "homeless" were again synonymous with the population of aging alcoholics in the nation's skid rows. Skid row neighborhoods shrank dramatically in size and population in the prosperous decades that followed the war. Overall, their population nationally was thought to have shrunk by 50 percent between 1950 and 1970. Most observers thought it was only a matter of time before these areas, and the homelessness associated with them, disappeared entirely.

That did not prove to be the case. By the early 1980s homelessness was once again an issue of major concern and debate in the United States. To understand the new crisis of homelessness, we will look first at the *perception* of homelessness that came to prevail in the course of the 1980s and then at the actual *causes* of homelessness.

THE EMERGENCE OF HOMELESSNESS AS A SOCIAL ISSUE

How did homelessness come to be regarded as a social problem in the first place? Though there have been persons without permanent shelter in our society since its earliest days, the designation of a distinct category of persons as "homeless" is a recent invention. It is important to understand the process through which "social problems" come to be designated as such. In the 18th century, for example, Americans were a hard-drinking group, consuming roughly three times as much alcohol annually as current per capita consumption. As historian Herbert Gutman noted in *Work, Culture, and Society in Industrializing America* (1976), workmen quaffed their ale or rum at regular intervals throughout the working day, often in the company of their employers. And no public gathering, such as a militia drill or an election, was considered complete without the jug of hard cider or whiskey to pass around. And yet court records from the era record virtually no crimes of "public drunkenness." It was only in the 19th century (when alcohol consumption actually began to decline) that "demon rum" emerged into public consciousness as one of the most important problems facing the nation.

The change in the *perception* of the meaning of the use of alcohol reflected the requirements of an emerging industrial order, as the evangelically minded middle and upper classes worried over the control of the immigrant workforce crowded into the nation's cities. As a result, the consumption of alcohol, which caused little notice or concern in the 18th century, came to be regarded in the 19th century as a matter both of sin and of concern for the public authorities.

Closer to our own time, the fact that a crisis of "juvenile delinquency" emerged as a leading concern of newspaper reporters, congressional investigators and social workers in the 1950s, followed by the crisis of "poverty" in the 1960s, does not mean that either of these two problems had been unknown or unimportant previously. The reasons why and the ways in which various social problems come to the fore in certain periods are too complex to explore here; but what is important to note is that the seriousness of a "social problem" is not necessarily the reason why it becomes a part of the public policy agenda.

In a seminal essay on homelessness published in 1984, Mark J. Stern argued that the emergence of homelessness as a social issue was part of the conservative political reaction that brought Ronald Reagan to the presidency in 1980. Reagan campaigned for office with the promise to get government "off the back" of the American people. As he declared in a speech introducing his "Program for Economic Recovery" in February 1981, a month after his inauguration:

The goal of this administration is to nurture the strength and vitality of the American people by reducing the burdensome, intrusive role of the federal government; by lowering tax rates and cutting spending; and by providing incentives for individuals to work, to save, and invest. It is our belief that only by reducing the growth of the government can we increase the growth of the economy.

A combination of high unemployment and high inflation in the late 1970s, combined with public doubts about the ability of President Jimmy Carter to stand up to America's foreign enemies, eroded an already damaged "New Deal coalition" that had kept the Democrats in control of the White House for most of the time since the Great Depression. When Reagan asked a national television audience during the 1980 campaign to answer the question "Are you better off today than you were four years ago?" few could answer in the affirmative. Many listened sympathetically to Reagan's charges that irresponsible federal spending on social welfare programs had unbalanced the budget, unleashed inflation and undermined individual initiative and the nuclear family.

The impact of the Reagan administration's policies on the lives of poor Americans was dramatic. Cutbacks in social programs such as Aid to Families of Dependent Children (AFDC) and Social Security Disability Insurance (SSDI) often made the difference in determining whether a poor family, or a mentally ill or otherwise disabled person, could continue to afford to pay rent in urban neighborhoods where rent costs were rising steeply and rapidly. From 1981 through 1988 all funds for federally subsidized housing programs were cut over 69 percent. The number of low-income housing starts, including public housing, Section 8 construction and rehabilitation and Section 202 housing for the elderly and handicapped dropped from 183,000 units in 1980 to 28,000 by 1985. New York City alone lost approximately $12 billion in federal assistance during the Reagan years. The New York City Housing Authority, the largest landlord in the United States, had a waiting list of approximately 200,000 families at the end of the 1980s. The 1989 United States Conference of Mayors survey of homelessness in 27 major cities concluded, "With the decline in federally-assisted housing programs, none of the survey cities expect to be able to meet the housing needs of low-income households in the forseeable future."

Stern noted that the social policies adopted by the Reagan administration represented:

a return to a "traditional" American approach to poverty. Yet, at the same time, they go against fifty years of government action flowing out of the New Deal . . . The response to the homeless emerged as an issue that suited the situation by allowing the better off in society to affirm their continued belief in New Deal tradition, while reimposing an older vision of the relationship of the poor to the nonpoor.

Stern suggested that the very term *homeless* implies a kind of traditional relationship between affluent and dependent classes that affirms the values of the dominant class. To understand his point, consider the story of Rosemary Pritchett, a black 31-year-old homeless mother of three, who was living in an emergency shelter in Kansas City, Missouri. One day, in 1990, Pritchett happened to find a lost paycheck. Instead of forging a signature and cashing it for her own use, she tracked down the nurse who had lost it and returned it to her. The nurse, a woman named Cheryl Wood, was immensely grateful to Pritchett and dismayed to learn of her homelessness.

Pritchett did in fact own a home, of sorts. She had scraped together $1,200 on her own, which she put in a bid on an abandoned house in Jackson County, Missouri. When the county accepted her offer, Pritchett discovered that the house she had purchased was uninhabitable, with no heating, electricity or plumbing. She was in despair when Cheryl Wood, grateful and impressed by Pritchett's honesty, decided to make the rehabilitation of the Pritchett house a personal crusade. She contacted the newspapers and local television stations to report Pritchett's good deed. The response was overwhelming. Donations of work, building materials, cash and even a used car from a local dealer poured in. As a result, the story made the national newspapers. Pritchett and her family were able to move into their rehabilitated house, complete with a new furnace, plumbing, electrical fixtures, doors, windows and furnishings.

The *New York Times* noted that Pritchett's "Christmas-season story has added a human face, and a rare happy twist, to a seemingly endless procession of grim news about poverty and homelessness in America." Pritchett struck such a responsive chord because she had proven herself a deserving individual (honest and self-improving). Her problems seemed finite, her needs specific and easily addressed by other individuals, without the impersonal involvement of government bureaucracies. And she was immensely grateful for the gifts bestowed upon her. "It's like a rebirth of some sort," she said of her experience. "It's moving to see so many caring people trying to help me do what I thought I could only do alone. It's like having an extended family—something I didn't have the first time around."

The Pritchett Christmas story tells us something about the instinctive generosity of Americans. But it also tells us something about the limits of the American social imagination when called upon to think about such issues as homelessness. By calling certain people "homeless," in a sense, we domesticate them. The "homeless" are a dependent class, to be pitied and nurtured. The term *homeless* draws upon our sympathies because it reminds us of the virtues of the opposite condition: "home" with its associations of warmth, unconditional acceptance and love. "It's like having an extended family," Ms. Pritchett said of the gifts she received from strangers—and that's the kind of response people want to get when they give.

By saying people are "homeless" we acknowledge that, within certain limits, they have a claim on our conscience and generosity. As a way of thinking about social problems, it is an example of what social scientists and historians have called the "gift relationship," an exchange between individuals that affirms (in the eyes of the donor) the worthiness of both the donor and the recipient, the donor for his or her generosity in offering the gift (of soup, blankets, time, cash) and the recipient for being judged "worthy" of the privilege of receiving the gift. The gift, British historian Gareth Stedman Jones has written, "generally serves as a method of social control. To give, from whatever motives, generally imposes an obligation upon the receiver. In order to receive one must behave in an acceptable manner, if only by expressing gratitude and humility. . . ."

Consider again Mark Stern's linkage of the emergence of homelessness as a public problem and the triumph of Reaganism. Despite the assurances of the Reagan administration that a "safety net" would protect the deserving poor, it was difficult to avoid evidence of increasing social misery in the early 1980s. During the "Reagan Recession" of 1981–82, newspapers and television news shows carried stories about unemployed "rust-belt" workers, sleeping in their cars or on the streets as they searched for employment in the "sun-belt" communities of the Southwest. Parallels were drawn between the experience of these homeless workers and the "Okies" of the 1930s. "Homeless Crisscross U.S., Until Their Cars and Their Dreams Break Down," the *New York Times* reported in December 1982, noting in the story that followed that the House Subcommittee on Housing and Economic Development had scheduled "the first Congressional hearing on homelessness in America since the Depression. . . ." Within a few years however, the homeless were no longer being portrayed in the media as the reincarnation of the Great Depression's displaced "Okies." For if the 1980s were the 1930s reborn, then it followed that it was the responsibility of the federal government to return to the philosophy and programs of the New Deal era. But that was not a message that many Americans were prepared to hear, especially since the Democratic opposition to the Reagan administration was stressing its own willingness to discard the supposedly failed and discredited liberal policies of the Carter years. By Reagan's second inaugural, the maxim that "you can't solve problems by throwing money at them" had become the conventional wisdom.

To think of the increasingly visible legions of the poor as "the homeless" offered Americans in the 1980s a way of reaffirming their own sense of living in a good and fair society, even as federal social welfare programs were cut back or eliminated. "After two decades of guilt and worry," Stern concluded, "the framing of the homeless issue served to reestablish the gift relationship of a by gone era." Distinctions between the "deserving" and "undeserving" poor were once again in vogue. Soup kitchens and shelters, rather than expensive government entitlement programs, were celebrated in the media. The homeless benefited, to the extent that hot soup and a warm bed in a church basement were better than not having a meal or a place to sleep. "Docility and gratitude," Stern wrote, ". . . were the general images of the homeless. [T]he reestablishment of a 'proper' gift relationship was one element of the popularity of the homeless."

"Popularity" may be too strong a word. Even in the early 1980s, a competing vision of the homeless as a dangerous class overlapped with the more favorable image of the grateful recipients of free soup and blankets. In many parts of the country the existence of home-lessness was treated by the local authorities as primarily a law enforcement problem, which could be solved by "getting tough" on the homeless themselves. In 1983 in Tucson, Arizona, the city's mayor ran for reelection on a platform that included the pledge he would get "the transients the hell out of town." Police attempted to drive away homeless people through verbal and physical harassment and arrests for a variety of misdemeanors such as trespass, squatting, public indecency and loitering. In Santa Barbara, California, antihomeless ordi-nances prohibited sitting, sleeping or lying down in public parks. Trash-bin refuse was defined as public property, making foraging in garbage a criminal act. Zoning ordinances were used to close down religious missions providing food and shelter to the homeless or to prevent churches from running homeless shelters in their buildings. In some cities the authorities sponsored "clean sweeps" to rid the community of unsightly homeless people before some event likely to attract tourists, such as the 1984 Olympics in Los Angeles or the annual Mardi Gras celebration in New Orleans. Seating was redesigned in airports, bus terminals and city parks specifically to prevent people from sleeping on benches. A Fort Lauderdale, Florida councilman proposed spraying rat poison in trash cans and dumpsters as a way of discouraging people from rummaging through them for food. In some communities authorities attempted to solve the problem by providing the homeless with bus tickets to neighboring cities or states.

As should be evident, perceptions of the homeless are complex and sometimes self-contradictory. Urban policies and the causes of homelessness are equally complex and are often highly controversial.

URBAN CHANGE IN POSTWAR AMERICA

The United States emerged out of World War II in a strong economic position. The European industrial infrastructure had been severely damaged by the war, while the war had greatly strengthened American industrial capacity. In the late 1940s and 1950s the United States was in a position both to rebuild the European economies and to enter those markets in Third World countries that had once been controlled by European industry. The United States became the commanding economic power in the world.

At home, Americans were faced with a potentially severe housing shortage at the close of the war. The nation's housing stock was aging, and there had been few resources available during the war (and the Depression before it) to build new housing or rehabilitate older buildings. With two decades of insecurity behind them and economic expansion promising hope for the future, millions of servicemen returned to civilian life expecting to marry and raise families. The postwar "baby boom" was under way, a population explosion that rapidly generated the demand for new housing.

A comparable situation emerged in other nations that had been involved in the war effort, but governmental responses differed. In Britain the housing shortage was addressed through a massive program of investment in public housing construction. Private housing construction was actually banned for a time in postwar Britain, as the Labour Party government sought to focus all construction activity in the public sector toward a comprehensive policy to provide housing for the whole of the British working class. New towns were created outside of the large cities, high-rise apartment complexes were constructed and generous rent subsidies were provided to keep rents below the level of controlled rents in the private sector.

While some public housing was made available in the United States, the emphasis of the government's postwar housing policy was on strengthening the private housing market and private ownership of the single-family home. Though the cultural imagery of the yeoman farmer and the homesteading family of the West had been a part of traditional American folklore, prior to the 1950s there were limited possibilities for many Americans actually to own their own home. After the war, a combination of factors, including federal loan programs, new construction techniques, federal funding for the expansion of the highway system and the promotion of middle-class cultural values in the mass media, awarded a home of one's own a central place in the American Dream. The American suburb, previously the preserve of the most prosperous classes, was increasingly regarded as the natural habitat of the broad American middle class.

Prefabricated housing techniques, tested during the war in the construction of barracks for GIs, were widely used to create vast tracts of low-cost suburban houses in an assembly-line fashion. Supported by federal housing loans and promoted by low down payment demands, many working and middle-class Americans were able to purchase their own modest homes outside of the largest cities.

Meanwhile, an effort was under way to remake America's cities. As mandated by the National Housing Act of 1949 (and revised in 1954), the federal government began a program of urban renewal to rebuild the downtown areas of American cities. Commercial and financial interests supported urban renewal because two-thirds of the cost of the program was borne by the federal government. These interests viewed renewal areas as providing a buffer against the expansion of "slums" and as a magnet to attract retail trade to downtown areas. The urban renewal program essentially provided for the use of public funds to buy, clear and improve renewal sites, after which land ownership would revert to the private sector.

Urban renewal policies proved controversial. The labeling of neighborhoods as "slums" and as "blighted" often provoked heated arguments. Residents of low-income communities did not always agree with the politicians and developers who sought to target their neighborhoods for "renewal." Through the 1950s large numbers of low-income families were displaced without adequate provision for their relocation. With the sanction of legal and political authorities, 250,000 families were evicted every year in the urban renewal program. Compensation averaged $80 per family. Urban renewal served to accelerate suburban migration from the cities as well as to concentrate the poor (often minorities) who could not afford suburban tract housing or who were excluded from it by racially segregated housing policies.

In his 1964 State of the Union Address, President Lyndon Johnson unveiled a program to confront urban poverty. Spurred to action by the civil rights movement, Johnson called for an "unconditional war on poverty in America" while promoting a substantial legislative agenda that culminated in passage of the Civil Rights Act of 1964 and the Voting Rights Act of 1965. The War on Poverty, which won congressional approval in August 1964, consisted of a variety of programs designed to prepare individuals to take advantage of those economic opportunities that were provided in the expanding economy of the 1960s (including the Job Corps, the Neighborhood Youth Corps, Work-Study programs, Operation Head Start and the Elementary and Secondary Education Act).

A variety of housing programs were advanced as part of the War on Poverty. A Cabinet-level Department of Housing and Urban Development (HUD) was created to serve as the principal federal agency responsible for housing needs, fair housing opportunities and community improvement and development. A wide range of new housing measures was enacted to benefit low- and moderate-income families, including funding for 240,000 units of low-income housing; a program of federal rent supplements for low-income families; and the Model Cities program, which sought to concentrate and coordinate diverse federal programs in order to focus reform in some of the poorest urban neighborhoods in the country. The War on Poverty reaffirmed the commitment made in the 1949 National Housing Act guaranteeing "a decent home and a suitable living environment for every American family" and set a target of construction of 26 million new and rehabilitated housing units for low- and moderate-income families over the following decade.

Johnson's war on poverty soon ran into difficulties. Its loosely drafted legislation and hastily organized programs sometimes led to examples of waste and corruption, providing ammunition for conservative critics who attacked the programs for exploiting taxpayers and expanding the government bureaucracy. Model Cities funds, controlled by city mayors, were sometimes used to benefit affluent neighborhoods, and this led to power struggles between local officials and federal administrators. And poor black communities, where expectations had been steadily raised by the promise of economic opportunity, exploded in rebellion and frustration in the mid-1960s. The "Long Hot Summers," in turn, fueled a rising "white backlash" against federal efforts to ameliorate poverty among the urban poor. Finally, the Vietnam war increasingly diverted attention from domestic reconstruction and drained the funds that might have continued it. Richard Nixon, benefiting from the white backlash against federal poverty programs and widespread frustration with the war effort, was elected president in 1968. Though he cut back on many elements of the War on Poverty, rebellions in hundreds of black urban communities convinced him to maintain and even expand some social welfare programs, most notably the Aid to Families of Dependent Children program.

By the mid-1970s existing conditions of poverty were exacerbated by several factors: the continued loss of urban manufacturing jobs in the private sector; political resistance to the enactment of large-scale government social programs to tackle poverty (compounded by the Nixon administration's preoccupation with the Watergate crisis as well as the costs of the Vietnam war); and an increasing inability of municipal governments to maintain basic services. The problem was that the continuing suburban migration of large numbers of middle and working-class whites from American cities was eroding the tax base upon which basic city services, such as education, fire and police protection, sanitation and recreational facilities, depended. By 1975 many cities found themselves in a serious financial crisis as the eroding tax base forced city governments to cut services, which further fueled the migration of those who could afford to leave (and who had sustained the tax base) while making life increasingly difficult for those who could not.

Though poverty was widely recognized in the 1970s, it was not until the 1980s that homelessness emerged as a distinct problem in American society. Paradoxically, the problem of homelessness in the 1980s has its roots partly in the attempt to solve the urban fiscal crisis of the 1970s. That is, the very strategies employed by many municipal administrations to revitalize the cities in the wake of the fiscal crises of the 1970s, such as the accelerated destruction of "skid row" areas, the construction of waterfront hotel/restaurant/shopping complexes, the development of high-rise corporate office space, condominium development and the "gentrification" of urban neighborhoods, have had a powerful impact on the nature of the housing market and on the ability of the poor to sustain affordable housing. Strategies of urban "revitalization," combined with the sharp cutbacks in federal spending on public housing and other housing programs for the poor, made rental housing for low-income persons an increasingly rare and expensive commodity throughout the 1980s and contributed to the rise in homelessness on urban streets.

An example of this shift is the decline of SROs, or "single-room occupancy hotels," institutions that once represented the shelter of last resort for the poorest Americans. Such hotels rented rooms by the day, week or month at low rates. Over the past two decades there has been a rapid decline in the number of housing units in the least expensive segments of the housing market. (One survey of 12 large cities from 1978 to 1983 found that rental housing available to the poor dropped by an average of 30 percent.) Part of this decline is the result of the demolition of SROs in cities across the country due to downtown redevelopment of the skid row areas in which they are located. From 1975 to 1981 over 30,000 rooms in SROs were eliminated in New York City. Nationwide, over 1 million single-room units, nearly half of the total stock, disappeared between 1970 and 1982.

Other factors played a role in the rise of contemporary homelessness. Consider the process of "gentrification," which transformed the core of many, if not most, American cities throughout the 1980s. Gentrification is a process whereby upper-income people displace lower-income residents, on a house-by-house basis, thus changing the social class and/or racial composition of a neighborhood and causing the price of local housing stock to rise. Gentrification was often encouraged by municipal officials as a means of redeveloping city neighborhoods in order to help revitalize downtown commercial districts and sustain the middle-class tax base of cities. Waterfront redevelopment projects in cities such as Boston, Baltimore, Portland and Seattle have served as magnets for retail trade and have encouraged the gentrification of nearby residential neighborhoods.

It is impossible to fully understand the process of gentrification without considering the social class (socio-economic background, occupational position, lifestyle) of the people involved. One important group has been the young urban professionals ("yuppies") whose tastes and consumption patterns are reflected in many of the outward forms of gentrification. Ironically, these young professionals are often the children of middle-class parents who migrated out of the cities to the suburbs in the postwar decades. They represent the large middle-class segment of the "baby boom" generation. In demographic and cultural terms, they differ from their middle-class parents in significant ways. While their parents moved to the suburbs in the 1950s and 1960s seeking "good" schools, green grass and room to raise their children, the current generation is often made up of two-career couples, who tend to marry later in life, have fewer children (and have them later in life), while preferring the variety and vibrancy of urban cultural amenities to the child-centered emphasis and social homogeneity of suburban living.

The changing economic basis of American cities has created a context for gentrification. Manufacturing industries that once provided reasonably stable and well-paid employment for working-class Americans have declined. Low-paying clerical, sales, restaurant and health-care occupations have become the main sources of employment at one end of the new "service economy," while high-paying financial, legal and corporate executive professions have expanded at the other. Such economic changes have been manifested in spatial terms at the neighborhood level, by enclaves of urban "gentry" (or middle-class professionals) forming in inner-city working-class neighborhoods. Once a neighborhood begins to change in this way, housing costs rise, local homeowners sell their properties for windfall profits and low-income tenants (particularly the elderly and others living on fixed incomes) are displaced from rental housing. Just as important, the social and cultural character of neighborhoods is altered by this market activity.

Powerful pressures are brought to bear on city officials to encourage such changes. A declining urban tax base and cuts in federal funding for local programs force city officials to develop ways to attract residents who pay higher taxes and who do not draw upon already underfunded social service programs. Gentrification can serve as a magnet for upper-income residents and can encourage commercial investment. Residential rehabilitation is only one aspect of the process, however. Residential gentrification is linked to a more general transformation of the urban political economy. As the manufacturing sector has declined, other sources of investment have been found in the growth of the tourist industry and construction of urban hotel and convention complexes, corporate office-space development and the growth of "trendy" retail and restaurant districts.

Gentrification can be encouraged in subtle ways. For example, in the mid-1980s artists in New York City were offered subsidized housing in a declining neighborhood in lower Manhattan. Though artists were literally "starved" for low-cost housing and work space, some opposed the offer, arguing that they were being used as "point men" or "pioneers" to make the neighborhood attractive (in cultural terms) to affluent investors. The fear was that once low-income residents were evicted and the neighborhood renovated, only very wealthy residents would be able to live there. And the artists themselves might ultimately be displaced and forced to seek inexpensive space elsewhere, effectively serving as "pioneers" in another neighborhood in need of redevelopment.

Despite the role of city officials in the process, proponents of gentrification often consider it a good example of the role of the "free market" and the "individual" in urban redevelopment (as opposed to public initiatives). In recent years a mythology has been woven about the young professional as an "urban pioneer," or "urban homesteader," who courageously moves into an uncharted urban territory and with a small down payment and a great deal of "sweat equity" becomes the first of many to renovate the neighborhood's old Victorian homes. The frontier is thus "tamed," and it becomes "safe" for others to follow.

Though some may find it reasonable to think of middle-class professionals venturing into communities that are inhabited by relatively poor people (with "alien" ethnic cultural ways) as "pioneers," neighborhood residents might consider "colonizer" a more accurate term. In the initial stage of neighborhood gentrification, middle-class newcomers move into a neighborhood seeking moderate housing prices and a rich ethnic street life. But their very presence begins to transform the social, cultural and economic character of the neighborhood. In the context of the private real estate market, their move can signal others (including speculators) that a neighborhood is "on the way up" and begin to attract a flood of investment.

While investment is clearly good for housing stock in any community, it also forces up housing costs, displacing longtime neighborhood residents and small businesses. Gourmet yogurt shops and sushi bars catering to the new residents begin to replace the local shoe repair store and butcher shop. The threat of displacement and neighborhood change may generate deep social tensions when affluent newcomers appear in a declining urban neighborhood. Ultimately, many of the structures in the community may be renovated with very few of the original residents able to remain.

Advocacy groups for the homeless consider gentrification a major problem because of its role in shrinking the supply of low-cost housing. Previously low-cost rental housing units are lost as investors buy buildings for conversion to condominiums and cooperatives. The loss of rental units drives up the price of the remaining apartments, while those who cannot afford to buy the renovated condominiums are forced to move to more crowded and dilapidated quarters or are made homeless. It has been estimated that 500,000 apartment buildings were converted into condominiums and cooperatives between 1977 and 1982 in the United States. There are as yet no reliable national estimates of the number of people made homeless directly through gentrification. But in a study of displacement in New York City, Peter Marcuse, professor of urban planning at Columbia University, estimated that from 1970 to 1980, between 10,000 and 40,000 households were displaced annually by gentrification alone (while an additional 30,000 to 60,000 households were displaced by the abandonment of buildings).

While most commentators agree that the shrinkage of low-cost housing has been a major factor in the rise of homelessness, other factors are often cited as well. The "deinstitutionalization" of patients suffering from mental illness is often noted as a cause for the spread of homelessness. The history of the deinstitutionalization movement begins just after World War II. In 1946 Congress established the National Institute of Mental Health (NIMH) to study the causes and possible cures of mental illness. At the same time new drugs such as Thorazine were being developed that stabilized symptoms of the mentally ill, permitting patients to live outside of hospital settings. By 1955 nearly 2 million people were being given Thorazine. Public outcry against the often squalid or brutal conditions prevailing in U.S. mental hospitals, whose population peaked at over 550,000 in the 1950s, led to demands for reform. In 1963 President John F. Kennedy proposed to Congress to phase out the custodial care of the mentally ill. Congress passed the Mental Retardation Facilities and Community Mental Health Centers Construction Act later that year, providing federal funding for outpatient and emergency treatment centers for the mentally ill.

In response to public pressures and the federal government's initiative, state mental hospitals began to discharge large numbers of their patients. Their patient population was cut to less than 138,000 by 1980. The states welcomed the new policies, because they saw the opportunity to shift the burden of caring for mentally ill from their own treasuries to the federal government. The passage of the Medicaid and Medicare bills, providing federal health insurance benefits for the poor and the elderly, also shifted the burden of supporting the mentally ill from the states to the federal government. But the federal government did not follow through on its commitment to provide new forms of treatment for the former state hospital patients. Only 700 of what was originally planned to be 2,500 community mental health centers were opened in the 1960s and 1970s, and these often wound up serving a more affluent and less severely disturbed clientele than the population previously confined to state mental hospitals.

Calls for reinstitutionalization began to be heard in the 1980s. The importance of "deinstitutionalization" in and of itself as a cause of homelessness can, however, easily be exaggerated. Through most of the 1960s and 1970s, the recently discharged mentally ill (and those who were never admitted to mental hospitals due to more stringent entry requirements) were not, in fact, reduced to homelessness. New regulations for public assistance in the 1960s made federal money available to support people with mental illness outside of a hospital setting. Housing was available for them in single-room occupancy hotels, for example. These were often not ideal settings for psychiatric recovery, but they were sufficient to keep the mentally ill out of the elements and away from the dangers of the street.

In fact, relatively few of today's homeless are drawn from the ranks of the "deinstitutiona-lized." As sociologist James Wright pointed out in his book *Address Unknown* (1989), "By the late 1970s, most of the people destined ever to be 'deinstitutionalized' already had been. So as a direct contributing factor to the rise of homelessness in the 1980s, deinstitutionaliza-tion cannot be that important." According to one study, only 3 percent of the homeless came directly from mental institutions to homelessness. Many more have passed through one or another form of transitional setting, such as halfway houses or SROs. But cutbacks in social welfare spending have eliminated many halfway houses, while the forces of urban gentrification eliminated the SROs. When the administration of President Ronald Reagan slashed federal spending on welfare programs in the early 1980s, nearly a half million recipients were cut from the rolls of the Social Security Disability Insurance program. Nearly a third of these were people suffering from psychiatric disabilities, and many of them wound up living on the street.

As should be clear, the relationship between homelessness and other social problems, such as the treatment of the mentally ill, is a complex one. It is also one that is sometimes misconstrued by politicians and administrators eager to escape responsibility for the social and economic problems festering within their jurisdiction. For example, if Americans are persuaded that homelessness is primarily a matter of the deinstitutionalization of the mentally ill, then problems with the supply of housing and the adequacy of social welfare programs will be ignored. Dealing with homelessness then becomes primarily a matter of mental health and the policies surrounding it, rather than a multicausal social problem to be addressed by those with the power to mobilize political and financial resources. In other words, home-lessness becomes defined as a problem caused by malfunctioning individuals rather than as a problem of a malfunctioning system of housing, employment and social welfare. Not only is the definition of the problem subject to varying interpretations depending on the political interests at stake, but so are the means of counting those afflicted with homelessness.

THE "NUMBERS GAME": A MATTER OF DEFINITION

The number of homeless persons in the United States varies with every study, every interest group and every government agency that addresses the question. Estimates have varied from 250,000 to 3 million. The numbers vary so greatly because the definitions of who ought to be included vary, and definitions embody particular sets of values with their own social implications. Thus, any attempt to quantify the homeless population immediately confronts the question: Just who ought to be considered homeless? In other words, what circumstances constitute the condition of homelessness? Underlying all issues of definition are social and political values that reflect different views of the role of the state in relation to social problems, the sense of social solidarity in society and the responsibility of the community to those needing shelter, as well as the responsibility of those without shelter to the rest of the community.

Definitions of homelessness have been more or less inclusive. Everyone might agree that a family living in a car or an individual sleeping nightly on a park bench or under a bridge ought to be considered homeless. But what about a family living in a shelter, or an individual living in a "flophouse"? And what about the person living on the couch of a friend, or a family forced to live in the already overcrowded apartment of a relative? Though these are also people without permanent shelter, not all experts or government officials would agree that they ought to be counted as part of the homeless population.

Some researchers have distinguished between the "literally homeless," those sleeping on the streets or in emergency shelters and missions, and the "marginally housed," those people who live "doubled up" in the homes of others, in their definition of the problem. Once this distinction is made, there is a tendency to concentrate research and policy only on the "literally homeless" as the focus population, while ignoring, at least for the time being, the "marginally housed." The most reliable estimates of the number of persons who are "literally homeless" *on any given night* in the United States still vary considerably, from 350,000 estimated by sociologist Peter Rossi, to 600,000 estimated by the nonprofit research organization the Urban Institute, to the estimate of 735,000 advanced by The National Alliance to End Homelessness, an advocacy group. The phrase "on any given night" is important because there are many more families and individuals who may become homeless "during the course of any given year." For example, while the National Alliance to End Homelessness estimated 735,000 homeless Americans "on any given night," it also estimated that between 1.3 and 2 million people will become homeless at some point during the course of a year and thus claims to have identified a group that ought to be considered central for public policy attention.

On the other hand, some researchers and advocacy groups favor combining both the "marginally housed" and the "literally homeless" in their estimates of the homeless population. They argue that all those without permanent shelter must be the focus of social policy since "literal homelessness" will be prevented only if the problem of the "marginally housed" is addressed simultaneously. That is, since the "marginally housed" are in constant danger of being made "literally homeless" and since the source of literal homelessness is the imminent loss of shelter for those who have been precariously housed, a comprehensive policy must address both conditions if there is to be any hope of overcoming the problem of homelessness.

Obviously, when this advice is taken, estimates of the number of homeless will be much higher than if the more narrow definition ("literal homelessness") is employed. For example, the estimate of 3 million homeless that was advanced by the National Coalition for the Homeless several years ago was ridiculed by some commentators for dramatically overestimating the number of homeless. But the National Coalition did not limit its estimate to people living on the streets or in emergency shelters, as conservatives and many social scientists are wont to do. It also included those precariously housed with friends or relatives in overcrowded conditions; those living in tents, campers, makeshift shacks and chicken coops in rural areas; and generally those who cannot afford to sustain what most Americans would recognize as a permanent shelter. The number of Americans living in such conditions is considerable. The *New York Times* reported in September 1991 that in New York City alone, over 100,000 people were living "doubled up" with relatives or friends. If we add to this the "literally homeless" population in New York City, which some have estimated to be in the range of between 70,000 and 90,000, then New York City would appear to have a homeless population approaching 200,000. If this is accurate, then the national figure of 3 million advanced by the National Coalition for the Homeless may not be completely unrealistic.

There are no precise figures on the number of homeless people in America because the problems of achieving an accurate count are formidable. Conventional censuses and surveys are designed with the assumption that the respondents have an address through which they can be contacted and counted. Clearly, such an assumption cannot be made about the homeless.

On March 20, 1990, the U.S. Bureau of the Census attempted to quantify the homeless in a project named "Shelter and Street Night." Though homeless persons had been counted in previous censuses, because homelessness had become such a prominent public issue in the 1980s, the Census Bureau sought to make an especially focused and systematic nationwide effort to, in their words, "improve the count and to identify selected components of the homeless population." Notice that the claim was not to count the homeless population, but "to improve the count," an important difference.

Advocates for the homeless had complained for years that the Bush and Reagan administrations, as part of their effort to cut back and contain federal spending on social services, had misrepresented the causes and had sorely understated the extent of homelessness in America. When the Bureau of the Census announced its plans to "improve the count," organizations that had spent the better part of a decade trying to convince two administrations that homelessness was a serious and growing social problem were skeptical. Many advocacy groups voiced concerns that insufficient resources were being provided, that the methods used in the effort would be flawed and that even though Census officials and others might warn against it, much of the media, the political establishment and the general population would treat the published numbers as an officially sanctioned figure on the number of homeless Americans. In short, they feared a serious underestimate that would then be used as "scientific" justification for minimizing the problem and maintaining funding at inadequate levels.

The Census Bureau's plan to quantify homelessness in 1990 was twofold. The first part was a focused effort to spend one full night counting persons in previously identified public and private emergency shelters and "open locations in the streets or other places not intended for habitation." This was the main element of "Shelter and Street Night," or "S Night." The second part was to enumerate persons often considered homeless who could be identified within the regular census operation, such as "doubled-up families" or homeless persons living in tents at commercial campgrounds.

In order to identify emergency shelters for the project, letters were sent to 39,000 officials in urban and rural areas across the country requesting that they work with local service providers, advocates for the homeless and homeless persons in order to identify the shelters and street locations that would be visited during the night of the operation. The plan called for sending 7,500 two-person teams of census takers to interview and count the homeless in three settings during three different periods of the night. Counting began at shelters from 6 P.M. to midnight (when, it was presumed, the homeless would be settled for the night). From 2 A.M. to 4 A.M. the census takers counted the homeless on the streets, and from 4 A.M. to 8 A.M. the census takers stood outside of abandoned buildings to count the homeless people as they exited in the morning. Altogether, 11,000 shelters and 11,000 open-air sites were visited. The sites had all been identified previously, and there was no attempt to search cars or enter abandoned buildings, roofs or dumpsters. In addition to S Night, the Census expected to be able to use the regular census process to count households that were "doubled up" or that resided in commercial campgrounds, two groups that are often included in the homeless population. S Night was widely recognized as the most ambitious effort by the federal government to gain information on the homeless population, but it was also the subject of considerable controversy.

Though most recommended full participation in the effort, advocates for the homeless offered a range of criticisms even before S Night took place. They argued that the budget provided was much too low to do a reasonable survey and that the time allotment would not allow the enumerators to reach any more than a fraction of the homeless, especially in large cities such as New York. While officials in some cities responded to the bureau's mailing, critics noted that only 10 percent of those contacted actually responded, thus making it difficult to properly locate the homeless in many cities. Advocates raised questions about the times of the count, the impact of weather on that night and the fact that enumerators could count only those who were visible on the streets, though the safety and survival of the homeless often depends on not appearing or admitting to being homeless. Except in a few instances, no cities with populations of less than 50,000 were visited on S Night.

In April 1991 the Census Bureau reported that its census takers had counted 230,000 people on S Night, which included 180,000 in shelters and 50,000 more at selected street sites. When the figures were released, homeless advocates felt that their warnings of a significant undercount of the homeless population had proven true. Maria Foscarinas of the National Law Center on Homelessness and Poverty declared: "My fear is that this is an effort by the Federal Government to diminish the plight of the homeless by minimizing their numbers." Paula Schneider, director of the Population Division at the Census Bureau, denied that there had been a deliberate undercount: "We admitted all along that you can't count everybody. Those who hide from the census can't be counted. There is no way you can count them. And some of the homeless are among them." Over a dozen cities, fearing that federal aid to the homeless would be cut because of the Census figures, sued to force an adjustment in the final count.

The number of homeless in America, as should now be evident, is extremely difficult to estimate with a reliable degree of accuracy. Depending on how we define what we mean by homeless, the estimates may vary wildly, from a low of about one-quarter of a million persons, to a high of 3 million nationally.

THE HOMELESS IN AMERICA

Some have argued that too heavy an emphasis on numbers is beside the point, that the problem of homelessness is widespread and is caused by a range of overlapping social problems. Moreover, the emphasis on numbers, it is argued, tends to objectify people by classifying them on the basis of specific attributes, such as physical disability, mental illness, veteran status and so on and then implying, without offering any evidence, a causal relationship between the attribute and the condition of being homeless. Generally speaking, the characteristics of the homeless population essentially mirror the characteristics of America's poor population. Being homeless is but one of many conditions associated with being poor, and poverty is an enduring feature of our society. But poverty has never been distributed evenly throughout our society. And, until quite recently, one could be poor and still maintain reasonably secure shelter. Today poverty increasingly means the risk of losing one's home. Moreover, a job is no guarantee against homelessness: An estimated 18 percent of the homeless are actually employed full or part time. Throughout the country, millions of Americans work but remain poor, and many cannot afford shelter.

In the nation's largest cities, the homeless population is disproportionately a minority population. In the 1980s African Americans and Hispanics represented nearly half of the national homeless population. A 1984 study of the homeless by the Department of Housing and Urban Development (HUD), perhaps the most comprehensive survey of the decade, estimated that 44 percent of the homeless shelter population consisted of minorities (compared to the 20 percent minorities represented in the national population as a whole). In larger cities the proportion of minorities among the homeless ran much higher. Richard Ropers's study of the Los Angeles homeless in 1983–84 found that minorities made up 51 percent of the homeless population. African Americans comprised 32 percent of his sample population; Hispanics, 11 percent; Native Americans, 5 percent; Asians, 1 percent; and others, 2 percent. The proportion of minorities among the homeless, especially African Americans, seems to have increased in the course of the 1980s; estimates of the proportion of minorities among the homeless population in the late 1980s varied from 65 percent in Chicago, to 80 percent in Los Angeles, to 90 percent in New York City.

According to the 1992 *Status Report on Hunger and Homelessness* issued by the United States Conference of Mayors, cities in which African Americans comprised two-thirds or more of the homeless population include Alexandria, Chicago, Cleveland, Detroit, Los Angeles, Miami, New York and Philadelphia. Though African Americans account for only about 12 percent of the population of the United States, they comprise a third or more of the nation's homeless population. (When the Hispanic and Native American homeless are also considered, minorities add up to a majority of the homeless.)

The disproportionate share of African Americans in the homeless population is startling. Although African Americans have always been overrepresented among the poor in the United States, they were traditionally underrepresented in "skid row" populations earlier in the century. While the civil rights movement and the War on Poverty programs in the 1960s produced some genuine victories, in recent years the condition of African Americans as a group has either stagnated or declined. The enactment of a range of programs to improve and equalize educational opportunity helped to expand the black middle class in the 1970s, and the civil rights movement proved remarkably successful in striking down discriminatory legislation that had stood for a century or longer. But other forms of racial discrimination, enshrined in custom if not in law, have persisted.

African Americans have always faced discrimination in the urban housing market and have always had to spend a higher proportion of their income in order to secure adequate housing. African Americans were locked out of homeownership by prejudice and also by government policy. Federal mortgage loan guarantees, such as those provided by the Federal Housing Administration, were largely unavailable to African Americans until the 1960s.

Problems of inadequate housing in African-American neighborhoods were exacerbated in the 1980s by cuts in social welfare spending initiated by the Reagan administration. Longer-range economic changes have also had a disproportionate impact on minority, and particularly black, communities. The shift in the American economy away from manufacturing to "service" industries has left urban minority communities without a secure economic base. While the overall national unemployment rate has moved into double digits only once since the Great Depression (reaching 10.7 percent in the recession of 1982), African-American unemployment has rarely dropped below double digits in recent years. Between 1981 and 1986 the annual African-American unemployment rate averaged 17 percent; it peaked at 19.5 percent in 1983 (over double the unemployment rate of whites). As the industrial base of urban America declined through the 1970s and 1980s, millions of black families and individuals remained locked in poverty. While the number of white people living in poverty is much greater than the number of African Americans, the percentage of whites is 10 percent, while it is 32 percent for African Americans. So, while African Americans have always been forced to contend with a much higher poverty rate than whites, it is only recently that large numbers of African Americans have become homeless.

Along with African Americans and other minorities, the presence of a significant proportion of women among today's homeless population is a new and disturbing trend. In 1958 a study estimated that no more than 3 percent of the nation's skid row population was women. Currently at least 25 percent of homeless people are women, and women and children together comprise nearly 40 percent of the total homeless population. Women are in general overrepresented among the ranks of the poor. A 1990 study by the Low Income Housing Coalition's Women and Housing Task Force confirmed the Census Bureau's statistics that more than two-thirds of all poor—hence at risk of becoming homeless—households in the United States are maintained by women.

The economic status of women has changed significantly in recent decades. More and more women have joined the workforce. In 1960 there were 22 million female workers, comprising about one-third of the workforce. By 1985 there were 47 million female workers, comprising 44 percent of all employees. The increase has included women with children as well as childless women. In 1950 only about a fifth of all women with children were in the labor force. By 1985, 68 percent of all mothers of children in the six- to 17-year range were employed, as were just over half of those with children under the age of six.

At the same time, more and more women have become poor. Between 1969 and 1985 a substantial increase occurred in the numbers of those living below the poverty line in families headed by women (from 10.4 million to 16.4 million). Every year between 1969 and 1978, 100,000 additional women with children fell below the poverty rate. In 1982 two of every three poor adults were women, and women headed over half of all poor families, a phenomenon that is often termed the "feminization of poverty." The fact that increasing numbers of women are in the workforce and increasing numbers of women are in poverty is not as puzzling as it may seem. Despite the attention paid in the media to female lawyers, stockbrokers, coalminers and other pioneers in traditionally male occupations, the continuing strength of occupational sex segregation means that women continue to find the readiest employment in low-paying service sector, clerical or light manufacturing jobs. Women on average earn only about three-fifths of what men earn. The decline in American manufacturing has led to a steady reduction in well-paying blue-collar jobs. Women have entered the job market to supplement the uncertain earnings of their spouses or, increasingly, to replace those earnings as best they can. More women are thus entering the labor force at a time when the number of well-paying jobs available for all workers has been decreasing. Increasing rates of divorce, male desertion and unmarried women having children on their own (including a sharp increase in the pregnancy rate of unmarried teenaged girls) have left many women the sole support of their children. Eighty-five percent of all American women can expect to support themselves, as a result of divorce, separation or death, at some point in their lives. Less that two-thirds of divorced fathers pay anything toward child support. These factors, combined with the low wages and insecurity of women's jobs and the cutbacks in spending on social programs in the 1980s, have left many women and their children at risk of losing their housing in an increasingly expensive housing market.

Homeless women differ from homeless men in a number of ways. They are found to be less transient, less likely to be substance abusers and more likely to remain part of family units. They also tend to have been homeless for shorter periods on average than men. As with homeless men, there are many different subgroups among the population of homeless women.

One large group of homeless women are mothers caring for dependent children. More than half of homeless families are single-parent units, generally female-headed. In a 1984 study of homeless families in Boston, 80 homeless mothers and 151 children living in family shelters were interviewed. With a median age of 27 years, 45 percent of the women were single and another 45 percent were separated, divorced or widowed. Each mother had an average of 2.4 children. Nine out of ten of the mothers received Aid to Families of Dependent Children. Most cited eviction, nonpayment of rent, overcrowding and housing conversion as their primary reasons for homelessness.

Abuse by male partners is also a significant cause of homelessness among women. In the 1970s and 1980s the women's movement made domestic violence an issue that drew increasing media and legal attention. Battered women's shelters and safe houses opened up in many communities, providing temporary refuge for women and their children fleeing domestic violence. Between 1983 and 1987 the number of women seeking shelter at battered women's shelters increased 100 percent. In 1988 over 300,000 women and their children sought refuge in 1,100 shelters and safe houses. These shelters could not, however, take in all of those who sought refuge in them. The Coalition Against Domestic Violence reported that in 1987, 40 percent of women with children seeking such shelter had to be turned away because of lack of space. And many shelters and safe houses have limits of a few days or weeks in which battered women and their children can stay. As a result, many women and children fleeing domestic violence end up in the homeless population. Researcher Ellen Bassuk and her colleagues conducted a study of the characteristics of the homeless staying in Massachusetts family shelters in 1986 and found that although it was not always the immediate cause of their homelessness, 45 percent of the women they interviewed had experienced domestic violence.

Children are the most tragic victims of the homeless crisis. Sociologist James Wright estimated in his book *Address Unknown* (1989) that one in every seven homeless persons is under 19 years of age, while the U.S. Conference of Mayors put the figure at one in every four. That adds up to something on the order of a half to three-quarters of a million children living in shelters, in welfare hotels or on the streets. Jonathon Kozol wrote in *Rachel and Her Children: Homeless Families in America* (1988) that if all the homeless children in the United States "were gathered in one city, they would represent a larger population than that of Atlanta, Denver, or St. Louis. Because they are scattered in a thousand cities, they are easily unseen."

In the 1990s families with children represent the most rapidly growing segment of the homeless population. A 1992 study sponsored by the Children's Defense Fund and the Center for Labor Market Studies at Boston's Northeastern University showed that a disproportionate number of Americans who lost their jobs in the recession of the early 1990s were 16 to 24 years old. According to Marian Wright Edelman, president of the Children's Defense Fund: "Job losses among young workers, often the parents of America's youngest and most vulnerable children, are creating a devastating cycle of declining earnings, declining family incomes and rising child poverty." In 1990 alone, according to the Children's Defense Fund, 841,000 children lived in families that slipped below the poverty line.

Poverty and homelessness are widespread in America, but they are not exclusively urban phenomena. Rural homelessness, although less visible than its urban counterpart, was a serious and mounting problem throughout the 1980s. High interest rates, mounting energy costs and stagnant or declining prices for farm products all contributed to the worst economic crisis in American agriculture since the years of the Great Depression. There were over 650,000 foreclosures on farms in the "farm crisis" of the 1980s, a decade that saw an average of 2,000 farmers giving up farming every week. Loss of a farm often represented to a family loss of both home and income. America's rural economy was also hard hit by economic downturns in timber, mining, petroleum and other extractive industries. As a result, the rural population declined in the 1980s, while rural poverty rates increased. In 1985 the poverty rate for nonmetropolitan areas of the United States was 18.3 percent, compared to 12.7 for metropolitan areas.

Studies of homelessness in California and Maryland in 1986 estimated that in each state 18 percent of their respective homeless populations resided in rural areas. The rural homeless tend to be overlooked because they are less concentrated than the urban homeless and spend less of their days in visible public spaces. Rather than sleeping on the streets, the rural homeless are more likely to sleep in their cars or in state and federal campground areas, or to double up with friends and relatives. The rural homeless tend to be younger, more likely to live in families and maintain stronger ties to local communities than the urban homeless. They include more women and fewer minorities in their ranks. The rural homeless also include migrant and seasonal farm workers. Despite such demographic differences, the rural homeless suffer from many of the same ills as the urban homeless, including hunger, alcohol and drug abuse, poor physical and mental health and the denial of education for their children. A special problem faced by the rural homeless is the lack of government or private services available to them.

In both rural areas and in cities, veterans make up a disproportionate share of the homeless population. It has been estimated that veterans comprise between a third and a half of the male homeless population in the United States. That is, using a conservative estimate of total homelessness, anywhere from 150,000 to 250,000 veterans are homeless on any given night, according to the Department of Veterans Affairs. Twice that number is likely to be homeless for some period during the course of a year.

Homeless veterans are certainly not new. Veterans of American wars have been a visible component of unemployed and homeless populations during earlier episodes of economic distress. The problems of World War I veterans were dramatized by the Bonus Army encampment in Washington, D.C. in 1932. World War II veterans had fewer difficulties, enjoying the generous support of the GI bill and returning to their civilian lives in a time of unprecedented prosperity and economic growth.

Things have been different for many Vietnam veterans. As a group they tended to be drawn from lower socioeconomic groups than in past wars, and consequently they had fewer occupational options upon returning to civilian life. Many had difficulty readjusting to civilian life because they felt that they were not honored by their communities for their service in a war that was unpopular and divisive. Many veterans of the Vietnam war suffered from posttraumatic stress disorder and other mental and physical problems connected with their time in the service. For many, these problems included drug abuse. An outreach program run by the Veterans Administration (VA) interviewed 7,800 homeless veterans in 1987. The survey revealed that 31 percent of the homeless veterans had had combat experience, 1.7 percent had been prisoners of war, 37.8 percent had served during Vietnam era, and 86 percent revealed symptoms of mental illness.

While some may argue that it is because of their sometimes bizarre appearance and public behavior that the mentally ill have been cited as emblematic of the homeless population, as we noted earlier, it has also proved convenient for some in power to focus on "deinstitutionalization" as the cause for the emergence of the homeless crisis. Estimates of the proportion of the chronically mentally ill among the homeless vary widely, from 10 percent to a majority of the total homeless population, but the focus on mental illness has more often been used to explain away the problem rather than understand it more thoroughly. That is, some observers have portrayed the problem of homelessness largely as a problem of mental health. Conservatives favor this argument, because it suggests that cuts in social welfare spending or the high cost of urban housing have had little to do with the emergence of the contemporary homeless crisis. For example, President Ronald Reagan told a television interviewer in December 1988 that a "large percentage" of the homeless were "retarded" people who had voluntarily left the institutions in which they had earlier been housed. And the neo-conservative columnist Charles Krauthammer, writing in 1985, claimed that a "majority of the homeless" were "near either psychosis or stupor." His main source for this claim was Ellen Bassuk's frequently cited study of the homeless in a Boston shelter, published in *Scientific American* in 1984, which found a "90 percent incidence of diagnosable mental illness: psychoses, chronic alcoholism and character disorders."

Other estimates of the percentage of the mentally ill among the homeless population run much lower, and Bassuk herself disagreed with the conclusions Krauthammer drew from her study. Estimates of the percentage of the homeless population with chronic mental illness gathered by the U.S. Conference of Mayors in a 1986 survey varied from a high of 60 percent in Louisville to a low of 15 percent in Philadelphia, Los Angeles, and New Orleans. New York governor Mario Cuomo's report to the National Governors' Association Task Force on the Homeless in 1983 contended:

> Lest there be any misunderstanding, the bulk of research to date indicates that (1) the majority of the homeless poor are not seriously mentally disabled; and that (2) even for those with severe disabilities, preferable alternatives to re-hospitalization exist, although in far too short a supply. Moreover, it is often not a simple matter to judge to what degree an observed disorder should be considered a cause, and to what degree a consequence of street-living.

Since the beginning of the 1980s, homelessness has been featured prominently in the media, in the public pronouncements of politicians and on the research agenda at "think tanks," foundations and social science departments of universities. But while many words have been produced, just how successful has anyone been in actually doing anything about the problem of homelessness? In the next section we consider some examples of what has actually been done, practically, to address the problem of homelessness in American society.

HOMELESSNESS AND SOCIAL ACTION

As we have seen, the problem of homelessness in American society is a complex, multidimensional one. This is as true for the solutions to the problem as it is for its causes and its victims. In the relatively short time that homelessness has been a part of the national consciousness, a myriad of organizations and initiatives have formed to address the problem in one way or another. In pages that follow we briefly review these efforts, realizing that none of them alone represent an ultimate solution.

Advocacy groups, impatient with the lack of governmental initiative, have played an important role in stirring the public conscience, pressuring policymakers and organizing the homeless and their supporters for social, political and legal action. One of the most active and effective advocacy groups for the homeless has been the National Coalition for the

Homeless. Founded in 1982 in New York City as the Coalition for the Homeless, in 1985 the organization changed its name and opened its headquarters in Washington, D.C. The Coalition, affiliated with some 500 local groups throughout the country, advocates permanent housing for all and a system of supportive services as the best long-term response to the problem of homelessness. To this end, it has conducted educational and legislative analysis, organized lobbying efforts and sponsored legal suits on behalf of the homeless.

Legal advocacy on behalf of the homeless has set some important precedents but has not always been the most effective means of addressing the problem. Because the U.S. Constitution does not guarantee the right to shelter, legal advocates for the homeless have focused their attentions at the state and local levels, where such a right can sometimes be found to be at least implied in statutes and constitutions. Perhaps the most famous case was *Callahan v. Carey* in New York City where, unlike most cities, shelter was provided for homeless persons before the 1980s. The suit was brought on behalf of one homeless man, Robert Callahan. It was settled in 1981 under a consent decree that stated: "The City . . . shall provide shelter and board to each homeless man who applies for it provided that (a) the man meets the need standard to qualify for the home relief program established in New York State; or (b) the man by reason of physical, mental or social dysfunction is in need of temporary shelter." A subsequent legal decision held that this decree applied equally to homeless women, and under the provisions of the consent decree, the city was required to expand the number of beds available for the homeless from 1,750 in 1979 to 7,000 by the mid-1980s. Though the total number of homeless in the city was then estimated to be many times larger than the expanded shelter capacity and was to expand rapidly in subsequent years, the decision proved to be an important precedent-setting legal victory for the homeless. Similarly, in a 1983 decision in *Hodge v. Ginsberg* (a class action suit brought on behalf of West Virginia's homeless by the United Mine Workers Union), the Supreme Court of Appeals of West Virginia declared that under the state's Social Services for Adults Act of 1981, the state was obligated to provide shelter, food and medical care for its homeless population.

A 1983 Superior Court decision in Los Angeles *(Eisenham v. County Board of Supervisors)* ruled that Los Angeles County could no longer restrict eligibility for emergency local shelter relief (in the form of housing vouchers or housing checks) by demanding the presentation of identification and imposing a waiting period of several days. Also in Los Angeles, the American Civil Liberties Union (ACLU) in 1987 filed suit and won an injunction to prevent the city from conducting "sweeps" to demolish homeless shantytowns built on vacant lots, without giving at least 12 hours' notice. In 1986 the American Bar Association (ABA) resolved to support enactment of federal, state and local laws that would "Prohibit discrimination on the basis of transient or homeless status in government assistance programs . . . and prohibit interference with the exercise of civil rights solely on the basis of transient or homeless status." And by 1989, an ABA "Representation of the Homeless Project" had organized pro bono legal services for the homeless in 20 cities.

But while lawsuits have been clearly successful in some cases and have kept public attention on the problem, often they have had only minimal impact on the social conditions of the homeless. Though the problem of homelessness has not been substantially reduced through legal efforts, by fighting for the homeless in the court system legal advocacy groups have helped maintain the focus of political leaders on the problem and have served to gain a measure of protection for those without shelter. Similarly, groups involved in direct action have played an important role in focusing the nation's attention on homelessness. Through imaginative and militant protests, groups of political activists have thrust the issue into the media spotlight while making life difficult for political leaders slow to respond to the needs of the homeless.

Perhaps the best known of these activist groups is the Community for Creative Non-violence (CCNV), a non-violent direct action group based in Washington, D.C. Dedicated to the fight to overcome poverty and homelessness, the organization was initially formed in 1970 to oppose the war in Vietnam. Mainly through educational activities, self-help programs and nonviolent social protest, CCNV increasingly focused its attention on the problems of the urban poor as the war in Vietnam drew to a close. For example, in 1973 the CCNV established a free medical clinic and a "community kitchen" to feed the poor. Soon the CCNV was feeding 400 people daily. And on New Year's Eve, 1976, on one of the coldest nights of the coldest winter in 50 years, the group took in its first homeless person, and then began to drive throughout the city to offer the homeless warm shelter.

Since then the CCNV has been in the forefront of action on behalf of the homeless, pressuring religious organizations and political leaders to do more. For example, in the mid-1970s the CCNV, joined by several socially conscious religious groups, launched a joint appeal to all 1,100 churches, synagogues and mosques in the Washington, D.C. area requesting that they open their buildings to the homeless. While a few responded with money and clothing, only one church offered actual shelter space. And during the winter of 1977–78, the organization responded to the freezing deaths of three homeless men by mounting a pressure campaign against city officials, who, after meeting with the CCNV agreed to open a vacant city-owned building to 75 homeless men as an asylum.

After other homeless people died from exposure on the streets of the nation's capital, the CCNV threatened to camp out on the street in front of city hall unless additional beds were provided. The city responded to the threat and to the pleas of religious leaders by expanding its facilities for the homeless to 500 beds. And after CCNV members occupied the National Visitor Center in Washington's Union Square station and invited people to sleep there, the city was pressured to agree to open a vacant school, which it had previously promised to use as a backup shelter. Through such acts of civil disobedience, the CCNV maintained pressure on the city, which expanded its facilities for the homeless.

In addition, members of the CCNV (which include homeless people as well as nonhomeless in its ranks) have fasted, petitioned and demonstrated outside supermarket chains that refuse to make available the discarded food from dumpsters. They have, in general, been a thorn in the side of city administrators, federal legislators and even the President of the United States. On Thanksgiving Day, 1981, in the midst of a dispute with the National Park Service over the right of the homeless to sleep in tents in Layfayette Park, the CCNV erected a tent community across from the White House, naming it "Reaganville" after the president.

Similarly, building occupations (or "squatting"), though infrequent, have been one direct action method by which the homeless have been able collectively to take the initiative and force cities to provide housing. Community activists have organized the poor and homeless to occupy and renovate abandoned government-owned buildings in Philadelphia, New York City, and elsewhere and in some cases have won permanent concessions from authorities fearful of engaging in a bitter eviction process. Because collective action is dramatic and disruptive, its practical effect may be too easily underestimated; collective action has often been an effective way to spur authorities who have the power and resources to make a difference yet lack the will to do so.

Some groups have sought to provide services directly to the homeless in the form of shelter programs and social service assistance. One such program is the Partnership for the

Homeless, a coalition of more than 300 churches and synagogues in New York City that, along with assistance from local and federal government, jointly manage about 100 private shelters for the homeless. The city provides supplies and technical assistance; the Federal Emergency Management Administration (FEMA), supplemented by private foundations, provides money for food; while the religious communities provide shelter sites (most in churches and synagogues), volunteers, and day-to-day management. In addition to shelter, the partnership helps people find child care, health, and social programs in local neighborhoods, while providing furniture and other household goods to those homeless people who move into city-owned apartments. The shelters established by the coalition have proved successful because they are small, communal environments and tend to involve local community residents (drawn from the church and synagogue congregations) in their planning and operating. The Partnership has served as a model for other community-based efforts in other cities across the country.

In addition to private and quasi-public efforts to provide needed services for the homeless, in recent years an increasing number of nonprofit organizations have been created to find permanent solutions to the problem. These initiatives have often sought to mobilize financial and human resources to try to increase the pool of housing stock available to those who have been squeezed out of the housing market. Thus, in the past decade a number of national organizations and grass-roots community groups have collaborated to draw upon both private and public sources of funding in efforts to initiate nonprofit housing development.

One of the most prominent of such groups is the Local Initiatives Support Corporation (LISC), founded by the Ford Foundation in 1979 to channel private-sector monies to community-based housing groups. In an era of government cutbacks for public and subsidized private housing, the LISC and similar groups were able to take up some of the slack through innovative "social investment banking." Under the provisions of the 1986 Federal Low-Income Housing Tax Credit, passed as part of that year's Tax Reform Act, the LISC and similar groups have been able to sell federal tax credits to corporations willing to invest in low-income housing. For a $2 million investment a participating corporation can receive up to $3 million in tax credits spread over the course of ten years. The LISC sponsors the National Equity Fund (NEF), which raised $77 million in 1989 from 35 corporations to create $200 million worth of affordable housing for 2,000 low-income households. This proved to be the largest single corporate investment in community-based low-income housing ever made in the United States. The LISC has been involved in building and rehabilitation projects from the South Bronx to the Tenderloin district of San Francisco. It has also financed the building or rehabilitation of commercial and industrial real estate in neighborhoods that are in physical decline, such as a new shopping center in Miami's Liberty City district.

The LISC has worked closely with existing community development groups. For example, by 1990 groups in New York City such as the Banana Kelly Community Improvement Association, Bronx United in Leveraging Dollars (Build), and Asian-Americans for Equality had produced more than 1,000 new apartments, with 2,000 more under construction or being designed. In the projects sponsored by these groups, rents in the late 1980s ranged from $400 to $450, with 10 percent of units in the buildings set aside for the homeless who paid the welfare shelter allowance, $312 a month for a family of four. The Banana Kelly Community Improvement Association began in the mid-1970s to fight housing abandonment in the Longwood section of the South Bronx. By 1990 Banana Kelly managed buildings with more than 700 apartments and had supervised the reconstruction of eight large abandoned apartment buildings through "sweat equity," as well as five smaller abandoned buildings and 20 occupied but rundown buildings taken over by the city from defaulting landlords.

Though community nonprofit groups have developed viable housing programs and have established a reliable record of providing long-term management for the projects they have constructed or rehabilitated, in our view the scale of the homeless in the United States is so great that substantial government resources will be essential for any comprehensive solution to the problem. But for all of its importance, the problem of homelessness cannot be reduced to a simple matter of housing. The problem is inextricably bound to a range of social issues; an effective comprehensive policy will have to entail a broader effort to provide jobs at a living wage, employment training, health care, drug and alcohol treatment, child care for working parents and other human needs that are currently unmet in our society. In short, homelessness will be solved only as part of a comprehensive social policy, one that simply does not exist at present. This is a tall order, particularly because in recent years a backlash against the homeless has developed in many communities.

Increasingly, the presence of the homeless on the streets has stirred feelings of anger and fear among the many Americans forced to pass by them on a daily basis. Frustration over this problem may be beginning to have political consequences. For example, in the fall of 1991 Art Agnos, mayor of San Francisco, was defeated for reelection in a campaign that turned largely on the issue of whether he had been too slow to dislodge an encampment of homeless people from in front of city hall. It symbolized the growing frustration of voters toward the persistence of homelessness and may have been suggestive of the direction that Americans elsewhere will choose in channeling their frustrations over this issue.

Further evidence of the backlash was reported in 1991 by the United States Conference of Mayors in its anual *Status Report on Hunger and Homelessness*. Officials in 48 percent of the cities surveyed reported that they had seen evidence that public sentiment toward the homeless had become increasingly negative in the past year. One city official in Boston reported: "People have become more concerned with the increasing numbers of mentally ill people on the streets. They are also concerned with the apparent increase of panhandlers." An official in New York City spoke of "compassion fatigue" among the public, while a Kansas City official reported: "We are beginning to get backlash reactions, especially in the downtown area, as more homeless aggressively beg and try to sell homeless newspapers on the streets. Reactions include the public closing their pocketbooks to shelters, or blaming the victim because the problem has not gone away. Economic problems of the middle class have also resulted in less tolerance."

Feelings of hostility to the homeless have given rise to what policymakers have termed *NIMBY*, "Not-In-My-Back-Yard" syndrome. Politicians and community residents often obstruct efforts to place homeless shelters in their own community. The NIMBY syndrome was much in evidence in New York City in the fall of 1991 when Mayor David Dinkins announced a $258 million program to decentralize the shelter system. His administration had listed 35 potential sites for smaller shelters that would have created 2,500 sorely needed additional shelter beds. Three new sites were proposed in Manhattan, seven on Staten Island, seven in Brooklyn, seven in the Bronx, and 11 in Queens, but public protest from the affected neighborhoods was immediate and angry. Peter Vallone, a councilman from Queens and the City Council speaker, declared: the "[Dinkins' plan is] unnecessarily frightening all the people of the city, and it doesn't make any sense. It's spreading homelessness and hopelessness throughout. It's almost as if you're saying we have a serious disease and we'll spread it so everybody will suffer from it."

Countervailing sentiments can also be heard. The Reverend Thomas J. Harvey, president of Catholic Charities, told a reporter in 1991 that "During the Reagan administration the responsibility for many social welfare programs was shifted from the Federal level to the states, and now with some 40 states facing budget deficits, the government role is really contracting." The onset of a severe economic recession in the early 1990s stretched the resources of Catholic Charities, but it also created a new awareness, according to Harvey, of the seriousness of the plight of the homeless. "This kind of downturn reminds people that there are capricious forces at work," Harvey declared in December 1991. "It explodes the myths that the poor are poor out of choice because people see their neighbors going unemployed due to circumstances beyond their control." Similarly, events such as the Los Angeles riots of 1992 have served to focus national attention on the conditions of poverty and unemployment in urban America. But translating the social concerns of individuals into thoughtful and effective government policy has never been simple or direct. It seems that political leaders often speak of pressing social needs with great eloquence and compassion, only to acquiesce later to the pressures of powerful lobbies whose narrow interests may require that they obstruct or limit social reform.

For example, in 1949 the National Housing Act was passed as part of the Fair Deal programs of President Harry Truman, who declared that it should be federal policy to guarantee "the goal of a decent home and a suitable living environment for every American family, thus contributing to the development and redevelopment of communities and to the advancement of the growth, wealth, and security of the nation." The bill was passed, but endured stiff opposition from conservatives in Congress, who forced significant concessions on behalf of the powerful real estate lobby. While the act pledged the support of the federal government in the construction of 810,000 units of public housing, it also limited the design of public housing buildings to unattractive, boxlike structures without ornamental features, in order that this housing would not compete with the private rental market. In this and other ways, residing in public housing in the United States became a source of stigmatization, reserved for the poorest sector of the population, rather than a viable source of attractive and secure housing for a large portion of the population (as it was in Britain, for example). Moreover, those provisions in the act that called for slum clearance and urban renewal were used by real estate interests in many cities to tear down older but affordable housing, replacing it with luxury apartments, government buildings, or commercial development. Low-income urban dwellers were usually left out "in the cold." Generally speaking, despite the good intentions of those who formulate social programs on behalf of the powerless, the actual policies themselves have often tended to reflect the concerns and the interests of the powerful.

Recent social policy toward homelessness reflects this paradox at least as clearly as it did in 1949 when the National Housing Act was passed. The first federal legislative effort to address the contemporary homeless problem was the Steward B. McKinney Homeless Assistance Act, signed into law in July 1987. President Reagan opposed the bill, objecting to both its cost and what he called its "duplicative programs." Because the measure had such strong support in both houses of Congress, he did not, however, threaten a veto. The legislation authorized the spending of over $400 million in homeless aid for 1987 and over $600 million for 1988 (although the amounts actually appropriated were far less). The purpose of the bill was defined as meeting "the critically urgent needs of the nation's homeless," and included 20 different provisions for emergency shelter funds, health care, job training and other programs, with seven federal agencies participating. Though the McKinney Act bolstered and coordinated shelters and other services for the homeless, because the administration had severely cut funding for federal housing programs (from $39 billion annually at the beginning of the decade to $8 billion at its close) and had sharply reduced grants to states, cities, and local communities as well as other social welfare programs that had been relied on for programs for the poor, the result was a sharp drop in the overall resources available to address many of the causes of homelessness.

Government social policy on homelessness that concentrates on strengthening the shelter system while simultaneously cutting funding for low-income housing construction is not designed as a long-range strategy to solving the problem of homelessness. Though there may be more shelter beds available than at any time in American history, homeless advocates emphasize that shelters are not the answer to the problem. They are at best a temporary expedient, a stopgap measure of last resort. Not only does the emphasis on the shelter system fail to address the problem of permanent housing for the homeless, but it stigmatizes those who turn to it. Like "poor relief" in the last century, and public housing, the food stamp program, and other public welfare programs, the shelter system seems to foster shame, helplessness and dependency on the part of those who enter it, instead of a sense of power, control and confidence in one's ability to shape one's own life. While providing people with protection from the elements, the rituals of obtaining food and a bed in the shelter system also reinforce a sense of powerlessness.

Despite the goodwill displayed by many Americans and initiatives undertaken by advocacy groups and nonprofit organizations, the problem of homelessness in America remains acute. Indeed, the severe recession of 1992 forced tens of thousands of Americans to discover anew the fear and pain of living without permanent shelter. Such insecurities may become a permanent feature of our social and economic landscape. The competitive jostling between businesses will result in the continual "downsizing" of firms, which for the forseeable future means an increase in unemployment and stagnation of occupational mobility for workers at all levels.

The notion of the "American Dream" once conjured up images and hopes of upward mobility, if not in one's own lifetime, then certainly in the lives of one's children. The possibility of owning one's own home used to be at the very center of that dream: For many it was a virtual expectation, and for most it was at least a reasonable and reachable goal. But this is changing. After years of steady increases, the rate of homeownership began to turn down at the end of the 1980s as stagnating incomes and rising housing costs prevented ever larger numbers of young workers and their families from being able to afford their own homes. Because the cultural symbolism of the home is so central and because its meaning is so bound to a sense of security, community and family, widespread homelessness has been jarring to the American consciousness since the early 1980s. It reminds us of the fragility of those things that we value as well as of our own vulnerability.

A *New York Times*/CBS News poll taken in January 1992 reported some disturbing findings. People were asked to respond to the question: "Do you think that when most people see the homeless they feel upset, or do you think that most people have gotten so used to seeing the homeless that they don't feel upset by them?" Forty-two percent of respondents asked felt that people were upset by the sight of the homeless; 44 percent felt that people were not upset. By age group, 45 percent of people 65 and older responded that people felt upset by the sight of the homeless, compared to only 35 percent of people 18 to 29 years old. Fifty-five percent of those 18 to 29 years old felt that "People have gotten so used to seeing the homeless that they don't feel upset by them." In other words, people who came of age in the 1980s were considerably more likely to accept the existence of homelessness as a normal part of the social landscape than those who reached adulthood in preceding decades. This suggests that the longer homelessness is allowed to exist in our society, the more difficult it will become to mobilize the public to do something about the problem.

The continued growth of homelessness raises fundamental questions about our values as a society. Are we willing to be our brothers' and sisters' keepers? In 1630 the Puritan leader John Winthrop delivered a sermon to his followers aboard the *Arabella*, the flagship of the expedition that was carrying settlers to New England. The new settlement, he declared, would be like "a city on a hill." President Reagan was fond of citing this phrase. Less often remembered in the 1980s were the conditions that Winthrop laid down for the realization of this dream:

> For this end, we must be knit together in this work as one man, we must entertain each other in brotherly affection, we must be willing to abridge ourselves of our superfluities, for the supply of others necessities, we must uphold a familiar Commerce together in all meekness, gentleness, patience and liberality, we must delight in each other, make others Conditions our own, rejoice together, mourn together, labor and suffer together, always having before our eyes our Commission and Community in the work, our Community as members of the same body. . . .

Can we solve our problems collectively, "as members of the same body," or have we become so alienated and cynical and despairing as a nation that we have no choice but to grow hardened and callous to the suffering in our midst? Can we come to grips with the problem of homelessness, recognizing that people sleeping on subways and begging in the streets may be symptoms of a systemic illness? Such self-scrutiny may prove uncomfortable. It will raise disturbing questions about the distribution of wealth in our society and the ways in which we allocate resources for such basic necessities as health care, nutrition, education, child care, jobs, and, of course, housing. It will raise questions about how we reconcile our values of equal opportunity with our reliance on market principles to allocate our resources. These are not easy questions, and they do not have easy solutions. But we gain nothing by ignoring them. To confront the problem of homelessness is to confront who we are as a people and what kind of "city on a hill" we wish to construct as we enter the 21st century.

A

abandonment A process generally occurring in low-income neighborhoods in which a landlord abandons those properties that no longer provide an acceptable profit, thus giving up title to the property without compensation. Abandonment is often the final step in the process of disinvestment, whereby landlords allow buildings to deteriorate by witholding necessary services and maintenance. Abandonment often results in the DISPLACEMENT of low-income residents. (See also GENTRIFICATION; REDLINING.)

ACORN The Association of Community Organizations for Reform Now (ACORN) was founded in 1970 in Little Rock, Arkansas. Its purpose was to build a multiracial, statewide, neighborhood-based organization and mobilize low- and moderate-income people to fight for and defend their collective interests. Currently the organization is the largest low-income membership organization in the country, with 75,000 African-American, Hispanic and white families in 26 states.

Wade Rathke, a community organizer, introduced the name ACORN (which originally stood for "Arkansas Community Organizations for Reform Now") in the midst of the group's first organizing effort, a "furniture for families" campaign. In this struggle, Rathke organized hundreds of welfare recipients to storm the state welfare office to demand free furniture, a previously mandated state welfare benefit that was not being provided to the poor. With the state government completely unprepared for direct action protest and with his reelection bid pending, Governor Winthrop Rockefeller established a new agency to distribute used furniture, appliances and clothing for over 1,000 families. This initial success served to draw large numbers of low-income families to ACORN.

Between 1975 and 1980 ACORN spread to over 40 communities nationwide, fighting urban renewal schemes, toxic chemical dangers, tenant evictions and bank DISINVESTMENT. In the early 1980s ACORN in Philadelphia organized a SQUATTING campaign to take over and renovate vacant city-owned properties. ACORN activists had been organizing to force the city to make low-income households eligible for the city's Gift Property Program of urban HOMESTEADING. When the city failed to respond, ACORN recruited hundreds of low-income families to seize, occupy and repair the abandoned structures. In May 1982 the Philadelphia city council passed a bill allowing abandoned tax-delinquent properties to be deeded to resident squatters, provided they agreed to make the repairs necessary to bring houses up to code. By 1982 ACORN had organized 200 squatters in 13 cities. The tactics sometimes succeeded and sometimes did not: Squatters were evicted and arrested in Pittsburgh, St. Louis and Dallas, but also forced concessions from city officials in Ft. Worth, Detroit and Tulsa.

The purpose of ACORN has shifted periodically. At certain points its emphasis has been on organizing low-income communities, while at others it has mobilized moderate-income working-class people; sometimes its focus has been to expand the membership, at other times it has sought to consolidate itself. It is known as an innovative organization, employing a broad range of tactics, from lobbying, petitioning and legal suits, to militant confrontation (including marches, picketlines, sit-ins and squatting). The organization is largely self-sufficient, with 80 percent of its expenses covered by membership dues, staff-run canvassing campaigns, raffles, dances and small businesses run by the organization.

advocacy groups See Appendix I.

acquired immune deficiency syndrome (AIDS) Among the many health problems besetting the homeless, acquired immune deficiency syndrome (AIDS) is perhaps the most deadly. AIDS is a disease caused by the human immunodeficiency virus (HIV), which attacks the immune system and damages its ability to fight other diseases. People with AIDS are vulnerable to infection by bacteria, protozoa, fungi and other viruses and malignancies that may cause life-threatening illness such as pneumonia, meningitis or cancer, including some otherwise rare types. People with AIDS-related complex (ARC) have symptoms of AIDS but not the full-blown disease. Common symptoms included swollen glands or fever, weight loss or persistent diarrhea. AIDS was first diagnosed in the United States in 1981. By the spring of 1992, 218,301 Americans had been diagnosed with AIDS; of these 141,223 had already died. The Centers for Disease Control estimate that an additional 1 million to 1.5 million Americans are infected with HIV. HIV, a transmissible bloodborne virus, can be spread through sexual intercourse in which blood, semen, preseminal fluid or vaginal secretions are exchanged; injection with blood-contaminated needles; blood transfusions; or from infected mothers to their newborn infants. No cure presently exists for AIDS, but some experimental medicines can prolong the lives of some infected people.

In some countries in Africa, HIV infection and subsequent cases of ARC and AIDS have been found primarily among heterosexual populations. In contrast, in the United States AIDS was found initially among urban gay men. By the end of the 1980s, however, AIDS was on its way to becoming a disease of the urban minority poor, spreading rapidly among intravenous drug users, their sexual partners and their offspring. According to a 1990 report issued by the National Coalition for the Homeless, in Newark, New Jersey, where a third of the city's population lives at or below the poverty line, a fifth of the population may be HIV-seropositive. The incidence of AIDS among African Americans and Hispanics is three times that of the incidence in the white population in the United States. According to the Centers for Disease Control, African Americans make up 12 percent of the U.S. population, 27 percent of adult AIDS cases and 53 percent of pediatric AIDS cases; Hispanics make up 6 percent of the U.S. population, 15 percent of adult cases and 23 percent of pediatric cases.

AIDS is a disease increasingly associated with homelessness. In New York City as many as 10 percent of homeless shelter residents may be infected. Homeless advocates estimated in 1991 that there are 13,000 people with AIDS or AIDS-related illnesses in the city who lack permanent housing. A 1987 study of 16 U.S. cities estimated the incidence of AIDS and AIDS-related complex at 185 per 100,000 homeless persons in those cities, compared to 144 per 100,000 for the U.S. population as a whole. Many homeless people contract AIDS because they are intravenous drug users, but AIDS is also a *cause* of homelessness. People with AIDS may lose employment and housing because they have the disease, and federal welfare regulations require them to "spend down" their financial resources to become eligible for SOCIAL SECURITY DISABILITY INSURANCE (SSDI) benefits. Homeless people with AIDS tend to become even sicker than the general population of people with AIDS, because of their exposure to secondary infections and the stress of life on the streets or in crowded emergency shelters. Despite the fact that AIDS cannot be spread by casual contact, AIDS-infected homeless people seeking shelter sometimes find themselves shunned, assaulted and even excluded from public shelters. One homeless man with AIDS, who lived for three years in the Fort Washington Men's Shelter in New York City, told a reporter from the *New York Times* in 1991 that he would take showers in the middle of the night so that no one could see the evidence of his illness. "If they were to know you're HIV-positive, the other clients would be flipping over your bed, breaking into your personal locker, to get you out."

A by-product of the AIDS epidemic has been the growing number of hospitalized "boarder babies" who are suffering from AIDS and whose parents are dead or unable or unwilling to care for them at home. The Centers for Disease Control reported 1,432 cases of pediatric AIDS (children with AIDS under 13 years of age) were known to exist in 1989, and by 1992, that number had risen to 3,471, with estimates for the number of HIV-infected children ranging from 10,000 to 20,000. Pediatric AIDS is already the ninth leading cause of infant death in the United States, and a report provided to the U.S. House of Representatives Committee on Appropriations in 1992 stated a 24 percent increase in pediatric AIDS cases in 1989–90, compared with a 15 percent increase in adult cases during the same period. Infants can acquire the AIDS virus from their mothers during pregnancy, labor and delivery, or through their mother's breast milk. Four out of five children infected with the HIV virus are born to parents who are intravenous drug abusers. AIDS leads to death much more quickly in infants than in adults. The average age of diagnosis of AIDS in infants is 9 months, and the average age at the time of death is 18 months. In 1989 First Lady Barbara Bush helped publicize the plight of boarder babies through a visit to Grandma's House, a privately sponsored home in Washington, D.C. for children infected with HIV or with AIDS. She played with and kissed several of the children, in an effort to counter irrational fears of these young victims of the disease.

Older homeless children are often at risk of acquiring AIDS, since many of them are forced into prostitution or "survival sex" to survive on the streets. In New York City an estimated 6.5 percent of homeless youth from the age of 16 to 20 are HIV-seropositive, a percentage that jumps to 17 percent of the 20-year-olds.

Few resources are yet available to serve the special needs of the homeless AIDS population. Getting people with AIDS off the street can, in itself, lead to an improvement in their condition. A woman suffering from the disease who was able to leave the shelters and move into a city-provided two-bedroom apartment in Brooklyn regained 19 pounds in a year and was able to care for her son again for the first time in three years. "I don't think I would have made it this long," she told a reporter from the *New York Times*, without the apartment. When she lived in a shelter, "I wasn't happy and that's all part of this disease. If there's too much on you, stress, it brings you down." But in New York City, with its estimated 13,000 homeless people with HIV-related illnesses, there are just 1300 housing units available with the necessary services.

As growing numbers of HIV-infected individuals progress to later stages of the disease, the AIDS population is expected to represent a steadily larger part of the total homeless population. By 1995 the number of homeless people with AIDS in the United States is expected to grow to 100,000. In October 1990 Congress approved the National Affordable Housing Act, which included the AIDS Housing Opportunity Program. The legislation authorized the spending of $156 million to set up community residences or offer rent subsidies to people with AIDS. Peter Smith, president of the Partnership of the Homeless, responded to the bill's passage by commenting that the money authorized "isn't anywhere near what is really needed to meet this swiftly growing need, but it is a giant step forward considering that funding such programs has been completely ignored almost a decade into the epidemic." The Bush administration's budget for fiscal year 1992 did not include any funding for this program.

affordable housing   According to the definition used by the Department of Housing and Urban Development (HUD), housing is "affordable" for low-income people if it costs no more than 30 percent of the household's income.

Affordable Housing Act   See CRANSTON-GONZALEZ NATIONAL AFFORDABLE HOUSING ACT.

African-Americans   Blacks account for about 10 percent of the population of the United States but for a third or more of the nation's homeless population. (Together with Hispanics and Native Americans, minorities add up to a majority of the homeless.) According to the 1991 *Status Report on Hunger and Homelessness* issued by the United States Conference of Mayors, African-Americans comprised two-thirds or more of the homeless population of Detroit, Los Angeles, Louisville, New Orleans, Portland, San Antonio and San Diego.

The disproportionate share of African Americans in the homeless population is startling. Although African Americans have always been overrepresented among the poor in the United States, they were underrepresented in SKID ROW populations earlier in the century. As the bright hopes of the civil rights movement and the WAR ON POVERTY faded in the 1970s and 1980s, social commentators spoke of the emergence of an urban minority UNDERCLASS, mired in poverty, criminality and addiction. In many respects, the same social forces were at work in recent decades to generate the "underclass" and the "homeless."

The presence of a large number of minorities within the general homeless population has complicated public attitudes toward the problem of homelessness. John Coleman, former president of Haverford College, spent ten days on the streets and in the emergency shelter system in New York City pretending to be a homeless person. He reported his own discomfort with the "many young, intensely angry blacks" he encountered in the Men's Shelter on East 3rd Street:

Hatred pours out in all of their speech and some of their actions . . . Hundreds and hundreds of men here have been destroyed by alcohol or drugs. A smaller, but for me more poignant, number are being destroyed by hate. Their loudest message—and because their voices are so strong it is very loud indeed—is "Respect me, man." The constant theme is that someone or some group is putting them down, stepping on them, asking them to conform to a code they don't accept, getting in their way, writing them off.

The civil rights movement and the war on poverty programs in the 1960s enjoyed some genuine victories and helped close the social gap between whites and minorities. The movement was remarkably successful in striking down discriminatory legislation that had stood for a century or longer. But other forms of racial discrimination, enshrined in custom if not in law, persisted. Minorities have always faced discrimination in the urban housing market and have always had to spend a higher proportion of their income in order to secure adequate housing. African Americans were locked out of homeownership by prejudice and also by government policy. Federal mortgage-loan guarantees, such as those provided by the Federal Housing Administration (FHA), were largely unavailable to African Americans. The FHA's 1938 *Underwriting Manual* offered this guideline to bank officers: "If a neighborhood is to retain stability, it is necessary that properties shall continue to be occupied by the same social and racial classes." Less than 2 percent of all housing financed with federal mortgage insurance was made available to blacks between 1946 and 1959. The Reverend Martin Luther King, Jr. led protest marches in Chicago in the mid-1960s, demanding an end to discriminatory real estate and rental practices, but this campaign was one of his least successful. Problems of inadequate housing in African-American neighborhoods were exacerbated in the 1980s by cuts in social welfare spending initiated by President Ronald Reagan.

Longer-range economic changes have also had an impact, especially the shift in the American economy away from manufacturing to "service" industries. While the overall national UNEMPLOYMENT rate has moved into double digits only once since the Great Depression (reaching 10.7 percent in the "Reagan recession" of 1982), the African-American unemployment has rarely dropped below double digits in recent years. Between 1981 and 1986 the annual African-American unemployment rate averaged 17 percent, and peaked at 19.5 percent in 1983. Sociologist William Julius Wilson argued in 1986:

> Blacks have borne the brunt of deindustrialization with their heavy concentration in the steel, automobile, rubber and textile industries. If you look at the data on blacks moving out of poverty throughout the 1940s, the 1950s, the 1960s, you see that much of that movement was due to getting higher-paying jobs in the industrial sector. That has all been reversed.

Blacks made striking economic gains because of the civil rights movement. In 1960 African-American men earned about 31 percent as much as whites; by 1986 they were earning on average 73 percent of white income. But as the industrial base of urban America declined through the 1970s and 1980s, millions of black families and individuals remained locked in poverty. The 1980 Census revealed that the overall poverty rate for the country was 10 percent for whites and 32 percent for African Americans. A 1989 study by the National League of Cities showed that African Americans and other minority Americans were more likely than whites to live in extremely poor neighborhoods, and that poverty among African Americans was more persistent than for other groups. More than 21 percent of African Americans living in big cities were poor throughout the ten years from 1974 to 1983, compared to less than 3 percent average for other groups.

Agnos, Art   Art Agnos was elected mayor of San Francisco in 1987 and defeated for reelection in 1991. His defeat was attributed to public dissatisfaction with his reluctance to use the police to close down an encampment of the homeless in the park outside of San Francisco's city hall. He was the first major political figure to lose office for, in effect, being "soft" on the homeless.

AIDS   See ACQUIRED IMMUNE DEFICIENCY SYNDROME.

Aid to Families with Dependent Children (AFDC)

Aid to Families with Dependent Children (AFDC) is one of the cornerstones of the federal social welfare system. Established in 1935 as Aid to Dependent Children, a relatively minor program within the Social Security system, the number of AFDC recipients increased markedly in the 1960s and 1970s (from just over 3 million in 1960 to over 11 million by 1975). In the early 1980s, one out of every eight children in the United States was dependent on AFDC. However, AFDC eligibility and payment standards were tightened three times by the Reagan administration. Between 1981 and 1988, $3.6 billion in AFDC funds was cut, with over 440,000 families dropped from the average monthly caseload. By 1988 the average monthly caseload was just under 11 million recipients, with a cost to the federal government and the states of $16.6 billion. Between 1989 and 1992, caseloads rose by 27 percent, and in a report in the December 13, 1993 *U.S. News and World Report,* 14.2 million Americans were said to be recipients of AFDC, with one in seven children receiving funds.

AFDC is administered within the Department of Health and Human Services. The federal government pays at least half of the cost of the AFDC program, while states and localities pay the rest. Since each state administers the program separately and sets its own benefit levels, the level of AFDC support varies dramatically from state to state: In 1983 the monthly payment to an incomeless single parent with two children amounted to nearly $700 a month in Washington state, but to less than $100 a month in Mississippi. Two-thirds of the recipients of AFDC benefits are children. Most of them come from female-headed families. Women who are divorced or who have been abandoned by their male partners make up the majority of AFDC clients, though in some states families with unemployed fathers present in the household are also eligible. While the program is not specifically targeted to the homeless, homeless families are included among its broader clientele. AFDC provides cash benefits to families in which a needy child has been deprived of support due to death, incapacitation, continued absence or unemployment of a parent. Some states including California, Illinois and New York provide special needs allowances under the AFDC program for such items as training and educational expenses, child care costs, special diets and shelter for the homeless.

AFDC came under attack from conservative politicians in the 1980s. President Reagan declared in a 1986 speech that "under existing welfare rules a teen-age girl who becomes pregnant can make herself eligible for welfare benefits that will set her up in an apartment of her own, provide medical care, and feed and clothe her. She has to fulfill only one condition—not to marry or identify the father." A prevalent stereotype of AFDC recipients regards them as "welfare queens" from the nation's inner cities, who bear one illegitimate child after another in order to remain on and increase their AFDC benefits. It is true that the proportion of households headed by single females has markedly increased in recent decades, up from 6 percent of all households in 1950 to nearly 25 percent in the 1980s. By 1988, 12.9 percent of white families and 42.8 percent of African-American families were female-headed. In 1988 African Americans made up 40 percent and Hispanics accounted for 15 percent of those receiving AFDC benefits; 39 percent were white.

Most mothers on AFDC bore their children out of wedlock. Contrary to stereotypes, however, three-quarters of all AFDC households have two or fewer children. Only 25 percent of AFDC recipients have received benefits for five or more years, and less than 10 percent have received benefits for over a decade. More than half of all recipients of AFDC leave the program voluntarily before their third year.

AFDC provides, at best, a minimal level of comforts to families dependent on the program. Average AFDC stipends amount to about a seventh of the average American family income, and most households receiving AFDC and related benefits subsist at below the POVERTY LEVEL. In most states the combined value of AFDC and food stamps benefits will bring a family income up only to about 75 percent or less of the poverty level. Because AFDC payments, unlike the Social Security system's Old Age Insurance payments, have not been indexed to the Consumer Price Index, they have lost much of their value in recent years. Between 1970 and 1991, the average value of real benefits fell by 41 percent. In the most generous states, AFDC benefits for a family of three put their annual income at only about four-fifths the official poverty level; in many states the benefits for such a family fall beneath 50 percent of those at the poverty level. Public and legislative hostility to AFDC recipients has also led to an increasing number of states requiring recipients to participate in so-called WORKFARE programs. In 1988 Congress passed the Family Support Act, which requires states to initiate job search, training or work programs enrolling at least one-fifth of their AFDC recipients by 1995.

The National Coalition for the Homeless contends that the inadequate level of AFDC benefits is a direct cause of homelessness. Emergency shelter operators have reported that they often encounter homeless families already receiving AFDC payments. Sixty-eight percent of AFDC families live in urban areas where housing costs are likely to be higher than average. Nearly two-thirds of AFDC families spend half or more of their income for housing. Cutbacks in federal subsidized housing have also made it more difficult for AFDC families to find adequate housing; only 18.7 percent of AFDC recipients in 1988 were in public housing or receiving a HUD SECTION 8 subsidy. The record of AFDC lends support to the saying among social service providers that "programs for poor people are poor programs."

Albrecht, Chris   See COMIC RELIEF.

alcoholism   It has been estimated that up to 40 percent of the homeless are alcohol abusers. Alcoholism, the excessive use of alcohol either periodically or continuously, is one of the nation's major health problems, afflicting at least 10 million people. Attitudes toward the use of alcohol have changed periodically and dramatically in American history. In the 17th and 18th centuries alcohol consumption per capita was considerably higher than any time thereafter. Alcohol was a common feature of public gatherings, such as militia training days, and workmen drank steadily through their working day. Drunkenness was not regarded as either a sin or a crime. But in the 19th century the consumption of alcohol came to be associated with new immigrant groups such as the Irish and Germans and the dangers of a rapidly urbanizing society. The temperance movement, closely associated with evangelical Protestant revivalism, sought to limit or eliminate the consumption of alcohol. In 1919 Congress passed the 18th Amendment to the Constitution, outlawing the possession, sale or consumption of alcoholic beverages. Prohibition in the 1920s led to the widespread violation of the law, with alcohol smuggled in or illegally produced in the country and illegally sold and consumed in "speakeasies." Gangsters such as Al Capone got rich on the proceeds, while violence between gangsters and police and between rival gangs of "bootleggers" broke out in the streets. The country grew weary of the flawed experiment of prohibition, and in 1933 Congress repealed the 18th Amendment.

In recent years alcoholism has come to be seen as a disease rather than a crime. Among the health problems associated with alcoholism are cirrhosis of the liver, cancer, diabetes and diseases of the heart, stomach and pancreas. Alcoholism is a contributing factor in tens of thousands of traffic deaths, murders and suicides every year. When pregnant women drink alcohol, even in moderate amounts, it can impair the development of the fetus and the newborn child, resulting in fetal alcohol syndrome (which can include growth deficiencies, physical malformation and mental retardation). Alcoholics have a life expectancy ten to 12 years shorter than the average. While the popular image of the alcoholic has been the Skid Row "drunken bum" lying unconscious in the gutter, the overwhelming majority of alcoholics do have homes, jobs and families. But alcoholism is also widespread among those living near or below the POVERTY LINE, affecting an estimated 15 percent to 35 percent of the poor. Among the homeless population, alcoholism is sometimes the cause of homelessness. But as homeless advocates point out, alcoholism can also be a consequence of the despair associated with poverty and homelessness. (See the figure under MENTAL ILLNESS, for the prevalence of alcohol/drug problems among the adult homeless. See also SUBSTANCE ABUSE.)

Alexandria, Virginia   According to the 1991 *Status Report on Hunger and Homelessness* issued by the United States Conference of Mayors, Alexandria, Virginia had an estimated homeless population of 1,516. The city had 223 beds available in emergency shelters and 134 beds available for families seeking shelter. On a typical day in the fall of 1991, 160 individuals sought shelter in the city. The average length of stay in a shelter in the city increased. According to a city official quoted in the report:

The City of Alexandria is located in a metropolitan area with an extremely high cost of living which makes it extremely difficult for those households with marginal incomes. Already these households pay a disproportionately high percentage of their income for basic necessities (shelter, utilities, food, clothing). Any unforeseen loss of income or additional expenses place these households at risk of homelessness. Further, the recession [of 1990–91] affects these households the greatest and has resulted in the loss of jobs for many in the construction, retail and food service industries.

almshouses See WORKHOUSES.

Altman, Drew See ROBERT WOOD JOHNSON FOUNDATION.

American Bar Association Representation of the Homeless Project (AB-ARHP) The Representation of the Homeless Project sponsored by the American Bar Association is based in Washington, D.C. and assists state and local bar association in the implementation and maintenance of programs for the homeless. It has published a Research Guide on Bar Homeless Programs. (See also LEGAL RIGHTS.)

American Civil Liberties Union (ACLU) The American Civil Liberties Union (ACLU) grew out of efforts by anti-war opponents to protect the rights of conscientious objectors and other opponents of World War I. It was established as a permanent organization in 1920, under the leadership of Roger N. Baldwin. In the 1920s and 1930s the ACLU defended labor organizers, radicals and members of minority religious groups against attempts by legal authorities to deny them freedom of speech. In the 1950s the ACLU fought a defensive battle against the abuses of "McCarthyism," the hysterical fear of domestic communism. Beginning in the 1960s the ACLU expanded its concerns beyond traditional civil liberties issues, into such areas as the rights of women, homosexuals, prisoners and the

mentally ill. It was the concern over the latter that brought the ACLU into the Joyce Brown case in New York City in 1987, a case involving a homeless woman who was taken off the streets by the authorities and hospitalized against her will. The ACLU has been involved in a number of other cases around the country involving the rights of the homeless. In 1987, for example, the ACLU filed suit in Los Angeles and won an injunction to prevent the city from conducting "sweeps" to demolish homeless shantytowns built on vacant lots without giving at least 12 hours' notice. In 1988 the ACLU brought suit against the City of Miami to stop the police from arresting homeless people for sleeping, standing or otherwise occupying public sidewalks, parks or buildings and to prevent the practice of rounding the homeless up and destroying their property. In 1991 Federal District Judge C. Clyde Atkins held Miami in contempt after finding that the police had violated his ban on destroying the possessions of homeless people camped in parks and beneath overpasses. He also directed the city to allow lawyers from the ACLU to attend any meetings where officials discussed matters affecting the homeless. (See also LEGAL RIGHTS; MENTAL ILLNESS; VAGRANCY.)

American Institute of Architects The American Institute of Architects, based in Washington, D.C., sponsors the Search for Shelter program. The program assists the development of local coalitions of providers, professionals, government officials and others to foster education and action around the issue of homelessness.

American Red Cross The American Red Cross, which has its headquarters in Washington, D.C., provides services to those made homeless by disaster. Local chapters also provide services to the homeless through funding by the Stewart B. McKinney Homeless Assistance Act. (See MCKINNEY ACT.)

Anti-Drug Abuse Act of 1986 See
HOMELESS ELIGIBILITY CLARIFICATION ACT.

Antonio G. Olivieri Center for Homeless Women See DROP-IN CENTERS.

Arson The purposeful burning of rental
housing stock has become a significant
source of displacement of low-income
households. According to the National Fire
Protection Association (NFPA), the number
of arson cases reported by local fire departments
increased by over 3,000 percent from
1951 to 1977, from 5,600 cases to 177,000
cases. Between 1977 and 1980 there were
over 1,000 deaths and 34,000 injuries of
civilians and firefighters each year. Arson
does not take place randomly, but tends to
be concentrated in low-income communities
with most victims made up of the poor,
members of minority groups, children and
the elderly. In 1975, 13,000 fires broke out
in the 12-square-mile area of New York City
known as the South Bronx, and over half
were recorded as "cause unknown."

Though deadly, arson is a profitable way
for dishonest landlords to dispose of properties.
The Legal Services Anti-Displacement
Project estimated the yearly property damage
from arson to be $1.5 billion and most
of this is covered in insurance policies. In
declining communities that have a potential
for GENTRIFICATION, arson can be a cost-effective
means of clearing a decaying or
unprofitable residential site for the development
of commercial properties, of removing
tenants for condominium conversion, or,
where rent control only allows unlimited rent
increases when tenants change, for evicting
existing tenants. According to a study conducted
by James Brady, director of the City
of Boston Arson Strike Force, in Boston
arson for profit is closely related to ABANDONMENT
and DISINVESTMENT. That is, over
half of the 3,000 arson cases between 1978
and 1982 in Boston took place in abandoned
buildings, and patterns of abandonment were
linked to bank policies of REDLINING and

disinvestment. By displacing low-income
tenants, gutting the building's interior and
therefore eliminating some of the cost of
conversion, and then being able to use the
insurance settlement to finance renovation,
arson has been a deadly element of urban
redevelopment.

In New York City in 1991 charges that
the homeless people had been responsible
for fires in city-owned buildings led the
administration of Mayor David Dinkins to
order that the homeless be evicted from all
city-owned buildings and property. A fire in
September 1991 in the Staten Island Ferry
Terminal at Battery Park was attributed to
homeless people smoking crack cocaine; less
than a week later a firefighter was killed
in Brooklyn, when the burning roof of an
abandoned building collapsed on him.
Homeless people had been squatting in the
building before the fire, and one of the
squatters was arrested and charged with
arson and second-degree murder. (See also
DISPLACEMENT.)

Asian-Americans for Equality See
NONPROFIT HOUSING PROGRAMS.

Asians According to the 1991 *Status Report
on Hunger and Homelessness* issued by
the United States Conference of Mayors,
Asians accounted for 1.5 percent of the
homeless population of San Francisco and 1
percent in Los Angeles, Minneapolis, Phoenix,
Salt Lake City, and Seattle. (See also
MINORITIES.)

B

baby boom See GENTRIFICATION.

back-to-the-city movement See GENTRIFICATION.

bag lady One common stereotype of the

homeless is that of the "bag lady"—a woman who lives on the street and carries all her possessions with her in plastic bags or shopping carts. Often these women display bizarre personal behavior, which is not always the product of mental illness. A 1979 study of "bag ladies" argued that some of the negative characteristics associated with them, such as poor personal hygiene or verbal abusiveness, could be understood as a conscious defense mechanism against sexual or other assault on the streets. (See also MENTAL ILLNESS; WOMEN.)

Baldwin, Roger N. See AMERICAN CIVIL LIBERTIES UNION (ACLU).

Banana Kelly Community Improvement Association The Banana Kelly Community Improvement Association began in the mid-1970s to fight housing abandonment in the Longwood section of the South Bronx in New York City. By 1990 Banana Kelly managed buildings with more than 700 apartments and had supervised the reconstruction through "sweat equity," of eight large abandoned apartment buildings as well as five smaller abandoned buildings, and 20 occupied but rundown buildings taken over by the city from defaulting landlords. (See also NONPROFIT HOUSING PROGRAMS.)

battered women Domestic violence is a significant cause of homelessness among women. According to Federal Bureau of Investigation (FBI) statistics, a woman is beaten by her male partner in the United States every 30 seconds, for a total of 1.5 million reported cases of wife beating or "battering" every year. However, since many women blame themselves for their partner's violence, or for emotional or financial reasons see no alternative but to remain with an abusive partner, battering may be the most underreported crime in the United States. Domestic violence can continue for

years, and sometimes ends only in the deaths of the women involved. Forty-one percent of all women murdered in the United States are killed by their husbands. Police are often reluctant to involve themselves in domestic violence cases, and in the past courts have often proven unsympathetic to women requesting protection from abusive partners.

In the 1970s and 1980s the women's movement made domestic violence an issue that drew increasing media and legal attention. Battered women's shelters and safe houses opened up in many communities, providing temporary refuge for women and their children fleeing domestic violence. Between 1983 and 1987 the number of women seeking shelter at battered women's shelters increased 100 percent. In 1988 over 300,000 women and their children sought refuge in 1,100 shelters and safe houses. These shelters could not, however, take in all of those who sought refuge in them. The Coalition Against Domestic Violence reported that in 1987, 40 percent of women with children seeking such shelter had to be turned away because of lack of space. And many shelters and safe houses have limits of a few days or weeks in which battered women and their children can stay. As a result, many women and children fleeing domestic violence end up in the homeless population. Sociologist Ellen Bassuk's 1984 study of the homeless staying in Massachusetts family shelters revealed that 45 percent of the women they interviewed had experienced domestic violence, though this was not always the immediate cause of their homelessness. (See also WOMEN.)

beggarshouses See WORKHOUSES.

begging See PANHANDLING.

Bellevue Hospital See BROWN, JOYCE.

Berkeley, California The area around the University of California at Berkeley attracted a large homeless population in the 1980s, some of whom camped out in the rundown "People's Park" area or begged for spare change along Telegraph Avenue. An innovative approach to the problem of panhandling was launched in Berkeley in 1991. In a program called Berkeley Cares, sponsored by city merchants, social service providers and the University of California, Berkeley residents were encouraged to purchase vouchers from local stores that can be given in place of money to street beggars. The vouchers could then be used to pay for food, laundry, bus fare or showers. Other cities, inspired by Berkeley's example, set up similar programs. Berkeley's mayor, Loni Hancock, cautioned, however, that the program was by no means a solution to homelessness. "It's impossible for any city to really solve the homeless problem within its borders because the problem doesn't originate locally. Homelessness is a national problem."

blight   See URBAN BLIGHT.

Block Grant Program for Services to Homeless Individuals Who Are Chronically Mentally Ill   This program, administered within the Alcohol, Drug Abuse, and Mental Health Administration in the Department of Health and Human Services (HHS), was established by Section 611 of the Stewart B. McKinney Homeless Assistance Act. It provides funds to states and territories for outreach services, community mental health treatment, referrals to health services and substance-abuse treatment, staff training, case management, and supportive and supervisory services in residential settings to benefit mentally ill homeless individuals. (See also MENTAL ILLNESS.)

blood plasma   One source of income for homeless people is the sale of their blood. According to a study by R. Bruce Wiegand (1990), there are over 400 blood plasma

centers in 225 American cities where blood is bought and sold. These centers, sometimes referred to by homeless people as "stab labs," are usually found near the SKID ROW sections of town. Over 11 million donations take place each year, with homeless and unemployed people among the most frequent donors. Government regulations require potential donors to be screened for hepatitis, syphilis and acquired immune deficiency syndrome (AIDS). Blood plasma is sold by donors for $10 to $15 a pint. Some of the men Wiegand interviewed sold up to eight pints of their blood a month.

Bonus Army   Among the unemployed in the early days of the Great Depression of the 1930s were many veterans of World War I. Under provisions of an act passed by Congress in 1923, veterans of the American Expeditionary Force in France in 1917–18 would be paid bonuses of between $50 and $100 in 1945. Early in 1932 a movement sprang up among unemployed veterans to "march" on Washington to demand an early payment of their bonuses. The march, spontaneously organized, was reminiscent of COXEY'S ARMY of 1894, with contingents gathering and setting off for Washington from many different parts of the country. The press started calling them the Bonus Expeditionary Force.

The first contingent of 300 Bonus marchers left Portland, Oregon in the spring of 1932, traveling most of the way by railroad freight cars, depending on donations from sympathizers along the way for food. Their slogan was a bitter one: "Heroes in 1917— Bums in 1932." By June more than 15,000 veterans had arrived in Washington. The "army" maintained itself with a semblance of military discipline, occupying abandoned buildings on Pennsylvania Avenue as temporary barracks, while another camp of rough huts and tents was set up on the Anacostia Flats across the Potomac River. Congress appropriated $100,000 to help pay for the veterans to return to their homes. The House passed the Bonus aid bill, which was defeated in the Senate. Congress adjourned for its summer recess on July 17 without taking any further action on the Bonus Army's demands.

Most of the disappointed veterans gave up and returned to their home communities, but about 2,000 of them, feeling they had nothing to return to, remained. After two veterans occupying the buildings on Pennsylvania Avenue were killed by District police, General Douglas MacArthur, acting on his own initiative, decided to clear the veterans out of Washington. MacArthur's soldiers, some of them on horseback with sabers, some carrying rifles and bayonets, and some in tanks, moved into Anacostia Flats, burning huts and driving away the veterans and their families. A seven-year-old boy trying to rescue a pet rabbit was stabbed in the leg, and an 11-week-old baby suffocated from tear gas thrown by the soldiers. An editorial response by the *Washington News* summed up the public's reaction to the eviction of the Bonus Army: "What a pitiful spectacle is that of the great American government, mightiest in the world, chasing unarmed men, women, and children with army tanks."

MacArthur, justifying his actions, declared that "the mob was a bad-looking one. It was one marked by signs of revolution." There was actually very little sentiment for revolution or any kind of political radicalism among the homeless veterans, who simply had no other place to go and no other source of help to appeal to. President Herbert Hoover took responsibility for MacArthur's actions, though he had not authorized the attack on Anacostia Flats. The incident contributed to Hoover's overwhelming defeat in the fall 1932 presidential election. President Franklin Delano Roosevelt attempted to aid homeless veterans by enrolling them in the Civilian Conservation Corps, a NEW DEAL program that put unemployed youth and others to work on a variety of conservation projects. (See also HOOVERVILLE; UNEMPLOYMENT; VETERANS.)

Boston, Massachusetts According to the 1991 *Status Report on Hunger and Homelessness* issued by the United States Conference of Mayors, Boston had an estimated homeless population of 3,641 for the year. (Other estimates put the number significantly higher.) On an average day in the fall of 1991, 1,456 people sought emergency shelter in the city, which had 3,661 beds available in emergency shelters and 636 beds available for homeless families. Boston is the second most expensive city in the nation in rental costs, after San Francisco. In 1991 a worker would need hourly wages of $16.71 to be able to afford rent on a two-bedroom apartment. The city also has a high unemployment rate, due to the prolonged recession that gripped the New England economy in the late 1980s and early 1990s. In August 1991, 9 percent of the city's population was unemployed. URBAN RENEWAL and GENTRIFICATION in the Boston-Cambridge area led to a steep decline in the number of affordable housing units in the 1960s and 1970s, and was a major cause for the increase in homelessness in the 1980s. While president of the United States Conference of Mayors, former Boston mayor Raymond Flynn was a strong advocate for the homeless.

bottle and can redemption In the 1970s and 1980s a number of states passed so-called bottle bills requiring consumers to pay deposits on bottled and canned soft drinks and beer, and requiring retail stores selling those items to accept the empty bottles for recycling and return the deposit. The bills were designed to protect the environment, clean up roadsides and reduce the pressure on landfills. An unintended benefit of such bills was the income they provided for many homeless people who rummaged through garbage pails for deposit bottles thrown out by consumers. In some cities homeless people carrying large plastic sacks of bottles they had picked up during the day became a familiar sight. Some retailers were reluctant to accept bottles and cans from the homeless, feeling that the presence of homeless people in their stores would deter other customers. In New York City, the WE CAN program on West 43rd Street was set up in 1987 to accept all bottles brought in by "self-employed bottle and can redeemers."

Bowery Bowery is a New York City street that runs along 16 blocks in lower Manhattan, bounded by East Greenwich Village on the north and Chinatown on the south. It is one of the oldest streets in Manhattan, dating back to the days of Dutch settlement, when it was the site of large country estates. The area commonly referred to as the Bowery includes the street and the side streets and avenues that run parallel to it. Since the 1870s the Bowery has been the center of New York's skid row, a neighborhood populated mostly by single men, many of them alcoholics, who patronized the local bars, vaudeville houses, FLOPHOUSES and religious missions. The Bowery's population dropped precipitously in the aftermath of the Second World War, as skid rows around the country began to disappear. Today there are a few remaining flophouses and missions, but many of the buildings now have been converted to commercial use, artist's lofts, and cooperative apartments. (See GENTRIFICATION.)

Bradley, Tom   See LOS ANGELES.

Bridge Over Troubled Waters   See RUNAWAYS.

Britain The British government has played a much more significant role in creating housing than the government in the United States. However, in the 1980s, under the leadership of Conservative prime minister Margaret Thatcher, the government's role in providing housing was cut back dramatically. The Thatcher government carried out policies designed to encourage the "privatization" of the public housing sector. Those policies, combined with economic hard times, led to a significant increase in homelessness in Britain. As Major John Boyd, a Salvation Army official in London, told an American reporter in 1992:

> The intent was never malicious, but all the decisions [taken by the Thatcher government] involved a certain kind of financial calculation. So you cut back housing subsidies and encouraged renters to take over their own homes, you eliminated welfare benefits for teenagers in the hopes of reducing welfare dependency, and you closed down mental hospitals with the idea that it is cheaper to keep people in [bed and breakfast establishments.]

The result, he concluded, as that Britain no longer had enough affordable rental housing. "We failed to measure the social costs when we looked at the monetary savings."

Although the framework for British housing policy was set in the 1930s, it wasn't until the end of World War II that a comprehensive housing policy was enacted. Immediately after the war, a popular Labour Party government began a massive expansion of public housing to address a wartime housing shortage and redevelop deteriorating housing stock. Private housing construction was banned and the government embarked on a program that created completely new towns outside of the large cities, built high-rise apartment complexes and provided generous rent subsidies (which kept rents below private-sector controlled rents). Popular demand and political consensus kept even Conservative Party governments heavily involved in the housing market through the 1960s.

But in the 1970s, this consensus began to break down as high inflation rates generated calls for cuts in public spending, while the physical condition of many public housing "estates" were allowed to deteriorate. By the time Margaret Thatcher was elected prime minister in 1979, political support for public housing was much weaker than it had been previously, paving the way for the privatization of a large portion of the public housing sector. (Despite this, in 1986, 27 percent of the housing stock in Britain was still in the public sector, compared to 1.5 percent in the United States.)

While housing policy has shifted dramatically in recent decades, the notion of housing rights for the homeless has been sustained, in part, by the Homeless Persons Act of 1977. The act obligated local housing authorities to secure accommodation for households that were "unintentionally homeless" and that had "priority need" (defined in the act as families with dependent children, retirees, pregnant women and those with serious physical or mental disability). Though criticized by advocacy groups for minimizing the plight of single homeless persons (as opposed to those with dependent children), the act was significant in that it shifted responsibility for the homeless from social service departments to housing departments, thus recognizing homelessness as primarily a problem of providing adequate housing rather than as a problem to be treated by social workers.

Currently over 100,000 homeless households are accepted each year for housing under the act, double the rate when the law was first enacted. But since this figure refers only to those homeless people in "priority need," it does not reflect the total number of homeless households in Britain. (Assessing that number would depend on resolving issues of definition.) As in the United States, there is an enormous range of experiences that lie between being "literally homeless" (that is, sleeping on the streets) and living in secure housing. Temporary shelter in hostels and bed-and-breakfast hotels, "doubling up" with others and extremely precarious private rental housing are all part of the mix in quantifying homelessness in Britain. For example, in London alone in 1984–85, 42,000 homeless households were placed in temporary accommodation, and 75,000 were granted official "priority need" status. There were from 150,000 to 200,000 people "doubling up" with others (80 percent of whom would have preferred to live separately) while another 300,000 low-income households were in immediate danger of being made homeless.

Housing shortages are generally recognized as the underlying cause of homelessness. The British housing shortage has been the result of a decline in the numbers of public and private rental units (much as in the United States), while increasing levels of unemployment have generated demand for low-cost housing. According to Shelter, a British homeless advocacy group, the annual government investment in public housing declined from $6.3 billion in 1980–81 to $2 billion in 1989–90.

Recent studies of homelessness in Britain have identified family conflict as another important source of the recent wave of homelessness. Spouse abuse, divorce and the inability of parents, relatives and friends to accommodate the homeless are reported as the immediate reasons for homelessness much more often now than in previous periods.

The growth of homelessness in Britain has been increasingly managed by the use of temporary shelter, often in bed-and-breakfast hotels. The numbers of homeless people housed in such hotels increased from 32,000 in 1980 to 41,000 in 1986. Problems associated with temporary shelters in Britain are not substantially different from those in the United States. Inadequate cooking and toilet facilities are linked to nutritional and other health problems, and hotel locations are not typically in the areas where the families once resided, thus severing community and support networks.

In the early 1990s the Salvation Army estimated that as many as 2,000 people were sleeping on the streets of London on any given night, which was more than double the government's tally. In addition, 18,000 single people slept in hostels and shelters run by churches or charity organizations, and an additional 25,000 people were sleeping in government-subsidized bed-and-breakfast establishments. About 30,000 people were illegally SQUATTING in buildings in London. Homelessness had also become a problem in many smaller cities in Britain, such as Basingstoke, Croydon, Eastbourne and Hastings. (See also POOR LAWS; PUBLIC HOUSING.)

Bronx United in Leveraging Dollars (Build) See NONPROFIT HOUSING PROGRAMS.

Brown, Joyce In New York State, as in many other states, police are authorized to take people who are mentally ill and cannot survive on the street or who are dangerous to themselves or others to a mental hospital, where the people will be evaluated and either admitted or released. This policy has raised questions about the civil liberties of the homeless mentally ill, which were dramatized by the case of Joyce Brown. The Brown case is sometimes cited as justification for a policy of REINSTITUTIONALIZATION of the mentally ill homeless.

Brown was a homeless, mentally disturbed person who came to national attention in 1987 when she filed suit against Bellevue Hospital in New York City. Brown, a former secretary, had first been hospitalized for mental problems in 1984, at the age of 37. Her sisters brought her to the emergency room, saying that she was aggressive and threatening violence. She was released after 15 days in the hospital with a diagnosis of paranoid personality disorder. In the winter of 1986 Brown's case came to the attention of social workers from Project Help, a New York City group that works with the homeless. At that time she was living on the streets by a hot-air vent, wearing dirty and inadequate clothing. She angrily rejected offers of help. On subsequent occasions in the spring and summer of 1987 she was ob-

served urinating and defecating on the streets, shouting at strangers and placing piles of torn-up currency around her. In July 1987 she was taken to Bellevue Hospital against her will and admitted as a patient. Her subsequent legal suit, backed by the American Civil Liberties Union (ACLU), was heard in New York Appellate Court. While the case was being heard, the court allowed her hospitalization to continue, but barred doctors from forcing her to take medication.

The court eventually decided that Brown could not be held against her will. She was released from Bellevue in January 1988, interviewed on *60 Minutes* and the *Donahue* show, and addressed classes at Harvard Law School. Although she was no longer living on the street, her mental condition soon relapsed, and she returned to panhandling and yelling at passersby in the street. The Brown case came to symbolize without finally resolving the difficult issue of whether mentally disturbed people are capable of judging their best interests, or whether government agencies and medical evaluators should have the power to deny freedom to such individuals. In 1993, she was readmitted to Bellevue for psychiatric evaluation. (See also MENTAL ILLNESS.)

Buchanan v. Warley In 1917 the U.S. Supreme Court ruled in *Buchanan v. Warley* that the use of ZONING ordinances to mandate racial residential segregation was unconstitutional.

Bureau of Indian Affairs See NATIVE AMERICANS.

Bush, Barbara See ACQUIRED IMMUNE DEFICIENCY SYNDROME (AIDS).

Bush, George George Bush was elected as the 41st president of the United States in November 1988. Before his election to the White House, Bush had established a career record as the consummate Washington,

D.C. "insider." The son of a U.S. senator, Bush served two terms in the U.S. Congress as a representative from Texas. He served as U.S. ambassador to the United Nations, chief of the U.S. Liason Office in the People's Republic of China and director of the Central Intelligence Agency (CIA) before being selected as the vice presidential running mate of Ronald Reagan in 1980. Bush campaigned in 1988 on the slogan of creating a "kinder, gentler" America, which some observers interpreted as an implied criticism of his predecessor. Among other campaign pledges, Bush promised to seek full funding for Stewart B. McKinney Homeless Assistance Act programs. He also called for "a THOUSAND POINTS OF LIGHT," continuing the Reagan administration's emphasis on nongovernmental voluntary action and private charity as the solution to social problems. Bush proposals for solving the nation's housing and homeless problems included various programs to encourage homeownership by those with low and moderate incomes; tax incentives for both housing and community/economic development in "enterprise zones"; preservation of existing Department of Housing and Urban Development (HUD)-subsidized, privately owned housing; additional assistance for helping homeless persons; and reformation of the FEDERAL HOUSING AUTHORITY (FHA) insurance program. The centerpiece of the program is the "Home Ownership Opportunities for People Everywhere" program (HOPE), first advocated by Bush in a speech in Dallas to the National Association of Realtors in November 1989, which would provide grants for public housing ownership; grants for buying distressed FHA properties; and grants to assist nonprofit groups in acquiring government-owned housing for home ownership. Critics have complained that, regardless of the merits of tenant ownership, HOPE does not add a single new unit to the nation's supply of housing. Bush signed into law the CRANSTON-GONZALEZ NATIONAL AFFORDABLE HOUSING ACT in 1991, provid-

ing some new funds for public housing. Bush was defeated by Demorcratic challenger Bill Clinton in the 1992 presidential election.

C

Callahan v. Carey One of the most famous and significant court cases involving the legal rights of the homeless was that of *Callahan v. Carey* in New York City. New York, unlike most cities, was providing shelter for homeless before the 1980s. But its Men's Shelter, located at 8 East Third Street, was overcrowded, unsanitary and dangerous; those who could not be fit into the shelter or given a voucher for a bed in one of the "welfare hotels" the city used to shelter homeless people were turned away. An attorney named Robert Hayes brought suit on behalf of one homeless man, Robert Callahan, against the city and state of New York. Callahan, a one-time short order cook who had been without work for four years, had been evicted from his apartment and had fruitlessly sought shelter at the Men's Shelter. Hayes sued the city on behalf of Callahan and two other homeless men in a class action suit. He argued that under a clause in New York State's Constitution adopted in 1938, there was a legally enforceable right to shelter. The clause held that "the aid, care, and support of the needy are public concerns and shall be provided by the state." In 1979 the New York Supreme Court granted a preliminary injunction requiring New York City to provide "shelter (including bedding, wholesome food and adequate security and supervision) to any person who applies for shelter at the Men's Shelter." This was a precedent-setting ruling that had an immediate effect on New York City's policies regarding the homeless. To meet this new requirement, the city opened a new shelter at an abandoned mental institution on Wards Island. The case was finally settled in 1981 under a consent decree that stated: "The City . . . shall provide shelter and board to each homeless man who applies for it provided that (a) the man meets the need standard to qualify for the home relief program established in New York State; or (b) the man by reason of physical, mental or social dysfunction is in need of temporary shelter." (A subsequent legal decision held that this decree applied equally to homeless women.) Under the provisions of the consent decree, the city expanded the number of beds available for the homeless from 1,750 in 1979 to 7,000 by the mid-1980s.

Campaign for Human Development
See CATHOLIC CHURCH.

Canada
Homelessness is a growing problem in Canada. As in the United States, the exact size of the homeless population is difficult to determine. A 1987 study by the Canadian Council on Social Development (CCSD) estimated that somewhere between 130,000 and 250,000 homeless individuals had sought shelter during the year. Many of the ills that beset American communities, including a depressed national economy, the DEINSTITUTIONALIZATION of patients suffering from mental illness, substance abuse, and the deterioration or disappearance of low-cost housing, can also be found in Canadian cities. According to a 1991 report by the Big City Mayors' Caucus of the Federation of Canadians Municipalities, "Roomers and boarders, people suffering from mental health or psychiatric problems, alcohol and drug addicts, young runaways, the unemployed, immigrants and refugees, and victims of family violence have now joined the ranks of the more 'traditional' homeless." The CCSD survey found that roughly 20 percent of those seeking shelter on a typical night in 1987 were current or ex-psychiatric patients, one third were alcohol abusers and 15 percent were drug abusers (these categories overlapped in some instances.) In some

western provinces, like Saskatchewan, Native Americans constituted a significant proportion of the homeless population. The social programs provided by the Canadian government, including a national health program, have helped to ease the plight of Canada's homeless.

The Canadian national housing agency (Canada Mortgage and Housing Corporation) sponsors a number of programs aimed at providing low cost housing. The corporation provides funding, for example, to the Homes First Society in Toronto. A nonprofit developer, Homes First built an 11-story, 77-unit rooming house near Toronto's SKID ROW district, were apartments with separate bedrooms and shared kitchens, dining rooms and living rooms are available at low cost to qualified applicants. Provincial governments have also addressed the problem of homelessness through such programs as Ontario's Project 3000, designed to provide 3,000 rental units for the neediest.

Carter, Jimmy
James Earl ("Jimmy") Carter was elected the 39th president of the United States in November 1976. Carter, a former naval officer and peanut farmer from Plains, Georgia, served one term as governor of Georgia before launching a bid for the U.S. presidency. His attempt might have seemed quixotic had it not been for the anti-"insider" mood that gripped the country in the aftermath of the Watergate scandal and the resignation of President Richard M. Nixon in 1974. Carter promised that he would "never lie" to the American people. His domestic agenda was considerably vaguer; during the campaign, liberals perceived him as a liberal and conservatives as a conservative. Once in office, despite his sensitivity to racial issues and his human rights initiatives abroad, he came to be seen as the most conservative Democratic president to hold office in the 20th century. While scorned by Republican opponents as a freespending antibusiness liberal, Carter in fact anticipated the policies of the more conser-

vative administrations to come by launching the deregulation of cargo airlines in 1977, commercial airlines in 1978, natural gas prices in 1978 and the trucking industry in 1980. He signed into law the Humphrey-Hawkins Full Employment Act in 1978, which set an economic goal of obtaining 4 percent unemployment level by 1983, but the act was no more than a pious gesture that cost nothing in federal expenditures. (The goal of reducing unemployment to that level has yet to be achieved under any subsequent administration.) Carter offered no significant legislative initiatives in the field of housing. He did create the Department of Health and Human Services (HHS), which administers a wide variety of programs, including the Social Security system. (The old Department of Health, Education and Welfare (HEW) was divided into two new departments: HHS and the Department of Education.)

It was during Carter's tenure in office that homelessness first began to emerge as a major social problem. There were protests by homeless advocates at the Democratic national convention in New York City in 1980. At that convention, Carter beat off a liberal insurgency to nominate Senator Edward M. Kennedy of Massachussetts as president. In November 1980, beset by economic problems at home and by the hostage crisis in Iran, Carter went down to defeat. In the years since leaving office, Jimmy Carter has been an active supporter of the Christian housing group HABITAT FOR HUMANITY.

Cartoonists' Homeless Project The Cartoonists' Homeless Project, a Los Angeles-based group, consists of artists who dedicate panels on editorial and comic pages to the subject of homelessness in America.

Catholic Charities Catholic Charities, USA was founded in 1910 as the National Conference of Catholic Charities, the central organization for Catholic human services in the United States. With national headquarters in Washington, D.C., Catholic Charities offers membership to charter groups, such as the Society of St. Vincent de Paul, to local parishes and to individuals. Its federation represents the largest private provider of human services in the United States. In recent years it has turned its attention increasingly to the issue of homelessness. Its 1986 policy statement on housing declared that "the commitment of Catholic Charities to decent and affordable housing rests upon the Church's teaching on the dignity of the human person and the value of family." In addition to providing services directly to the homeless, Catholic Charities has also advocated expanded local, state and federal government efforts to solve the housing crisis. The Reverend Thomas J. Harvey, president of Catholic Charities, told a reporter in 1991 that "during the Reagan administration the responsibility for many social welfare programs was shifted from the Federal level to the states, and now with some 40 states facing budget deficits, the government role is really contracting." The onset of a severe economic recession in the early 1990s stretched the resources of Catholic Charities, but also created a new awareness, according to Harvey, of the seriousness of the plight of the homeless. "This kind of downturn reminds people that there are capricious forces at work," Harvey declared in December 1991. "It explodes the myths that the poor are poor out of choice because people see their neighbors going unemployed due to circumstances beyond their control." (See also CATHOLIC CHURCH, ROMAN.)

Catholic Church, Roman The Roman Catholic Church has been deeply involved with the issue of homelessness. In a letter to the Vatican's Pontifical Commission entitled *Justitia et Pax* in 1987, Pope John Paul II declared that the church had an obligation "to find concrete and urgent solutions to the housing problem and to see that the homeless receive the necessary attention and concern on the part of public authorities." The Pontifical Commission's 1988 statement on housing and homelessness *(What Have You Done to Your Homeless Brother?)* declared that decent housing was a "fundamental human right." The National Conference of Catholic Bishops and other church groups in the United States have also issued calls for action on the issue of homelessness. CATHOLIC CHARITIES, religious orders, dioceses and local parishes have provided shelters for the homeless and the church's Campaign for Human Development has provided assistance for self-help groups working to build low-income housing. The church has also called on government to recognize its own responsibility for solving the homelessness crisis. The U.S. Catholic Conference's 1988 statement, *Homelessness and Housing: A Human Tragedy, A Moral Challenge,* declared that private efforts alone, including those by religious groups, were not sufficient: "[T]here is no substitute for an involved, competent, and committed federal government providing resources, leadership and direction for a broad and flexible attack on homelessness and poor housing . . . What is missing are leadership and commitment." (See also CATHOLIC WORKER.)

Catholic Worker   Since the 1930s the Catholic Worker movement has provided food and shelter to the urban homeless. The history of the movement is bound up with the biography of journalist and radical activist Dorothy Day. Day was born in Brooklyn in 1897, the daughter of a newspaper sportswriter. She attended the University of Illinois, where she was attracted to the then rapidly growing socialist movement. She returned to New York City shortly before the start of World War I as a reporter for the New York *Call,* a daily socialist newspaper. She also worked for the *Masses,* a radical literary magazine published in Greenwich Village. In the 1920s she was married and divorced, published a novel and bore a daughter out of wedlock. Shortly after her

daughter's birth she underwent a religious crisis and coverted to Catholicism. She remained a political radical, however, and, in 1933, along with the French religious mystic and social critic Peter Maurin, founded the *Catholic Worker* newspaper.

The *Catholic Worker,* which sold for a penny a copy, combined spiritual essays with radical reporting. Its politics was a mixture of pacifism, anarchist utopianism and Catholic social thought. Its circulation climbed to a peak of 185,000 by 1940. The Catholic Worker soon developed into a movement as well as a newspaper. Day and her followers opened a soup kitchen and shelter for the homeless on the Lower East Side of New York City in 1933, at the lowest point of the GREAT DEPRESSION, and were feeding 1,200 people a day by 1938. Members of the Catholic Worker movement practiced a "voluntary poverty" similar to that of many purely religious orders, living and eating with the poor they sought to serve, dressing in cast-off clothing and accepting no salary. By 1941 there were 32 Catholic Worker "Houses of Hospitality" located in 27 cities and several rural farming communes. The Catholic Worker lost many supporters during World War II due to its unyielding pacifist opposition to the war, and many of the Houses of Hospitality were forced to close. But the movement continued to exercise considerable influence over a later generation of Catholic activists.

Perhaps the most famous alumni of the Catholic Worker movement, apart from Dorothy Day herself, was Michael Harrington, who spent two years in the early 1950s living in the Chrystie Street House of Hospitality in New York's Bowery district. "Our ideal," Harrington recalled in his memoir *Fragments of a Century* (1973), "was 'to see Christ in every man,' including the pathetic, shambling, shivering creature who would wander in off the streets with his pants caked with urine and his face scabbed with blood." Harrington's 1962 book, *The Other America,* described the destitution he had

seen in his Catholic Worker days and afterward, and did much to influence the federal
government's war on poverty in the mid-
1960s. Harrington remained a recognized
authority on poverty and social policy as
well as a prominent socialist activist. Others
have carried the Catholic Worker tradition
down to the present. At the start of the
1990s, about 100 Catholic Worker houses
and farms operated nationally in very loose
affiliation. There are two Catholic Worker
houses in New York City, St. Joseph House
on East First Street and Maryhouse on East
Third Street, which together provide residences for about 70 people. St. Joseph's
feeds lunch to 300 or so people every day,
and both houses also distribute clothing and
groceries. The *Catholic Worker* newspaper
still appears, from its editorial offices in
New York.

Homeless activist Robert Hayes, a
founder of the National Coalition for the
Homeless, said of Day's example: "Dorothy
Day wrote that those of us who labor on
behalf of the poor need not see results.
'Our work is to sow,' she said. 'Another
generation will be reaping the harvest.'
That, in large measure, must be the credo
of those of us working for and with the
homeless." Dorothy Day died on November
29, 1980 in the House of Hospitality she had
founded on Manhattan's Lower East Side.

**Center on Budget and Policy Priorit-
ies** This Washington, D.C.-based group
issues reports analyzing data and policy issues affecting poor Americans. It published
a series of reports on the housing crisis in
the 1980s and 1990s under the general title
A Place to Call Home. (See also GENERAL
ASSISTANCE, WORKING POOR.)

Centers for Disease Control   See AC-
QUIRED IMMUNE DEFICIENCY SYNDROME
(AIDS).

charities   See Appendix I.

Charleston,   South   Carolina According to the 1991 *Status Report on Hunger
and Homelessness* issued by the United
States Conference of Mayors, Charleston
had an estimated homeless population of
369. On an average day in October 1991,
341 people would seek emergency shelter in
the city, which has a total of 390 emergency
shelter beds available. Due to the economic
recession gripping the city in the early
1990s, a Charleston official reported, "There
has been a significant increase in the numbers of those needing services, an increase
in the severity of their needs and a significant
decrease in funding to provide those services." (See also HISTORIC PRESERVATION.)

Chicago,   Illinois Estimates of Chicago's homeless population vary widely,
from a few thousand to as many as 40,000.
The city has 4,354 beds in emergency shelters and 636 beds available for families.
With a large minority population and a high
percentage of families living below the POV-
ERTY LINE, the city of Chicago has also been
suffering from the effects of deindustrialization. The 1991 *Status Report on Hunger and
Homelessness* issued by the United States
Conference of Mayors did not provide an
updated estimate of Chicago's homeless
population. It did report that on a typical
day in October 1991, 3,130 people requested
emergency shelter. A Chicago city official
was quoted in the Status Report as saying:

There has been no significant improvement in
the economic status of the City's poor and near
poor. In fact, the economy has entered what
may be a deep and long recessionary period.
Because of the recession, many are facing the
expiration of the unemployment compensation
benefits. . . . [C]hanges in the GENERAL AS-
SISTANCE program in Illinois will have a major
impact in early '92 when new regulations may
cause tens of thousands to become ineligible
for assistance. There seems to be little that can
prevent the anticipated increase in demand for
emergency shelter.

children Children are the most tragic victims of the homeless crisis. Sociologist James Wright has estimated that one in every seven homeless persons is under 19 years of age, while a 1988 study of 27 cities by the United States Conference of Mayors put the figure at one in every four. (See ELDERLY for a figure depicting age distribution among the homeless.) That adds up to something on the order of a half to three-quarters of a million children living in SHELTERS, in WELFARE HOTELS or on the streets. Jonathon Kozol wrote in *Rachel and Her Children: Homeless Families in America* (1988) that if all the homeless children in the United States "were gathered in one city, they would represent a larger population than that of Atlanta, Denver, or St. Louis. Because they are scattered in a thousand cities, they are easily unseen."

Families with children represent the most rapidly growing segment of the homeless population. A 1992 study sponsored by the Children's Defense Fund and the Center for Labor Market Studies at Boston's Northeastern University showed that a disproportionate number of Americans who lost their jobs in the recession of the early 1990s were 16 to 24 years old. According to Marian Wright Edelman, president of the Children's Defense Fund: "Job losses among young workers, often the parents of America's youngest and most vulnerable children, are creating a devastating cycle of declining earnings, declining family incomes and rising child poverty." In 1990 alone, according to the Children's Defense Fund, 841,000 children lived in families that slipped below the POVERTY LINE. Thirteen million children were living in poverty in that year.

Homeless children carry a heavy burden of disadvantages, beginning with the state of their health. Poor women in general, and homeless women in particular, do not get the prenatal care necessary to ensure that they give birth to healthy children. Babies born to homeless mothers characteristically suffer from low birth weight and high infant mortality rates. Homeless children are almost twice as likely to suffer chronic physical disorders as children in the general population. A 1987 report revealed that homeless children had twice the incidence rate of upper respiratory infections and serious skin disorders as other children, and were four times more likely to suffer from gastrointestinal disorders. Anemia, malnutrition and asthma were found to be much more common among homeless children. Over 50 percent of homeless children are not properly immunized, making them more vulnerable to illnesses such as diptheria, tetanus, measles and polio, all of which are disappearing among the general population. Infant mortality rates in New York City welfare hotels are nearly 25 per 1,000 live births, compared to a rate of under 11 per 1,000 for the nation as a whole. Homeless children in welfare hotels and shelters live in a climate where substance abuse is a common affliction, and drugs and alcohol are readily available. Sexually transmitted diseases and pregnancy are also common problems of homeless adolescents.

Though access to adequate nutrition is a problem for homeless people of all ages, it is especially critical for children and young adults. Welfare hotels, where many homeless families reside, have no cooking or refridgerator facilities available. Families must either violate safety codes by bringing a hot plate to their room, or eat in restaurants (which uses more of their scarce income than if they could prepare their own meals). Consequently, homeless families must rely upon nonperishable foods for nourishment (canned goods, dry cereals, etc.). For mothers with infants, the lack of refrigeration makes it difficult to keep milk or infant formula cold, except through such improvised techniques as using toilet tanks as coolers.

In addition to physical health problems and inadequate nutrition, homeless children suffer greater emotional and developmental problems than other children. They often live surrounded by chaos and squalor. Members of the New York City Council who visited the notorious Martinique welfare hotel in 1986 reported:

People passing by the hotel have no sense of the tragic dimensions of life inside. Upon entering the hotel, one is greeted by a rush of noise, made in large part by the many small children living there. These children share accommodations with a considerable cockroach and rodent population. The nearly 400 families housed at the Martinique are assisted by just seven [social work] caseworkers, whose efforts to keep in touch with each family—at least once each month—often amount to no more than a note slipped under a door.

Children growing up in such settings, or on the street, often suffer from an acute sense of loss due to separation from a familiar home and belongings, friends and relatives, and both reasonable and unreasonable anxieties that grow out of a situation where they may not know where their next meal or bed is coming from. They may also suffer shame and embarrassment over their family's poverty, resentment and envy of those more privileged and frustration that they are unable to help improve their family's living situation. "School is bad for me," a child living in the Martinique hotel told Kozol. "I feel ashamed. They know we're not the same. My teachers do not treat us all the same. They know which children live in the hotel." According to a 1987 study by sociologist Ellen Bassuk of children living in family shelters and welfare hotels in Massachusetts, nearly half of all the preschoolers in the sample showed at least one developmental delay (in language, motor skills and coordination, and personal/social development), and half of all the school-age children were extremely depressed and anxious.

Homeless families with children are at considerable risk of breaking up. (See also figure under WOMEN, which lists mental health indicators of homeless single women with children versus other homeless adults.) Some families voluntarily divide up temporarily, as parents leave children with friends or relatives while they seek permanent housing. In congressional testimony, Diana Pearce of the National Low-Income Housing Coalition cited a 1980 study by the Department of Housing and Urban Development (HUD) of homeless families with children that showed that 20 percent of these families split up, and half of those families remained apart for four months or more. Some emergency shelters will not accept teenagers or members of both sexes, forcing families to separate at least temporarily to gain a night's shelter. Children have been taken away from parents for no other reason than family homelessness. In New Jersey, according to a study conducted by the state's child welfare agencies, over 1,200 children were placed in foster homes in 1986 because their parents lacked housing, representing almost 18 percent of children placed in FOSTER CARE in the state. (In 1987 New Jersey began work on a program called Transitional Support Home Program, which would allow single parents and their children to stay together as a family with foster families on a short-term basis.)

Because of fears of being broken up, many homeless families avoid shelters. Homeless children are thus less "visible" to service providers and the general public than single men, the mentally ill, and other subgroups of the homeless population. (See also EDUCATION; FAMILIES; RUNAWAYS; YOUTH.)

Children's Defense Fund The Children's Defense Fund, based in Washington, D.C., seeks to educate policymakers about the needs of poor and minority children. It monitors federal and state policy on a variety of issues pertaining to children and young people. It publishes an annual report, the *Children's Defense Budget,* analyzing federal budget proposals and their effects on children.

Time Adult Homeless Persons Had Already Spent Homeless When Surveyed

Source: Interagency Council on the Homeless (1990 Annual Report)

Child Welfare Demonstration program When Congress reauthorized the Stewart B. McKinney Homeless Assistance Act in 1990, it added a new provision establishing the Child Welfare Demonstration program, intended to prevent the inappropriate separation of homeless families. The act, adminstered by the Department of Health and Human Services, provides competitive grants to public child welfare agencies in areas where homelessness or inadequate housing is resulting in the initial or prolonged placement of children in FOSTER CARE, or is delaying the discharge of older youth from foster care without adequate living arrangements. Grantees must provide joint training for staff of the participating agencies on the relationship between inadequate housing and out-of-home care and the resources available to address this problem. Funds also can be used to hire staff to assist families or youth awaiting discharge with their housing needs; to provide training and technical assistance to staff of homeless shelters in preventing the abuse and neglect of homeless children; and to develop materials to advise homeless families of available resources.

Child Welfare League of America The Child Welfare League of America (CWLA), founded in 1920 and headquartered in Washington, D.C., is a national association representing over 600 public and voluntary child welfare agencies. Concerned with a variety of issues involving the welfare of children, in recent years the CWLA also has taken up the cause of providing shelter and education for homeless children.

chronic homeless The chronically homeless are persons who are more or less permanently without fixed residence. Many of these are homeless due to mental illness or substance abuse. They are often the most visible component of the homeless population, both on the streets and in SHELTERS. And yet, according to sociologist James Wright, the chronically homeless in the late 1980s accounted for less than a third of the total homeless population. Far more homeless people are part of the EPISODIC HOMELESS population.

Cisneros, Henry G. In January 1993, Henry Cisneros became secretary of Housing and Urban Development in the administration of President Bill Clinton. Formerly the four-term Mayor of San Antonio, Texas, where he served from 1981 to 1989, Cisneros was prominent for having been the nation's first Hispanic mayor and for the vibrant economic development of San Antonio during his tenure, particularly in the high technology industry and tourism.

As Secretary of HUD, Cisneros has been an active and vocal member of the Clinton

Cabinet. For example, while President Clinton himself has had relatively little to say about the often volatile subject of race in the United States, Cisneros has been bold in asserting the centrality of racism in shaping many of our social problems. For example, in a July 8, 1993 *New York Times* article entitled "Housing Secretary Carves Out Role As a Lonely Clarion Against Racism," Cisneros stated that "race is at the core of the problems which confront America's urban areas" and noted previous federal housing policy not only tolerated but promoted racial segregation. Part of his strategy to reverse such practices is to begin to locate federally subsidized housing in predominantly white suburbs rather than in central city areas, over the expected opposition of middle-class suburbanites who have put up fierce resistance to subsidized low-income housing in the past. He has begun negotiations with some suburban governments outside Detroit to encourage them to accept a larger portion of the metropolitan area's subsidized housing in exchange for financial incentives. But widespread implementation of this policy and Cisneros' view of urban poverty generally are likely to encounter resistance within the Clinton administration itself, given that Clinton and the conservative Democratic Leadership Council, with which Clinton has been associated, campaigned hard to secure the votes of middle class suburbanites in the presidential election.

Secretary Cisneros is considering other reforms aimed at addressing the problems of urban poverty and homelessness, including an expanded housing voucher program aimed at giving the residents of public housing the opportunity to move into private apartments in the suburbs; stricter enforcement of the nation's fair housing laws to make it more difficult for landlords and realtors to discriminate against minorities; and more scrutiny of banks and insurance companies to prevent discrimination against minority groups. In addition, in May 1993 Cisneros announced that he had been in consultation with the leadership of the AFL-CIO about using $500 million in investments from union pension funds to help finance housing for poor families and urban business development in 27 cities across the nation. According to the pension director of the AFL-CIO, Stephen Coyle, the labor federation would invest the pension money for construction projects, creating union jobs, and the investment would provide "safe, competitive and secure returns" to the pension programs. Already, the AFL-CIO's housing and building trusts produced 3,000 units of housing in 1992, and the future projects under consideration would be aimed at producing rental apartment buildings or town houses; single-room occupancy hotels; new or renovated single family-homes; work on HUD properties gained in foreclosure; and commercial development, like shopping centers and grocery stores.

Such a project would draw upon the financial resources of the private sector, rather than the federal government. But though the Clinton Administration has not offered substantial budgetary commitments to the fight against homelessness, as chairman of the Federal Interagency Council on the Homeless, Secretary Cisneros is responsible for implementing a presidential executive order, signed May 19, 1993, that requires the Council to develop a plan to end homelessness. The plan will be designed to coordinate federal activities to better facilitate programs for the homeless, and will require consultation with state and local governments, nonprofit homeless service providers, and homeless individuals and families, both currently and formerly homeless. (See CLINTON, WILLIAM JEFFERSON.)

city sleeper In 1987 a San Francisco architect built a prototype of a cheap and easily constructed street shelter for homeless individuals, which he called a "city sleeper." The plywood crate, which was tall enough for a man to sit up in, contained a mattress, closet, shelf and window. Access was gained by a door that could be hooked open so the person could crawl into and out of the crate. The architect estimated that each shelter could be constructed for less than $800, and would represent a potential savings of millions of dollars over the cost of emergency shelters and welfare hotels. San Francisco's city hall denounced the plan, since the shelter provided neither running water or a toilet and did not meet the city's building code.

Civilian Conservation Corps (CCC)

The Civilian Conservative Corps (CCC) was the first relief program established by the NEW DEAL in 1933. Its passage was a measure of the importance that President Franklin D. Roosevelt attached to both conservation and the welfare of American youth during the GREAT DEPRESSION. When Roosevelt was elected president, an estimated 250,000 young people were roaming the nation, unsure of where their next meal or night's lodging would come from. The CCC enlisted young unemployed men (women were not included in the program) between the ages of 18 and 25 for six-month periods. CCC recruits lived in rural camps administered by the War Department and worked on conservation-related projects including reforestation, erosion control, wildlife preservation and national park improvement. In addition to their room and board, enlistees were paid $30 a month, $25 of which was sent home to their families. After their initial six-month enlistments expired, recruits could renew their enlistments for up to a total of two years. At its height the CCC enlisted 500,000 young men who lived and worked in a system of 2,500 camps.

The CCC was one of the most popular of the New Deal programs. It left its mark on the American landscape: Three-quarters of all the trees planted in the United States in its entire history up until 1942 were planted by the CCC. It also left its mark on a generation of young Americans, who found in it a measure of hope and material well-being they otherwise would have been denied. By the time the program ended in 1942 (when most men in the eligible age brackets were going into military service), more than 3 million young men had passed through its ranks, along with 250,000 military veterans who were eligible to join.

Civil Rights Act of 1964

Title VI of the Civil Rights Act of 1964, passed during the administration of President Lyndon Baines Johnson, offered a broad guarantee of nondiscrimination in federally assisted programs, declaring "No person in the United States shall, on the ground of race, color, or national origin, be excluded from participation in, be denied the benefits of, or be subjected to discrimination under any program or activity receiving Federal financial assistance." One result of the passage of the Civil Rights Act of 1964 was a dramatic increase in the percentage of minorities living in public housing, climbing to over 60 percent in the next decade and a half.

Civil Rights Act of 1968

Title VIII of the Civil Rights Act of 1968, passed during the administration of President Lyndon Baines Johnson, stated: "It is the policy of the United States to provide, within constitutional limitations, for fair housing throughout the United States." The act extended the guarantee of nondiscrimination in housing from public housing to private, nonfederally assisted housing, with some exceptions in the case of owner-occupied rental units or houses sold or rented without the use of a real estate broker. With the passage of the Civil Rights Act of 1968, nearly 80 percent of the nation's housing units became subject to federal nondiscrimination regulations.

civil rights movement See AFRICAN AMERICANS; KENNEDY, JOHN F.; MINORITIES; PUBLIC HOUSING.

Clearing House on Homelessness Among Mentally Ill People

Based in Silver Spring, Maryland, the Clearing House on Homelessness Among Mentally Ill People (CHAMP) collects and disseminates in-

formation through its database of published
and unpublished materials and also produces
technical briefs, concise descriptions of programs serving homeless mentally ill people.
CHAMP also publishes a quarterly newsletter highlighting recent database acquisitions,
news from federal and state governments
and innovative program models. (See also
MENTAL ILLNESS.)

Clinton, William Jefferson   In the November 1992 election, William Jefferson
"Bill" Clinton defeated George Bush, becoming the 42nd president of the United
States. Previously, he had been the governor
of Arkansas for five terms, had served as
Arkansas' attorney general, and had practiced and taught law in Arkansas after gradu-
ating from the Yale University Law School
in 1973.

During the 1992 presidential campaign
both candidates generally avoided discussion
of urban problems in general and homelessness in particular. In the very few times
that the problem of homelessness was raised
during the campaign, Clinton sought to appeal to this new constituency base by pledging to give preference to homeless veterans
by using closed military bases to house the
homeless.

Shortly after taking office, President Clinton's administration followed up on his
pledge by beginning to draw up plans to
convert de-commissioned military bases and
other unused federal property into living
places for the homeless and for low-income
families. As part of this effort, the Department of Housing and Urban Development
began drawing up plans to contact nonprofit
groups to let them know how they might be
able to locate and gain the use of such
properties, as well as foreclosed properties
belonging to the Farmer's Home Administration and the Veterans Administration. Mech-
anisms for releasing unused federal
properties were actually drawn up as part of
the McKinney Homeless Assistance Act of
1987, but were never pursued under the

previous administration. Advocacy groups
for the homeless, who filed lawsuits to try
to force full compliance with the McKinney
Act, and who view this plan as only part
of what should be a more comprehensive
program, are nevertheless hopeful that the
Clinton Administration will finally make unused federal property available to the
homeless.

In May 1993, President Clinton ordered
that a plan be drawn up to find a long-
term solution to the problem of homelessness. The secretary of Housing and Urban Development, Henry G. Cisneros, who
was elected chairman of the Federal Interagency Council on the Homeless, explained
that the president had issued an executive
order that directed the 17 principal federal
agencies that comprise the Interagency
Council to develop a coordinated plan within
nine months that would make efforts on
behalf of the homeless more effective than
they had been. The executive order included
a call for administrative and legislative initiatives, for recommendations on how current funding programs might be redirected
to provide links between housing, support
and education services, and a plan for promoting coordination and cooperation among
local housing and support service providers,
school districts and advocates for homeless
individuals and families. The order sought
recommendations on "ways to encourage
and support creative approaches and cost-
effective, local efforts to break the cycle of
existing homelesssness and prevent future
homelessness, including tying current homeless assistance programs to permanent housing assistance, local housing affordability
strategies, or employment opportunities." In
addition, Cisneros has been in consultation
with the leadership of the AFL-CIO about
the investment of $500 million in union
pension funds to build low-income housing
in 27 cities across the nation, an initiative
that reflects President Clinton's preference
for using private sector resources rather than
public funds. Though advocacy groups for

the homeless have been somewhat encouraged by President Clinton's attention to the problem since taking office, most believe that the problem of homelessness will not be substantially reduced without significant amounts of new federal funds specifically designed to address the various aspects of the problem. (See CISNEROS, HENRY; MCKINNEY ACT.

Coalition Against Domestic Violence
See BATTERED WOMEN.

Comic Relief
Comic Relief, a live benefit fund-raising program, produced by the cable television company Home Box Office (HBO), was first broadcast on March 29, 1986. Bob Zmuda, a comedy writer and producer, and Chris Albrecht, a senior vice president of HBO, initiated the idea. Billy Crystal, Whoopi Goldberg and Robin Williams hosted the performance. That broadcast raised more than $2.5 million. Since then, Comic Relief has become an annual event. There have also been regional fundraising efforts in comedy clubs in cities across the United States. In its first three broadcasts, Comic Relief raised $8.7 million for Health Care for the Homeless projects in 23 cities.

commodities
Commodities are surplus agricultural products purchased under the Price Support Program by the federal government and distributed through school lunch programs, soup kitchens, food banks and social service programs for individuals and families.

Common Cents
Common Cents is a fund-raising effort to benefit the National Coalition for the Homeless, started by Theodore Gross, a playwright living on the Upper West Side of Manhattan in New York City. Canvassers for Common Cents go apartment to apartment, asking their neighbors to donate their pennies to help the homeless. From each household that contributes, Gross

estimated, an average of $13 in pennies was donated. "I realized that pennies and the homeless were the same," Gross told a reporter in 1991, "wasted capital, scorned and ignored."

Communist Party
See TENANT ACTIVISM; UNEMPLOYED COUNCILS.

Community for Creative Nonviolence (CCNV)
The Community for Creative Nonviolence is a nonviolent direct action group based in Washington, D.C. and dedicated to the fight to overcome poverty and homelessness. The organization was formed in 1970 to oppose the war in Vietnam through educational activities and nonviolent social protest. As the war came to a close, the CCNV increasingly focused its attention on the problems of the urban poor. In 1973, the CCNV organized a "Community Kitchen" to feed the poor and homeless. Soon it fed 400 people daily, while maintaining a free medical clinic. And on New Year's Eve, 1976, on "one of the coldest nights of the coldest winter in 50 years," the group took in its first homeless person. Thereafter members began driving throughout the city to offer the homeless warm shelter.

The CCNV has been in the forefront of action on behalf of the homeless, keeping pressure on city officials and church leaders for over 15 years. Along with a small group of socially conscious religious groups, in the mid-1970s CCNV launched a joint appeal to all 1,100 churches, synagogues and mosques in the Washington, D.C. area requesting that they open their buildings to the homeless. (While a few responded with money and clothing, only the Luther Place Memorial Church offered shelter.) The CCNV placed direct pressure on city officials in the winter of 1977–78 when, after three homeless men froze to death on one night, the director of the city's Department of Human Resources made a public statement attributing the deaths to weather, alcohol and bad luck rather than to a lack of warm shelter. After meeting with the CCNV, the city agreed to open a vacant city-owned building as an asylum to 75 homeless men. But homeless people continued to die of exposure on the streets of the nation's capital that winter, and the CCNV responded with a threat to camp out in front of city hall unless additional beds were provided. In response to the threat (and to the pleas of a Catholic priest), the city expanded its facilities for the homeless to 500 beds. The CCNV kept the pressure on the city through such acts of civil disobedience. In November, after occupying the National Visitor Center in Washington's Union Square station and inviting homeless people to sleep there, the city agreed to open a vacant school that it had previously promised to use as a backup shelter.

Many of these sorts of civil disobedience actions have continued to punctuate the activities of the CCNV. Members have gone on well-publicized fasts, have launched petition campaigns, have demonstrated outside those supermarket chains that refuse to make available the discarded food from dumpsters and have been a thorn in the side of city administrators, federal legislators and the president himself. For example, on Thanksgiving Day, 1981, in the midst of a struggle with the National Park Service over the right of the homeless to sleep in tents in Lafayette Park, the CCNV erected a tent community across from the White House, naming it "Reaganville" after President Ronald Reagan.

Currently, the Community for Creative Nonviolence is a multiracial group of about 50 activists, many of whom live together in a large house on Euclid Street. The household, organized as a cooperative, is furnished with donated (and scavenged) furniture, while the work of the group is sustained by donations that are, according to the group, not "encumbered in ways that could impair, reduce, or delay our ability to respond to the dictates of conscience or the needs of others." (See also SNYDER, MITCH.)

Community Demonstration Grant Projects for Alcohol and Drug Abuse Treatment of Homeless Individuals Community demonstration grants, authorized by the Stewart B. McKinney Homeless Assistance Act and awarded by the National Institute on Alcohol Abuse and Alcoholism, are designed to implement and evaluate innovative approaches to community-based alcohol/drug treatment and rehabilitation services for homeless individuals (or persons at risk of becoming homeless) from alcoholism and/or other substance abuse problems. Nine two-year demonstration grants were awarded in 1988. These grants provided for sobering-up stations for homeless men in Louisville and Anchorage, a residential alcohol/drug treatment center for homeless women and their children in Philadelphia, outreach and engagement teams in two welfare hotels in New York City to provide social and treatment services to women and children, a program of intensive case management for homeless clients in transitional care facilities and shelters in Boston and jail liaison services in Louisville. (See also DEPARTMENT OF HEALTH AND HUMAN SERVICES.)

Community Development Block Grant (CDBG) Program Established by Title I of the Housing and Community Development Act of 1974 and administered by the Department of Housing and Urban Development (HUD), the Community Development Block Grsnt (CDBG) Program awards grants to communities for neighborhood revitalization, economic development and provision of community facilities and services. The funds are intended for the benefit of low- and moderate-income communities and can be used for the acquisition of property, demolition or rehabilitation of buildings, provisions for public facilities and planning activities. CDBG regulations require that the bulk of the funds be used for activities that benefit low- and moderate-income persons. In recent years HUD has encouraged local grantees to use entitlement funds to acquire and rehabilitate buildings as homeless shelters and to provide social services to the homeless. Between 1983, and 1988, $202 million in CDBG funds were used for homeless assistance.

Community Mental Health Centers Act of 1963 See DEINSTITUTIONALIZATION; MENTAL ILLNESS.

Community Mental Health Services Demonstration Projects for Homeless Individuals Who Are Chronically Mentally Ill Funds for the Community Mental Health Services Demonstration Projects were authorized by Section 612 of the Stewart B. McKinney Homeless Assistance Act and are awarded by the National Institute for Mental Health (NIMH). The demonstration projects are intended to develop and evaluate comprehensive, community-based mental health service systems for homeless mentally ill adults. The projects are required to provide outreach, case management, mental health treatment, supportive housing and coordination of services in a comprehensive system of care. Of the 12 projects awarded funds by the NIMH in 1988, nine were designed for homeless mentally ill adults and three for homeless children and adolescents at high risk of emotional disturbance. As of the spring of 1989, these projects had provided direct services to 865 adults and approximately 500 children and youth. (See also DEPARTMENT OF HEALTH AND HUMAN SERVICES.)

Community Service Society (CSS)
The Community Service Society (CSS) of New York, a private social welfare agency, was founded in 1939. The CSS was formed from the merger of two prominent charitable groups, the Association for Improving the Condition of the Poor, incorporated in 1848, and the Charity Organization Society, founded in 1882. The earlier organizations were concerned with housing for the poor in New York City, among other issues, and sponsored pioneering studies of conditions in the tenement districts of the Lower East Side. Since its merger in 1939 the CSS has sponsored a variety of social welfare programs, including direct service, educational programs, training for community organizers and research and advocacy on behalf of the city's poor and elderly populations.

Early on, the CSS entered the debate over the homeless issue. In 1981 it published "Private Lives/Public Spaces: Homeless Adults on the Streets of New York City," an influential study by Kim Hopper and Ellen Baxter, and the following year it published "One Year Later: The Homeless Poor in New York City, 1982." The CSS criticized New York City's homeless shelter system for being the "place of last resort for many homeless men" because of "deplorable conditions." The CSS was the source of the widely quoted estimate of 36,000 homeless living in New York City in 1982. In a 1987 report entitled "Alternatives to the Welfare Hotel," the CSS described how shelters run by nonprofit agencies, using the same emergency assistance funds paid by the city in rent to often squalid WELFARE HOTELS, have managed to provide decent family shelters.

In addition to its research and advocacy activities, the CSS sponsors an Ownership Transfer Project that helps arrange the transfer of ownership of residential buildings from private landlords to tenant cooperatives, to prevent their abandonment or sale to speculators and gentrifiers. The CSS was also instrumental in creating The Heights, a single-room-occupancy (SRO) housing project built in New York City. Opening in 1986, the building provides housing for 55 formerly homeless men and women.

Community Support Program The
Community Support Program, authorized by the Public Health Service Act and administered within the Department of Health and Human Services (HHS), provides grants to state mental health authorities to develop comprehensive, community-based systems of care for severely mentally ill adults with

special emphasis on individuals who are homeless or at risk of becoming homeless.

Comprehensive Homeless Assistance Plan (CHAP)   In order to be eligible to receive Department of Housing and Urban Development (HUD)-administered funds for emergency shelter grants, participating states, metropolitan cities and urban counties must submit a Comprehensive Homeless Assistance Plan (CHAP) that includes: a description of the applicant's need for assistance under the homeless programs; a description of the available services that assist the homeless within the applicant's jurisdiction; a strategy to match needs with available services and to recognize the special needs of families with children, the elderly, the mentally ill, and veterans; an explanation of how federal assistance will complement and enhance available services; identification of a CHAP contact person or agency; and an assurance that each grantee, recipient and project sponsor will administer, in good faith, a policy designed to ensure that the homeless facility is free from the illegal use, possession or distribution of drugs or alcohol by its beneficiaries. In 1989, 50 states, Puerto Rico, 323 cities and counties and five territories were eligible to receive assistance; all but two of the territories submitted and had approved a Comprehensive Homeless Assistance Plan. Critics of HUD policies have argued that the CHAP guidelines for counting local homeless populations will lead to a serious understatement of the dimension of the problem.

congregate shelter   A congregate shelter is a large, undivided barrackslike shelter for the homeless. Some congregate shelters in New York City have beds for as many as 1,400 people. Although New York state law requires that no city shelters house more than 200 people, the city has routinely obtained waivers allowing it to continue to use its larger shelters. The cost of running the shelters is heavy. It costs New York City about $39 per person to provide each with a bed and basic services. Generally the larger the shelter, the worse its reputation for crime, disease and disorder. According to a report in the *New York Times* in November 1991: "Rife with tuberculosis, bronchitis, and other infections, congregate adult shelters . . . have become dumping grounds for men without homes who have been released from prisons, hospitals, and other institutions." (See also SHELTERS.)

Council of State Community Affairs Agencies (COSCAA)   The Council of State Community Affairs Agencies (COSCAA) is a national network of state-level community affairs officials working on homeless programs. COSCAA, headquartered in Washington, D.C., monitors federal and state legislation on homelessness and housing. It publishes a newsletter entitled "States and Housing."

court decisions   See LEGAL RIGHTS.

Covenant House   Covenant House, headquartered in New York City, is a religious social service agency that offers shelter and services for homeless teenagers in New York City, Houston, Fort Lauderdale, Toronto, New Orleans, Los Angeles and Anchorage. In an average year 28,000 homeless young people find temporary shelter with the Covenant House program. Covenant House maintains a telephone hotline (1-800-999-9999) where runaway children or their parents can call in for counseling or to leave messages.

Coxey's Army   Coxey's Army was one of several loosely organized "industrial armies" that set off from around the country to march on Washington in 1894. Its aim was to petition Congress to provide federal works projects to relieve the plight of the unemployed. Estimates of the numbers of marchers who set off for Washington in the spring of 1894 vary from between 6,000 to as many as 20,000.

The Panic of 1893 had unleashed what would be the worst depression in U.S. history until the Great Depression of the 1930s. It lasted for four bitter years, and several million workers lost their jobs. There was no federal or state relief for the unemployed, and private charities could do little to take up the slack. Many of the unemployed took to the road in search of employment, leading to widespread (and exaggerated) fears of social upheaval and banditry. "We cannot disguise the truth that we are on the verge of revolution," Kansas senator John J. Ingalls told his colleagues in Washington in 1893. "Labor, starving and sullen in the cities, aims to overthrow a system under which the rich are growing richer and the poor are growing poorer."

Jacob Sechler Coxey (1854–1951), a successful quarry owner from Massilon, Ohio, believed that the nation could be delivered from economic hardship through a combination of monetary reform and public works employment. Coxey's proposal to put the unemployed to work improving the nation's roads was endorsed by the American Federation of Labor (AFL) at its 1893 convention. Teaming up with Carl Browne, a showman, political agitator and religious enthusiast, Coxey assembled an "army" of 100 unemployed workers, who set out from Massilon on Easter Sunday, 1894 for Washington. Similar groups of 500 to 1,000 men set off independently from a number of West Coast cities. Some of the groups commandeered trains to carry them eastward. Coxey's small band attracted considerable publicity along the route of the march and aroused fears of insurrection, but gained relatively few recruits. Coxey's followers were at pains to insist that they were respectable citizens, despite their lack of employment. "We are not tramps nor vagabonds that's shirking honest toil / But miners, clerks, skilled artisans and tillers of the soil," went a refrain from their marching song "Marching with Coxey." On May 1, 1894 Coxey's 500-strong "army" paraded peacefully through the streets of downtown Washington to present their "petition in boots," cheered by a crowd of 30,000 spectators. When they reached the Capitol grounds, Coxey, Browne and another of his followers were arrested for walking on the grass and sentenced to 20 days in jail. Coxey's followers camped out in Washington for several months afterwards but were dispersed before the end of summer without incident. On May 1, 1944 the 50th anniversary of the original march, Coxey delivered the speech from the Capitol steps that he had intended to give in 1894, at the invitation of Speaker of the House Sam Rayburn and Vice President Henry Wallace.

crack   See DRUG ABUSE.

Cranston, Alan   See CRANSTON-GONZALEZ NATIONAL AFFORDABLE HOUSING ACT.

Cranston-Gonzalez National Affordable Housing Act

The Cranston-Gonzalez National Affordable Housing Act, named for its sponsors Senator Alan Cranston of California and Representative Henry B. Gonzalez of Texas, was passed by Congress in October 1991 and signed into law by President George Bush the following month. The bill reversed a decade-long trend, which had begun in the administration of President Ronald Reagan, to reduce government spending on housing. The bill passed by overwhelming majorities in both houses of Congress and authorized $27.5 billion to affordable housing programs in fiscal 1991 and $29.9 billion in fiscal 1992. Under the HOME Investment Partnerships Act, $3 billion was to be spent over two years in block grants to state and local government to fund the construction and rehabilitation of public housing. The HOMEOWNERSHIP AND OPPORTUNITY FOR PEOPLE EVERYWHERE (HOPE) program to encourage public housing tenants to purchase their apartments, a strategy favored by President Bush and Housing and Urban Development (HUD) Secretary Jack

Kemp, also received substantial funding. The bill also shored up the financially troubled Federal Housing Administration (FHA).

crime In the 19th century the poor, the homeless and the vagrant were considered deviant, evil and a "dangerous class" by the middle classes, who often harbored wildly exaggerated fears of crime, disorder and rebellion by those who were victims of the new industrial order. Such fears are evident today as well, as some cities treat homelessness primarily as a law enforcement problem. The rhetoric of that earlier age is often heard again as cities with large homeless populations face political pressure from property owners to prevent the homeless from sleeping in parks and town squares and other public spaces, while the rise of aggressive panhandling on urban streets reinforces fears of the homeless as a menacing "dangerous class."

Deciding the extent to which such fears are legitimate is not a simple task. Violent and well-publicized crimes by homeless people such as JUAN GONZALEZ have created an association in the minds of many between the presence of the homeless and a high crime rate. The homeless do have a higher rate of arrest and incarceration than the non-homeless. According to a 1987 survey of soup kitchen and shelter users by the Urban Institute, 60 percent of the single men, 23 percent of the single women and 15 percent of the women with children had spent more than three or four days in a county jail. Moreover, 29 percent of the single men reported serving time in state or federal prison, as did 2 percent of the single women and women with children.

Such figures need to be considered carefully, however. Shelter residents are only one segment of a larger homeless population for whom comparable data is lacking. (Many homeless families can be found "doubling up," sleeping on the floors in the home of a friend or relative, living in tents in the woods or in a van on the side of a road.) Even more important, however, is that time spent in county jails is often for misdemeanors, including those connected with the condition of homelessness itself (vagrancy, public drunkenness, urinating in public and so on). Homeless people with histories of hospitalization for mental illness or treatment for substance abuse (drugs or alcohol) had much higher rates of criminal records than other homeless people, and it is likely that being on the streets increases the odds that a mentally unstable or drug- or alcohol-addicted person will be arrested by the police; they are at greater risk than a person who is mentally ill or addicted in the privacy and safety of his or her own home. Arrest records themselves do not tell us very much about the "criminal tendencies" of a population, particularly when the main characteristic of that population (in this case, homelessness) is itself treated as a criminal act. For example, in 1990 the U.S. Supreme Court upheld a ban against begging in the New York City subway system. This ban will most likely lead to an increase in the arrest rates of beggars in the city and make "criminals" of those with these arrest records.

The average homeless person is more likely to be the victim than the perpetrator of a violent crime. The homeless have found themselves victims of violent attack by non-homeless persons who fear or resent their presence. Teenagers in California have boasted of being "troll-busters," beating up homeless men who sleep under bridges. On Halloween night in 1990, masked young men wielding clubs and knives attacked homeless men living in a shelter on New York City's Wards Island, leaving one homeless man dead and others seriously injured. "They treat us like we're dogs, or dirt," complained one of the survivors of the attack. And in the winter and spring of 1992, there were a series of attacks by youth gangs on homeless people sleeping in the New York City subway system. Robert Walther, a 39-year-old homeless man, was set on fire by a gang in March, sustaining third-degree burns over 95 percent of his body, and dying several days later. His assailants were not captured.

The homeless are also preyed upon by other homeless people. Many of the homeless refuse to go into emergency shelters because of the danger of violence or theft. Experienced shelter residents tell of sleeping with their shoes clutched in their hands so that the shoes won't be stolen from them while they sleep. Women are particularly vulnerable to theft and sexual assault by those preying on the homeless. (See also LEGAL RIGHTS.)

culture of poverty See HARRINGTON, MICHAEL; WAR ON POVERTY.

Cuomo, Andrew Andrew Cuomo, the son of New York governor Mario Cuomo, started a private nonprofit housing group in 1986 called HOUSING ENTERPRISE FOR THE LESS PRIVILEGED (HELP). HELP's transitional housing projects are often cited as models of what can be accomplished to help homeless families prepare to move on to permanent housing. In 1991 Cuomo was appointed by Mayor David Dinkins to head up a commission to make recommendations on the homeless problem in New York City. The Cuomo commission report, released in February 1992, called for the city to move its homeless population out of large barracks-style shelters into smaller, intensive social service programs, and whenever possible into permanent housing. The commission made headlines when it reported that two-thirds of homeless single men and nearly a third of adults in families who lived in city shelters tested positive for drug or alcohol use. "You have to be honest about a problem before you can do anything about it," Cuomo told reporters when the commission's report came out. "There was a decade of denial in the 1980's [on the part of homeless advocates], an insistence on the simplistic 'housing, housing, housing' slogan. But

the problem was always deeper than that." In 1993 Cuomo joined the administration of President Bill Clinton as assistant housing secretary in the Department of Housing and Urban Development. He was principal author of a report written in early 1994 entitled *Priority: Home! The Federal Plan to End Homelessness,* which argued that the dimensions of the homeless problem were far greater than suggested in the statistics relied on by federal officials under Presidents Ronald Reagan and George Bush. (See also TRANSITIONAL HOUSING.)

Cuomo, Mario Mario Cuomo, born in Queens, New York in 1932, was the son of Italian immigrant parents. He was elected governor of New York state in 1982, after serving as secretary of state and lieutenant governor. Under Cuomo's leadership in the 1980s, New York State's spending on homeless shelters and other programs increased dramatically. Known as one of the most charismatic liberal politicians of his time, Cuomo was an outspoken critic of the Reagan administration's cutbacks in social welfare spending. Cuomo's son, Andrew Cuomo, initiated a widely praised program to create nonprofit housing in New York.

cyclical homeless See EPISODIC HOMELESS.

D

Day, Dorothy See CATHOLIC WORKER.

day labor See SPOT LABOR.

definition of homelessness The 1987 Stewart B. McKinney Homeless Assistance Act defined a homeless person as "a person who 1) lacks a fixed, regular, and adequate nighttime residence, or 2) lives in: a) a shelter, b) an institution other than a prison, or c) a place not designed for or ordinarily used as a sleeping accommodation for human beings." The National Coalition for the Homeless has argued that the definition should be broadened to include the " 'invisible' homeless, those who move from one improvised setting to another, DOUBLING UP with friends and family, and making use of emergency lodging only on rare occasion." (See also EPISODIC HOMELESS.)

deinstitutionalization   The "deinstitutionalization" of patients suffering from MENTAL ILLNESS is often cited as a cause for the spread of homelessness. The history of the deinstitutionalization movement begins just after World War II. In 1946 Congress established the National Institute of Mental Health (NIMH) to study the causes and possible cures of mental illness. At the same time new drugs, such as Thorazine, were developed that stablized symptoms of the mentally ill, permitting patients to live outside of a hospital setting. By 1955 nearly 2 million people were being given Thorazine. Public outcry against the often squalid or brutal conditions prevailing in U.S. mental hospitals, whose population peaked at over 550,000 in the 1950s, led to demands for reform. In 1963 President John F. Kennedy proposed to Congress the phasing out the custodial care of the mentally ill. Congress passed the Mental Retardation Facilities and Community Mental Health Centers Construction Act later that year, providing federal funding for outpatient and emergency treatment centers for the mentally ill.

In response to public pressures and the federal government's initiative, state mental hospitals began to discharge large numbers of their patients. The over 500,000 state mental hospital patient population of 1955 was cut to less than 138,000 patients by 1980. The states welcomed the new policies, because they saw the opportunity to shift the burden of caring for mentally ill from their own treasuries to the federal government.

The passage of the Medicaid and Medicare bills, providing federal health insurance benefits for the poor and the elderly, also shifted the burden of supporting the mentally ill from the states to the federal goverment. But "reform" again prepared the way for a new social crisis. The federal government largely reneged on the commitment it had made to providing new forms of treatment for the former state hospital patients. Only 700 of what was originally planned to be 2,500 community mental health centers were opened in the 1960s and 1970s, and these often wound up serving a more affluent and less severely disturbed clientele than the population previously confined to state mental hospitals.

Well-publicized cases, such as those involving JOYCE BROWN and JUAN GONZALEZ, inflamed public sentiment against the homeless mentally ill in the 1980s and contributed to the belief that deinstitutionalization had gone too far. Calls for REINSTITUTIONALIZATION began to be heard.

The importance of "deinstitutionalization" in and of itself as a cause of homelessness can, however, easily be exaggerated. As sociologist James Wright pointed out in 1989, "By the late 1970s, most of the people destined ever to be 'deinstitutionalized' already had been. So as a direct contributing factor to the rise of homelessness in the 1980s, deinstitutionalization cannot be that important." Through most of the 1960s and 1970s, the recently discharged mentally ill (and those who were never admitted to mental hospitals due to more stringent entry requirements) were not, in fact, reduced to homelessness. New regulations for public assistance in the 1960s made federal money available to support people with mental illness outside of a hospital setting. Housing was available for them—in SINGLE-ROOM-OCCUPANCY HOTELS (SROS), for example. These were often not ideal settings for psychiatric recovery, but they were sufficient to keep mentally ill persons out of the elements and away from the dangers of the street.

In fact, relatively few of today's homeless are drawn from the ranks of the "deinstitutionalized." According to one study only 3 percent of homeless came directly from mental institutions to homelessness. Many more have passed through one or another form of transitional setting, such as halfway houses or SROs. But cutbacks in social welfare spending have eliminated many halfway houses, while the forces of urban GENTRIFICATION eliminated the SROs. When the administration of President Ronald Reagan slashed federal spending on welfare programs in the early 1980s, nearly 500,000 recipients were cut from the rolls of the SOCIAL SECURITY DISABILITY INSURANCE program. Nearly a third of these were people suffering from psychiatric disabilities, and many of them wound up living on the street.

Denver, Colorado According to the 1991 *Status Report on Hunger and Homelessness* issued by the United States Conference of Mayors, Denver, Colorado had an estimated homeless population of 1,050. Other estimates placed the number between 1,500 and 3,500. The city received an average of 1,050 requests for emergency shelter in the fall of 1991. The city had 1,005 emergency shelter beds available in that year and 270 beds available for families seeking shelter. A Denver city official was quoted in the *Status Report* as saying: "The problems have increased, particularly in terms of housing and shelter. While needs are increasing, resources are decreasing."

Department of Agriculture The United States Department of Agriculture (USDA) provides assistance to homeless individuals as part of more broadly targeted nutrition programs administered by its Food and Nutrition Service (FNS). These include the food stamp program, the Special Supplemental Food Program for Women, Infants, and Children (WIC), the National School Lunch Program, and the School Breakfast Program. In addition, the Hunger Prevention

Act of 1988 provided $40 million to the USDA to purchase surplus commodities for SOUP KITCHENS, food banks, and other institutions that provide meals to the homeless. (See also FOOD STAMPS.)

Department of Defense Since the passage of the 1984 Department of Defense Authorization Act, the Department of Defense (DOD) has opened 15 shelters for the homeless in unused buildings on military installations. The DOD has also provided surplus cots, pillows, sheets and blankets to other shelter operators, and surplus food to private food banks. The DOD does not provide any of the cost of running the shelters, which must be borne by local governments.

Department of Education The Stewart B. McKinney Homeless Assistance Act (See MCKINNEY ACT) of 1987 authorized the Department of Education to conduct special programs for the education of the homeless. These include the Adult Education for the Homeless Program, the Education for Homeless Children and Youth—State Grants Programs, and Exemplary Programs. (See also CHILDREN.)

Department of Health and Human Services Health and Human Services (HHS) is the Cabinet-level department that is most concerned with issues of health, welfare and income security. Its subagencies administer a wide variety of programs, including the Social Security system. HHS was created in 1979 under the administration of President Jimmy Carter, when the old Department of Health, Education and Welfare (HEW) was divided into two new departments: HHS and the Department of Education.

HHS administers programs authorized by the Stewart B. McKinney Homeless Assistance Act (See MCKINNEY ACT) and other assistance programs that are specifically targeted to provide health care, mental health care, substance abuse treatment, emergency services, and shelter for homeless individuals and families. These include the HEALTH CARE FOR THE HOMELESS (HCH) Grant Program, the BLOCK GRANT PROGRAM FOR SERVICES TO HOMELESS INDIVIDUALS WHO ARE CHRONICALLY MENTALLY ILL, the COMMUNITY MENTAL HEALTH SERVICES DEMONSTRATION PROJECTS FOR HOMELESS INDIVIDUALS WHO ARE CHRONICALLY MENTALLY ILL, the COMMUNITY SUPPORT PROGRAM, the COMMUNITY DEMONSTRATION GRANT PROJECTS FOR ALCOHOL AND DRUG ABUSE TREATMENT OF HOMELESS INDIVIDUALS, the EMERGENCY COMMUNITY SERVICES HOMELESS GRANT PROGRAM (EHP), the McKinney AFDC Transitional Housing Demonstration Program, the Runaway and Homeless Youth Program and the DRUG ABUSE PREVENTION PROGRAM FOR RUNAWAY AND HOMELESS YOUTH. In addition, homeless individuals also may be entitled to benefits under more broadly targeted programs administered by HHS, including EMERGENCY ASSISTANCE, AID TO FAMILIES WITH DEPENDENT CHILDREN (AFDC), MEDICAID, MEDICARE, SOCIAL SECURITY Old Age and Survivors Insurance, SOCIAL SECURITY DISABILITY INSURANCE (SSDI) and SUPPLEMENTAL SECURITY INCOME (SSI), and SOCIAL SERVICES BLOCK GRANTS (SSBG).

Department of Housing and Urban Development (HUD) See HUD.

Department of Labor The Department of Labor has funded several pilot programs directed toward homeless people. Among these are the Job Training for the Homeless Demonstration Program (JTHDP), which provided funding to 21 public and private groups in 1989 to operate employment and training projects for the homeless. After nine months of operation, these groups reported having enrolled 1,956 homeless people in training and placing 1,546 homeless people in jobs. The Department of Labor administers the Homeless Veterans Reintegration Project (HVRP), authorized by the Stewart B. McKinney Homeless Assistance Act (See

MCKINNEY ACT). In 1988 this project awarded 15 grants to local demonstration projects to develop employment and training services such as job counseling, resume preparation, job-search assistance, remedial and vocational education, job placement and on-the-job training that will "expedite the reintegration of homeless veterans into the labor force." Some demonstration projects also provide additional services, such as transportation, clothes or tools needed for employment, alcohol and drug-treatment referrals, and posttraumatic stress disorder counseling.

In 1988 and 1989 the Labor Department also cosponsored a pilot project with the New York City Human Resources Administration (HRA) called Shelter Corps. The project set aside 50 slots the first year and 75 the second year at the Glenmont Job Corps Center near Albany for youth and young adults living in shelters. The center provides room and board, education, vocational training, counseling, medical care, driver education and support services to program participants. The former shelter inhabitants were reported to be highly motivated, with a smaller dropout and discharge rate than other program participants.

Department of Veterans Affairs In October 1988 President Ronald Reagan signed the bill creating the Department of Veterans Affairs (VA), which took the place of the Veterans Administration, an independent federal agency. The Department of Veterans Affairs provides services to nearly 30 million American veterans of military service. It runs a system of 172 VA hospitals, 231 outpatient clinics, 58 regional offices, 117 nursing homes, 27 domiciliaries and 189 outreach centers for Vietnam-era veterans. The VA also administers disability compensation and pensions, guarantees home loans to eligible veterans and operates 111 national cemeteries.

In addition to the general services it offers to all veterans, the VA runs two programs specifically targeted to homeless veterans. (Over 30 percent of homeless persons are believed to be veterans.) The first, created in 1987, is known as the Homeless Chronically Mentally Ill Veterans Program. Through the program, 43 VA medical centers provide: outreach to homeless chronically mentally ill veterans in shelters and soup kitchens and on the streets; medical and psychiatric examinations to determine veterans' health and mental status; and, where needed, treatment and rehabilitation in community-based facilities for limited periods. In a preliminary evaluation of the program, the VA concluded that half the veterans involved in the program "show improvement in their health care problem areas and their residential situations." For veterans placed in community-based residential treatment, the success rate was judged to be considerably lower: 25.6 percent were judged to have completed the program successfully, but another 53 percent left against medical advice or were discharged for violation of program regulations. The other program provided by the VA is known as the Domiciliary Care for Homeless Veterans (DCHV) Program, also begun in 1987. Under this program, 20 VA medical centers have provided a total of 913 beds for temporary domiciliary care for homeless veterans. The veterans enrolled in the program are offered medical and psychiatric care, "incentive therapy" designed to "re-establish work habits" and follow-up help in housing and job placement. (See also VETERANS.)

Detroit, Michigan   The 1991 *Status Report on Hunger and Homelessness* issued by the United States Conference of Mayors did not offer an estimate of the total homeless population of Detroit, but reported that on an average 1991 fall day, 15,200 people sought emergency shelter. Estimates of the number of homeless in the city from other sources range as high as 60,000. There are 1,200 to 1,300 emergency shelter beds available in the city, and 500 beds available for families seeking shelter. The decline of the auto industry has been a major factor in increasing the number of homeless people in Michigan. Since 1968 the city has lost over 200,000 jobs, one-third of its total employment. Cutbacks in welfare spending have also contributed to the increase in homelessness. Nearly a quarter of the city's populations subsists on welfare payments. A Detroit city official was quoted in the 1991 *Status Report* as saying:

> The state [of Michigan] eliminated the General Assistance and Emergency Needs programs in October, 1991. This is affecting approximately 40,000 people in Detroit, and it is estimated that as many as 5,000 of them could become homeless through evictions. There is definitely a direct relation between the state cuts and increasing homelessness in our city.

(See also DEINSTITUTIONALIZATION; GENERAL ASSISTANCE.)

Deukmejian, George   See WORKFARE.

Dinkins, David   David Dinkins, born in Trenton, New Jersey in 1927, was elected mayor of New York City in 1989, after serving as city clerk and Manhattan borough president, and served one four-year term. A graduate of Howard University and Brooklyn Law School, Dinkins was New York's first African-American mayor. As borough president, Dinkins had been a staunch critic of the homeless policies of his predecessor, Edward Koch. But once in office, severe financial and political constraints limited Dinkins's ability to do away with CONGREGATE SHELTERS and WELFARE HOTELS, as he promised in his election campaign. (See also ARSON; SHANTYTOWNS; SUBWAYS; TOMPKINS SQUARE PARK.)

Disability Benefits   See SOCIAL SECURITY DISABILITY INSURANCE (SSDI).

disinvestment   Banks and other financial institutions sometimes take the funds from checking and savings deposits from branches in one community and move the money elsewhere instead of reinvesting that money in the community where it was deposited. The result is a shift of capital from lower- to higher-income areas, creating the conditions for the ABANDONMENT of property in poorer neighborhoods by landlords and the eventual DISPLACEMENT of its residents.

Disinvestment may also refer to the process by which an individual landlord finds it profitable to let property deteriorate by withholding services and maintenance. For some landlords disinvestment may reflect the inability to maintain an adequate financial investment in the property, but for many others it is a conscious strategy to "milk" the property for profit before abandoning it altogether. (See also GENTRIFICATION, REDLINING).

displacement Displacement refers to the forced, involuntary dislocation of low-income households from existing housing units or the removal of housing stock from neighborhoods. It is a particularly severe problem where low-income housing is scarce. Some experts considered displacement to be one of the most frequent causes of homelessness.

From 1950 to 1980 URBAN RENEWAL projects were thought to have displaced well over a million low-income residents while reducing substantially the supply of low-cost housing. More recently displacement has been associated with the process of neighborhood GENTRIFICATION and has been viewed by many as one of its major costs. As housing costs rose more rapidly than incomes from the mid 1970s through the 1980s, rental housing became prohibitively expensive for low-income persons in many cities across the nation.

While the Department of Housing and Urban Development (HUD) issued an official "Displacement Report" in 1979 that minimized the significance of the problem, more recent empirical studies suggest otherwise. For example, Legates and Hartman

(1981, 1986) estimated that 2.5 million persons were being displaced annually by gentrification in the United States while suggesting that the figure may actually have been much higher. In his case study of displacement caused by ABANDONMENT and gentrification in New York City, Peter Marcuse (1986) estimated that abandonment caused between 31,000 and 60,000 households to be displaced and gentrification caused between 10,000 and 40,000 households to be displaced annually in the decade prior to 1986. That is, between 41,000 and 100,000 households were displaced from both causes together (or 102,500 to 250,000 individuals, assuming an average household size of 2.5 persons) in New York City yearly. (See also EVICTION.)

Doe Fund See READY, WILLING AND ABLE.

domestic violence See BATTERED WOMEN.

Domestic Volunteer Service Act Amendments of 1983 Under these amendments to the Domestic Volunteer Service Act, VOLUNTEERS IN SERVICE TO AMERICA (VISTA), the federal volunteer program, was authorized to provide its workers to homeless-related projects.

Domiciliary Care for Homeless Veterans Program In 1987 the Department of Veterans Affairs (VA) launched a program known as Domiciliary Care for Homeless Veterans (DCHV). Under this program, 20 VA medical centers have provided a total of 913 beds for temporary domiciliary care for homeless veterans. The veterans enrolled in the program are offered medical and psychiatric care, "incentive therapy" designed to "re-establish work habits" and follow-up help in housing and job placement.

doubling up The practice of two or more families sharing a living space designed for one family is known as doubling up. The result is overcrowded living conditions, with overcrowding generally defined as a household with more than one person per room. Families resort to doubling up in order to hold down housing costs. In public housing projects alone, the number of two- and three-family households doubled from 1983 to 1990. In New York City, it was estimated that 35,000 people in public housing and 73,000 in private housing were doubled up in the mid-1980s. Doubling up can be a cause for eviction of both the original and the "doubled up" tenants, and thus a cause of homelessness. A 1987 survey of New York City shelter residents found that between 50 and 60 percent were doubled up before they arrived in the shelter. The *New York Times* reported in 1990 that while doubling up was once mainly a problem for the poorest people in the city, by 1990 it was a severe problem for the city's working class as well. In cities across the nation, the 1980s saw housing costs rise precipitously, with little or no increase (and in some regions a decrease) in income. Doubling up became the only option for working families.

downtown redevelopment See GENTRIFICATION; URBAN RENEWAL.

Downtown Women's Center See DROP-IN CENTERS.

drop-in centers While many cities have developed shelter programs to provide homeless people a place to sleep at night, relatively few have considered the problems that homeless people have finding a place to spend their daytime hours. Drop-in centers have been established in several cities to provide a place for homeless to spend their days. The privately supported Downtown Women's Center in Los Angeles offers showers, meals, a place to nap and psychiatric services to homeless women, as does the Antonio G. Olivieri Center for Homeless Women in New York City.

drug abuse Use of illegal and addictive drugs is rampant in the United States. Federal authorities estimated in 1990 that there were more than 4 million people addicted to drugs in the country. Estimates of drug abuse by the homeless vary widely. See the figure under MENTAL ILLNESS for the prevalence of drug/alcohol problems among adult homeless. In February 1992 a commission appointed by New York City mayor David Dinkins released the results of a survey that estimated that 80 percent of the homeless men housed in the city's large shelters and 30 percent of the adults in family shelters abused drugs or alcohol. Commission chairman Andrew Cuomo told reporters that homeless advocates had made a serious error in underplaying the extent of drug abuse among the homeless. The Cuomo commission report, released in February 1992, called for the city to move its homeless population out of large barracks-style shelters, where drug and alcohol abuse was rampant, into smaller, intensive social service programs, and whenever possible into permanent housing.

The federal government's "drug war" has thus far emphasized law enforcement over prevention and cure of drug addiction. In 1991 President George Bush outlined a "National Drug Control Strategy" that included a request for $1.6 billion for drug treatment programs. But for every dollar the administration has requested for such programs, it has requested four dollars for interdiction, law enforcement and prisons designed to interfere with the supply of drugs. As of 1990 there were only 400,000 treatment slots nationwide to cope with an addict population that was at least ten times that number.

New York City has a particularly serious problem with drug abuse, both in the general population and among the homeless. The widespread availability of crack cocaine has exacerbated the problem. Crack was introduced in the United States in the mid-1980s. It is available at low cost and smoked in cigarettes or water pipes. (In 1992 the cost of getting high on crack in Harlem was about three dollars.) There may be as many as 500,000 users of cocaine and other illegal drugs in New York City. The city also has an estimated 250,000 intravenous drug users (who inject drugs into their blood with intravenous needles), who are at special risk of being infected with the human immunodeficiency virus (HIV), the infectious agent that causes acquired immune deficiency syndrome (AIDS). Crack users are also at risk of AIDS, because many female crack addicts exchange sex for drugs to support their habits. New York City's clinics, long-term rehabilitation centers and drug counseling services have been underfunded and understaffed to meet the emergency; only about 37,000 treatment slots are available for drug users. The National Coalition for the Homeless brought suit against New York City and New York State in 1989 in a case called PALMIERI V. CUOMO on behalf of homeless men who had sought and been denied drug treatment. The Coalition hoped to repeat its earlier success in the 1981 settlement of *CALLAHAN V. CAREY*, which required New York City to provide shelter for all who seek it. But a New York State trial court dismissed the lawsuit in December 1989, declaring that there was no enforceable right to treatment for drug addiction.

One New York state-funded program, the Jericho Project, provides housing and rehabilitation services for homeless substance abusers. Jericho provides housing for 57 single adults, substance abuse treatment in conjunction with Alcoholics Anonymous and Narcotics Anonymous. If participants in the project are able to go for a full year without relapsing into alcohol or drug abuse, Jericho will provide them with interest-free loans for down payments on housing. Jericho provides its services at cost of under $5,000 a year, one-third the cost of housing a homeless person in a city shelter. (See also CUOMO, ANDREW; SUBSTANCE ABUSE.)

Drug Abuse Prevention Program for Runaway and Homeless Youth This program, authorized by the Anti-Drug Abuse Act of 1988 and administered within the Department of Health and Human Services (HHS), seeks to educate RUNAWAYS and homeless youth about the dangers of substance abuse. Program activities include comprehensive services projects, community networking projects and demonstration projects for runaway and homeless youth. (See also CHILDREN; DRUG ABUSE; SUBSTANCE ABUSE.)

Dukakis, Michael See WORKFARE.

E

Earthwise Education Center The Earthwise Education Center is a nonprofit group located on an organic farm 40 miles northeast of Syracuse, New York that trains homeless people to become organic farmers.

Edelman, Marian Wright See CHILDREN.

education Education has traditionally been regarded in the United States as a vehicle for social mobility. By taking advantage of the free gift of public education, the children of the poor would be able to train themselves to be qualified for better jobs and a better way of life than their parents knew. But the rapid increase in homelessness in the 1980s provided the nation's public schools with challenges they were ill-prepared to meet, coming at a time when the schools themselves were facing financial hardship. As a result, homeless children living in shelters, welfare hotels, abandoned buildings or on the streets are often deprived of the benefits of education.

In the late 1980s Congress passed legislation designed to overcome the hardships homeless children face in pursuing their educations. The Stewart B. McKinney Homeless Assistance Act requires that "each State educational agency shall assure that each child of a homeless individual and each homeless youth access to a free, appropriate public education." Under the provisions of the act, state education departments may apply for federal funds to develop programs for homeless children. As the authors of the MCKINNEY ACT and homeless advocates have recognized, the question of education for homeless children has important long-range implications for American society, since hundreds of thousands of children may be growing up ill or uneducated because of their lack of housing. And while education in itself is not a solution to homelessness, it could be one element of a comprehensive attack on its causes. Lorraine Friedman, a lawyer at the National Law Center on Homelessness and Poverty (a homeless advocacy group), argued in 1991: "Education is the way to insure that homeless children don't become homeless adults. Only through education will they become productive, employable members of society. It's the only chance they have to break out of the cycle of poverty they are now stuck in."

A 1989 federal report estimated that there were 241,700 homeless children of school age and that nearly 28 percent of them, or 67,500 school-age children, were not attending school. A report issued in May 1991 by the National Association of State Coordinators for the Education of Homeless Children and Youth, the group charged with implementing the educational provisions of the McKinney Act, put the number much higher. It estimated that anywhere between 310,000 and 1.6 million children of school age were homeless. The parents of these children, preoccupied with the difficulties of securing shelter, jobs and food, are often forced to give priority to such basic elements of survival over the educational needs of their children.

In addition, despite the provisions of the McKinney Act requiring that all homeless children receive access to public schools, common bureaucratic procedures often block their enrollment. The lack of previous school records or delays in transferring records, the lack of a birth certificate and of proper immunization or immunization records or the confused legal guardianship of an individual child can make school enrollment for the homeless child a difficult process. Moreover, school districts have sometimes tried to escape the burdens of educating the homeless through other legal devices. In Wrightstown, New Jersey, for example, local officials passed a municipal ordinance restricting motel stays by homeless families to 30 days to keep homeless children out of their schools. This policy was successfully challenged in a lawsuit in 1987, *Vingara et al. v. Borough of Wrightstown.*

Even when parents and school districts are willing to have homeless children attend school, other obstacles remain. Homeless parents' financial constraints may mean there is no money available to pay for school supplies or adequate clothing. Many homeless children are reluctant to attend a strange school, feeling discouraged that they have fallen behind their peers through frequent transfers or absences from school and ashamed to enter a setting where their family's poverty will be evident to other children. Lee Hines, a homeless teenager living in Queens, New York, told a reporter in 1992 of an incident that had happened to him when he was in sixth grade, living in a welfare hotel. He had carefully kept his homelessness a secret until one day his math teacher, learning of his residence, stood in front of class and announced: "I didn't know we had a shelter kid in here; give a hand for the shelter kid." Hines recalled his overwhelming humiliation at being singled out:

"Everybody started laughing. I cried, and I ran out of the classroom." Hines nearly dropped out of school, and took to selling crack on streetcorners, but eventually returned to the classroom.

Data from the New York City Board of Education showed in 1990 that the average homeless elementary school pupil attended class just under three-quarters of the time, compared with a schoolwide average of nearly 90 percent attendance. The attendance rate for homeless high school children drops to only about half time. A 1989 study by Advocates for Children, an educational advocacy group, found that homeless students in New York City were twice as likely as their classmates to be forced to repeat a grade. Only 42 percent of homeless children in grades three through ten were reading at grade level, compared to 68 percent of students citywide, and only 28 percent of homeless children could meet grade-level requirements in math compared to 57 percent of students citywide.

Children who have become homeless because of domestic violence may be in danger of kidnapping or physical harm from an abusive parent if they are at school. Even if they do enroll in school, sleep deprivation, hunger, stress, frequent illness and inadequate socialization can interfere with their academic performance. A 1987 study of children living in family shelters and welfare hotels in Massachusetts showed that 43 percent of the school-age children in the sample had failed a grade, and nearly half were currently failing or performing below-average work in school. The National Association of State Coordinators for the Education of Homeless Children and Youth argued in a 1990 report that American schools would have to learn to address the special needs of homeless children: "In opening the schoolhouse doors without addressing these needs, we may find that we are opening a revolving door through which homeless children enroll, experience failure, and prematurely exit."

Innovative programs designed to help homeless students have been launched in a number of states. In Maryland the Helping Hands Homework Assistance Program matches public libraries with homeless shelters in their area. In Baltimore two libraries in 1989 provided quiet places for homeless children to study and to receive homework assistance from tutors. The New York City Board of Education established a Students Living in Temporary Housing Unit (SLTHU) that, among other things, arranged for teaching GED preparation and English as a second language in selected welfare hotels and emergency shelters. The Madison, Wisconsin Metropolitan School District established a Transitional Education Program that maintains a "transition room" in a local elementary school, where homeless students can receive school materials and supplies and meet with the principal and teachers before moving into the general school population. The Orlando [Florida] Coalition for the Homeless offered an after-school tutoring program as part of its shelter services, which incorporated art, videos, creative writing and stress management in its curriculum. Similarly innovative programs from around the country were described in a report issued by the Department of Education in 1990. In 1991 Congress appropriated $7.2 billion for the education of homeless children and called for greatly stepping up such federal support. Federal money is used to identify homeless children, enroll them in school, defray the cost of transportation and other services. Representative Louise Slaughter of Rochester, New York wrote amendments to the McKinney Act in 1990 strengthening the federal commitment to homeless education. She charged that the administration of President George Bush was failing to aggressively enforce the provisions of the McKinney Act to protect homeless children, despite Bush's vow to be the "education President." "The biggest mistake that the United States can make now," Slaughter argued in 1991, "is to ignore the education needs of these homeless children."

educational level of homeless people

According to a 1989 study conducted by sociologist James Wright, nearly one in five homeless people has attended one or more years of college; over half have a high school degree. Younger homeless people generally have higher educational levels than older ones.

Eisenheim v. County Board of Superiors

A 1983 Superior Court decision in Los Angeles in the case of *Eisenheim v. County Board of Superiors* ruled that Los Angeles County could no longer restrict eligibility for emergency local shelter relief (in the form of housing vouchers or housing checks) by demanding the presentation of identification and imposing a waiting period of several days' duration. (See also LEGAL RIGHTS.)

Eisenhower, Dwight D.

Dwight David Eisenhower was the 34th president of the United States. He was first elected in November 1952 and reelected in 1956. He came to the White House after a distinguished military career that included the command of Allied forces in Western Europe during World War II. His years in office saw the development of several trends that contributed in the long run to the emergence of homelessness, including federally subsidized URBAN RENEWAL programs, authorized by the NATIONAL HOUSING ACT OF 1949, and the passage of the Interstate Highway Act, which by providing easier access to urban employment from residential suburbs contributed to the flight of the white middle class and working class from the nation's cities.

elderly

During the 1970s and 1980s the average age of the homeless population dropped considerably. In the 1950s and 1960s the homeless population was largely an older population, associated with ALCO-HOLISM and SKID ROW neighborhoods. In 1968 half the clients of New York City's Men's Shelter were over the age of 50. By 1979 only 17 percent of first-time clients of the Men's Shelter were that old. Today, while 12 percent of American males are over 65 years of age, only 3 percent of homeless males are that age. The availability of Medicare, SOCIAL SECURITY and other entitlement programs targeted for the elderly is part of the explanation for this discrepancy. More than for most groups, something resembling a "safety net" does exist for the elderly poor. In addition, homeless males have an average life expectancy of only 51 to 53 years, about 20 years below the normal male life expectancy, so that fewer long-term homeless men are likely to survive until age 65.

But if the elderly are underrepresented proportionately among the homeless, the elderly homeless are a particularly vulnerable and hard-hit group. Sister Mary Ann Luby, a staff member at a private women's shelter in Washington, D.C., offered this vivid description of the life of the homeless elderly to the House Select Committee on Aging in 1984:

Let me describe for a minute what I have learned to be the experience of homeless women. What I would ask you to do is to keep in mind the additional stress that is present when one is older. For those women who live in the shelters the day begins about 7:00 a.m. with movement out onto the streets. Within an hour the women arrive at the day centers. There are two in the District. Usually the older women remain at the centers for the day. At the closing time which is 4:00 p.m., the women move to the Library and wait there until 6:30 p.m. when the evening feeding site opens. Upon completion of the evening meal which is served at the Congregational Church the women make their way back to the shelters. The next day is a repeat performance . . . and this regardless of weather—in heat, cold, rain, snow. No easy routine for a young person! What must it be like for those who are physically ailing or feeble? What must it be like for those who use walkers, canes? For older

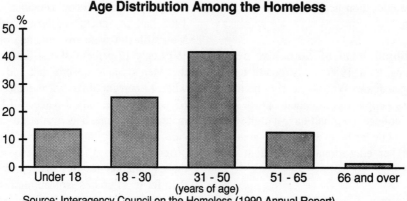

Age Distribution Among the Homeless

(years of age)
Source: Interagency Council on the Homeless (1990 Annual Report)

women, the routine has to be exhausting and devastating—limited energy, health complications (physical or mental) make it so.

Despite the existence of Social Security benefits, many elderly people still are vulnerable to losing their places of residence and find it difficult to find alternative housing. In many large cities, Social Security benefits provide only the barest kind of subsistence, unless supplemented by other sources of income. New York City and Philadelphia are the cities with the largest proportion of elderly residents. According to the 1980 Census, one in every five New Yorkers over the age of 60 lived on incomes below the poverty line. Mayor W. Wilson Goode of Philadelphia, testifying before the House Select Committee on Aging in 1984, reported that 16 percent of older Philadelphians lived on incomes below the poverty line. For Philadelphia's elderly whose only source of income was Social Security, the median yearly income was $4,173, leaving less than $11.50 per day to pay for all basic necessities.

The elderly face the danger of outliving their resources, as their savings run out or are diminished in value by inflation, spouses and other relatives die, their health grows worse and their housing deteriorates. They then face the cruel choice of life on the streets or in the shelters (where they are often the preferred targets of criminals) or

accepting institutionalization in a nursing home.

Eldredge v. Koch   In *Eldredge v. Koch*, the New York Superior Court affirmed that the decree in CALLAHAN V. CAREY requiring New York State and New York City to supply adequate SHELTER to homeless men also applied to homeless women.

Emergency Assistance (EA)   Federal Emergency Assistance funds, authorized by the Social Security Act and administered by the Department of Health and Human Services (HHS), are used by state welfare agencies to pay for the cost of providing temporary shelter, for storing or replacing household goods and for reimbursing the expenses of moving a family to a new home or returning a family to a former home. In 1988, 25 states made some use of EA funds to shelter families or to prevent evictions, and eight states used EA funds to provide temporary shelter in hotels or motels.

Emergency Community Services Homeless Grant Program (EHP)   The Emergency Community Services Homeless Grant Program, authorized by the Stewart B. McKinney Homeless Assistance Act and administered within the Department of Health and Human Services (HHS), allocates funds to states and Indian tribes for distribution to agencies such as community action agencies and migrant farm worker organizations to provide services for the homeless. The funds are used to expand comprehensive services to enable homeless persons to make the transition from poverty, to provide social and maintenance services and to promote private-sector assistance to the homeless.

Emergency Food and Shelter National Board Program   See FEDERAL EMERGENCY MANAGEMENT AGENCY (FEMA).

Emergency Jobs Appropriations Act   See FEDERAL EMERGENCY MANAGEMENT AGENCY (FEMA).

Emergency Shelters   See SHELTERS.

Emergency Shelter Grants Program   Under the Emergency Shelter Grants Program (ESG), created by the Stewart B. McKinney Homeless Assistance Act, the Department of Housing and Urban Development (HUD) was authorized to provide grants to states, cities and counties to increase the number and improve the quality of emergency shelters for the homeless. Congress appropriated $46.5 million for the program for fiscal 1989 and $73.8 million for fiscal 1990.

episodic homeless   The episodic homeless are persons who are usually homeless for a brief period of time, because of poverty or circumstances such as the loss of a job, a house burning down or abuse in the home. A closely related phenomenon is that of cyclical homelessness, where people are left without a home routinely and predictably, such as people on fixed and limited incomes who can afford to pay rent only three out of four weeks every month. Sociologist James Wright estimated that in the late 1980s more than 750,000 Americans living at or near the poverty line were forced out of housing each year because of some temporary financial crisis. These episodically homeless people account for about half of the total homeless population. Of the remaining homeless population, Wright argued that 29 percent were chronically homeless (due to mental illness, substance abuse or some other cause) and the remaining 19 percent recently homeless for the first time. Rather than homelessness being a permanent condition, it is probably more useful to think of it as a kind of revolving door that most homeless people pass through either occasionally or frequently. For example, in a 1987 study in Wisconsin that tracked a sample of homeless persons over six months, the majority of the sample had found and lost housing twice in that short period of time. (See also PRECARIOUSLY HOUSED.)

eviction   Eviction is the removal of a tenant from rented premises by a landlord, through court action, physical removal or disturbance of the tenant's enjoyment of the premises by cutting off services that contribute to the habitability of the rented unit. Urban evictions sharply increased in the 1970s and 1980s. In New York City half a million eviction cases were initiated in the Housing Courts each year in the 1980s, with an average of 25,000 to 27,000 households actually evicted, roughly double the rate of 20 years earlier. Housing advocates report that the most common cause of eviction is the inability of tenants to pay rent due to the loss or inadequacy of wages or government benefits. From 1975 to the 1990s the income of those in the poorest 40 percent of the population remained stagnant or actually declined, while rental costs rose dramatically in many regions of the country. In addition, landlords and real estate developers have pressed for eviction of their tenants as a means of replacing them with higher-income groups and as a means of removing them for the redevelopment of property. (See also DISPLACEMENT, GENTRIFICATION.)

F

Fair Deal   See NATIONAL HOUSING ACT OF 1949; TRUMAN, HARRY S.

families   Families with children, according to the National Low-Income Housing Coalition, "most of which are women alone with their children—are the fastest-growing segment of the homeless." The coalition estimated that the proportion of homeless people who are in families varies from 25 percent in some cities to 70 percent in others. Estimates of the number of homeless families by other groups and agencies vary widely. Surveys conducted in particular cities report that the ratio of those turned away from shelters and soup kitchens to those served is highest for families with children. For example, in Minneapolis, families with children are 28 percent of the homeless served by the shelters and soup kitchens surveyed, but are 72 percent of those turned away for lack of space. In New York City the number of homeless families receiving temporary shelter grew from 800 in 1978 to 5,600 in 1993.

The estimates of homeless families drawn from studies that count only those homeless on the streets or in shelters (such as the 1990 Census) are bound to be low because homeless families often struggle to avoid being "counted." To be counted is to become known as homeless, and for a family to be known as homeless is to risk having the children taken away and placed into foster homes. A baby born to a homeless mother is, according to policies in some jurisdictions, by definition considered to be neglected by her since shelter and adequate nutrition are not being provided.

In congressional testimony in 1989, Diana Pearce of the National Low-Income Housing Coalition described five strategies used by homeless families to cope with their situation, all of which tend to contribute to their "invisibility." Many homeless families with children "DOUBLE UP" in apartments already occupied by relatives or friends. In 1986 a third of all children living in Washington, D.C. were believed to be living in doubled up households. A second strategy is to find "hidden housing," in parks, campgrounds, abandoned cars and empty buildings. A third strategy for women with abusive partners is to go to battered women shelters or safe houses. In 1988 over 300,000 women and children found temporary refuge in 1,100 shelters and safe houses in the United States. These women and children are usually not thought of as part of the "homeless" population, even though they often have no permanent housing to which they can return safely. Fourth, homeless families will temporarily divide up, with children left in the care of relatives or friends while parents seek permanent housing. Finally, some homeless parents voluntarily place their children into FOSTER CARE.

A city official from Providence, Rhode Island reported in 1988 to the U.S. Conference of Mayors that the emotional impact of homelessness on families included "fighting, fear, depression (acute or chronic), feelings of failure, and lack of stability. . . . These families are so beaten, it's almost to the point of self-abuse."

The effect of homelessness on families is clearly demonstrated in an increase in the number of single-parent households, domestic violence referrals and, perhaps the most tragic, reported abuses of children. Children are perhaps the most victimized group. Their adjustment to an often chaotic and rootless lifestyle strips them of their own individuality and leaves them with a sense of hopeless acceptance of their circumstances.

Cities surveyed by the U.S. Conference of Mayors in 1988 identified affordable, permanent housing as the resource most needed by homeless families, followed by services such as transitional housing, emergency shelters, child care and job training.

Family Support Act See AID TO FAMI-
LIES OF DEPENDENT CHILDREN (AFDC).

Family Support Centers When Congress reauthorized the Stewart B. McKinney
Homeless Assistance Act in 1990, it included a new provision for the establishment
of Family Support Centers, under the direction of the Department of Health and Human
Services (HHS). These centers were to be
established in poverty areas and in or near
public housing projects to provide intensive
and comprehensive supportive services to
low-income individuals and families, especially individuals in very low-income families who were previously homeless or were
at risk of becoming homeless. Services to
be provided include case management, nutritional services, child care, education, counseling, substance abuse services, and
eviction and foreclosure prevention assistance. Up to 30 demonstration grants were
to be awarded. Congress authorized spending for the program at $50 million in fiscal
1991, but failed to appropriate any funds for
that year. (Also see FAMILIES.)

farm crisis See RURAL HOMELESSNESS.

Farmers Home Administration The
Farmers Home Administration (FmHA),
which is part of the Department of Agriculture, administers a Homes for the Homeless
Program, intended to provide vacant rural
single-family dwellings to community-based
organizations to house homeless persons.
However, as of 1989, according to the *Annual Report of the Interagency Council on
the Homeless:* "no homeless people are being served by this program."

farm workers See MIGRATORY LABOR;
RURAL HOMELESSNESS.

**Federal Emergency Management
Agency (FEMA)** In 1983 Congress
passed the Emergency Jobs Appropriation
Act, granting the Federal Emergency Man-

agement Agency (FEMA) $100 million to
aid the homeless by providing grants to nonprofit groups that were feeding and sheltering them. (Prior to this, FEMA had
restricted its aid to victims of natural disas-
ters such as hurricanes and floods.) This
Emergency Food and Shelter National Board
Program was the first legislation passed by
Congress in the 1980s specifically targeted
to benefit the homeless, and it passed over
the opposition of President Ronald Reagan.
The program was set up to draw upon the
resources and expertise of voluntary agencies. A national board consisting of representatives from the United Way, the
Salvation Army, the Red Cross, the National
Council of Churches, the National Conference of Catholic Charities, and the Council
of Jewish Federations oversaw the distribution of the funds to communities around the
country. Local boards spent the money to
subsidize SOUP KITCHENS; add beds to emergency SHELTERS; make rent, utility, or rental
payments to keep people from being evicted
from existing housing; or provide housing
vouchers for hotel or motel space for homeless families. In its first year of operation
the program funded about 3,000 agencies in
approximately 1,000 communities. Although an additional $200 million was ap-
propriated for the program by 1986, the
program was unable to keep pace with the
expanding homeless population in the mid-
1980s. A study by the EFSP National Board
revealed that even with the program's funds,
local shelters were turning away more people than ever for lack of beds. The 1987
Stewart B. McKinney Homeless Assistance
Act renewed the mandate of the EFSP program to supplement and extend ongoing efforts to provide shelter, food and supportive
services for the homeless. By 1989 the EFSP
program funded 9,000 agencies in over
2,300 communities.

federal funding Federal spending on behalf of the homeless increased substantially

in the course of the 1980s. The passage by Congress of the Stewart B. McKinney Homeless Assistance Act in 1987 was intended both to coordinate federal efforts and to increase the level of federal funding for homeless funding. Funding for MCKINNEY ACT programs was set at $400 million in its first year. By 1993, under President Bill Clinton, funding had increased to nearly $1.4 billion.

Federal Housing Administration (FHA)   The Federal Housing Administration (FHA) insures market-rate loans for mortgages for qualified families. This agency has been a cornerstone of federal housing policy since the 1930s and represents one of the most important ways in which the federal government has stimulated housing construction and private homeownership. The FHA program was established by the National Housing Act of 1934. This act, the first direct federal involvement in housing, was part of the NEW DEAL legislation passed under President Franklin Delano Roosevelt, designed to cope with the effects of the GREAT DEPRESSION. But the passage of the act had long-range implications for American housing and indeed for American

society. The FHA, along with the Veterans Administration (VA) mortgage-guarantee system, played a major role in the postwar suburban boom by reducing the risk faced by banks in private housing development, thus serving as a subsidy for the private lending system. The program has insured more than 11 million mortages, worth nearly $200 billion, and in doing so has standardized the long-term, low-down-payment, fully amortizing mortgage. The program also, to a considerable degree, shaped the character of postwar housing choices by favoring the construction of new, single-family housing units in suburban districts and discriminating against the rehabilitation of older, multiple-unit dwelling units in urban settings. FHA insurance policies thus served to hasten the decline of urban housing stock, encouraging the migration of the white middle and working classes out of the cities to the suburbs and setting the stage for URBAN RENEWAL programs in the 1950s and urban GENTRIFICATION in the 1970s and 1980s. In the 1950s about one-third of all homes purchased had mortgages insured by either the FHA or Veterans Administration loan guarantees. FHA policy in the 1930s and 1940s was to preserve the racial segregation of residential neighborhoods, preventing Af-

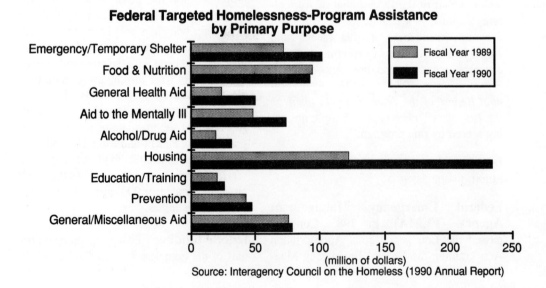

Federal Targeted Homelessness-Program Assistance by Primary Purpose

Source: Interagency Council on the Homeless (1990 Annual Report)

Federal Funding Specifically Targeted to Homelessness
(Fiscal Years 1987–1993)

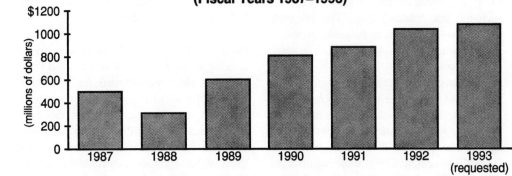

Source: *Federal Progress Toward Ending Homelessness.* Interagency Council on the Homeless (1991/1992 Annual Report)

Proposed Appropriations for Federal Homelessness-Specific Programs
Fiscal Year 1993 (by department)

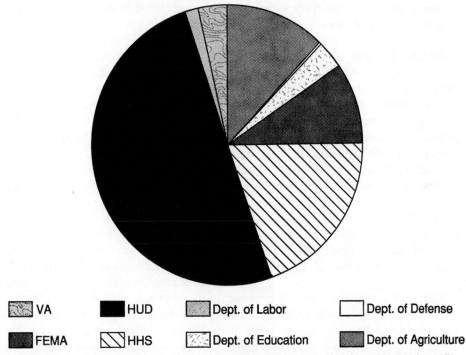

VA   HUD   Dept. of Labor   Dept. of Defense

FEMA   HHS   Dept. of Education   Dept. of Agriculture

Source: *Federal Progress Toward Ending Homelessness.* Interagency Council on the Homeless (1991/1992 Annual Report)

rican Americans from taking advantage of federally insured mortgages.

Federal Transient Program   This NEW DEAL program was established as part of the Federal Emergency Relief Administration (FERA) in 933 to cope with the effects of the GREAT DEPRESSION. It offered federal grants to states to be used to provide relief to homeless people. By July 1934 the program was funding 189 camps for transients, which provided food, shelter and a small cash allowance in exchange for work on camp maintenance and outside projects, such as park improvements. The program ran for two years and, at its peak, provided shelter to nearly 400,000 people. The term *transient* was deliberately chosen by the program's directors to remove the stigma associated with life on the road. FERA director Harry Hopkins defended the men and women who found shelter in these camps against charges that they were "bums" or "hobos" by emphasizing their willingness to work. They were, he said, "industrial workers, artisans, laborers who . . . were forced by necessity to seek employment in new places." With the establishment of the Works Progress Administration (WPA) in 1935, which provided public employment for the unemployed, the Federal Transient Program was closed down.

Feinstein, Dianne   See SAN FRANCISCO.

flophouses   A "flophouse" is a derogatory term for hotels in SKID ROW sections of cities offering a minimal form of shelter (often just a cot in a small, windowless cubicle), rented on a nightly basis. The term originated in the 19th century when commercial flophouses, located in the poorer sections of cities, provided a crude canvas hammock or a bit of floor space on which to sleep for a few cents. Those who slept beyond their time had the ropes holding their hammock untied so that they would "flop" to the floor.

Flynn, Raymond   Boston's former mayor Raymond Flynn was a staunch advocate of the homeless during his terms in office, serving as chairman of the Task Force on Hunger and Homelessness of the United States Conference of Mayors. Flynn was elected mayor in 1984 and oversaw an expansion of the city's shelter system (made up of two public shelters and several others run under city contract by nonprofit agencies) from 972 beds to 2,754 in 1989. Flynn has also been an influential advocate of fed-

eral legislation to aid the homeless. In 1993 he resigned as Boston's mayor to become U.S. ambassador to the Vatican.

food bank   A food bank is a nonprofit clearinghouse for surplus or salvaged food, which is then redistributed for a nominal fee to SOUP KITCHENS, SHELTERS and other nonprofit social service agencies that have on-site meal or food distribution programs. Changes in the federal tax laws in 1976 made voluntary food contributions tax deductible, creating an incentive for food companies and supermarket chains to donate surplus products to food banks. Many food banks are affiliated with a group called Second Harvest, a national food bank network. There were over 70 food banks in existence in the United States in the 1980s. (See also NUTRITION.)

Food Security Act   The Food Security Act of 1985 specifically required states to have a method of certifying and issuing FOOD STAMPS to homeless people.

food stamps   The Food Stamp Program administered by the United States DEPARTMENT OF AGRICULTURE (USDA) provides a monthly supplement to the food purchasing power of low-income individuals in the form of coupons that can be used in lieu of cash to purchase food for home consumption from retail food stores. Initiated by President John F. Kennedy in 1961, the program has been controversial since its expansion under the WAR ON POVERTY of the later 1960s. Conservatives such as President Ronald Reagan contended that the program was prone to abuse by its recipients. According to these critics, rather than providing basic nutrition for the truly needy, food stamps were being used to provide luxuries for welfare spongers. In fact, many recipients of the program do have jobs, but their incomes fall beneath the official POVERTY LINE. Food stamp recipients are allowed to own assets equal to $2,000 in value, excluding their homes, and a car worth less than $4,500. The average benefit per person per meal is about 65 cents. Eighty percent of those who receive food stamp benefits are families with children. The percentage of Americans using food stamps has climbed dramatically since the program's inception. In 1970 only about 2 percent of the American population received food stamps. By January 1992 that percentage had grown to nearly 10 percent, or 25 million all told, an all-time record number. The Food Stamp program cost over $19 billion in 1991, about half of the Agriculture Department's total budget.

President Reagan attempted to roll back the program, slashing its budget by $6.8 billion between 1982 and 1986. One million recipients lost their benefits and 20 million more had their benefits reduced. The Reagan administration also cut all funding for outreach programs.

Among those denied the benefits they were entitled to under the program were many homeless people. Congress took several steps in mid-decade to restore benefits to them. The Food Security Act of 1985 specifically required states to have a method of certifying and issuing food stamps to homeless people. Recognizing that homeless persons without kitchen facilities or food storage capacity are limited in the kinds of foods they can purchase and make proper use of, the Homeless Eligibility Clarification Act of 1986 (HECA) gave those individuals the option of using their benefits to purchase prepared meals from specially authorized providers. However, the Prepared Meals Provision Evaluation undertaken by the USDA in 1988 reported that fewer than 50 food and shelter providers nationwide had been authorized by the USDA's Food and Nutrition Service to accept food stamps in exchange for prepared meals. The evaluation also estimated that only 18 percent of service-using homeless individuals (those who use meal or shelter services) in cities of 100,000 or more were receiving food stamp benefits.

Ford, Gerald R. Gerald Rudolph Ford was the 38th President of the United States. He was the first man to become both vice president and president without being elected to either office. Ford was elected to the U.S. House of Representatives from Michigan in 1948 and elected House minority leader in 1965. On December 6, 1973 he was confirmed as vice president, after being nominated for the post by President Richard Nixon under the provisions of the 25th amendment to the Constitution, following the resignation from office of vice president Spiro Agnew. On August 9, 1974, when Richard Nixon resigned from the presidency to avoid impeachment for his role in the Watergate affair, Ford was sworn in as president. His was a short, unhappy administration, marred by the highest unemployment rate since 1941 and high inflation. He continued the housing policies of his predecessor, signing the HOUSING AND COMMUNITY DEVELOPMENT ACT OF 1974, which included the provision for SECTION 8 certificates. He was defeated for election by his Democratic challenger Jimmy Carter in the 1976 presidential election.

foster care Many studies have shown that a disproportionate number of the homeless population consists of people who were in foster care during their childhood or adolescence. In cases where CHILDREN are abused or neglected by their natural parents, state welfare agencies can take custody of the children away and commit them to the care of other families, called foster families, or place them in group homes. Families are paid a stipend by the state (about $4,400 a year per child in New York City, one of the highest rates in the country) to care for foster children. In 1991 there were more than 360,000 children in foster care across the United States.

Because homeless children have been taken away from their parents and placed in foster care, many homeless FAMILIES with children avoid shelters or other services where they might come to the attention of social workers, thus leading to an undercounting of the extent of homelessness among families. In other cases, homeless parents have voluntarily committed their children to foster care, believing that the children will be better cared for by strangers, than in the conditions prevailing in many SHELTERS and WELFARE HOTELS. While foster care may be a preferable alternative for children growing up in genuinely abusive or neglectful natural families, it can also have costs in terms of the emotional development and social adjustment of children. These problems can lead to homelessness in adult life. In studies conducted in 1990, the percentage of people formerly in foster care among the homeless population ranged from 38 percent in Minneapolis to about 13 percent in rural Ohio. The foster care systems in the 1980s were overwhelmed by budgetary cutbacks that eliminated other programs to aid troubled families. Many young people were then placed in incompatible foster care settings by overworked Family Court judges or social workers. According to Rich Gordon, executive director of Youth and Family Assistance, a private group in Redwood City, California concerned with the foster care issue: "Youngsters in foster care have never had the kind of childhood we think of as normal. They have not completed the task of being children, and yet the system demands they become independent at 18." Many of the children placed into foster care have been physically or sexually abused by their parents. Diane Flannery, executive director of the Larkin Street Youth Center in San Francisco, a private social service agency providing food, medical care and counseling to young people, told a reporter in 1991: "These kids are a lot harder to handle because of the psychological damage they've suffered. They don't trust adults, so for the foster care relationship to get going is almost impossible." Many of those who were sexually abused at home wind up practicing "survival sex" or prostitution to sup-

port themselves once they have left foster care for life on the streets.

Most states require children who turn 18 to leave foster care programs. (New York State is an exception, having raised its age limit to 21 in the 1980s under pressure from homeless advocates.) Left to their own resources, these former foster children often lack the skills to secure employment and housing.

France Though France, along with the other Western European countries, provides a more extensive system of social security than the United States, homelessness remains a pressing social problem. While authorities are required to provide a bed for those in need, establishing "need" is not always a simple matter, and the conditions in some of the homeless shelters are reportedly so poor that homeless people avoid staying in them. In France, the homeless can be found sleeping in subway stations, in cars, under bridges and "SQUATTING" in abandoned buildings in large cities and rural villages. Estimates of the number of homeless persons (including those in emergency shelters, hotels, and other forms of temporary accommodation) in 1993 range from 200,000 to 500,000.

There has been an increase in homelessness in France in recent years, largely attributed to a shortage of low-income rental housing. Public housing amounts to 16 percent of the housing stock in France (in contrast to 27 percent in Britain and 1.5 percent in the United States) so that most housing is obtained through the private housing market. Approximately 2 million low-wage households are precariously housed, on the edge of homelessness at any given time. Such households find it difficult to pay monthly rent and housing expenses. Unemployment in France in 1993 was close to 12 percent of the workforce, also contributing to the rise of homelessness. Though social programs were established by the Socialist government elected in 1981 to prevent evictions and to protect the rights of tenants, these protections have been slowly eroded in recent years. Private and religious organizations provide a strong network of charitable programs to address the problems of the homeless.

G

General Assistance General Assistance is a form of welfare program that provides aid to poor, able-bodied adults without children. Unlike such programs as Aid to Families with Dependent Children (AFDC), the General Assistance programs are funded entirely with state and local money. Recipients are typically single men with little education and few job skills. Many are homeless. The amount of benefits vary widely from state to state. In New York, where the program is called home relief, it provides up to $352 a month to eligible persons, who can also receive food stamps and medical benefits. Facing budget deficits, Michigan and Maryland eliminated general assistance programs in 1991; Ohio followed suit in 1992, and a dozen states cut back significantly on the funding of such programs.

General Assistance is a politically vulnerable program, because of widespread public sentiment against providing welfare benefits to able-bodies adults and because each state is free to continue or abolish the program as it chooses. Some 83,000 people lost benefits in Michigan in 1991. A spokesman for Michigan's governor John Engler declared that ending General Assistance was a step toward ending "welfare dependency." For able-bodied workers, he contended, "The jobs are out there. They may be minimum wage, but most people will be able to find one." With Michigan's unemployment rate in mid-1991 standing at 9.7 percent (or over 400,000 unemployed), others were more pessimistic. Jessi Young, an unemployed

and homeless man in Detroit who received General Assistance payments, contrasted his job prospects with those of his father who had worked as an autoworker for 40 years. "Those days are gone, long, long gone. Those jobs are gone. Robots do that work now." As for himself, he thought he could at best find a job "distributing handbills, cutting grass, washing windows. This is a slow death." Julie Strawn of the Center on Budget and Policy Priorities, a liberal research organization in Washington, commented in 1991: "I don't think the public really understands how important G.A. [General Assistance] is as the program of last resort. There is nothing else for people when G.A. goes away. Nothing." In the spring of 1992 the Salvation Army estimated that the ending of Michigan's General Assistance program had increased homelessness in Detroit by 30 percent.

General Services Administration The General Services Administration (GSA) was authorized by the Stewart B. McKinney Homeless Assistance Act to identify federally owned surplus real estate and buildings, for lease to groups providing housing for the homeless. Other surplus real property identified by the GSA, including beds, kitchen equipment and appliances, have been donated for use by the homeless under the Surplus Federal Personal Property Donation Program.

gentrification The term *gentrification* originated in Britain in the 1960s to refer to the restoration of declining urban property, particularly in low-income and working-class neighborhoods, by upper-middle-class professionals. Other terms that have been used to refer to the same process are the "back-to-the-city movement," urban "invasion" or "reinvasion" and "urban revitalization." Individuals engaged in the gentrification of neighborhoods have sometimes been called "urban pioneers." In the United States, the process of gentrification has been underway since the mid-1960s in many cities and has been one key factor in the rise of homelessness. It is a complex process made up of political-economic, demographic and sociocultural factors.

Gentrification has generally been encouraged by municipal officials as a means of redeveloping inner-city neighborhoods in order to revitalize downtown commercial districts and sustain the middle-class tax base of the city. Waterfront redevelopment projects in cities such as Boston, Baltimore, Portland or Seattle, have served as magnets for retail trade and have encouraged the gentrification of nearby residential neighborhoods. Gentrification can be encouraged in subtle ways. For example, in the mid-1980s artists in New York City were offered subsidized housing in a declining neighborhood in lower Manhattan. Though artists were literally "starved" for low-cost housing and work space some opposed the offer, arguing that they were being used as "point men" or "pioneers" to make the neighborhood attractive (in cultural terms) to affluent investors. The fear was that once low-income residents were evicted and the neighborhood renovated, only very wealthy residents would be able to live there. And the artists themselves might ultimately be displaced and forced to seek inexpensive space elsewhere, effectively serving as "pioneers" in another neighborhood in need of redevelopment.

It is impossible to fully understand the process of gentrification without considering the social class (socioeconomic background, occupational position, lifestyle) of the players involved. One important group has been the young urban professionals ("yuppies") whose tastes and consumption patterns are reflected in many of the outward forms of gentrification. Ironically, these young professionals are the children of middle-class parents who migrated *out* of the cities to the suburbs in the postwar decades. That is, they represent the large middle-class segment of the "baby-boom" generation. In demographic and cultural terms, they differ from

their middle-class parents in significant ways. While their parents moved to the suburbs in the 1950s and 1960s seeking "good" schools, green grass and room to raise their children, the current generation is often made up of two-career couples, who tend to marry later in life, have fewer children (and have them later in life) and prefer the variety and vibrancy of urban cultural amenities to the child-centered conformity of suburban life.

The changing economic basis of American cities has created a context for gentrification. With the decline of the manufacturing industries that once provided reasonably stable and well-paid employment for working-class Americans, in recent years urban economies have been sustained by a somewhat polarized service sector. Low-paying clerical, sales, restaurant and health care occupations have become the main sources of employment at one end; and the high-paying financial, legal and corporate executive professions have expanded at the other. Such economic changes have been manifested in spatial terms at the neighborhood level, by enclaves of urban "gentry" (or middle-class professionals) forming in inner-city working-class neighborhoods. Once a neighborhood begins to change in this way, housing costs rise, local homeowners sell their properties for windfall profits and low-income tenants, particularly the elderly and others living on fixed incomes, are displaced from rental housing. Just as important, the social and cultural character of neighborhoods is altered by this market activity.

Powerful pressures are brought to bear on city officials to encourage such changes. A declining urban tax base and cuts in federal funding for local programs force city officials to develop ways to attract residents who pay higher taxes and who do not draw upon already underfunded social service programs. Gentrification can serve as a magnet for upper-income residents and can encourage commercial investment. Residential rehabiliation is only one aspect of the process, however. Residential gentrification is linked to a more general transformation of the urban political economy. As the manufacturing sector has declined, other sources of investment have been in the redevelopment of urban waterfronts for recreational and commercial functions; the growth of the tourist industry and construction of urban hotel and convention complexes; corporate office-space development; and the growth of "trendy" retail and restaurant districts.

Despite the role of city officials in the process, proponents of gentrification often consider it a good example of the role of the "free market" and the "individual" in urban redevelopment (as opposed to public initiatives). In recent years a mythology has been woven about the young professional as an "urban pioneer" or "urban homesteader" who courageously moves into an uncharted urban territory and, with a small down payment and a great deal of "sweat equity," becomes the first of many to renovate the neighborhood's old Victorian homes. The frontier is thus tamed and others are safe to follow.

Though it may be reasonable to think of middle-class professionals venturing into communities that are inhabited by relatively poor people (with "alien" ethnic cultural ways) as "pioneers," for many analysts a more accurate analogy is that of "colonizer." In the initial stage of neighborhood gentrification, middle-class newcomers move into a neighborhood seeking moderate housing prices and a rich ethnic street life. But their very presence begins to transform the social, cultural and economic character of the neighborhood. In the context of the private real estate market, their move can signal others (including speculators) that a neighborhood is "on the way up" and begin to attract a flood of investment. While investment is clearly good for housing stock in any community, it also forces up housing costs, displacing longtime neighborhood residents and small businesses. Gourmet yogurt shops and sushi bars catering to the new residents begin to replace the local shoe repair stores and butcher shops. The threat of displacement and neighborhood change may generate deep social tensions when affluent newcomers appear in a declining urban neighborhood. Ultimately, most of the structures in the community may be renovated, with very few of the original residents able to remain.

Advocacy groups for the homeless consider gentrification a major problem because of its role in shrinking the supply of low-cost housing. Previously low-cost rental housing units are lost as investors buy buildings for conversion to owner-occupied housing—condominiums and cooperatives. The loss of rental units drives up the price of the remaining apartments while those who cannot afford to buy the renovated condominiums are forced to move to more crowded and dilapidated quarters or are made homeless. It has been estimated that nationwide 500,000 apartment buildings were converted into condominiums and cooperatives between 1977 and 1982 alone. There are as yet no reliable national estimates of the number of people made homeless directly through gentrification. In a study of displacement (though not necessarily homelessness) in New York City, Peter Marcuse (1986) estimated that from 1970 to 1980, between 10,000 and 40,000 households were displaced annually by gentrification alone. (Another 30,000 to 60,000 households were displaced by the abandonment of buildings.) Out of these, the number of households made homeless or forced into "DOUBLING UP" with other families is thought to be substantial. (See also ABANDONMENT; DISINVESTMENT; DISPLACEMENT; REDLINING.)

Gonzalez, Henry B. See CRANSTON-GONZALEZ NATIONAL AFFORDABLE HOUSING ACT.

Gonzalez, Juan Juan Gonzalez was a mentally disturbed homeless man who was released from a 48-hour confinement in New York City's Columbia Presbyterian Medical Center in 1986, despite the fact that he was crying "Jesus wants me to kill" and had signed a voluntary commitment form. The center had to release him because its psychiatric facilities were already overcrowded. Two days later Gonzalez killed two passengers on the Staten Island ferry with a sword. The Gonzalez case contributed to public fears of the homeless and the belief that the DEINSTITUTIONALIZATION of the MENTALLY ILL had gone too far in recent years.

Goode, W. Wilson   See ELDERLY.

Grandma's House   See ACQUIRED IMMUNE DEFICIENCY SYNDROME (AIDS).

Grate American Sleepout   In March 1987 the "Grate American Sleepout" was organized to dramatize the condition of the homeless in America and to protest the social welfare policies of the administration of President Ronald Reagan. The event was timed to draw support for the proposed Stewart B. McKinney Homeless Assistance Act, which was then being considered in the Congress. Several celebrities from the world of politics and entertainment, including Senator John Kerry and actor Martin Sheen, joined with activists and homeless people to sleep on the streets of the nation's capital for three nights. The demonstration received nationwide publicity, successfully drawing attention to the plight of the homeless, though a few media commentators criticized the event as tending to glamorize a difficult social problem. (See also HANDS ACROSS AMERICA.)

Great Depression   Ellen Bassuk's often-cited 1984 *Scientific American* article entitled "The Homelessness Problem" began with the sentence: "More Americans were homeless last winter than at any time since the Great Depression." The Great Depression of 1929 to 1941 has long been the benchmark for human suffering caused by economic disaster. The worst depression in American history, it spread overseas as well, with dramatic political consequences. In the United States, the Depression ushered in the era of Franklin Delano Roosevelt and the NEW DEAL; in Germany it contributed to the political victory of Adolf Hitler and the Nazi movement. Millions of Americans lost both their jobs and their homes as a result of the Great Depression. At the worst moment of the Depression, the spring of 1933, over 12 million Americans, a quarter of the total workforce, were unemployed. Millions of others were working only part time or for reduced wages.

Homelessness was one of the worst social consequences of the Great Depression. The actual size of the homeless and wandering population of the United States in the 1930s is difficult to estimate, but one good indicator of the dimensions of the crisis can be found in testimony given before a U.S. Senate subcommittee by a railroad detective in 1933. He testified that in 1929 the railroads counted a total of 13,875 "trespassers" on their property (walking along the rails, sleeping in boxcars, and so on); by 1931 that number had jumped to 186,028. A survey of emergency relief agencies in 60 cities undertaken by the Department of Labor's Children's Bureau in 1932 revealed that various agencies, mostly private, were sheltering almost 400,000 homeless people. A contemporary and conservative estimate of the homeless population in 1933 put the figure at 1,250,000, half of whom were on the road looking for work. Some of the homeless found shelter in religious missions or public buildings turned into temporary shelters, or slept under bridges. Others threw up shelters where they could, using whatever materials were at hand. Whole neighborhoods of these flimsy structures, called "Hoovervilles" after President HERBERT HOOVER, sprang up in some cities. In New York City, for example, the "Hooverville" stretched along the Hudson River all the way from 72nd Street north to 110th Street. In the western United States families of migrant laborers lived in cars, trucks, tents and makeshift shelters near the fields in which they worked.

The Great Depression made a lasting impression on those who lived through it, and also provided American historical memory with some of its most vivid images of hopelessness and despair, in the photographs of migrant farmworkers in California taken by Dorothea Lange and other photographers from the New Deal's Farm Security Agency and in works of fiction such as John Steinbeck's *Grapes of Wrath*. These memories were revived for some during the early years of the administration of President Ronald Reagan. In the "Reagan recession" of 1981–82, the media carried many stories about unemployed "rustbelt" workers, sleeping in their cars or on the streets as they searched for unemployment in the "sunbelt" communities of the Southwest. Parallels were drawn between the experience of these homeless workers and the "Okies" of the 1930s. "Homeless Crisscross U.S., Until Their Cars and Their Dreams Break Down," a headline in the *New York Times* reported in December 1982, noting in the following story that the House Subcommittee on Housing and Economic Development had scheduled "the first Congressional hearing on homelesssness in America since the Depression." Within a few years, however, the media no longer portrayed the homeless as the reincarnation of the Great Depression's displaced "Okies." New images of the homeless, including one as a dangerous urban underclass, came to dominate media treatment of the topic. One important and ironic difference between the 1930s and the 1980s is that when prosperity returned to the United States at the start of World War II, homelessness virtually disappeared as a problem, except among the shrinking population of the nation's SKID ROWS. When prosperity returned to the United States in the mid-1980s, homelessness continued to increase. (See also UNEMPLOYMENT.)

Great Society   The term *Great Society* was used by President Lyndon Baines Johnson in a speech to students at the University of Michigan on May 22, 1964. It became the slogan for his administration, as the "New Deal" had earlier been used to characterize Franklin Roosevelt's administration. Johnson used the term to describe the ultimate goal of his legislative proposals, which included programs for improving American education, protecting the environment, ending racial discrimination and, most important, ending poverty. Earlier that year Johnson had gone to Congress calling for a WAR ON POVERTY. Johnson's ambitious plans for domestic reform ran afoul of the escalating war in Vietnam as well as the outbreak of ghetto rioting during the "long hot summers" of the mid-1960s. In 1968 Johnson decided not to seek reelection. His successor, Republican Richard Nixon, cut some Johnson programs but left much of the structure of the Great Society intact. When President Ronald Reagan took office in 1981, one of his domestic priorities was to cut spending by the federal government, which effectively rolled back the relatively generous social welfare policies that were a legacy of Johnson's Great Society. And in spring of 1992 the George Bush administration blamed the "destructive" Great Society programs of the 1960s for making social problems worse rather than better and for being the indirect cause of the race rioting that year in Los Angeles that left 51 dead and millions of dollars in property damage.

Greyhound therapy   "Greyhound therapy" is the ironic term applied to the policy of some cities of "solving" the problems of mentally ill homeless people by offering them one-way bus tickets out of town. (See MENTAL ILLNESS.)

Guthrie, Woody   See HOBO.

H

Habitat for Humanity   Habitat for Humanity is a nonprofit, Christian ministry that sponsors projects using volunteer labor and donated materials to build housing for low-income families. The houses are sold to their new owners on a nonprofit basis with a 20-year interest-free mortgage. Each family is also expected to donate "sweat equity" in the construction of the home. The group, founded in 1976, based in Americus, Georgia, has 450 affiliated projects in the United States, Canada and Australia and has sponsored additional projects in 26 developing countries. By 1987 Habitat for Humanity had built over 2,500 homes. Former President Jimmy Carter has publicly supported Habitat for Humanity's efforts. Each summer the group sponsors the "Jimmy Carter Work Project," a weeklong building blitz program in a chosen city.

halfway houses   Halfway houses are transitional living settings for the mentally ill, designed to smooth the transition from institutional care to community life. Several hundred have been established in the United States since the beginning of the movement for DEINSTITUTIONALIZATION of mental patients in the 1960s. Studies of former residents of halfway houses indicate that they have a good rate of success in establishing themselves in school, employment and independent living settings. Other forms of community residences for the mentally ill include community lodges (designed for long-term care for those unable to move on to fully independent households), satellite housing (small groups of patients live together without live-in staff, but with a measure of supervision from a sponsoring agency) and board and care homes (larger dormitory-type settings, with meals and housekeeping service, and supervision of medications by a physician). There are not enough of these institutions available to absorb the population of deinstitutionalized or never-institutionalized mentally ill homeless people. (See also MENTAL ILLNESS.)

Hancock, Loni   See BERKELEY, CALIFORNIA.

Hands Across America   On May 25, 1986 over 5 million people grasped hands in a human chain that stretched across the United States from lower Manhattan in New York City to the Pacific Ocean at Long Beach, California. Hands Across America was organized to raise money and focus the nation's attention on poverty, hunger and homelessness. Though it was not a completely unbroken chain (sections of the Arizona desert were not covered), it stretched over 4,000 miles across 16 states and over 500 cities. Planners of the event had hoped to raise over $50 million dollars from participants (who were asked to pay $10 dollars each) and from contributors. Approximately $33 million was actually raised and, after expenses, $16 million was distributed as grants to groups aiding the poor and the homeless.

While Hands Across America may not have been the financial success its planners had hoped, it successfully focused the attention of the media and the American people. Publicity for the event built for weeks prior to the event, and celebrities such as Bill Cosby, Steven Spielberg, Lily Tomlin, and Frank Sinatra lent their names and time to the event as planners and as participants. Although President Ronald Reagan participated, he was criticized by many advocates for the homeless who they felt that his policies had actually contributed to the problem of hunger and homelessness in the country. (See also GRATE AMERICAN SLEEPOUT.)

HandsNet   HandsNet, with its headquarters in Santa Cruz, California, is a computer information and communications network begun in 1987 that links hundreds of social service and advocacy groups across the nation. HandsNet's founder, Sam Karp, a student activist in the 1960's, served as the California coordinator of the 1986 Hands Across America demonstration for the homeless. Among other information provided on-line to its subscribers, HandsNet summarizes articles of interest from major newspapers and wire services and carries policy analysis, statistics, abstracts of studies and reports, and information on available resources and services. Subscribing agencies can communicate with and transmit material to one another quickly through computer hookups. Many homeless advocacy and service groups are involved in the HandsNet network.

Harrington, Michael Michael Harrington was widely regarded as one of the nation's leading social critics and experts on poverty from the 1960s through the 1980s. Moving to New York City in 1950 hoping to become a writer, Harrington soon joined the radical CATHOLIC WORKER movement led by Dorothy Day. He spent the next two years living in the Chrystie Street House of Hospitality in New York's BOWERY district. After leaving the Catholic Worker, Harrington joined the socialist movement. Harrington's 1962 book, *The Other America: Poverty in the United States*, argued that the poor, while a minority, were actually a much larger group than most middle-class Americans assumed. He estimated that the size of the poor population in the United States was between 40 and 50 million. Borrowing a concept from anthropologist Oscar Lewis, he argued that the poor were bound to their condition by a "culture of poverty." Without the assistance of government programs, most poor people would be unable to rise out of poverty through the time-honored means of pulling themselves up by their own bootstraps. "The other Americans," Harrington argued, "are those who . . . are so submerged in their poverty that one cannot begin to talk about free choice." Harring-

ton's book came to the attention of several key advisors in the administration of President John F. Kennedy and helped shape the policies of the WAR ON POVERTY.

Hayes, Robert Robert Hayes became a pioneering advocate of the LEGAL RIGHTS of the homeless in New York City in the late 1970s. Raised on Long Island, Hayes attended Georgetown University as an undergraduate and completed a law degree at New York University in 1977. While employed as a lawyer for a prestigious Wall Street law firm, Hayes became interested in the plight of the homeless people he saw on his way to work in the morning. Appalled by the conditions he found during a visit to the city-run Men's Shelter on East Third Street (which at that time was the only public shelter providing beds for homeless men in the city), Hayes filed suit against the city of New York in October 1979 in what became a landmark legal case CALLAHAN V. CAREY. The case led to a court injunction in December 1979 and to a consent decree in 1981 that recognized the existence of the right of homeless people in New York to public shelter. The settlement of the case led to a dramatic expansion of the New York City shelter system. Hayes remained a prominent spokesman for the interests of the homeless in subsequent years, founding the Coalition for the Homeless in New York City, and the National Coalition for the Homeless, for which he serves as legal counsel. (See also MOONEY, DAVID.)

Health Health problems of the homeless are difficult to measure. Because the homeless are less likely to be able to afford or to seek medical care, their medical problems are hard to calculate and evaluate. Impressionistic evidence supported by small-scale studies suggests that the nation is suffering a medical emergency among its homeless population. Emergency rooms and clinics that treat homeless patients report high levels of trauma and related infections, sexual assault, substance abuse (including alcohol and drugs), malnutrition, parasite infestation (LICE and SCABIES) and diseases such as ACQUIRED IMMUNE DEFICIENCY SYNDROME (AIDS), TUBERCULOSIS, cardiovascular disease, PERIPHERAL VASCULAR DISEASE, cancer, hepatitis and venereal diseases. Overall mortality rates for the homeless may run from ten to 40 times those of the general population. Homeless pregnant women often receive inadequate prenatal care: Their children are born underweight and suffer higher than usual rates of infant mortality.

The task of treating the illnesses of the homeless is complicated by the usually stressful, unsanitary, physically wearing conditions that they endure on a daily basis, in the streets or in shelters. Philip Brickner, director of the Health Care for the Homeless program of St. Vincent's Hospital in New York City, reported to the House Select Committee on Aging in 1984:

> Homeless patients are usually the poorest of the poor, the most destitute of the disenfranchised in our complex world. We live in a society which demands much of healthy people, and considerably more of those burdened with even a minor and self-limiting disease. Poverty prevents patients from acquiring medicines unless they have the motivation to make the bureaucracy of the welfare system work for them. Where there is cash available for medicines, priorities of homeless people for spending may differ from those of health care providers. Often, shelter, food, or substances of abuse come first.

Even those homeless people fortunate enough to have seen doctors for their ailments may find it very difficult to follow a doctor's advice. Homeless people who use prescribed medications have problems storing them properly. Diabetics, for example, may not be able to refrigerate their insulin and/or protect their syringes from theft in emergency shelters. Specially prescribed diets present other difficulties. People at risk of hypertension or cardiovascular disease, for example, need to reduce their sodium

intake, which is difficult to do on the kinds of meals available in emergency shelters, heavy as they are on potato chips, luncheon meats, franks and beans and other foods loaded with salt. As Sister Mary Ann Luby of Rachael's Women's Center in Washington, D.C. testified before the House Select Committee on Aging in 1984: "Though those of us who serve meals attempt to provide nutritious ones, our ability to accommodate special diets is nil."

Private charitable foundations, such as the Robert Wood Johnson Foundation and the Pew Memorial Trust, have taken initiatives to begin to meet these medical needs, funding the Health Care for the Homeless Project. The federal government has also taken some steps to ease the crisis. The Stewart B. McKinney Homeless Assistance Act established the Primary Health Services and Substance Abuse Services Program, which makes direct grants to community health centers, nonprofit health groups, inner-city hospitals and local public departments, to provide primary health, mental health and substance abuse treatment to the poor. Some clinics funded through the program provide outreach in shelters and soup kitchens, or use outreach vans to seek out homeless people living in parks, under bridges or in abandoned buildings. Some 230,000 homeless people were served by the program during its first year. But funding support from Congress has been uneven; in 1990, 40 large cities and nine states had no health care projects for the homeless. (See MCKINNEY ACT.)

Health Care for the Homeless (HCH) Grant Program   The HCH grant program, administered by the Public Health Service (PHS), was created as part of the Stewart B. McKinney Homeless Assistance Act to provide primary health care and substance abuse services, emergency health services, referrals to necessary hospital services, mental health services, outreach and case management services and aid in establishing eligibility for and obtaining services under entitlement programs for homeless individuals. The program funds 109 Health Care for the Homeless projects, which serves over 350,000 patients. Fifty-three percent of these patients were residents in emergency shelters, 84 percent were male, 60 percent were minorities and 40 percent were either runaway youths or children and their parents living as a family unit. (See also DEPARTMENT OF HEALTH AND HUMAN SERVICES [HHS]; HEALTH.)

Health Care for the Homeless Program
In 1985 the Robert Wood Johnson Foundation and the Pew Charitable Trusts funded the 19-city Health Care for the Homeless Program (HCHP), a program co-sponsored with the United States Conference of Mayors. This four-year, $28 million program provided primary care services, health assessments and referrals to the homeless. The program demonstrated the feasibility of delivering health care services to the homeless and helped lay the groundwork for the health care provisions of the Stewart B. McKinney Homeless Assistance Act of 1987. (See also HEALTH; HEALTH CARE FOR THE HOMELESS [HCH] GRANT PROGRAM.)

The Heights
See COMMUNITY SERVICE SOCIETY.

hermits
See RURAL HOMELESSNESS.

hidden homeless
Homeless advocates use the term *hidden homeless* to describe people who have lost their own housing but who do not turn up on the streets, in shelters or in the official estimates of the homeless population. These are people who are DOUBLING UP or tripling up with friends or relatives in temporary housing arrangements. New York governor Mario Cuomo estimated in the mid-1980s that New York State alone may have had as many as 500,000 hidden homeless people. The Housing and Community Development Act of 1990 noted that one in five of the almost 16 million displaced

homemakers in the United States were part of the "hidden homeless."

Hispanics
The 1991 *Status Report on Hunger and Homelessness* issued by the United States Conference of Mayors reported that Hispanics comprised one-fifth or more of the homeless population in Hartford, Kansas City, Miami, New York City, Phoenix and San Francisco. (See MINORITIES.)

historic preservation
Historic preservation refers to the organized efforts to conserve examples of antique buildings or to preserve the original architectural integrity of aging urban districts. All states and many local communities maintain some version of "historic district zoning," which provides a legal basis to control property development and redevelopment, often through a screening process of new building designs by an architectural review board. While this would appear to be a useful mechanism to preserve architectural integrity, it also can serve to determine the "social integrity" of a neighborhood as well. Historic preservation efforts sharply define the character of a neighborhood and buttress that definition with a legally defensible set of sanctions. Once defined as having a "significant historical character," a changing neighborhood is then "stabilized" for investors seeking out areas for real estate investment. That is, historic preservation can signal that a particular neighborhood is a good investment, thus furthering the process of GENTRIFICATION. In a case study of the role of historic preservation in the city of Charleston, South Carolina, Robert E. Tournier found that while much of the architectural value of historical districts was indeed protected, the poor were displaced and the affluent were drawn in, polarizing the city along clear social and economic class lines.

hobo
The word *hobo* is a corruption of "hoe boy," a 19th-century term for a migra-

tory worker. Hobos helped harvest the nation's crops, pick its fruit and chop down its trees. In the early 20th century the term hobo came to have a romantic connotation (as opposed to the TRAMP, who was seen as a threatening figure in the late 19th century). The hobo, wandering the countryside in search of work, companionship and adventure, traveling on foot or in a railroad boxcar, was treated in song and literature as a kind of free-spirited American folk hero. Singers such as Woody Guthrie and Jimmy Rodgers dedicated songs to the hobo's life (although Guthrie's lyrics, in particular, also captured the harsher aspects of the hobo's existence). As late as the 1950s, in Jack Kerouac's novel *On the Road*, the hobo was celebrated as someone who stood apart from and above the trivial concerns of those who lived more conventional lives. (See also MIGRATORY LABOR; SKID ROW.)

Hodge v. Ginsberg In a 1983 decision in a case called *Hodge v. Ginsberg* (a class action suit brought on behalf of West Virginia's homeless by the United Mine Workers Union), the Supreme Court of Appeals of West Virginia declared that under the state's Social Services for Adults Act of 1981, the state was obligated to provide shelter, food and medical care for its homeless population. The case was similar to that of CALLAHAN V. HAYES in establishing legal precedent for the claim by homeless advocates to a right to shelter in some states. (See also LEGAL RIGHTS.)

Homeless Chronically Mentally Ill Veterans Program In 1987 the Department of Veterans Affairs (VA) launched the Homeless Chronically Mentally Ill (HCMI) Veterans Program. Through the program, 43 VA medical centers provide: outreach to homeless chronically mentally ill VETERANS in shelters, soup kitchens and on the streets; medical and psychiatric examinations to determine the health and mental status of the veterans; and, where needed, treatment and

rehabilitation in community-based facilities for limited periods. In a preliminary evaluation of the program, the VA concluded that half the veterans involved in the program "show improvement in their health care problem areas and their residential situations." For veterans placed in community-based residential treatment, the success rate was judged to be considerably lower: 25.6 percent were judged to have completed the program successfully, but another 53 percent left against medical advice or were discharged for violation of program regulations. (See also MENTAL ILLNESS.)

Homeless Eligibility Clarification Act Congress enacted the Homeless Eligiblity Clarification Act in 1986 as part of the Anti-Drug Abuse Act. The Clarification Act removed the bar to FOOD STAMP eligibility for shelter residents and permitted the homeless to use food stamps to buy prepared meals from soup kitchens and shelters. It also required the Department of Health and Human Services, the Social Security Administration, the Department of Agriculture and the Department of Veterans Affairs to develop procedures to make their programs and benefits more accessible to people without fixed home or mailing addresses. It also made the homeless eligible for job training programs authorized by the Job Training Partnership Act.

Homeless Families Program In 1989 the Robert Wood Johnson Foundation and the Department of Housing and Urban Development (HUD) initiated the Homeless Families Program, which offered two-year grants to enable cities to design and implement comprehensive health and supportive services systems tied to suitable permanent housing for homeless families.

Homelessness Exchange The Homelessness Exchange, with its headquarters in Washington, D.C., is a central collection point for information on homelessness around the country. The exchange disseminates information and technical assistance on various programs for homeless persons. It publishes a quarterly newsletter called *Homewords*.

homelessness prevention programs By the end of the 1980s a number of states (including New Jersey, Pennsylvania, and Massachusetts), and cities (including New York City and St. Louis, Missouri), had developed programs designed to prevent homelessness by making timely short-term loans and grants to households at risk of homelessness. New York's Housing Alert Program, for example, helps people who cannot pay their utility bills avoid eviction; in New Jersey the Housing Assistance Program for the Homeless makes loans to eligible households to pay off up to three months' back rent. In doing so, it forestalled the eviction of roughly 8,000 tenants in 1987. The economic rationale for such programs is that it is a lot less expensive in the long run to provide a few hundred dollars to keep a family in its present home than to provide the tens of thousands of dollars it would cost to house the same family for months or years in emergency shelters or welfare hotels.

Homeless Persons Act of 1977 See BRITAIN.

Homeless Veterans Reintegration Project The Department of Labor administers the Homeless Veterans Reintegration Project (HVRP), authorized by the Stewart B. McKinney Homeless Assistance Act (see MCKINNEY ACT). In 1988 this project awarded 15 grants to local demonstration projects to develop employment and training services such as job counseling, resume preparation, job-search assistance, remedial and vocational education, job placement and on-the-job training that will "expedite the reintegration of homeless veterans into the labor force." Some of the demonstration projects also provide additional services,

such as transportation, clothes or tools needed for employment, alcohol and drug-treatment referrals and posttraumatic stress disorder counseling.

home mortgage tax deduction The home mortgage tax deduction, which allows interest paid on mortgages for homeowner's residences to be deducted from their income tax, is in effect the largest subsidy the federal government provides for housing. The deductions have stimulated both private homeownership and private construction by making owning a home affordable for a greater proportion of the population than would otherwise be the case. But the advantages offered by the deduction are skewed to the benefit of upper- and middle-class families. In 1988 federal tax deductions for mortgage income cost the federal Internal Revenue Service (IRS) about $54 billion, compared to less than $14 billion in direct expenditures on federal low-income housing assistance programs that year.

homeownership After years of steadily increasing, the rate of homeownership turned down at the beginning of the 1990s. In 1950, 55 percent of Americans owned their own homes. By 1980 that figure had grown to 66 percent. In 1990 the rate dropped to 64 percent. A Bureau of the Census study released in 1991 showed that 57 percent of all owners and renters could not afford to buy a median-priced house with a conventional 30-year, fixed-rate mortgage. That figure included 36 percent of current homeowners, and 91 percent of renters. Mark Obrinsky, an economist with the Federal National Mortgage Association, commented on the Census Bureau report that: "This seems to be telling us that the step from renting to home ownership is a big step for a large number of households and perhaps a bigger step than was generally realized." Minorities found it particularly difficult to purchase homes. Seventy-seven percent of African-American families and

Homeownership Rates

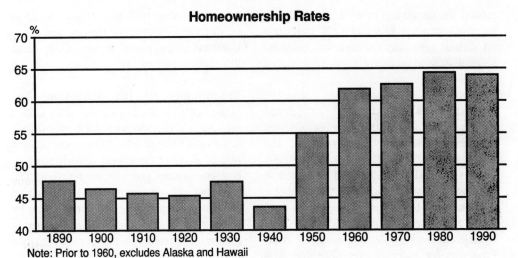

Note: Prior to 1960, excludes Alaska and Hawaii

Source: *The State of the Nation's Housing.* Joint Center for Housing Studies of Harvard University, 1992. p.3

74 percent of Hispanic families could not afford to buy a median-priced home, compared to 43 percent of white families.

Homeownership and Opportunity for People Everywhere (HOPE)

HOPE is a plan announced by President George Bush in 1989 to address housing issues. The plan includes initiatives encouraging homeownership for low- and moderate-income people (including tenant purchase of public housing); URBAN ENTERPRISE ZONES tax incentives for housing; community and economic development, Federal Housing Administration insurance reforms and preservation of existing government-subsidized privately owned housing units. (See also HUD; KEMP, JACK.)

homeownership rate

The rate of homeownership has been considered an important measure of social and economic growth throughout the 20th century in the United States. And in the postwar period in particular, the concept of the "American Dream" has largely hinged on homeownership as a key measure of middle-class status for three generations of Americans. The rate of homeownership remained at aproximately 47 percent of the population between 1890 and

1930, dropping several percentage points during the Great Depression. (See figure.) As the result of federal policies, the steady growth in income and modest mortgage interest rates, the homeownership rate then grew quite dramatically in the decades following World War II, to a high of 64.4 percent in 1980. Between 1960 and 1980, the number of homeowners increased by 18 million. The 1990 Census showed the rate of homeownership beginning to "flatten" at 64 percent of the population.

According to the Joint Center for Housing Studies of Harvard University, a fairly sharp decline in homeownership rates among young households accounted for most of the downward pressure on overall rates, the result mainly of weak incomes and rising housing prices. The homeownership rate for blacks and Hispanics has declined more substantially than for whites over the past decade, and minority rates continue to trail behind the rates for the white population. (See table.) (See also HOUSING MARKET.)

Homeowners Refinancing Act of 1933

This temporary emergency piece of NEW DEAL legislation passed under the administration of President Franklin Delano Roosevelt established the Home Owners Loan

Corporation (HOLC) to refinance home mortgage debts for nonfarm owners. When the act was passed in 1933 at the height of the GREAT DEPRESSION, more than 40 percent of U.S. home mortgages were in default, threatening the well-being of the nation's banks as well as private homeowners. The HOLC allowed homeowners to pay off their previous mortgage debt with new 15-year mortgages at 5 percent interest. Homeowners who had defaulted on their mortgages could redeem ownership of properties lost by foreclosure anytime after January 1, 1930. (A similar bill to protect farmowners, the Emergency Farm Mortgage Act of 1933, established the Federal Farm Mortgage Corporation.) Between 1933 and 1936, when the program came to an end, the HOLC made loans to 1 million homeowners, holding 20 percent of U.S. mortgages by 1936. The HOLC also provided cash advances for taxes and maintenance of homes.

home relief   See GENERAL ASSISTANCE.

homesteading   Homesteading is the legally sanctioned regulation of "squatting." Homesteading has a long history in the United States, although until recent years it was associated exclusively with rural life. The demand for free homesteads carved out of the public domain was heard with increasing frequency in the mid-19th century. Homestead measures were long blocked by pro-slavery advocates in Congress, who feared the spread of antislavery sentiment in the West. The coming of the Civil War provided the opportunity for the passage of the Homestead Act in 1862. The act provided federal land grants of 160 acres to any citizen, or to any immigrant intending to become a citizen who was the head of a family and over 21 years of age, provided that the person would cultivate the land and reside on it for a minimum of five years. Alternatively, land could be acquired under the Homestead Act after six months of residence at $1.25 an acre. By 1940 over 285

million acres of public land had been given away as homesteads. The act was designed to settle frontier lands and to provide an escape valve for poor people in the cities. Historians have argued that the Homestead Act worked more to the benefit of land speculators than to the poor. Urban laborers were unable to afford the price of setting up a homestead, even if the land was free. Mining and lumber companies filed fraudulent claims for individual stakes, acquiring valuable public land at bargain prices.

In recent years, homesteading has been used to resettle the "urban frontier." That is, in order to respond to the rapid DISINVEST-MENT of urban neighborhoods, some cities sold abandoned houses for a nominal price to "homesteaders" who would rehabilitate them. In addition, community organizations, such as ACORN, have often pressured government into releasing vacant federally owned houses to low-income homesteaders. When unsuccessful in winning concessions in the political arena, such community groups have resorted to "SQUATTING" in those vacant houses.

Hoover, Herbert   Herbert Clark Hoover, a Republican, was the 31st President of the United States. He was elected to the White House in 1928, after having served as secretary of commerce in the administrations of Warren G. Harding and Calvin Coolidge. The 1920s was the era of "normalcy," a conservative reaction to what were perceived as the excesses of the PROGRESSIVE ERA in American politics. When Hoover won the White House, few observers doubted that the Republicans were destined to remain the majority party for the forseeable future. But within a year of his election, the stock market crashed, ushering in the Great Depression.

In the 1932 presidential election campaign, Democratic Party strategists stigmatized Hoover's policies as the source of all the nation's economic ills, including the growing homeless population. They coined the term Hoovervilles to describe the ramshackle communities of cardboard and scrapwood shacks that had grown up on the edge of many cities and towns since the start of the Depression, and the term soon entered the popular vocabulary. Variations such as "Hoover blankets" (old newspapers) and "Hoover heaters" (campfires) soon appeared.

Hoover was handily defeated for reelection in 1932 by the Democratic challenger Franklin Delano Roosevelt. Roosevelt greatly expanded the federal government's role in stimulating the construction of both private and public housing construction. Hoover's name remained a byword for economic hard times and political hard-heartedness for decades afterward. (See also NEW DEAL.)

Hooverville See GREAT DEPRESSION; HOOVER, HERBERT.

Hope Foundation The Hope Foundation, a Dallas-based national nonprofit foundation, provides funds to shelters that "demonstrate their effectiveness in servicing the homeless in their communities."

Hopkins, Harry See FEDERAL TRANSIENT PROGRAM.

Houses of Hospitality See CATHOLIC WORKER.

Housing Act of 1934 See NATIONAL HOUSING ACT OF 1934.

Housing Act of 1937 See NATIONAL HOUSING ACT OF 1937.

Housing Act of 1949 See NATIONAL HOUSING ACT OF 1949.

Housing and Community Development Act of 1974 Signed into law by President Gerald R. Ford on August 22, 1974, the Housing and Community Development Act of 1974 authorized the spending of $11.1 billion in federal funds to promote low-cost housing, URBAN RENEWAL, water and sewer facilities construction and other programs. As part of the New Federalism initiated under Ford's predecessor in the White House, President Richard Nixon, the funds were to be distributed to local government as block grants that could be spent at the discretion of the community for its urban development needs. Section 8 of the Housing and Community Development Act authorized the Department of Housing and Urban Development (HUD) to provide federal funds to subsidize rentals in the private housing market by qualified low-income renters.

Housing and Urban Development Act of 1965 See HUD; WAR ON POVERTY.

Housing and Urban/Rural Recovery Act of 1983 (HURRA) Passed during the administration of Ronald Reagan, the Housing and Urban/Rural Recovery Act of 1983 (HURRA) represented a two-year program of federal subsidies for 100,000 housing units, part of which was a program for the construction or rehabilitation of 30,000 to 40,000 rental units. Other elements of this legislation provided an experimental voucher program to subsidize rents, continued a program of community block grants, and expanded housing assistance to the elderly and handicapped. Housing advocates in Congress successfully attached this initiative to a bill on funds for the International Monetary Fund, favored by the administration. In order to pass the bill, the Reagan administration was forced to seek a compromise on the housing section of the bill despite its ideological opposition to government involvement in housing.

Housing Assistance Council The Housing Assistance Council (HAC), founded in 1971, is a national nonprofit corporation that is concerned with rural housing issues. The HAC provides seed money and technical assistance to rural housing sponsors, conducts research into rural housing needs and resources, and provides program and policy analysis, training and information services to public, nonprofit and private organizations. The HAC issued several reports in the 1980s on the issue of rural homelessness.

Housing Enterprise for the Less Privileged (HELP) Housing Enterprise for the Less Privileged (HELP) is a private nonprofit housing group started in 1986 by Andrew Cuomo, the son of New York governor Mario Cuomo. HELP's TRANSITIONAL HOUSING projects are often cited as models of what can be accomplished to help homeless families prepare to move on to permanent housing. The HELP projects have proven that they can house homeless families more cheaply than the welfare hotels, and in far less dehumanizing circumstances. By 1991 there were nine HELP projects open or nearing completion, providing housing for about 1,000 families in New York City, Albany, and Suffolk and Westchester counties. In Greenburgh, a suburban community in Westchester County, HELP constructed a $10 million facility on six wooded acres of land, providing apartments for 108 families with preschool-age children. The facilities include day care rooms, a library, a medical unit, offices and a playground. Laurie Nudi, a formerly homeless mother with a five-month-old son, told a reporter from the New York Times in 1991 that the HELP housing was "very supportive. It's one step at a time. Right now, I want to get the work background so I can get a job, and then I'll concentrate on housing. It's much easier to get motivated when you have an attractive environment." The project met with less enthusiasm from residents of Greenburgh, who saw it as an intrusion into a peaceful suburban community.

HELP has also broken ground for what will be its first venture in permanent hous-

ing, a 150-apartment complex in East New York, where half the apartments will be reserved for formerly homeless families. Another project, combining market-rate low-income and homeless housing, is planned for the Union Square area of Manhattan.

housing market Over the past 15 years, the private housing market has failed to supply low-income housing to an increasing number of poor and low-wage workers in a time when the number of urban poor has continued to increase. The result has been a crisis in low-cost housing and a homeless problem of substantial dimensions. This is not to say that the entire problem of homelessness can be reduced to a matter of housing supply but, as sociologist James Wright has argued, "An inadequate low-income housing supply is probably not the proximate cause of homelessness in most cases, but it is the ultimate cause of homelessness in all cases."

According to data compiled in 1985, about one in every three households in the United States live in physically substandard, overcrowded or unaffordable housing. (Costs exceeding 30 percent of income are considered unaffordable.) Of these three, excessive costs are the most prevalent. While the costs of housing (land, mortgage costs, materials, operating expenses) and the increase in the low-wage sectors of the economy are important parts of the reason for the problem, the fate of previously existing low-cost housing is crucial. Large numbers of low-rent housing units were demolished by federal urban renewal and highway programs between 1950 and 1980. Through the 1980s GENTRIFICATION has replaced tens of thousands of low-rent housing units with luxury housing in the form of rental or condominium units. In addition, inexpensive urban residential hotels (SROs or SINGLE-ROOM-OCCUPANCY HOTELS) have been demolished through downtown redevelopment projects, while tens of thousands of other

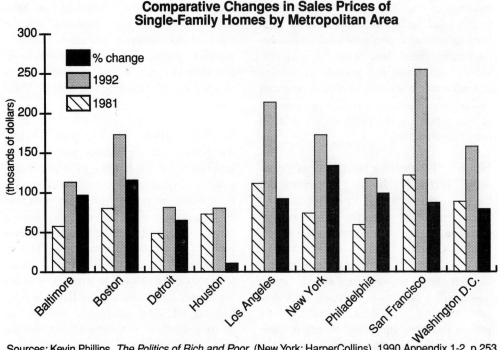

Comparative Changes in Sales Prices of Single-Family Homes by Metropolitan Area

Sources: Kevin Phillips, *The Politics of Rich and Poor* (New York: HarperCollins), 1990 Appendix 1-2, p.253, and National Association of Realtors (February 1993)

low-rent housing units have been allowed to deteriorate, abandoned, or the victims of arson.

The actions of government officials have aided the decline in low-cost housing. Lucrative tax incentives for costly real estate properties (such as the J-51 TAX ABATEMENT PROGRAM in New York City), the lack of organized political power of the poor and the lack of political will on the part of local and national politicians have all contributed to the DISINVESTMENT in low-cost housing.

The private housing market is by no means a "free market." Government has been deeply involved in shaping this market since the days of the New Deal and the postwar GI bill. The immense federal support for suburban homeownership in the 1950s represented an intervention into the private market through Federal Housing Administration (FHA) and Veterans Administration (VA) lending assistance programs, serving to lessen the investment risks taken by banking institutions. Similarly, the income tax system amounts to an indirect subsidy to homeowners, as every homeowner may deduct property tax payments and mortgage interest payments from their taxable income base. This encourages private homeownership and represents a subsidy to middle- and upper-income groups that amounts to about $50 billion per year. The government's role in shaping the housing market is less a matter of whether the government should intervene in the private market and more a question of which groups and which sorts of housing are deemed worthy of government intervention and encouragement. (See also HOME MORTGAGE TAX DEDUCTION.)

Housing Now On October 7, 1989, 250,000 people traveled to Washington, D.C. to demand federal help for the homeless, under the slogan "Housing Now!" After the rally, ongoing Housing Now groups remained active in a number of cities across the United States. On October 5, 1991 Housing Now sponsored a rally in front of the Kennebunkport, Maine vacation home of President George Bush to protest continued government inaction.

Hubbard, Jim   Jim Hubbard, a former White House photographer for United Press International, started a workshop in 1988 in Washington, D.C. for young homeless people interested in photography. An exhibit of the photographs taken by the young people, called "Shooting Back: Photography by and About the Homeless," opened a three-year national tour of galleries in 1991. Hubbard's own photographs of the homeless were published in a book in 1991 entitled *American Refugees*. Of the photographs taken by his students, Hubbard said:

> When I saw their pictures I realized I had somewhat distorted the lives of the poor by showing only squalor and misery. If you're trying to raise the issue of homelessness, and trying to provoke an emotional response, you show things that are a disaster. You bring back what you know the editor wants. But poverty is not only about despair. With the kids' pictures, we're talking about a full range of human emotion. Kids are unbiased. They're honest about their world.

HUD (Department of Housing and Urban Development)   The Department of Housing and Urban Development (HUD) administers a variety of development grant, subsidy, loan, insurance and other programs designed to improve the quality of the nation's urban housing stock. Among the most important of these are the COMMUNITY DEVELOPMENT BLOCK GRANT PROGRAM and the SECTION 8 rental subsidy program. The EMERGENCY SHELTER GRANTS PROGRAM was established to aid the urban homeless population. HUD has also leased or sold over 500 single-family homes to homeless providers for nominal fees since 1985.

HUD was established by a vote of Congress in 1965 during President Lyndon

Baines Johnson's administration, intended as an integral part of Johnson's plans for a Great Society. Prior to HUD's establishment, federal housing programs were administered by the Housing and Home Finance Agency (HHFA), which was not a Cabinet-level department. Robert C. Weaver, the administrator of HHFA, was appointed as HUD's first secretary. (Weaver was also the first African American to hold a Cabinet-level post.) The creation of HUD and Weaver's appointment symbolized federal commitment to revitalizing the inner cities during Johnson's "war on poverty." The Housing and Urban Development Acts of 1965 and 1968 gave HUD responsibility for a rent supplement program for low-income families and the Model Cities program to rebuild the inner city. The 1968 act set a target of 26 million new and additional units of housing to be built over the next ten years, with 6 million units designed for low- and moderate-income households. Johnson decided not to seek reelection in 1968. His successor, Republican Richard Nixon, initially stepped up production of federally subsidized low-income housing. But during his second term in office, Nixon shifted gears and sought to dismantle HUD, ending the Model Cities program and declaring a moratorium on federal housing programs.

HUD programs enjoyed a modest revival under President Jimmy Carter, only to be decimated under the administration of President Ronald Reagan. HUD's budget of $35.7 billion in fiscal 1980 was reduced to $14.2 billion by fiscal 1987. An internal HUD audit and a subsequent investigation by the House Banking Committee uncovered evidence that Samuel Pierce, HUD's secretary under Reagan, had practiced political favoritism in awarding contracts for HUD-subsidized federal housing developments. Prominent Republicans such as former Nixon administration attorney general John Mitchell received huge "consulting fees" from developers who won HUD contracts. Former Reagan administration secretary of the interior James G. Watt was paid $400,000 for making eight phone calls and attending one half-hour meeting. As much as $6 billion may have been misspent for the benefit of politically influential consultants and developers. President George Bush, who appointed Jack Kemp as his HUD secretary, promised to clean up the scandal-ridden department.

human immunodeficiency virus (HIV)
See ACQUIRED IMMUNE DEFICIENCY SYNDROME (AIDS).

Humphrey-Hawkins Full Employment Act   See CARTER, JIMMY.

hunger   See NUTRITION.

Hunger Prevention Act of 1988   The Hunger Prevention Act of 1988 was federal legislation that provided $40 million to the U.S. Department of Agriculture to expand the availability and improve the quality of shelter and soup kitchen meals for the homeless. (See also FOOD STAMPS.)

I

illegal aliens   See MIGRATORY LABOR.

Indians   See MINORITIES; NATIVE AMERICANS.

indoor relief   Indoor relief refers to aid given to people requiring that they live in almshouses or other institutional settings. This was a common form of support for the poor in the United States in the 19th century. (See also POORHOUSE.)

Industrial Workers of the World (IWW)   See MIGRATORY LABOR.

Institute for Community Economics (ICE)   The Institute for Community Economics (ICE), based in Greenfield, Massachusetts, provides technical and financial assistance to housing and economic development projects in low-income communities via a community loan fund.

Interagency Council on the Homeless
The Interagency Council, an independent agency within the executive branch of the federal government, was established in 1987 by Title II of the Stewart B. McKinney Homeless Assistance Act (see MCKINNEY ACT). The agency consisted of the ten Cabinet secretaries and the heads of five independent agencies (Action, Federal Emergency Management Agency, General Services Administration, Department of Veterans Affairs and the Postmaster General). Its purpose was defined as reviewing federal activities and programs for the homeless; reducing duplication among those programs; monitoring and evaluating federal, state, local and private programs and activities; providing technical assistance to state, local and private groups; collecting and disseminating information; and coordinating regional homeless programs. The council was required to provide annual reports to Congress and the president regarding the nature and extent of homelessness and the activities of the federal government in meeting the needs of the homeless.

Critics, such as the National Coalition for the Homeless, charged that under the administration of President Ronald Reagan the Interagency Council failed to fulfill its mandate. These criticisms were echoed by the General Accounting Office, which charged that the agency had deliberately omitted the "lack of affordable housing" as a cause of homelessness in its annual report, because that conclusion clashed with the ideological assumptions of the Reagan administration. The agency's seeming ineffectiveness in its first years of operation was seen by critics as a deliberate policy. Illinois congresswoman Cardiss Collins, chair of the House Government Activities and Transportation Subcommittee, charged in 1989 that the council "didn't hold meetings. It didn't set policy. It didn't coordinate Federal programs. It didn't assess the needs of the homeless. It didn't recommend legislative changes or funding." The administration of President George Bush responded to such criticisms by replacing all the members of the agency's professional staff. Homeless advocates had hoped that the council would play a stronger role under President Bill Clinton, who appointed HUD secretary Henry Cisneros as its chairman in 1993. But that same year Congress voted to defund the agency.

Interagency Task Force on Homelessness and Severe Mental Illness The Interagency Task Force on Homelessness and Severe Mental Illness was established by Louis Sullivan, secretary of the Department of Health and Human Services (HHS), in May 1990. The task force, which included representatives from various agencies within HHS, including the Social Security Administration, Health Care Financing Administration, Public Health Service and the National Institutes of Mental Health and of Alcohol Abuse and Alcoholism, along with the White House, the Interagency Council on the Homeless, the Department of Housing and Urban Development (HUD), the Department of Labor, the Justice Department and the Department of Veterans Affairs, was charged with three tasks: reviewing methods of treatment and service coordination; documenting the extent, cause and means of arresting homelessness among severely mentally ill persons; and identifying barriers to housing, treatment, income support and services.

Interfaith Assembly on Homeless and Housing Founded in 1984, the Interfaith Assembly on Homeless and Housing has attempted to mobilize the resources of the religious community in New York City on behalf of the homeless through education, training, organization and advocacy. It publishes a quarterly political update.

Internal Revenue Service (IRS) See HOME MORTGAGE TAX DEDUCTION; LOW-INCOME HOUSING TAX CREDIT; REHABILITATION INVESTMENT CREDIT.

International Year of Shelter for the Homeless The General Assembly of the United Nations (UN) proclaimed 1987 to be the International Year of Shelter for the Homeless in order to focus the world's attention on adequate shelter as one of the basic human necessities. According to the UN, nearly every government, 25 UN organizations and bodies, several bilateral agencies and financial institutions and over 1000 nongovernmental organizations concerned with shelter and services for the poor responded to the call for participation in this effort. The declaration was designed to follow-up on "Habitat," a UN conference on human settlements, held in Vancouver in 1976. The project had two main objectives: first, to improve the housing and neighborhoods of some of the poor by 1987, and second, to develop the means of improving housing and neighborhood conditions for all of the poor by the end of the 20th century. The initiative sought: a political commitment on the part of national governments for an improvement of shelter for the poor; to share knowledge and experience gained by member states in order to have a range of alternative housing programs made available; and to develop new approaches to assist the efforts of the poor and homeless to secure their own shelter.

Though many important activities took place in 1987, the program was not conceived as a single-year project. Rather it was designed as a three-phase process. In phase 1, from 1983 to 1986, 600 local projects throughout the world were identified for the purpose of finding innovative approaches to improving shelter for the poor. Phase 2 was in 1987, during which time the results of the review and evaluation of relevant knowledge, experiences and innovative projects were to be made available to all countries through publications, seminars and conferences. Strategies and methods were to be examined during this phase. Phase 3, implementation, was launched in 1988.

J

J-51 Tax Abatement Program   The J-51 Tax Abatement is a controversial New York City tax incentive program providing property tax abatements to landlords to encourage them to renovate their buildings. The program was instituted in 1955 in order to encourage single-unit renovation, but it wasn't until the mid-1970s, when housing costs were skyrocketing, that it began to have a significant impact on the supply of low-income housing in New York City and to receive attention from the critics of GEN-TRIFICATION. In 1975 the program was extended to cover the conversion of SINGLE-ROOM-OCCUPANCY hotels (SROs) and other large structures into apartment buildings, essentially changing the intent of the original law. Almost immediately, many landlords took advantage of the J-51 tax abatement to force out their low-income tenants in order to convert their structures into high-rent luxury apartments or high-priced condominiums and cooperatives. The profits to be made from the combination of tax abatements and high rents were so great that some landlords used illegal means, including lockouts, physical assault and even arson in order to remove low-income tenants from their SROs and other properties. Though the J-51 program was not the only cause of the loss of SRO housing stock in New York City, it certainly hastened the decline. It has

been viewed as one important factor in the shrinking supply of inexpensive housing and the increasing numbers of homeless people in New York City. (See also DIS-PLACEMENT).

Jericho Project   See DRUG ABUSE.

Job Training for the Homeless Demonstration Program   The Job Training for the Homeless Demonstration Program, created by the Stewart B. McKinney Homeless Assistance Act, is administered by the Department of Labor. It is designed to provide information and direction for job-training programs for the homeless. The program awards one-year grants to state and local public agencies and private nonprofit organizations to demonstrate innovative approaches to job training for the homeless. In 1988 the program awarded grants totaling $7.7 million to 33 public and private groups to operate employment and training projects for the homeless.

John Paul II   See CATHOLIC CHURCH.

Johnson, Lyndon Baines   Lyndon Baines Johnson was the 36th president of the United States. As vice president, he succeeded John F. Kennedy in the White House when Kennedy was assassinated on November 22, 1963. Johnson was a consummate politician, who was first elected to Congress from Texas in 1937, then to the Senate in 1948 and finally to the vice presidency in 1960. Following Kennedy's death, Johnson embraced and greatly expanded Kennedy's proposals for an antipoverty program, launching what he called a WAR ON POVERTY as part of his GREAT SOCIETY Programs in 1964. Johnson secured the legislation that created the Department of Housing and Urban Development (HUD) as well as the passage of MEDICARE, MEDICAID and a host of other social welfare measures. Johnson was elected to the White House in a landslide victory over challenger Barry Goldwater in November 1964, which he took as a mandate for his Great Society programs. But by the end of the following year, the escalating war in Vietnam drew Johnson's attention away from domestic issues and led to a steady decline in his popularity. At the end of March 1968 Johnson announced that he would not be a candidate for reelection, avoiding almost certain defeat at the polls. His successor, Richard Nixon, preserved some war on poverty programs while abolishing others.

K

Kansas City, Missouri   According to the 1991 *Status Report on Hunger and Homelessness* issued by the United States Conference of Mayors, Kansas City had an estimated homeless population of 11,264 in 1991. Kansas City has 842 emergency shelter beds available and 489 beds available for families seeking shelter. According to a city official quoted in the *Status Report:* "Due to the continued recession, there are large waiting lists for Section 8 housing and public housing. One large agency reports that as services in mental health facilities, prisons, substance abuse treatment centers and hospitals that work with indigents all decrease, the call for shelter (and food) from our homeless agency will increase at an alarming rate."

Karp, Sam   See HANDSNET.

Kemp, Jack   Jack Kemp was appointed secretary of the Department of Housing and Urban Development (HUD) by President George Bush. His promise to make housing a priority in domestic policy in the new administration initially raised the hopes of homeless advocates. Under Bush's predeces-

sor, Ronald Reagan, HUD had been racked with scandals. The HUD secretaryship was thus a sensitive and important political appointment for the Bush administration. In his first years in office Kemp, a former professional football player and former congressman from the suburbs of Buffalo, New York, was able to remove some of the tarnish from the department's reputation and played a high-profile role in the Bush administration.

In order to create "economic opportunity" in poverty-stricken urban communities, Kemp favored the creation of "urban enterprise zones," industrial enclaves in inner city areas to attract business investment through favorable tax incentives and lower wage rates for young workers. A similar plan was proposed for creating more affordable housing through "Housing Opportunity Zones" in which cities would remove such barriers to construction as restrictive zoning and building codes in addition to regressive property taxes and rent control. Kemp also favored the selling of public housing units to individuals, the use of housing vouchers to help low-income tenants afford the cost of market-level rents and the creation of tax incentives for developers to encourage low and moderate income housing construction. For Kemp, the sale of public housing to tenants was part of a larger strategy for solving the problems of the nation's poor and minorities. He told an interviewer in 1991: "I do believe we can make a tremendous contribution to changing behavior in our inner cities by giving people a greater stake in their neighborhood." Following the devastating Los Angeles riots in the spring of 1992, Kemp's proposals received renewed attention within the Bush administration and in the national press. Ultimately, however, Kemp disappointed homeless advocates, as he loyally defended administration policies and budgets, which did little to increase the nation's supply of affordable housing. (See HOUSING AND URBAN DEVELOPMENT.)

Kennedy, John F. John Fitzgerald Kennedy was the 35th president of the United States. He was elected to the White House in November 1960, defeating his Republican opponent Richard M. Nixon. Kennedy came to the presidency after serving in Congress and as U.S. senator from Massachusetts. Kennedy had campaigned on the promise of getting America "moving again," but in the early part of his administration he was far more interested in foreign policy than in domestic issues. Historians have argued that Kennedy's legacy as liberal reformer was more a matter of image than reality. Nevertheless, his election encouraged liberals, civil rights advocates and others to believe that a new era of reform, similar to the Progressive Era and the New Deal, had begun. Although early in his administration Kennedy launched the FOOD STAMPS program, he was only mildly interested in social welfare issues. The civil rights movement pushed Kennedy to begin paying more attention to the problems of the poor and minorities. For example, in the 1960 campaign Kennedy had promised to eliminate discrimination in public housing with a "stroke of the pen," by issuing an executive order. For nearly two years he stalled on the promise, but on November 20, 1962 he signed Executive Order No. 11063, which required federal housing agencies to "take all action necessary and appropriate to prevent discrimination because of race, color, creed, or national origin." Until that time, the integration of public housing was left to the discretion of local public housing authorities. In the years that followed the dropping of racial barriers, the percentage of minorities living in public housing increased dramatically.

In his last year in office Kennedy set in motion the planning that would lead to the WAR ON POVERTY legislation of the mid-1960s. During Kennedy's administration the MENTAL RETARDATION FACILITIES AND COMMUNITY MENTAL HEALTH CENTERS CONSTRUCTION (CMHC) ACT, which contributed to the DEINSTITUTIONALIZATION of mental

patients over the next decade, was passed. The act is often cited as a cause for the emergence of homelessness. Kennedy was assassinated in Dallas, Texas on November 22, 1963, and succeeded in office by his vice president, Lyndon Baines Johnson.

Kerouac, Jack See HOBO.

Kerry, John See GRATE AMERICAN SLEEP OUT.

King, Martin Luther, Jr. See AFRICAN AMERICANS.

Koch, Edward Edward Koch was elected mayor of New York City in 1977. The years he served in office, from 1978 through 1989, saw the emergence of the city's homeless crisis. Born in New York in 1924, Koch attended City College and New York University law school. He was a leader of New York City's liberal Democratic Party reform movement, before being elected to the City Council in 1966 and to Congress in 1968. He served in Congress for four terms, then ran for mayor in 1977, winning the Democratic Party nomination in September and defeating the Liberal Party candidate Mario Cuomo in the general election in November. From his first days in office, Koch was plagued with a severe budget deficit. His reputation as a liberal faded during his administration. When David Dinkins successfully challenged Koch for the Democratic nomination for mayor in 1989, one of the main issues in the campaign was Koch's homeless policies, which Dinkins described as inhumane and ineffective.

Kreimer, Richard Richard Kreimer, a homeless man living in Morristown, New Jersey, won extensive media coverage as a legal gadfly by filing lawsuits against local officials on behalf of the legal rights of the homeless. A former house painter, mechanic and landscaper who grew up in Morristown, Kreimer became homeless in the 1980s, sleeping in parks and abandoned vehicles and spending his days around the town municipal building and library. One of Kreimer's lawsuits won a guarantee from the state of New Jersey of voting rights for homeless people. In a second, highly publicized case in federal court, the judge agreed with Kreimer's argument that he should not be barred from the Morristown library, even if other patrons were annoyed by his presence. Kreimer received an $80,000 payment from the library's insurer to settle claims for compensatory damages. But the decision was overturned by a federal appeals panel in Philadelphia in the spring of 1992. Kreimer planned further appeals. Kreimer also filed a suit against a number of Morristown officials and policemen, charging personal harassment, and received $150,000 from the town to settle the suit. (See also LIBRARIES.)

L

legal rights Homeless people are frequently denied the legal rights enjoyed by other Americans. In fact, in many parts of the country the existence of homelessness has been treated by the local authorities as if it were primarily a law enforcement problem that could be solved by "getting tough" on the homeless themselves. In 1983 in Tucson, Arizona, for example, the city's mayor ran for reelection on a platform that included the pledge he would get "the transients the hell out of town." Police in some cities have attempted to drive away homeless people through verbal and physical harassment and through arrests for a variety of misdemeanors, such as trespass, squatting, public indecency and loitering. In Santa Barbara, California antihomeless ordinances prohibited sitting, sleeping or lying down in public parks. Trash-bin refuse was defined as public property, making foraging in gar-

bage a criminal act. ZONING ordinances have been used in some cities to close down religious missions providing food and shelter to the homeless or to prevent churches from running homeless shelters in their buildings. In some cities the authorities have sponsored "clean sweeps" to rid the community of unsightly homeless people before some event likely to attract tourists, such as the 1984 Olympics in Los Angeles or the annual Mardi Gras celebration in New Orleans. Airports and bus shelters have revamped their seating to prevent people from sleeping on benches, and a Fort Lauderdale, Florida councilman proposed spraying rat poison in trash cans and dumpsters as a way of discouraging people from rummaging through them for food. Authorities in some communities attempted to solve local problems by making it clear to the homeless that they were not wanted, then providing them with bus tickets to neighboring cities or states. Homeless advocates also complain of inadequate police protection for the homeless, who are often the victims of random violence.

Homeless people are, almost by definition, people without clout. They don't pay property taxes, and they often are denied voting rights. (Court decisions in California, the District of Columbia, New Jersey and New York have upheld the right of local homeless people to register and vote, but many communities and states still require potential registrants to list a "residence" in order to be allowed to vote.) The homeless lack powerful advocates and the skills or the means to influence public opinion.

Homeless people are entitled to many federal benefit programs, including FOOD STAMPS, benefits for elderly and disabled persons, medical benefits, veterans' benefits, AID TO FAMILIES WITH DEPENDENT CHILDREN (AFDC), and public education for their children. They have often encountered difficulties in applying for and receiving these benefits. Sometimes they are unaware of the benefits that are available to them.

Elderly, poorly educated or mentally disabled homeless persons often find the complex application procedures for federal benefits too intimidating or baffling to complete without assistance, which is not always forthcoming from overworked social workers or clerks. (A 12-page application form is required for SUPPLEMENTAL SECURITY INCOME [SSI] payments.) Federal legislation such as the Homeless Eligibility Clarification Act of 1986, amendments to the Social Security Act passed in 1987, the rewriting of regulations governing the policies of individual agencies and outreach programs by individual agencies are intended to make it easier for homeless persons and families to receive the benefits they are entitled to. Advocacy groups, such as the National Law Center on Homelessness and Poverty and the National Coalition for the Homeless, have brought suit on behalf of the homeless to force the federal government to make benefits more easily accessible. Persons applying for food stamps, Supplemental Security Income, SOCIAL SECURITY DISABILITY INSURANCE, Medicaid, veterans' benefits, or AFDC do not have to have a permanent residence or address to qualify. Title VII of the Stewart B. McKinney Homeless Assistance Act provides that homeless children may not be denied access to public schools by residency requirements or other other legal bars. Homeless children must be granted equal access to special education and after-school programs.

The U.S. Constitution does not guarantee the right to shelter, but homeless legal advocates have argued that some state statutes and constitutions do imply such a right. The right to shelter has been tested through courts at the local level in several communities. The most famous case was *Callahan v. Carey* in New York City. New York, unlike most cities, was providing shelter for homeless before the 1980s. But its Men's Shelter, located at 8 East Third Street, was overcrowded, unsanitary and dangerous; those who could not be fit into the shelter or given

a voucher for a bed in one of the "welfare hotels" the city used to shelter homeless people would be turned away. Robert Hayes, an attorney and director of New York City's Coalition for the Homeless (CFTH), brought suit on behalf of one homeless man, Robert Callahan, against the city and state of New York. He argued that under New York State's Constitution, there was a legally enforceable right to shelter. In 1979 the New York Supreme Court granted a preliminary injunction requiring New York City to provide "shelter (including bedding, wholesome food and adequate security and supervision) to any person who applies for shelter at the Men's Shelter." To meet this requirement, the city opened a new shelter at an abandoned mental institution on Wards Island. The case was finally settled in 1981 under a consent decree that stated: "The City . . . shall provide shelter and board to each homeless man who applies for it provided that (a) the man meets the need standard to qualify for the home relief program established in New York State; or (b) the man by reason of physical, mental or social dysfunction is in need of temporary shelter." (A subsequent legal decision held that this decree applied equally to homeless women.) Under the provisions of the consent decree, the city vastly expanded the number of beds available for the homeless (although the total number of homeless in the city was still estimated at many times larger than the expanded shelter capacity).

Similar lawsuits filed by homeless advocates in other cities and states met with mixed results. In a 1983 decision in *Hodge v. Ginsberg* (a class action suit brought on behalf of West Virginia's homeless by the United Mine Workers Union), the Supreme Court of Appeals of West Virgina declared that under the state's Social Services for Adults Act of 1981, the state was obligated to provide shelter, food and medical care for its homeless population. A 1983 Superior Court decision in Los Angeles *(Eisenheim v. County Board of Superiors)* ruled that

Los Angeles County could no longer restrict eligibility for emergency local shelter relief (in the form of housing vouchers or housing checks) by demanding the presentation of identification and imposing a waiting period of several days' duration. And in 1987 the American Civil Liberties Union (ACLU) filed suit in Los Angeles and won an injunction to prevent the city from conducting "sweeps" to demolish homeless shantytowns built on vacant lots, without giving at least 12-hours notice.

In 1986 the American Bar Association (ABA) resolved to support enactment of federal, state and local laws that would "prohibit discrimination on the basis of transient of homeless status in government assistance programs . . . and prohibit interference with the exercise of civil rights solely on the basis of transient or homeless status." In 1988 the ABA launched its "Representation of the Homeless Project." Local bar programs in 20 cities had organized by 1989 to offer pro bono legal services for the homeless.

Some homeless people have won reputations as legal gadflies. In Morristown, New Jersey, a homeless man named Richard Kreimer won a series of legal victories on behalf of the homeless, including one famous case establishing the rights of the homeless to use local libraries. In a Connecticut case, a formerly homeless man named David Mooney successfully sued to have his conviction on robbery and murder charges overturned, on the grounds that the police violated his Fourth Amendment rights when they searched his belongings, which he kept under a highway overpass, without a search warrant.

Lessard v. Schmidt   A 1972 Wisconsin court decision called *Lessard v. Schmidt* helped establish the legal principle that involuntary commitment of the mentally ill was justified only in cases where the behavior of mentally ill individuals represented a danger to themselves or others. It was one of a series of court decisions that strengthened the legal rights of the mentally ill and contributed to the move toward DEINSTITUTIONALIZATION of mental patients. (See also MENTAL ILLNESS.)

Lewis, Oscar   See WAR ON POVERTY.

libraries   In many communities homeless people have sought shelter during the day in local libraries. Their presence has sometimes created conflicts with other patrons who object to their appearance, behavior or personal hygiene. Librarians have been torn between respecting the rights of homeless people to make use of public facilities and their traditional concern for preserving peace and decorum. The courts have sent out conflicting signals to librarians on this question. In May 1991, in a case involving the public library in Morristown, New Jersey, Federal District Judge H. Lee Sarokin ruled in favor of a suit by a homeless man named Richard Kreimer, who had been barred from using the library. "Libraries cannot and should not be transformed into hotels or kitchens, even for the needy," Sarokin declared in his decision overturning the library's rules that were specifically designed to keep out Kreimer. But he argued that keeping Kreimer out was a violation of his First Amendment rights to have access to the books and newspapers in the library. Some patrons had complained that Kreimer had made them uncomfortable by staring at them. Librarians complained that homeless people had been falling asleep at tables and hiding bags of clothing in closets. The mayor of Morristown, Norman Bloch, argued after the judge's ruling that "it's not an issue of bad people going after down-and-out people. It's a library wanting a modicum of civility in their building. If the trend goes against the library and they can't have reasonable rules, then, somewhere down the road, you're talking about a bus depot type of place with books in it." Judge Sarokin declared in his ruling, "If we wish to shield our eyes and noses from the homeless, we should revoke their condition, not their library cards." In March 1992 a three-judge federal appeals panel in Philadelphia upheld the Morristown library's rules on patron behavior, overturning Judge Sarokin's ruling. Under the latest ruling, homeless people with offensive body odor could be excluded from libraries, if they interfered with other patrons' use and enjoyment of the libraries.

lice   Lice are a common affliction of the homeless. These small, flattened, wingless insects have three pairs of legs ending in claws and spend their entire life cycle on the skin or in the clothing of human beings. Three different species of lice affect humans: the crab or pubic louse, affecting the pubic area and other hairy parts of the body; head lice, found on the scalp or the back of the neck; and body lice, which spend most of their life cycle in garments worn by infested people. Female lice lay their eggs at the base of hairs or in clothing. The eggs hatch in five or ten days and grow quickly into adult form. The adults pierce the skin of their human carriers, feeding on their blood. The saliva they deposit in the wounds creates inflammations. Head and body lice grow to three to four millimeters in size and can be seen in clothing or on the body. Body lice, which are especially common, are spread among the homeless through the exchange of clothing or from people huddling close together. Effective treatment is available through the use of lindane and the fumigation of clothing and bedding, but reinfestation is difficult to avoid as long as patients remain homeless. (See also HEALTH.)

Local Initiatives Support Corporation (LISC)   See NONPROFIT HOUSING PROGRAMS.

Los Angeles, California   According to the 1991 *Status Report on Hunger and Homelessness* issued by the United States

Conference of Mayors, Los Angeles had an estimated homeless population of 15,200. Other estimates of the number of homeless persons in Los Angeles have ranged as high as 70,000. (The National Coalition for the Homeless estimates that there are 50,000 homeless persons.) In any case, by most estimates Los Angeles is second only to New York in the size of its homeless population. In 1991 the city had a total of 8,000 emergency shelter beds, and 3,000 beds available for families seeking shelter.

The homeless in Los Angeles tend to be far less visible than their counterparts in other cities, at least as far as the general population is concerned. Unlike New York or San Francisco, there is no subway system, around which the homeless can gather. Apart from clusters of the homeless in Santa Monica and near Los Angeles City Hall, much of the city's homeless population is scattered in poorer neighborhoods around the city. Like the homeless population in many cities, that in Los Angeles consists largely of minorities: As many as 80 percent of the homeless in the city may be African Americans. Approximately 35 percent of Los Angeles's homeless population consists of families with children, 40 percent are single men, and 25 percent are single women and unaccompanied youth. Approximately 30 percent of the homeless population are mentally ill, and 30 percent are substance abusers. The number of homeless who are employed is estimated to be 35 percent. The main cause of homelessness in Los Angeles is a shortage of affordable housing. Los Angeles is the third most expensive city in the United States to rent housing in, after San Francisco and Boston. According to the findings of a commission appointed by Mayor Tom Bradley, one out of every four renters in the city was paying over half of his or her monthly income for rent. The average monthly rent more than doubled between 1980 and 1988. In 1988 the average rent in Los Angeles was $525 per month, which amounted to 70 percent of the income of a worker being paid the minimum wage. In 1991 a worker would need to earn at least $14.37 per hour to be able to afford to rent a two-bedroom apartment in Los Angeles. The city was hit by both the economic recession of the early 1990s and by cuts in government funding. A city official was quoted in the 1991 *Status Report* as saying that there has been "increasing homelessness due to loss of work. There are insufficient funds to cover demand. Cutbacks in state-funded social services have decreased agencies' ability to respond."

In Los Angeles in the 1970s and early 1980s over 2,000 units of housing in SINGLE-ROOM-OCCUPANCY hotels (SROs) were lost to conversion and demolition, reducing the supply of low-cost shelter in the city's skid row area. In 1986 the city passed a five-year moratorium on the destruction of SROs and since then has worked with various nonprofit organizations to preserve and renovate existing SROs.

In 1990 there were 8,368 reported cases of AIDS virus in Los Angeles. The serious shortage of affordable, low-income housing resulted in an increase in the number of homeless persons with AIDS and HIV-related illnesses. The specific needs of homeless persons infected with the AIDS is increasingly being recognized in Los Angeles, where advocacy groups such as AIDS Project Los Angeles (APLA), the Los Angeles Homeless Health Care Project and Aid for AIDS have brought the issue to the attention of city officials and the general public.

There have been several well-publicized clashes between the homeless and city officials who regard homelessness as chiefly a law enforcement problem. In 1987 the city's Department of Public Works launched a bulldozer-equipped sweep against the "cardboard condominiums" (refrigerator boxes and other makeshift shelters) in which some homeless people were living on downtown streets. Later Police Chief Daryl Gates gave the homeless seven days to move off skid row. But city attorney James Hahn announced that he would not prosecute those Gates arrested because "personally, I don't think it's the right thing to do." A city official reported in the 1991 *Status Report* that public sentiment was turning against the homeless: "There seems to be an atmosphere of increasing negative sentiment which appears to be in direct correlation with an increase of homeless people on the streets." In April 1992 poor neighborhoods in Los Angeles were devastated by the worst racial rioting of the century, in response to a verdict acquitting police officers of using excessive force in subduing a man suspected of drunken driving. One of the by-products of the riots was to increase Los Angeles homeless population, since many people were burned out of their homes.

Louisville, Kentucky   According to the 1991 *Status Report on Hunger and Homelessness*, Louisville had an estimated homeless population of 11,442. The city had 615 emergency shelter beds, and 45 beds available for families seeking shelter. A Louisville city official was quoted in the *Status Report* as saying: "Louisville is a very caring community, but homelessness is an overwhelming issue which is unending. . . . As [Louisville] Mayor Abramson says: 'The problem will continue to grow until it is placed on the national agenda.'"

Low Income Housing Information Service   See NATIONAL LOW INCOME HOUSING COALITION.

low-income housing tax credit   The low-income housing tax credit is a general business tax credit allowed by the Internal Revenue Service (IRS) in order to encourage low-income housing development. The credit is granted against expenditures on qualified low-income buildings placed in service after 1986. The credit is allowed each year over the course of a ten-year period at a rate determined yearly by the IRS. Various requirements must be satisfied before a building can qualify for a tax credit. (See also NONPROFIT HOUSING PROGRAMS.)

M

MacArthur, Douglas See BONUS ARMY.

Maryhouse See CATHOLIC WORKER.

Maticka v. Atlantic City In *Maticka v. Atlantic City* the New Jersey Superior Court ruled in 1987 that the state protective services law guaranteed a right to shelter for general assistance applicants who were homeless.

Maurin, Peter See CATHOLIC WORKER.

McKinney Act The Stewart B. McKinney Homeless Assistance Act (PL 100–77), signed into law on July 22, 1987 by President Ronald Reagan, was the first comprehensive federal legislation designed to counter the homeless crisis. Reagan was opposed to the passage of the Democratic-initiated bill, raising objections to both its cost and its "duplicative programs," but he did not threaten a veto because the measure had strong support in both houses of Congress. The legislation authorized the spending of over $400 million in homeless aid for 1987 and over $600 million for 1988 (although the amounts actually appropriated were far less). The purpose of the bill was defined as meeting "the critically urgent needs of the nation's homeless," with special emphasis on elderly and handicapped persons, families with children, Native Americans, and veterans.

The bill that became the McKinney Act was first introduced in Congress on January 8, 1987 by House Majority Leader Thomas S. Foley of Washington, under the title Urgent Relief for the Homeless Act. House Speaker Jim Wright of Texas endorsed the bill the next day. In March the House passed the bill by a vote of 264 to 121, dividing along partisan lines. Democrats supported the bill, which won votes from only 43 Republicans. On March 23 a similar although less costly bill was introduced in the Senate, jointly sponsored by Senate Majority Leader Robert C. Byrd of West Virginia and Senate Minority Leader Robert Dole of Kansas. The bill passed the Senate by a vote of 85 to 12 on April 9. Senate and House conferees agreed on a compromise measure on June 19. The conferees also agreed to name the bill after the late Connecticut representative Stewart B. McKinney who had died on May 7. (McKinney, a Republican who had represented Connecticut's 4th district for 16 years, had been an opponent of the Reagan administration's attempts to cut back domestic programs in the 1980s.) The Senate voted its approval of the final bill on June 27 by a vote of 65 to 8, and House approval followed three days later by a vote of 301 to 115.

The initial authorization for the McKinney Act was for two years and expired on September 30, 1988. On November 7, 1988 Reagan signed the Omnibus McKinney Homeless Assistance Act of 1988, which reauthorized the McKinney Act for another two years. In 1990 Congress reauthorized the McKinney Act, extending its housing programs for another two years and its education, health, and support service programs for three or more years. The 1990 reauthorization also added new programs, such as the SHELTER PLUS CARE PROGRAM, the CHILD WELFARE DEMONSTRATION PROGRAM and FAMILY SUPPORT CENTERS.

The McKinney Act includes 20 different provisions for emergency shelter funds, health care, job training and other programs, with seven federal agencies participating. Among other major provisions, the act established an Interagency Council on the Homeless to coordinate federal programs to assist the homeless. It created an Emergency Food and Shelter National Board, under the direction of the Federal Emergency Management Agency (FEMA), to disburse funds to local private nonprofit organizations and local government. The funds were to be used to expand ongoing efforts to provide shelter, food and supportive services to the homeless as well as to pay for "minimum rehabilitation" of existing mass shelters and feeding facilities. The McKinney Act established the Emergency Shelter Grants program, authorizing the Department of Housing and Urban Development (HUD) to distribute block grants to states (and through states to local governments, cities, counties and private nonprofit organizations) for capital improvements to and operating expenses of new and existing emergency shelters. The grants could also be used to fund services, including employment, health, drug abuse counseling and educational services. HUD was authorized to set up a Supportive Housing Demonstration Program to provide loans, grants and other support for transitional housing designed to assist homeless persons move from shelters to permanent housing, and for permanent housing for handicapped persons.

The McKinney Act also established the Health Care for the Homeless program to be administered by the Department of Health and Human Services (HHS), providing grants to public and private non-profit organizations to deliver primary health care and substance abuse services to homeless persons. Similarly, the act established the Community Mental Health Services for the Homeless program administered by HHS, providing grants to states for provision of community mental health services to chronically mentally ill homeless persons. The Department of Education was authorized to make grants to state education agencies for programs of literacy training for homeless persons. The Department of Agriculture was authorized to provide matching funds to states for providing outreach to assist eligible homeless persons applying for FOOD STAMPS. The department was also authorized to expand an existing Temporary Emergency Food Assistance Program to provide surplus food to states requesting assistance to feed the homeless. The Labor Department and the Department of Veterans Affairs were also authorized to set up programs to benefit the homeless.

When the bill that became the McKinney Act was first introduced in Congress in January 1987, it was hailed by homeless advocates. The Community for Creative Non-Violence, which had maintained a vigil at the Capitol's East Front since Thanksgiving of 1986, called off their protest the next day, saying that further protest was unnecessary. Since the passage of the McKinney Act, however, homeless advocates have renewed their criticisms of federal policy. While acknowledging some progress, they have argued that the act has been grossly underfunded to meet the needs of an ever-increasing homeless population. In a time of fiscal restraint, with a swelling federal deficit and political pressure against federal tax increases, congressmen are more willing to pass ambitious-sounding programs than to fully fund them. Although Congress authorized the spending of over $1 billion for fiscal years 1987 and 1988 under the provisions of the McKinney Act, it appropriated considerably less: In 1987 only $350 million of the authorized $430 was actually appropriated; in 1988 only $360 million of the authorized $615 million was appropriated. For some of the mandated programs, this level of funding represented virtual elimination: The Emergency Shelter Grants program, for example, was authorized at $120 million for 1988 and actually received only $8 million; the Section 8 SRO rehabilitation program was not funded for 1988.

During the 1988 presidential campaign George Bush pledged to support full funding of the McKinney Act. Funding did increase after his election, but the appropriated funds for 1990 were still $68.3 million below authorization levels. In the first year of President Bill Clinton's administration, funding for McKinney Act programs approached the $1.4 billion level, an increase of 21 percent over the previous fiscal year funding.

McKinney AFDC Transitional Housing Demonstration Program   This program, authorized by the Stewart B. McKinney Homeless Assistance Amendments Act of 1988 and administered within the Department of Health and Human Services (HHS), funds demonstration projects to place homeless families receiving Aid to Families with Dependent Children (AFDC) in transitional facilities instead of in commercial or other transient facilities. Funds may be used to rehabilitate or construct transitional facilities that can be converted to permanent housing and to provide on-site social services.

Medicaid   Medicaid, part of President Lyndon Baines Johnson's WAR ON POVERTY legislation passed by Congress in 1965, provides health insurance protection to indigent people 65 years or older, as well as to recipients of AID TO FAMILIES OF DEPENDENT CHILDREN (AFDC) and SUPPLEMENTAL SECURITY INCOME (SSI). The Department of Health and Human Services estimates that "approximately 25 percent of homeless individuals and families receive Medicaid."

Medicare   Medicare, part of President Lyndon Johnson's WAR ON POVERTY legislation passed by Congress in 1965, provides comprehensive health insurance protection to the aged, disabled and suffers of chronic kidney disease. Homeless elderly people are eligible for Medicare, provided that have paid Social Security taxes for minimum periods that vary according to individual work histories.

mental illness   The chronically mentally ill are persons who experience severe and persistent mental or emotional disorders, such as schizophrenia or major depression, that interfere with their functioning and require prolonged professional care. Estimates of the proportion of the chronically mentally ill among the homeless vary widely, from 10 percent to a majority of the total homeless population. The mentally ill are perhaps the most visible subpopulation among the homeless, because of their sometimes bizarre appearance and antisocial behavior in public places. The DEINSTITUTIONALIZATION of former inmates of mental hospitals is frequently cited as a cause for the emergence of the homeless crisis.

Some observers have portrayed the problem of homelessness largely as a problem of mental health. Conservatives favor this argument because it suggests that cuts in social welfare spending or the high cost of urban housing have little to do with the emergence of the homeless crisis. President Ronald Reagan told a television interviewer in December 1988 that a "large percentage" of the homeless were "retarded" people who had voluntarily left the institutions in which they had earlier been housed. The neo-conservative columnist Charles Krauthammer, writing in 1985, claimed that a "majority of the homeless" were "near either psychosis or stupor." His main source for this claim was sociologist Ellen Bassuk's frequently cited study of the homeless in a Boston shelter, published in *Scientific American* in 1984, that found a "90 percent incidence of diagnosable mental illness: psychoses, chronic alcoholism and character disorders."

Other estimates of the percentage of the mentally ill among the homeless population run much lower, and Bassuk herself disagreed with the conclusions Krauthammer drew from her study. Estimates of the percentage of the homeless population with chronic mental illness gathered by the United States Conference of Mayors in a 1986 survey varied from a high of 60 percent in Louisville to a low of 15 percent in Philadelphia, Los Angeles, and New Or-

Indicators of the Prevalence of Mental Illness and Drug/Alchohol Problems Among Adult Homeless
(Please note that a person may fall into more than one category)

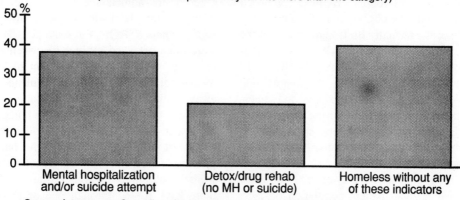

Source: Interagency Council on the Homeless (1990 Annual Report)

leans. New York governor Mario Cuomo declared in his report to the National Governors' Association Task Force on the Homeless in 1983:

> Lest there be any misunderstanding, the bulk of research to date indicates that (1) the majority of the homeless poor are not seriously mentally disabled; and that (2) even for those with severe disabilities, preferable alternatives to rehospitalization exist, although in far too short a supply. Moreover, it is often not a simple matter to judge to what degree an observed disorder should be considered a cause, and to what degree a consequence of street-living.

The mentally ill have historically found themselves the victims of fear and superstition. In the Middle Ages mental illness was widely regarded as a sign that an individual was the victim or the practitioner of witchcraft. In the Enlightenment era in Europe, medical reformers argued that mental illness could be cured by humane and scientific methods and that the mentally ill should not be punished for their disability. "Insane asylums" were established in Europe and America to house the mentally ill. In the United States Dorothea Dix, a humanitarian reformer, launched a crusade in the 1840s to improve the treatment of the mentally ill. At that time many of the mentally ill were

confined in jails and almshouses under primitive and sometimes brutal conditions. In 1841 Dix presented a statement to the Massachusetts state legislature protesting the confinement of "Insane Persons" in "cages, closets, cellars, stalls, pens! Chained, naked, beaten with rods, and lashed into obedience!" Dix's crusades led to widespread reforms and the establishment of mental hospitals across the country.

Ironically, one generation's "reform" often has a way of becoming another generation's "crisis." Conditions in the new system of insane asylums were sometimes as deplorable as those they were designed to cure. Asylums became warehouses for keeping the mentally ill out of sight, not places where they could be cured, as Dix had hoped. In 1946 Congress established the National Institute of Mental Health (NIMH) to study the causes and possible cures of mental illness. At the same time new drugs were being developed that stabilized symptoms of the mentally ill, permitting patients to live outside hospital settings. A public outcry against conditions in U.S. mental hospitals (whose population peaked at over 550,000 in 1955) led to demands for reforms and alternative forms of treatment. Critics charged that "total institutions" such as mental hospitals shaped the behavior of their inmates in ways that had little to do with promoting their return to mental health. In 1963 President John F. Kennedy proposed to Congress the phasing out of the custodial care of the mentally ill. Congress passed the Mental Retardation Facilities and Community Mental Health Centers (CMHC) Construction Act later that year, providing federal funding for outpatient and emergency treatment centers for the mentally ill.

In response to public pressures and the federal government's initiative, state mental hospitals began to discharge large numbers of their patients. The over 500,000 state mental hospital patient population of 1955 was cut to less than 138,000 patients by 1980. The states welcomed the new policies, because they saw the opportunity to shift the burden of caring for mentally ill from their own treasuries to the federal government. But "reform" again prepared the way for a new social crisis. The federal government largely reneged on the commitment it had made to providing new forms of treatment for the former state hospital patients. Only 700 of the originally planned 2,500 community mental health centers were opened in the 1960s and 1970s, and these often wound up serving a more affluent and less severely disturbed clientele than the population previously confined to state mental hospitals.

Well-publicized cases, such as those involving JOYCE BROWN and JUAN GONZALEZ, inflamed public sentiment against the homeless mentally ill in the 1980s and contributed to the belief that deinstitutionalization had gone too far. The importance of deinstitutionalization in and of itself as a cause of homelessness can, however, easily be exaggerated. As sociologist James Wright pointed out in 1989, "By the late 1970s, most of the people destined ever to be 'deinstitutionalized' already had been. So as a direct contributing factor to the rise of homelessness in the 1980s, deinstitutionalization cannot be that important." Through most of the 1960s and 1970s, the recently discharged mentally ill (and those who were never admitted to mental hospitals due to more stringent entry requirements) were not, in fact, reduced to homelessness. Housing was available for them—in single-room-occupancy hotels (SRO), for example. These were often not ideal settings for psychiatric recovery, but they were sufficient to keep mentally ill persons out of the elements and away from the dangers of the street.

In fact, relatively few of today's homeless are drawn from the ranks of the deinstitutionalized. According to one study, only 3 percent of homeless moved directly from mental institutions to homelessness. Many more have passed through one or another form of transitional setting, such as halfway houses or SROs. But cutbacks in social welfare spending have eliminated many halfway houses, while the forces of urban gentrification eliminated the SROs. In the cutbacks in federal spending on welfare programs in the early 1980s, nearly half a million recipients were dropped from the rolls of Social Security Disability Insurance program. Nearly a third of these were people suffering from psychiatric disabilities, and many of them wound up living on the street.

Confronted with the unpleasant spectacle of the homeless mentally ill living filthy, disordered lives on the streets, some people have argued for a policy of "reinstitutionalization." A series of state and federal court decisions, such as the 1972 Wisconsin case *Lessard v. Schmidt*, established the legal principle that involuntary commitment of mentally ill persons was justified only in cases where their behavior represented a danger to themselves or others. Critics of deinstutionalization have responded that commitment laws should be rewritten to make it easier to commit the mentally ill to asylums against their will. They argue that the benefits of institutionalization (regular meals, shelter, supervised therapy and the protection of the public from potentially dangerous individuals) outweigh an individual patient's right to absolute freedom of choice in how to live his or her life. The American

Psychiatric Asssociation, while opposed to any mass reinstitutionalization of the mentally ill, supports the power of state authorities to commit anyone "likely to suffer substantial mental or physical deterioration" if left uncommitted. Apart from civil libertarian and legal objections to reinstitutionalization, there is also a question of cost effectiveness. Costs for maintaining a patient in a mental hospital run about $70,000 a year. In transitional housing, such as group homes and SROs, the costs drop to $13,000 a year, including the cost of case worker supervision. But cities are reluctant to take on the expense of providing such facilities. New York City and the State of New York agreed in 1990 to begin construction of some 5,000 SROs with caseworkers and social programs. In February 1991 a state supreme court justice ruled that New York City needed to expand its system of stable housing and outpatient services to provide beds and services for 10,000 mental patients discharged by city hospitals into the shelter system. New York City officials indicated they would appeal the ruling.

Marjorie Hope and James Young have called for an integrated strategy of housing and treatment for the homeless mentally ill, including emergency shelters, halfway houses, outreach programs and supportive services. They contend that the

> much-discussed failure of deinstitutionalization has really been a failure for low-income and moderate-income deinstitutionalized people. Excellent mental health care and supportive services, as well as adequate housing, existing in this country—for those who can afford to pay for them. . . . [T]he crux of the problem is the unwillingness of society to pay for good services for all who need them. . . .

The Franciscan religious order runs a residence for former mental patients in New York City that could serve as a model for public and other private agencies. Seventy-five men and 25 women live in the center, where room rentals cost between $35 and $50 a week, and meals are provided for

under a dollar a day. Psychiatric, medical and crisis intervention services are supplied on site. The emphasis of the community is on tolerance and establishing a homelike atmosphere in which, for example, residents' birthdays are remembered and celebrated.

While mental illness is in some cases a cause of homelessness, in its most debilitating forms it is often a consequence of homelessness. Some "crazy" people on the street would seem a good deal less crazy if, as Ellen Baxter and Kim Hopper argued in 1982, they enjoyed the benefit of "several nights of sleep, an adequate diet, and warm social contact." The failure of deinstitutionalization, in other words, is not necessarily a good argument for reinstitutionalization. Other alternatives do exist and can work. For mental health indicators of homeless single women with children verus other adults, see the figure under WOMEN.

Mental Retardation Facilities and Community Mental Health Centers (CMHC) Construction Act In 1963 President John F. Kennedy proposed to Congress the phasing out of the custodial care of the mentally ill. Congress passed the Mental Retardation Facilities and Community Mental Health Centers (CMHC) Construction Act later that year, providing federal funding for outpatient and emergency treatment centers for the mentally ill. The passage of the act was followed by the widespread DEINSTITUTIONALIZATION of mental patients, often cited as a cause for the increase in homelessness. (See also MENTAL ILLNESS.)

Miami, Florida According to the 1991 *Status Report on Hunger and Homelessness* issued by the United States Conference of Mayors, there are an estimated 2,000 homeless people in Miami. Other estimates of the city's homeless population range as high as 10,000 people. Dade County has 1,189 emergency shelter beds and 333 beds available for families seeking shelter. A Miami city offical was quoted in the *Status Report* as predicting a rise in homelessness due to "increasing unemployment and the increasing influx of refugees."

Concerned about the city's appeal to tourists, Miami has responded to the crisis of homelessness in the 1980s and early 1990s largely as a problem of law enforcement, using its police force to arrest and harass the city's homeless population for a variety of minor offenses, in order to sweep them off the city's streets. In November 1992 Federal District Judge C. Clyde Atkins ordered the city of Miami to create "safe zones" where the homeless could eat, sleep, bathe and cook without fear of arrest. In response to the judge's order, and his criticisms of excessive and unconstitutional police harassment of the homeless in 1993, Miami imposed a 1% tax on restaurant meals served in the city to finance new programs for the homeless. (See also LEGAL RIGHTS.)

migratory labor   In 17th- and 18th-century America, skilled artisans such as shoemakers and weavers, transporting the tools of their trade with them, often moved from place to place in search of new markets for the products of their labor. By the late 19th century they made up a sizable proportion of the U.S. workforce, many of whom were immigrants. According to a 1910 study, 3.5 million male workers moved frequently enough to be classified as migratory laborers, over one-tenth of the total male workforce. Migratory labor continued to be a feature of the American economy in the 19th and 20th centuries. By then most migratory laborers were unskilled or semiskilled workers who moved from place to place in order to sell their labor. Many seasonal and extractive industries depended on migratory labor, including agriculture, construction, fishing, mining and lumbering in the late 19th century.

The numbers of migratory laborers varied with the business cycle. The Panic of 1873 and subsequent depressions in the mid-1880s and 1890s sent hundreds of thousands of men on the road in search of employment. Although necessary to the functioning of many enterprises, migratory laborers were often looked down on and feared by those who enjoyed stable employment and more permanent homes. Migratory laborers were referred to by derogatory terms such as *bum*, *tramp* or *hobo;* were believed to be dirty, dishonest and lazy; and were harassed by local authorities who charged them with vagrancy, drunkenness and other offenses against the public order. The fact that many migratory laborers were foreign-born only added to the public hysteria. Many people associated the existence of tramps with labor disturbances in the United States, such as the 1877 railroad strike, and foreign revolutions, such as the Paris Commune of 1871. Many states passed "tramp acts" in the late 19th century, providing for the imprisonment of vagrants, and outlawing the earlier practice of providing shelter to the homeless in urban police stations. (In the 1880s the New York City police department provided lodging in its jails to an estimated 150,000 men a year.) Religious missions, such as those run by the Salvation Army, often filled the gap left by the abolition of police lodging. Other migratory laborers found shelter in flophouses on urban skid rows.

Migratory laborers were usually unable to vote, because they never settled long enough in one place to qualify, and were rarely afforded the protections of union organization.

A radical labor federation, the Industrial Workers of the World (IWW), made a determined effort to organize agricultural, lumber and other migratory laborers between 1905 and 1917 but was all but destroyed by government repression during World War I. The IWW's chief legacy today are the songs written by IWW bard Joe Hill, including the classic "Hallelujah, I'm a Bum." Typically, migratory laborers traveled from place to place by "riding the rails," catching rides on freight trains. In between jobs they could be found living in hobo "jungles," temporary encampments near railroad junctions. Mechanization of agriculture, construction and extractive industries lowered demand for migrant labor.

Today many migratory laborers are "illegal aliens" who enter the United States across the Mexican border to find work in agriculture or other enterprises. They often stay only long enough to acquire land or pay off debts in their home country. Other foreign workers are brought in on seasonal contracts to harvest crops. A 1980 study by the Farmers Home Administration (FmHA) found an unmet need nationally for 800,000 units of migrant shelter. Between 1980 and 1987 the FmHA financed 5,721 units of farmworker housing, primarily for year-round workers. (See also COXEY'S ARMY; SKID ROW; VAGRANCY.)

minimum wage The passage of the Fair Labor Standards Act of 1938 under the NEW DEAL administration of President Franklin Delano Roosevelt established for the first time a uniform minimum wage for most if not all nonagricultural workers. In the decades that followed the minimum wage was extended to cover more and more workers. Congress periodically raised the minimum wage, until it reached $3.35 an hour in 1981. But for the next eight years of the administration of Ronald Reagan, the minimum wage remained unchanged, declining in real value to its lowest level since the 1950s. This meant that earnings from a full-time, year-round minimum wage job were several thousand dollars below the poverty line for a family of four throughout the 1980s, a decade that saw housing costs rise sharply in many regions of the nation. As the American economy shifted from away from manufacturing and toward the service industry, more and more jobs offered only the minimum wage or a little more. President George Bush vetoed a bill that would have raised the minimum wage to $4.55 an

hour, but in 1991 finally agreed to legislation raising it to $4.25. At that rate, a family of three with one breadwinner earning the minimum wage would have an income reaching only 80 percent of the official POVERTY LINE.

Minneapolis, Minnesota According to the 1991 *Status Report on Hunger and Homelessness* issued by the United States Conference of Mayors, there were an estimated 792 homeless people in Minneapolis. The average number of requests for emergency shelter in the fall of 1991 was 792. Other estimates of the homeless population in the city run much higher. The city had 998 emergency shelter beds and 130 beds available for families seeking shelter.

minorities In the nation's largest cities, the homeless population is primarily composed of minorities. This fact represents a significant demographic change, because African Americans and Hispanics, though always representing a disproportionate number of the poor, were underrepresented in skid row populations earlier in the century. In the 1980s African Americans and Hispanics represented nearly half of the national homeless population. A 1984 study of the homeless by the Department of Housing and Urban Development (HUD) estimated that 44 percent of the homeless shelter population consisted of minorities. In the national population as a whole, minorities represented only 20 percent. In larger cities the proportion of minorities among the homeless ran much higher. Richard Ropers's study of the Los Angeles homeless in 1983–84 found that minorities made up 51 percent of the homeless population: African Americans comprised 32 percent of his sample population, while 11 percent were Hispanics, 5 percent Native Americans, 1 percent Asians and 2 percent others. The proportion of minorities, especially African Americans, among the homeless seems to have increased over the course of the 1980s. Estimates of the proportion of minorities among the homeless population in the late 1980s varied from 65 percent in Chicago, to 80 percent in Los Angeles, to 90 percent in New York City.

Minorities have traditionally suffered from discrimination in both the private housing market and in PUBLIC HOUSING. In some communities, zoning ordinances legally mandated segregation based on race, even after such ordinances were declared unconstitutional by the U.S. Supreme Court in *Buchanan v. Warley* in 1917. After 1917 the use of restrictive covenants, private contractual arrangements in which a buyer of a house promised not to sell, rent, or transfer the property to members of racial or religious minorities, came into widespread use. Restrictive covenants were found unconstitutional by the U.S. Supreme Court in *Shelley v. Kraemer* in 1948, but as in the case of zoning segregation, their use continued long after the decision. The federal government acquiesced in and sometimes promoted racial discrimination in housing. Federal Housing Administration mortgage insurance policies were designed to insure against the mixing of "inharmonious racial groups." And in public housing, the decision on whether to integrate housing projects was left to the discretion of local public housing authorities.

The civil rights movement won some dramatic victories in the field of housing in the 1960s. On November 20, 1962 President John F. Kennedy signed Executive Order No. 11063, which required federal housing agencies to "take all action necessary and appropriate to prevent discrimination because of race, color, creed, or national origin." Title VI of the Civil Rights Act of 1964, passed during the administration of President Lyndon Baines Johnson, offered a broad guarantee of nondiscrimination in federally assisted programs, declaring, "No person in the United States shall, on the ground of race, color, or national origin, be excluded from participation in, be denied the benefits of, or be subjected to discrimination under any program or activity receiving Federal financial assistance." Title VIII of the Civil Rights Act of 1968 stated: "It is the policy of the United States to provide, within constitutional limitations, for fair housing throughout the United States." The act extended the guarantee of nondiscrimination in housing from public housing to private, nonfederally assisted housing, with some exceptions in the case of owner-occupied rental units or houses sold or rented without the use of a real estate broker. With the passage of the Civil Rights Act of 1968, nearly 80 percent of the nation's housing units became subject to federal nondiscrimination regulations.

The civil rights movement was remarkably successful in pushing the nation to fulfill its promise of equality of all citizens before the law. It was less successful in its attempts to lessen economic inequality of the races. One of the ironic consequences of the civil rights movement was the departure of the middle class from minority neighborhoods, leaving behind communities more uniformly and desperately poor than those that had existed under conditions of segregation. As the bright hopes of the civil rights movement and the war on poverty faded in the 1970s and 1980s, social commentators spoke of the emergence of an urban minority "underclass," mired in poverty, criminality and addiction. The 1980 Census revealed that the overall poverty rate for the country was 10 percent for whites, 25 percent for Hispanics and 32 percent for African Americans. The 1990 census reported the same overall poverty rate for whites, 28.1 percent for Hispanics, and 31.9 percent for African Americans. A 1989 study by the National League of Cities showed that African American and Hispanic Americans were more likely than whites to live in extremely poor neighborhoods and that poverty among African Americans was more persistent than for other groups. More than 21 percent of African Americans living in big cities were poor throughout the ten years from 1974 to 1983, compared to less than 3 percent average for other groups.

Minority households spend a higher proportion of their income on housing than nonpoor households and are much more likely to be renters rather than homeowners. While 68 percent of white households owned their own homes in 1985, only 40 percent of Hispanic households and 44 percent of African-American households owned their own homes. Minority populations were thus very vulnerable to rising prices in the urban housing market and cutbacks in government social welfare spending.

missions Religious groups such as the Salvation Army have run shelters and soup kitchens in SKID ROW neighborhoods since the 19th century. Their purpose has been both to serve the needs of the transient and sometimes homeless population of those neighborhoods and to spark the religious conversion of those who come to them for help. Typically, missions have required attendance at a Bible meeting or sermon in order to qualify for a meal or a night's shelter. Because of this requirement, missions have developed a bad reputation among skid row populations. As Samuel Wallace noted in his 1965 study *Skid Row as a Way of Life:*

> It is all right to attend mission services now and then when one is really desperate or perhaps simply in need of some diversion. To make such attendance a regular habit, however, to take active part in the services, or even worse, to take up regular lodging in a mission—to become a mission stiff—makes one an outcast on skid row, possibly the lowest stage imaginable.

By the 1980s many religious missions had abandoned the heavy-handed evangelism of earlier days, concentrating more on providing a range of social services to the needy and homeless.

model cities See WAR ON POVERTY.

Mooney, David In a Connecticut case, a homeless man named David Mooney who was imprisoned for robbery and murder filed suit in state court to have his conviction overturned. The evidence in the case against him included items found by police in a box and a duffel bag that Mooney kept under an overpass on Interstate 91 in New Haven, where he slept. Mooney's lawyers argued that under the Fourth Amendment to the Constitution, which protects the right of individuals to be "secure in their persons, houses, papers, and effects against unreasonable searches and seizures," the police should have obtained a search warrant before searching Mooney's "residence." Homeless advocate Robert Hayes called Mooney's position "legally right" but also commented that it was "a miserable, wretched right to win. It suggests a social acceptance of homelessness, which should be resisted to the grave." Mooney won his case in the state court, and in the fall of 1991 the U.S. Supreme Court refused to hear the state's appeal. The Connecticut prosecuting attorney decided that it would be difficult to convict Mooney a second time, given the court's ruling, so Mooney was freed from prison in 1992 under a plea-bargain agreement in which he pleaded no-contest to charges of first-degree manslaughter. At the time of his release he had served five years in prison.

N

Nashville, Tennessee According to the 1991 *Status Report on Hunger and Homelessness* issued by the United States Conference of Mayors, there were an estimated 1,031 homeless people in Nashville. The city had 998 emergency shelter beds and 130 beds available for families seeking shelter. Other estimates of Nashville's homeless population run as high as 2,000. A Nashville city official was quoted in the *Status Report* as saying that many homeless people were turned away from shelters: "There is a lack of space and/or bed capacity. Very few are placed temporarily in motels. Most go without shelter. They stay on the streets or in parks, libraries, the Service Center for the Homeless or their cars."

National Affordable Housing Act See CRANSTON-GONZALEZ NATIONAL AFFORDABLE HOUSING ACT.

National Alliance to End Homelessness Founded in 1983 and headquartered in Washington, D.C., the National Alliance to End Homelessness (NAEH) seeks the cooperation of citizens, corporations, foundations and the government to develop long-term solutions to the problem of homelessness. The alliance acts as an information clearinghouse and conducts research and advocacy on behalf of the homeless. It published a report in 1988 called "Housing and Homelessness" and publishes a monthly newsletter called "Alliance."

National Anti-displacement Project See NATIONAL LOW INCOME HOUSING COALITION.

National Association of Community Health Centers (NACHC) The National Association of Community Health Centers (NACHC), headquartered in Washington, D.C., represents Health Care for the Homeless projects funded by the Stewart B. McKinney Homeless Assistance Act (see MCKINNEY ACT) as well as health care providers at migrant health centers. It publishes a quarterly newsletter called "Streetreach."

National Association of Social Workers (NASW) The National Association of Social Workers (NASW), headquartered in Silver Spring, Maryland, attempts to raise public awareness of the problem of homelessness through a program called "There's No Place Like Home."

National Association of State Coordinators for the Education of Homeless Children and Youth The National Association of State Coordinators for the Education of Homeless Children and Youth is the group charged with implementing the educational provisions of the Stewart B. McKinney Homeless Assistance Act of 1987 (see MCKINNEY ACT). (See also EDUCATION.)

National Coalition for the Homeless Founded in 1982 in New York City as the Coalition for the Homeless, the organization changed its name to National Coalition for the Homeless and opened its headquarters in Washington, D.C. in 1985. The Coalition advocates permanent housing for all and a system of supportive services as the best long-term response to the problem of homelessness. It has sponsored law suits on behalf of the homeless as well as educational, legislative analysis and lobbying efforts. Some 500 local groups are affiliated with the National Coalition for the Homeless, and in 1990 the coalition also began enrolling individual members. The coalition publishes a monthly newsletter called "Safety Network."

National Conference of Catholic Bishops See CATHOLIC CHURCH, ROMAN.

National Equity Fund See NONPROFIT HOUSING PROGRAMS.

National Fire Protection Association See ARSON.

National Governors' Association The National Governors' Association, with its headquarters in Washington, D.C., is the organization through which the nation's governors attempt collectively to influence the development and implementation of federal policies that affect the states. The association's members include the governors of the 50 states; the commonwealths of the Northern Mariana Islands and Puerto Rico; and the territories of American Samoa, Guam and the Virgin Islands. In 1991 the National Governor's Association released a report entitled *Addressing Homelessness: Status of Programs under the Stewart B. McKinney Homeless Assistance Act and Related Legislation.*

National Highways Act The National System of Interstate and Defense Highways Act, proposed by the administration of President Dwight D. Eisenhower and passed by Congress in 1956, was the most ambitious public works project ever sponsored by the federal government. It would have profound though unintended effects on the future of life and housing in American cities.

The superhighway system accelerated the flight of the white middle classes, and the businesses that catered to them, from the city to the suburbs. Suburban shopping malls flourished, while downtown business districts languished. Commuters traveled by private automobile into the cities to work in the morning and returned home to suburbs every evening. Public transportation systems were allowed to atrophy. Urban residential districts were increasingly left to the minorities and the poor. Banks, eager to lend money to suburban housing developers, were reluctant to put money into new construction or rehabilitation of the decaying housing stock of the inner cities. America's love affair with the private automobile in the era of cheap energy prices would thus ultimately contribute to both the energy crisis and the homeless crisis.

National Housing Act of 1934 Passed during the GREAT DEPRESSION, this NEW DEAL legislation established the Federal Housing Administration (FHA) to insure loans by banks and other private lending institutions for housing construction and improvements. FHA regulations reduced the size of down payments and lengthened the repayment time for mortgages. By 1939 the FHA had insured 400,000 housing units,

nearly a quarter of the units financed since the passage of the National Housing Act. By providing creditors with insurance against default, the act made it possible for Americans of relatively modest means to afford to buy a house.

FHA insurance was one of the factors contributing to the enormous expansion of homeownership over the next half century, which increased from under 48 percent of American households in 1930 to 65 percent 50 years later. FHA policies had other social consequences. Reflecting President Franklin Delano Roosevelt's own antipathy to urban life, FHA policies favored construction of suburban single-family homes rather than urban apartment dwellings and until 1948 deliberately fostered racially segregated neighborhoods. FHA policies thus contributed to the postwar flight of the white middle classes from the cities and the continued neglect of the urban housing stock. The Housing Act of 1934 also established the Federal Savings and Loan Insurance Corporation (FSLIC) to insure mortgages offered by federally chartered savings and loan associations.

National Housing Act of 1937 (Wagner-Steagall Act) Passed during the GREAT DEPRESSION, this NEW DEAL legislation established the United States Housing Authority (USHA) as an agency of the Department of the Interior. The USHA extended low-interest federal loans to local agencies for slum clearance and public housing projects. It also provided rent subsidies for low-income renters. U.S. Senator Robert Wagner of New York was instrumental in securing the passage of the bill, along with Congressman Henry Steagall of Alabama. By 1940 the Wagner-Steagall Act had provided funding for 334 public housing projects, amounting to over 118,000 housing units. The establishment of the USHA represented the first ongoing peacetime federal commitment to the construction of public housing.

National Housing Act of 1949 The National Housing Act of 1949, passed as part of the Fair Deal programs of President Harry S Truman, declared that it should be federal policy to guarantee "the goal of a decent home and a suitable living environment for every American family, thus contributing to the development and redevelopment of communities and to the advancement of the growth, wealth, and security of the nation." The housing bill was passed over stiff opposition from conservatives in Congress and only at the cost of significant concessions to the real estate lobby. The act pledged the support of the federal government in the construction of 810,000 units of public housing. The act also contained provisions to increase Federal Housing Administration mortgage insurance and new provisions for slum clearance and URBAN RENEWAL. Many cities used the federal support for slum clearance provided in the National Housing Act of 1949 to tear down older but affordable housing, replacing it in many instances with luxury apartments, government buildings or commercial buildings.

National Housing Association See PROGRESSIVE ERA.

National Housing Conference The National Housing Conference (NHC), which has its headquarters in Washington, D.C., is an independent lobbying group that works to promote federal support for housing programs for low- and moderate-income Americans. The conference publishes a newsletter called "Reports from Washington."

The National Housing Conference has undergone a significant shift in orientation in its more than half-century existence. In its early years the NHC was part of a reform-minded social movement concerned primarily with securing decent housing for poor and working class tenants. In more recent years the NHC has evolved into a special-interest coalition of builders, construction unions and real estate developers, representing groups that profited from federal housing programs. The NHC was founded as the Public Housing Conference (PHC) in New York City in 1932, in the midst of the GREAT DEPRESSION. The new organization could trace its own concerns with housing issues to the reformist sentiments that had stirred many Americans during the PROGRESSIVE ERA. Among the founders of the PHC was Mary Kingsbury Simkovitch, a settlement house director. The PHC called on state governments to help finance new housing projects. It also appealed to Congress to authorize federally sponsored public housing projects, which was a role that the federal government had never before played. When President Franklin Delano Roosevelt initiated his NEW DEAL policies, the PHC began to get a respectful hearing in Washington. Although Roosevelt himself preferred programs that favored single-family home ownership, such as the mortgage insurance offered by the Federal Housing Authority (FHA), public housing supporters found an ally in New York Senator Robert Wagner. The organization (which in 1933 had changed its name to the National Public Housing Conference [NHPC]) effectively mobilized support for federal housing legislation, a campaign that climaxed with the passage of the NATIONAL HOUSING ACT OF 1937. The NHPC continued to lobby for federal housing programs in the years that followed, opening its Washington office in 1944. It helped bring about the passage of the NATIONAL HOUSING ACT OF 1949 but in general proved less effective in the postwar years. In the conservative political atmosphere of those years, the real estate lobby mounted an effective resistance to further public housing experiments. In 1949 the NHPC changed its name to the National Housing Conference (NHC), to indicate that its concerns were not confined to public housing alone. In the 1950s the NHC lobbied for the creation of a Cabinet-level department of housing, realizing that goal with the creation of the Department of Housing and Urban Development (HUD) in 1965 as part of President Lyndon Baines Johnson's GREAT SOCIETY programs. By the 1970s the leadership of the movement was firmly in the hands of builders and real estate developers.

National Housing Institute (NHI)
The National Housing Institute, based in Orange, New Jersey, is an education and research organization focused on low-income housing. The Institute publishes *Shelterforce* magazine six times a year.

National Housing Law Project (NHLP) The National Housing Law Project, based in Berkeley, California, advises and assists local Legal Services lawyers working on housing and community development issues, including homelessness. The NHLP publishes the bimonthly *Housing Law Bulletin*.

National Institute of Mental Health (NIMH) The National Institute for Mental Health was established in 1946 by Congress to study the causes and possible cures of mental illness. The NIMH awards funds for the COMMUNITY MENTAL HEALTH SERVICES DEMONSTRATION PROJECTS FOR HOMELESS INDIVIDUALS WHO ARE CHRONICALLY MENTALLY ILL, as authorized by Section 612 of the Stewart B. McKinney Homeless Assistance Act (see MCKINNEY ACT). The demonstration projects are intended to develop and evaluate comprehensive, community-based mental health service systems for homeless mentally ill adults. The projects are required to provide outreach, case management, mental health treatment, supportive housing and coordination of services in a comprehensive system of care. Of the 12 projects awarded funds by the NIMH in 1988, nine were designed for homeless mentally ill adults and three for homeless children and adolescents at high risk of emotional disturbance. As of the spring of 1989, these projects had provided direct services to 865 adults and approximately 500 children and youth. (See also DEPARTMENT OF HEALTH AND HUMAN SERVICES; MENTAL ILLNESS.)

National Institute on Alcohol Abuse and Alcoholism The National Institute on Alcohol Abuse and Alcoholism awards Community Demonstration Grants for Alcohol and Drug Abuse Treatment of Homeless Individuals, as authorized by the Stewart B. McKinney Homeless Assistance Act. These grants are designed to implement and evaluate innovative approaches to community-based treatment and rehabilitation services for homeless individuals (or persons at risk of becoming homeless) from alcoholism and/or other substance abuse problems. Nine two year demonstration grants were awarded in 1988. These included sobering-up stations for homeless men in Louisville and Anchorage, a residential alcohol/drug treatment center for homeless women and their children in Philadelphia, outreach and engagement teams in two welfare hotels in New York City to provide social and treatment services to women and children, a program of intensive case management for homeless clients in transitional care facilities and shelters in Boston and jail liaison services in Louisville. (See also DEPARTMENT OF HEALTH AND HUMAN SERVICES.)

National Law Center on Homelessness and Poverty The National Law Center is a Washington, D.C.-based legal advocacy group that acts as a clearinghouse for information for local groups concerned with the issue of homelessness, monitors government compliance with existing legislation on behalf of the homeless and advocates the expansion of homeless rights through new legislation. The center has brought several successful suits to enforce the provisions of the Stewart B. McKinney Homeless Assistance Act.

National Low Income Housing Coalition

The National Low Income Housing Coalition (NLIHC), which has its headquarters in Washington, D.C., lobbies for federal support to solve the low-income housing crisis. The coalition's slogan is "Housing is a human right!" The coalition is affiliated and shares offices with the Low Income Housing Information Service (LIHIS), which publishes a monthly *Low Income Housing Round-Up* and an occasional special memoranda on topics of special interest. The NLIHC also sponsors several projects, including the National Mutual Housing Network, which provides technical assistance and financial intermediary support to nonprofit sponsors of limited-equity, low-income housing cooperatives; the National Anti-displacement Project, which provides networking and technical assistance support to individuals and organizations fighting involuntary displacement; and the National Support Center for Low-Income Housing, which provides information resources on state and local housing initiatives to grassroots advocates and organizations. The NLIHC sends out regular updates on federal legislative events through the *Memo to Members* and *Calls to Action,* alerting members when action is necessary to influence critical legislative events in Washington.

National Network of Runaway Youth Services

The National Network of Runaway Youth Services, based in Washington, D.C., provides more than 1,000 local shelter programs for runaway youth with training, information and other services.

National Student Campaign Against Hunger and Homelessness

The National Student Campaign, which has its headquarters in Boston, was founded in 1985 by the Public Interest Research Groups (PIRGs) in cooperation with USA for Af-

rica. At first concerned with hunger issues, the National Student Campaign soon took on the issue of homelessness as well. With chapters or contacts at 500 high school and college campuses across the nation, the campaign is the largest student group working on homelessness. It sponsors educational, lobbying and fund-raising activities around the issues of hunger and homelessness. In 1989 the National Student Campaign raised $150,000 for the hungry and homeless through its annual Student Hunger Cleanup, where student volunteers take pledges and donate their time to activities such as cleaning up local homeless shelters, food banks and the like. The campaign publishes a monthly newletter called "Students Making a Difference." (See also STUDENT ACTIVISM.)

National Support Center for Low Income Housing

See NATIONAL LOW INCOME HOUSING COALITION.

National Union for the Homeless

Founded in 1986, with its headquarters in Philadelphia, the National Union for the Homeless is a network of 14 local chapters representing 30,000 homeless individuals. The group seeks to guarantee shelter and provide other assistance to homeless people.

National Welfare Rights Organization (NWRO)

The National Welfare Rights Organization was founded in 1967 to represent the interests of welfare recipients. The NWRO grew out of both the civil rights movement and the concerns for the conditions of America's poor that had resulted in the passage of President Lyndon Baines Johnson's WAR ON POVERTY legislation. By 1969 the NWRO had 30,000 members and chapters in about 100 cities. The NWRO used a variety of tactics, from marches, to legal suits, to disruptive protests, to push for more benefits for welfare recipients. The NWRO's aggressive championing on the rights of welfare recipients was one factor in the vast expansion of programs, such as Aid to Families of Dependent Children (AFDC). The NWRO dramatized the needs of welfare recipients, but it was unable to transform itself into a stable and ongoing organization. Nor was it able to link its advocacy of welfare rights with the concerns of a broader constituency. As a result, the welfare rights movement found itself fighting a defensive and losing struggle against welfare cutbacks. The NWRO's militant style was rapidly going out of fashion as the turbulence of the 1960s was replaced by the conservative reaction of the 1970s. The resignation of its founding director, George Wiley, at the end of 1972 weakened the group, as did a series of internal factional battles. The NWRO finally disbanded in 1975.

Native Americans Native Americans make up a significant proportion of the homeless population in some American cities. According to data gathered by Richard Ropers, Native Americans made up 1.4 percent of the general population of Los Angeles County in the mid-1980s and 6 percent of the local homeless population. In Chicago, according to sociologist Peter Rossi, Native Americans make up 0.2 percent of the general population and 7.1 percent of the local homeless population. The 1991 *Status Report on Hunger and Homelessness* issued by the United States Conference of Mayors reported that Native Americans comprised 18 percent of the homeless population in Phoenix; 12 percent of the homeless population in Nashville; and 8 percent in Denver, Salt Lake City, and Seattle. Many urban Native Americans come from rural backgrounds where substandard housing is the norm. The Bureau of Indian Affairs (BIA) surveyed federally recognized tribes in 1987 and found that 97,970 Native American families, over half of all families living on reservations, needed new, replacement or substantially rehabilitated houses. (See also MINORITIES.)

new asylum movement The new asylum movement refers to a recent trend among human services providers and psychiatric and penal workers who seek to establish "humane asylums" for chronically ill homeless people. The movement represents a reaction to problems perceived to have been generated by the DEINSTITUTIONALIZATION of patients from mental hospitals since the 1950s and to the seemingly intractable problems of substance abuse and mental illness among today's homeless.

New Deal "New Deal" is the term used to describe the first one-and-a-half terms that Franklin Delano Roosevelt served in the White House, from 1933 through roughly mid-1938. Coming into office in the midst of the GREAT DEPRESSION, Roosevelt secured the passage of an enormous amount of reform legislation and laid the groundwork for the modern American welfare state.

In his acceptance speech for the presidential nomination at the 1932 Democratic national convention, Roosevelt pledged a "new deal for the American people." Roosevelt took office in March 1933, at the absolute pit of the Great Depression, when more than 25 percent of the workforce was unemployed and the nation's industrial output was a third of its 1929 level. In the first famous "100 days" of his administration in the spring of 1933, Roosevelt persuaded Congress to pass a blizzard of legislation establishing the new "alphabet soup agencies" intended to counter the effects of the depression, including the National Recovery Administration (NRA), the Agricultural Adjustment Adminstration (AAA), the Federal Emergency Relief Administration (FERA) and the Civilian Conservation Corps (CCC). As it emerged over the next half decade, the New Deal was anything but a unified set of programs or philosophies. Roosevelt prided himself on his pragmatic attitude; if one program didn't work, he discarded it for another that might.

Some historians have argued that there were two new deals, an early relatively con-

servative New Deal (1933–34) that emphasized federally encouraged price-fixing and
the restriction of production by private enterprise (as embodied in the NRA and the
AAA) as a way of ending the economy's
"overproduction," and a later, more liberal
New Deal (1935–38) that emphasized income redistribution through government
spending and social insurance (as embodied
in the Works Progress Administration
(WPA) and the Social Security system) as a
way of ending the economy's "undercon-
sumption." In reality, the two approaches
overlapped, and Roosevelt never made a
clear choice between the sometimes contradictory and sometimes complementary strategies promoted by his various advisors for
ending the depression.

In a famous phrase in his second inaugural
speech in 1937, Roosevelt declared that "I
see one third of the nation ill-housed, ill-
clad, ill-nourished." The order in which he
listed the nation's "ills" was not accidental.
Roosevelt came from New York, an urban
state where housing issues had always been
a high priority for reformers. Roosevelt was
a firm believer in the private ownership of a
single-family home, preferably in a rural or
suburban setting, as the cornerstone of the
American Dream. Robert Wagner, U.S. senator from New York, worked diligently to
persuade Roosevelt of the importance of
public housing for the future of American
cities. Private organizations, such as the National Public Housing Conference, also lobbied effectively for federal public housing
programs.

The housing legislation passed during
Roosevelt's first and second terms in office
were among the most innovative and far-
reaching in their impact of all the New
Deal's reform measures. New Deal housing
initiatives during Roosevelt's first term included the Home Owners Refinancing Act of
1933, which established the Home Owners
Loan Corporation (HOLC), and the National
Housing Act of 1934, which established the
Federal Housing Administration (FHA). The

National Industrial Recovery Act of 1933
provided a limited amount of funding for
construction of PUBLIC HOUSING (about
22,000 housing units would be built with
NRA funds during Roosevelt's first term).
The passage of the National Housing Act of
1937, also known as the Wagner-Steagall
Act, during Roosevelt's second term in office committed the federal government to an
ongoing program of providing subsidized
low-income public housing facilities for the
first time in U.S. history. The New Deal's
Resettlement Administration (RA), established in 1935, sought to resettle rural people
on better land in new communities through
its subsistence homestead program. Eventually 100 of these homestead communities
were established. The RA also sponsored an
experiment in suburban community planning
and development in three federally constructed "greenbelt" towns, in Greenbelt,
Maryland, Greenhills, Ohio, and Greendale,
Wisconsin. Reflecting Roosevelt's streak of
pastroal romanticism as well as the ideas
of British and American housing reformers,
these communities were intended as models
of integrating agricultural, industrial, residential and recreational space. The Resettlement Administration (later renamed the
Farm Security Administration) also provided
temporary shelter for migrant farm laborers
in a system of camps in California and Florida, an experiment warmly praised in John
Steinbeck's 1939 novel *The Grapes of
Wrath*. The Federal Transient Program, a
subagency of the Federal Emergency Relief
Administration, provided temporary housing
to homeless transients from 1933 to 1935,
and the Civilian Conservations Corps (CCC)
provided work and housing to unemployed
(and often homeless) young Americans during the 1930s.

Although the New Deal provided welcome relief to millions of Americans who
benefited from its programs, it failed to end
the depression. By 1938 New Deal programs
were facing heavy opposition from conservative congressmen, and Roosevelt himself

was increasingly preoccupied with a threatening international situation. At the beginning of 1941, 14 percent of the U.S. workforce was still unemployed. It was World War II that finally brought back American prosperity. Nevertheless, the New Deal did have a lasting impact on the American economy, society and politics, not least through its housing policies. (See also NATIONAL HOUSING CONFERENCE.)

New England Shelter for Homeless Veterans   Ken Smith, who served as an army medic in Vietnam, helped found the New England Shelter for Homeless Veterans in Boston in 1989. He decided to do so after a visit to the Vietnam Memorial in Washington, D.C., where he saw the reflection in the monument's black granite of homeless veterans of the war camped in nearby bushes. With the help of two partners he acquired an abandoned ten-story federal building in Boston and turned it into a shelter. It is one of the few shelters in the country run exclusively by veterans for veterans. The shelter provides beds for 200 of Boston's estimated 1,500 homeless veterans, some of whom stay for months. More than 2,000 veterans have stayed in the New England Shelter since it opened. It provides counseling on drugs and alcohol abuse, and help in finding housing and work as well as beds and a familiar military atmosphere. The men who stay in the shelter are organized into squads and platoons; the cook for the shelter is called the mess sergeant. The shelter has benefited from favorable public attention and support. Playwright David Mamet helped raise $250,000 to start the shelter by staging a benefit performance in 1988 called *Sketches of War,* featuring Al Pacino, Michael J. Fox and other actors. President George Bush cited the shelter as "Point of Light No. 142" in his growing list of volunteer-sponsored "points of light." Ken Smith believes that many of the men who stay in the New England shelter can trace the problems that led to their homelessness to

their military combat duty: "The common denominator that I find," he told a newspaper reporter in 1991, "is the effect of combat violence on the human psyche." (See also VETERANS.)

New Orleans, Louisiana   According to the 1991 *Status Report on Hunger and Homelessness* issued by the United States Conference of Mayors, there were an estimated 10,000 homeless people living in New Orleans. The city had 787 emergency shelter beds and 188 beds available for families seeking shelter. A New Orleans city official was quoted in the *Status Report* as saying: "The recession has increased the number of homeless and has reduced the amount of resources available to address the problem. Private donations as well as local and state revenues have been reduced. The recession has changed the composition of the homeless from the image of the wino to those who were gainfully employed until the last few years."

New York City, New York   For many reasons, New York City has played a prominent role in shaping the nation's image of the homeless problem. New York City may have as many as 70,000 to 90,000 homeless people, the largest homeless population of any American city. As the nation's network news headquarters, New York City news—including news about the homeless—often becomes national news. The contrast between New York City's extremes of wealth and poverty underlines the extent of the problem of homelessness and has been the source of much ironic commentary. Large numbers of the homeless congregate in rail and bus terminals and in subways, which often makes them among the first people visitors to the city see. And, unlike the more concentrated homeless populations of some cities, the homeless of New York are distributed across much of the metropolitan area. According to a 1989 poll, 82 percent of New Yorkers reported seeing homeless people in their neighborhoods or while traveling on the way to work every day. Several well-publicized struggles over the condition of the homeless have been fought in New York City. These include physical battles such as the recurrent clashes between police and homeless people over control of public space in TOMPKINS SQUARE PARK in lower Manhattan and legal battles such as the case involving JOYCE BROWN, a homeless mentally ill woman temporarily hospitalized against her will.

New York City has mobilized more resources than any other city to contend with the problems of the homeless. In 1992 the city spent more than $400 million to shelter more than 20,000 homeless people. Private groups have spent millions more. But the beds provided by the city's 270 emergency shelters and the meals provided in 130 private soup kitchens have not been enough to meet the overwhelming needs of the homeless population. On any given night, thousands of homeless people sleep in subways or in the parks or doubled up with other families in crowded housing. Gentrification has resulted in spiraling rents. Over 30,000 rooms in SINGLE-ROOM-OCCUPANCY HOTELS were lost between 1975 and 1981 alone, due to gentrification and official policies such as the J-51 tax abatement program. The deinstitutionalization of mental patients, the high proportion of poverty-stricken minorities among the city's population, the attraction New York City holds for youthful runaways and the steady loss of manufacturing jobs over several decades have all contributed in varying degrees to the city's homeless problem. The poverty rate in New York City reached record highs in the 1980s, with 25.2 percent of all New Yorkers living in poverty in 1990, which was about twice the national poverty rate.

Federal policies also have had a dramatic impact on the city's housing crisis. Under the cutbacks in federal housing programs initiated by President Ronald Reagan, including public housing, SECTION 8 construction and rehabilitation and SECTION 202 housing for the elderly and handicapped, New York City lost approximately $12 billion in federal assistance. As a result, the New York City Housing Authority, the largest landlord in the United States, had a waiting list of approximately 200,000 families at the end of the 1980s.

The existence of so many homeless people in New York amounts to a public health crisis of menacing proportions. Tuberculosis and other diseases that doctors thought had long since ceased to trouble Americans have reappeared among the city's homeless. Drug abuse among the city's poor and homeless population has also led to the spread of acquired immune deficiency syndrome (AIDS): It has been estimated that as many as 10 percent of the residents of New York City's public shelters may be suffering from the effects of the disease.

Homeless people had been a familiar feature on New York City's streets since the 19th century, but only in certain districts. The Bowery area of Manhattan's Lower East Side had long been the site of New York's "SKID ROW." Like most skid rows, the Bowery was home to a population that was largely male, white, aging and often alcoholic. But in the early 1970s homeless people began to be seen in other parts of the city and the homeless population took on a new demographic appearance. By 1971 a homeless population had begun to congregate around Grand Central Terminal, and in the course of the 1970s more and more homeless people began to be seen along Broadway as it ran up Manhattan's West Side. The new homeless population was younger than the traditional Bowery population, more racially diverse, with many more women and children and including many deinstitutionalized mental patients.

Homelessness reached crisis proportions during the mayoral administration of Edward Koch, who served as the city's mayor from 1977 until he was defeated for reelection in 1989. The city moved reluctantly, under legal pressure in the case of *Callahan v. Carey*, to expand its system of homeless shelters. In 1981 the city and state agreed in a out-of-court settlement of *Callahan v. Carey* to "provide shelter and board to each homeless man who applies for it." The agreement was later extended to include homeless women.

Today approximately 75 percent of the homeless of New York City reside in shelters. The city's Human Resources Administration runs a system of 14 shelters for men. These include the Shelter Care Center for Men (or Men's Shelter) on 8 East 3rd Street, which was opened after World War II, to provide meals, social services and tickets to lodging houses for approximately 1,050 men daily. Additional shelters are located in armories and other buildings located throughout the city's five boroughs. New York maintains 11 shelters for women, generally smaller in scale than the men's shelters, and shelters families in a number of commercial "WELFARE HOTELS" and "Tier II" shelters (shelters with private bedrooms and support services, run by not-for-profit agencies). The city also runs a system of battered women's shelters and maintains contracts with non-profit agencies to run six DROP-IN CENTERS in Manhattan and Brooklyn to provide meals, showers and other services to the homeless. Outreach services are made available to the homeless in train, bus and ferry terminals, offering transportation to shelters, emergency food and referral information.

Koch was defeated for renomination in the Democratic primary in September 1989 by David Dinkins, the former borough president of Manhattan. Dinkins then won the November election, becoming the city's first African-American mayor. One of the central themes of his campaign was Dinkins's promise to have the city offer a more humane response to the problems of the homeless. He criticized the Koch administration for its inaction and commissioned a report entitled "A Shelter Is Not a Home," which was sympathetic to the plight of the homeless.

Soon after Dinkins took office, the city made several changes in its policies toward the homeless, including giving priority to the "hidden homeless" (families doubled up in apartments) when new apartments became available. The city hoped to keep families out of its shelter system through its "Alternative Pathways" plan, which was a $13 million program to provide legal services to help prevent the eviction of families. Another program, which would have cost $12.4 million, would help pay the unpaid rent of thousands of other families. Another $1.4 million was to be spent on hiring teams of city workers to help prevent families who had been DOUBLING UP from becoming homeless. Mayor Dinkins and New York governor Mario Cuomo also announced a plan in 1990 to provide 5,200 new beds for mentally ill people in group homes and SRO. But in Dinkins's first years in office, a time of fiscal hardship for the city, his administration wound up following many of the same policies as those of its predecessor. A shortage of funds delayed the start of the antieviction program. Of the over 600 city-owned apartments that were to be set aside for housing doubled-up families, only half were available by 1991, a year and a half after Dinkins took office. After her first year in office, Nancy G. Wackstein, appointed by Dinkins as director of the Mayor's Office on Homelessness, acknowledged how difficult the problem of dealing with the homeless was:

Homelessness is really the end result of a whole lot of failed systems. When people talk about eradicating homelessness, we also have to talk about eradicating poverty, drug abuse, mental illness and family problems. Homelessness becomes the catch-all phrase, and behind it is the whole range of social problems, plus the housing shortage. I think we in this administration are beginning for the first time to deal with these complexities. The disappointing part is that I don't know where we will be able to find the money to do these wonderful things.

Wackstein eventually resigned in frustration, complaining of the lack of direction in Dinkins administration policies toward the homeless. Dinkins also came under heavy criticism from homeless advocates outside his administration. Robert Hayes complained in 1990 that "By and large, Dinkins says kinder things [than former New York City mayor Edward Koch], but Dinkins, like Koch, is not moving toward any solution."

Shantytowns, built by the homeless out of cardboard boxes, scraps of wood and other refuse, had sprung up in dozens of locations across the city by the early 1990s. Neighborhood residents find them eyesores, and city officials have been particularly concerned about the impression such sights make on visiting dignitaries. In 1991 the Dinkins administration oversaw the expulsion of the homeless from Tompkins Square Park, Riverside Park and the area around Columbus Circle; ordered the bulldozing of other homeless encampments on abandoned lots in the East Village; barred the homeless from sleeping in city-owned buildings; and cautiously embraced the Transit Authority's decision to evict panhandlers and people who sleep in subway stations or on subway trains from the transit system.

One of the main criticisms of the New York City shelter system under Koch's administration had been its reliance on huge barrackslike shelters, some with as many as 1,400 beds. In the fall of 1991 Dinkins announced a $258 million program to decentralize the shelter system, listing 35 potential sites for smaller shelters of up to 150 beds each, for a total of 2,500 additional beds. Three new sites were proposed in Manhattan, seven on Staten Island, seven in Brooklyn, seven in the Bronx and 11 in Queens. Public protest from the affected neighborhoods was immediate and angry. Peter Vallone, a councilman from Queens and the City Council speaker, declared of Dinkins's plan: "You're unnecessarily frightening all the people of the city, and it doesn't make any sense. It's spreading homelessness and

hopelessness throughout." Vallone, criticized by homeless advocates and the Dinkins administration for comparing the presence of the homeless to a "disease," modified his tone, but there is no doubt that he accurately reflected the sentiments of many of his constituents. The controversy typified the mixed feelings that many New Yorkers, like other Americans, were developing toward the homeless. Public opinion might sympathize with the plight of the homeless, but few people welcomed the presence of institutions designed to serve the homeless in their own neighborhoods.

The Dinkins administration came under attack again from an unexpected quarter when a blue-ribbon commission appointed by the mayor to investigate homelessness released its report in February 1992. The commission, headed by ANDREW CUOMO, was sharply critical of the city's record in providing service and shelters to the homeless, arguing that reliance on huge homeless shelters had proven a social disaster. In place of current policies, the commission advocated a system of smaller shelters, offering intensive social service programs that would be administered by nonprofit agencies. The commission hoped that communities would be more willing to accept homeless shelters run by nonprofit groups than the city-run shelter system. The commission also recommended that drug treatment centers for the homeless be located in nonresidential areas of the city.

Both the Koch and Dinkins administrations were criticized for their reliance on commercial "welfare hotels" to shelter homeless families at exorbitant monthly costs (approximately $3,000 per month per family). Poorly maintained, offering little security or services for residents, these hotels have been the dreaded "last resort" for homeless families, some of whom prefer to live on the street or "doubled up" to life under such conditions. Both Koch and Dinkins pledged to phase out the use of commercial welfare hotels. Indeed, the number of families housed in welfare hotels dropped from a peak of more than 3,600 in 1987 to 147 in July 1990. But that same summer the number of families housed in the hotel's began to climb again. By December 1990 over 600 families were housed in the hotels. Some observers attributed the increase to the new city policy of giving families in the hotels priority in getting new apartments in public housing. This may have created an incentive for some families to leave doubled-up apartments for the city's shelter system.

In a front-page article in December 1990 the *New York Times* declared: "A decade after vast numbers of homeless people began to be seen on New York City's streets, officials and advocates fear that homelessness has become embedded in the city's life for the foreseeable future." Despite the millions of dollars the city spends on its homeless shelters; the valuable efforts by such voluntary agencies as the Catholic Worker, the Community Services Society and the Partnership for the Homeless; and inspirational record of self-help and "sweat equity" programs such as the Ready, Willing and Able program and the Banana Kelly Community Improvement Association, there seems no good reason to dispute the judgment.

In 1993 David Dinkins was defeated in his bid for re-election by Republican challenger Rudolph W. Giuliani. During the campaign Giuliani proposed cutting services to New York's homeless population, including setting a 90-day limit on shelter stays. The continued homeless problem contributed to Dinkins' defeat. As *New York Times* columnist Anna Quindlen commented on the day after the election: "In the minds of many voters, [Giuliani] came to represent a vision of a different New York, a former New York in which a pile of rags on the street was a sanitation worker's oversight and not a human being." (See also ACQUIRED IMMUNE DEFICIENCY SYNDROME [AIDS]; J-51 TAX ABATEMENT PROGRAM; LEGAL RIGHTS; MENTAL ILLNESS; NONPROFIT HOUSING PRO-GRAMS; PROGRESSIVE ERA; TENANT ACTIVISM.)

New York City Housing Authority

See NEW YORK CITY; PUBLIC HOUSING; REAGAN, RONALD.

Nixon, Richard   Richard Milhous Nixon was the 37th president of the United States. Elected in November 1968 and reelected in 1972, Nixon was forced to resign from the presidency on August 9, 1974 to avoid impeachment for his role in the Watergate affair. Nixon came to office at a moment when the WAR ON POVERTY launched by his predecessor, Lyndon Baines Johnson, had lost much of its political support in Washington, D.C. Some federal social welfare programs, such as Aid to Families of Dependent Children, Medicaid and Medicare, survived and even expanded dramatically under the Nixon administration. Others, such as the Model Cities program, were done away with. In the name of the "New Federalism" Nixon redesigned many social welfare programs to take the form of block grants, in what was called REVENUE SHARING. The Nixon administration proposed the legislation that became the Housing and Community Development Act of 1974, which authorized the spending of $11.1 billion in federal funds to promote low-cost housing, urban renewal, water and sewer facilities construction and other programs. Gerald R. Ford, Nixon's vice president and successor, signed the bill into law.

nonprofit housing programs   In the 1980s a number of national organizations and grassroots community groups collaborated to draw on both private and public sources of funding to create new housing for low- and moderate-income renters. As economics columnist Robert Kuttner noted in *Business Week* in 1987:

> A decade ago, the idea of relying on nonprofit developers for a massive new housing strategy would have been ridiculed. But in the past

several years a network of competent, dedicated, community-based developers has gained stature and sophistication. Much of the affordable housing that gets built in the Reagan era is the result of their good work.

At the national level, one of the most important groups promoting the growth of such nonprofit housing programs has been the Local Initiatives Support Corporation (LISC). LISC was founded by the Ford Foundation in 1979 to channel private-sector monies to community-based housing groups. In an era of government cutbacks for public and subsidized private housing, LISC and similar groups have been able to take up some of the slack through innovative "social investment banking." Under the provisions of the 1986 federal low-income housing tax credit, passed as part of that year's Tax Reform Act, LISC and similar groups have been able to sell federal tax credits to corporations willing to invest in low-income housing. For a $2 million investment a participating corporation can receive up to $3 million in tax credits spread over ten years. LISC sponsors the National Equity Fund (NEF), which raised $77 million in 1989 from 35 corporations to create $200 million worth of affordable housing for 2,000 low-income households. This money was the largest single corporate investment in community-based low-income housing ever made in the United States. LISC has been involved in building and rehabilitation projects for low-cost urban housing from the South Bronx to the Tenderloin district of San Francisco. It has also financed the building or rehabilitation of commercial and industrial real estate in blighted neighborhoods, such as a new shopping center in Miami's Liberty City district.

LISC works closely with existing community development groups. By 1990 groups in New York City such as the Banana Kelly Community Improvement Association, Bronx United in Leveraging Dollars (Build) and Asian-Americans for Equality had produced more than 1,000 new apartments,

with 2,000 more under construction or being designed. In the projects sponsored by these groups, rents in the late 1980s ranged from $400 to $450, with 10 percent of units in their buildings set aside for the homeless, who paid the welfare shelter allowance, $312 a month for a family of four. The Banana Kelly Community Improvement Association began in the mid-1970s to fight housing abandonment in the Longwood section of the South Bronx. By 1990 Banana Kelly managed buildings with more than 700 apartments and had supervised the reconstruction of eight large abandoned apartment buildings through "sweat equity," as well as five smaller abandoned buildings, and 20 occupied but rundown buildings taken over by the city from defaulting landlords. Community nonprofit groups have established a reliable record of providing long-term management for the projects they have constructed or rehabilitated. According to New York City's acting commissioner of housing preservation and development, Felice Michetti: "The not-for-profits bring something that dollars and cents can't measure. They know neighborhoods as no private developer could know them. They look at tenants as neighborhood residents; there's a difference between a tenant and a neighborhood resident."

Homeless advocates have been appreciative of the efforts by the nonprofit housing groups, but critical of the idea that, in and of themselves, they can do much to end the crisis of homelessness. The National Alliance to End Homelessness noted in its 1988 report, "Housing and Homelessness," that nonprofit groups "will be one of the primary providers of low-income housing." But the alliance concluded that "even the strongest advocates" of this approach "recognize that nonprofits can supply only a small number of annual units required. . . . "

Norfolk, Virginia   The 1991 *Status Report on Hunger and Homelessness* issued by the United States Conference of Mayors reported that on an average day in 1991, 1,628 people sought emergency shelter in Norfolk. The city had 247 emergency shelter beds available and 243 beds for families seeking shelter. A Norfolk city official quoted in the *Status Report* predicted an increased problem with homelessness: "Anticipated cuts in the military should have a direct impact on requests for shelter, as will the continuation of the recession."

nutrition Homeless Americans are, more often than not, also hungry Americans. Relative to the rest of the population, the diets of homeless people are inadequate in terms of the frequency and regularity of eating as well as the quality and the nutritional balance of the foods eaten. The homeless are usually too poor to purchase adequate food and have no place to prepare it, so nutrition is an important concern in relation to the homeless (especially infants, children, pregnant women and chronically ill adults). The Institute of Medicine found homeless children under two years old at higher risk of iron deficiency than poor children with shelter, while malnutrition rates among homeless children and prenatal problems caused by poor nutrition have been the source of particular concern. Many homeless families reside in welfare hotels that provide no cooking facilities or refrigerators. Consequently, homeless families are forced to violate the safety codes by bringing a hot plate into their room (thus risking eviction), spend the little money they have on restaurant meals (not cost effective), or depend on nonperishable foods for their diet (i.e. canned goods and dry cereals).

According to a report by the Urban Institute, 75 percent of homeless people eat only twice daily or less, and 36 percent do not eat at all for one day or more per week. The study found that of those interviewed, 65 percent had eaten no milk or milk products the day before the interview, 43 percent had eaten no fruits or vegetables, 30 percent had

eaten no grain products and 20 percent had eaten no meat or meat alternates. The report concluded that the amounts of emergency food available to the homeless do not meet the need. According to the estimates of the number of homeless in cities of over 100,000, the number of available meals would provide an average of only 1.4 meals per day for each homeless person. Since cities this large might be expected to devote more resources to the homeless than smaller cities and rural areas, even less food may be available to the homeless outside of the large cities.

Meals provided at SHELTERS and SOUP KITCHENS are an important source of nutrition for the homeless. Many soup kitchens serve only one meal per day and are less likely to offer meals seven days a week than are shelters that serve meals. However, only 11 percent of shelters serve food at all. According to the Urban Institute study, homeless people who manage to eat some of their meals in shelters and soup kitchens are provided with substantial nutritional variety. Over 50 percent of lunches and dinners contained at least four out of five of the essential food groups, and the average meal provided a good measure of essential nutrients. Those supplying meals for the homeless tend to provide as much food of a high nutritional value as possible because they understand that the meal may very well be the homeless person's only meal of the day.

The demands on food banks, soup kitchens and other suppliers of emergency food assistance are steadily increasing. A survey of 27 major cities by the United States Conference of Mayors revealed that in 1988, requests for emergency food assistance increased by an average of nearly 20 percent in the majority of the cities. More than three out of five persons requesting emergency food assistance were members of families with children. An average of 15 percent of requests for emergency food assistance had to be turned down because the demand outstripped the available supply. The Southeastern Michigan Food Coalition estimated that in 1988, 1,100 clients were turned away each month in their area from private agencies that had run out of food. The resources of many food programs are being overtaxed, because they have come to be a regular source of food rather than a resource of last resort for many of the poor and homeless. A Boston city official quoted in the 1989 Conference of Mayors report declared "the inadequacy of public benefits and the chronic unemployment of some force them to rely on 'emergency' food assistance in a continuing way."

The 1993 Conference of Mayors survey of 26 cities indicated that the demand for emergency food assistance increased approximately 13 percent, that almost three quarters of the cities surveyed turned away people because of "lack of resources," and that two-thirds of the requests for emergency food assistance were from families with children. Two-thirds of the 26 cities surveyed reported inadequate quantities of food to satisfy all requests. (See also CHILDREN; FAMILIES; HEALTH.)

O

Omnibus McKinney Homeless Assistance Act of 1988   On November 7, 1988 President Ronald Reagan signed the Omnibus McKinney Homeless Assistance Act of 1988, which reauthorized the Stewart B. McKinney Homeless Assistance Act (see MCKINNEY ACT) for another two years.

Open Hearts—Open Homes   Open Hearts—Open Homes is a program sponsored by the Greater Kansas City Community Foundation and the Metropolitan Lutheran Ministry to help the local homeless by placing them in volunteer private homes, where they can live in exchange for provid-

ing child care, elderly care, cooking or housekeeping.

outdoor relief   Before the institutional poorhouse system became firmly established at the end of the 18th and beginning of the 19th centuries, funds were provided by local communities to help local poor people, a form of assistance known as outdoor relief. Outdoor relief consisted of money, firewood, food and provisions, and in early New York City (and its predecessor, New Amsterdam) funds were available to enable poor immigrants to return to Europe. Such assistance was often grudgingly provided and those who received it were stigmatized. Moreover, outdoor relief was not extended to all who were needy, but was strictly reserved for "neighbors" or longtime town residents. No matter how needy, the newcomer or the stranger passing through town in the 18th century would receive no outdoor relief and could often expect to be transported to the town limits and expelled. (See also POORHOUSE.)

outreach   Outreach is a technique used by service providers to bring services or information to homeless people who might otherwise find it difficult or would be reluctant to take advantage of the services available to them. Outreach means bringing help to individuals in need rather than waiting for them to approach an agency for help. Outreach workers have to know where to find homeless people and have the personal skills to overcome their suspicions or hostility. Outreach workers are trained to display a "no-questions-asked" demeanor to avoid frightening or antagonizing individuals who may be fearful of police or bureaucracies. Outreach can take place in the streets or in shelters or drop-in centers, or wherever homeless people congregate. Agencies concerned with nutrition, mental health, acquired immune deficiency syndrome (AIDS) prevention and general health care often use outreach teams to establish contact with the homeless population. In New York City a group of psychiatrists have banded together in the Project for Psychiatric Outreach to provide psychiatric care to the homeless in shelters and group homes.

overcrowding Overcrowding is a condition of having more people living in an apartment or home than is safe or healthy. According to the standards set by the Department of Housing and Urban Development (HUD), a housing unit is overcrowded if it houses more than one person per room. In 1985, the last year overcrowding was measured, nearly 1 million households—7.5 percent of poor households—fit that definition. Homeless advocates have argued that the true extent of homelessness in the United States is hidden because of the "doubling up" of individuals and families in inadequate living space. (See DOUBLING UP.)

Ownership Transfer Project See COMMUNITY SERVICE SOCIETY.

P

Palmieri v. Cuomo The National Coalition for the Homeless brought suit against New York City and New York State in 1989 in a case called *Palmieri v. Cuomo* on behalf of homeless men who sought and had been denied drug treatment. The coalition hoped to repeat its earlier success in the 1981 settlement of *Callahan v. Carey*, which required New York City to provide shelter for all who seek it. But a New York State trial court dismissed the lawsuit in December 1989, declaring that there was no enforceable right to treatment for drug addiction. (See also DRUG ABUSE.)

panhandling In the 1980s and 1990s a growing public antipathy toward the home-

less stemmed in part from the fact that for many people, their only encounter with the homeless was as panhandlers or street beggars, asking for spare change on the subways or street corners. In the 1991 *Status Report on Hunger and Homelessness*, a city official in Philadelphia reported that "homeless people are categorized as 'panhandling substance abusers' without regard for situational homelessness," while a Kansas City official noted, "We are beginning to get backlash reactions, especially in the downtown area, as more homeless aggressively beg and try to sell homeless newspapers on the streets." Panhandlers are often regarded by the public as too assertive in their requests for help. Some panhandlers offer an unwanted "service," such as wiping the windshields of cars pulled up at traffic lights, and then demand a handout as payment. Such encounters can be annoying and even frightening. Even among the homeless, panhandling is sometimes regarded with disdain. Joseph Kovacs, who had lived for 16 years in a railroad tunnel along New York City's Riverside Drive, told a reporter for the *New York Times* in 1991: "There's too many people walking the streets—you turn around there's always someone in your face with a cup asking for money. I tell them to get a job. Panhandling's a little too low for me. I would never do something that degrading."

Some of those approached by panhandlers fear that whatever they give will only go to pay for alcohol or drugs. The fact that panhandlers are often young, male and from minority backgrounds also adds to the perception of threat. The sheer volume of requests for help tends to increase public hostility not only to panhandlers but to all homeless people. As Joel Blau astutely argued in *The Visible Poor* (1992): "Some people are generous and do not mind occasional requests for money. Too many requests, though, soon exhaust their generosity. Losing their capacity to engage in single charitable acts, they are increasingly inclined to see homelessness as a disfigurement of the landscape, and begging as a personal assault." Merchants in urban downtown areas worry that panhandling scares away tourists and potential suburban customers. Panhandling is often treated as a law enforcement problem. In Atlanta Mayor Maynard Jackson proposed a "public nuisance" law designed to give the police the power to arrest beggars. In New York City the Transit Police stepped up the ejection of beggars from the city's subways in the 1990s, ejecting 28,000 beggars in the first six months of 1991 alone. Some cities, such as Berkeley, California, have tried another approach to contend with the presence of panhandlers. In 1991 Berkeley initiated a voucher system. Instead of giving money to homeless panhandlers, residents are encouraged to hand out paper vouchers purchased from local merchants, which can be traded in for food, laundry services, bus fare or showers.

Panic of 1873   The Panic of 1873 began with the collapse of Jay Cooke and Company, a major investment house. The five-year depression that followed the panic left a million workers without work, with unemployment in some cities approaching 25 percent of the workforce. It was the worst depression in American history until that point. Many people lost their homes. "Thousands of homeless men and women are to be seen nightly sleeping on the seats in our public parks, or walking the streets," reported a New York City labor newspaper. Protests by the unemployed were sometimes met with fierce repression, as in the 1874 clash in TOMPKINS SQUARE PARK. The Panic and its aftermath also saw the rise of the TRAMP phenomenon in the countryside.

Panic of 1893   See COXEY'S ARMY.

Papachristou v. City of Jacksonville
In *Papachristou v. City of Jacksonville* in 1972, the U.S. Supreme Court declared the Jacksonville, Florida vagrancy ordinance unconstitutional because of its vagueness. The Jacksonville statute defined vagrants as, among other things, "persons wandering or strolling around from place to place without any lawful purpose or object. . . ." Justice William Douglas, author of the Court's decision in the case, declared "Persons 'wandering or strolling' from place to place have been extolled by Walt Whitman and Vachel Lindsay. The qualification 'without any lawful purpose or object' may be a trap for innocent acts." (See also LEGAL RIGHTS; VAGRANCY.)

Partnership for the Homeless   A successful shelter program founded by Peter Smith, the Partnership for the Homeless is a coalition of more than 300 churches and synagogues in New York City that, along with government assistance, jointly manage about 100 private shelters for the homeless. The city provides supplies and technical assistance; the Federal Emergency Managment Administration (FEMA) provides money for food, supplemented by private foundations; while the religious communities provide shelter sites (most in churches and synagogues), volunteers and day-to-day shelter management. In addition to shelter, the partnership helps people find child care and health and social programs in local neighborhoods, while providing furniture and other housewares to those homeless people who move into city-owned apartments. According to Marjorie Hope and James Young (1986), the two main reasons for the success of this coalition effort are that "its shelters are not warehouses but small communal type places" and "no shelters are opened without involving community residents in planning." The former is a result of a policy of limiting the number of clients to 19 per shelter (with an average of 11), while the latter is due to the community-based nature of the program and the thousands of committed volunteers who are directly recruited from the congregations of the involved churches and syna-

gogues. The partnership has established the National Technical Assistance Project in an effort to organize religious communities across the nation to address the problem of homelessness in similar ways.

Pediatric AIDS   See ACQUIRED IMMUNE DEFICIENCY SYNDROME (AIDS).

People's Park   See BERKELEY, CALIFORNIA.

peripheral vascular disease   A familiar sight on many city streets is the homeless man or woman with enormously swollen legs. Homeless people often develop varicose veins (venous stasis of the lower extremities) through prolonged periods of standing, sitting or sleeping with the legs down. Blood pools in their feet, leading to swelling of tissues and compression of circulation in skin capillaries. Symptoms of peripheral vascular disease include swollen feet and legs, cellulitis and skin ulcers. (See also HEALTH.)

Pew Charitable Trusts   The Pew Charitable Trusts, based in Philadelphia, was established in 1948. It is one of the nation's largest general foundations, making more than $50 million in grants annually in the areas of health care, education, culture and human services. In 1984 the Pew Charitable Trusts co-funded the HEALTH CARE FOR THE HOMELESS PROGRAM with the ROBERT WOOD JOHNSON FOUNDATION.

Philadelphia, Pennsylvania   According to the 1991 *Status Report on Hunger and Homelessness* issued by the United States Conference of Mayors, Philadelphia had an estimated 18,993 homeless people living in the city. The city has 2,819 emergency shelter beds and 1,300 beds available for families seeking shelter. In the 1980s Philadelphia maintained a relatively generous system of shelters and services for the homeless, but during the city's fiscal crisis

at the end of the decade these were cut back significantly. As in other cities, attitudes toward the homeless have been hardening. A Philadelphia city official was quoted in the *Status Report* as saying: "Homeless people are categorized as 'panhandling substance abusers' without regard for situational homelessness."

Phoenix, Arizona   The 1991 *Status Report on Hunger and Homelessness* did not report the number of homeless people in Phoenix (a 1988 study estimated the city's homeless population at 6,000). The *Status Report* did note that on an average day in the fall of 1991, 997 people sought emergency shelter in Phoenix. The city had 900 emergency shelter beds and 380 beds available for families seeking shelter.

Photography   See HUBBARD, JIM; PROGRESSIVE ERA.

Pierce, Samuel   See HUD.

poorhouse   Because their familiarity with the institution comes largely through the writings of 19th-century novelist Charles Dickens, many Americans assume that the poorhouse has been a distinctly English institution. But prior to the NEW DEAL of the 1930s, the poorhouse served as the basic mechanism of public welfare policy for well over a century in the United States. The poorhouse (also called the almshouse, county farm or workhouse) was an institution for the poor designed to minimize the expense of pauperism to the local community and to closet destitute people away from family and friends in order to deter others from asking for poor relief in a rapidly industrializing nation. In 19th-century America, agriculture was rapidly mechanizing and home work was declining, forcing laboring people to seek industrial jobs in urban areas. A developing capitalist system produced unemployment along with its profits, and a downturn in a company, a recession or a depression would swell the population of poorhouses, particularly in the winter months when it was more difficult for people to survive on their own.

The poorhouse was designed as an institution for the "unworthy poor," those who were thought to be poor for their lack of discipline, laziness and sinfulness. Often built in areas that were segregated from the rest of society, poorhouses were organized with a strict regimen that would, social reformers thought, "rehabilitate" the poor. Inmates were required to work in poorhouse workshops where "the threat of punishment, decreased rations, and solitary confinement hung over those who did not fulfill their assignments," according to historian David J. Rothman (1987). Poorhouse overseers dealt harshley with attempts to leave the institution, have visitors, waste or pilfer food and other transgressions. According to Rothman, the system incorrectly viewed the poor as morally corrupt and lazy, whereas the actual inmates were more often "the enervated, exhausted, and enfeebled elderly or the very young and mentally handicapped, either by reason of insanity or retardation. . . . The institutional routine was designed for the wrong clientele." Nevertheless, by the mid 19th-century nearly every rural county and urban neighborhood had its poorhouse.

From the latter half of the 19th century to well into the 20th, public policy toward the homeless was built on the practices of the poorhouse: to differentiate between the "worthy" (infirm) and "unworthy" (able-bodied) in the various needy and homeless populations, to incarcerate them in specialized institutions isolated from the larger society. The programs of the New Deal are said to have represented a decisive break with the era of the poorhouse. However, many contemporary critics of public policy toward the poor and homeless argue that many current social welfare policies and institutions, such as the homeless shelter, the public old-age home and the system of

stigmatizing welfare recipients, differ very little from the logic and practice of the poorhouse. (See also OUTDOOR RELIEF; POOR LAWS; VAGRANCY.)

poor laws The poor laws were a series of parliamentary measures enacted in Britain from the 16th through the 19th centuries, intended to provide relief for the poor while distinguishing between the "worthy" and "unworthy" poor and controlling the movements of "vagabonds." Until the 19th century in Britain, poor relief was a religious responsibility, administered through local parishes of the Church of England, by means of taxes levied by the government. Many of the provisions of the poor laws were punitive in character. The poor and homeless could be punished for idleness or for moving to new communities. Beggars were licensed by an act of 1530–31; unlicensed beggars could be punished by whipping, and those who gave to them could be fined or imprisoned. "Vagrants" could be deported to the place of their birth or shipped to one of Britain's overseas colonies to serve a term of involuntary servitude. (Vagrants accounted for a high proportion of the early settlers in British North America.) The Elizabethan Poor Law Act of 1601 did away with some of the harsher punishments of the old poor laws but still maintained the distinction between worthy and unworthy poor. The aged and infirm were granted OUTDOOR RELIEF, which allowed them to remain in private home settings; the able-bodied poor could be confined against their will to WORKHOUSES (which were to gain literary notoriety in Charles Dickens's 1838 novel *Oliver Twist*). In the 19th century, parish control of relief was replaced by a system of boards of elected guardians. The punitive character of the poor laws had not changed, however. The Poor Law Reform of 1834 declared that "the fundamental principle with respect to the legal relief of the poor is, that the condition of the pauper ought to be, on the whole, less eligible than that of the independent laborer." In other words, public relief programs should never be more attractive than even the poorest paid jobs in the private sector. This tradition has had a decisive impact on both British and American systems of welfare. In Britain in the 20th century, old-age pensions and other forms of social insurance substituted for the poor laws, with the last vestiges of the system abolished in 1948. (See also POORHOUSE; VAGRANCY.)

Portland, Oregon   The 1991 *Status Report on Hunger and Homelessness* issued by the United States Conference of Mayors estimated that 11,607 homeless people were living in Portland. On an average day in the fall of 1991, 1,365 people would seek emergency shelter in the city. Portland had 556 emergency shelter beds and 80 beds for families seeking shelter. High unemployment and the destruction of SINGLE-ROOM-OCCUPANCY HOTELS in the city's traditional SKID ROW neighborhoods contributed to a dramatic expansion of the homeless population in the 1980s.

postal service   Lacking fixed addresses or the funds to rent post office boxes, many homeless people have difficulty in receiving mail, including benefits from welfare agencies. Recognizing this problem, the U.S. Postal Service began in the late 1980s to allow homeless people to designate shelters or other service-providing facilities as their mailing address. Homeless people also may receive mail through general delivery for up to 30 days or longer at the discretion of the local postmaster.

Potter's Field   Homeless people who die in New York City and whose bodies are unclaimed, or whose relatives cannot afford to pay for burial, are buried in a 45-acre public burial ground called Potter's Field. Potter's Field is located on Hart's Island in Long Island Sound. The island is also home to a prison facility, and the inmates do the

burials. The unembalmed bodies are buried in trenches in rough wooden boxes, with 20 to 30 boxes buried at a time. Friends and relatives are not allowed to attend the burial or to visit the unmarked graves. According to a study by the New York Coalition for the Homeless, about a third of those buried in Potter's Field between 1981 and 1984 were infants.

poverty level   See POVERTY LINE.

poverty line   The poverty line is an official U.S. government income threshold, updated annually, that is designed to identify the point below which a family is poor. Eligibility for certain government benefits programs, such as food stamps, is tied to whether individual or family income falls below the poverty line. In 1992 the poverty line for a three-person household, $11,186; and for a four-person household income, $14,335. According to the United States Census Bureau 36.9 million Americans fell below the poverty line in 1992. It is important to understand that *all* poverty thresholds are set arbitrarily and ultimately represent a subjective determination. That is, there is simply no agreed-upon, objective and scientific way to determine who in a society is poor. For example, a relative definition of poverty could be employed by defining the poor as those earning less than half of the median income. This definition would include those whose very survival may not be at stake, but whose incomes are substantially below the average and who have a difficult time "making ends meet."

Another way to define the poor is to include only those whose survival is at stake. These poor would be at risk of not being able to maintain a minimal diet, to keep a roof over their head and to gain other absolute necessities. This definition informs the offical poverty line in the United States. It is important to remember that whatever definition is chosen will determine how many people are counted as "poor" and will

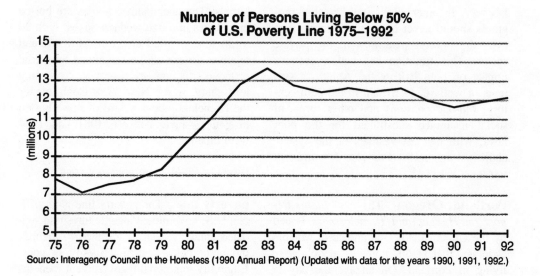

**Number of Persons Living Below 50%
of U.S. Poverty Line 1975–1992**

Source: Interagency Council on the Homeless (1990 Annual Report) (Updated with data for the years 1990, 1991, 1992.)

always reflect certain social, cultural and political values held by those who are doing the defining. Social scientists in the United States have frequently argued that the poverty line is set too low to account for those living under conditions that they believe *ought* to be recognized as conditions of poverty, such as substandard housing, inadequate health care or poor nutrition; while some argue that the line is set too high, thus including persons who are not really poor.

President Lyndon Baines Johnson established the official poverty line in 1964 in order to be able to count the number of poor people in the United States for his WAR ON POVERTY. The Social Security Administration developed two possible measures of the poverty line, and Johnson chose the lower one. His choice then became the measure employed to determine "poverty." It is a measure designed to identify those with less than the minimum income required to obtain the necessities for living in American society. The formal definition of the poverty line notes that it is "based on the amount [of money] needed by families of different size and type to purchase a nutritionally adequate diet on the assumption that no more than a third of the family income is used for food."

Sociologist James D. Wright has explained how the federal poverty line is determined and its relationship to homelessness in his book *Address Unknown* (1989). The U.S. Department of Agriculture publishes an "emergency temporary low-budget diet," which Wright defines as "the minimum nutrient intake necessary to sustain human life over short periods." The department then has employees go to various supermarkets in a sample of major cities to determine the cheapest possible way to purchase foods with the nutrient components of this diet. After comparing their shopping results, analysts determine the minimum amount a family can spend to purchase this diet. Analysts for the Social Security Administration then calculate the poverty line by multiplying the cost of the diet (reasoning that the average poverty family spends about one-third of its income on food, as studies in the 1960s showed). The poverty line is then adjusted to account for family size, region of the country and urban/rural differences. (Food prices vary by region and size of city.)

Calculating the poverty line in this fashion is controversial. For example, in 1992 the government formulated a poverty line of $11,186 in annual income for a three-person household by calculating what it costs this family to purchase an "emergency low-budget diet" for a year and then multiplying by three. (Again, the assumption is that food makes up one-third of the household budget.) The yearly food budget then would have been $3,729. This amount translates into a food budget of only $3.40 *per day* for each person in the family (or if we assume three meals a day, only $1.13 per meal). Besides pointing out that the poor are not professional dieticians and thus will not always receive the highest nutritional value for the lowest cost, critics argue that by calculating the poverty line at such a low level of subsistence, the government considerably understates the extent of poverty in the society.

The relationship between the determination of the poverty line and homelessness brings us to a consideration of the percentage of income that poor households spend on housing. In 1983 one-third of the nation's poverty population spent 70 percent or more of its income on housing costs alone. If the household mentioned spent only 40 percent of its income on housing (or $373 per month), each family member would only have $2.72 per day for *all* other expenses combined (transportation, clothing, entertainment, and so on). If we recall that these figures are based on a household income set *at* the poverty line and not *below* it, we can get a sense of the difficulties for those with a poverty-level income. Since the median income for all poverty households is about half of the official poverty line, most poor households are worse off than the household considered here. Moreover, the arbitrariness of the official poverty line seems apparent if we consider that the difference between being "poor" by official standards and not being poor is only one dollar. That is, in 1989 the poverty level was $6,870 for a single person. Using the official definition a person whose income was $6,871 would not have been considered poor even though his

or her ability to survive would have been essentially the same.

The poverty line should be treated as a rough "benchmark" figure rather than a clear scientific determination of who is or is not actually poor. When used judiciously, it can provide us with some important trends. For example, between 1964 and 1969 the number of Americans below the poverty line dropped from 36 million to 24 million, or from 19 percent to 12.5 percent of the population. Between 1969 and 1980 the number below the poverty line increased from 24 million to 29 million, but the poverty rate remained virtually constant, with 12.9 percent of Americans below poverty in 1980. In 1983 the figure had grown to 15.2 percent; the number of Americans below the poverty line grew from 29 million to 35 million. Cuts in social programs, the effects of the recession of 1981–82, the trade deficit and the continued shrinkage of the manufacturing sector of the economy all contributed to the rise in poverty. An economic boom of the latter portion of the 1980s brought the numbers of Americans living in poverty down. In 1989, 12.8 percent of Americans lived below the poverty line. But the number rose again with the recession of the early 1990s. Between 1991 and 1992 the number of poor people in the United States increaed by 1.2 million, three times as fast as the overall increase in population, to a total of 36.9 million, or 14.5 percent of the U.S. population.

People move in and out of being officially defined as poor. Over a ten-year period, it is estimated that 25 percent of the U.S. population will slip under the poverty line at one time or another. Children are the most likely people in our society to be poor; those under 18 years of age make up more than 40 percent of those below the poverty line. Minorities are also overrepresented among the nation's poor. For example, the 1992 poverty rate for whites was 11.6 percent; for African Americans, 33.3 percent; for

Hispanics, 29.3 percent and for Asian Americans 12.5. The poverty rate for female-headed households within all groups is higher than it is for male-headed households, a process that sociologists have termed a *feminization of poverty.*

Though poverty is extensive in rural areas, it is more concentrated in cities. A study by the National League of Cities in 1989 reported that an increasing number of poor lived in neighborhoods where at least 40 percent of residents were below the poverty line. This study led some observers to speak of the growth of an "underclass" in the 1980s, trapped in an endless cycle of poverty, poor education, low aspirations, crime and substance abuse. (See also AID TO FAMILIES WITH DEPENDENT CHILDREN [AFDC]; WORKING POOR.)

precariously housed   The precariously housed are persons who live in conventional dwellings but whose connection to those domiciles is temporary or tenuous. The precariously housed include persons doubled up with relatives or friends and often may include persons temporarily housed in institutions such as jails and hospitals. (See also EPISODIC HOMELESS.)

prevention   of   homelessness   See HOMELESSNESS PREVENTION PROGRAMS.

Program for the Chronically Mentally Ill Homeless   The Program for the Chronically Mentally Ill Homeless was initiated by the Robert Wood Johnson Foundation in cooperation with the Department of Health and Human Services (HHS) and the Department of Housing and Urban Development (HUD) to support community projects aimed at coordinating and expanding services for homeless mentally ill individuals. Nine cities were awarded grants and low-interest loans totaling $28 million from the Robert Wood Johnson Foundation to provide health, mental health and social services, while HUD provided 1,125 Section 8 cer-

tificates to local housing authorities to house mentally ill clients. As of 1989, more than 35,000 people with chronic mental illness had participated in the program. (See also MENTAL ILLNESS.)

Progressive era   The progressive era was a period in the early 20th century when reform movements of all kinds were on the rise in the United States. Reformers influenced local, state and federal governments to address many pressing social issues in innovative ways. The era is considered to have lasted, roughly, for the decade and a half between Theodore Roosevelt's taking the oath of office as president (replacing William McKinley, who fell victim to an assassin's bullet in 1901) and President Woodrow Wilson's decision to lead the United States into World War I in the spring of 1917. It was a time when an urgent desire for reform swept the nation, symbolized by muckraking reports in newspapers and magazines about political corruption and corporate misdeeds and by the efforts of earnest settlement workers, such as Chicago's Jane Addams, to improve the lives of residents of the nation's crowded urban immigrant neighborhoods. The roots of the movement reach back at least a decade earlier, as a generation of journalists, scholars and reformers perfected new techniques of social investigation and advocacy.

Among the chief concerns of Progressive era reformers was the lack of decent housing for the urban poor. New York City, with its crowded immigrant neighborhoods, gave rise in the late 19th and early 20th centuries to an influential movement for housing reform. By 1900 the most crowded wards on the Lower East Side had population density levels of 350,000 people to a square mile, the highest urban population density in the world. Many of New York's newest and poorest residents were housed in so-called dumbbell tenements built between 1879 and 1900, narrow five-story walk-up apartment buildings with little light and poor air circulation. Immigrant families crowded into them, many taking in boarders for extra income, or using homes for sewing garments and other forms of industrial homework.

Jacob Riis, a veteran New York newspaperman, began experimenting in 1880s with flash photography as way of opening up the view of life in tenements to a middle-class audience, by means of magic lantern shows, books and newspaper photographs. In his classic 1890 book, *How the Other Half Lives*, he described how he followed home an immigrant worker carrying a bundle of clothing through the streets of the Lower East Side:

> Let us follow one to his home and see how Sunday passes in a Ludlow Street tenement. Up two flights of dark stairs, three, four, with new smells of cabbage, of onions, of frying fish, on every landing, whirring sewing machines behind closed doors betraying what goes on within, to the door that opens to admit the bundle and the man. . . . Five men and a woman, two young girls, not fifteen, and a boy who says unasked that he is fifteen, and lies in saying so, are at the machines sewing knickerbockers, "knee-pants" in the Ludlow Street dialect. . . . In the alcove, on a couch of many dozens of "pants" ready for the finisher, a barelegged baby with pinched face is asleep. . . .

Progressives were often drawn from elite Anglo-Saxon Protestant backgrounds. However, they represented an important parting of the ways with the tradition of 19th-century evangelical Protestant reform. Nineteenth-century reformers had often been more concerned with the souls than with the physical well-being of the poor, administering charity only to the "worthy" poor in the guise of "friendly visitor." As Riis told one audience who came to view his show of photographs from New York City tenements, "We have dropped the talk of infant damnation in the hereafter and are devoting ourselves to the salvation of the child from the damnation of the gutters here and now." His exposés helped spark a housing reform

movement. The great successes of Progressive era reformers lay in establishing the principles of government regulation, particularly at the local and state levels.

Another important figure in progressive era housing reform was Lawrence Veiller. Employed as a caseworker by the New York Charity Organization Society (COS), secretary of its Tenement House Committee, Veiller organized an exhibit of maps, photographs and cardboard models of tenements in 1900 that attracted national attention and led to the passage of New York State's Tenement House Law of 1901, which established minimum standards for tenement house construction. Veiller went on to influence housing reform movements in a number of cities as organizer and first director of the National Housing Association (NHA). A number of other prominent Progressives, including Jane Addams, became honorary vice-presidents of the NHA. The NHA held annual conferences and published numerous reports urging states and cities to adopt housing reforms. But its activism decreased in the 1920s, and the organization disbanded in 1936.

While progressive era reformers were successful in arousing public concern over the issue of inadequate housing and in passing valuable regulatory legislation, they did not succeed in eliminating city slums. But their efforts laid the groundwork for later NEW DEAL initiatives in PUBLIC HOUSING.

prohibition   See ALCOHOLISM.

Project for Psychiatric Outreach   The Project for Psychiatric Outreach is a group of psychiatrists who volunteer their time to provide care to mentally ill homeless people in shelters and group homes in New York City. Since its founding in 1986 by Dr. Katharine Falk, the project's psychiatrists have treated over 2,000 people. The psychiatrists involved in the project found that many of their homeless patients were unlikely to find their way to public hospitals and clinics and, even if they had been pre-scribed medication, were unlikely to take it, without direct and frequent reminders from caregivers. The project's outreach tech-niques have proven a valuable supplement to more conventional approaches to mental health care.

Project Help　See BROWN, JOYCE.

public housing　In the United States pub-lic housing accounts for 1.5 percent of the nation's housing stock. This is a small per-centage compared with that of other indus-trial nations, such as Great Britain (27 percent) and Sweden (35 percent). Reform-ers in the PROGRESSIVE ERA and the NEW DEAL placed high hopes on plans for public housing to replace or supplement the na-tion's dilapidated stock of low-rent urban housing. But these hopes have been disap-pointed over the years. As social critic Jane Jacobs wrote in her 1961 study *The Death and Life of Great Cities.* "Low-income proj-ects" have "become worse centers of delin-quency, vandalism, and general social hopelessness than the slums they were sup-posed to replace."

The National Housing Act of 1937 estab-lished the first ongoing federal program of public housing construction. The National Housing Act of 1949 stated a federal com-mitment to guarantee "a decent home and suitable living environment for every Ameri-can family." The passage of these bills, in the face of strong opposition from real estate lobbyists, marked a recognition that the pri-vate market was not meeting the needs of lower-income urban renters. Although feder-ally sponsored public housing programs were limited in significant ways, by the 1980s such housing represented 5 percent of the nation's rental units, with over 3.5 mil-lion people living in 1.3 million units of public housing.

Public housing never enjoyed the level of support from the federal government or the public esteem reserved for private home-ownership. In fact, in order to lessen the impression that public housing would com-pete with the private market, the Housing Acts of 1937 and 1949 both included provis-ions to destroy one substandard unit of pri-vate housing for every new unit of public housing created, to limit the total supply. In the conservative political atmosphere of the postwar era, the real estate industry was able to block any significant federal initiatives in the field of public housing. Because of a lack of funding for building new public units, the Housing Act of 1949 actually resulted in the destruction of more central city housing than

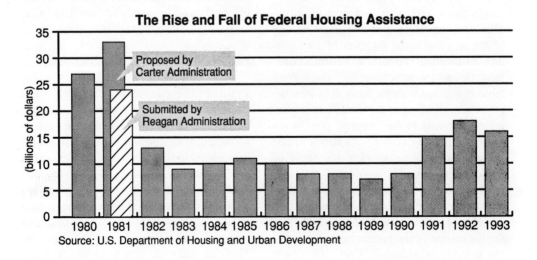

The Rise and Fall of Federal Housing Assistance

Source: U.S. Department of Housing and Urban Development

the amount added between 1949 and 1965. "Slum clearance" took precedence over the creation of public housing. At the same time, the availability of low-interest Veterans Administration and Federal Housing Administration mortgages, along with the development of the federally financed interstate highway system, made ownership of single-family houses in suburbs more attractive and possible for larger numbers of potential buyers, leaving urban public housing to the poor and minorities. In the early years of public housing, the overwhelming majority of tenants were working class or lower middle class. But already in the 1950s the number of tenants on public assistance began to increase. In the 1960s that trend accelerated dramatically, particularly as the barriers of racial discrimination dropped away. In 1962, acting in response to the pressure of the growing civil rights movement, President John F. Kennedy issued Executive Order No. 11063 on equal opportunity in federally sponsored housing, which called on all federal housing agencies to "take all action necessary and appropriate to prevent discrimination because of race, color, creed, or national origin." Until that time the integration of public housing was left to the discretion of local public housing authorities. Title VI of the Civil Rights Act of 1964, passed during the administration of President Lyndon Baines Johnson, offered a broad guarantee of nondiscrimination in federally assisted programs, declaring "No person in the United States shall, on the ground of race, color, or national origin, be excluded from participation in, be denied the benefits of, or be subjected to discrimination under any program or activity receiving Federal financial assistance." As a result of Kennedy's executive order and the passage of the Civil Rights Act, the percentage of minorities living in public housing increased dramatically in the years that followed, climbing to over 60 percent by 1978. The civil rights movement also lessened, although it did not eliminate, discrimination in the private housing market. Like the whites before them, middle-class and working class minorities left the projects for private housing as soon as they could afford to. Public housing became the housing of last resort for the poorest of the urban population. By the beginning of the 1990s, only about 40 percent of public housing tenants were employed.

In most public housing projects, tenants pay rents amounting to 30 percent of their income, with the difference between rental income and actual cost of maintenance made up by funds administered by Department of Housing and Urban Development (HUD). Projects are administered on the local level by Public Housing Authorities (PHAs). Some of these projects are well managed and provide decent, comfortable shelter for people who would otherwise have difficulty finding suitable housing in the private rental market. The public housing program in New York City has long enjoyed a reputation as one of the best-run programs in the country, with its apartments 100 percent occupied. But some well-publicized projects, such as the high-rise Pruitt-Igoe buildings in St. Louis, have created a negative public image of all public housing projects. The Pruitt-Igoe apartments admitted their first tenants in 1954 and were soon home to nearly 3,000 families. But by 1971, because of catastrophic problems in design, maintenance and crime, only 600 families remained in the complex. In the mid-1970s the 33 buildings in the complex were torn down by housing authorities, leaving a barren 70-acre plot of rubble behind as a memorial to a failed social policy. Two best-selling studies of life in Chicago public housing projects, Alex Kotlowitz's *There Are No Children Here* (1991) and Nicholas Lehmann's *The Promised Land* (1991), make it clear that the problems associated with Pruitt-Igoe were by no means unique and had not disappeared. In some cities the spread of drugs

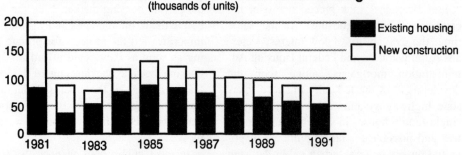

Net New Government Commitments for Rental Housing
(thousands of units)

Existing housing

New construction

Source: *The State of the Nation's Housing.* Joint Center for Housing Studies of Harvard University, 1992. p.3

and gang-related violence have driven all but the most desperate tenants out of public housing. In Detroit, for example, public housing had a vacancy rate of 44 percent in 1992.

The administration of President Ronald Reagan slashed spending on public housing in the 1980s, from $7.3 billion in 1981 to under $2.5 billion in 1988. New construction and most rehabilitation of public housing projects were halted. As of the spring of 1990, approximately 200,000 families were on waiting lists for public housing in New York City; 60,000 waited in Chicago and 17,000 were listed in Washington, D.C. In New York City, eligible families faced waits of eight to ten years to move into public housing apartments.

Calls for the privatization of public housing were first heard during the Reagan administration. Jack Kemp, secretary of Housing and Urban Development (HUD) under President George Bush, was an enthusiastic supporter of privatization. The Kenilworth-Parkside Project in Washington, which was sold to the Kenilworth-Parkside Resident Management Corporation for $1 in 1988, was scheduled to begin selling apartments to its residents by 1995. In November 1991 the New York City Housing Authority announced that families would be able to apply some of their rent toward the purchase of apartments in some new developments to be built over the next few years. The Bush Administration saw this

announcement, which came from the largest housing authority in the nation, as sending a forceful signal to other cities to consider similar programs. In the spring of 1992 the Bush administration proposed to eliminate $547.7 million from the federal budget that was designated to pay for public housing construction, arguing that the private market and other government housing programs should be relied on to provide housing for low-income tenants. (See also NATIONAL HOUSING CONFERENCE.)

public housing authorities See PUBLIC HOUSING.

public opinion Public opinion polls reveal that many Americans are aware and concerned about homelessness but that it is not the nation's leading concern. A 1992 *New York Times*/CBS poll showed that 58 percent of Americans reported seeing homeless people on a daily basis. Seven out of ten people who responded to the poll believed that homelessness is "something the Government can do a lot about," while only three in ten regarded it as a problem "beyond the Government's control." Polls indicate that many Americans are reluctant to see increased spending on social programs, including programs benefiting the homeless, if that spending means higher taxes. But they are not opposed to spending more money on such programs if it can be done without increasing taxes. A 1990 Gallup poll posed the question of what to do with the savings from a hypothetical cut in defense spending. Sixty-two percent of respondents answered that the savings should be used "to increase spending on social problems such as homelessness, poverty, drugs, and education"; 27 percent believed it should be used to reduce the federal budget deficit.

Attitudes toward the homeless seemed to harden in the late 1980s and early 1990s. On the one hand, the onset of economic recession in 1990 made people more aware of their own economic vulnerability. The Reverend Thomas J. Harvey, president of Catholic Charities USA, told a reporter in December 1991 that "this kind of downturn reminds people that there are capricious forces at work. It explodes the myths that the poor are poor out of choice because people see their neighbors going unemployed due to circumstances beyond their control." On the other hand, the presence of the homeless stirred feelings of anger and fear among many Americans forced to pass by them every day. In the fall of 1991 ART AGNOS, mayor of San Francisco, was defeated for reelection in a campaign that turned largely on the issue of whether he had been too slow to dislodge an encampment of homeless people from in front of city hall. According to the 1991 annual status report on hunger and homelessness of the United States Conference of Mayors, officials in 48 percent of the cities surveyed reported that they had seen evidence of public sentiment toward the homeless becoming negative in the past year. A city official in Boston reported: "People have become more concerned with the increasing numbers of mentally ill people on the streets. They are also concerned with the apparent increase of panhandlers." A Kansas City official reported:

We are beginning to get backlash reactions, especially in the downtown area, as more homeless aggressively beg and try to sell homeless newspapers on the streets. Reactions include the public closing their pocketbooks to

shelters, or blaming the victim because the problem has not gone away. Economic problems of the middle class have also resulted in less tolerance.

An official in New York City spoke of "compassion fatigue" among the public. Many people were increasingly taking for granted the presence of the homeless. The January 1992 *New York Times*/CBS poll revealed that 42 percent of Americans polled agreed with the statement "that most people have gotten so used to seeing the homeless that they don't feel upset by them." A plurality of 44 percent disagreed with that statement. But, significantly, a majority of 55 percent of 18- to 29-year-olds (in other words, those who had reached adulthood after the onset of the homeless problem in the early 1980s) agreed that most people were not upset at the sight of the homeless. The Reverend Joan B. Campbell, executive director of the National Council of Churches, commented on the results of the polls: "The daily encounters harden many of us to some degree. You do walk past [the homeless.] I've often said, 'What is this doing to me?' "

R

Rathke, Wade See ACORN.

Ready, Willing and Able The Ready, Willing and Able program is a self-help project for the homeless, sponsored by the Doe Fund (a nonprofit group concerned with homelessness) and the New York City Department of Housing Preservation and Development. The program was launched in 1990. Homeless single adults signed up in the program are paid to help renovate apartments in New York City for homeless families. Part of their pay every week is set aside; at the end of nine months, their savings are matched by a grant from the Doe Fund to help them find and furnish their own apartments. Those enrolled in the program are trained in construction skills, and a referral network helps them get jobs in construction or elsewhere after they have completed nine months with the program. Ready, Willing and Able workers were also renovating a large single-room-occupancy residence in New York's Bedford Stuyveysant section where enrollees will live while in the program. Felice Michetti, New York City's acting housing commissioner, said of the program, "The thing that makes this so appealing is that here you have homeless people building for homeless families."

Reagan, Ronald Ronald Wilson Reagan was the 40th president of the United States. A former movie star who made his debut in Hollywood in 1937, and who served as governor of California from 1967 through 1975, Ronald Reagan was a prominent spokesman for conservatives for two decades before his election to the presidency. The years of his administration coincided with the emergence of homelessness as a major social and political crisis for the nation. Some argued that his administration's policies significantly worsened the crisis.

Reagan was elected president in 1980 promising to get government "off the back" of the American people. He declared in a speech introducing his "Program for Economic Recovery" in February 1981, a month after his inauguration:

The goal of this administration is to nurture the strength and vitality of the American people by reducing the burdensome, intrusive role of the federal government; by lowering tax rates and cutting spending; and by providing incentives for individuals to work, to save, and to invest. It is our belief that only by reducing the growth of the government can we increase the growth of the economy.

A combination of high unemployment and high inflation in the late 1970s, combined with doubts about the ability of President Jimmy Carter to stand up to America's for-

eign enemies, eroded an already damaged "NEW DEAL coalition" that had kept the Democrats in control of the White House for most of the years since the Great Depression. When Reagan asked a national television audience during the 1980 campaign to answer the question "Are you better off today than you were four years ago?" few could answer in the affirmative. Many listened sympathetically to Reagan's charges that irresponsible federal spending on social welfare programs had unbalanced the budget, unleashed inflation and undermined individual initiative and the nuclear family.

Reagan proved far more committed to and successful in delivering a conservative political agenda than such other recent Republican presidents as Dwight Eisenhower, Richard Nixon and Gerald Ford. A man who was always most comfortable when speaking to a camera, celebrated in the media as the "Great Communicator" and the "Teflon President" (it was said that bad news didn't stick to him), Reagan was genuinely popular with millions of Americans who hoped he could turn the clock back to what they imagined had been a simpler golden age of American power abroad and individual self-sufficiency at home, before the 1960s brought along military defeat in the form of Vietnam and a swollen government bureaucracy in the form of the war on poverty programs for the poor. Reagan's policies would have profound effects on federal housing and welfare programs. Critics argued that those policies exacerbated the trends leading to the expansion of America's homeless population and that the Reagan administration was painfully slow in taking any measures to relieve the plight of the homeless.

Cutbacks in social programs such as AID TO FAMILIES WITH DEPENDENT CHILDREN (AFDC) and SOCIAL SECURITY DISABILITY INSURANCE (SSDI) often made the difference in determining whether a poor family or a mentally ill or otherwise disabled person could continue to afford to pay rent in rapidly gentrifying urban rental markets. The "Reagan Recession" of 1981–82 led to widespread unemployment and further increased the ranks of the homeless. But the most direct link between the Reagan administration's policies and the increase in homelessness can be found in the cutback of federally supported housing programs. From 1981 through 1988 all funds for federally subsidized housing programs were cut over 69 percent. The number of low-income housing starts, including PUBLIC HOUSING, SECTION 8 construction and rehabilitation, and SECTION 202 housing for the elderly and handicapped, dropped from 183,000 units in 1980 to 28,000 units by 1985. New York City alone lost approximately $12 billion in federal assistance during the Reagan years. The New York City Housing Authority, the largest landlord in the United States, had a waiting list of approximately 200,000 families at the end of the 1980s. The 1989 United States Conference of Mayors survey of homelessness in 27 major cities concluded that "with the decline in federally-assisted housing programs, none of the survey cities expect to be able to meet the housing needs of low-income households in the forseeable future."

Believing that the "free market" would eventually make up for the lack of housing without government intervention, the Reagan adminstration introduced only one new housing program in the 1980s. The system of VOUCHERS allowed low-income renters to rent an apartment on the open market, with some financial assistance from the Department of Housing and Urban Development (HUD).

Reagan's own attitudes toward the homeless were perhaps best summed up in an offhand analysis of the problem he offered in 1986: "What we have found in this country, and we're more aware of it now, is one problem that we've had, even in the best of times, and this is the people who are sleeping on the grates, the homeless who are homeless, you might say, by choice."

Homeless advocates charged that HUD deliberately undercounted the homeless in its 1984 survey to minimize the problem. Despite the hostility of the administration, Congress finally did turn to the problem of homelessness in the form of the Stewart B. McKinney Homeless Assistance Act. Reagan opposed its passage and only reluctantly signed it into law in 1987. The administration proposed drastic cuts in the act's authorized programs for both fiscal year 1988 and 1989. For fiscal year 1988 the administration tried to eliminate the act's emergency shelter funding provision. In fiscal year 1989 the administration proposed $200 million to fund the entire act, although $600 million had been authorized. (Congress eventually appropriated $378 million for the year's funding.) Critics accused the Department of Education, and the Interagency Council on the Homelessness (the latter established by the act to coordinate government programs for the homeless) of dragging their feet in implementing homeless relief programs authorized by Congress. Reagan's successor in office was his vice-president, George Bush. Though many interpreted Bush's 1988 campaign pledge to create a "kinder, gentler" America as an implicit criticism of Ronald Reagan, the Bush administration continued to uphold many of the policies and attitudes of the Reagan years.

real estate lobby The housing industry, including builders, real estate agents and mortgage bankers, is one of the most powerful and influential lobbies in Washington. According to a report in *Congressional Quarterly*, in 1987–88 the Realtors Political Action Committee was "the No. 1 contributor to federal candidates," with over $3 million in political contributions. The National Association of Home Builders' political action committee (PAC) gave nearly a $1.5 million, and the Mortage Bankers Association of America PAC gave over $300,000. The real estate lobby favors federal aid to the private housing market but is unsympathetic to proposals for public housing. (See also NATIONAL HOUSING CONFERENCE.)

redlining Redlining is the practice in which banks and other financial institutions refuse to make loans in certain urban districts by drawing an unofficial "red line" on city maps around areas where residents are projected to be at high risk of not fulfilling loan obligations. Through this practice, whole areas are made ineligible for loans for mortgages or property improvement, thus exacerbating the deterioration and neglect of low-income urban districts and decreasing the supply of adequate housing stock. Redlining is an illegal institutional form of ABANDONMENT. In recent years banking regulations have been established to stop the practice of redlining, while programs have been developed to encourage interstate banks to support reinvestment in community housing programs. (See also DISINVESTMENT; DISPLACEMENT; GENTRIFICATION.)

rehabilitation investment credit The rehabilitation investment credit is an income tax credit available for rehabilitation of qualified older buildings. Generally, the credit equals 10 percent of the qualified expenditures and results in a direct reduction of federal tax.

reinstitutionalization From the 1950s through the 1970s several hundred thousand mental patients were deinstitutionalized. DEINSTITUTIONALIZATION is often cited as a major factor leading to the spread of homelessness in the 1980s. Confronted with the unpleasant spectacle of homeless people suffering from mental illness living filthy, disordered lives on the streets, some have argued for a policy of reinstitutionalization. A series of state and federal court decisions, such as the 1972 Wisconsin case *Lessard v. Schmidt,* established the legal principle that involuntary commitment of the mentally ill was justified only in cases where the behavior of such individuals represented a danger

to themselves or others. Critics of deinstitutionalization have responded that commitment laws should be rewritten to make it easier to commit the mentally ill to asylums against their will. These critics believe that the benefits of institutionalization (regular meals, shelter, supervised therapy and protecting the public from potentially dangerous individuals) outweighs patients' rights to absolute freedom of choice in how to live their lives. The American Psychiatric Asssociation, while opposed to any mass reinstitutionalization of the mentally ill, supports the power of state authorities to commit anyone "likely to suffer substantial mental or physical deterioration" if left uncommitted. But apart from civil libertarian and legal objections to reinstitutionalization, there is also a question of cost effectiveness. Costs for maintaining a patient in a mental hospital run about $70,000 a year. In transitional housing, such as group homes and single-room-occupancy residences (SROs), the costs drop to $13,000 a year, including the cost of supervision by case workers.

religious   groups See   CATHOLIC CHURCH, ROMAN.

religious missions See MISSIONS.

rent control Approximately 200 cities and counties in the United States have some form of rent regulation or control, estimated to cover about 10 percent of the nation's rental housing stock. Rent controls are designed to permit landlords to raise rents in order to maintain a reasonable return on their investment while protecting tenants from unreasonably sharp rent increases. Controls generally link yearly rent increases to increases in the landlord's costs and require adequate maintenance in order for rent to be raised. Newly built rental housing is often exempted from rent controls, and landlords often are allowed to raise rents to market levels when current tenants vacate a dwelling.

The real estate industry has lobbied forcefully against rent control, arguing that it discourages investment in rental housing by limiting the returns on investment, and conservative policy analysts have linked rent control to the shortage of affordable housing and a consequent rise of homelessness. An analysis by the liberal Economic Policy Institute found that the data do not support a causal link between rent control and homelessness; the institute posits that declining incomes at the lower end of the income scale, rising housing costs and shortsighted federal policies are the primary causes of homelessness. Rent control, it argues, is a mechanism available to localities to maintain a stock of affordable housing by addressing the dramatic rise in rental housing costs.

restrictive covenants Restrictive covenants, private contractual arrangements in which a buyer of a house promised not to sell, rent or transfer property to members of racial or religious minorities, were in widespread use in the United States in the first decades of the 20th century. Restrictive covenants were found unconstitutional by the U.S. Supreme Court in SHELLEY V. KRAEMER in 1948, but their use continued down through the 1960s when the Civil Rights Act of 1968 made discrimination in the private housing market illegal. The federal government contributed to racial segregation through its mortgage insurance policies. The *Underwriting Manual* issued to banks by the Federal Housing Administration in 1938 declared that "If a neighborhood is to retain stability, it is necessary that properties shall continue to be occupied by the same social and racial classes." Although officially abandoned in 1950, these views continued informally to guide federal mortgage guarantee policies through the next decade.

revenue sharing In the second term of the presidency of Richard Nixon, the federal government shifted toward a new funding philosophy for social programs that Nixon called the "New Federalism." Nixon was responding to the perceived failure of the war on poverty programs of his predecessor, Lyndon Baines Johnson. Rather than provide categorical grants to states and cities, in which federal money could be used only in specifically designated ways, under the New Federalism the federal government engaged in "revenue sharing." Revenue sharing meant providing federal aid in the form of general or block grants to be used in ways determined by state or local governments, with relatively few strings attached. Under Nixon and his successors Gerald Ford and Jimmy Carter, revenue sharing became one of the principal strategies of the federal government for coping with the problems of housing the urban poor. Under President Ronald Reagan federal outlays for revenue sharing declined sharply, contributing to the fiscal crisis that overtook many cities and states in the late 1980s.

revitalization See GENTRIFICATION.

Riis, Jacob See PROGRESSIVE ERA.

Robert Wood Johnson Foundation The Robert Wood Johnson Foundation is a Princeton-based health care–oriented charitable foundation established as a local charity in 1936 and expanded to a national enterprise in 1972. Disbursing nearly $100 million a year in grants, it is one of the largest private philanthropies in the United States. Its main focus is on health care problems. The foundation has sponsored a number of innovative programs for the homeless. In 1985 it helped establish the 19-city Health Care for the Homeless Program (HCHP), co-funded by the Pew Charitable Trusts and co-sponsored with the United States Conference of Mayors. HCHP was a four-year $28 million program to provide primary care services, health assessments and referrals to the homeless. The program demonstrated the feasibility of delivering health care services to the homeless and helped lay the groundwork for the health care provisions of the Stewart B. McKinney Homeless Assistance Act of 1987.

In 1986 the foundation launched a grant program to provide housing for the mentally ill homeless, co-sponsored by the U.S. Department of Housing and Urban Development (HUD), the National Governor's Association, the U.S. Conference of Mayors and the National Association of Counties. In 1989 it co-sponsored with HUD the Homeless Families Program to make eight two-year grants to enable cities to design and implement comprehensive health and supportive services systems tied to suitable permanent housing for homeless families. While proud of the accomplishment of the Robert Wood Johnson Foundation, its president, Drew Altman, has warned that such private philanthropic efforts are not in themselves the solution to homelessness:

> We believe that our program shows that groups can come together and that something can be done. But we also know that it is a drop in the bucket. It cannot even pretend to solve the problems of the homeless in any big city—nor can any private initiative alone. The resources available from philanthropy, churches, and voluntary organizations pale in comparison to what is needed to do the job.

Rockefeller, Winthrop   See ACORN.

Roman Catholic Church   See CATHOLIC CHURCH, ROMAN.

Roosevelt, Franklin D.   Franklin Delano Roosevelt was the 32nd president of the United States. Roosevelt had served in the New York state senate and as assistant secretary of the navy before running unsuccessfully as the Democratic nominee for vice-president in the 1920 election. He gained election as governor of New York State in 1928. He was first elected to the White House in November 1932 in the midst of the GREAT DEPRESSION and won reelection

to the presidency three times. His NEW DEAL policies reshaped the American economy and American society in significant ways, laying the groundwork of the modern welfare state. Homelessness was a major problem during the depression, which Roosevelt attempted to counter through such temporary measures as the CIVILIAN CONSERVATION CORPS and the FEDERAL TRANSIENT PROGRAM. Long-lasting precedents and policies also were established. His administration saw the first significant federal initiatives in stimulating the construction of private housing and public housing, through such measures as the NATIONAL HOUSING ACT OF 1934 (which established the Federal Housing Administration) and the NATIONAL HOUSING ACT OF 1937. Roosevelt died in office on April 12, 1945 and was succeeded by his vice-president, Harry S Truman.

Runaway and Homeless Youth Program   The Runaway and Homeless Youth Program, authorized by the Juvenile Justice and Delinquency Prevention Act of 1974 and administered within the Department of Health and Human Services (HHS), provides financial assistance to establish and strengthen community-based centers serving runaway and homeless youth and their families. Federal funding in 1988 supported approximately 315 runaway and homeless youth projects as well as a national hot line serving runaway and homeless youth and their families. Approximately one-third of the youth seeking services from these projects identified themselves as homeless. (See also CHILDREN; RUNAWAYS.)

runaways   Statistics vary widely, depending on sources. According to estimates by the U.S. Department of Health and Human Services (HHS) and the National Network of Runaway Youth Services, as many as a million young Americans ran away from home annually during the 1980s, with the U.S. Department of Justice putting that annual figure at 450,000 in 1990. Twenty-five percent of them remained on their own, surviving on the streets. According to the survey of 27 major cities conducted by the United States Conference of Mayors in 1988, "unaccompanied youth" accounted for 10 percent or more of the homeless population in Denver, Los Angeles, New Orleans, Providence, San Antonio, San Francisco and San Juan. In New York City alone there were estimated to be 20,000 young street people. A report made to the U.S. Senate Committee on the Judiciary estimated that 100,000 runaways were arrested in 1992.

Runaways face lives of danger and deprivation on the streets. Virginia Price, clinical coordinator of Bridge Over Troubled Waters, a private agency in Boston providing assistance to runaways, described how young people living on Boston's streets banded together and furtively lived in what they called "empties," abandoned buildings:

As more youth find out about a new empty they must be included, since anyone denied admission might disclose the building to the authorities. Thus, to discover another's empty is tantamount to gaining entry to the group. . . . As the group expands, it moves into less safe parts of the building, bringing the danger of physical injury. The electricity has usually been disconnected, so candles are used for lighting. Since the youth are often high or drunk, the risk of fire is increased; in recent years a number of fires in downtown Boston have begun this way. Finally, these youth have limited social skills with which to sustain cooperative living, most of them having grown up in families where violence is routinely used to handle interpersonal conflict. Thus the increase in group size brings an increase in the incidence of violence.

When the group becomes too large, Price noted, the original founders of the "empty" often abandon it, fearing that a large group will attract the attention of the authorities.

Runaways are vulnerable to physical violence, sexually transmitted diseases, including acquired immune deficiency syndrome (AIDS), psychiatric disorders and emotional disturbances, substance abuse, pregnancy and more than their share of the "normal" adolescent illnesses, including dental and skin problems.

Homeless youth are often "voluntarily" homeless and are usually not counted as part of the general homeless population. A study of runaway youth in New York City youth shelters in 1984 revealed that of the 118 subjects interviewed, none had a currently homeless parent. Most could find their parents if they wanted to, but nearly half said they could not return home and over half said they would not want to go home. Runaway youth are generally drawn from the lower end of the social spectrum. A 1984 New York City study reported that 44 percent of homeless youth surveyed had mothers receiving public assistance. One-half had been in foster homes. Sixty percent reported that their parents had drug or alcohol problems or were involved in criminal activity. Half reported physical abuse. Another study indicated that 73 percent of female runaways and 38 percent of male runaways were the targets of parental abuse, many of the females in particular the subject of sexual abuse. (See also CHILDREN; COVENANT HOUSE; THROWAWAYS.)

rural homelessness Rural homelessness, although less visible than its urban counterpart, was a serious and mounting problem throughout the 1980s. High interest rates, mounting energy costs and stagnant or declining prices for farm products all contributed to the worst economic crisis in American agriculture since the years of the GREAT DEPRESSION. There were over 650,000 foreclosures on farms in the "farm crisis" of the 1980s, a decade that saw an average of 2,000 farmers giving up farming every week. Loss of a family farm often represented loss of both home and income. America's rural economy was also hard hit by economic downturns in timber, mining, petroleum and other extractive industries. As a result, the rural population declined in the 1980s, while rural poverty rates increased. In 1985 the poverty rate for nonmetropolitan areas of the United States was

18.3 percent, compared to 12.7 percent for metropolitan areas. By 1992, 38 percent of the nation's poor lived in rural areas that contained 25 percent of the U.S. population. Eighteen percent of the homeless population lived in rural America, where 67 percent of all substandard housing could be found.

Studies of homelessness in California and Maryland in 1986 estimated that in each state 18 percent of the homeless populations were rural. The rural homeless tend to be overlooked because they are less concentrated than the urban homeless, and spend less of their days in visible public spaces. Rather than sleeping on the streets, the rural homeless are more likely to sleep in their cars, or in state and federal campground areas, or double up with friends and relatives. The rural homeless tend to be younger and more likely to live in families and maintain stronger ties to local communities than the urban homeless. They include more women and fewer minorities in their ranks. The rural homeless also include migrant and seasonal farm workers.

Despite such demographic differences, the rural homeless suffer from many of the same ills as the urban homeless, including hunger, alcohol and drug abuse, poor physical and mental health and the denial of education for their children. A special problem faced by the rural homeless is the lack of government or private services available to them. (See also HOUSING ASSISTANCE COUNCIL; MIGRATORY LABOR.)

S

safe houses   See BATTERED WOMEN.

Safe Space   In 1991 St. Mary the Virgin Church opened a teenage center called Safe Space in its adjoining Mission House on West 46th street, near Times Square in New York City. Safe Space was co-sponsored by the Center for Children and Families in Jamaica, Queens, a nonsectarian social agency. Its purpose was to provide a refuge for runaway teenagers, where they could find a hot meal, clean clothing, laundry service and counseling. Counselors at the center encouraged teenagers to be tested for acquired immune deficiency syndrome (AIDS). One of the parishioners of the church, a nurse at Roosevelt Hospital, said: "The more programs for teen-agers to take care of their health, the less chance I'll be seeing them at the hospital in their 20's and 30's."

Saint Joseph's House   See CATHOLIC WORKER.

St. Paul, Minnesota   The 1991 *Status Report on Hunger and Homelessness* issued by the United States Conference of Mayors estimated that in St. Paul 1,040 people were homeless. On an average day in the fall of 1991, 274 people sought emergency shelter. The city had 312 emergency shelter beds and 134 beds available for families seeking shelter. A St. Paul city official was quoted in the *Status Report* as saying: "At times all shelter beds and motel beds are full. People then stay in cars, or abandoned and condemned buildings." As in other cities, attitudes toward the homeless have begun to harden. The same official also said: "Most people seem 'tired' of homelessness in our midst. The continued exposure to the reality is complicated by the fact that political leadership on a national level has 'no vision' and no plan for dealing with the issue."

Salvation Army   The Salvation Army is a religious and charitable movement, organized on a paramilitary pattern, and providing a variety of services to the poor and homeless, including SOUP KITCHENS and SHELTERS. The Salvation Army was founded in England by William Booth, an ordained Methodist minister, who left the pulpit in

1861 to become a free-lance evangelist. In 1865 he moved to London's impoverished East End, where he founded the Christian Mission, which changed its name to Salvation Army in 1878. Booth designated himself "general" of his religious army; his followers became soldiers or officers, his mission stations became corps, and so forth. Converts to the Salvation Army are required to signs its "Articles of War," pledging volunteer service to the poor. Through its elaborate system of social services, the Salvation Army hoped to attract those who were needy in both the physical and spiritual realm and lead them to salvation. Salvation Army missions spread over the British Isles, and in 1880 the movement reached the United States. Here the Salvation Army quickly built up a system of missions in poor neighborhoods: Four were built in the Bowery district of New York City alone between 1891 and 1903. The Army's work in the United States was hindered in the early days by factional squabbles among its leadership; several disaffected leaders broke away to found the rival VOLUNTEERS OF AMERICA in 1896.

Today the Salvation Army has missions in 82 countries with some 25,000 officers preaching in 111 languages to a membership of about 2 million believers. The Salvation Army is perhaps best known to the general public for the brass bands that play on city streets at Christmastime to attract donations to the Army's work among the poor. It is best known to the poor and homeless for its social institutions, including a network of soup kitchens and missions in urban SKID ROW neighborhoods. In the years since World War II the Salvation Army has become known within the social service community for the scope and increasing professionalism of its activities. In addition to its services to the homeless, the Salvation Army runs homes and hospitals for unwed mothers; camps for children, mothers and senior citizens; boys and girls clubs; meals-on-wheels programs for the elderly; family service bureaus; adult rehabilitation centers; day care centers; and other services and agencies.

San Francisco, California San Francisco has the nation's most expensive housing rental market. In 1991 a worker would need hourly wages of $17.67 to be able to afford the rental of a two-bedroom apartment in the city. San Francisco's homeless population is estimated to be about 6,500. Under the administration of Mayor Dianne Feinstein, the city was slow to respond to the growing problem of homelessness in the 1980s. With the election of Art Agnos in 1988, however, the city began to expand its services to the homeless. The number of beds available in city shelters increased from 2,900 to 4,395 in 1991. The city also invested millions of dollars in acquiring and renovating five hotels in the Tenderloin district.

Agnos was defeated for reelection in 1991 because of widespread public dissatisfaction with his reluctance to send in the police to remove an encampment of the homeless in front of San Francisco's city hall. Belying the "liberal" reputation of the San Francisco electorate, Agnos was in effect the first major political figure in the country turned out of office for being "soft" on the homeless.

scabies Scabies is a common medical problem among homeless people congregated in shelters. Human scabies is caused by a mite known as *Sarcoptes scabei,* a white eyeless creature with small brown spines and eight short legs. The male is about .2 millimeters in length; the female, .3 millimeters. They live a parasitic existence on their human hosts. The female mite burrows into the skin to lay its eggs, which hatch in three to four days. The mite completes its entire life cycle in about 30 days. Allergic responses to scabies infestation causes itching and skin eruptions. Scabies can be transmitted through sexual intercourse, but the primary means of transmission is through people sharing sleeping space or clothing. Scabies can be treated by the application of lindane cream and the washing of clothing and bed linen. Reinfestation is difficult to prevent as long as the patient remains homeless however. (See also HEALTH.)

Search for Shelter program See AMERICAN INSTITUTE OF ARCHITECTS.

Seattle, Washington The 1991 *Status Report on Hunger and Homelessness* issued by the United States Conference of Mayors estimated that 13,405 people were homeless in Seattle. The city has 2,341 emergency shelter beds and 884 beds available for families seeking shelter. Under Mayor Norm Rice, Seattle has adopted relatively generous policies toward the treatment of its homeless population. The city was honored in 1989 by the National Alliance to End Homelessness as a community "in which cooperation, not confrontation, is the norm." But even in Seattle, the problem of homelessness has outstripped the capacities of local government and private charities to deal with it. A Seattle city official was quoted in the *Status Report* as saying: "Single adults often sleep in doorways, alleys and parks. There is an increasing number of women who do the same. Families and youth often stay in poor housing situations, and are sleeping in cars in outlying neighborhoods and parks. This is a growing problem."

Seattle Housing and Resource Effort (SHARE) The Seattle Housing and Resource Effort (SHARE) is a homeless self-help organization organized in 1990 by homeless people in Seattle. During the Goodwill Games, an international sporting event that Seattle was hosting in the summer of 1990, SHARE sponsored an event known as the Goodwill Gathering, which featured music, art exhibits and booths for job recruiters and housing specialists. On the day before Thanksgiving in 1990, SHARE set

up a tent city to house homeless people. After three weeks the city donated an old bus barn to the group and helped refurbish it as a homeless shelter. About 100 homeless people moved into the shelter, which is one of only a few in the country that is run entirely by its residents, without government, church or social service agency supervision. One homeless resident of the shelter told a reporter in December 1990, soon after it opened, "What we have here is a unique opportunity to set a standard not just for Seattle, but for the whole country. This is a historic experiment, and if it fails we can only blame ourselves."

Second Harvest See FOOD BANKS.

Section 8 Section 8 of the Housing and Community Development Act of 1974 authorized the Department of Housing and Urban Development (HUD) to provide federal funds to subsidize rentals in the private housing market by qualified low-income renters. Eligible households pay 30 percent of their income toward the rent and HUD pays the difference with a Section 8 certificate. Chosen households receive a certificate, funded for five to 15 years, that allows them to rent an existing apartment from a private landlord at the fair market rent. HUD regulations govern the health and safety requirements of the rental units and set "fair market prices," which Section 8 renters cannot exceed. Section 8 also has a program to provide contracts to developers to build or rehabilitate apartments designated as Section 8 units for low-income tenants.

Many problems have been identified with the program of Section 8 certificates and housing vouchers for low-income tenants. Such certificates are not given to all who qualify on the basis of income. Only a certain number are available, to be given out to those on a very long waiting list. In the mid-1980s, about one-fifth of all eligible households were receiving low-income housing vouchers through Section 8. Housing advocates report that it is often difficult for people to find housing that meets the strict quality standards of the program, while still being within the amounts specified, and that the "fair market rents" are often unrealistic figures in the recent housing market. Because tenants are given only two months to find housing in the program, most households selected to participate forgo the benefit because they cannot find housing that qualifies. It has also been reported that in some areas the Section 8 program has driven up rents to match the amount allowed.

Funding for Section 8 housing was dramatically cut under the administration of President Ronald Reagan. In addition, more than 300,000 Section 8 certificates expired in 1991, and thousands more will in following years. Congress and the White House have pledged to renew all expiring contracts. Though the Section 8 program has helped many low-income people to cope with the rapidly rising costs of the housing market, it is only a short-term and partial solution. As Joel Blau argued in his book *The Visible Poor,* "Section 8 temporarily equips poor people to obtain housing, but consistent with its market orientation, it makes no permanent contribution to the supply of affordable apartments." (See also SECTION 8 ASSISTANCE FOR SINGLE-ROOM OCCUPANCY DWELLINGS).

Section 8 Assistance for Single-Room Occupancy Dwellings Section 8 Assistance for Single-Room Occupancy Dwellings is a program, administered by the Department of Housing and Urban Development (HUD), which subsidizes low-income renters in nonpublic housing. Eligible households pay 30 percent of their income toward the rent charged for standard (nonpublic) housing, and HUD pays the difference with a "Section 8 certificate." (See also SECTION 8.)

Section 201 Program The Section 201 Program is a Department of Housing and Urban Development (HUD) program that provides assistance in restoring or maintaining the financial and physical soundness of privately owned, federally assisted, multifamily housing projects.

Section 202 Program The Section 202 Program is a Department of Housing and Urban Development (HUD) program that authorizes 50-year direct loans at a below-market interest rate to finance the development of housing for elderly and/or disabled persons of low and moderate income.

Section 236 Interest Reduction (or Subsidy) Program The Section 236 Interest Reduction Program was a Department of Housing and Urban Development (HUD) program enacted and terminated in 1968. The program provided tax breaks and direct payments of subsidies to mortgage lenders and provided mortgage insurance to specified sponsors for rental and cooperative housing for low- and moderate-income persons. The program also provided interest-reduction payments to eligible families and individuals to lower their housing costs. Many developers made high profits by building housing and then failed to manage the projects. HUD wound up repossessing a third of the half-million units that had been constructed with federal subsidies under Section 236.

shantytown In the 1980s homeless encampments—collections of tents, lean-tos and flimsy shelters constructed from cardboard, scrap wood and refuse—began to spring up in American cities. The word shantytown, a term usually associated with the slums surrounding Third World cities, is sometimes used to describe such an encampment. A front-page headline in the *New York Times* in October 1991 read "In the Shadow of Skyscrapers Grows a Shantytown Society." In New York City, by the early 1990s, there were dozens of such shantytowns in parks, beneath bridges, alongside roadways and on vacant lots. Many homeless residents of such encampments preferred such flimsy shelter to the dangers and overcrowding of the available public shelters. Some even took pride of "ownership" in their hand-built shelters. "I feel like I'm in my own house, my own apartment," a homeless person in a shantytown near the Port Authority Terminal told a reporter from the *New York Times* in 1991. And although nearby residents often blamed the homeless living in shantytowns for bringing crime and dirt into the neighborhood, some shantytowns enforced their own rules of behavior. "We don't tolerate no drugs," a homeless person living in a shantytown beneath the Manhattan Bridge told the same reporter. "And if you have to go to the bathroom, you don't do it here. This is our home. You go across the street to that other lot and use the sand pile and cover it up."

Although sleeping in the open is usually a violation of local ordinances, police and city officials often turn a blind eye to the existence of the shantytowns. Sometimes they crack down on them, if the complaints of neighbors grow too vocal to ignore, or if special events or visiting dignitaries make the untidy appearance of the shantytowns too great an embarrassment. In 1991 the administration of New York City mayor David Dinkins sent the police to close down the homeless encampment in Tompkins Square Park. Bulldozers later knocked down the new shantytown erected by some of those who formerly slept in the park on empty lots on the Lower East Side. (See also LEGAL RIGHTS.)

Shared Housing Resource Center

The Shared Housing Resource Center, based in Philadelphia, offers information and technical assistance in promoting the use of shared housing as a solution to the lack of affordable housing for low-income people.

Shelley v. Kraemer   See MINORITIES; RESTRICTIVE COVENANTS.

Shelter and Street Night (S Night)   As an additional component of its decennial census, the Bureau of the Census (a division of the U.S. Department of Commerce) undertook on March 20, 1990 to collect demographic, social and economic data on "selected components" of the homeless population. This special effort was called "Shelter and Street Night" (or "S Night") and, according to the Bureau, was designed to "improve the count" of homeless persons in previously identified public and private emergency shelters as well as "in open locations in the streets or other places not intended for habitation." In order to identify emergency shelters, letters were sent to 39,000 officials in urban and rural areas across the country requesting that they work with local service providers, advocates for the homeless and homeless persons in order to identify the shelters and street locations that would be visited during the night of the operation.

The plan called for sending 7,500 two-person teams of census takers to interview and count the homeless in three settings during three different periods of the night. Counting began at shelters from 6 P.M. to midnight (when, it was presumed, the homeless would be settled for the night). From 2 A.M. to 4 A.M. the census takers counted the homeless on the streets, and from 4 A.M. to 8 A.M. the census takers stood outside of abandoned buildings to count homeless people as they exited in the morning. Altogether, 11,000 shelters and 11,000 open-air sites were visited. The sites had all been identified previously, and there was no attempt to search cars or enter abandoned buildings, roofs or dumpsters. In addition to S Night, the Census expected to be able to use the regular census process to count households that were "doubled up" or that resided in commercial campgrounds, two groups that were often included in the count of the homeless. S Night was widely recognized as the most ambitious effort by the federal government to gain information on the homeless population, but it was also the subject of a great deal of controversy.

Though most recommended full participation in the effort, advocates for the homeless offered a range of criticisms even before S Night took place. They argued that the budget provided was much too low to do a reasonable survey and that the time allotment would not allow the enumerators to reach any more than a fraction of the homeless, especially in large cities such as New York. While officials in some cities responded to the bureau's mailing, critics noted that only 10 percent of those contacted actually responded, thus making it difficult to properly locate the homeless in many cities. Advocates raised questions about the times of the count, the impact of the weather on that night and the fact that enumerators could count only those who were visible on the streets, though the safety and survival of the homeless often depends on not appearing or admitting to being homeless. Except in a few instances, no cities with populations of less than 50,000 were visited. Generally, critics argued that S Night was bound to underestimate the number of homeless people and that despite warnings by the bureau that S Night would not yield an accurate accounting, policymakers at all levels would use the figures to slow or lower funding for the homeless.

In April 1991 the Census Bureau reported that its census takers had counted 230,000 people on S Night, which included 180,000 in shelters and 50,000 more at selected street sites. When the figures were released, homeless advocates felt that their warnings of a significant undercount of the homeless population had proven true. Maria Foscarinas of the National Law Center on Homelessness and Poverty declared: "My fear is that this is an effort by the Federal Government to diminish the plight of the homeless by minimizing their numbers." Paula Schneider, director of the Population Division at the Census Bureau, denied that there had been a deliberate undercount: "We admitted all

along that you can't count everybody. Those who hide from the census can't be counted. There is no way you can count them. And some of the homeless are among them." Over a dozen cities, fearing that federal aid to the homeless would be cut because of the Census bureau figures, sued to force an adjustment in the final count.

Shelter Corps Shelter Corps was the working title for a pilot project launched by the U.S. Department of Labor and the New York City Human Resources Administration in 1988. The program continues as the "special project" at the Glenmont Job Corps Center located near Albany, New York. The program recruits young homeless shelter residents, ages 16 to 24, from New York City. The Job Corps center provides room and board, education, job training, counseling, medical care, driver education and support services to those enrolled in the program. Approximately 50 slots are set aside for the program.

Shelter-Pak The Shelter-Pak is a hooded, waterproof, full-length coat, designed by faculty and students of the Philadelphia College of Textiles and Sciences. The coat is intended to serve as a combination outer garment and sleeping bag for homeless people. In warm weather it can be folded up and used as a backpack or pillow. Fashion design students have produced dozens of the coats since 1990 and distributed them through social service agencies to homeless people in Philadelphia. One feature of the coat is its simple lines and somber colors, which act as a kind of camouflage for the homeless in the sometimes hostile environment of the city streets.

Shelter Plus Care program In 1990, as part of the reauthorization of the Stewart B. McKinney Homeless Assistance Act, Congress created the Shelter Plus Care program. This is a competitive grant program that provides rental housing assistance and support services for homeless people (and their families) who are seriously mentally ill, are chronic substance abusers or have acquired immune deficiency syndrome (AIDS) or related diseases. At least 50 percent of the funds must be used for homeless individuals who are seriously mentally ill or have chronic problems with alcohol, drugs or both. The housing assistance can be provided in three forms: the Rental Housing Assistance program (authorized at $167.2 million), the Section 8 Single Room Occupancy (SRO) moderate rehabilitation program (authorized at $54.2 million) and the Section 202 rental assistance program (authorized at $37.2 million). The program requires that each dollar of housing assistance be matched with a dollar of support services from any other source, including other federal programs. The program did not receive any appropriated funds for fiscal 1991. (See also ALCOHOLISM; MENTAL ILLNESS; SUBSTANCE ABUSE.)

shelter poverty   When an inordinate portion of one's monthly income must be spent for shelter, leaving very little left for other expenses, one may be considered "shelter poor." That is, a household can be considered "shelter poor" if, after housing expenses, it cannot afford to pay for what the U.S. Bureau of Laboar Statistics defines as a minimum amount of nonhousing necessities. Mishel and Frankel, researchers at the Institute for Policy Studies, estimate that approximately one-third of all households are shelter poor. Until the 1980s, 25 percent of a household's income was considered the standard for housing affordability, but that standard has increased to 30 percent of income in recent years.

The condition of being poor by virtue of the high cost of housing became a particularly widespread problem in the mid-1980s, as rents and home prices in many parts of the United States rose more rapidly than income. According to data provided by the Joint Center for Housing Studies of Harvard

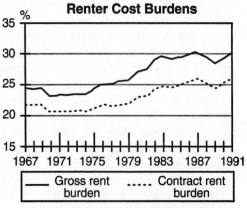

Renter Cost Burdens

Source: *The State of the Nation's Housing.*
Joint Center for Housing Studies
of Harvard University, 1992. p.3

University, by 1989 20 percent of all renters were paying at least 50 percent of their income for housing, a situation placing many low- and middle-income families in shelter poverty. With renter incomes remaining stagnant, the "rent-cost burden" has shown an overall increase (despite temporary dips) between 1974 and 1991, the latest year for which data is available. (See figure.) The figure shows two inflation-adjusted measures of the cost burden for renters. The median contract rent refers to the actual payment to the landlord, while gross rent consists of the contract rent plus payments for fuel and utilities.

Though shelter poverty is a condition faced by even middle-income households, those households whose income places them under the official poverty line (and who are unsubsidized) have been especially hard hit in recent years. Median gross rents for poverty households have risen substantially since the mid-1970s, causing particularly serious problems of shelter poverty. For example, measured in 1989 dollars, rents for poor households rose between 1974 and 1989 from $258 to $350 nationally, with even more significant increases in some regions of the country. (For example, in the West rents paid by the poor rose from $299 to $444.) As the Joint Center for Housing

Studies noted in reporting this data, "the unsubsidized poor must pay rents far in excess of what they can afford." (See also HOUSING MARKET; POVERTY LINE.)

shelters   Since the 1970s a variety of shelters—buildings providing temporary nighttime lodging for the homeless—have been set up in most large and many smaller American communities. The number of people housed in such shelters increased dramatically in the 1980s, jumping in New York City from an average of 2,000 adults a night in January 1980 to over 9,000 in January 1988. By the end of the 1980s, New York City operated 25 shelters for the homeless. Nationally, over 120,000 beds were available by the end of the decade.

Apart from New York City, few municipalities run their own shelters. In most communities shelters for the homeless are run by voluntary or religious organizations, funded by a mixture of private and public funding. This funding mixture changed in the later 1980s as new sources of federal funding, such as the Stewart B. McKinney Homeless Assistance Act, appeared. According to a 1983 Department of Housing and Urban Development (HUD) report, 63 percent of shelter operating expenses that year were paid for by private funds, with the additional 37 percent coming from government funds. A 1988 HUD report found, in contrast, that the government provided 65 percent of shelter funding, with the remaining 35 percent coming from private sources. In both 1983 and 1988 volunteers provided a significant proportion of the labor necessary to operate the shelters: In 1983 there were four volunteers for every three paid staff persons employed by shelters, while in 1988 the ratio was two volunteers for each paid staff person employed.

Shelters differ from the WORKHOUSES of the 19th century in that no one is legally compelled to stay in them and usually there is no work requirement. New York City opened its first shelter, the Sailors' Snug Harbor, in 1833. By 1840 Boston, Philadelphia and New Orleans had similar shelters for homeless sailors. New York City opened a municipal shelter on an old barge to all comers in the 1890s and built a more permanent shelter in 1909.

Despite the fact that shelter bed capacity almost tripled between 1983 and 1988, in no major city at the end of the decade did the number of beds available to the homeless in shelters match the needs of the homeless populations. In 1989 alone, according to a survey of major cities by the United States Conference of Mayors, requests for emergency shelter by the homeless increased by an average of 25 percent. In Los Angeles, for example, there were approximately 5,000 shelter beds available in 1989 for a homeless population estimated at 50,000.

In 1993, the Conference of Mayors reported that the overall number of shelter beds increased by an average of 4 percent, the rate of increase ranging from 48 percent in New Orleans to 5 percent or less in Chicago, Cleveland, Los Angeles, Phoenix and Salt Lake City. Despite the increase in the number of shelter beds, the mayors' survey showed, according to a report in the *Los Angeles Times* in late December 1993, that the ability of cities to meet families' needs for shelter had declined over the years and was worse in 1993 than at any time since the Conference of Mayors began keeping the data in 1988. The percentage of families being denied shelter jumped radically from 15 percent in 1991 to 20 percent in 1992, to 29 percent in 1993.

Shelters have encountered many problems as the demands on them increased. They have had to deal with a heterogenous population, with more women, children and minorities seeking shelter during the 1980s. A 1984 HUD survey of shelter users found they included 13 percent single women, 21 percent family members and 44 percent minorities. Fifty percent of the shelter population was found to suffer from chronic disabilities (alcoholism, drug abuse, and chronic mental illness). A 1990 survey of New York City shelter residents found that over 43 percent reported a health problem, over a fifth had received counseling for emotional or nervous problems and nearly 11 percent had been hospitalized for such problems.

Many homeless people shun shelters, fearing violence, theft, unsanitary and overcrowded conditions and the lack of privacy. John Coleman, a former president of Haverford College who impersonated a homeless person in the streets of New York City for ten days in 1983, described his first impression of the New York City Men's Shelter at 8 East 3rd Street as reminiscent of "London's workhouses and asylums in the times of Charles Dickens":

> The lobby and the adjacent "sitting room" were jammed with men standing, sitting, or stretched out in various positions on the floor. It was as lost a collection of souls as I could have imagined. Old and young, scarred and smooth, stinking and clean, crippled and hale, drunk and sober, ranting and still, parts of another world and parts of this one. The city promises to take in anyone who asks. Those rejected everywhere else find their way to East 3rd Street. The air was heavy with the odors of Thunderbird wine, urine, sweat, and above all, nicotine and marijuana. Three or four Human Resources Administration police officers seemed to be keeping the violence down to tolerable levels, but barely so.

Little had changed in the course of the next decade, according to the testimony of a resident in the Atlantic Avenue Armory shelter in Brooklyn in 1991. "I've been threatened and I've seen people pull out razors," he told a reporter from the *New York Times*. "You never know when a guy with a mental problem or someone smoking crack is going to go off. You have people in here who use drugs in the bathrooms, and the guards and institutional aides do nothing about it."

In the fall of 1991 more than 7,000 men and 1,300 women were seeking shelter nightly in New York City, at a cost to the city of $39 per person a night. In New York, smaller shelters generally enjoy better reputations than larger barrackslike shelters, which are also referred to as congregate shelters. Although New York State law requires that no city shelters house more than 200 people, the city has routinely obtained waivers allowing it to continue to use its larger shelters where 900 to 1,000 men sleep on cots in a single giant room. In the fall of 1991 New York's Mayor David Dinkins proposed to decentralize the shelter system in the city, identifying 35 neighborhoods in the city's five boroughs as potential sites for new and smaller shelters of no more than 150 beds. But the plan met vociferous protest from residents and politicians representing the affected neighborhoods, and by year's end it was politically doomed.

Shelters differ in their philosophy and goals. Some, such as Boston's Pine Street Inn, which provides facilities for over 300 homeless people, avoid elaborate intake procedures, rules or provision of services or treatment. Other shelters, such as Boston's Parker Street shelter, which has beds for 50, admit only those homeless people identified as mentally ill, with a clinical evaluation as part of the intake process and a treatment plan developed for each homeless person. In New York City there is no restriction on length of time a homeless person may stay in shelters; a 1986 survey indicated that one-half of the residents had spent one year or more in the shelters. Despite the generally bad reputation of public shelters among New York City's homeless population, some homeless people have adapted to the conditions, a process that social scientists called "shelterization." Tony Branch, the director of the large, dimly lit and unheated Atlantic Avenue Armory shelter in Brooklyn, told the *New York Times* in 1991 that some shelter residents had started to call the place "home," a fact that he found very disturbing.

> Some people say it's cleaner than the environment they grew up in. They have guaranteed breakfast, lunch and dinner. They get clothing and a place to sleep. By court decision we

have to offer shelter to anyone who asks for it. To be honest with you, a lot of guys come in here who need mental repair. They lose faith in themselves. They've been put down by a lot of people.

Public shelters in other cities limit stays to a few days or weeks at the most. Many shelters do not allow homeless people to stay on the premises during daylight hours; they must leave the building until nightfall.

Homeless advocates have often criticized the shelter system for its inadequacies. The Community Service Society of New York, for example, criticized New York City's homeless shelter system for being the "place of last resort for many homeless men" because of "deplorable conditions." Anthropologist Kim Hopper termed the shelters "zones of discard," a place to "throw away" people who can't support themselves. Other people are less concerned with the conditions that the homeless find within the shelters than they are with the very existence of the shelter system. In 1983 the *Wall Street Journal* complained editorially that upgrading New York City's public shelters would only lure many people who were "not really homeless" into the shelters. Conservatives often argue that public shelter should be offered only with work requirements attached, such as New York City's Work Experience Program, which offers shelter residents $12.50 a week in exchange for 20 hours of work cleaning subway platforms and toilets and maintaining city parks. And as Mayor Dinkins discovered when he proposed to expand the shelter system, very few people welcomed the possible presence of a homeless shelter in their own neighborhood. New York City Council Speaker Peter Vallone described the building of new shelters as an epidemic: "It's almost as if you're saying we have a serious disease and we'll spread it so everybody will suffer from it."

Homeless advocates emphasize that shelters are at best a temporary expedient, not a solution for homelessness. Whatever the long-term solution to homelessness may prove to be, there is no question that, for the foreseeable future, shelters will provide the only alternative for many people to sleeping in the streets. (See also PARTNERSHIP FOR THE HOMELESS; POORHOUSE)

shopping-bag ladies See MENTAL ILLNESS.

Sinatra, Frank See HANDS ACROSS AMERICA.

single-parent families See WOMEN.

single-room-occupancy hotels (SRO)
"Single-room-occupancy," or SRO, hotels rent single rooms, generally by the day, the week or the month, at low rates. SROs once served as an important source of inexpensive shelter, especially for single persons living in poverty. But in the past two decades there has been a sharp decline nationally in the number of housing units in the least expensive segments of the housing market. A survey of 12 large cities from 1978 to 1983 found that rental housing available to the poor dropped by an average of 30 percent. Part of this decline is the result of the demolition of SROs in cities across the country due to downtown redevelopment and gentrification. For example, in Chicago 18,000 dwelling units in SROs were demolished between 1973 and 1984; in Los Angeles fully one-half of the SRO rooms were eliminated between 1970 and 1985. In 1975 New York City extended its J-51 TAX ABATEMENT PROGRAM to cover the renovation of SRO buildings, thus providing a strong financial incentive for landlords to evict low-income tenants in order to renovate the buildings into luxury housing. From 1975 to 1981 over 30,000 rooms in SROs were eliminated in New York City. Nationwide, over 1 million single-room units, nearly half of the total stock, disappeared between 1970 and 1982. By 1993, the Conference of Mayors reported a reversal of this trend, with SRO units increased by 16 percent in 26 cities surveyed. New York City's SRO units increased 20 percent in 1993, San Antonio's

by 100 percent and Los Angeles by 56 percent.

Though SROs have not generally represented high-quality housing (in terms of comfort or aesthetic appearance), almost no housing of comparable function or price has been built to replace them over the past several decades. As sociologist Phil Kasinitz noted in 1984:

> There is a danger in romanticizing the SRO. . . . Many of these buildings provided—and provide—the most squalid conditions of the housing market. Landlords have at times abused tenants with few options. . . . Nevertheless, it is a housing stock that does provide shelter for persons who might otherwise lack shelter. It is being destroyed. It is not being replaced.

The loss of SRO hotels had clearly been a significant factor in the rise of homelessness in the 1980s. Moreover, the elimination of large numbers of SRO units caused rental rates to increase substantially in those SROs that remain, thus placing this housing option beyond the reach of many homeless people. The 1993 Mayors' report indicate cities are addressing this problem. (See also HOUSING MARKET; SKID ROW.)

skid row　The term *skid row* refers to run-down sections of cities inhabited by unskilled, transient men, with a high percentage of alcoholics among them. The term originated in the Pacific Northwest in the 19th century, although it did not come into common usage until the 1930s. (Until that time, the transient neighborhoods of a city were commonly referred to as the "main stem.") A "skid row" (originally a "skid road") was a road constructed of greased logs over which lumbermen would drag, or "skid," their logs to the mills. The lumber industry workforce consisted largely of single transient workers. Because of the seasonal nature of their employment, they would spend the winters in such cities as Seattle, Tacoma and Portland, waiting for the return of spring and a new cutting season. The areas in which they lived acquired a rough-and-tumble reputation, known for their concentration of saloons, brothels, religious missions, cheap hotels and eating establishments, pawnshops and employment agencies recruiting casual labor.

Skid rows began to appear in many cities in the 1870s, associated with the appearance of tramps. In the 20th century skid rows shrank in size and changed in character. Increasing mechanization in agriculture and extractive industries reduced the demand for migratory labor. The tramping workers who moved from place to place in search of work became less common. While life on skid row was never as romantic as some literary observers liked to believe, the quality of life undoubtedly worsened in the 20th century. Increasingly skid rows came to be associated in the public mind with a more or less permanent population, a "home guard" of alcoholics and other "derelicts," although as late as the early 1970s studies reported that between one-third and one-half of all skid row residents worked, usually at menial jobs.

After a temporary expansion during the GREAT DEPRESSION, the skid row population continued to decrease in numbers in the postwar years. A 1950 survey of skid rows in 41 cities estimated their total population at under 100,000. A survey of New York City's Bowery district in the mid-1960s estimated a total homeless population of less than 7,000, down from 14,000 in 1949. Overall, the population of skid rows nationally was thought to have shrunk by 50 percent between 1950 and 1970. Although contemporary studies often referred to the population of skid rows as "homeless," the term was used to refer to transients without any fixed place of abode as well as to those who lacked any kind of shelter at night. Most skid row residents did have a roof over their head at night, however shabby their quarters in missions and FLOPHOUSES might have been. The population of skid rows remained overwhelmingly male and white, though it increasingly shifted to older men. In the 1950s and 1960s, URBAN RENEWAL programs were often targeted at skid row areas. Although skid row populations were often simply shunted from one dilapidated neighborhood to another through the urban renewal process, many observers assumed in those years that skid rows would soon disappear from the urban scene. (See also HOBO.)

slum "Slum" is a subjective term referring to a run-down, neglected quarter of a city. In the urban renewal programs of the 1950s and 1960s planners, developers and urban renewal agencies defined slums by assessing the viability of a residential community in relation to the "higher use" to which the land might be put. Essentially "slum" is a state of residential substandardness.

S Night Every 10 years, the U.S. Census Bureau conducts a census of population and housing. As part of the 1990 Census, the bureau attempted to count America's homeless population; this portion of the census was commmonly referred to as the "S Night" Count. The *Christian Science Monitor* reported in late December 1992 that results of the March 20 and 21 "S Night" Count were criticized by homeless advocacy groups and state and local governments. The 1990 Census S Night Count found more than 200,000 homeless, but the National Coalition for the Homeless in Washington, D.C. claims the number of homeless people ranges from 600,000 to 3 million. (See SHELTER AND STREET NIGHT.)

Snyder, Mitch A native of New York City, Mitch Snyder left his job as an advertising executive in 1969 at age 26 to campaign for the rights of the homeless in Washington, D.C. Snyder, an atheist who became an activist Roman Catholic, cofounded the Community for Creative Non-Violence (CCNV), a Washington group that has engaged in a range of nonviolent protest

activities against homelessness. As a leader of the group, Snyder was arrested for praying on the front lawn of the White House. He also set cockroaches loose in the White House dining room and played tape-recorded laughter at City Council meetings when officials insisted they were doing enough to help the homeless. Mitch Snyder worked without pay and lived in the homeless shelter run by the group. The CCNV had acquired the building that housed the shelter from the federal government several days before the 1984 presidential election and several hours before the television program *60 Minutes* was due to air a segment on a hunger strike that Snyder had undertaken to protest government inaction. Though the Reagan administration transferred the building to the CCNV, it did not provide the funds to renovate it as, according to Snyder, it had promised. A television film *Samaritan* about Snyder's life was produced in 1985 and 1986. In June of 1990 the Internal Revenue Service demanded that Snyder turn over $90,000 in back taxes and penalties from the $150,000 he had been paid for rights to his story. His coworkers claimed that Snyder had contributed all of his proceeds to the CCNV and that he had planned to turn the IRS demand into a public issue about the federal government's priorities. Snyder's suicide on July 4, 1990 put an end to the planned campaign.

Social Security The Social Security Act, passed in the midst of the GREAT DEPRESSION during the administration of President Franklin Delano Roosevelt, was one of the NEW DEAL's most popular achievements. The Social Security Act of 1935 was a legislative package including unemployment insurance and grants-in-aid to states to provide funds for dependent mothers and children, the blind and public health services. Its best known feature was its provision for old-age insurance, funded by payroll taxes. Social Security Old Age and Survivors Insurance (OASI) benefits are payable directly to retirees at age 62 or to dependents and survivors of retirees.

While not specifically targeted to the homeless population, OASI payments have provided the elderly with a minimum level of income support that has enabled many to avoid homelessness, especially since (unlike most benefit programs) Social Security pension payments have been linked to the consumer price index. Since the late 1960s, with the introduction of the GREAT SOCIETY's Medicare program to complement Social Security pensions, the poverty rate among the elderly has dropped dramatically in the United States. In 1967 nearly 30 percent of the elderly lived below the POVERTY LEVEL, but by 1976 the rate had fallen to about 15 percent and, by 1985, to less than 13 percent. The 1990 Census put the figure at 10.7 percent. The American welfare state works best when its benefits are available not just to the poor but to all groups in society, without eligiblity being tied to income levels. (See also SOCIAL SECURITY DISABILITY INSURANCE.)

Social Security Disability Insurance (SSDI)

The Social Security Disability Insurance (SSDI) program, authorized by the Social Security Act, pays monthly disability benefits to disabled workers under age 65 and their families. Persons are considered disabled if they have a severe physical or mental condition that prevents them from working and that is expected to last (or has lasted) for at least 12 months or is expected to result in death. SSDI payments can start at the beginning of the sixth full month of a disability and continue as long as the person remains disabled and unable to perform gainful work. Starting in 1981, under the administration of President Ronald Reagan, the Social Security Administration began pruning the rolls of SSDI recipients by an aggressive review of recipients' eligibility. By 1985, when the reviewing process was ruled illegal, 491,300 recipients had

been dropped from SSDI's rolls. Of these, some 200,000 were able to regain benefits after often-lengthy administrative and court proceedings. (See also SOCIAL SECURITY.)

Social Services Block Grants (SSBG)

Social Services Block Grants, authorized by the Social Security Act and administered within the Department of Health and Human Services, are awarded to states to furnish a variety of social services, including the prevention, reduction or elimination of dependency; the prevention of child neglect, abuse or exploitation; and the reduction of inappropriate institutional care. While not directly targeted to the homeless population, the homeless are among a broader clientele who can benefit from the program. Emergency food and shelter for the homeless may also be funded through Social Services Block Grants.

South Bronx, New York   See ARSON; BANANA KELLY COMMUNITY IMPROVEMENT ASSOCIATION.

soup kitchens   Privately sponsored soup kitchens providing free meals to hungry, homeless and unemployed people have long been a fixture in American urban life. The CATHOLIC WORKER movement has maintained a soup kitchen on the Lower East Side of New York City since the Great Depression. In the 1980s many churches and charitable groups organized soup kitchens in response to the growing crisis of homelessness. The meals provided at soup kitchens are an important source of nutrition for the homeless. According to a study by the Urban Institute, homeless people who manage to eat some of their meals in shelters and soup kitchens are provided with substantial nutritional variety. Over 50 percent of lunches and dinners contain at least four out of five of the essential food groups, and the average meal provides a good measure of essential nutrients. Soup kitchen sponsors strive to provide as much food of a high nutritional value as possible; they know that the meal they provide may very well be the only meal the homeless person eats that day. By the early 1990s an estimated 24,000 meals were being served every day at 130 private soup kitchens across New York City. In a Legal Action Center for the Homeless survey of soup kitchen users, only 25 percent of those interviewed said they averaged three meals a day over the preceding three days. One-third said they averaged two meals a day, and 42 percent said they averaged one meal or less a day.

spot labor   One source of income for the homeless is spot labor, temporary jobs that last for a few hours or a few days and that pay in cash at the end of the day's work. These manual labor jobs include such tasks as loading and unloading trucks, doing yardwork or minor repair or maintenance jobs, or filling in on a factory assembly line. Sometimes these jobs are filled through temporary hiring halls, located in SKID ROW sections of many cities. According to a study by R. Bruce Wiegand (1990), there were 8,000 such halls in the United States in 1985. In some cities job seekers wait at designated streetcorners for potential employers to drive up and ask for workers. Spot labor usually pays the minimum wage, or about $25 a day (or a take-home pay of around $18 once Social Security tax is deducted). Sometimes temporary laborers are hired to take the place of permanent workers who go on strike. Spot labor offers no benefits, and workers are sometimes exposed to unsafe working conditions.

squatting   Squatting is the act of occupying abandoned or otherwise unused buildings in order to satisfy the immediate need for shelter. In agrarian societies squatting has long been a tactic used by impoverished landless peasants as a form of illegal "land reform," whereby they seize for cultivation unused lands on large estates. But since the late 1960s, squatting has become a fixture in the cities of many industrial societies as well, particularly in Europe. In the urban context squatting is an unlawful response by the homeless to the lack of affordable housing.

The forcible eviction of squatters sometimes has turned into violent conflicts between police and squatters, as has occurred in Holland and West Germany. Yet in many cities authorities have tolerated squatting to a greater or lesser degree as a way of relieving the pressure of homelessness. For example, in the 1960s authorities in Britain often sought to prevent squatting by tightening security on vacant properties, cutting gas and electrical links to property inhabited by squatters, removing squatters' names from waiting lists for public housing and evictions. But by the middle of the 1970s the number of squatters in London and its immediate suburbs had risen to 25,000 and the local authorities increasingly became resigned to the practice of squatting. The squatter's movement in London became so large that it spawned a citywide organization, the Family Squatting Advisory Service, to coordinate movement activities to negotiate with the local authorities and even to "license" squatters by accepting responsiblity for specific acts of squatting.

Though not as widespread as in Europe, in the United States urban squatting has become evident in response to the shortage of low-cost housing. ACORN, the Association of Community Organizations for Reform Now, a national organization of low-income activists, has won concessions from authorities in a number of cities by organizing squatting campaigns. An example of one squatter's movement in the late 1970s is illustrative. In Philadelphia, community organizers began placing homeless families in vacant government-owned houses, an act that reportedly evoked considerable public sympathy and support, particularly by those who viewed the abandonment of buildings as a threat to their own properties. Though federal government officials moved to evict the squatters because the issue was so politically sensitive, evictions were processed only very slowly and selectively. City officials, dealing with a public housing waiting list of over 14,000, were even more reluctant to see the squatters evicted, and consequently handled the situation in a relatively conciliatory fashion.

Community organizations used these well-publicized squatting actions to pressure city officials into including low-income households in an ongoing "homesteading" program. In 1982 the Philadelphia city council passed legislation allowing resident squatters to acquire tax-delinquent private houses and government-owned houses in exchange for performing repairs necessary to meet minimum housing codes.

In New York City squatters live in a number of neighborhoods. In December 1990 two dozen squatters, mostly immigrants from Latin America or the Caribbean, were evicted from the abandoned city-owned building in the Bronx where they had lived for three years. During that time they had done considerable renovation work including installing bathrooms and kitchens and rewiring. A larger community of about 500 squatters lived in 32 city-owned buildings on the Lower East Side in the early 1990s. In October 1991 the squatters held a Squatters Day parade, carrying banners reading "Defend the Squats" and "No Evictions of Squatters." Some neighbors blamed a group of the squatters known as "the anarchists" for the violent protests that had taken place over the preceding year in Tompkins Square Park. City authorities periodically threaten to evict the squatters, but so far have refrained from doing so for fear of appearing insensitive to the plight of the homeless. (See also HOMESTEADING.)

Staten Island Ferry Terminal See ARSON.

Steve the Tramp Steve the Tramp was a five-inch high plastic toy figure of a tramp sold by the Walt Disney Company, until pressure from the National Coalition for the Homeless and other homeless advocates forced the company to withdraw it from the market. The tramp, based on a character in the movie *Dick Tracy,* was described on its package as "hardened and bitter after a life on the mean streets," as "a lout who would just as soon take your life as your wallet" and as someone who "will use and abuse any young helpless prey he comes across." The Reverend Christopher Rose, rector of Grace Episcopal Church in Hartford, Connecticut, denounced Steve the Tramp "as one of the most offensive toys of the 1990 Christmas season," because of its stereotyping of homeless people. Toy stores began withdrawing Steve the Tramp from the shelves after homeless advocates set up picket lines protesting its sale. (See also TRAMPS.)

Steward B. McKinney Homeless Assistance Act (PL100–77) See MCKINNEY ACT.

Street News *Street News* is a biweekly newspaper produced in New York City and distributed by unemployed homeless people. It is published by the staff of Street Aid, a not-for-profit organization that was formed in 1988 to organize a series of benefit concerts for Hunger Awareness Day, seeking to raise money, consciousness, and canned food for the poor. *Street News,* which describes itself as "America's Motivational Non-Profit Newspaper," is edited by Hutchinson Persons and has a circulation of over 350,000 per month. Paid advertisements help to support the publication of the paper, while over 800 homeless men and women sell it. The content of the paper ranges from articles on homelessness, poverty, public policy and the housing market in New York City, to poetry, letters, photography, book reviews and human interest stories. Articles by and interviews with movie stars, famous rock stars and sympathetic politicians are often featured, as are articles written by homeless persons themselves. Despite periodic attempts by the police to crack down on *Street News* vendors, the newspaper continued to be sold in the subways.

student activism   In the late 1980s students on a number of college campuses became involved in homeless advocacy campaigns. An estimated 20,000 students from 300 colleges and universities traveled to Washington, D.C. for the October 7, 1989 Housing Now! march and rally. (See also NATIONAL STUDENT CAMPAIGN AGAINST HUNGER AND HOMELESSNESS.)

substance abuse   Substance abuse is an addictive dependence on drugs or alcohol. According to the United States Conference of Mayors, about one-third of the homeless population are estimated to be substance abusers. Critics of government programs to help the homeless sometimes cite the statistics on substance abuse as evidence that the homeless brought their plight on themselves and thus are undeserving of the taxpayers' dollars. Homeless advocates respond that substance abuse is itself often the product of poverty, not its cause. When people find themselves in the street, they pick up the vices of the street. Poor people turn in despair to drugs and alcohol as compensation for other deficiencies in their lives. Selling illegal drugs offers some of the homeless a source of income, while using the drugs offers a means of temporary escape. (See also ALCOHOLISM; DRUG ABUSE.)

substandard housing   The Department of Housing and Urban Development (HUD) and the Bureau of the Census classify housing units as suffering from "severe" physical problems if they have one or more of the following five deficiencies: lacking hot or cold water or a flush toilet, or both a bathtub and a shower; the heating equipment has

broken down at least three times in the previous winter for six hours or more, resulting in the unit being uncomfortably cold for 24 hours or more; the unit has no electricity, or the unit has exposed wiring and has a room with no working wall outlet and also has had three blown fuses or tripped circuit breakers in the last 90 days; the unit has, in public areas (such as hallways and staircases), nonworking light fixtures and loose or missing steps and loose or missing railings and no elevator; the unit has at least five basic maintenance problems, such as water leaks, holes in the floors or ceilings, peeling paint or broken plaster or evidence of rats or mice in the last 90 days. The Census Bureau and HUD classify a housing unit as suffering from "moderate" physical problems if it has one or more of the following five deficiencies: on at least three occasions in the last three months, all flush toilets were broken down at the same time for at least six hours; the unit has unvented gas, oil or kerosene heaters as its primary heating equipment; the unit lacks a sink, refrigerator or either burners or an oven; the unit has three of the four hallway or staircase problems listed above; or the unit has at least three of the basic maintenance problems listed above. The percentage of Americans living in substandard housing has increased in recent years, after a period of decline. In 1950, 35 percent of American families lived in substandard housing. By 1970, after the WAR ON POVERTY had been launched, that percentage declined to 7 percent. But in 1985 just under one in ten American households lived in what HUD classified as substandard housing. One in five poor households in the United States (2.7 million households) lived in housing with "moderate" or "severe" physical problems. (See also SLUM.)

subways   Homeless people have become a familiar sight in and around many of the nation's subway systems, including the Metro system in Washington, D.C. and the

BART system in the San Francisco Bay Area. The New York City subway system has been home to a large homeless population for more than a decade. By the end of the 1980s the Metropolitan Transit Authority estimated that about 2,500 homeless people were sleeping in New York City's subways, while homeless advocates put the figure at closer to 5,000.

In the fall of 1989 the Metropolitan Transit Authority launched "Operation Enforcement" to prevent the city's homeless population from living, sleeping and panhandling in the subway system. Transit Authority police arrested beggars and loiterers, and benches were removed from several subway stations where the homeless congregated. The program was controversial and the label "Operation Enforcement" was soon dropped. Program defenders argued that the subway system was a dangerous place for homeless people to seek shelter. According to Transit Authority figures, 79 homeless people died in the subway system in 1989, including 15 crushed by trains and nine through electrocution and other accidents. Critics of the operation argued that it was a callous attempt to push the homeless out into the streets. Some homeless people preferred the subway to the city's emergency shelters, which they felt were even more dangerous. In 1990 the U.S. Supreme Court upheld a ban against begging in the New York City subway system.

Another issue that involved the subways was the lack of public rest rooms. The Legal Action Center for the Homeless filed a class action suit against New York City and the Transit Authority in the fall of 1990 demanding that lavatories be provided in parks and in subways. Doug Lasdon, director of the Legal Action Center, argued that the homeless had no other facilities available to them. As a result, "New York is turning into a literal sewer." City officials responded that it was hard to keep public facilities from being vandalized and that the homeless were using the available facilities to bathe, making them unavailable for others to use.

In the fall of 1991 the Transit Authority renewed its drive to remove the homeless from the subways. Transit police were instructed to offer transportation to shelters to homeless people caught panhandling or sleeping in the subways. If they refused the offer, they were to be evicted, regardless of the weather, so long as they appeared to be adequately dressed. William J. Bratton, chief of the New York City Transit police, defended the policy against critics: "Transit police officers," he wrote in a letter to the *New York Times*, "are not just saying 'get out.' By enforcing rules they are helping to guide desperate and vulnerable people to shelters and rehabilitation programs where many get help." The fact that so many people apparently preferred to sleep in subway trains or tunnels than to take their chances in the shelter system reflected poorly on the city's homeless program. (See also STREET NEWS.)

Sullivan, Louis See INTERAGENCY TASK FORCE ON HOMELESSNESS AND SEVERE MENTAL ILLNESS.

Supplemental Security Income (SSI)

The Supplemental Security Income program, which is part of the Social Security system, makes monthly payments to people who are at least 65, disabled or blind and have little or no income and assets. About 4.6 million people received SSI benefits in 1989. The Department of Health and Human Services estimates that "approximately 10 percent of the homeless population receives SSI." However, the General Accounting Office (GAO) estimates that "about 30 to 50 percent of those eligible" for SSI are not enrolled in the program. Unlike old-age pensions, SSI payments have not been linked to the consumer price index and have declined in value considerably in recent years.

Surplus Federal Personal Property Donation Program See GENERAL SERVICES ADMINISTRATION.

sweat equity See BANANA-KELLY COMMUNITY IMPROVEMENT ASSOCIATION; NONPROFIT HOUSING PROGRAMS.

Sweden Sweden has gone farther than other countries in the world in securing decent housing for all of its residents, and homelessness has not been a problem as it has in other industrialized societies, particularly the United States. Sweden, a relatively large country with a relatively small population, has had rapid economic growth and urbanization. A strong commitment to universal social welfare and the powerful trade union movement that supports it have combined to spare Swedes many of the ills of homelessness. One Swedish housing analyst noted:

> Facing winter, social authorities in Gothenburg, our second largest city, scanned the city for outdoor sleepers. Their total findings were one man sleeping in his car as a victim of a raging wife rather than housing policy. In Stockholm, comparable to Hamburg in size, conditions are somewhat harsher and in a recent TV-programme social authorities estimated the number of outdoor lodgers to less than 100.

Basically three categories of homeless persons have been identified in Sweden: alcoholics and drug abusers, those mentally ill people who refuse to accept homes offered by social agencies and refugees from other countries who have not been accepted as immigrants.

The Swedish government sponsors a range of nonprofit housing strategies combined with strong regulation of private investment and management, in order to limit the role of the market as the sole determinant of the availability of high-quality, low-cost housing. Direct government financial support in the form of housing allowances, interest allowances, loans and other benefits are the main reasons why homelessness has not become a major problem in Sweden. For much of the postwar period the state has fashioned social policy specifically to protect the poorest members of the population from housing shortages and high rents. In recent years, however, as Swedes have become more affluent, tax deductions on owner-occupied housing have increased, while the proportion of government funds devoted to housing allowances has decreased. Though social conditions have not deteriorated to any significant degree, such changes suggest a possible weakening of the Swedish commitment to firm social welfare programs and an equitable housing policy. Social welfare activists are monitoring events in Sweden closely.

T

temporary hiring halls See SPOT LABOR.

tenant activism Tenant activists seek to organize tenants to defend their interests. Through negotiations, rent strikes and other tactics they try to convince landlords to respond to the grievances of their renters. Tenant activists also have turned to political action, to push for rent control and other legislative gains.

Unlike the labor movement, tenant activism has been largely localized in its focus and organization. Ongoing tenant organizations have proven difficult to sustain because of the transient nature of tenancy and because of the common assumption that housing, unlike employment, is part of a family's private existence and should not become "politicized." Nevertheless, tenant movements have repeatedly sprung up in this century. New York City has a long history of tenant activism. In 1904 several hundred tenants on the Lower East Side banded together to resist rent increases, picketed the homes of their landlords and formed the short-lived New York Rent Protective Association. The Socialist Party organized rent strikes in a number of New York City neighborhoods in the years leading up to World War I. During the Great Depression and for some years afterward the Communist Party organized a significant tenants' movement in New York City. The Communist-led tenants' organizations fell apart as the party came under attack during the McCarthy era of the 1950s and as the largely Jewish neighborhoods that had been the traditional basis of support for tenant-organizing were transformed by an influx of black and Puerto Rican residents. The rise of the civil rights movement in the 1960s sparked a renewal of urban tenant activism, including a dramatic rent strike led by the Harlem Tenants Council in 1963.

In the 1970s and 1980s tenant activism was once again on the upswing, and over a broader geographical area than in the past. A national magazine, *Shelterforce*, was founded in 1975 to encourage tenant activism, and the National Tenants Union (NTU) was organized in 1980 to coordinate local tenant activism. Several statewide coalitions of tenant activists, such as the New Jersey Tenant Organization (NJTO), the California Housing Action and Information Network (CHAIN), the New York State Tenants and Neighborhood Coalition and the Massachusetts Tenants Organization, have launched ongoing campaigns to defend tenants' rights, and have won important court and legislative victories. In New Jersey more than 100 communities passed rent control laws, as did 25 communities in California. Other groups, such as ACORN (the Assocation of Community Organizations for Reform Now) have successfully organized low-income residents, including some homeless people, to pressure city governments to establish "sweat equity" programs, in which poor people can gain title to condemned and abandoned buildings by fixing them up for their own use.

Thatcher, Margaret   See BRITAIN.

Thorazine   See   DEINSTITUTIONALI-ZATION.

thousand points of light   In the 1988 presidential campaign, presidential candidate George Bush called for a "kindler, gentler" America and praised the tradition of charity and voluntary service, the "thousand points of light," that had eased the burdens of poor and disadvantaged Americans in past years. Indeed, throughout the 1980s there was an upsurge of volunteer service, through such groups as Habitats for Humanity. The number of volunteers working in Catholic Charities programs increased from 23,000 in 1980 to just under 200,000 in 1990. Critics argued that such voluntary efforts, however admirable, could not substitute for sustained government involvement in dealing with problems such as homelessness. The Reverend Thomas J. Harvey, executive director of the national coordinating office for local Catholic Charities programs, told a reporter from the *New York Times* in January 1992: "I favor encouraging voluntarism, but it's no substitute for social policy." He was frustrated that religious organizations were being forced to assume the role of "safety net," with the elimination of many government social welfare programs. The economic recession that began in the early 1990s stretched the resources of private charities to the breaking point. Individual giving to charitable groups such as the United Way and the Salvation Army increased in 1991, but not nearly enough to keep up with the growing needs of the poor and homeless. Potential donors were also facing financial hardships and insecurity. The United Way saw its contributions increase by 2 to 3 percent in 1991, the smallest increase in giving in more than 30 years. The Salvation Army was forced to cut back on some programs for the homeless, despite the increased need. "When Americans see their neighbors in trouble, they give more," Colonel Leon Ferraez, director of national communications for the Salvation Army, told a reporter in December 1991, "so our income is up nationwide by as much as 16 percent, and that's not unusual in a recession. The downside is that demand for services has increased by more than 25 percent."

throwaways Throwaway children are children abandoned by their parents, or forced to leave home by their parents. It has been estimated that between 10 and 20 percent of children in shelters for runaway youth are actually throwaways. (See also CHILDREN; RUNAWAYS.)

Tier I shelter In the New York City homeless shelter system, a Tier I shelter is a barracks-type shelter where many individuals or families share a single, large room.

Tier II shelter In the New York City homeless shelter system, a Tier II shelter is a small apartment, intended as interim or TRANSITIONAL HOUSING for families until they can be placed in more permanent housing.

Tompkins Square Park In the 1980s Tompkins Square Park on the Lower East Side of New York City became home to an encampment of dozens of homeless people. The area around the park has long been one of New York's poorer neighborhoods, home to generations of new immigrants, but in the 1960s also attracting a countercultural element. In the 1980s neighborhood groups complained of increased crime, drug-dealing, garbage and noise because of the presence of a number of homeless people who lived in and around the park. The Tompkins Square Park Coalition charged that the presence of the homeless was keeping other neighborhood residents from using the park. There was also a controversy over the role of so-called anarchists who were leading protests on behalf of the homeless. For three summers in a row, conflicts between police, the homeless and their supporters turned violent. In August 1988 a riot in the park left 50 injured and 31 arrested. In May 1991 another riot led to 13 arrests and more injuries.

The 1980s and 1990s were not the first time in the city's history that Tompkins Square Park had been the scene of clashes between police and citizens. On January 13, 1874, in the midst of the prolonged depression that followed the Panic of 1873, mounted police charged into a demonstration of unemployed workers, dispersing it with great violence.

Antonio Pagan, a founder of the Tompkins Square Park Coalition who was elected to City Council in 1991, declared that "No one should have a God-given right to public property. The infamous minority creating havoc around Tompkins Square Park are living out their revolutionary fantasies." In June 1991 Mayor David Dinkins ordered police to remove the homeless and temporarily close the park.

Homeless advocates charged that Dinkins had adopted a "hard line" against the homeless. New York City's deputy mayor Bill Lynch denied the charges. Lynch said,

> we tried a number of things and then the realization came to us that we weren't going to get people out of the park, so we had to remove them from the park. Where the debate has to be is over the quality of the facilities that we provide for the homeless and not whether they can sleep in parks or on streets or in vacant lots. That is not an acceptable policy for the homeless or for the people who have to use the parks and streets.

Even after the homeless were removed from the park, the Tompkins Square area remained a center of homeless activism. In 1991 about 500 squatters were estimated to live in buildings in the neighborhood. The squatters denied that they were a threat to their neighbors and staged events such as a "Squatters Day parade" in October 1991 defending their right to shelter.

tramps The term *tramp* dates to the 1870s, when large numbers of wandering homeless men began to appear in American cities and towns, seeking employment, public relief or a handout. These were, for the most part, young, unmarried men, many of them immigrants to the United States. The social disruption of the Civil War, the resumption of large-scale immigration after the war and the economic Panic of 1873 and subsequent depression have all been cited as causes for the appearance of tramps in large numbers in the 1870s. The five-year depression that followed the Panic of 1873 left a million workers without work, with unemployment in some cities approaching 25 percent of the workforce. "Thousands of homeless men and women are to be seen nightly sleeping on the seats in our public parks, or walking the streets," reported a New York City labor newspaper. The tramp phenomenon was the cause of great concern among the better-off and more stable classes, particularly as tramps came to be associated with labor unrest and protest. Speaking in 1877 at a charity conference in Boston, Professor Francis Wayland of Yale University described the tramp as "a lazy, shiftless, incorrigible, cowardly, utterly depraved savage. . . . Having no moral sense, he knows no gradations in crime. . . . He has only one aim—to be supported in idleness." The reformer Henry George, writing in 1879, explained the tramps' appearance as the by-product of an industrial society in which the divisions between rich and poor were becoming ever more pronounced. "The 'tramp' comes with the locomotive, and almshouses and prisons are as surely the marks of 'material progress' as are costly dwellings, rich warehouses, and magnificent churches." An unemployed mechanic wrote a letter to the *National Labor Tribune* in 1875 describing his experiences:

Twelve months ago, left penniless by misfortune, I started from New York in search of employment. . . . During this year I have traversed seventeen states and obtained in that time six weeks' work. I have faced starvation; been months at a time without a bed, when the thermometer was 30 degrees below zero. Last winter I slept in the woods, and while honestly seeking employment I have been two and three days without food. When, in God's name, I

asked for something to keep body and soul together, I have been repulsed as a "tramp and vagabond."

Though scorned for their alleged unwillingness to work, tramps actually played a vital economic role as a mobile reserve labor force in late 19th-century America. Many were skilled artisans, such as carpenters, while the unskilled provided labor for seasonal industries such as agriculture and extractive industries such as lumbering. (See also MIGRATORY LABOR.)

transitional housing   Transitional housing is a form of shelter for homeless people, which is intended to give them a setting in which they can develop the skills necessary to move on to permanent housing. Transitional housing is usually a multifamily institituion, on a smaller scale than emergency shelters. A good example of a transitional housing program is the Westhelp program in Mount Vernon, New York, which is funded through a combination of county, state and federal money. Westhelp is part of the Housing Enterprise for the Less Privileged (HELP) program established by Andrew Cuomo. Westhelp runs a 46-unit complex providing shelter to homeless families in Westchester County. Families enrolled in the program are provided furnished apartments. They must agree to abide by strict rules, including being in by midnight, and are not permitted to have visitors in their apartments. The program provides recreation, day care, high school equivalency classes and classes on finding and keeping a home, among other activities. Those who move on to permanent apartments are visited by the program's social workers every three months during the first year and twice in the second year to check up on their progress. The cost of maintaining a family in the Westhelp program is cheaper than the cost of housing a family in a motel room, which is where most of Westchester County's homeless families are sent. Similar programs have been established in other New York communities, including Albany and Brooklyn.

trauma Life on the streets exposes the homeless to many threats to their health, including the dangers of accidents and assaults. Hospitals in major cities report seeing large numbers of homeless patients with stab wounds and other puncture wounds, burns, abrasions, bruises, fractures, concussions, dislocations, eye injuries and other trauma. Because of poor medical treatment and sanitation, even minor wounds suffered by homeless people can turn into major medical problems; an infected cut on the foot, for example, can turn gangrenous and require amputation of the foot.

Travelers Aid The Travelers Aid society is a nonprofit organization with national headquarters in Washington, D.C. whose local volunteers serve people who are in crisis due to homelessness or other disruptive circumstances. Travelers Aid was formed as a national organization in 1917, uniting local Travelers Aid societies, some of which could trace their origins back to the 1850s and the days of the western migration of the covered wagons. In the 1930s Travelers Aid societies helped transient unemployed workers; during World War II it provided services to the millions of military personnel who were crisscrossing the country; in the 1960s it initiated programs to help migrant workers and their families and also youthful runaways. In recent years local Travelers Aid societies have found that homelessness has become the primary cause that sends people to apply to them for aid. In 1988–89 local Travelers Aid agencies provided casework services to 210,948 people. Of these, 40 percent sought the aid of Travelers Aid either because they were homeless or because they were homeless and unemployed. Many local Travelers Aid societies have developed specialized programs to serve the homeless. Travelers Aid

in Tucson, for example, operates transitional apartments to ensure that evicted families or newcomers have a place to stay while they seek employment and permanent housing, while in Rhode Island the Travelers Aid society sponsors a runaway prevention program that provides homes with local host families for teenagers at risk of running away, allowing them time in a protected environment away from home to resolve conflicts with parents.

troll-busters See CRIME; LEGAL RIGHTS.

Truman, Harry S Harry S Truman was 33rd president of the United States. Truman had been selected by Franklin Delano Roosevelt as his running mate in the 1944 presidential election, and succeeded Roosevelt in the White House when Roosevelt died on April 12, 1945. Truman's attempts to continue the reform agenda of the NEW DEAL ran into heavy conservative opposition. The high point of Truman's "Fair Deal" legislative achievements came with the passage of the NATIONAL HOUSING ACT OF 1949. In general Truman's housing policies, which included new federal commitments to slum clearance and URBAN RENEWAL, increased the destruction of affordable housing in the cities and encouraged the flight of the white middle and working classes to the suburbs. Facing near certain defeat, Truman declined to run for reelection in 1952.

tuberculosis Among other health problems, homeless people have been affected by the spread of tuberculosis (TB). Once widespread in the United States, tuberculosis had been virtually eliminated until it began to appear again in the 1970s and 1980s. Tuberculosis is spread by a bacillus *Mycobacterium tuberculosis,* which can be carried in the air to new victims from the coughing or breath of an infected person. Tuberculosis causes coughing, fever, pleurisy, shortness of breath and weight loss, and in the past was often fatal.

In the 19th century, when the disease was popularly referred to as consumption, tuberculosis was often associated with poverty, as close, poorly ventilated living quarters facilitated the spread of the disease. Improved living conditions and the use of antibiotics to treat the disease led to a dramatic drop in its incidence. Yearly mortality from tuberculosis dropped from 200 per 100,000 people in the United States in 1900 to 10 per 100,000 by the mid-1950s. In the late 1970s, however, the decline in frequency of new cases began to slow, in part due to influx of refugees from Southeast Asia who had been exposed to disease before they came to this country.

In 1986 an increase in the number of TB cases was reported for the first time since national reporting on the disease started in 1953. Many of the new cases were found among the homeless population. The homeless are particularly vulnerable to the disease, due to their exposure to unsanitary and crowded living conditions in shelters, and malnutrition. A 1986 study showed that 1.6 to 6.8 percent of the homeless people selected had clinically active tuberculosis, 150 to 300 times the national average. Shelter staff members have also proven vulnerable to the increase in tuberculosis infection. In 1990 new cases of tuberculosis rose by more than 38 percent in New York City over the previous year's rate. According to a health department spokesman, 15 to 20 percent of the city's tuberculosis cases were found in the homeless population. African Americans, who make up 28.7 percent of the city's population in 1990, accounted for 58 percent of the tuberculosis cases. That year New York City began a program of testing all students entering the school system for the disease. The city also provides tuberculosis testing and treatment at homeless shelters, and maintains an 85-bed shelter for homeless tuberculosis patients.

Migrant laborers also have proven vulnerable to an increase in tuberculosis in recent years. A study of African-American migrant farm workers in eastern North Carolina, conducted in the late 1980s, showed a rate of tuberculosis infection 300 times the national average. The workers were often housed in crowded and dirty camps and had limited access to medical care.

turnaways See RUNAWAYS.

U

underclass The term underclass was originally used by academics studying poverty to refer to segments of the population that remained in conditions of deep poverty, even during periods of general economic expansion and a decline in the rate of unemployment. The underclass was considered to represent those suffering from the seemingly intractable joblessness caused by economic dislocation and were thought to be made up of largely, though not exclusively, racial minorities. The term was popularized by the 1982 book by Ken Auletta, *The Underclass*, and by articles in a range of popular newsmagazines. While originally a term that referred to the objective conditions of poverty and joblessness, gradually it was used to refer to the behavioral characteristics of the poor themselves, independent of economic conditions. That is, increasingly "underclass" became a term distinguishing behaviors such as unwed parenting, dependency on welfare, school dropout rates and crime from the behaviors of the middle class. Areas with high rates of such behaviors were sometimes designated as "underclass areas."

In recent years sociologists have been increasingly concerned about the misuse of the term and the value assumptions that sometimes underlie its usage. The concept tends to blur distinctions and leave unanalyzed the causal relations of economic structure, race, class and culture, thus allowing middle-class prejudices about the poor to be given a scientific veneer. The danger is that the focus of concern and action can become the behaviors of the poor rather than the economic conditions that create and shape those behaviors. Indeed, William Julius Wilson, past president of the American Sociological Association and a prominent social researcher who employed the term in two of his most well-known books, *The Declining Significance of Race* and *The Truly Disadvantaged*, announced in 1990 that he would no longer use the term *underclass* because of the tendency of others to misconstrue it.

underemployment See WORKING POOR.

Unemployed Councils In the early 1930s, as the United States sank into the pit of the GREAT DEPRESSION, 25 percent of the American work force was unemployed. In some industrial cities, such as Chicago, Detroit and Cleveland, the rate of unemployment reached 50 percent of the workforce or higher. Millions of other workers were reduced to part-time employment, or had to accept pay cuts as the price of continuing employment. Despite the mass scale of suffering, many of the unemployed blamed themselves for their own plight, lapsing into despair and apathy. But hundreds of thousands of the unemployed, through spontaneous acts of protest or under the leadership of various radical groups, sought collective solutions to economic hard times and built the most significant movement of the unemployed in American history.

The Communist Party played a key role in organizing the unemployed. Their efforts often met with a violent response from officials. On March 6, 1930 a nationwide protest organized by the Communists brought out hundreds of thousands of demonstrators in a score of cities demanding relief or jobs for the unemployed. The largest protest took place in New York City, where between 35,000 and 100,000 gathered in Union Square. When the crowd attempted to march on city hall, they were attacked by squads

of mounted police and dispersed. A Communist-led march of the unemployed on the Ford River Rouge plant in Dearborn, Michigan in March 1932 was turned back by police firing machine guns, with four of the marchers killed. Despite such attacks, the Unemployed Councils organized by Communists in many cities were often quite effective in gaining a measure of relief for the unemployed. In the early 1930s demonstrations by the Unemployed Councils at city halls and local welfare agencies were a common occurrence. The councils organized "gas squads" to turn back on utilities shut off for nonpayment. They also mobilized their supporters to block evictions. Two sociologists studying the black community in Chicago in the 1930s reported that when local residents received eviction notices, "it was not unusual for a mother to shout to the children, 'Run quick and find the Reds!' " The Communists also led two "hunger marches" of several thousand unemployed workers on Washington, D.C. in 1931 and 1932 demanding the passage of a bill providing unemployment insurance.

Although they enjoyed a measure of success, the Unemployed Councils were never able to develop a stable organizational base. Unemployed workers might join a single protest or help block an eviction, but generally drifted away from ongoing involvement in the work of the councils. The Communists contributed to the instability of the Unemployed Councils through their rigid political control of the movement, including their insistence that demonstrators "link" the issues of unemployment with others that most of the unemployed may have considered to be irrelevant, such as support for the Soviet Union's foreign policies. The Socialist Party and the "Musteites" (followers of the radical minister A.J. Muste) organized their own movements of the unemployed, which were less sectarian and violence-prone than the Communist Unemployed Councils. In 1936 the Communist- and Socialist-led unemployed organizations merged to form a new group, the Workers Alliance. By this time the NEW DEAL administration of Franklin Delano Roosevelt had initiated a number of programs, such as the Works Progress Administration (WPA), to provide relief and jobs for the unemployed. In the later 1930s the focus of the Workers Alliance shifted from local organizing to lobbying in Washington for increased WPA expenditures. In some cities the Workers Alliance also functioned as a kind of trade union of WPA workers. As the depression wound down in the late 1930s, the unemployed movement lost momentum: The Workers Alliance itself collapsed as a result of the signing of the Nazi-Soviet Pact, which divided the Socialists and Communists in the group's leadership. Apart from the short-term benefits the movement managed to win for individual unemployed workers, it also trained a number of organizers who would play important roles in the organization of the new industrial unions established in the late 1930s. The movement also helped to popularize the idea of unemployment insurance, which became part of the package of social welfare legislation passed in 1935 as the Social Security act. (See also BONUS ARMY; UNEMPLOYMENT.)

unemployment The loss of a job is often, but not always, the precipitating event causing an individual or family to become homeless. According to a 1989 Urban Institute report, most of the homeless have been unemployed longer than they have been homeless, with over half of those surveyed reporting that they had not held a steady job (defined as three months with the same employer) for more than two years. In the past, homelessness has always been associated with unemployment. In times of general economic distress, such as the Great Depression of the 1930s, when thousands of people lost their jobs, families were turned out of their homes and breadwinners went on the road in a search for new employment. But the correlation between the two social ills of

joblessness and homelessness is no longer as direct as it once was. From the 1970s through the 1990s unemployment rose and fell and then rose again, but the homeless problem continued to rise regardless. In fact, some homeless people are employed, but at wages that make it impossible for them to find housing for themselves and their families.

The term *unemployed* first came into wide usage in the United States during the depression of the 1870s. Carroll Wright, a pioneering labor statistician, defined the word in 1878 as meaning "out of work and seeking it." Before that time, as historian Alexander Keyssar has noted, the term often carried connotations of "sloth and willfull idleness." Unemployment has been a grim fact of life for wage-earners for much of American history. Recurrent "panics" and depressions in the 19th century (in 1819, 1837, 1857 and the mid-1870s, 1880s and 1890s) threw hundreds of thousands of workers out of work, sometimes for years on end. The impact of such periodic episodes of mass unemployment was heightened as the United States shifted from a primarily agricultural to a primarily industrial nation. Farming had its good and its bad years, but to the extent that it provided a subsistence livelihood, it shielded Americans from the full impact of business downturns. In the early 19th century many farmers were also part-time artisans, drawn into "putting out" system in rural New England. But by the late 19th century the American workforce had largely become one of wage-earners who had no other resources to fall back upon in hard times.

The 20th century brought no relief from the business cycle: There were brief but sharp economic downturns in 1907–8, 1913 and 1920–21. The "Coolidge prosperity" of the 1920s brought with it the illusion that the United States had reached a kind of permanent plateau of prosperity, but those illusions were dispelled at decade's end with the onset of the worst depression in U.S.

history. The Great Depression of the 1930s was finally brought to an end though heavy military expenditures in 1941, though its worst social effects were earlier relieved to an extent by the NEW DEAL programs set up under President Franklin Delano Roosevelt. Unlike most of Western Europe, where plans for state-sponsored unemployment insurance were established in the late 19th century, in the United States unemployed workers had to rely on their own resources, on a patchwork network of private relief agencies or on the meager benefits provided by some states and cities until the 1930s. The Great Depression swamped the resources of existing care providers. Families on relief in New York City in 1931–32 received only $2.39 a week, well below the minimum income necessary to sustain existence.

The plight of the unemployed was a major factor in the realignment of American party politics in the 1930s. For the next 30 years, Democrats ran against the memory of Herbert Hoover. With creation of the New Deal, which established unemployment insurance as part of the Social Security Act of 1935, Democrats emerged as the majority party for the first time in the 20th century.

Unemployment not only represents loss of income. Particularly for men in American culture, it also can deal a serious blow to self-esteem. Fragmentary evidence from the 19th century and sociological and psychological studies of the unemployed in 1930s revealed that prolonged unemployment resulted in depression, physical illness, alcoholism, loss of appetite, impotence, family abandonment, suicide and other ills. The hundreds of thousands who left or were forced from their homes in the 1930s for life on the road were sometimes motivated by hope of finding work elsewhere, but also by shame and the desire to flee the communities in which they had lost their jobs. Such feelings often led to broken families: A 1940 survey revealed that over 1.5 million women had been abandoned by their husbands during the Great Depression.

Unemployment peaked during the 1930s at 25 percent of workforce. For 25 years after American entry into World War II, the United States approached a condition of what economics textbooks called "full employment" with a "normal" unemployment rate of about 3 percent. The worst year for unemployment in the 1960s was 6.5 percent in 1961. For the remainder of the decade the number never exceeded 5.5 percent; it remained under 4 percent for four consecutive years from 1966 through 1969, fueled in part by Vietnam War spending. In the 1970s the unemployment rate crept upward, because of economic difficulties caused by the energy crisis and the long-term restructuring of the U.S. economy away from manufacturing to service sector industries. (Between 1960 and 1980 the percentage of the labor force employed in manufacturing dropped by 20 percent.)

When Ronald Reagan entered office in 1981, the unemployment rate stood at 7.4 percent. Unemployment rose steeply during the "Reagan recession" of 1981 to 1983, reaching 10.7 percent in 1982 and remaining in double digits for ten months in 1982–83. In the same period, the percentage of unemployed collecting unemployment insurance dropped to 25.8 percent, the lowest percentage in the history of the program, due to longer periods of joblessness and tighter eligiblity requirements introduced by the cost-cutting Reagan administration. The average duration of unemployment in the recession of 1973 to 1975 was 15 weeks; in 1983 it was 22 weeks. In 1985 the Reagan administration terminated the Federal Supplemental Compensation program, which had lengthened the amount of time the unemployed could collect benefits for an extra eight to 14 weeks. As a result, 340,000 unemployed workers lost their benefits.

Rates of minority unemployment have always been much higher than for the general population. This was true even during the boom years of the 1960s, when the African-American unemployment rate varied between 6.4 and 7.4 percent. In 1985 the jobless rate for whites was 5.9 percent; for blacks, 14.7 percent; and for black youth, 41.6 percent. One of the consequences of unemployment in the 1980s was an accelerated shift in population away from the industrial Northeast and Midwest to the nation's Sunbelt, in the South and Southwest. But migrants to the Sunbelt were often unsuccessful in their quest for new jobs, and many joined the ranks of the homeless as a result.

Unemployment was on the rise again in the early 1990s, approaching 7 percent at the end of 1991. In that year President George Bush twice vetoed bills that would have extended jobless benefits to 3 million unemployed Americans whose benefits had run out, asserting first that the recession had ended and then that the measure would increase the federal deficit. But in November 1991 Congress and the White House agreed on a measure extending benefits to the unemployed for between six and 20 weeks, depending on unemployment rates in individual states. (See also UNEMPLOYED COUNCILS.)

United Homeless Organization (UHO)

The United Homeless Organization (UHO) was founded in 1988 by Steve Riley, a homeless man. Riley enlisted homeless people on the soup lines near Grand Central Terminal in New York City in an effort to provide services to other homeless people. The UHO solicits donations of money and goods and distributes food, clothing, blankets and toiletries for the homeless in train terminals, bus stations and the World Trade Center. The UHO offers legal advice and referrals to make sure that the homeless know their rights and what benefits are available to them.

United Nations   See INTERNATIONAL YEAR OF SHELTER FOR THE HOMELESS.

United States Conference of Mayors

Since the mid-1980s the United States Conference of Mayors, headquartered in Washington, D.C., has issued an annual report on the status of hunger and homelessness in its member cities. This annual report is considered one of the most reliable sources of information on homeless issues. The mayors drafted a five-point plan, submitted to Congress in 1982, calling for emergency federal relief for the homeless. The request helped bring about in December 1982 the first congressional hearings on the problem of homelessness since the GREAT DEPRESSION. Five years later the U.S. Conference of Mayors played an important role in the passage of the Stewart B. McKinney Homeless Assistance Act. The conference has since lobbied for full funding for the act's programs. The conference also cosponsored the HEALTH CARE FOR THE HOMELESS PROGRAM with the Robert Wood Johnson Foundation and the Pew Charitable Trusts.

The Conference of Mayors' *Status Report on Hunger and Homelessness in America's Cities* for 1991 found that requests for emergency shelter had increased an average of 13 percent in the survey cities over the preceding year, that 15 percent of such requests were estimated to have gone unmet and that in three out of four cities homeless families and individuals are turned away from shelters due to lack of resources. Officials in nearly half the cities reported that public sentiment toward the homeless had grown increasingly negative over the preceding year. The report listed "the lack of affordable housing" as the leading cause of homelessness in the nation's cities. (See also MCKINNEY ACT.)

United Way of America   The United Way of America, with its national headquarters in Alexandria, Virginia, helps fund and coordinate local and national programs for the homeless, among many other concerns. The United Way has been a pioneer in the

field of volunteer fund-raising efforts, techniques that many other groups have emulated. The origins of the United Way can be traced to the late 19th century, when local charitable, social welfare and health organizations began to pool their fund-raising efforts rather than to compete with one another for philanthropic donors. One such effort in Cleveland, Ohio in 1913 set the model for other cities; the Cleveland Federation for Charity and Philanthropy developed a budget program to allot funds to participating agencies. Two dozen other communities developed similar plans in the next few years, and in 1918 what became the United Way of America was established in Chicago under the name of the American Association for Community Organization. It took the name United Way in 1970.

urban blight "Blight" is a term that has been used by urban planners, developers and urban renewal agencies to identify a set of land-use patterns considered worthy of redevelopment. Thus, a "blighted" area might include certain physical characteristics, such as structures in disrepair; environmental factors, such as noise, odors or dust; and a lack of certain community facilities, such as schools, playgrounds or adequate drainage facilities. The term has been generally used to mean the "substandard quality of structures," on land that could be put to "higher use." But rarely is there agreement on what standard is being brought to bear; thus it could be argued that the term *blight* is essentially a subjective value judgment rather than an agreed-upon set of physical, social or economic characteristics. (See also DISPLACEMENT; SLUM; URBAN RENEWAL.)

Urban Development Action Grant Program (UDAG) The Urban Development Action Grant Program was developed by the adminstration of President Jimmy Carter in 1977 to supply federal financial support for economic development projects in depressed urban areas. By spending one dollar of federal money, it was claimed that four dollars of private money could be leveraged. Critics charged that the program amounted to a welfare plan for rich commercial developers since it funded many luxury hotels and shopping malls in urban centers while displacing low- and moderate-income residents.

Urban Enterprise Zones The concept of the Urban Enterprise Zone was developed by the administration of President Ronald Reagan, who described it as his remedy for high levels of unemployment among urban blacks. Jack Kemp, secretary of the Department of Housing and Urban Development (HUD) in the George Bush administration, also viewed Urban Enterprise Zones as an important aspect of urban policy. The concept is based on using the market by relying primarily on private corporations, rather than federal funding, to solve urban problems. Generous tax incentives would induce corporations to invest capital, particularly manufacturing capital, in inner cities. These incentives would eliminate 75 percent or more of corporate income taxes and all capital gains taxes for companies that establish plants in inner-city areas. Initial proposals also called for a waiver of federal minimum wage laws for workers under 21 years of age, arguing that if the minimum wage were eliminated, corporations would have more of an incentive to hire the unemployed.

Urban Institute The Urban Institute was founded in 1968 as massive urban unrest and rebellion forced the problems of the urban poor onto the national agenda. Requested by Congress and encouraged by President Lyndon Baines Johnson, the institute was formed to mobilize intellectual resources against the social and economic problems facing U.S. cities. Its task was to evaluate the effectiveness of various courses of action and to develop solutions that might be put into practice nationally. Though the problems of the city remain a major focus of the institute's concerns, its research is not restricted to urban problems. Policy research at the Urban Institute is conducted in the areas of housing, welfare and poverty, employment and labor, transportation, immigration, program evaluation and management, simulation modeling of proposed policies as well as the application of U.S. models to less developed countries.

The Urban Institute sponsored the first nationally representative survey of homeless people and providers in large cities, published as Martha Burt and Barbara Cohen's *America's Homeless: Numbers, Characteristics, and Programs That Serve Them* (1989). This survey provided new estimates of the numbers of homeless people, their social characteristics and the state of their health, as well as information on local and state programs that provide emergency food and shelter to the homeless.

Though the studies conducted by researchers at the Urban Institute are widely regarded as unbiased and of high quality, the institute has sometimes been criticized for defining those social and economic problems that are primarily of concern to America's elite. Prominent policymaking elites on the governing board of trustees are part of the reason for such criticism, while the fact that half of the approximately $12 million yearly budget is provided by private and corporate grants probably accounts for the rest. Such grants are awarded either to support specific research projects on domestic policy questions or to provide general support to the institute. In addition, the institute conducts contract research for individual state governments, departments of the U.S. government and various international bodies.

urban renewal   Mandated by the NA-TIONAL HOUSING ACT OF 1949 (and revised in 1954), the federal government began a massive and somewhat controversial pro-

gram of urban renewal in the 1950s to rebuild large portions of America's deteriorating cities. Attention to cities had waned in the two decades prior to the program, as the Great Depression and World War II prevented investment in aging housing stock. The urban renewal program transformed the downtown areas of most American cities.

Proposals to the federal government for urban renewal projects were initiated at the local level by municipal authorities and developers. Two-thirds of the cost of the program was borne by the federal government. Commercial and financial interests tended to support urban renewal because they viewed renewal areas as providing a buffer against the expansion of slums and as a "magnet" attracting retail trade.

The program essentially provided for the use of public funds to buy, clear and improve renewal sites, after which landownership would revert to the private sector. Though urban renewal rebuilt deteriorating central city retail districts and improved "blighted" neighborhoods, in the first decade of the programs large numbers of low-income families were displaced without adequate provision for their relocation. Under the political authority of eminent domain, 250,000 families were evicted every year with compensation averaging $80 per family. With no requirement that low-cost housing be provided on the renewal site, low-income residents were generally replaced by middle- and upper-middle-class groups. Often vibrant, well-functioning communities were destroyed and cohesive ethnic subcultures were dispersed after having their neighborhoods labeled "slums" by urban renewal planners. Urban renewal sometimes generated vigorous collective resistance by neighborhood groups in an effort to preserve their neighborhoods, and these movements had a positive impact on later urban renewal policies. (See also DISPLACEMENT; EVICTION; URBAN BLIGHT.)

V

vagrancy Vagrancy is defined in *Black's Law Dictionary* as "the act of going about from place to place by a person without visible means of support, who is idle, and who, though able to work for his or her maintenance, refuses to do so, but lives without labor or on the charity of others." Laws against vagrancy or idleness have existed since the time of ancient Athens, if not earlier. The British poor laws were attempts to control the wandering of the poor as well as to provide a minimal level of support for the needy. In the United States, vagrancy laws vary considerably from state to state and city to city. Police have often used such laws to punish people who, while not having committed a crime, are considered socially undesirable. In 1960 over half of all arrests made in the United States were for vagrancy, disorderly conduct and public drunkenness. Prostitutes, alcoholics and members of racial minorities found in the wrong part of town have all been rounded up under vagrancy statutes. The homeless have also been targets of the enforcement of vagrancy laws. The courts have erected some barriers to the overzealous application of vagrancy laws. In *Papachristou v. City of Jacksonville* in 1972, the U.S. Supreme Court declared the Jacksonville, Florida vagrancy ordinance unconstitutional because of its vagueness. The Jacksonville statute defined vagrants as, among other things, "persons wandering or strolling around from place to place without any lawful purpose or object. . . . " Justice William O. Douglas, author of the Supreme Court's decision in the case, declared "Persons 'wandering or strolling' from place to place have been extolled by Walt Whitman and Vachel Lindsay. The qualification 'without any lawful purpose or object' may be a trap for innocent acts."

Vallone, Peter F. See NEW YORK CITY, NEW YORK; SHELTERS.

veterans Veterans are estimated to make up between a third and a half of the male homeless population in the United States. Anywhere from 150,000 to 250,000 veterans are homeless on any given night, according to estimates by the Department of Veterans Affairs (VA), and twice that number may be homeless in the course of a year.

Homeless veterans are nothing new. Veterans of American wars have been a visible component of unemployed and homeless populations during previous times of economic distress. The problems of World War I veterans were dramatized by the BONUS ARMY encampment in Washington, D.C. in 1932. World War II veterans had fewer difficulties, enjoying the generous support of the GI bill, which provided low-cost mortgages and other benefits, and returning to their civilian lives in a time of unprecedented prosperity and economic growth. Many Vietnam veterans have displayed serious readjustment problems to civilian life. As a group they were drawn from lower socioeconomic groups than in past wars. They felt that they were not honored by their communities for their service in an unpopular war. Many suffered from post-traumatic stress disorder or other mental or physical problems connected with their time in the service. Many of them became drug abusers, sometimes picking up the habit while in service in Vietnam.

An outreach program run by the VA interviewed 7,800 homeless veterans in 1987. The survey revealed that 31 percent of the homeless veterans had combat experience, 1.7 percent had been prisoners of war, 37.8 percent had served during Vietnam era and 86 percent had symptoms of mental illness. According to other studies, 50 to 60 percent of homeless veterans are drug or alcohol abusers.

A number of specialized programs have been organized in recent years to provide shelter and services to homeless veterans. The New England Shelter for Homeless Veterans, set up in 1989 in Boston, offers beds, counseling and a familiar military atmosphere. (The 200 men who sleep in the shelter are organized into "squads" and "platoons.") A group called Vietnam Veterans of San Diego is using a federal grant to convert an abandoned motel into a temporary home for veterans. The group also sponsors an annual "Standdown" encampment on the grounds of a San Diego high school. In 1990 about 700 homeless veterans took part in the three-day encampment, where they could receive medical care, apply for food stamps and appear before a municipal judge to dispose of outstanding misdemeanor warrants. Groups working with homeless veterans around the country have formed a confederation called the National Coalition of Homeless Veterans Service Providers, with affiliates in 39 cities.

In a time when public sentiment has turned against the homeless in many communities, homeless veterans still receive considerable sympathy, Robert Van Keuren, director of Vietnam Veterans of San Diego, said in 1991. "People all over the country are saying, 'My God, how could we have so many people who served our country out on the streets?' "

Vietnam Veterans of San Diego   See VETERANS.

Vingara et al. v. Borough of Wrightstown   *Vingara et al. v. Borough of Wrightstown* was a lawsuit that in 1987 successfully challenged a municipal ordinance in Wrightstown, New Jersey restricting motel stays by homeless families to 30 days. The ordinance was used as a device to keep homeless children out of the Wrightstown public schools. (See also EDUCATION; LEGAL RIGHTS.)

Volunteers in Service to America (VISTA)   Under the amended Domestic Volunteer Service Act of 1983, Volunteers in Service to America (VISTA), the federal volunteer program, was authorized to provide its workers to homeless-related projects.

Volunteers of America   Volunteers of America, with national headquarters in Metairie, Louisiana, operates more than 400 local programs for the homeless, the elderly, alcoholics and drug users. The organization was founded in New York City in 1896 by Maud and Ballington Booth, daughter-in-law and son of William Booth, the founder of the Salvation Army. After breaking with Booth, they founded an organization that was in many ways similar to the Salvation Army, with its own paramilitary structure, ranks and terminology, but one that incorporated more democratic control in its structure, including an elected leader. Like the Salvation Army, the Volunteers of America combine religious evangelicalism with services to the poor, including shelters for the homeless, and food and clothing distribution. In the 1960s the Volunteers of America built more than 20 senior citizen housing complexes, and other housing for low- and middle-income families, in one of the largest nonprofit housing programs in the nation. The Volunteers of America also sponsors daycare centers, programs for the handicapped, aid to released prisoners programs and rehabilitation programs for alcoholics.

voting   Although the right to vote is considered one of the most fundamental legal rights enjoyed by American citizens, the homeless are often are denied the right to vote. Court decisions in the District of Columbia, New Jersey, New York and California have upheld the right of local homeless people to register and vote, but many communities and states still require potential registrants to list a "residence" in order to be allowed to vote. In some communities all that is required to register to vote is a mailing address (which can be a post office box, or in care of a shelter or a workplace), or a street address (which can be the intersection of two streets, where homeless people camp or live in a car). The National Coalition for the Homeless undertook a voter registration project, "You Don't Need a Home to Vote," for the 1992 elections. In 1992 Illinois became the first state in the nation to pass a law guaranteeing homeless people the right to vote. Under the law, a homeless person may vote if he or she has two forms of identification, and a mailing address, such as a shelter.

vouchers The voucher system, administered by the Department of Housing and Urban Development (HUD), is the only housing program created by the administration of President Ronald Reagan. Like the existing SECTION 8 program, vouchers enable qualified low-income renters to rent apartments from private landlords. Unlike the Section 8 program, there is no requirement that the apartment rent for the "fair market" rent. The HUD voucher supplies the difference between 30 percent of the tenant's income and what is judged to be the fair market rent. (The tenant must make up any difference between the fair market and the actual rent.) The program assumes that there is no shortage of housing, only that people are unable to pay for it. Thus it creates no new low-income housing units while the number of low-income housing units constructed or renovated in the United States declined from 203,113 units in 1979 to 55,120 in 1983, according to HUD. One study in New York City revealed that nearly half of all voucher recipients returned them to local housing authorities because they could not find rental units they could afford even with the vouchers.

W

Wackstein, Nancy G. Nancy G. Wackstein was director of the Mayor's Office on Homelessness and Single-Room-Occupancy Housing Services in Mayor David Dinkins' administration in New York City, until she resigned the post in frustration. In 1987, when Dinkins was a mayoral candidate, Wackstein wrote a report entitled "A Shelter Is Not a Home" which criticized the homeless policies of the administration of Mayor Edward Koch. The report called for closing down large CONGREGATE SHELTERS and ending the use of WELFARE HOTELS to shelter families. Attempts to carry out these policies ran into difficulties soon after Dinkins took office in 1990, because of the city's fiscal crisis. After initially reducing the number of families in welfare hotels, the city's Human Resources Administration was forced to increase use of such shelters in 1991, due to the fiscal crisis. As spokeswoman for the mayor's homeless policies, Wackstein came under heavy criticism from homeless advocates. Finally in September 1991 she resigned her position declaring: "It is a reasonable thing to say that I have been frustrated. We cannot go on with the homeless family system the way we have. We have to look at what the folks really need. They need social services. It's a mistake to think that a shelter is the answer." Upon her resignation, Wackstein took on a new position as executive director of the Lenox Hill Neighborhood Association, a settlement house on the Upper East Side of Manhattan that provides social services for homeless people in the neighborhood.

Wagner, Robert See NATIONAL HOUSING CONFERENCE; NEW DEAL.

war on poverty The "war on poverty" was an ambitious set of federal programs launched in the mid-1960s, designed to eliminate the conditions that kept millions of Americans in economic distress. In the late 1950s and early 1960s Americans for the first time since the Great Depression began to express concern about the issue of poverty in the United States. Unlike the 1930s, with its massive unemployment and homelessness, the issue of poverty in the early 1960s was thought of largely as one of bringing the remaining minority of the underprivileged into the mainstream of American prosperity. Economist John Kenneth Galbraith's 1958 book, *The Affluent Society*, referred to the existence of "insular poverty" in such places as the poor mining communities of West Virginia. Michael Harrington's 1962 book, *The Other America: Poverty in the United States*, argued that the poor, while a minority, were actually a much larger group than most middle-class Americans assumed. He estimated that the size of the poor population in the United States was between 40 and 50 million. Borrowing a concept from anthropologist Oscar Lewis, he argued that the poor were bound to their condition by a "culture of poverty." Without the assistance of government programs, most poor people would be unable to rise out of poverty through the time-honored means of pulling themselves up by their own bootstraps. "The other Americans," Harrington argued, "are those who . . . are so submerged in their poverty that one cannot begin to talk about free choice." Harrington's book came to the attention of several key advisors in the administration of President John F. Kennedy. Kennedy, largely preoccupied with foreign policy issues, succeeded in winning congressional passage of only a few initiatives on behalf of the nation's poor, such as a pilot food stamp program and a manpower development and training program. His administration also launched a number of programs to combat urban juvenile delinquency. These programs, relying heavily on organizing "community action" programs, would have a significant influence on the shape of antipoverty efforts later in the 1960s.

Kennedy had been considering an antipoverty program in the fall of 1963. After his assassination in November, several of his advisors with backgrounds in the juvenile delinquency programs approached the new president, Lyndon Johnson, with a proposal for an experimental antipoverty program.

Johnson transformed their limited plans into a much more ambitious effort. In his State of the Union address in January 1964, Johnson called for an "unconditional war on poverty in America." In his commitment to reform, Johnson was spurred to action by the civil rights movement, which was gaining impressive political victories from 1963 to 1965 in campaigns in Birmingham and Selma, Alabama and in the Mississippi Delta. Johnson responded by proposing and winning congressional passage of the Civil Rights Act of 1964 and the Voting Rights Act of 1965. Johnson, who had come to Washington, D.C. as a congressional aide during the New Deal, wanted to win a place in American history similar to that of his early hero Franklin Delano Roosevelt.

Johnson's war on poverty, which won congressional approval in August 1964, consisted of a variety of programs designed to train individuals to take advantage of the economic opportunities provided by an expanding economy (including the Job Corps, the Neighborhood Youth Corps, Work-Study Programs, Operation Head Start and the Elementary and Secondary Education Act). More controversial were programs intended to organize and empower the poor ("maximum feasible participation" of the poor was the term used). Community Action Agencies and later the Model Cities program were part of this effort. Medical insurance for the elderly (Medicare), for the poor (Medicaid) and an expanded FOOD STAMPS program were also part of Johnson's strategy to end poverty.

Unlike the New Deal, where Roosevelt had been careful to design programs to provide equivalent benefits to both the cities and the countryside (in order to appeal to congressmen from rural constituencies), the war on poverty's emphasis was on the cities. Johnson's special concern for the problems of urban America led to creation of the Cabinet-level Department of Housing and Urban Development (HUD) in November 1965. HUD was designed to be the principal federal agency responsible for programs concerned with housing needs, fair housing opportunities and improving and developing communities. Over the next few years Johnson pushed a variety of housing measures designed to benefit low- and moderate-income families through Congress. The Housing and Urban Development Act of 1965 provided funding for 240,000 units of low-income housing and authorized spending $2.9 billion over four years for urban renewal projects. In 1966 Congress passed a program of federal rent supplements for low-income families. Johnson declared at the signing of this measure that "While every man's house cannot be a castle, it need not be a hovel." The Model Cities program, established in 1966, sought to concentrate and coordinate diverse federal programs to benefit some of the poorest urban neighborhoods in the country. Under the program, housing for the urban poor would be part of a comprehensive effort to improve social and material conditions in poverty-stricken neighborhoods. The Housing and Urban Development Act of 1968 reaffirmed the goal of the 1949 National Housing Act of guaranteeing "a decent home and a suitable living environment for every American family." To attain this goal, the act set a target of constructing 26 million new and rehabilitated units over the next ten years, with six million of the units designed for low- and moderate-income households.

Johnson's war on poverty soon ran into serious difficulties. Its hastily drafted legislation and hastily organized programs led to some instances of waste and corruption. Conservative critics attacked the "poverty pimps" and "welfare queens" allegedly exploiting the taxpayers. Model Cities funds, controlled by city mayors, were sometimes used to benefit nonslum neighborhoods, setting off power struggles between local officials and HUD administrators. The "Long Hot Summers" of ghetto rioting in the mid-1960s sparked a white backlash against the civil rights movement. This backlash spilled over into hostility to Johnson's programs, which were popularly perceived as mainly benefitting urban blacks. The Vietnam war distracted Johnson's attention from his domestic programs and drained funds from the war on poverty. Richard Nixon was one of the political beneficiaries of popular disenchantment with the war on poverty, defeating Johnson's chosen successor, Vice President Hubert Humphrey, in the 1968 presidential election.

When Nixon came into office he cut back on many war on poverty programs, eliminating the Model Cities program and the Office of Economic Opportunity. But he maintained and even expanded other programs in the 1970s (in particular overseeing the expansion of AID TO FAMILIES WITH DEPENDENT CHILDREN [AFDC], from 4.4 million recipients in 1965 to 11 million in 1973). In housing, the Nixon administration saw fulfillment of some of the goals set by the Housing and Urban Development Act of 1968. Subsidized housing starts, including new and rehabilitated buildings, jumped from under 163,000 in 1969 to over 384,000 in 1970, though they dropped off dramatically in Nixon's troubled second term in office. The levels of subsidized housing starts rose again under President Jimmy Carter in the late 1970s, before being heavily cut by the administration of President Ronald Reagan in the 1980s.

In the end, Johnson's war on poverty achieved a mixed record of success and failure. Programs such as Medicare, Medicaid and the Women with Infants and Children (WIC) nutritional program improved the health and reduced the level of hunger and infant mortality among the poor, while Operation Head Start improved the educational records of poor children. The nation's overall poverty level declined dramatically, although the general prosperity of the 1960s contributed to that change. Between 1962 and 1969 the number of people living below the POVERTY LINE dropped by 2 million each year, from roughly 40 million to 25 million in the course of the decade, from 19 percent of the population to 12.5 percent of the population. But the failure of some war on poverty programs, especially those concerned with "community action," led to a popular disapproval all welfare programs. The conventional wisdom in Washington after the 1960s became "You can't solve problems by throwing money at them," an attitude that contributed to Ronald Reagan's election in 1980 on an antiwelfare spending program. In the aftermath of the spring 1992 riots in Los Angeles, President Bush's spokesman, Marlin Fitzwater, declared, "We believe that many of the root problems that have resulted in inner-city difficulties were started in the 60's and 70's, and that they have failed." The Great Society programs, according to the White House, had actually worsened problems of inner-city poverty and other social problems. Defenders of social welfare programs charged that the Republicans, who had been in power for the past dozen years, were engaging in election-year politics when they attacked the legacy of the Great Society.

Washington, D.C. Estimates of the number of homeless persons in the nation's capital range from 10,000 to 18,000. Most are African Americans in a city where African Americans make up nearly 70 percent of the population. The primary cause of homelessness in Washington, D.C. is the shortage of low-income housing in a city with a high rate of unemployment and inadequate social benefits for the poor and for the mentally disabled. Between 1970 and 1980 the District of Columbia lost over 25,000 units of rental housing as a result of conversion, abandonment and demolition, and rents for existing apartments increased by almost 50 percent during the same period. In 1986 there were over 11,000 families waiting for public housing and housing assistance, and the wait was expected to be seven years long.

Many Washington, D.C. neighborhoods have experienced GENTRIFICATION. In the course of two decades Washington has become a major convention site, while it continues to draw many young urban professionals to stock high-status white-collar occupations in government, law and the lobbying industry. Most of the newcomers have been white, while most of those displaced have been African American. As in other cities that have experienced a measure of gentrification, condominium conversions lead to displacement and increased rental costs resulting from a decrease in the supply of rental units. Though there were less than 1,000 condominium units in the metropolitan area in 1970, by July of 1981 there were almost 95,000 condominium units.

In 1987 there were approximately 2,500 beds available for the homeless, but at the time the city's largest shelter was turning away an average of 50 people per day. There are approximately 30 shelters in Washington, with 70 percent allocated to single men, 15 percent to single women and 15 percent to families. Church-affiliated missions run most of the shelters for men; the city funds two men's shelters and one women's shelter. In 1990 voters in Washington repealed a law guaranteeing homeless people the right to shelter. The length of stay permitted the homeless in public shelters is now limited to 30 days for single people and 90 days for families. Voluntary organizations, many church-affiliated, run drop-in centers and soup kitchens for the homeless population, while the Coalition for the Homeless has been active organizing for rent control and rent subsidies in addition to lobbying and maintaining several centers for the homeless. The advocacy group best known nationally for its activities on behalf of the homeless is the Community for Creative Non-Violence, based in Washington, D.C. This group, led by activist Mitch Snyder until his death in 1990, has made headlines throughout the country for its dramatic non-violent protest activities.

Watt, James G.   See HUD.

Weaver, Robert C.   See HUD.

WE CAN program   See BOTTLE AND CAN REDEMPTION.

welfare hotels   Families receiving AID TO FAMILIES WITH DEPENDENT CHILDREN (AFDC) payments are also eligible for federally funded emergency assistance (EA). A number of states use EA programs to pay for providing temporary shelter to homeless families in hotels, motels and similar accommodations. These are often referred to as "welfare hotels." They are an expensive alternative to conventional housing. In New York City the Martinique Hotel charged rates of $34 to $41 a night for a family of four; monthly costs for a family of six ran as high as $3,000, or much more than it would cost to keep a family housed in public housing or even in a private apartment, were such apartments and the funds to pay the rent for them available. The owners of the Martinique Hotel received $8 million from the City of New York in 1985 for housing about 400 families. These welfare hotels have many problems, as they are not designed to house families with children for extended periods. They lack facilities for food storage and preparation, among other amenities. They are often located in neighborhoods where prostitution and drug abuse are common and are often in deteriorating condition.

Jonathon Kozol interviewed a number of families living in the Martinique for his book *Rachel and Her Children: Homeless Families in America* (1988). The children living in the hotel were surrounded by crime and chaos. "Last week a drug addict tried to stab me," one 12-year old child told Kozol. "With an ice pick. Tried to stab my mother too. Older girls was botherin' us. They try to make us fight." And a child in a neighboring apartment, six-years old, reported, "Those girls upstairs on the ninth floor, they be

bad. They sellin' crack." A 12-year-old girl named Yvette Diaz, in testimony before the House Select Committee on Children, Youth and Families in 1987, offered this portrait of life in the Martinique:

> We can't cook in the apartment. My mother sneaked a hot plate in, because we don't have enough money to eat out every night. They, the hotel, warned us that if we are caught cooking in the rooms, we could be sent to a shelter. I play in the hallways with my friends from other rooms on the floor. Sometimes, even this isn't safe. A boy, about fifteen or sixteen, came over to me and wanted to take me up to the sixteenth floor. I got frightened and ran into my room and told my mother. She went to the police and she was told this same boy was showing his private parts to girls before, and that it was reported to them. If he bothered me again, I was to tell the police. The five of us live in two rooms at this hotel.

Given such conditions, welfare hotels have not proven an effective form of TRANSITIONAL HOUSING to move people from homelessness to permanent housing. In response to a suit by the Legal Aid Society's Homeless Family Rights Project, New York City agreed in 1988 to stop putting homeless families in welfare hotels by the summer of 1990. The deadline passed without effect; in fact, the city increased the number of families it placed in welfare hotels. (See also CHILDREN.)

Westhelp program   See TRANSITIONAL HOUSING.

Wiley, George   See NATIONAL WELFARE RIGHTS ORGANIZATION (NWRO).

women   The presence of a significant proportion of women among today's homeless population is a new and disturbing trend. In 1958 a study estimated that no more than 3 percent of the nation's SKID ROW population were women. Currently at least 25 percent of homeless people are women. Women and children together comprise nearly 40 percent

Mental Health Indicators of Homeless Single Women with Children Versus Other Homeless Adults

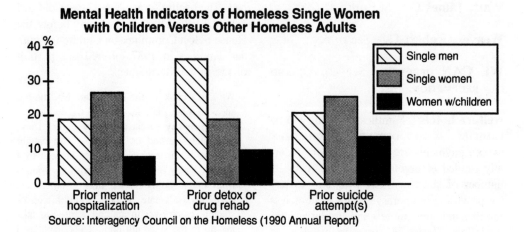

Source: Interagency Council on the Homeless (1990 Annual Report)

of the total homeless population. Women are in general overrepresented among the ranks of the poor. A 1990 study by the Low Income Housing Coalition's Women and Housing Task Force confirmed the Census Bureau's statistics that more than two-thirds of all poor—hence at risk of becoming homeless—households in the United States are maintained by women.

The economic status of women has changed dramatically and in several important ways in recent decades. More and more women have joined the workforce. In 1960 there were 22 million female workers, comprising about one-third of the workforce. By 1985 there were 47 million female workers, comprising 44 percent of all employees. The increase has included women with children as well as childless women. In 1950 only about a fifth of all women with children were in the labor force. By 1985, 68 percent of all mothers of children in the six- to 17-year range were employed, as were just over half of those with children under the age of six.

At the same time, more and more women have become poor. Between 1969 and 1985 a substantial increase occurred in the numbers of those living below the poverty line in families headed by women (from 10.4 million to 16.4 million). Every year between 1969 and 1978, 100,000 additional women

with children fell below the poverty rate. In 1982 two of every three poor adults were women. Women headed over half of all poor families. Social scientists have termed this phenomenon the "feminization of poverty." The facts that increasing numbers of women are in the workforce and that increasing numbers of women are in poverty are not as contradictory as may seem the case at first glance. Despite the attention paid in the media to female lawyers, stockbrokers, coalminers and other pioneers in traditionally male occupations, the continuing strength of occupational sex segregation means that women continue to find the readiest employment in low-paying service sector, clerical or light manufacturing jobs. Women on average earn only about three-fifths of what men earn. The decline in American manufacturing has led to a steady reduction in well-paying blue-collar jobs. Women have entered the job market to supplement the uncertain earnings of their spouses or, increasingly, to replace those earnings as best they can. Thus more women are entering the labor force at a time when the number of well-paying jobs available for all workers has been decreasing. Increasing rates of divorce, male desertion and unmarried women having children on their own (including a sharp increase in the pregnancy rate of unmarried teenage girls), have left many women the sole support of their children. Eighty-five percent of all American women can expect to support themselves, as a result of divorce, separation or death, at some point in their lives. More than one third of divorced fathers pay nothing toward child support. These factors, combined with the low wages and insecurity of women's jobs, and exacerbated by cutbacks in spending on social programs in the 1980s under President Ronald Reagan, have left many women and their children at risk of losing their housing in an increasingly expensive housing market.

Homeless women differ from homeless men in a number of ways. They seem to be less transient, less likely to be substance abusers and more likely to remain part of family units. They also tend to have been homeless for shorter periods on average than men. As with homeless men, there are many different subgroups among the population of homeless women.

One large group of homeless women are mothers caring for dependent children. More than half of homeless families are single-parent units, generally female-headed. In a study of homeless families in Boston, 80 homeless mothers and 151 children living in family shelters were interviewed. With a median age of 27 years, 45 percent of the women were single and another 45 percent were separated, divorced or widowed. Each mother had an average of 2.4 children. Nine out of ten of the mothers received AID TO FAMILIES WITH DEPENDENT CHILDREN (AFDC). Most cited eviction, nonpayment of rent, overcrowding and housing conversion as their primary reasons for homelessness. Abuse by male partners is also a significant cause of homelessness among women. A survey of homeless women in Portland, Oregon revealed that two-thirds of the women reported having been abused at some point in their lives. About one-third explained their current homelessness as the result of their escape of an abusive relationship.

A study by the Health Care for the Homeless Program indicates that roughly one third of homeless mothers suffer from some psychiatric impairment and one in five is a substance abuser. One common stereotype of the homeless is that of the "bag lady." Bag ladies are older women who live on the street and carry all their possessions with them in plastic bags or shopping carts. Often they display bizarre personal behavior. But such behavior is not always the product of mental illness. A 1979 study of bag ladies argued that some of the negative characteristics associated with them, such as poor personal hygiene or verbal abusiveness, could be understood as a conscious defense mechanism against sexual or other assault on the streets. The incidence of rape in the homeless population is estimated to be 20 times higher than for the rest of the population. In a nine-month period in 1983 in San Francisco, homeless women made up 9 percent of all adults treated as sexual assault victims.

The Women's Institute for Housing and Economic Development The Women's Institute for Housing and Economic Development, based in Boston, provides expertise in housing and business development to grassroots women's organizations and other service groups that recognize the need to provide housing and economic self-sufficiency opportunities for low-income women and their children.

Workfare In the 1980s many proposals surfaced for so-called workfare programs, which would link individual eligibility for social welfare benefits to the willingness of the recipient to accept employment in the private or public sector. Advocates of workfare contend that it will discourage those who are not truly in need from applying for public assistance, that it will reduce the cost of public assistance and that it will provide those enrolled in the program with needed skills and enhance their employability. Opponents deny the validity of these arguments and contend that workfare will serve only to stigmatize the poor. An early experiment with workfare took place in California when Ronald Reagan was governor. Subsequent studies showed that there was no decline in county welfare rolls during the years of the Reagan-initiated workfare program. Workfare requirements have begun to appear in such programs as Aid to Families with Dependent Children (AFDC) and in some homeless shelter programs. During the 1980s both conservatives, such as California governor George Deukmejian, and liberals, such as Massachusetts governor Michael Dukakis, proposed workfare programs.

workhouses   Workhouses appeared in Britain in the 17th century as a solution to the problem of VAGRANCY. The Elizabethan poor laws required able-bodied vagrants to be sent to workhouses, where they were provided shelter and sometimes small wages in exchange for industrial or agricultural work. Workhouses were sometimes referred to as beggar houses, almshouses, or labor colonies. The institution spread to the New World, and the first workhouse was established in New York City in 1735.

working poor   According to the official definition, the "working poor are people who work at least 27 weeks of the year, but have family incomes below the POVERTY LINE." It has been estimated that one-third of all homeless adults work full or part time. Over the last decade industries that once provided stable employment at a living wage have reduced their workforces and closed aging factories, eliminating over 850,000 jobs. Though even more jobs have been created, they have been in industries that are non-union and thus pay less, provide fewer benefits and more frequently than before offer only part-time employment. Thus the numbers of "working poor" have increased substantially as the economy has been restructured and unions have declined. According to the Center on Budget and Policy

Priorities in Washington, the number of workers whose incomes fell below the poverty level ($12,675 for a family of four in 1990 and $14,335 in 1992) has increased by 28 percent since 1978.

The working poor have a distinct set of problems, frequently earning too much to be eligible for limited welfare benefits, such as Medicaid or FOOD STAMPS, while working for companies that provide no employee medical benefits. A poverty-line income is not eligible for Medicaid in 33 states, and 37 million working Americans have no health insurance whatsoever. One serious illness for a worker without health insurance can make it impossible for a family with one working adult to pay rent, placing all family members in immediate danger of homelessness. In recent years administrators of food banks and soup kitchens have reported an increase in the number of working people forced to rely on charity to survive. The working poor are thought to be a large portion of those who avoid homelessness by living "doubled up" in the homes of relatives and friends. (See also DOUBLING UP; MINIMUM WAGE.)

Y

youth   See CHILDREN.

yuppies   See GENTRIFICATION.

Z

zoning   Zoning is the division of a community into districts for the purpose of controlling and directing the use of properties within those districts. It is a basic tool of urban planning. Zoning is concerned with such questions as the use of land and buildings, the density of population, and the height and bulk of buildings. In many towns and cities municipally elected or appointed zoning boards are given the power to divide communities into districts for specified uses, such as residential, commercial or industrial. Specific requirements also may be set for the kind of housing or other buildings that can be erected in a given zone. New York City was the first American community to adopt zoning ordinances that districted an entire city.

The official uses of zoning are to conserve the value of property, to insure orderly community growth and to safeguard the general public welfare. Zoning also has sometimes been used to enforce social distinctions. In some communities before World War I, zoning mandated residential segregation, with some blocks reserved for whites and others for racial minorities. In *Buchanan v. Warley* in 1917 the U.S. Supreme Court ruled that this kind of zoning was unconstitutional. In more subtle ways, zoning can still be used to separate races or classes. For example, zoning restrictions that exclude multifamily housing units or set a minimum lot size can eliminate the possibility of providing affordable housing to low- and moderate-income people in some neighborhoods. Zoning ordinances also have been used in some cities to drive out the local homeless population.

APPENDIX I
GROUPS AND RESOURCES FOR
THE HOMELESS

Resources

American Affordable Housing Institute
P.O. Box 118
New Brunswick, NJ 08903

American Bar Association Commission on
  Homelessness and Poverty
1800 M Street, NW
Washington, DC 20036
(202) 331-2291

American Institute of Architects
1735 New York Avenue, NW
Washington, DC 20006
(202) 626-7468

American Public Welfare Association
810 First Street, NE
Suite 500
Washington, DC 20002
(202) 682-0100

American Red Cross
17th & D Streets, NW
Washington, DC 20006
(202) 639-3610

Arizona Coalition for the Homeless
  Community Housing Partnership
P.O. Box 25312
Phoenix, AZ 85002
(602) 253-6905

Arlington/Alexandria Coalition for the
  Homeless
3103 N. 9th Road
Arlington, VA 22201
(703) 525-7177

Association of Community Organizations
  for Reform Now (ACORN)
522 8th Street, SE
Washington, DC 20003
(202) 547-9292

Bread for the World
802 Rhode Island Avenue, NE
Washington, DC 20018
(202) 269-0200

California Homeless and Housing Coalition
1010 South Flower, Suite 500
Los Angeles, CA 90015
(213) 746-7690

Cartoonists' Homeless Project
c/o Senator David Roberti
6150 Van Nuys Blvd., Suite 400
Van Nuys, CA 91401
818-901-5588

Catholic Charities USA
1319 F Street, NW
4th Floor
Washington, DC 20004
(202) 639-8400

Center for Policy Alternatives
1875 Connecticut Avenue, NW
Suite 710
Washington, DC 20009
(202) 387-6030

Center on Budget and Policy Priorities
236 Massachusetts Avenue, NE
Suite 305
Washington, DC 20002
(202) 408-1080

Chicago Coalition for the Homeless
P.O. Box 2751
Chicago, IL 60690
(312) 435-4548

Child Welfare League of America, Inc.
440 First Street, NW
Suite 310
Washington, DC 20001-2085
(202) 638-2952

Children's Defense Fund
25 E Street, NW
Washington, DC 20001
(202) 628-8787

Coalition for the Homeless
500 Eighth Avenue
Room 510
New York, NY 10018
(212) 695-8700

Coalition for the Homeless for Central
  Florida
P.O. Box 482
Orlando, FL 32802
(407) 425-5307

Coalition for the Homeless, Louisville-
  Jefferson County
Box 4462
Louisville, KY 40204
(502) 589-0190

Comic Relief
2049 Century Park East, Suite 4250
Los Angeles, CA 90067
(301) 201-9317

Common Cents New York, Inc.
500 Eighth Avenue
New York, NY 10018
(212) 736-6437

Community for Creative Non-Violence
425 Second Street, NW
Washington, DC 20001
(202) 393-4409

The Community Outreach Team
63 Fountain Street
Framingham Resource Center
Framingham, MA 01701
(508) 872-0765

Community Service Society of New York
105 East 22nd Street
2nd Floor
New York, NY 10010
(212) 254-8900

Connecticut Coalition to End Homelessness
30 Jorday Lane
Weathersfield, CT 06109
(203) 721-7876

Council of Jewish Federations
227 Massachusettts Avenue, NE
Suite 220
Washington, DC 20002
(202) 547-0020

Covenant House
460 West 41st Street
New York, NY 10036
(212) 613-0300

Dignity Housing
7208 Germantown Avenue
Philadelphia, PA 19119
(215) 242-3140

Emergency Food & Shelter National Board
  Program
701 N. Fairfax Street
Suite 310
Alexandria, VA 22314-2064
(703) 706-9660

Food First
Institute for Food and Development Policy
145 Ninth Street
San Francisco, CA 94103
(415) 864-8555

Friends of the Homeless
924 E. Main Street
Columbus, OH 43205
(614) 253-2770

Fund for the Homeless
Boston Foundation
One Boston Place, 24th Floor
Boston, MA 02108
(617) 723-7415

Goodwill Industries, Inc.
9200 Wisconsin Avenue
Bethesda, MD 20814
(301) 530-6500

Greater Cincinnati Coalition for the
   Homeless
1510 Elm Street
Cincinnati, OH 45210
(513) 421-7803

Greater Wheeling Coalition for the
   Homeless
P.O. Box 406
Wheeling, WV 26003
(304) 232-6105

Habitat for Humanity
121 Habitat Street
Americus, GA 31709
(912) 924-6935

HOME (Housing Opportunities in
   Massachusetts for Everyone) Coalition
25 West Street
Boston, MA 02111
(617) 728-9100

HomeBase
870 Market Street
Suite 1228
San Francisco, CA 94102
(415) 788-7961

The Homeless and Housing Coalition of
   Kentucky
141 Pike Street
Covington, KY 41011
(606) 431-8717

Homeless Economic Development Fund
Roberts Foundation
873 Sutter Street
San Francisco, CA 54109
(415) 771-4300

Homeless Family Rights Projects
11 Park Place
18th Floor
New York, NY 10007
(212) 267-4642

Homeless on the Move for Equality
   (HOME)
1325 South Wabash, Suite 205
Chicago, IL 60605
(312) 435-4548

Homelessness Information Exchange
1830 Connecticut Avenue, NW
4th Floor
Washington, DC 20009-5732
(202) 462-7551

Housing Assistance Council
1025 Vermont Avenue, NW
Suite 606
Washington, DC 20005
(202) 842-8600

Illinois Coalition for the Homeless
1325 S. Wabash Avenue
Chicago, IL 60605
(312) 435-4548

Innovative Youth Services
1030 Washington Ave
Racine, WI 53403
(414) 637-9559

Institute for Policy Studies
1601 Connecticut Avenue, NW
Washington, DC 20009
(202) 234-9382

Interagency Council on the Homeless
451 7th Street, SW
Suite 7274
Washington, DC 20410
(202) 708-1480

Interfaith Assembly on Homeless and
  Housing
1047 Amsterdam Avenue
New York, NY 10025
(212) 316-3171

Interfaith Coalition for Housing
United Methodist Church
100 Maryland Avenue, NE
Washington, DC 20002
(202) 488-5653

Iowa Coalition for the Homeless
921 Pleasant Street
Des Moines, IA 50309
(515) 244-9748

Legal Action Center for the Homeless
220 E. 74th Street
New York, NY 10009
(212) 529-4240

Local Initiatives Support Corporation
733 Third Avenue
New York, NY 10017
(212) 455-9800

Manhattan Bowery Corporation
275 Seventh Avenue, 5th Floor
New York, NY 10001
(212) 620-0340

Minnesota Coalition for the Homeless
122 West Franklin Street
Suite 318
Minneapolis, MN 55404
(612) 870-7073

National Advocacy Program Paralyzed
  Veterans of America
801 18th Street, NW
Washington, DC 20006
(202) USA-1300

National Alliance for the Mentally Ill
2101 Wilson Boulevard
Suite 302
Arlington, VA 22201
(703) 524-7600

National Alliance to End Homelessness
  (NAEH)
1518 K Street, NW
Suite 206
Washington, DC 20005
(202) 638-1526

National Association of Community Action
  Agencies
1775 T Street, NW
1st Floor
Washington, DC 20009
(202) 264-7546

National Association of Community Health
  Centers
1330 New Hampshire Avenue, NW
Suite 122
Washington, DC 20036
(202) 659-8008

National Association of Counties
440 First Street, NW
8th Floor
Washington, DC 20001
(202) 393-6226

National Association of Home Builders
1201 15th Street, NW
Washington, DC 20005
(202) 822-0200

National Association of Housing and
  Redevelopment Officials
1320 18th Street, NW
Washington, DC 20036
(202) 429-2960

National Association of Social Workers
7981 Eastern Avenue
Silver Springs, MD 29010
(301) 565-0333

National Clearinghouse for Legal Services,
   Inc.
407 S. Dearborn
Suite 400
Chicago, IL 60605
(312) 939-3830

National Coalition for the Homeless (NCH)
1621 Connecticut Avenue, NW
Suite 400
Washington, DC 20009
(202) 265-2371

National Coalition for the Homeless
311 South Spring Street
Suite 520
Los Angeles, CA 90013
(213) 488-9137

National Community Action Foundation
2100 M Street, NW
Suite 604
Washington, DC 20037
(202) 775-0223

National Conference of State Legislatures
444 North Capitol Street, NW
Suite 515
Washington, DC 20001
(202) 624-5400

National Council of Community Mental
   Health Centers
12300 Twinbrook Parkway
Suite 320
Rockville, MD 20852
(301) 984-6200

National Council of State Housing
   Agencies
444 North Capitol Street, NW
Suite 438
Washington, DC 20001
(202) 624-7710

National Governors Association
444 North Capitol Street, NW
Suite 267
Washington DC 20001
(202) 624-7819

National Housing Conference
1126 16th Street, NW
Suite 211
Washington, DC 20036
(202) 223-4844

National Housing Institute
439 Main Street
Orange, NJ 07050
(201) 678-3110

National Housing Law Project
122 C Street, NW
Suite 680
Washington, DC 20001
(202) 783-5140

National Law Center on Homelessness and
   Poverty
918 F Street, NW
Suite 412
Washington, DC 20004
(202) 638-2535

National League of Cities
1301 Pennnsylvania Avenue, NW
6th Floor
Washington, DC 20004
(202) 626-3000

National Low-Income Housing Coalition
1012 14th Street NW
Suite 1200
Washington, DC 20005
(202) 662-1530

National Mental Health Association
1021 Prince Street
Alexandria, VA 22314
(703) 684-7722

National Resource Center on Homelessness
   and Mental Illness
262 Delaware Avenue
Delmar, NY 12054
(518) 439-7415

National Student Campaign Against
   Hunger and Homelessness
29 Temple Place
Boston, MA 02111-9907
(617) 292-4823

National Volunteer Hotline
425 2nd Street, NW
Washington, DC 20001
1-800-HELP-664

New York Coalition for the Homeless
90 State Street
Albany, NY 12207
(518) 436-5612

New York Coalition for the Homeless
500 8th Avenue, 9th Floor
New York, NY 10018
(212) 695-8700

Northern California Grantmakers Task
   Force on Homelessness
116 New Montgomey Street
Suite 742
San Francisco, CA 94105
(415) 777-5761

Partnership for the Homeless
110 West 32nd Street
New York, NY 10001
(212) 947-3444

Philadelphia Committee for the Homeless
802 N. Broad Street
Philadelphia, PA 19130
(215) 232-2300

Program for the Homeless Mentally Ill,
   National Institute of Mental Health
Room 7c-08
Fishers Lane
Rockville, MD 20857
(301) 443-3706

Salvation Army
1007 K Street, NW
Washington, DC 20005
(202) 639-8414

Shared Housing Resource Center
431 Pine Street
Burlington, VT 05401
(802) 862-2727

Task Force for the Homeless
363 Georgia Avenue, SE
2nd Floor
Atlanta, GA 30312
(404) 589-9495

Travelers Aid International
918 16th Street, NW
Suite 201
Washington, DC 20006
(202) 659-9468

United States Conference of Mayors
1620 I Street, NW
4th Floor
Washington, DC 20006
(202) 293-7330

United Way of America
701 North Fairfax Street
Alexandria, VA 22314
(703) 836-7100

Urban Institute
2100 M Street, NW
5th Floor
Washington, DC 20037 .
(202) 833-7200

Virginia Coalition for the Homeless
7825 Cherokee Road
Richmond, VA 23225
(804) 320-4577

Volunteers of America
3900 N. Causeway Blvd.
Suite 700
Metairie, LA 70002
(504) 836-5225

West Virginia Coalition for the Homeless
1205 Quarrier St.
Charleston, WV 25301
(304) 344-3970

Women's Institute for Housing &
    Economic Development, Inc.
43 Kingston Street
Boston, MA 02111
(617) 423-2296

APPENDIX II
COUNT OF PERSONS IN SELECTED LOCATIONS WHERE HOMELESS PERSONS ARE FOUND

Count of Persons in Selected Locations Where Homeless Persons Are Found: 1990 Census of Population

	Selected Locations																	
	Shelter and Street Enumeration (S-Night) 1/						Special Place Enumeration for Persons with no Usual Home Elsewhere 2/											
	Emergency Shelters		Shelters for Runaway, Neglected, and Homeless Youth		Visible in Street Locations		Shelters for Abused Women		Homes for Unwed Mothers		Drug/Alcohol Centers, Group Homes		Agricultural Workers' Dorms on Farms		Group Homes for the Mentally Ill		Other Non-household Living Situations	
State	Number	Percent	Number	Percent	Number	Percent	Number	Percent	Number	Percent	Number	Percent	Number	Percent	Number	Percent	Number	Percent
United States	168,309	100.0	10,329	100.0	49,728	100.0	11,768	100.0	1,682	100.0	52,038	100.0	35,280	100.0	32,348	100.0	97,727	100.0
Alabama	1,367	0.8	163	1.6	364	0.7	127	1.1	29	1.7	546	1.0	15	0.0	161	0.5	743	0.8
Alaska	402	0.2	45	0.4	79	0.2	157	1.3	27	1.6	237	0.5	0	0.0	111	0.3	43	0.0
Arizona	2,600	1.5	135	1.3	1,897	3.8	279	2.4	4	0.2	885	1.7	675	1.9	540	1.7	4,306	4.4
Arkansas	398	0.2	91	0.9	62	0.1	105	0.9	29	1.7	473	0.9	29	0.1	306	0.9	1,777	1.8
California	29,830	17.7	976	9.4	18,081	36.4	1,257	10.7	150	8.9	8,950	17.2	7,542	21.4	5,372	16.6	17,963	18.4
Colorado	2,444	1.5	110	1.1	393	0.8	167	1.4	0	0.0	746	1.4	181	0.5	540	1.7	470	0.5
Connecticut	3,965	2.4	229	2.2	221	0.4	155	1.3	14	0.8	899	1.7	81	0.2	171	0.5	1,088	1.1
Delaware	302	0.2	11	0.1	19	0.0	36	0.3	0	0.0	75	0.1	47	0.1	357	1.1	201	0.2
District of Columbia	4,419	2.6	263	2.5	131	0.3	49	0.4	7	0.4	447	0.9	0	0.6	190	0.6	182	0.2
Florida	6,275	3.7	835	8.1	3,189	6.4	601	5.1	46	2.7	3,319	6.4	10,477	29.7	1,481	4.6	22,512	23.0
Georgia	3,697	2.2	233	2.3	450	0.9	192	1.6	0	0.0	924	1.8	3,859	10.9	285	0.9	1,799	1.8
Hawaii	773	0.5	81	0.8	1,071	2.2	73	0.6	0	0.0	349	0.7	248	0.7	14	0.0	633	0.6
Idaho	390	0.2	71	0.7	19	0.0	78	0.7	0	0.0	120	0.2	733	2.1	103	0.3	622	0.6
Illinois	7,002	4.2	479	4.6	1,755	3.5	536	4.6	120	7.1	1,225	2.4	860	2.4	2,702	8.4	3,107	3.2
Indiana	1,902	1.1	349	3.4	268	0.5	279	2.4	26	1.5	448	0.9	43	0.1	143	0.4	415	0.4
Iowa	780	0.5	209	2.0	148	0.3	164	1.4	12	0.7	320	0.6	70	0.2	514	1.6	617	0.6
Kansas	797	0.5	143	1.4	158	0.3	60	0.5	15	0.9	406	0.8	4	0.0	210	0.6	131	0.1
Kentucky	1,127	0.7	157	1.5	118	0.2	190	1.6	18	1.1	293	0.6	5	0.0	19	0.1	581	0.6
Louisiana	1,321	0.8	238	2.3	184	0.4	244	2.1	101	6.0	441	0.8	0	0.0	110	0.3	1,239	1.3
Maine	389	0.2	30	0.3	7	0.0	43	0.4	10	0.6	157	0.3	0	0.0	189	0.6	202	0.2
Maryland	2,365	1.4	142	1.4	523	1.1	199	1.7	0	0.0	665	1.3	290	0.8	175	0.5	1,024	1.0
Massachusetts	5,948	3.5	259	2.5	674	1.4	269	2.3	57	3.4	2,154	4.1	53	0.2	802	2.5	1,317	1.3
Michigan	3,442	2.0	342	3.3	262	0.5	506	4.3	67	4.0	2,048	3.9	575	1.6	1,484	4.6	1,136	1.2
Minnesota	2,152	1.3	101	1.0	138	0.3	230	2.0	27	1.6	1,768	3.4	0	0.0	1,681	5.2	224	0.2
Mississippi	223	0.1	160	1.5	83	0.2	125	1.1	0	0.0	401	0.8	0	0.0	327	1.0	672	0.7
Missouri	2,154	1.3	122	1.2	215	0.4	117	1.0	100	5.9	1,079	2.1	3	0.0	890	2.8	685	0.7
Montana	419	0.2	26	0.3	17	0.0	49	0.4	14	0.8	51	0.1	9	0.0	3	0.0	92	0.1

1. Includes persons counted the evening of March 20th in sites listed as shelters for the homeless; women and children counted the evening of March 20th in shelters and safe houses for abused counted during the early morning hours of March 21st at pre-identified street sites, abandoned buildings and open public locations where homeless persons were likly to congregate.

2. A separate count of persons who reported they had "no usual home elsewhere" during the standard enumeration of special places and group quarters. Also includes persons who reported home elsewhere but did not provide enough address information to locate the usual home elsewhere. When this happened, the persons were counted at the group quarters.

Count of Persons in Selected Locations Where Homeless Persons Are Found: 1990 Census of Population

Selected Locations

| | Shelter and Street Enumeration (S-Night) 1/ | | | | | | Special Place Enumeration for Persons with no Usual Home Elsewhere 2/ | | | | | | | | | |
| | Emergency Shelters | | Shelters for Runaway, Neglected, and Homeless Youth | | Visible in Street Locations | | Shelters for Abused Women | | Homes for Unwed Mothers | | Drug/Alcohol Centers, Group Homes | | Agricultural Workers' Dorms on Farms | | Group Homes for the Mentally Ill | | Other Non-household Living Situations | |
State	Number	Percent	Number	Percent	Number	Percent	Number	Percent	Number	Percent	Number	Percent	Number	Percent	Number	Percent	Number	Percent
Nebraska	719	0.4	45	0.4	20	0.0	41	0.3	57	3.4	270	0.5	0	0.0	116	0.4	154	0.2
Nevada	978	0.6	35	0.3	436	0.9	49	0.4	0	0.0	185	0.4	0	0.0	91	0.3	2,542	2.6
New Hampshire	334	0.2	43	0.4	8	0.0	27	0.2	0	0.0	207	0.4	15	0.0	211	0.7	79	0.1
New Jersey	7,299	4.3	171	1.7	1,639	3.3	255	2.2	8	0.5	1,474	2.8	639	1.8	869	2.7	1,508	1.5
New Mexico	642	0.4	25	0.2	164	0.3	108	0.9	0	0.0	298	0.6	0	0.0	81	0.3	786	0.8
New York	31,436	18.7	1,036	10.0	10,732	21.6	756	6.4	242	14.4	6,993	13.4	550	1.6	5,386	16.7	6,085	6.2
North Carolina	2,453	1.5	184	1.8	259	0.5	315	2.7	56	3.3	937	1.8	876	2.5	112	0.3	1,932	2.0
North Dakota	279	0.2	0	0.0	30	0.1	36	0.3	0	0.0	49	0.1	0	0.0	5	0.0	35	0.0
Ohio	3,814	2.3	463	4.5	188	0.4	496	4.2	31	1.8	1,093	2.1	86	0.2	391	1.2	1,103	1.1
Oklahoma	2,025	1.2	197	1.9	340	0.7	113	1.0	12	0.7	586	1.1	28	0.1	404	1.2	1,601	1.6
Oregon	3,170	1.9	84	0.8	564	1.1	251	2.1	3	0.2	515	1.0	2,114	6.0	329	1.0	2,322	2.4
Pennsylvania	7,815	4.6	422	4.1	1,312	2.6	603	5.1	76	4.5	2,055	3.9	1,464	4.1	1,027	3.2	1,479	1.5
Rhode Island	433	0.3	36	0.3	44	0.1	33	0.3	0	0.0	422	0.8	0	0.0	116	0.4	11	0.0
South Carolina	814	0.5	159	1.5	102	0.2	87	0.7	24	1.4	173	0.3	547	1.6	139	0.4	1,313	1.3
South Dakota	329	0.2	67	0.6	71	0.1	41	0.3	4	0.2	86	0.2	0	0.0	70	0.2	0	0.0
Tennessee	1,644	1.0	220	2.1	357	0.7	230	2.0	12	0.7	546	1.0	26	0.1	426	1.3	948	1.0
Texas	7,082	4.2	734	7.1	1,442	2.9	1,049	8.9	213	12.7	3,113	6.0	415	1.2	1,346	4.2	7,892	8.1
Utah	894	0.5	31	0.3	276	0.6	49	0.4	8	0.5	340	0.7	75	0.2	168	0.5	536	0.5
Vermont	232	0.1	0	0.0	10	0.0	29	0.2	0	0.0	48	0.1	0	0.0	155	0.5	12	0.0
Virginia	2,544	1.5	113	1.1	319	0.6	185	1.6	23	1.4	1,069	2.1	321	0.9	406	1.3	968	1.0
Washington	4,493	2.7	72	0.7	772	1.6	297	2.5	0	0.0	1,015	2.0	2,142	6.1	936	2.9	2,237	2.3
West Virginia	404	0.2	47	0.5	33	0.1	128	1.1	36	2.1	74	0.1	12	0.0	14	0.0	29	0.0
Wisconsin	1,464	0.9	91	0.9	71	0.1	258	2.2	4	0.2	1,028	2.0	160	0.5	665	2.1	288	0.3
Wyoming	129	0.1	54	0.5	13	0.0	45	0.4	0	0.0	36	0.1	11	0.0	0	0.0	86	0.1

APPENDIX III

A STATUS REPORT
ON
HUNGER AND HOMELESSNESS
IN AMERICA'S CITIES: 1993

A 26-CITY SURVEY
DECEMBER, 1993

THE UNITED STATES
CONFERENCE OF MAYORS

THE UNITED STATES CONFERENCE OF MAYORS

Jerry E. Abramson, Mayor of Louisville
President

Freeman Bosley, Jr., Mayor of Saint Louis
James Scheibel, Mayor of Saint Paul
Co-Chairs, Task Force on Hunger and Homelessness

J. Thomas Cochran, Executive Director

This report was prepared by Laura DeKoven Waxman, Assistant Executive Director, The U.S. Conference of Mayors, with the assistance of Jenell Williams, a Bethel College intern at the Conference of Mayors. Additional copies are available for $15 each (payable in advance) from The U.S. Conference of Mayors, 1620 Eye Street, NW, Washington, DC 20006 (202) 293-7330.

TABLE OF CONTENTS

SUMMARY

To assess the status of hunger and homelessness in urban America during 1993, The U.S. Conference of Mayors surveyed 26 major cities whose mayors are members of its Task Force on Hunger and Homelessness. The survey sought information and estimates from each city on 1) the demand for emergency food assistance and emergency shelter and the capacity of local agencies to meet that demand; 2) the causes of hunger and homelessness and the demographics of the populations experiencing these problems; 3) the availability of affordable housing for low income people; 4) the outlook for the future; and 5) the most important federal actions that need to be taken to prevent and respond to homelessness.

Among the findings of the 26-city survey:

HUNGER

* Officials in the survey cities estimate that during the past year requests for emergency food assistance increased by an average of 13 percent, with 83 percent of the cities registering an increase. The number of families with children requesting assistance increased by an average of 13 percent, with 83 percent of the cities registering an increase. Two out of every three people requesting emergency food assistance in the survey cities were members of families -- children and their parents. Thirty percent of the adults requesting assistance were employed.

* On average, 17 percent of the requests for emergency food assistance are estimated to have gone unmet. In 72 percent of the cities emergency food assistance facilities may have to turn away people in need due to lack of resources.

* The overall level of resources available to emergency food assistance facilities increased by seven percent. Two out of three of the survey cities reported that emergency food assistance facilities are unable to provide an adequate quantity of food. The number of bags of food provided and/or the number of times people can receive food are limited in 88 percent of the cities. Eighty-three percent of the survey cities reported that the food provided is nutritionally balanced.

* In 84 percent of the cities emergency food assistance facilities were relied on by families and individuals both in emergencies and as a steady source of food over long periods of time.

* Unemployment and/or underemployment lead the list of causes of hunger identified by the city officials. Other causes frequently cited include poverty and the high cost of housing.

* During the last year 85 percent of the survey cities supported local emergency food assistance efforts. Fifty-four percent used locally generated revenues; 31 percent used Stewart B. McKinney Homeless Assistance funds; 27 percent used Community Development Block Grant funds; 23 percent used state grants; and 23 percent used Community Services Block Grant funds.

HOMELESSNESS

* During the past year requests for emergency shelter increased in the survey cities by an average of 10 percent, with just over four out of five of the cities registering an increase. Requests for shelter by homeless families alone increased by 13 percent, with just over two-thirds of the cities reporting an increase.

* An average of 25 percent of the requests for emergency shelter by homeless people and 29 percent of the requests by homeless families are estimated to have gone unmet. In 85 percent of the cities emergency shelters may have to turn away homeless families due to lack of resources. In 77 percent of the cities shelters may have to turn away other homeless people due to lack of resources.

* People remain homeless for an average of seven months in the survey cities. Sixty-two percent of the cities said that the length of time people are homeless increased during the last year.

* The lack of affordable housing leads the list of causes of homelessness identified by the city officials. Other causes frequently cited include unemployment and other employment-related problems, substance abuse and the lack of needed services, mental illness and the lack of needed services, poverty and domestic violence.

* Officials estimate that, on average, single men and families with children each comprise 43 percent of the homeless population, single women comprise 11 percent and unaccompanied minors four percent. Children account for 30 percent of the total. The homeless population is estimated to be 56 percent African-American, 27 percent white, 13 percent Hispanic, three percent Native American and one percent Asian. An average of 27 percent of the homeless population in the cities is considered mentally ill; 48 percent are substance abusers; nine percent have AIDS or HIV-related illness. An average of 18 percent of homeless people are employed in full- or part-time jobs; 21 percent are veterans.

* During the last year the number of emergency shelter beds increased overall in the survey cities by an average of four percent. Transitional housing units increased by an average of 20 percent, Single Room Occupancy units by 16 percent.

* Families with children and substance abusers each were identified by 65 percent of the cities as a group of homeless people for whom shelter and other needed services are particularly lacking. Mentally ill persons were identified by 58 percent of the cities as being in particular need of shelter and other services.

* Every survey city used city government funds during the last year to support shelters or other services for homeless people. Seventy-seven percent used locally generated revenues; 77 percent used Stewart B. McKinney Homeless Assistance Act funds; 61 percent used Community Development Block Grant funds; 39 percent used Community Services Block Grant funds; and 42 percent used state grants.

HOUSING

* Requests for assisted housing by low income families and individuals increased in 70 percent of the cities during the last year. An average of 28 percent of eligible low income households are currently served by assisted housing programs.

* Applicants must wait an average of 21 months for public housing in the survey cities. The wait for Section 8 housing is 35 months; for vouchers it is 31 months. Fifty-eight percent of the cities have stopped accepting applications for at least one assisted housing program due to the excessive length of the waiting list.

* Among those with special needs, it is most difficult to find assisted housing for large families and mentally ill persons in the survey cities.

THE OUTLOOK AND NEEDED ACTIONS

* Officials in every survey city expect requests for emergency food assistance to increase during 1994. Requests for emergency shelter -- by all homeless persons and by homeless families in particular -- are expected to increase in 88 percent (all but three) of the cities next year.

* Providing affordable housing was identified most frequently by the city officials as the single most important federal action to address the housing needs of homeless people. Providing transitional housing and coordinated case management also were cited by the city officials as needed actions.

* Raising the minimum wage and providing job training were identified most frequently as the most important actions the federal government can take to address the income needs of homeless people. These were followed by increasing employment opportunities, stimulating the economy and increasing welfare payments.

* Providing comprehensive case management was cited most frequently by the city officials as the single most important federal action to address the service needs of homeless people. This was followed by increasing funding for substance abuse treatment and mental health services, fully funding existing services and increasing job training.

* Creating additional employment opportunities was identified most frequently as the single most important action the federal government can take to prevent homelessness from occurring in the first place. Providing more housing with supportive services and improving the economy also were frequently cited.

INTRODUCTION

In October 1982, The U.S. Conference of Mayors and The U.S. Conference of City Human Services Officials brought the shortage of emergency services -- food, shelter, medical care, income assistance, energy assistance -- to national attention through a 55-city survey. That survey showed that the demand for emergency services had increased in cities across the nation, and that on average only 43 percent of that demand was being met.

Since that time the Conference has done numerous reports on hunger, homelessness and poverty in cities. These reports have documented the causes and the magnitude of the problems, how cities were responding to them and what national responses were required. They include:

* Hunger in American Cities, June, 1983
* Responses to Urban Hunger, October, 1983
* Status Report: Emergency Food, Shelter and Energy Programs in 20 Cities, January, 1984
* Homelessness in America' Cities: Ten Case Studies, June, 1984
* Housing Needs and Conditions in America' Cities, June 1984
* The Urban Poor and the Economic Recovery, September, 1984
* The Status of Hunger in Cities, April, 1985
* Health Care for the Homeless: A 40-City Review, April, 1985
* The Growth of Hunger, Homelessness and Poverty in America's Cities in 1985: A 25-City Survey, January, 1986
* Responding to Homelessness in America's Cities, June, 1986
* The Continued Growth of Hunger, Homelessness and Poverty in America's Cities in 1986: A 25-City Survey, December, 1986
* A Status Report on Homeless Families in America's Cities: A 29-City Survey, May, 1987
* Local Responses to the Needs of Homeless Mentally Ill Persons, May, 1987
* The Continuing Growth of Hunger, Homelessness and Poverty in America's Cities: 1987, A 26-City Survey, December, 1987
* A Status Report on The Stewart B. McKinney Homeless Assistance Act of 1987, June, 1988
* A Status Report on Hunger and Homelessness in America's Cities: 1988, A 27-City Survey, January, 1989
* Partnerships for Affordable Housing, An Annotated Listing of City Programs, September, 1989
* A Status Report on Hunger and Homelessness in America's Cities: 1989, A 27-City Survey, December, 1989
* A Status Report on Hunger and Homelessness in America's Cities: 1990, A 30-City Survey, December, 1990
* A City Assessment of the 1990 Shelter and Street Night count, A 21-City Survey, June 1991
* Mentally Ill and Homeless, A 22-City Survey, November 1991
* A Status Report on Hunger and Homelessness in America's Cities: 1991, A 28-City Survey, December 1991
* A Status Report on Hunger and Homelessness in America's Cities: 1992, A 29-City Survey, December 1992
* Addressing Hunger and Homelessness in America's Cities, June 1993

To spearhead the Conference's efforts to respond to the emergency services crisis in cities, the President of The Conference of Mayors appointed 20 mayors to a Task Force on Hunger and

Homelessness in September, 1983. That Task Force is no chaired by Saint Paul Mayor James Scheibel and Saint Louis Mayor Freeman Bosley, Jr., and the number of mayors serving on it has increased to 33. The Task Force meets at least twice each year; many of its members have testified before Congress; and the cities represented on it have provided information to Conference staff on conditions relating to hunger and homelessness for the various reports that have been prepared.

Methodology

This report provides information on the current status of hunger, homelessness and the conditions which have affected them in 26 of the cities represented on the Task Force. A copy of the survey instrument sent to the cities is contained in the Appendix.

To respond to the survey, the city officials consult with and collect data from community-based provider and government agencies. The data is compiled by the individual or agency in the city government designated to be the Conference of Mayors' contact for the survey and it is reviewed by a senior-level manager before it is submitted to the Conference of Mayors.

The data was collected from the cities for the period of November 1, 1992 to October 31, 1993 during November and December, 1993. It was supplemented with data on population, poverty and unemployment available from the Bureau of the Census and the Bureau of Labor Statistics. The reader should note that in no case do the percentages reported for a survey question include a city unable to respond to that question. Tables which provide city-specific data appear at the back of chapters on Hunger, Homelessness and Housing.

HUNGER

During the last year, the demand for emergency food assistance increased by an average of 13 percent across the survey cities, and it increased in 83 percent of those cities. The demand remained the same in four. The demand by families with children increased by 13 percent in the survey cities, with 83 percent of them reporting an increase. Two-thirds of those requesting emergency food assistance were families with children. In 72 percent of the survey cities emergency food assistance facilities may turn away people in need because of lack of resources. The city officials estimate that 17 percent of the requests for food assistance went unmet during the last year. The overall level of resources available to such facilities is estimated to have increased by seven percent during the last year. In two out of three of the cities emergency food assistance facilities are unable to provide adequate quantities of food.

THE PROBLEM

The Demand for Emergency Food Assistance

During the last year, requests for emergency food assistance increased in 83 percent of the survey cities. Across all of the cities, requests increased by an average of 13 percent. Increases ranged from 28 percent in Santa Monica, 25 percent in St. Louis, 20-25 percent in Alexandria and 23 percent in New Orleans to under 10 percent in Louisville, Minneapolis and St. Paul. Emergency food requests remained the same in Cleveland, Nashville, Portland and Seattle.

Among the comments by the city officials on the increase in requests for emergency food assistance:

* **Alexandria:** The response to requests per day represents an estimate compiled by contacting all emergency food providers in the city. Two providers actually noted a decrease; this can be attributed in one case to reduced hours of operation for renovation, and in the other to the permanent loss of one provider mid-way through the year. Other providers reported substantial increases as workers turned to alternatives to fill the void. Service agencies involved with Information and Referral programs also noted an increase in inquiries about emergency food.

* **Boston:** A survey of 20 emergency food assistance agencies conducted by the Greater Boston Food Bank obtained the following results: 75 percent of the agencies report an increase in clients served; 70 percent have an average increase of 21 clients, 15 percent have twice as many clients, five percent have 50 percent more clients, and 10 percent have 30 percent more clients.

* **Los Angeles:** The 10 percent increase reported is based on agencies served by the Los Angeles Regional Food Bank, not individuals served by the agencies. The number of people requesting emergency food assistance is increasing, although the number of people served has not increased at the same rate.

* **Louisville:** Client records of Dare to Care, the local food bank, reflect 97,000 persons served in 1992 and project 100,000 in 1993. We estimate that Dare to Care provides 75 percent of food orders in metropolitan Louisville, with the food bank assisting other programs.

* **New York City:** The percentage reported is an estimate. Our last survey was conducted in November 1992. Based on a 40 percent response rate, we concluded that 1,783,000 meals were provided each month – or approximately 90,000 per day -- and that 2,000 individuals were turned away each month.

* **Philadelphia:** The recession has made it more difficult for low income families to pay their bills and has resulted in higher unemployment, especially for single males. Grandparents raising their grandchildren utilize food assistance programs because their fixed incomes are too small to support a family.

* **Portland:** An agency which provides a substantial amount of food locally is serving 35 percent more people than last year. Last year they served 1,641 households, this year 2,531 households.

* **Saint Louis:** Some notable causes of the increase in requests for emergency food assistance are: unemployment, lack of affordable day care, child welfare and support issues, health care needs, and lack of education on, or knowledge of, available resources.

* **Salt Lake City:** Soup kitchens and food banks report an 8-12 percent increase in the number of requests for emergency food assistance this year over last year. They also report a significant increase in requests for food assistance among poor people in general, in addition to those who are homeless.

* **San Antonio:** The number of food requests has increased substantially over the last 12 months. This is indicative of the fact that the economic recovery has been slow in reaching low income people.

* **Santa Monica:** Approximately 700 persons are served each day through meal programs at social service agencies, parks and local churches. An additional 2,000 persons per day receive food from local food pantries. Food pantries report an all-time high in quantity of food distributed.

Requests by Families for Emergency Food Assistance

The number of families with children requesting emergency food assistance increased in 83 percent of the survey cities. The average estimated increase was 13 percent, ranging from 35 percent in Portland and Santa Monica and 30 percent in Boston, Philadelphia and San Diego to 8-12 percent in Salt Lake City, 9.6 percent in Phoenix, five percent in Minneapolis and three percent in Louisville. The number of requests by families with children remained the same in Cleveland, Nashville and Seattle. It decreased by 43 percent in Trenton.

Across the survey cities it is estimated that two-thirds (67 percent) of those requesting emergency food assistance were either children or their parents. In Alexandria, Charleston, Cleveland,

Kansas City, Los Angeles, New Orleans, Phoenix, and Trenton, three-fourths or more of those requesting emergency food assistance were members of families with children.

Among the comments by the city officials on the increase in requests for emergency food assistance by families with children:

* **Louisville**: Client records show that 70 percent of all families seeking food assistance have dependent children in the home.

* **New York City**: Anecdotal reports from program directors suggest that families with children and employed individuals make up a growing portion of the caseload.

* **Salt Lake City**: Families with children are still a growing segment of the homeless/poverty population. Food distribution centers report a marked increase in requests for food assistance among poor families in general, in addition to those who are homeless.

* **San Antonio**: The increased number of families with children requesting emergency food assistance is a reflection of increased food costs.

* **Santa Monica**: Food pantries report a higher percentage of requests by families with children in 1993 and a higher percentage of persons requesting food for the first time.

Requests for Food Assistance by Employed Adults

Officials in the survey cities estimate that 30 percent of the adults requesting emergency food assistance are employed. The percentage of employed adults requesting food assistance ranges from 75 percent in Boston, 44 percent in Minneapolis and 40 percent in Louisville and Salt Lake City to 12 percent in Cleveland, 11 percent in New Orleans and Trenton and seven percent in Charleston.

The Causes

Officials in the survey cities say hunger is due to a number of factors, many of them inter-related. Those most frequently identified by the survey cities, in response to an open-ended question, are unemployment and other employment-related problems, poverty and lack of income and the high cost of housing. Other causes identified by the survey cities include the cost of food, inadequate federal benefit programs, substance abuse, mental health problems, lack of shelter and high medical costs.

* Twenty-one cities identified **unemployment and/or underemployment** as one of the main causes of hunger: Alexandria, Boston, Chicago, Cleveland, Denver, Kansas City, Los Angeles, Louisville, Miami, Nashville, New Orleans, New York City, Philadelphia, Phoenix, Portland, Saint Louis, Saint Paul, San Antonio, Salt Lake City, Seattle and Trenton.

* Thirteen cities cited **poverty or lack of income** as one of the main causes of hunger: Alexandria, Boston, Charleston, Chicago, Denver, Louisville, Miami, Minneapolis, New Orleans, Philadelphia, Portland, Salt Lake City and Santa Monica.

* Eleven cities identified **high housing costs** as a primary cause of hunger: Alexandria, Boston, Denver, Los Angeles, Minneapolis, Nashville, New York City, Philadelphia, Portland, San Antonio, San Diego and Seattle. **The cost of food** was identified as one of the main causes of hunger by four cities: Alexandria, San Diego, Seattle and Trenton.

* **Inadequate food stamp benefits** were identified by Portland, Saint Louis and Seattle as being among the main causes of the of hunger. Cleveland and Seattle identified **insufficient public assistance benefits**. Boston, Los Angeles and Salt Lake City cited **cuts in federal programs**.

* New Orleans, Philadelphia and Trenton identified **substance abuse** as a primary cause of hunger. Boston, Norfolk and Trenton cited **mental health problems or deinstitutionalization**. Minneapolis, Nashville and San Antonio cited **high medical bills**.

THE CAPACITY TO MEET THE NEED

The number of emergency food assistance facilities increased in one-half of the cities (12), remained the same in 43 percent (10) of the cities and decreased in four percent (one). Cities in which the number of facilities increased are Boston, Charleston, Louisville, Minneapolis, New York City, Norfolk, Philadelphia, Portland, Saint Louis, Saint Paul, San Antonio and Trenton. The number remained the same in Alexandria, Cleveland, Denver, Los Angeles, Nashville, New Orleans, Phoenix, Salt Lake City, Santa Monica and Seattle. Kansas City saw a decrease in emergency food assistance facilities.

During the last year, the level of resources, such as food, funds or volunteers available to emergency food assistance facilities, is estimated to have increased overall by seven percent. The level of resources increased in 29 percent (seven) cities, decreased in 50 percent (12) and remained the same in 21 percent (five). Those cities reporting an increase are New Orleans, Phoenix, Saint Paul, Salt Lake City, San Antonio, San Diego and Trenton. Those reporting a decrease are Charleston, Chicago, Cleveland, Denver, Kansas City, Minneapolis, New Orleans, Norfolk, Philadelphia, Portland, Saint Louis and Santa Monica. The level of resources remained the same in Alexandria, Boston, Los Angeles, Louisville and Nashville.

Among the comments of the city officials on increased levels of **resources**:

* **New York City**: The level of resources has remained constant, except for funds provided by the City. City funding has risen from $3.0 million in FY 1992 to $3.9 million in FY 1993 and $5.2 million in FY 1994.

* **Phoenix**: The impression is that there has been an increase in the number of volunteers; food supplies vary, but again, there seems to have been a concomitant increase in supplies to meet the basic demand.

* **Saint Paul**: The combination of funds from a State of Minnesota allocation, the Minnesota Food Drive and Flood Relief has increased resources available.

* **Salt Lake City:** Food donations, funds and volunteers have increased, but demand exceeds available supplies. There is still a need for additional funding and staffing.

* **San Antonio:** The local food bank has launched a number of public relations activities to increase the community's level of awareness of the increased incidence of hunger. This has resulted in an increase in the number of private/public partnership efforts to increase donations to the local food bank pantry distribution system.

* **Trenton:** Three new facilities (churches) are providing weekend meals under the Trenton Area Soup Kitchen.

Among the comments of the city officials on the **level of resources remaining unchanged:**

* **Alexandria:** The number of emergency food providers in Alexandria remains the same as in 1991-1992. One food closet closed, but a church was recruited to replace it. The United Way reports a loss of FEMA funds this year. In previous years, FEMA has been used to support feeding programs.

* **Boston:** Agencies received similar amounts of funding this year from programs such as Project Bread which, aside from donations, is the main source of money for pantries and soup kitchens.

* **Los Angeles:** Although funds have decreased, private foundation and volunteer efforts have helped maintain the existing system.

* **Louisville:** Sources are shifting, with income about the same but costs increasing. Corporate support generally has declined, while private donations are slightly higher. Food donations have increased slightly in poundage, but have declined in nutritional value.

Among the comments of officials in cities where **the level of resources declined:**

* **Charleston:** Needs have increased and as the local economic situation worsens, donations have been reduced.

* **Chicago:** Volunteerism (primarily among senior citizens and college students) has increased during the past year.

* **Cleveland:** We have experienced reduced private donations and termination of supermarket anti-trust settlement payments.

* **Denver:** There have been crucial reductions in Denver over the last two years in both federal and private funding for the homeless and for emergency food assistance.

* **Kansas City:** Resources have decreased in proportion to the amount of requests. NAAC reports that while the level of funds and food has increased, it has not kept pace with the increase in number of people seeking assistance. Churches are not able to open as often as necessary because of the lack of volunteers.

* **Minneapolis:** Individual and corporate giving have both decreased.

*   **New Orleans:** Donors have minimized their contributions due to the ongoing recession in our community.

*   **Norfolk:** United Way member agencies experienced a seven percent funding cut.

*   **Philadelphia:** State funding decreased by three percent during the period of this report.

*   **Portland:** Food assistance facilities report some increases in food donations this year, but decreases in funds donated, and many struggle to maintain sufficient volunteers.

*   **Saint Louis:** Volunteers have not increased. People do not realize that there is a constant need for food.

*   **Santa Monica:** The primary federal government source of funding is FEMA, which was reduced from $148,000 to $52,000 in 1993.

Emergency Food Assistance Facilities:
For Emergencies Only or as a Steady Source of Food?

Eighty-four percent of the cities reported that emergency food assistance facilities were used both for emergencies and as a steady source of food over long periods of time. Alexandria, Chicago, Nashville and New York City said they were used for emergencies only. Among the comments from the city officials where facilities were used both for emergencies and as a steady source of food:

*   **Boston:** Depending on the situation of the people receiving assistance, agencies adjust their policies concerning the provision of food. For instance, HIV/AIDS patients may use pantries as their regular suppliers of food.

*   **Charleston:** Clients often need a steady source of food to augment a meager diet. Many food providers must limit frequency and amounts to meet other client requests.

*   **Cleveland:** Many families use facilities as often as possible. Others only need emergency assistance.

*   **Kansas City:** A significant number of families return monthly to most pantries for assistance. However, there are also some individuals/families who come only in response to an infrequent "crisis" situation and are able to function without repeat visits.

*   **Los Angeles:** Pantries and shelters used to be short term -- addressing one-shot needs. Now emergency feeders in particular are becoming maintenance organizations and shelters. Also, there are more reported incidents of families giving aid and shelter to others.

*   **Louisville:** Emergency food programs limit service to four or five times yearly. Churches supplement this service and some vouchers are available from a few sources. Approximately 35 percent of the clientele need long term assistance with food.

*   **Minneapolis:** Most clients make four visits per year.

* **New Orleans:** Some people use food assistance for emergencies only. Some clients are steady repeaters in requesting emergency food assistance.

* **Norfolk:** Some families are served on a recurrent basis due to fluctuations in financial situations. Assistance facilities are used for emergencies most of the time. Some churches provide food to families on a monthly basis.

* **Philadelphia:** Although the primary use of the facilities is for emergencies, many people suffer from ongoing poverty and need food on a regular basis.

* **Phoenix:** The program is, of course, used for emergencies; but it is also used for periods of episodic need. If a family's income drops for some reason, then the "emergency" food is used to supplement what the family can afford.

* **Portland:** Emergency food box programs' frequency of service restrictions vary. The median number of times clients seek this type of service is three per year. Emergency meal programs provide meals on a regular basis to the homeless and elderly.

* **Saint Louis:** Food stamp recipients frequently use pantries toward the end of the month when their food stamps run out.

* **Salt Lake City:** Emergency food orders are limited at food banks but many persons rely on soup kitchens for a steady supply of food. In addition, more non-homeless poor individuals and families have been using these resources during the past year than previously.

* **San Antonio:** The local food bank pantry distribution system is designed to provide emergency food assistance and commodities on a monthly basis to eligible households.

* **Seattle:** Most food banks limit the allowable number of visits to one per week; those which do not set limits regularly run out of food or provide significantly smaller amounts to food bank clients.

* **Trenton:** Some agencies provide food on an emergency basis and others serve hot meals on a day-to-day basis.

Officials in the cities in which facilities were used for emergencies only commented:

* **Alexandria:** The providers we have surveyed for the report seek to provide emergency supplies only. Most attempt to provide a three- to five-day supply of food. Congregate meal programs can and often do provide longer term assistance with few if any restrictions, but have not been included in this year's survey.

* **Chicago:** The program funded and operated by the City is for emergency use only. Not-for-profit pantries may become a regular source of food over longer periods for some needy persons.

* **Nashville:** The Second Harvest Food Bank is strictly for emergency use.

*   **New York City**: There is not enough food to supply families for a long period of time.

The Quantity of Food Provided

Two-thirds of the survey cities reported that emergency food assistance facilities are unable to provide an adequate quantity of food. Those cities are Boston, Charleston, Cleveland, Kansas City, Los Angeles, Miami, Minneapolis, New Orleans, Norfolk, Philadelphia, Portland, Saint Louis, Saint Paul, Salt Lake City, Santa Monica and Seattle. Cities in which food assistance facilities are able to provide an adequate quantity of food are Alexandria, Chicago, Denver, Louisville, New York City, Phoenix, San Antonio and Trenton.

Among the comments from those cities in which emergency food assistance facilities are **unable to provide adequate quantities of food**:

*   **Boston**: Soup kitchens only provide food for a single meal and therefore must be visited on a regular basis for individuals to receive an adequate supply of food. Pantries provide an average of three to five days worth of food per visit. As a result, those who rely on these agencies as their regular source of meals do not receive an adequate supply of food.

*   **Charleston**: Food providers are distressed that to serve the increased number of clients they often must limit the amount and frequency of the food provided.

*   **Cleveland**: Public assistance benefits are so low that many recipients could use five days of food every month. Food assistance is now limited to three days of food every other month.

*   **Kansas City**: Based on Harvesters' monthly reports, 85 percent of the food pantries had enough food during this reporting period; 15 percent of the food pantries did not. Some pantries reduced the number of days for which food is provided.

*   **Los Angeles**: Lowest income communities often run out of food. Agencies never have enough but some manage to "make do." In many, the demand exceeds the supply.

*   **Minneapolis**: Resources are down, so food shelves have had to ration. This is the worst year in a long time.

*   **Nashville**: The situation depends on food availability. There usually are limited amounts of eggs, milk, meats and fresh produce.

*   **New Orleans**: There are not enough resources to keep up with the ongoing demand, and this is the reason clients can only return for assistance every three months.

*   **Norfolk**: A three to five day supply of food is usually all that is available. Expedited food stamp applications are processed within five days; regular food stamp applications can take up to 30 days.

*   **Portland**: Food assistance facilities are able to provide only a three or four day supply of food. This may be adequate to see some families through a temporary crisis, but it is not adequate for others who have no resources for food. Limited resources make it difficult to provide more sustained assistance.

*   **Saint Louis:** Many centers do not have proper refrigeration. Many centers limit the number of visits per month or the number of bags of food. There are more people in need but less food available. Many clients do not have transportation to pick up food.

*   **Saint Paul:** There is a need for more high protein foods and culturally sensitive meals.

*   **Salt Lake City:** Sometimes food supplies are limited and the number and frequency of visits are restricted. The problem is especially severe at the end of each month when food stamp allotments have been exhausted.

*   **Seattle:** Most emergency meal programs provide meals once or twice a week, and do not provide more than one meal during each day of operation. Most food banks are only able to supply enough food to feed a family for one or two days and must limit the number of food bank visits allowed. Even with food stamps and other sources of income/support, this is not sufficient to provide adequate food.

Among the comments of the officials in cities where emergency food assistance facilities are **able to provide adequate quantities of food:**

*   **Alexandria:** The mission of most emergency food providers in the City is to meet needs over a short-term. The providers successfully meet this goal. If longer-term assistance is necessary, persons are referred to congregate meal programs, public assistance or the food stamp program.

*   **Denver:** Food available is adequate, but considering funding cuts, supplies are much lower than in past years.

*   **San Antonio:** In emergency situations, food assistance facilities are able to provide an adequate quantity of food.

Eighty-eight percent (23) of the survey cities report that emergency assistance facilities have to **limit the number of bags provided and/or the number of times families and/or individuals can come to get food.**   Such limits are not necessary in Louisville, Miami and Trenton.

Among the comments by the city officials:

*   **Alexandria:** Emergency food providers report the quantity of food is generally based on the family size. Most provide food stocks to last for three days. Providers also have limitations on repeat usage due to high demand.

*   **Boston:** In an attempt to encourage independence of emergency food service, pantries serve clients only once a month; however, walk-in assistance is usually available.

*   **Chicago:** The city-funded and operated program limits each family/individual to one food box per year. Exceptions are allowed on a case by case basis whereas not-for-profits provide food strictly on a case by case basis.

*   **Denver:** Distribution is limited because resources are not abundant.

*   **Kansas City:** Most facilities provide a specific number of bags of food once a month. The number of bags is determined by family/household size. Many pantries will alter that pattern and provide food more often if there is a particularly dire situation or problem.

*   **Los Angeles:** The agencies do not have enough food to give out bags without a control system. Also, the number of times families/individuals can receive food in any given period of time is limited. The time period varies from center to center depending on availability of food.

*   **Louisville:** The Dare to Care Food Bank is the only community-wide organized network of food pantries, and must limit services to four to five times yearly. Families are given a four- to seven-day supply of food at each visit and, when available, receive store vouchers for fresh and refrigerated items.

*   **Minneapolis:** One time per month, clients receive a three-day supply for nine meals.

*   **Nashville:** Clients are limited to three boxes every six months or six boxes a year.

*   **New Orleans:** The limit the major emergency food facilities observe is a three-day supply of food every three months.

*   **New York City:** Program rules vary, but most pantries do not have enough food to permit multiple monthly visits by a household.

*   **Norfolk:** Most facilities limit assistance to once a quarter or four times a year.

*   **Philadelphia:** Most emergency food shelves distribute different amounts of food depending on family size. The majority have limits as to how often a person/family can return for food. Most facilities provide a two- or three-day supply of food and limit access to once a month, or twice in a six-month period.

*   **Phoenix:** The restrictions are primarily for the purpose of stopping abuse of the good programs by individuals/families who are identified through the networking of the feeding or food-providing agencies.

*   **Portland:** Agencies have to ration their supply of food due to lack of ability to always provide service when requested. Clients are forced to "make the rounds" of several agencies to "make do."

*   **Saint Louis:** There is variation here. Some centers limit the number of visits per month. Some limit as necessary. Many pantries set a goal for an emergency food package of a three-to-five-day supply of food.

*   **Saint Paul:** Food shelves are used one time per month and people get a three-to-five-day supply of food.

* **San Antonio**: This will vary from pantry to pantry. In some instances, an agency may supplement what it receives from the local food bank with its other resources and so be able to provide more food on a more regular basis. Those agencies with limited resources provide an adequate amount of food in emergency situations.

* **Seattle**: Most food banks limit the allowable number of visits to one per week; those which do not set limits regularly run out of food or provide significantly smaller amounts to food bank clients.

* **Trenton**: Most agencies have established guidelines which state the number of times a family can receive food. TASK stated that they serve anyone who comes to the agency.

The Quality of Food Provided

Eighty-three percent of the cities reported that emergency food assistance facilities are able to provide nutritionally balanced food. Those cities are Alexandria, Boston, Charleston, Chicago, Cleveland, Denver, Kansas City, Los Angeles, Minneapolis, Nashville, New Orleans, New York City, Philadelphia, Phoenix, Portland, Saint Paul, Salt Lake City, San Antonio, San Diego and Trenton. Four cities (17 percent) reported that emergency food assistance facilities are unable to provide nutritionally balanced food: Louisville, Norfolk, Saint Louis and Seattle.

City officials who indicated that emergency food assistance facilities are able to provide **nutritionally balanced food** explained their responses:

* **Alexandria**: We are confident that emergency providers in the City make every effort to provide wholesome food products that are safe for consumption and well-balanced. Many, if not most, buy goods from a central food bank.

* **Boston**: The food bank participates in a cooperative wholesale buying program in order to provide nutritious food. We also hold nutrition workshops to raise the awareness of those who actually prepare the meals.

* **Charleston**: While the meals are balanced they rarely include fresh vegetables, fruit or whole milk.

* **Chicago**: Food provided through the city-funded and operated program is reviewed annually by a DHS-designated health nutritionist, while not-for-profits are encouraged to participate in the nutrition/food handling certification classes offered by the Anti-Hunger Federation.

* **Kansas City**: Harvesters has assisted agencies that work with them by providing food bag "guides" and nutrition classes for emergency food assistance workers to increase their "nutrition knowledge." This has resulted in better nutritionally-balanced food bags. USDA commodities, when available, are included in the bags. Agencies not obtaining food from Harvesters must rely heavily on donations. These donations may not be the most nutritionally balanced foods.

* **Los Angeles**: Nutritional balance depends on the agency's resources. Every effort is made to supply a variety of foods but they are not necessarily nutritionally balanced.

*   **Nashville:** Food boxes are stocked with food from all food groups.

*   **New Orleans:** The food is nutritionally balanced, but the products vary because the available food items depend on what is donated.

*   **Norfolk:** The food is supplemental and is provided free of charge. Thus, fresh fruits, vegetables and meat are not always available. Every effort is made to provide nutritionally balanced food. The Foodbank has provided training to agencies on nutrition education and food preparation.

*   **Philadelphia:** The food provided at soup kitchens and shelters is nutritionally balanced. the nutritional balance of food provided through food cupboards and the neighborhood food program varies at times because of the variability of donated foods.

*   **Phoenix:** Nutritional balance varies from source to source, but generally the food is balanced. However, this will not necessarily be true for people who have special needs diets.

*   **Portland:** Every attempt is made to provide a nutritionally balanced food box. Success varies from one program to another. It is difficult to provide adequate dairy foods, particularly milk, for children, or to meet special dietary needs.

*   **Salt Lake City:** Food supplies are acquired primarily from donations and are nutritionally balanced to the greatest extent possible.

*   **San Antonio:** The local food bank works to provide a variety of food to its member agencies. While pantries have no control over the types of food donations they receive, every effort is made to ensure that a balanced food package is available.

*   **Santa Monica:** Nutritional balance is inconsistent.

*   **Seattle:** While food banks and meal programs attempt to provide nutritious food and meals, they must rely heavily on donated foods which are not always of the highest quality or nutritional value. Emergency food providers have made progress in improving the nutritional value of food distributed this year, through purchasing more nutritious foods.

Among the comments of city officials where emergency food assistance facilities are not able to provide nutritionally balanced food:

*   **Louisville:** Holiday food drives provide sufficient balance for the first quarter of the year; the food is sufficient but not very nutritious during the remainder of the year.

*   **Saint Louis:** There is some diversity here. Some of the larger distribution centers provide fresh fruits and vegetables, but overall there is a definite lack of dairy products, meats and fresh fruits and, therefore, a possible deficiency of Vitamin A and Vitamin C.

Child Nutrition Programs

Seventeen of the survey cities reported that 100 percent of their schools participate in the school lunch program. The average rate of participation of schools is 98.6 percent in all of the responding cities. Nine cities reported that 100 percent of the schools participate in the School Breakfast Program. The average rate of participation in this program across the cities is 89 percent.

THE FUNDING

During the last year 85 percent of the survey cities report using city government funds (either locally generated revenues or federal or state grants) to support local emergency food assistance efforts.

* Fifty-four percent (14) of the cities used **locally generated revenues** to support emergency food assistance efforts. Those cities and the amount of locally generated revenues expended during the last year are:

Alexandria	$ 25,000
Boston	350,000
Charleston	36,200
Chicago	1,475,000
Denver	20,000
Louisville	41,500
New Orleans	150,000
New York City	5,200,000
Norfolk	15,000
San Antonio	3,030
San Diego	1,680,628
Santa Monica	128,340
Seattle	1,205,543
Trenton	12,500

Boston, New York City, Norfolk, Santa Monica and Seattle reported that the amount of locally generated revenues spent for emergency food assistance had increased during the last year. Alexandria, Cleveland, Louisville, New Orleans, San Antonio and Trenton reported the amount had remained the same. Nashville reported that the amount had decreased.

* Six cities reported receiving **state grants** for food assistance efforts. These cities and the amount they spent are:

Minneapolis	$1,484,000
Nashville	12,000
New Orleans	158,174
New York City	456,000
Philadelphia	2,742,035
Portland	20,000

Minneapolis, New Orleans and Portland reported that the amount of state funding used for emergency food assistance increased during the last year. Nashville and Philadelphia reported that the amount decreased. While New York City and San Antonio reported that the amount of state funding remained the same, San Antonio indicated that it receives no state funds for emergency food assistance efforts.

*   Eight cities (31 percent) provided information on McKinney Act funds which they use to support emergency food assistance efforts. Those cities and the amount spent during the last year are:

Boston	$309,000
Denver	20,000
Louisville	45,000
New Orleans	245,000
New York City	262,000
San Antonio	186,950
San Diego	245,384
Trenton	6,100

New York City and San Antonio reported an increase in McKinney Act funds used for emergency food assistance during the last year. Boston, Denver, New Orleans and Trenton said the amount of McKinney Act funds decreased. In Louisville the amount remained the same.

*   Seven cities (27 percent) report using **Community Development Block Grant** funds to support emergency food assistance efforts. These cities and the amounts spent during the last year are:

Boston	$ 80,000
Chicago	1,622,824
Cleveland	708,491
Minneapolis	50,000
New Orleans	263,600
Salt Lake City	57,000
San Diego	206,616

The amount of Community Development Block Grant funds used increased during the last year in Boston, Chicago, Cleveland, Minneapolis, New York City and Salt Lake City.

*   Six cities report using **Community Services Block Grant** funds to support local food assistance efforts. These cities and the amounts spent are:

Alexandria	$ 34,962
Chicago	100,000
Denver	8,030
Louisville	6,137
Minneapolis	50,000
San Antonio	8,000

CSBG funds used for emergency food assistance efforts increased in Denver, Louisville and Minneapolis. They remained the same in Chicago and San Antonio.

THE UNMET NEED

An average of 17 percent of the demand for emergency food assistance is estimated to have gone unmet in the survey cities. The unmet need ranges from 50 percent in Cleveland and 38 percent in Santa Monica to 10 percent in San Antonio, seven percent in Norfolk and one percent in Trenton. Alexandria amd Minneapolis reported that none of the demand went unmet. Among the comments of the officials in cities able to meet the demand:

* **Alexandria**: Alexandria benefits from a strong community commitment by churches, synagogues, non-profit agencies, city government and businesses that assures families are not turned away due to lack of resources. When supplies run low food drives are initiated to replenish stocks.

* **Minneapolis**: A network is used to refer people if one location runs out of food.

Among the cities' comments on being unable to meet all of the demand for emergency food assistance:

* **Boston**: The number of people in need has increased and the resources have not.

* **Charleston**: Non-profit emergency food providers are entirely dependent on the community's contributions of food stuffs. Often the amount of food given is reduced because food stocks are limited. Emergency food providers frequently have to wait for houses of worship, civic groups and schools to conduct canned food drives that replenish food supplies.

* **Cleveland**: No facility has had to close because of insufficient supplies of food. However, it is necessary to limit clients to six visits a year.

* **Denver**: The City is not yet unable to meet demand, but the possibility exists if funding continues to be cut.

* **Kansas City**: Harvesters reports that of the agencies that receive their foods, some cannot meet needs of people who come due to lack of money, inadequate storage facilities or volunteers. Mid-America Assistance Coalition adds that some pantries underserve for the same reasons presented by Harvesters.

* **Los Angeles**: There isn't enough food to meet the demand all the time at all agencies. Some face worse conditions than others.

* **Louisville**: There are limitations, but in Louisville we have an excellent network of service providers who deal in emergency food assistance, from the terrific soup kitchens to one of the best food banks in the country. We also have a program called Kentucky Harvest in which

a growing core of volunteers takes left-over food donated by local restaurants, hotels, bakeries and caterers to the soup kitchens and shelters in the community. No one should go hungry in our city!

* **Nashville:** We are limited to the emergency food assistance we can give based on how much food is donated and available.

* **New Orleans:** Resources are decreasing while the need increases.

* **New York City:** Our last survey showed that 38,000 people per month were turned away for lack of food.

* **Norfolk:** Supply has not kept pace with demand. There is a shortage of volunteers to staff food pantries and soup kitchens.

* **Philadelphia:** In a survey of emergency food providers in the City, a majority reported that they run out of food at least once a month.

* **Phoenix:** On occasion the resources do not fit the need presented. This has been the only reason given. In general the feeling among providers is that there is usually enough food for all who seek it; the difficulties are more specific and occasionally programmatic.

* **Portland:** Some programs may have had to reduce the amount of food available to clients at certain times. People are not turned away unless they exceed the frequency limit.

* **Saint Louis:** In addition to the unmet need for emergency food assistance, most regular food assistance programs have waiting lists. As an example, the St. Louis Area Agency on Aging funded 62 senior meals out of an emergency fund and had a waiting list for home-delivered meals of 111.

* **Saint Paul:** At times when demand is great, some food shelves have cut hours or the amount of food handed out.

* **Salt Lake City:** Sometimes food supplies are limited and the number and frequency of visits are restricted. The problem is especially acute at the end of each month when food stamp allotments have been exhausted.

* **San Antonio:** Individual pantries do deplete their food resources from time to time, but they refer people to other agencies for assistance.

* **Santa Monica:** Food assistance facilities are providing less food and food less often due to a decrease in funding.

* **Seattle:** Because food donations are down this year, food banks have been forced to turn people away. Most, however, do attempt to serve all people requesting food, reducing the amount of food available to each household.

In 72 percent (18) of the cities, emergency food assistance facilities may have to turn away people in need due to lack of resources. Those cities are Boston, Kansas City, Los Angeles, Louisville, Nashville, New Orleans, New York City, Norfolk, Philadelphia, Phoenix, Portland, Saint Louis, Saint Paul, Salt Lake City, San Antonio, San Diego, Santa Monica and Seattle. In Alexandria, Charleston, Chicago, Cleveland, Denver, Minneapolis and Trenton, emergency food assistance facilities do not have to turn people away due to lack of resources. Among the comments of the city officials:

* **Charleston:** While people may not be turned away, they may receive only canned vegetables and fruit in limited supplies.

* **Cleveland:** Most families need assistance at the end of every month, not just six months a year.

* **Louisville:** Based on agency reporting and interviews, approximately 15 percent of applicants must be turned away or delayed because of unavailable resources.

* **Minneapolis:** A network is used to refer applicants to facilities with food.

* **Nashville:** Since we are limited as to how many boxes are given, some food needs may go unmet. Because of lack of transportation, many people who need assistance sometimes are unable to go to a site to pick up food.

* **New Orleans:** Some people are turned away because they return for more food before their three-month waiting period is over.

* **Portland:** Most (87 percent) persons on food stamps run out before the end of the month.

* **Phoenix:** The responses of need being unmet were based on the unavailability of food at the initial presentation, the need of some guests for food of a special nature, and the perennial problem of need generally exceeding resources. If there were more food, and it were more diverse, it could be utilized.

* **Saint Louis:** Resources are inadequate. Mostly there is not enough food for all families. Some agencies have limited hours. However, it is noteworthy that pantries which receive commodities are able to expand their food distribution when the monthly commodities are received.

* **Salt Lake City:** The biggest problems regarding the demand for emergency food assistance which go unmet relate to geographical access and lack of availability on weekends, holidays and in the evenings.

* **San Antonio:** The City has experienced a population increase, particularly in its elderly population. The recent Census indicates that the City has also continued to see growth among the young low-income population group.

CITY DATA ON HUNGER

| | Percentage Increase in Demand For Emergency Food | Percentage Increase In Families' Demand For Emergency Food | Percentage of Families Among Those Requesting Food | Percentage of Adults Requesting Food Who Are Employed | Level of Resources | Food Assistance Facilities Provide | | Are People Being Turned Away? |
						Adequate Quantity of Food	Nutritionally Balanced Food	
Alexandria	20-25	20	80	NA	SAME	YES	YES	NO
Boston	10-30	30	70	75	SAME	NO	YES	YES
Charleston	NA	NA	85	7	DECREASE	NO	YES	NO
Chicago	12.6	13	23	NA	DECREASE	YES	YES	NO
Cleveland	0	NA	80	12	DECREASE	NO	YES	NO
Denver	NA	NA	NA	NA	DECREASE	YES	YES	NO
Kansas City	NA	NA	87	30	DECREASE	NO	YES	YES
Los Angeles	10	15	75	18	SAME	NO	YES	YES
Louisville	3	3	70	40	SAME	YES	NO	YES
Miami	NA	NA	NA	NA	NA	NA	NA	NA
Minneapolis	5	5	66	44	DECREASE	NO	YES	NO
Nashville	0	0	30	NA	SAME	NO	YES	YES
New Orleans	23	13	75	11	DECREASE	NO	YES	YES
New York City	10	NA	NA	NA	INCREASE	YES	YES	YES
Norfolk	NA	NA	NA	NA	DECREASE	NO	NO	YES
Philadelphia	30	30	70	30	DECREASE	NO	NO	YES
Phoenix	9.5	9.6	92.5	18	INCREASE	YES	YES	YES
Portland	0	35	45	30	DECREASE	NO	YES	YES
Saint Louis	25	25	73	33	DECREASE	NO	NO	YES
Saint Paul	6	12	79	35	INCREASE	NO	YES	YES
Salt Lake City	8-12	8-12	65	40	INCREASE	NO	YES	YES
San Antonio	17	21	56	38	INCREASE	YES	YES	YES
San Diego	20	30	NA	NA	INCREASE	NA	YES	YES
Santa Monica	28	35	40	NA	DECREASE	NO	NA	YES
Seattle	0	0	45	NA	NA	NO	NO	YES
Trenton	-43	-43	90	11	INCREASE	YES	YES	NO

PARTICIPATION IN SCHOOL LUNCH, SCHOOL BREAKFAST AND SUMMER FOOD
PROGRAMS

CITY	CHILDREN IN SCHOOL LUNCH PROGRAM	CHILDREN IN SCHOOL BREAKFAST PROGRAM	SUMMER FOOD PROGRAM SITES	CHILDREN IN SUMMER FOOD PROG.
Alexandria	3,800	1,407	19	2,000
Boston	NA	NA	184	6,300 - 9,100
Charleston	45,246	24,477	87	6,742
Chicago	329,000	329,000	750	70,000
Cleveland	44,000	25,000	27	50,000
Kansas City	29,959	13,408	91	5,900
Louisville	31,562	12,462	77	5,000
New Orleans	55,329	21,000	51	21,000
New York City	517,500	126,000	400	190,000
Norfolk	16,500	7,500	18	1,295*
Philadelphia	87,250	16,000	975	48,000
Portland	14,780	6,948	43	2,100
Saint Louis	33,805	19,516	206	6,935
San Antonio	144,144	48,738	132	357,242
San Diego	64,000	35,000	47	45,000
Seattle	1,700	7,000	142	5,000
Trenton	NA	NA	85	3,500

*Average per day

HOMELESSNESS

During the last year overall requests for emergency shelter increased in just over four out of five of the survey cities. The average estimated rate of increase was 10 percent. Requests for shelter by homeless families alone are estimated to have increased by 13 percent, with an increase experienced in two-thirds of the survey cities. People remain homeless for an average of seven months in the survey cities. In 85 percent of the survey cities shelters may turn away families due to lack of resources. In 77 percent of the cities they may turn away other homeless people because of lack of resources. The city officials estimate that 29 percent of the requests for shelter by all homeless people as well as by homeless families alone went unmet. The number of emergency shelter beds in the survey cities increased by an average of four percent. Transitional housing units increased by 20 percent.

The Problem

The Demand for Emergency Shelter

Just over four out of five (81 percent) of the survey cities reported an increase in requests for emergency shelter during the last year. Charleston, Louisville and Saint Paul reported that the number of requests remained the same. New York City and Norfolk reported a decrease in requests for shelter.

Across the survey cities the average increase in requests was 10 percent. The percentage of increased requests ranged from 43 percent in Portland, 35 percent in Los Angeles, 24 percent in Kansas City, 21 percent in New Orleans and 20 percent in Miami to 5-10 percent in Denver, nine percent in Minneapolis, seven percent in Alexandria and Philadelphia, five percent in Phoenix and three percent in Seattle. Decreases in shelter requests were 29 percent in Norfolk and 2.5 percent in New York City.

Requests for shelter by homeless families alone increased in just over two-thirds (68 percent) of the cities during the last year. Five cities -- Alexandria, Charleston, New York City, Saint Paul and Trenton -- reported a decline in requests for shelter by homeless families. The number of such requests remained the same during the last year in Chicago, Louisville and Philadelphia. Shelter requests by homeless families alone increased by an overall average of 13 percent.

The average increase in requests by homeless families was 13 percent during the last year. Increases in requests for shelter by homeless families ranged from 88 percent in Portland, 50 percent in Los Angeles and 28 percent in Boston to 5-10 percent in Denver, seven percent in Saint Louis and five percent in Phoenix. Decreases in requests ranged from 30 percent in Saint Paul to eight percent in Alexandria and less than one percent in New York City.

The Length of Time People are Homeless

People remain homeless for an average of seven months in the survey cities. Sixty-two percent of the cities reported that the length of time people are homeless increased during the last year.

Twenty-nine percent (six) of the cities said that the length of time remained the same; two cities said the length of time decreased. In the 14 cities able to estimate the average length of homelessness, people remained homeless for an average of six months. The duration of homelessness ranged from 18 months in Miami and San Diego, 12 months in Louisville and 6-12 months in New Orleans to two months in Trenton, 1.5 months in Norfolk and one month in Saint Paul and Santa Monica.

Among the explanations of those cities reporting an **increase in the duration of homelessness:**

* **Louisville:** If families stay less than 30 days in an emergency shelter in Louisville, 80 percent of them will go back to an abusive or doubling-up arrangement. For many, quality support services are critical and a one-year to 18-month stay in a structured environment is necessary. Louisville's statistics show that there is an 85-90 percent success rate for families in stable permanent housing after they have completed their stay in a transitional housing program. It is important to know that over 80 percent of our homeless adults are developmentally disabled, mentally ill, chemically dependent or have more than one of these problems.

* **Miami:** Many people have become chronic substance abusers. The mentally ill do not have adequate housing.

* **Minneapolis:** The increase is probably due to decreased family income and increased housing costs.

* **Nashville:** The length of homelessness is four to six months for persons or families whose homelessness is largely economic and logistical (i.e. who merely need to locate jobs, entitlements and housing). It is 18 to 36 months for persons or families with one or more serious problems in addition to a lack of appropriate housing (i.e. experiences of violence, illness [including addiction], encounters with the criminal justice system, etc.)

* **New Orleans:** There is increased difficulty in finding adequate employment and affordable housing. Some shelters now provide housing for up to 24 months. Previously, it was up to 90 days.

* **Portland:** The length of time has increased for families due to the lack of affordable housing, especially public housing.

* **Saint Louis:** Providers report recidivism to be at the highest level ever, despite longer follow-up. All providers agree that clinical depression and substance abuse, especially of crack cocaine, is a leading cause. Patterns of usage due to homeless episodes appear to be three to four months at a stretch on average for families, eight to 12 months on average for single, primarily chronically mentally ill women, and 12 to 15 months for unaccompanied males.

* **San Antonio:** The lack of affordable housing and the freeze in the waiting list for subsidized housing continue to be major factors in the increased length of time a person remains homeless.

* **Trenton:** It is more difficult to obtain alternative housing due both to limited income and the lack of adequate affordable housing.

In **Saint Paul,** where the average is 11 days for families and single individuals, officials explain that emergency shelter is a back-up resource, not a way of life for the majority.

In **Philadelphia** the average length of time in a shelter has decreased due to the increase in transitional housing units. Stricter enforcement of policy where persons with substance abuse problems must seek treatment has also played a significant role.

The Population

Across the survey cities, it is estimated that single men and families with children each comprise 43 percent of the homeless population, single women 11 percent and unaccompanied youth four percent. (These percentages do not total 100 due to rounding.) Children account for 30 percent of the homeless population. City officials estimate that 56 percent of the homeless population is African-American, 27 percent is white, 13 percent is Hispanic, three percent is Native American and one percent is Asian.

It is estimated that persons considered mentally ill account for 27 percent of the homeless population in the survey cities; substance abusers account for 48 percent. in the survey cities, 18 percent of homeless persons are employed in full and part-time jobs; 21 percent of the homeless population are veterans. Nine percent have AIDS or HIV-related illness.

* Cities in which **single men** comprise 55 percent or more of the homeless population include Alexandria, Boston, Charleston, Louisville, Nashville, Salt Lake City and Seattle. They account for 35 percent in Philadelphia and Phoenix, 20 percent in Saint Louis, 19 percent in San Antonio, 16 percent in Trenton and 11 percent in Kansas City.

* **Families with children** account for 77 percent of the homeless population in Trenton, 75 percent in New York City, 73 percent in Kansas City, 66 percent in Saint Louis, 65 percent in San Antonio, 63 percent in Phoenix and 54 percent in Philadelphia. They account for one-fourth of the homeless population in Los Angeles and San Diego, 16 percent in Nashville and 14 percent in New Orleans.

  Children account for an average of 60 percent of homeless family members in the survey cities. Children account for 70 percent or more of homeless family members in Boston, Cleveland, Los Angeles, Saint Louis and Salt Lake City. They account for 20 percent of family members in New Orleans and 10 percent in Miami.

  Since homeless families comprise 43 percent of the homeless population in the survey cities, and 60 percent of family members are children, one can estimate that children who are members of homeless families comprise 26 percent of the homeless population. Since an addition four percent of the homeless population are unaccompanied youth, it can be estimated that **children** account for 30 percent of the homeless population.

  Among homeless families, 73 percent are headed by a single parent. More than 90 percent are headed by a single parent in Boston, Chicago, Cleveland, Philadelphia, Saint Paul and Trenton.

* **Single women** comprise 24 percent of the homeless population in New Orleans, 21 percent in Chicago and 20 percent in Santa Monica.

* **Unaccompanied youth** account for 13 percent of the homeless population in New Orleans and San Diego, 12 percent in Los Angeles, eight percent in Miami and seven percent in Louisville.

* Cities in which **African-Americans** comprise 70 percent or more of the homeless population include Alexandria, Charleston, Chicago, Cleveland, Norfolk and Philadelphia.

* **Whites** account for 40 percent or more of the homeless population in Nashville, Portland, Saint Paul, Salt Lake City and Santa Monica.

* **Hispanics** comprise 52 percent of the homeless population in San Antonio, 29 percent in New York City and one-fourth of the homeless population in Miami and Phoenix.

* Twenty-eight percent of the homeless population in Phoenix are **Native Americans**. They account for 10 percent of this population in Minneapolis.

* Cities in which **mentally ill persons** comprise 40 percent or more of the homeless population are Miami, Phoenix, Saint Louis and Salt Lake City. They account for under 10 percent of the homeless population in Chicago, Norfolk, Philadelphia and Seattle.

* **Substance Abusers** account for one-half or more of the homeless population in Boston, Louisville, Miami, Nashville, Saint Louis, San Diego, Santa Monica and Trenton.

* Cities in which 30 percent of more of homeless persons are **employed in full- or part-time jobs** are Alexandria, Charleston, Nashville, Portland and Salt Lake City.

* Cities reporting that 15 percent or more of the homeless population are persons with **AIDS or HIV-related illness** are Boston, Los Angeles, Miami, Philadelphia and San Diego.

* Thirty percent or more of homeless people are **veterans** in Los Angeles, Louisville, Nashville, New Orleans, Saint Louis, Salt Lake City and San Diego.

Veterans

The city officials were asked to describe the demographics of the homeless veterans' population and the extent to which they are being referred to services provided by the Department of Veterans Affairs. Their responses show the veterans population to be quite diverse with a wide range of problems; most frequently cited were substance abuse or mental illness. They are served by a variety of local agencies, some of which receive funding from the Department of Veterans Affairs, and by the DVA itself.

Following are the comments of the city officials in response to the open-ended question on homeless veterans:

* **Alexandria:** Veterans represent 12 percent of the adult population sheltered during the period October 1992 to June 1993. Shelters operate on a case management basis in which the service needs of the residents are identified and community resources, including services of the VA, are identified to meet those particular needs. The DVA has also provided outreach to the shelters.

* **Boston:** The local veterans' shelter serves between 40,000 and 50,000 men per year who come to Boston from around the country. Each night the shelter houses 150 men and provides day services to 100 more. The men are veterans of wars that span the century, from World War II to the Gulf War. Each week people from DVA come to the shelter to update the clients and workers on the latest opportunities and services. The clients of the shelter are referred to DVA services on a daily basis.

* **Charleston:** Based on a recent survey of 124 homeless men, we found that 35 percent were veterans. There is an outreach worker from the local DVA Hospital who works with veterans in all the area shelters.

* **Cleveland:** The average homeless veteran is a 39-year-old African-American male. Thirty percent of the vets have been homeless over six months. Fifty-five percent have been unemployed for over three years. Seventy-seven percent are substance abusing. The existing capacity of the Veteran's Administration is always filled.

* **Kansas City:** The Coordinator of the Health Care for Homeless Veterans Program reports the following: "Our best estimate is that there are between 1,200 and 1,500 homeless veterans in the Kansas City area. The majority of homeless veterans are single male adults and we took the number of shelter hotline calls from single adults and added approximately 3,000 to that for people on the streets, in cars, etc. The DVA uses a national standard which states that 30-33 percent of all homeless single adults are veterans. I took this percentage of the above numbers to arrive at an approximate number of 1,200 to 1,500."

  From November 1, 1992 to October 31, 1993, we received 550 referrals of homeless veterans to our Health Care for Homeless Veterans Program. We provided case management services to 150 of these veterans and arranged for DVA or community services for the remaining. We do not have accurate statistics, but many more homeless veterans received other services at the DVA Medical Center, including inpatient and outpatient medical treatment."

* **Los Angeles:** On veterans: 98 percent are male, two percent are female, 40 percent suffer from mental illness. More than half suffer from alcohol or other drug abuse problems. A small but rising percentage are the mobile homeless. These are individuals or families who have lost their jobs and homes and are living in their vehicles.

* **Louisville:** Louisville has an outstanding HCMI Veterans program which has been in operation since February 1987. It is an outreach program staffed by two outreach workers. They have done over 2,000 intakes of homeless veterans. It is estimated that 42 percent of the homeless in Louisville are veterans and 50 percent of those are from the Vietnam era.

  The purpose of the HCMI Veterans program is to identify homeless vets, establish their eligibility, assess and refer them to DVA for treatment and evaluation. Since 90 percent of the homeless are chemically dependent and 75 percent are mentally ill, extensive, long term treatment is required for rehabilitation. It is necessary, therefore, to provide long term residential treatment and education, which we do. The average stay in residential care is six months to a year.

The last stage of rehabilitation is vocational rehabilitation. Success rates have increased from 10 percent to 33 percent.

* **Nashville:** DVA staff working with homeless veterans estimate there are 660 homeless veterans in Nashville. At least 80 percent of these are males and at least 55 percent are Vietnam veterans. The DVA Medical Center has an intensive case management program and is presently working with 52 homeless veterans. There is an active outreach program and at least one to two veterans are admitted weekly into the hospital for a complete evaluation. At a recent Stand Down Operation, 140 homeless veterans participated.

* **New Orleans:** Of the homeless veterans in New Orleans, 62 percent are referred to the DVA. Of those, 30 percent are provided with health care, 42 percent with shelter, 92 percent are provided with clothing and 70 percent are provided personal hygiene assistance. Health Care for the Homeless takes care of the primary needs of the homeless veterans who come to them.

* **Norfolk:** The Homeless Chronically Mentally Ill Veterans Program at the DVA Medical Center in Hampton does outreach to homeless veterans, including initial assessments on approximately 40 first-visit veterans monthly. Veterans who are homeless, unemployed, eligible for care and want treatment for alcoholism, drug abuse and/or chronic mental illness are referred to the HCMI pre-placement program at the VAMC. If no beds are available, they are screened at the DVA for three other programs within their domiciliaries which treat homeless and other veterans for substance abuse, chronic mental illness and/or medical problems. The VAMC also provides income assistance and rehabilitation. Close to 400 beds in the DVA domiciliary are used for treatment and rehabilitation. Since the HCMI program began in May 1987, close to 3,000 homeless veterans have been identified in the Hampton Roads area.

* **Philadelphia:** Twenty-six percent of adult homeless men are veterans; 10.2 percent of the total homeless population are veterans. One shelter is designated to serve homeless veterans with substance abuse problems. The DVA is actively involved with outreach and service provision. A counselor from the DVA is available weekly at the Intake Center to process claims for benefits and other related issues.

* **Portland:** Because homeless families are very young (head of household is 30 or younger), very few veterans are represented in this population. Among homeless single males, veterans account for approximately 20 percent. Many receive services from the DVA. The largest mass shelter has an on-site representative from the DVA.

* **Saint Louis:** The largest group of homeless veterans is 22 to 44 years of age (primarily Vietnam era veterans). Over half have 12 or more years of education, resulting in high effectiveness in employability programs – 60 percent still employed after 12 months on the job; the average annual wage earned by that 60 percent is $12,600. Length of homelessness varies: 50 percent are homeless 60 days to one year while 25 percent are homeless for one to two years. Fifty

percent of homeless men have some kind of conviction history. Examples of convictions include old parking violations, vagrancy, assaults, and carrying a concealed weapon.

*   **Salt Lake City:** Veterans comprise about 35 percent of Salt Lake City's homeless population. Many homeless veterans do not take advantage of available DVA programs. They view the DVA as a very bureaucratic organization, and they don't deal well with bureaucracies.

*   **San Antonio:** The demographics of the homeless veterans population are: 50 percent white, 35 percent Hispanic and 15 percent African-American; two percent are women; 40 percent are Vietnam Veterans; 70 percent experience a substance abuse problem; 25-30 percent require intense psychiatric care. The average age is 40, and the majority are homeless for less than six months.

*   **Santa Monica:** Homeless veterans account for approximately 38 percent of the population of homeless men in Santa Monica. Several social service agencies have arrangements with DVA staff to provide on-site counseling services.

*   **Seattle:** Homeless veterans represent 15 percent of Seattle's shelter population, possibly up to 40 percent of all homeless persons. The average age for homeless vets is under 40; most are Vietnam-era vets. Ten to 15 percent are over age 50 and six percent are over age 60. Racial breakdown for homeless vets: approximately 51 percent white, 21 percent African-American, 13 percent Hispanic, 10 percent Native American and five percent Asian or other. Vietnam veterans are faced with life's most traumatic issues, e.g., post-traumatic stress disorder and alcoholism/drug addiction. Long term service to meet their needs often is not provided by the DVA or the local community.

*   **Trenton:** The City of Trenton's Office on Homelessness and Hunger, on average, sees three to four veterans a month. Most are in need of housing and are referred to the Veterans Center in Trenton.

Case Studies of Homeless Families and Individuals

The city officials were asked to describe the conditions faced by an actual homeless family or individual in their city. Following are brief **case studies of homeless families:**

*   **Alexandria:** Mr. and Mrs. A, both working, supported their family (a four-year-old daughter and three-year-old twin daughters) in an apartment until Mr. A was unable to work due to a job-related injury. Mr. A, who was a maintenance worker for the apartment complex in which they resided, subsequently lost his job. The family could not maintain their apartment on one part-time salary and public assistance. The family was evicted and entered a shelter.

While in the shelter, Mr. A entered an employment training program to acquire new skills. Mrs. A sought and secured full-time employment. After four months in a shelter, the family was approved for and relocated to a public housing unit. They have maintained their unit for over a year.

* **Boston:** A battered woman and her three children have been homeless for almost two years. They began with a one and a half year long stay at a "welfare" motel, followed by a brief time in a transitional housing program and then two months at a battered women's shelter. While at the shelter, the woman applied for public housing and section 8 at the Boston Housing Authority, as well as for an emergency Section 8 certificate available to battered women who can provide documentation from appropriate sources that they are in physical danger. Though the woman did obtain documentation that she had a restraining order, and a lawyer wrote a letter stating that she was still in danger from her batterer, the woman has yet to receive emergency help. When her time at the battered women's shelter expired, she was forced to return to a motel, even though her case manager strongly believes that she needs ongoing services, including possible Department of Social Services intervention. As of November 12, 1993, this woman and her three children remain homeless.

* **Cleveland:** This fall there was a family with five children who were not only unable to find affordable, permanent housing, but were also unable to be housed by the emergency shelter system, due to the large number of children, and to the fact that it was an intact family. This family was living in their car for most of the summer. The family did not want to be separated, as would have occurred if they went into the emergency shelters.

* **Kansas City:** The client is a 22-year-old single white female with three children. Her homelessness came about when she couldn't afford her apartment rent with her AFDC check. The client's case management goals were to obtain housing and schooling.

When the client entered our program she was already in training at the Job Corps. Day care was approved with the understanding that she would apply for state day care, which she did. The client entered the Futures program at a community college and is still studying nursing, with a graduation date of January 1994.

The client has applied and been approved for Section 8 housing. The client found and remains in Section 8 housing. She also began classes designed to help her earn a living and become more self-sufficient. This case is being closed as successful.

* **Louisville:** Lynn, a single parent with two children, recently left a transitional housing program and moved into a Section 8 apartment. Lynn grew up in an abusive family, married at 17 to a man who was an alcoholic, and physically and mentally abusive. She left her husband, assuming sole responsibility for caring for the family.

After spending a short time in an emergency shelter, Lynn and her children moved into a transitional housing program. Through extensive case management, therapy programs, and parenting classes, she has become a new person. While in the transitional housing program, she stated, "It is like a wonderful little apartment for me and my children and I feel safe here. I feel nurtured and because of the love and kindness that has been shown to me and my children, I am a much better person and I feel good about myself."

Lynn is presently attending college and enjoying taking care of her family.

* **Nashville:** The typical homeless family is a single, 23-year-old mother, either white or African-American, with two young children. The mother and at least one child have experienced violence, sexual or otherwise, during their lives. The mother's education, job training, employment and health care have been interrupted for any number of reasons, including pregnancy, insufficient child care, violence, depression, alcohol and/or other drug addiction.

* **New Orleans:** Jane is a 26-year-old mother of one. She and her daughter have both been diagnosed with AIDS. Jane is married and was living with her husband who has been physically abusive, especially since learning of his wife and child's diagnosis. Jane recently found the courage to leave her abusive situation and is living at a battered women's shelter. She has no family and her only means of support is food stamps (the SSI check for her child is under her husband's name). Jane is afraid to bring her child into C-100 for health care because of the risk of her husband locating her. She feels that if she could only find stable housing, her daughter's health could be much improved.

* **Norfolk:** A woman and her children had left their home for a second time because she had been beaten by her husband. While at the shelter the woman and her children were stalked by the husband. The man was jailed for a brief period for his continual harassment of the woman. A Section 8 certificate has been secured for the family and the woman is seeking housing. The family is receiving mediation services through the court and the woman has secured a job.

* **Philadelphia:** Ms. B. and her four children (ages three, four, seven and eight) were referred to emergency shelter by the Children's Protective Services worker due to severe overcrowding. Ms. B. and her children had moved into her mother's house after her 7-year-old daughter was sexually assaulted by a teenager while living in her sister's house. Ms. B. receives $589/month in AFDC benefits and food stamps. She stated that she used crack cocaine but has not used drugs for the eight months prior to shelter. The family was placed in shelter and was provided case management services and an array of support services over a 15 month period until placed in a one year transitional program. The family was provided case management services, drug and alcohol treatment, on-site drug and alcohol counseling, AA meetings, mental health treatment, health care information and referrals, day-care, a client savings program, advocacy, application assistance for public housing and Section 8 housing, training in parenting skills, and help in utilizing community resources. The family's public housing and Section 8 applications have been pending for over one year.

* **Portland:** Mary, age 24 and her 2-year-old son came to an agency in the Fall of 1992. Mary identified her needs as stable housing, stable income, improved family functioning and a more positive support system. Mary had health problems, but no alcohol or drug issues. Mary has many strengths and is clear about her goals. She has a strong will to succeed and cares deeply about her son's welfare. After the assessment was completed Mary and her son were housed in a church shelter for four weeks followed by a five-month stay in transitional housing. Mental health services began and a family counselor visits once per week. Her son was screened and referred to an early intervention program and is attending a special pre-school. With the help of a Family Advocate, Mary was accepted into a special long-term case management program with access to permanent subsidized housing. Rent assistance was provided to cover move-in costs. Mary is enrolled in a job training program. Mary and her son are doing well and will be self-sufficient in the near future.

* **Saint Louis:** Ms. "Jones," a single mother with three children sought shelter through our network intake and referral center. She was placed in a family shelter where it was discovered she had a drug problem. She was referred to an available out-patient program, but relapses occurred. She was referred out of state to a residential program and her children were placed in foster care. At the end of several months, the center placed the mother into a transitional program. While there, the mother made good progress and remained substance free and attended Narcotics Anonymous meetings regularly. After three to four months the children were returned to her when they successfully reintegrated as a family unit. Today, the family is in their own apartment receiving follow-up from the network housing provider and the State Division of Family Services, and regularly attends aftercare meetings for recovery from drugs. The mother is in nursing school and due to graduate in June 1994. The length of time from first request for services until now has been 44 months. It is anticipated that the family will need follow-up for an additional 12 months.

* **Saint Paul:** Mary has two children and receives $532 in AFDC. Her rent is $440. She faces an average monthly utility bill of $60. She has paid some of the bill, but not all of it. She is threatened with a gas and electric shut-off. Fuel assistance from a CAP agency will pay all but $300. She pays the balance but is short on the rent. The landlord evicts her, and she moves to a shelter.

* **San Antonio:** Annette, a 28-year-old female with two children ages three and four has been homeless for approximately one month. After suffering several months of abusive behavior and mismanagement of income by her husband, Annette finally fled with her children to a shelter. She remained in the shelter for four weeks before she was referred to and accepted into a transitional housing program. Annette has secured an income maintenance job and is working on following through with her self-sufficiency plan that addresses personal issues as well as education and job training strategies.

* **Seattle:** A single mother with three teenagers. This woman was employed as a secretary until she experienced pain in her forearm that became so severe she lost her job -- and eventually, her home. After staying in Seattle Emergency Housing Service's emergency and interim housing programs, the family moved into the permanent rental housing the week before Christmas. The mother received treatment for her arm and found a new job in January.

* **Trenton:** This is a single parent household headed by a 37-year-old father with four children, ages 12, 11, nine and eight. The father was employed for eight years but was laid off. His unemployment compensation has run out and he has not found employment. He went to the Mercer County Board of Social Services seeking monetary and housing assistance. His rent is $750 per month and his arrearage is $3700. His apartment is unaffordable since his income is an AFDC grant of $553. This family was placed in temporary shelter for the weekend and has found permanent housing, while not affordable on his current grant. Mercer County Board of Social Services will assist him with rent for 12 months or until he finds a job.

Below are brief **case studies of homeless individuals:**

* **Charleston:** Sam has been staying in a shelter off and on for five years. He doesn't want to live in a shelter; he hunts for employment almost every day. But Sam has several problems which make it difficult to keep a job, despite his bachelor's degree in biology. Sam is a 42-year-

old alcoholic with clinical depression and diabetes. Because of his illnesses and his age, employers hesitate to hire him. The work he finds is menial and always temporary. Sam's dreams never seem to come true and he doesn't understand why.

Sam receives shelter, food, clothing, counselling, health care and free medication; but until there is accessible, long-term, residential substance abuse treatment and creative job training and placement services available for him, Sam's situation is unlikely to change.

* **Chicago:** Mr. J is a Black male, 43 years of age. Mr. J. came to the Haymarket MISA unit in June 1993 after experiencing homelessness, major depression, an addiction to multiple substances, and a heart condition. Mr. J. became homeless after friends and family denied him access to their homes due to his depression and concurrent substance abusing behavior. Mr. J. had been hospitalized in psychiatric facilities four times with major depression and had attempted suicide twice. He was unable to maintain a place of residence due to the misuse of his social security disability allocation. Mr. J's possessions and identification were lost due to his homelessness.

At the MISA unit Mr. J. received intensive case management services provided by the Department of Human Services. These services included medical, psychiatric, housing, vision, dental, fiscal, and related services. Concurrently, transitional shelter services and substance abuse treatment services were provided by Haymarket Staff.

During Mr. J's stabilization period, he cooperated with efforts to treat his mental illness, addiction, and situation of homelessness. Mr. J. successfully completed graduation from the MISA unit in August 1993 and continued with planned services after discharge. Mr. J. maintained temporary housing while participating in Haymarket House's Intensive Outpatient Program. Mr. J. continues to keep up with his mental health treatment sessions, medical and psychiatric medication regimen, and addiction recovery. He is successfully living in independent housing at Lakefront SRO corporation, and has made inroads in re-establishing a healthy relationship with appropriate family and new stable friends.

* **Los Angeles:** "Brenda" is a mentally ill person who lives on a blanket surrounded by cardboard boxes. She is very suspicious of any authority figures. She refuses to seek treatment and it is difficult to get her to fill out even basic forms. She receives general relief and food stamps but then complains that they are stolen. She will not go to interviews for a hotel room. We continue to work with her toward the goal of getting her into a safe place.

* **Miami:** The person is mentally unstable. We facilitate the social services, but due to ineffective case management (no follow-up) he or she ends up on the street again.

* **Minneapolis:** Roger is a 23-year-old Native American male living with his mother, father and a younger sister in a transitional program in northern Minnesota. They have lived there for four months. He is not married and has no children. With a 10th grade education, no GED and no job training, he has a hard time holding a steady job. He has recently worked as a construction worker for 20 hours per week. He considers himself chemically dependent and has been in an alcohol treatment program. Roger has recently been told that he is schizophrenic. He has lived in a hospital for persons with mental health problems within the

last two years and is currently taking medication for his mental health problem. His main needs are to get a driver's license and a car.

Although not a case study, **Salt Lake City** officials provided a description of the conditions that homeless persons face: Crowded sleeping conditions, one free meal per day only, inadequate public transportation, hot in the summer/cold in the winter, difficulty obtaining basic necessities like showers, dental care, etc., difficulty obtaining clothes for work and job interviews, and access to various assistance programs can be frustratingly slow.

The Causes of Homelessness

A number of diverse and complex factors have contributed to the problems of homelessness in the survey cities. Many of those factors are interrelated. Listed in order of frequency, the following causes were identified by the cities in response to an open-ended question: The lack of affordable housing, unemployment and other employment-related problems, substance abuse and the lack of needed services, mental illness and the lack of needed services, poverty and low income, and domestic violence.

The lack of affordable housing -- Twenty-two cities identified the lack of affordable housing: Alexandria, Boston, Charleston, Chicago, Denver, Kansas City, Louisville, Miami, Minneapolis, Nashville, New Orleans, New York City, Norfolk, Philadelphia, Phoenix, Portland, Salt Lake City, Saint Louis, San Antonio, Santa Monica, Seattle and Trenton.

Unemployment and other employment-related problems -- A total of 19 cities identified unemployment, underemployment or other employment-related problems as one of the main causes of homelessness. Citing unemployment were Alexandria, Chicago, Cleveland, Denver, Los Angeles, New Orleans, Philadelphia, Portland, Salt Lake City, San Antonio, San Diego, Santa Monica and Trenton. Alexandria, Nashville, Norfolk, Philadelphia and San Antonio cited underemployment. Citing lack of unskilled jobs were Alexandria, Louisville, Kansas City, Nashville, Saint Louis and San Antonio. Charleston, Louisville, New Orleans and Portland identified lack of job training as a cause of homelessness.

Substance abuse and lack of needed services -- Fourteen cities identified substance abuse and the lack of available treatment and other needed services as a main cause of homelessness: Alexandria, Charleston, Cleveland, Denver, Kansas City, Los Angeles, Louisville, Miami, New York City, Philadelphia, Salt Lake City, Saint Louis, Seattle and Trenton.

Mental illness and the lack of available services for mentally ill people -- Ten cities cited mental illness and insufficient mental health services as a main cause of homelessness: Alexandria, Cleveland, Denver, Los Angeles, Louisville, Miami, New York City, Saint Louis, Seattle and Trenton.

Poverty and Low Income -- Nine cities -- Alexandria, Charleston, Chicago, Denver, Louisville, Minneapolis, New Orleans, Saint Louis and Saint Paul -- cited poverty or low income as a main cause of homelessness.

Domestic violence -- Six cities identified domestic violence and abuse as a primary cause of homelessness: Chicago, Portland, Saint Louis, Saint Paul, Salt Lake City and Seattle.

SERVICES FOR HOMELESS PEOPLE

Emergency Shelter Beds

Across the survey cities, the overall number of emergency shelter beds for homeless people is estimated to have increased by an average of four percent during the last year. The number of shelter beds increased in 57 percent of the cities: Boston, Charleston, Chicago, Cleveland, Los Angeles, Miami, Minneapolis, Nashville, New Orleans, Philadelphia, Phoenix, Salt Lake City, San Antonio, San Diego and Trenton. The number decreased in one-fifth of the cities: Denver, Kansas City, Louisville, New York City and Saint Louis. The number of shelter beds remained the same in 24 percent of the cities: Alexandria, Norfolk, Portland, Saint Paul, Seattle and Trenton.

The rate of increase ranged from 48 percent in New Orleans and 34 percent in Nashville to five percent or less in Chicago, Cleveland, Los Angeles, Phoenix and Salt Lake City. The rate of decrease ranged from 38 percent in Louisville to nine percent in Denver, eight percent in Kansas City and 4.1 percent in New York City.

The overall number of emergency shelter beds specifically for homeless families is estimated to have increased across the survey cities by three percent during the last year. The number of these beds increased in 31 percent of the cities: Boston, Los Angeles, Minneapolis, Nashville, New York City, Phoenix, Saint Paul, San Antonio and Trenton. The number decreased in 27 percent of the cities: Chicago, Denver, Kansas City, Louisville, New York City, Philadelphia and Saint Louis. The number of shelter beds specifically for homeless families remained the same during the last year in 42 percent of the cities: Alexandria, Charleston, Cleveland, Miami, Portland, Salt Lake City, San Diego, Santa Monica and Seattle.

The rate of increase in emergency beds specifically for homeless families ranged from 43 percent in San Antonio and 34 percent in Boston to 1.48 percent in Los Angeles. The rate of decrease ranged from 35 percent in Louisville and 17 percent in Kansas City to less than one percent in New York City. Louisville officials explained that one shelter converted most of its emergency beds to transitional housing.

Transitional Housing Units

The number of transitional housing units increased overall by an average of 20 percent across the survey cities. Seventy-four percent of the cities registered an increase: Alexandria, Boston, Chicago, Cleveland, Los Angeles, Louisville, Miami, Nashville, New Orleans, Norfolk, Philadelphia, Phoenix, Saint Louis, Salt Lake city, San Antonio, San Diego and Trenton. The number of transitional housing units remained the same in 26 percent of the cities: Charleston, Minneapolis, Portland, Saint Paul, Santa Monica and Seattle. No cities reported a decrease in the number of transitional housing units.

The rate of increase in transitional housing units ranged from 100 percent in Norfolk, 59 percent in New Orleans and 45 percent in Alexandria and Cleveland to 10 percent in Miami, Phoenix, Saint Louis, Salt Lake City and San Diego and one percent in Boston and Los Angeles.

The number of transitional housing units specifically for homeless families increased overall by an average of 15 percent in the survey cities. Sixty percent of the cities registered an increase: Alexandria, Boston, Chicago, Cleveland, Los Angeles, Louisville, New Orleans, Norfolk, Philadelphia, Phoenix, Portland, Saint Louis, Salt Lake City, San Antonio and Trenton. The number of such units remained the same in 36 percent of the cities: Charleston, Denver, Miami, Minneapolis, Nashville, Saint Paul, San Diego, Santa Monica and Seattle. New York City reported a decline in the number of transitional housing units for homeless families.

The increase in transitional housing units specifically for homeless families ranged from 72 percent in Chicago and 20 percent in San Antonio to five percent or less in Boston, Los Angeles, New Orleans and Saint Louis. New York City experienced a 5.5 percent decline in transitional units for homeless families.

Single Room Occupancy Units

Single room occupancy units increased overall by 16 percent in the survey cities during the last year. Thirty-nine percent of the cities saw an increase in this category: Boston, Charleston, Chicago, Los Angeles, Miami, New York City, Philadelphia, Salt Lake City and San Antonio. The number of such units remained the same in 48 percent of the cities: Alexandria, Cleveland, Denver, Louisville, Minneapolis, Nashville, New Orleans, Norfolk, Saint Paul, Santa Monica and Trenton. The number of SRO units decreased in Phoenix, Portland and Saint Louis.

The number of SRO units increased by 22 percent in New York City, 100 percent in San Antonio and 56 percent in Los Angeles, 32 percent in Chicago, 10 percent in Miami and five percent in Philadelphia. It decreased by 20 percent in Saint Louis and four percent in Portland.

Family Breakup -- A Requisite for Shelter

In 64 percent of the survey cities homeless families may have to break up in order to be accommodated in emergency shelters; Nine cities (36 percent) reported that families do not have to break up in order to be sheltered. The cities in which families may have to break up in order to be sheltered are Boston, Chicago, Cleveland, Denver, Kansas City, Louisville, Miami, Nashville, New Orleans, Norfolk, Philadelphia, Portland, San Antonio, Santa Monica, Seattle and Trenton. Among the city officials' explanations for **families not being able to be sheltered together:**

* **Boston:** Some shelters only accept women with children, while other shelters will not allow male children over a certain age.

* **Chicago:** Some shelters with the capacity to provide families with separate and private accommodations can keep the family together. However, some shelters have dormitory-type facilities. Male and female family members may be housed in the same facility (although not in the same area). Some shelters do not accommodate families. In addition, some shelters feel it is inappropriate for male children (e.g. age 14 and over) to share the same accommodations with the rest of the family.

*   **Denver:** Sometimes. There are not enough shelter beds to accommodate all of the families seeking emergency shelter.

*   **Kansas City:** There are some shelters that only take women and children, so a husband will have to go to a men's shelter. Some shelters will only take couples that are legally married. For married childless couples, the husband will have to stay at the men's shelter and the wife go to the women's shelter.

*   **Los Angeles:** Occasionally with two parent families, the men may have to sleep separated from the women and children or sleep in a different facility. Also males over 12 may be separated from the family.

*   **Louisville:** Women and children receive 24-hour services, but men are separated from families in two of the city shelters.

*   **Nashville:** The largest shelter in Nashville asks fathers to sleep in a mission approximately two miles away from where the family is being sheltered.

*   **New Orleans:** Women and children are housed separately from the men. Two-parent families are also separated when in need of emergency shelter. Many agencies attempt to place intact families in hotels or motels for short periods because they are not able to house them in their own facilities.

*   **Norfolk:** Some shelters keep the family together as a unit. Others allow family members of the same sex to stay together. If there is a mother and son and the son is over a certain age (seven in some cases, 12 in others), he is not allowed to share a room with his mother, but must stay in an all-male ward in the same facility.

*   **Philadelphia:** Every attempt is made to place families as intact units. Occasionally adult male members of a household are placed separately if there are not appropriate vacancies for the family; the family is reunited as soon as an appropriate vacancy can be found.

*   **Portland:** Couples cannot usually stay together. Domestic violence shelters cannot take boys over approximately 11 to 13. It is difficult to accommodate very large or extended families.

*   **Seattle:** Yes, although 637 of the 884 emergency beds available for families will accommodate two-parent families.

*   **Trenton:** Generally families do not have to be separated. However, if there is an adult male or sometimes an older teenage child, the family would have to be broken up to be accommodated in a shelter. Shelters are mainly for women and children or single males. Therefore, husbands and wives with children must be placed in motels.

Among the comments of the cities where **families are not required to break up to be sheltered:**

* **Alexandria:** As a rule, shelters do not separate families or require any break-up of the family unit. However, due to available beds and the configuration of the shelters, on occasion large families may not be sheltered together within the same room. This is rare.

* **Charleston:** Married couples without children sometimes have to split up to sleep in a shelter.

* **Phoenix:** At one time this was a common practice, now there are sufficient family shelters that one rarely hears of a family having to be broken up to stay in a shelter.

* **Saint Louis:** Since 1985 our priority for all shelters, especially City-funded family shelters, has been that families remain intact. In 1993 we only gave funding to family shelters that will accommodate entire families.

Limitations on the Use of Shelter Facilities/ Alternatives During the Day

Twelve (48 percent) of the survey cities reported that homeless families may have to leave shelters in which they are staying during the day. Thirteen (52 percent) said they do not. Those cities in which families may have to leave shelters during the day are Alexandria, Chicago, Cleveland, Denver, Kansas City, Miami, Nashville, New Orleans, Norfolk, Santa Monica and Trenton. Among the city officials' comments on the necessity of leaving shelters and where homeless people go during the day:

* **Alexandria:** Homeless families are encouraged to participate in service planning to alleviate barriers which precipitated homelessness. Services are designed to promote self-sufficiency and a relocation to permanent housing. Therefore, it is generally expected that families will be out of the shelter during the day pursuing individual goals (employment, job search, employment training, education, income maintenance, child care, counseling and treatment, housing search, etc.). Families are allowed to be in the shelter during the day if it is in accordance with their service plan or if other reasons (illness of a family member, infant care, etc.) make it necessary for them to remain in the shelter.

* **Chicago:** Families residing in transitional or second stage housing are not required to leave during the day. They are encouraged to look for jobs, permanent housing, to apply for entitlement or job training programs and/or obtain various supportive services. However, families residing in temporary overnight facilities (whether together or apart) are required to leave during the day. They are then referred to drop-in centers which housed them on a daily basis. These families/individuals are encouraged to pursue the same supportive services previously described.

* **Denver:** Homeless families are asked to leave overnight shelters due to the lack of resources and staff that would enable them to stay. Day shelters are available, but there are not enough to accommodate everyone.

* **Kansas City:** Some shelters will require that people leave during the day because staff is not at the facility during the day. One of the larger shelters does offer separate hospitality centers for men and for women and children, which people can use during the daytime hours.

* **Nashville:** Two family shelters provide shelter for only 12 hours during the evenings. Families must seek shelter wherever they can find it. There are several day shelters, however, where persons can go.

* **New Orleans:** Some walk the streets during the day seeking shelter vouchers. There is one day room at a mission that serves lunch and supper.

* **Norfolk:** Both. Some shelters require persons to leave during the day. When shelters require persons to leave, some frequent libraries, malls or bus stations while it is unknown where others go. In some of the homeless family shelters, adults must seek or maintain employment.

* **Saint Louis:** Depends. City-funded family shelters must be 24-hour shelters. There are four "independent" shelters that require families to leave during the day. In the city-funded 24-hour family shelters, support services, classes, counseling, etc. are brought to clients on site to reduce disruption.

* **Saint Paul:** Husbands and wives without children must split up, as must unmarried couples. Families with children, if accepted, are housed together.

* **San Antonio:** Shelters have designated family unit rooms, but when these are all occupied, families are separated into male and female dormitories.

* **San Diego:** Some emergency shelters have facilities for only women or women with children, while others are limited to men only. The availability of beds will determine whether a family can be housed as a single group, or must be split between facilities with gender limitations.

* **Trenton:** They do housing searches, attend training programs or do employment searches. Some go to visit family.

Among the comments from cities where families do not have to leave shelters during the day:

* **Charleston:** This depends on the rules of each individual shelter, but most family shelters do not require people to stay outside during the day.

* **Phoenix:** All shelters that serve families are 24-hour shelters.

* **Portland:** There are no mass shelters for families. Most are vouchered into a motel or into housing. A few families are in church shelters and have to leave during the day. A day shelter at a social service agency is available to these families.

* **Seattle:** Fewer and fewer shelters providing services to families require that they leave the shelter during the day if the children are sick or if the family has counseling or health appointments at the shelter. However, not all agencies have sufficient resources to hire staff to provide services to families over a 24-hour period. Families unable to stay at the shelter during the day are likely to spend the day on the street, in parks, and/or at public agencies seeking assistance. Day care and school are available for homeless children. However, all family shelters stretch resources to ensure that families are either referred or provided with other resources during the day.

THE FUNDING

During the last year every survey city used city government funds (either locally generated revenues or federal or state grants) to support local shelters or other services specifically for homeless people. The funds used by the cities come from a variety of sources:

* Seventy-seven percent of the cities used **locally generated revenues**. These cities and the amount expended during the last year are:

Alexandria	$ 726,671
Boston	4,100,000
Charleston	36,200
Chicago	5,292,100
Denver	445,168
Kansas City	113,261
Louisville	634,000
Minneapolis	500,000
Nashville	812,933
New Orleans	150,000
New York City	159,650,000
Norfolk	128,400
Philadelphia	12,863,705
Portland	928,219
Saint Louis	763,000
Saint Paul	38,000
San Antonio	98,000
San Diego	1,680,628
Santa Monica	1,013,057
Trenton	35,000

Louisville, Nashville, Norfolk, Philadelphia, Portland and San Antonio reported that during the last year locally generated revenues spent to provide assistance to homeless persons had increased. The amount remained the same in Boston, Charleston, Denver, New Orleans, Phoenix, Saint Louis, Saint Paul and Santa Monica and declined in Chicago, Kansas City and New York City.

* Forty-two percent of the cities (11) used **state grants**. Those cities and the amount expended during the last year are:

Alexandria	$241,666
Boston	3,000,000
Chicago	3,967,400
Cleveland	657,781
Minneapolis	300,000
New Orleans	158,174
New York City	160,000,000

Norfolk	55,340
Philadelphia	9,173,878
Portland	1,062,830
Trenton	35,000

Cleveland, New Orleans and Philadelphia report that the amount of state funding used for homeless assistance increased during the last year. In Chicago, Phoenix and Portland it decreased. In Boston, Charleston, New York City and Saint Louis it remained the same.

* Twenty cities (77 percent) reported using Stewart B. McKinney Homeless Assistance Act funds to provide services to homeless persons. These cities and the amount expended during the last year are:

Alexandria	$ 21,000
Boston	3,558,360
Chicago	1,863,300
Cleveland	390,000
Denver	175,000
Kansas City	189,449
Louisville	1,688,827
Miami	194,000
Minneapolis	477,000
Nashville	1,117,128
New Orleans	245,000
New York City	25,166,254
Norfolk	81,000
Philadelphia	120,800
Portland	523,681
Saint Louis	551,000
Saint Paul	107,000
San Antonio	424,086
San Diego	243,384
Trenton	420,588

Nashville and Portland reported that the amount of McKinney Act funds spent to provide homeless assistance increased during the last year, and Charleston said the amount remained the same. In 81 percent of the cities using McKinney Act funds the amount available declined. These cities are Boston, Chicago, Cleveland, Denver, Kansas City, Louisville, New Orleans, New York City, Norfolk, Phoenix, Saint Louis, Saint Paul and San Antonio.

* Sixteen cities (61 percent) used Community Development Block Grant funds to provide homeless assistance. These cities and the amount spent during the last year are:

Alexandria	$ 86,000
Boston	7,000,000
Charleston	35,000
Chicago	1,000,000
Cleveland	168,735

Los Angeles	5,767,085
Louisville	125,000
Miami	22,610
New Orleans	263,600
New York City	251,447,000
Portland	469,332
Saint Louis	476,000
Salt Lake City	138,000
San Antonio	50,000
San Diego	206,616
Seattle	5,420,624

Ten cities report that the amount of Community Development Block Grant funds spent on homeless assistance increased during the last year: Boston, Charleston, Chicago, Cleveland, Los Angeles, New Orleans, Phoenix, Portland, San Antonio and Seattle. In Louisville and Saint Louis the amount of CDBG funds used for homeless assistance remained the same. No city reported a decline.

Ten cities (39 percent) used **Community Services Block Grant** funds during the last year to provide assistance to homeless people. Those cities and the amounts spent are:

Alexandria	$ 34,778
Chicago	315,000
Denver	199,200
Louisville	39,571
Miami	9,876
Nashville	35,837
Portland	623,793
Saint Louis	145,000
San Antonio	128,000
San Diego	1,577,066

The amount of Community Services Block Grant funds used to provide assistance to homeless people increased in Cleveland and San Antonio, decreased in Denver, Nashville and Saint Louis and remained the same in Louisville and Phoenix.

THE UNMET NEED

On average, 25 percent of the requests by homeless people for emergency shelter are estimated to have gone unmet during the last year across the survey cities. Estimates of unmet requests range from 65 percent in San Diego, 60 percent in Los Angeles, 40-50 percent in Nashville and 41 percent in Charleston to 10 percent in Denver, 2.4 percent in Chicago and one percent in Trenton. Minneapolis and New York City reported that no shelter requests went unmet during the last year.

For homeless families specifically, it is estimated that 29 percent of the requests for shelter went unmet during the last year in the survey cities. The percent of unmet requests ranges from 70 percent in Los Angeles and 67 percent in Nashville to five percent in Philadelphia and two percent in Chicago. Minneapolis and New York City report that no shelter requests by homeless families went unmet during the last year.

People Turned Away from Shelters

In 85 percent (22) of the survey cities emergency shelters may have to **turn away homeless families** due to lack of resources. The cities in which shelters do not have to turn away homeless families are Chicago, Minneapolis and New York City. Among the city officials' comments:

* **Alexandria:** Alexandria's public and private sectors maintain an extremely high ratio of shelter beds per population (19.1 beds per 10,000 population). Still, the need for space outstrips available resources.

   When shelter beds are not available, homeless families and/or individuals may be housed in a motel for short periods of time (generally five to seven days) with discretionary funds or charitable contributions. Human services executives in the Northern Virginia region have also developed a regional coordination policy in which one jurisdiction may place a family or individual in available space in another jurisdiction with the intent to relocate them back to the original jurisdiction.

* **Boston:** Homeless family shelters often turn away families that are not EA eligible. Unfortunately, we do not know what happens to these families. Most of them may be accepted by other programs, and many families may remain in the homes of friends and family.

* **Charleston:** Charleston Interfaith Crisis Ministry, the largest shelter in the Charleston area, has a policy of never turning away any homeless person seeking shelter. But there are other shelters which do not have as large a capacity which do have to turn people away periodically. Homeless families who are not able to get into other shelters usually end up coming to Crisis Ministry.

* **Chicago:** The City operates not only a 24-hour emergency care system, but also a 24-hour communication center that acts as a clearinghouse for shelters that are full or have empty beds. Any shelter or homeless person can call an 800 number and be referred to the nearest available shelter. Mobile teams are available to provide counseling, referral, placement or transportation.

* **Denver:** Vouchers for motel rooms are given to families who are turned away from shelters.

* **Kansas City:** A draft of the 1993 Comprehensive Housing Affordability Strategy states that in calendar year 1992 an alarmingly high number of women and children were turned away from shelters for battered persons due to a lack of space. The Hotline provides information, when it is available, for emergency "overflow" accommodations, particularly during extreme weather conditions. Overflow refers to temporary make-shift sleeping space in non-bedroom space.

* **Louisville:** Four families were turned away from the shelters for every one family served. These families are not walking Louisville streets, but are doubled up with friends and relatives.

We are able to serve fewer families because those served receive comprehensive, long-term assistance.

* **Nashville:** Several family shelters would expand to serve greater numbers of homeless families if resources were available. Families either leave Nashville, sleep in cars or "double up" with friends and family.

* **New Orleans:** When funds are available, shelters are able to use shelter vouchers to house some families in hotels. Some shelters have a limited number of free nights during which families can stay.

* **Norfolk:** Some families turned away may be accommodated by another shelter provider. Some will continue to live in cars or on the street while others may be housed for a night in a motel by an agency.

* **Philadelphia:** On occasion, families are turned away due to a lack of vacancies, but every attempt is made to place the family with friends, relatives, or at a private shelter.

* **Phoenix:** During the months of inclement weather (December to March) the City provides overflow shelter space for any and all who wish who are forced by circumstance to live in open public space.

* **Portland:** In a single day, the one-night shelter count found 89 families had to be turned away due to lack of space. Families who are turned away stay in cars, remain in domestic violence situations, camp out, or stay in other undesirable locations not fit for families.

* **Saint Louis:** All truly "on-the-street" families are placed in shelter unless their shelter history has been so horrendous (violent, abusive, neglectful, etc.) that they have been banned from the network of providers. In those cases they would resume doubling up with friends or relatives. In our city we use shelter as a last resort only. Every attempt is made to prevent homelessness through removal of barriers to housing, case management, eviction prevention grants, condemnation dislocation and relocation grants, relocation from a volatile or unhealthy doubled up situation. Follow-up models have been developed ranging from three months to five years once individuals and families are in stabilized housing.

* **Saint Paul:** New guidelines have been enforced to make access to emergency shelter available for those who have a genuine need because available space is limited. Those not admitted stay with friends, or outside.

* **Salt Lake City:** The demand for emergency shelter has increased so much during the last several years that shelters have had to turn families and other people away at times because of lack of space to accommodate them.

* **Santa Monica:** If emergency shelter can be found, families are often separated. There is one mission with 44 beds and a small number of motel vouchers. Families can be found living in cars near the beach, in parks and in increasing numbers in garages.

*   **Seattle:** An estimated 30,260 members of families with children were turned away from shelters in 1992. The city has a program that provides emergency shelter to homeless families who are found sleeping on the streets. Homeless families that do not access the shelter system will often sleep in cars or doubled up in poor housing situations.

*   **Trenton:** There is very limited shelter space, and, therefore, few clients can be accommodated in shelter. Thus, they are placed in transitional housing or in a motel. The WomenSpace Shelter (Domestic Violence) reports that they turned away 194 individuals last year due to lack of space.

In 77 percent (20) of the survey cities, emergency shelters may have to **turn away homeless people other than families because of lack of resources.** Those cities in which shelters do not have to turn away other homeless people are Boston, Louisville, Minneapolis, New York City, Saint Paul and San Antonio. Among the comments of the city officials.

*   **Boston:** The Mayor has made a commitment to supply enough emergency beds for homeless men and women. The state controls access to beds from families.

*   **Chicago:** Some shelters are not equipped physically or financially to deal with the homeless mentally ill who are acting out or with people under the influence of mind altering substances. Some of these individuals are accommodated at detox centers, but others wind up in hospitals or with the police.

*   **Denver:** For the first time in many years we are facing a lack of shelter beds for single men.

*   **Kansas City:** In the summer months particularly, single men or women find it more difficult to find emergency housing. There is no documentation about what happens to people who are turned away. It can only be surmised that they take refuge in any area they can find, try to move in with any willing friend, etc.

*   **Los Angeles:** The typical shelter usually operates at full capacity. Often times there are no beds available. Referrals are made to other shelters and clients are asked to check daily for bed availability. More often than not they are turned away.

*   **Louisville:** Single males are served adequately. A Quality Assurance Program was initiated in 1992 by the Louisville Coalition for the Homeless for the entire shelter system. This program has made a big difference to the homeless population, especially single homeless men who for the first time will have the opportunity to receive professional case management.

*   **Nashville:** Several shelters would expand capacity to serve more homeless individuals if resources were available. During the winter, the Room-In-the-Inn provides night shelter for up to 200 persons. People who do not obtain shelter sleep outdoors.

*   **New Orleans:** Sometimes there are not enough beds, or the clients have used up their three free nights and do not have any money to pay for additional nights. Some homeless persons spend nights with friends or relatives or on the streets until they can return to a shelter.

* **Norfolk:** During the winter of 1992-93, a group of churches provided night shelter (on a rotating basis) and simple meals to homeless men, women and, on occasion, families. An estimated 75 were sheltered each night.

* **Philadelphia:** Some shelters are unable to serve homeless persons with physical disabilities. Arrangements are made to place disabled clients in personal care boarding homes.

* **Portland:** Youth are turned away because of lack of shelter space. Couples who wish to stay in the same place sleep where they can. Unfortunately, many end up on the streets.

* **Saint Louis:** They sleep in parks, cars, abandoned buildings, in underground caves, etc.

* **Saint Paul:** Not yet, but trends for single males suggest we may run out of space (i.e. chairs in a heated lobby) this winter.

* **San Antonio:** The shelter system that is in place allows for the easy referral between facilities. During extreme weather conditions the City has contingency plans to open city facilities.

* **Seattle:** The number of homeless persons turned away on any given night in Seattle exceeds the number of shelter beds available. Single adults often sleep in doorways, alleys and parks, and this includes increasing numbers of women. Families and youth often stay in poor housing situations, or sleep in cars in outlying neighborhoods and parks.

* **Trenton:** They are placed in motels.

Homeless People in Particular Need of Assistance

Officials in the survey cities were asked to identify in order of need three specific groups of homeless people for whom emergency shelter and other needed services are particularly lacking in their city, as well as the services most needed by each of these groups. Listed in order of frequency, these groups are families with children, substance abusers, mentally ill persons, single women, persons with AIDS or HIV-related illness, unaccompanied minors and single men.

Sixty-five percent (17) of the survey cities identified **families with children** as a group in particular need of services. Nine cities -- Boston, Denver, Kansas City, Miami, Minneapolis, New Orleans, New York City, Philadelphia and Saint Louis -- identified families as the group most in need of services. Saint Louis officials limited their response to homeless families experiencing substance abuse.

Substance abusers were also identified by 65 percent (17) of the cities as a group of homeless persons in particular need of service. Six cities -- Charleston, Cleveland, Phoenix, Saint Paul, Salt Lake City and Santa Monica -- said substance abusers were the group most in need of services.

Fifteen cities (58 percent) of the survey cities identified **mentally ill persons** as a group for whom emergency shelter and other needed services are particularly lacking. Four cities -- Chicago, Los Angeles, Louisville and Santa Monica -- said mentally ill persons were the group most in need of services.

Single women were identified by 38 percent (10) of the cities as a group of homeless persons in particular needed of services. Nashville and Seattle ranked single women first.

Six cities (23 percent) of the cities reported that persons with AIDS or HIV-related illness were a group of homeless persons in particular need of assistance. Alexandria, Norfolk and Trenton said they were the group for whom services were most lacking.

Unaccompanied minors were also cited by six cities as a group of homeless persons for whom services were particularly lacking. San Antonio ranked them first.

Five cities (19 percent) said that single men were a group of homeless persons for whom services are particularly lacking.

Services Most Needed

The city officials identified a wide range of services needed by the various groups of homeless people:

FAMILIES WITH CHILDREN -- Affordable permanent housing was the service most frequently identified as needed by homeless families. The seven cities identifying it are Boston, Cleveland, Louisville, Kansas City, New York City, Phoenix and Santa Monica. Emergency shelter was identified by Denver, Nashville, New Orleans, Philadelphia and Portland. Chicago, Cleveland, Kansas City, Los Angeles and Miami cited the need for transitional housing. Boston, Minneapolis, Los Angeles and Portland identified the need for jobs and job training.

SUBSTANCE ABUSERS -- A variety of treatment options were the services most frequently identified as needed by homeless substance abusers. Identifying this need were Charleston, Cleveland, Los Angeles, New York, Phoenix, Seattle and Trenton. Chicago and Minneapolis specifically cited the need for detoxification facilities. Emergency shelter was identified by Chicago, Philadelphia, Saint Paul, Salt Lake City and Santa Monica. Supportive housing was cited by Alexandria, Cleveland, Miami, Phoenix and Seattle as a service particularly needed by homeless substance abusers.

MENTALLY ILL PERSONS -- Case management and supportive services were identified by Chicago, Denver, Louisville, Miami, Nashville, New Orleans, New York City and Trenton as particularly needed by homeless mentally ill persons. Alexandria, Charleston, Louisville and Phoenix cited the need for housing. Los Angeles, Nashville, Saint Paul and Santa Monica identified a need for shelter. Boston, Charleston and Los Angeles cited the need for treatment.

SINGLE WOMEN -- Boston, Cleveland, Kansas City, Louisville, New Orleans and Seattle identified housing as a service particularly needed by homeless single women. Treatment and other services were identified by Boston, Kansas City, Louisville, Philadelphia, San Antonio and Seattle as needed by this group. Nashville and New Orleans identified the need for transportation.

PERSONS WITH AIDS OR HIV-RELATED ILLNESS -- Housing was identified by Alexandria, Kansas City and Norfolk as a service need by homeless persons with AIDS or HIV-related illness. Salt Lake City, San Antonio and Trenton identified the need for **shelter**. Kansas City, San Antonio and Trenton cited the need for **health care**.

UNACCOMPANIED MINORS -- **Emergency shelter** was identified by Portland, Salt Lake City, San Antonio and Seattle as the service most needed by homeless unaccompanied youth. Saint Paul cited the need for a **drop-in center**.

SINGLE MEN -- **Housing** was cited by Cleveland, Kansas City and New Orleans as the service most needed by homeless single men. Denver, Kansas City and San Antonio identified the need for **treatment and other supportive services**.

CITY DATA ON HOMELESSNESS

	Percent Increase in Request for Emergency Shelter	Percent Increase in Requests by Families For Emergency Shelter	Shelter Beds	Transitional Housing Units	Family Breakup For Shelter?	Family Leave During Day	Percentage Need Unmet	Families Turned Away	Others Turned Away
Alexandria	7	-8	SAME	INCREASE	NO	YES	21	YES	YES
Boston	18	28	INCREASE	INCREASE	YES	NO	NA	YES	NO
Charleston	0	NA	INCREASE	SAME	NO	NO	41	YES	YES
Chicago	11.25	0	INCREASE	INCREASE	YES	YES	24	NO	YES
Cleveland	10	10	INCREASE	INCREASE	YES	YES	NA	YES	YES
Denver	5-10	5-10	DECREASE	NA	YES	YES	10	YES	YES
Kansas City	24	24	DECREASE	NA	YES	YES	27	YES	YES
Los Angeles	35	50	INCREASE	INCREASE	NO	NO	60	YES	YES
Louisville	0	0	DECREASE	INCREASE	YES	NO	NA	YES	NO
Miami	20	25	INCREASE	INCREASE	YES	YES	NA	YES	YES
Minneapolis	9	15	INCREASE	SAME	NO	NO	0	NO	NO
Nashville	NA	NA	INCREASE	INCREASE	YES	YES	40-50	YES	YES
New Orleans	21	18	INCREASE	INCREASE	YES	YES	19	YES	YES
New York City	-2.5	-.4	DECREASE	NA	NO	NO	0	NO	NO
Norfolk	-2.9	NA	SAME	INCREASE	YES	YES	NA	YES	YES
Philadelphia	7	0	INCREASE	INCREASE	YES	NO	20	YES	YES
Phoenix	5	5	INCREASE	INCREASE	NO	NO	NA	YES	YES
Portland	43	88	SAME	SAME	YES	NO	13	YES	YES
Saint Louis	10	7	DECREASE	INCREASE	NO	YES	20	YES	YES
Saint Paul	0	-30	SAME	SAME	NO	NO	NA	YES	NO
Salt Lake City	8-12	8-12	INCREASE	INCREASE	NO	NO	NA	YES	YES
San Antonio	14	19	INCREASE	INCREASE	YES	NO	NA	NO	NO
San Diego	NA	10	INCREASE	INCREASE	NA	NA	65	YES	NO
Santa Monica	NA	NA	SAME	SAME	YES	YES	95	YES	YES
Seattle	3	NA	SAME	SAME	YES	NO	18	YES	YES
Trenton	NA	-16	INCREASE	INCREASE	YES	YES	1	YES	YES

COMPOSITION OF THE HOMELESS POPULATION (PERCENTAGE)

	Families	Single Men	Single Women	Unaccompanied Youth	Mentally Ill	Substance Abusers	Employed	Veterans	African Americans	White	Hispanic	Asian	Native Americans	Percentage Single Parent Families	Percentage Family Members Children
Alexandria	10	57	12	1	14	49	37	12	71	20	7	1	0	81	63
Boston	28	59	12	1	10.90	50	10	20	NA	NA	NA	NA	NA	98	70
Charleston	10	56	8	6	19	48	41	24	71	28	1	0	0	76	67
Chicago	425	36.4	21	NA	25	14.5	5	3	80.8	9.2	9.4	3	3	97.6	67.1
Cleveland	15	50	14	1	25	50	10	10	77	20	2	5	5	98	70
Denver	NA	NA	NA	NA	NA	NA	NA	NA	NA	NA	NA	NA	NA	NA	NA
Kansas City	71	11	13	3	NA	NA	NA	NA	NA	NA	NA	NA	NA	83	66
Los Angeles	25	50	13	12	30	40	NA	30	54	17	26	1	2	80	71
Louisville	32	55	6	7	13	70	14	35	NA	NA	NA	3	NA	78	65
Miami	40	40	14	8	50	75	20	20	59	15	25	2	2	15	10
Minneapolis	52	39	9	NA	19	35	15	25	58	25	5	2	10	74	66
Nashville	16	72	10	2	33	50	35	35	32	61	5	0	2	80	57
New Orleans	14	49	24	13	20	40	5	30	60	34	NA	5	NA	86	20
New York City	75	20	5	0	NA	NA	NA	NA	66	4	29	4	1	NA	56.5
Norfolk	35	54	10	1	.01	.02	3	.01	89	10.9	0	0	0	24	70
Philadelphia	541	14.8	11	1	6.7	45.4	9.4	10.2	88.84	7.67	3.37	.13	.05	91	70
Phoenix	63	35	2	NA	40	40	15	25	19	26	25	2	28	40	65
Portland	66	20	13	1	52	90	4	35	85	14	1	4	4	75	65
Saint Louis	44	43	9	4	NA	NA	30	NA	20	59	15	1	NA	68	75
Saint Paul	44.3	43.8	6.8	5	NA	NA	9	NA	38.6	40.2	15.5	9	39	95	69
Salt Lake City	28	60	10	2	57	32	39	35	8	70	13	1	8	67	70
San Antonio	65	19	12	4	NA	NA	NA	NA	26	22	52	NA	NA	49	56
San Diego	25	50	13	13	50	70	NA	40	NA	NA	15	NA	NA	NA	NA
Santa Monica	13	60	20	NA	27	60	NA	22	33	40	15	NA	NA	75	NA
Seattle	1084	56.32	11.65	.10	5.08	11.32	25	15.06	29.46	36.31	22.64	1.48	5.49	59	62
Trenton	77	16	6	1	22	85	NA	5	56	28	16	0	0	92	67

SHELTER BEDS, TRANSITIONAL HOUSING UNITS AND SRO HOUSING IN THE SURVEY CITIES

CITY	SHELTER BEDS	FAMILY SHELTER BEDS	TRANSITIONAL UNITS	FAMILY TRANSITIONAL UNITS	SINGLE ROOM OCCUPANCY UNITS
Alexandria	213	123	48	43	0
Boston	3,926	1,035	1,107	356	4,000
Charleston	350	112	34	4	50
Chicago	4,590	2,243	1,161	1,161	11,600
Cleveland	670	285	180	72	NA
Denver	919	28	NA	NA	NA
Kansas City	546	207	252	62	NA
Los Angeles	4,058	1,497	1,739	642	12,406
Louisville	379	53	472	60	70
Miami	1,400	NA	NA	NA	NA
Minneapolis	1,200	600	156	90	1,630
Nashville	885	165	181	89	184
New Orleans	1,398	67	814	105	0
New York City	23,973	17,359	3,771	NA	3,800
Norfolk	287	113	7	7	219
Philadelphia	2,460	1,227	1,571	286	1,150
Phoenix	3,000	470	1,000	145	100
Portland	650	40	376	126	4,147
Saint Louis	975	675	600	480	250
Saint Paul	NA	NA	187	187	642
Salt Lake City	850	45	50	50	NA
San Antonio	913	210	101	81	88
San Diego	1,397	319	708	319	NA
Santa Monica	336	44	43	3	NA
Seattle	2,632	884	519	201	NA
Trenton	212	72	40	32	26

HOUSING

Assisted Housing Requests

During the last year, requests for assisted housing by low income families and individuals increased in 70 percent (16) of the survey cities, remained the same in 17 percent (four) of the cities and decreased in 13 percent (three) cities. Requests increased in Boston, Chicago, Cleveland, Los Angeles, Miami, Minneapolis, Nashville, Norfolk, Philadelphia, Portland, Saint Louis, Salt Lake City, San Antonio, San Diego, Santa Monica and Trenton. They remained the same in Alexandria Charleston, Louisville and New Orleans. They decreased in Kansas City, New York City and Seattle. Among the city officials' comments on the increase in requests for assisted housing:

*   **Boston:** Cuts in programs like the Massachusetts Rental Voucher Program have increased the requests for the remaining housing assistance programs.

*   **Chicago:** Continued increases in rents and decreases in low and moderate housing units contribute to more requests for assistance.

*   **Los Angeles:** The increase in unemployment as well as a reduction in general relief created a greater demand for publicly subsidized housing.

*   **Nashville:** There has been an increase in public housing applications and an increased volume of calls from persons wanting Section 8 assistance.

*   **Philadelphia:** In Philadelphia, the demographic and employment trends have exacerbated the problem of poverty. Increasing poverty has intensified the need for housing and support services. The 1990 Census indicates that the need for affordable housing in Philadelphia is great. According to the CHAS Databook (a special tabulation prepared by HUD) the affordability crisis appears to affect renters more than homeowners: 46 percent of renter households pay more than 30 percent of their gross income for housing, and 26.3 percent pay more than 50 percent.

    Although the number of persons on PHA waiting lists severely under-represents the total number of households with such need, those waiting lists also indicate the need for low-income rental housing. According to PHA, there are currently 13,960 families on the Section 8 waiting list and 8,982 on the Public Housing waiting list (some families are on both lists). The number of persons on the waiting lists is relatively low for two reasons, First, not everyone who desires PHA housing is able to apply. PHA has recently opened its waiting lists for those homeless applicants who are in the preference Tier I, because their status can be certified by the City's Office of Services to the Homeless and Adults. Since 1981, however, the lists have been closed to all other applications needing a two bedroom or larger unit. Second, the general public knowledge that those on the list may wait two years to be placed in a public housing unit (and as long as three years for a Section 8 unit) has discouraged applications from families in immediate need of housing.

In contrast to the number of persons seeking PHA housing, many of whom must wait years for assistance, the number of available units has been diminishing over time. Several thousand units are unavailable because of substandard conditions.

*   **Portland:** The waiting list for Section 8 housing increased six percent, 60 percent for low rent public housing.

*   **Saint Louis:** The need for assisted housing is constant. Our entire jurisdiction only received 155 Section 8 certificates for a city with 396,000 people, more than 28 percent of whom are very low income.

Louisville officials explain that their city has seen an increase in low-cost housing units because the Abramson administration has worked diligently for the last eight years to address low cost housing. This was done by creating and developing partnerships with the private lending institutions in the housing industry. In Louisville, requests for assisted housing remained the same during the last year.

The Wait for Assisted Housing

Applicants in the survey cities must wait for public housing for an average of 21 months from the time of application until they actually receive assistance. For Section 8 housing the average wait in the cities is 35 months; for vouchers it is 31 months.

*   For **public housing** the average wait ranges from 42 to 48 months in Alexandria, 36 to 48 months in San Diego, 36 months in Chicago, Saint Louis and Trenton to six months in Cleveland and Louisville, three months in Nashville and one month in San Antonio.

*   The average wait for **Section 8** housing ranges from 132 months in Chicago, 48 months in New Orleans, 42 to 48 months in Alexandria, 36 to 60 months in San Antonio and 36 to 48 months in San Diego to nine to 12 months in Charleston.

*   For **vouchers** the average wait ranges from 132 months in Chicago, 42 to 48 months in Alexandria and 36 to 60 months in San Antonio to nine to 12 months in Charleston, six months in New Orleans and three months in Los Angeles.

Fifty-eight percent of the survey cities have stopped accepting applications for at least one assisted housing program due to the excessive length of the waiting lists. The 14 cities which have stopped accepting applications are Alexandria, Boston, Chicago, Cleveland, Denver, Minneapolis, Nashville, Norfolk, Philadelphia, Portland, Saint Paul, San Antonio, Santa Monica and Trenton.

Among the comments by the city officials on the closed waiting lists:

*   **Alexandria:** The Alexandria Redevelopment and Housing Authority closed its waiting list for one, two and three bedroom units in December of 1989. The waiting list for two bedroom units was opened in March of 1992 and closed again in April of 1992. In the one month period the Housing Authority received over 1,000 applications. The Housing Authority opened and closed the waiting list for one bedroom (non-elderly) in October of 1992. The waiting list for one bedroom (elderly) has remained open. The waiting list for three bedroom units has

remained closed since December of 1989. Currently, there are 1,079 households on the waiting lists.

* **Boston:** Lists are closed for the Section 8 and voucher programs.

* **Chicago:** Lists for non-elderly households have been closed since 1985 except for federal preference categories.

* **Minneapolis:** Waiting lists are closed for family housing and special needs housing.

* **Nashville:** Section 8 application taking was suspended in August 1991. On November 5, 1993, application taking was resumed on Fridays only of each week.

* **Norfolk:** The waiting lists are closed for Section 8, voucher and public housing.

* **Philadelphia:** The Philadelphia Housing Authority has stopped taking applications from the general public; only homeless persons within the Tier I preference are given a priority.

* **Portland:** Section 8 is closed. All other lists are open except two and three bedroom apartment units.

* **Saint Paul:** Waiting lists are closed for three and four bedroom public housing units and all Section 8 certificates and vouchers.

* **San Antonio:** The Section 8 and Moderate Rehabilitation Programs have closed their waiting lists.

* **Santa Monica:** The Section 8 waiting list is closed for all categories and it is not expected to open until 1994. This year 120 new certificates were awarded out of 5,000 requests.

* **Trenton:** Public housing and Section 8 are currently not accepting applications.

Applications for assisted housing are being accepted in Charleston, Kansas City, Los Angeles, Louisville, New Orleans, New York City, Saint Louis, Salt Lake City, San Diego and Seattle. Among the explanations by officials in these cities:

* **Kansas City:** The Missouri Housing Development Commission reports lists are closed for Section 8 certificates and vouchers (homeless). The Housing Authority of Kansas City reports lists have not been closed. Due to a consent decree, our waiting lists remain open.

* **New Orleans:** They continue to accept applications, but people stay on the waiting list for years. Our public housing has many vacancies, but very poor conditions and significant renovations are needed before renting many apartments. The waiting list for Section 8 has been closed.

* **Saint Louis:** Waiting lists are heavily dependent on the availability of funds. One and two bedrooms are more available than two and three bedrooms.

Special Needs Housing

Among those with special needs, it is most difficult to find assisted housing for large families and for mentally ill persons. Those next most difficult to find housing for are persons with AIDS and homeless people.

*   Twelve (55 percent) of the responding cities identified **large families** as a special needs population for whom it is particularly hard to find assisted housing: Alexandria, Boston, Charleston, Cleveland, Denver, New York City, Norfolk, Portland, Saint Louis, Santa Monica, Seattle and Trenton.

*   Twelve cities as well identified **mentally ill persons** as a special needs population difficult to house: Chicago, Cleveland, Denver, Los Angeles, Louisville, Nashville, New Orleans, New York City, Norfolk, Salt Lake City, San Antonio and Trenton.

*   Twenty-seven percent (six) of the cities reported that it is particularly hard to find housing for **persons with AIDS**: Chicago, Los Angeles, Minneapolis, New Orleans, New York City and Trenton.

*   Kansas City, Los Angeles and Philadelphia all reported that it is difficult to find housing for **homeless people**.

People Served by Assisted Housing

An average of 28 percent of eligible low income households are currently served by assisted housing in the survey cities. The percentage of those served ranges from 60 percent in Louisville and New Orleans, 39 percent in Portland and Saint Paul and 37 percent in Nashville to 20 percent in Los Angeles, 15 percent in Chicago, 13 percent in Norfolk and 10 percent in San antonio and Santa Monica.

CITY DATA ON HOUSING

CITY	HOUSING REQUESTS	PUBLIC HOUSING WAIT IN MONTHS	SECTION 8 WAIT IN MONTHS	VOUCHER WAIT IN MONTHS	STOPPED ACCEPTING APPS.	PERCENT OF NEED MET
Alexandria	same	42-48	42-48	42-48	yes	NA
Boston	increase	15	26	26	yes	30
Charleston	same	12-16	9-12	9-12	no	34
Chicago	increase	36	132	132	yes	15
Cleveland	increase	6	NA	NA	yes	33
Kansas City	decrease	12-26	12-26	12-26	no	NA
Los Angeles	increase	24	38	3	no	20
Louisville	same	6	24	30	no	60
Minneapolis	increase	9	24	24	yes	27
Nashville	increase	3	30	30	yes	37
New Orleans	same	28	48	6	no	60
Norfolk	increase	12	30	30	yes	13
Philadelphia	increase	6-25	14-20	14-20	yes	7
Portland	increase	3-36	18-36	NA	yes	39
Saint Louis	increase	36	36	36	no	14
Saint Paul	NA	12-60	24	24	yes	39
Salt Lake City	increase	1-24	6-24	6-24	no	NA
San Antonio	increase	1	36-60	36-60	yes	10
San Diego	increase	36-48	35-48	NA	no	NA
Santa Monica	increase	NA	24	NA	yes	10
Seattle	decrease	24	24-36	24-36	no	24
Trenton	increase	36	36	36	yes	NA

THE OUTLOOK AND NEEDED ACTIONS

EXPECTED REQUESTS FOR EMERGENCY FOOD AND SHELTER

Every survey city expects that requests for emergency food assistance will increase during 1994. Eighty-eight percent of the cities (all but three) expect that requests for emergency shelter, both by all homeless persons and by homeless families alone, will increase during 1994. Officials in Chicago and Miami expect requests for shelter to remain at the same level as in 1993; Trenton officials expect them to decrease below 1993 levels. Among the city officials comments on the outlook for 1994:

* **Alexandria:** Based on a stagnant economy, unemployment and the public assistance caseload, it is expected that the need for assistance will increase or hold steady.

* **Boston:** The trend of the past few years suggests this conclusion.

* **Charleston:** We expect it to increase because of the Naval Base closing and the city's high unemployment.

* **Chicago:** Trends for '92 and '93 are expected to continue into 1994, given the current economic conditions.

* **Cleveland:** There is no indication that the economic and social factors contributing to homelessness will not continue to expand. Even an end to the recession will not significantly increase economic opportunities for those with the least employment skills.

* **Denver:** People come to Denver expecting to find jobs, but the jobs that exist often require skills and education they do not have.

* **Kansas City:** We expect requests to increase due to loss of jobs in the area and the flood of 1993.

* **Los Angeles:** The depressed economy will continue. Also the number of jobs paying higher than subsistence wage aren't being targeted to the homeless population. Jobs capable of mainstreaming individuals aren't readily available.

* **Louisville:** We will continue to see homelessness increase until there is a stronger focus and emphasis on homeless prevention programs. There is a total of 37,319 families in danger of becoming homeless. Prevention programs for families at risk are critical. The largest percentage of families are at risk because they are unable to meet their financial obligations to pay rent and utilities. Families for the most part are without health insurance which places them at further risk. There is obviously a need for more subsidized housing, and good paying jobs with benefits.

* **Miami:** Poor families continue to grow in number. There is a lack of employment. Hopefully we will develop a good transitional housing system and people will be able to graduate from programs to affordable housing.

* **Minneapolis:** Requests will continue to increase due to the lack of employment opportunities and reduced resources available to provide help. Many households lack income to pay market rate rents. Families are a growing segment of our homeless population.

* **Nashville:** Jobs lost in other areas as a possible repercussion of NAFTA may result in more persons coming to Nashville for employment. This could increase demand for emergency food assistance.

* **New Orleans:** Poverty levels continue to skyrocket. Gambling casinos will attract more people in need of jobs.

* **New York City:** The slow recovery from a prolonged recession -- along with continued pressure on semi-skilled and service sector employment -- make it likely that this demand will increase, especially among families.

* **Norfolk:** The economic impact of possible military cut-backs could be severe in this area.

* **Philadelphia:** Philadelphia's significant economic and social changes in recent decades have intensified the demand for services, including emergency food assistance. These changes include the transformation of the economic base from industry and manufacturing to primarily a service economy, loss of population, an increased tax burden, unemployment and underemployment, relocation of industries, proliferation of drugs and crime, deinstitutionalization, domestic abuse and the scarcity of affordable housing.

* **Phoenix:** The expectations of increase or decrease in the demand for food or shelter are dependent on changes in the income of the clients, the availability of resources and their cost, and issues related to these two major items. Since no change is anticipated, except a greater disparity, the need will increase.

* **Portland:** Lack of full time employment at a livable wage will make more persons eligible for emergency food assistance.

* **Saint Louis:** The 1993 flooding in the Midwest has eventually led some to shelters, particularly those doubled-up with others.

* **Saint Paul:** We will see increased pressure from other states which are failing to address the needs of poor people, and people will continue to vote with their feet and move to more habitable cities.

* **Salt Lake City:** Soup kitchens and food banks report that requests for assistance continue to increase and that they do not anticipate any reversal in this trend during the coming year.

* **San Antonio:** The issue of an ever expanding poverty population in San Antonio is at the root of the general assistance needs and homelessness. Access to a quality education, jobs and income, and affordable housing are sorely lacking in San Antonio. As the San Antonio economy improves, some improvement will be seen in the employment rate and the income level of the poverty population, though raising education levels will and do require different

strategies. Unless and until all the above problems are seriously confronted and solved, these problems will only be changed incrementally, and unfortunately not positively.

*   **San Diego:** The current economic situation (high unemployment, high cost of living) is forcing more and more housed family groups to seek food assistance to supplement purchases. Many of these family groups are utilizing congregate feeding sites as an additional supplement for food needs.

*   **Santa Monica:** With the increase in poverty, there is expected to be an increase in the demand for food by homeless persons and the at-risk population.

*   **Seattle:** Inflation and a declining economy are indicators of the demand for emergency food assistance. Trends indicate that Seattle's low-income population is growing. Increasing rents paired with increased unemployment will force many of these households into homelessness.

WHAT NEEDS TO BE DONE

Many believe that if the problems of homelessness are to be solved three critical issues – housing, income and services – must be addressed. The city officials were asked to identify the single most important action relating to housing, income and services the federal government can take to meet the needs of homeless people.

Housing

The cities propose a range of federal housing initiatives which would increase the supply of permanent and transitional housing. Providing affordable housing was identified by officials in 14 of the survey cities as the single most important federal action to address the housing needs of homeless people. Five cities called for additional transitional housing, three for coordinated case management.

To address permanent housing needs they propose increased availability of housing subsidies and rental assistance; increased rehabilitation of existing units and construction of new units, including public housing units; the provision of sufficient operating subsidies to public housing authorities; and creation of community development banks to fund community development corporations to developed neighborhood-based programs. To address transitional housing needs they propose increased funding both for housing and for a comprehensive range of services to assist special needs populations to live within it.

Among the recommendations of the city officials:

*   **Alexandria:** The federal government should provide sufficient operating subsidies to public housing authorities to maintain units and guarantee funding for the replacement of subsidized units when mortgages are pre-paid or retired.

* **Boston:** We need more subsidies and rental assistance, help with the first and last month's rent and security deposits, and housing assistance coupled with services to provide a more holistic approach.

* **Charleston:** Federal funding for housing efforts should be increased. There is an urgent need for additional transitional housing and permanent housing for large families.

* **Cleveland:** The federal government should greatly expand the availability of housing programs such as Section 8 Certificates that provide a monthly rental subsidy.

* **Chicago:** There should be a funding mechanism that is equitable and flexible which allows the local housing entity to design housing that is both affordable and has the potential to offer supportive services to tenants that have special needs.

* **Denver:** The federal government should provide more subsidized transitional and permanent affordable housing.

* **Kansas City:** There should be provision of and access to more affordable permanent housing units. Also we need more transitional housing programs as a supportive measure between the shelter and independent living. With transitional housing there is a need for adequate funding for staff and services needed.

* **Los Angeles:** We need to build more affordable housing and/or offer more housing subsidies.

* **Louisville:** The federal government should provide more Section 8 certificates with comprehensive services. Many of our homeless people have enormous social disabilities and varied needs. Not only do we need more affordable housing, but the federal government should provide flexible funding for comprehensive services.

* **Miami:** We must construct affordable housing. We need approximately 38,000 units.

* **Minneapolis:** We should increase efforts to ensure fair housing opportunities for entire metropolitan geographic areas. We should also work with local Public Housing Authorities to increase local control over tenant selection and rights.

* **Nashville:** The federal government should provide service enriched transitional housing to help people transition from shelter to permanent housing. It should also make additional Section 8 certificates and voucher subsidies available, and increase the number of public housing units being built.

* **New Orleans:** The federal government should finance repairs on dilapidated houses and subsidize the rent on these homes.

* **New York City:** There should be increased flexibility governing rules for funding. For example, the federal government should allow cities to use emergency assistance funds for rent.

* **Norfolk:** The federal government should make decent affordable housing a goal for all Americans and provide funding to assist states and localities in reaching the goal.

* **Philadelphia:** The federal government should create more community development housing rehabilitation programs, assure that there is sufficient affordable low and moderate income housing and assure that existing public housing is maintained at a high level of quality and safety.

* **Phoenix:** We should give consideration to housing as a basic right.

* **Portland:** The federal government should give money to community development corporations to develop housing through community development banks.

* **Saint Louis:** A coordinated, managed plan which includes preparing to be a good tenant, managing money, parenting children, etc. is critical to a holistic plan. Increased rental subsidy is desperately needed. Increased housing construction funds are needed.

* **Saint Paul:** We need additional Section 8 certificates and vouchers.

* **Salt Lake City:** A major initiative to provide transitional and affordable permanent housing is critical.

* **San Diego:** We should encourage an increase in the amount of low-income housing.

* **Santa Monica:** The federal government should provide funding for the development of a range of low-cost permanent housing which is linked to a service continuum to address the specialized needs of homeless people and increase the Section 8 program.

* **Seattle:** The federal government should increase low income housing for all groups.

* **Trenton:** We need more affordable housing, both new and rehabilitated. We need to modify legislation to target temporary housing assistance programs for long-term housing.

Income

Raising the minimum wage and providing job training were identified most frequently as the most important actions the federal government can take to address the income needs of homeless people. Nine cities called for increasing the minimum wage, eight for increased job training. These were followed by increasing employment opportunities, stimulating the economy (by four cities) and increasing welfare payments (by three cities). Among the city officials' recommendations:

* **Alexandria:** We need to raise the minimum wage to guarantee "working families" income equal at least 150 percent of the poverty level.

* **Boston:** We need to increase welfare payments, raise the minimum wage, help the working poor to remain safely in their homes, help women exiting the welfare rolls with health care, child care and transportation costs until such aid is no longer necessary.

* **Charleston:** If the minimum wage was a living wage, all that would be necessary is a short-term general assistance program.

* **Cleveland:** The federal government should subsidize state welfare levels so that families' incomes would be brought up from poverty level. It should also develop a jobs program that reaches the chronic unemployed.

* **Chicago:** We must assure that the income entitlement meets the level of need, at the very least during the first two years of the first episode of homelessness. There should be an effort to link a gradual reduction in entitlements to decent paying employment when possible.

* **Denver:** We need to create more jobs that pay a wage that would enable people to become self-sufficient.

* **Kansas City:** We need job training and employment with the assurance that people will not be penalized for becoming employed. Once a person starts receiving more income, most of their benefits are either cut severely or taken away altogether. Housing officials also observe that as a result of reduced income, inadequate funds to provide medical care/coverage, transportation and child care problems impede persons from remaining stabilized if they do find housing. For those receiving assistance, perhaps a probationary period of six months to a year should be given to help with the transition.

* **Los Angeles:** The federal minimum wage should be increased.

* **Louisville:** We need to continue health and day care subsidies until a person's income can meet their financial obligations.

* **Minneapolis:** The federal government should create a "living wage jobs policy" and help central cities reclaim polluted land for job creation.

* **Nashville:** The federal government should increase the minimum wage and increase the number of job training programs.

* **New Orleans:** The federal government should provide more McKinney funds to cities, especially those with high poverty rates, to provide a continuum consisting of emergency, transitional and permanent housing.

* **New York City:** The federal government must concentrate on increasing economic activity so that more people can become self-sufficient. At the same time, the federal government must promote programs for economic development, job training and education.

* **Norfolk:** We need to improve the economy to provide increased employment opportunities with decent wages.

* **Philadelphia:** We need to stimulate the U.S. economy so that there will be sufficient jobs at all skill levels; provide job readiness to all those who need it; provide skill development programs to retrain persons with obsolete skills; and consider the economics of transition when formulating anti-trust, macroeconomic, fiscal, monetary, regulatory, trade and labor policies.

* **Phoenix:** We need a realistic minimum wage.

* **Portland:** We need to spur the economy to create jobs (e.g., provide technical assistance and funding to community development corporations to create job opportunities and employment training, fostering microenterprise). The federal government should provide start-up capital for community development banks.

* **Saint Louis:** A coordinated case management approach is best. Whether for acquiring benefits or embarking on job counseling and placement, all specialists need to be communicating and cooperating with a holistic plan.

* **Saint Paul:** Section 8 certificates and vouchers would make the most impact. Multi-state AFDC benefits might slow migration.

* **Salt Lake City:** We need to increase employment opportunities for the poor and less educated segments of our society, and provide incentives to businesses to hire and train homeless people.

* **San Diego:** The federal government should provide employer incentives to increase employment opportunities for members of the homeless community.

* **Santa Monica:** The minimum wage must be increased to provide "livable wages."

* **Seattle:** We need to increase public assistance grants for families and low-income persons.

* **Trenton:** We need training programs geared toward special needs of low-income families and individuals.

Services

A continuum of supportive services and case management lead the list of recommendations by city officials for addressing the service needs of homeless persons. Eight cities called for comprehensive case management, four for additional substance abuse treatment and mental health services, three for fully funding existing services and three for increasing job training. Among the city officials' specific recommendations relating to needed services:

* **Alexandria:** The federal government should fund a comprehensive, case management services program designed to enable the homeless to become self-supporting and obtain stable and affordable housing. It should include education, employment and training services, economic development and job creation, income supports, child care and other supportive services with transitional housing initiatives.

* **Boston:** We need to increase counseling and support services to battered women and the mentally ill. We need to target female-headed households to determine what services they need to avoid homelessness and target a campaign at young women living in inner-cities to prevent out-of-wedlock births.

* **Charleston:** Comprehensive job training and re-training and placement are needed on a national level to benefit single adults. These services are needed to assure that our citizens earn a living wage with comprehensive benefits (health insurance and day care).

* **Chicago:** Funding for services, especially from HHS, is highly competitive and research oriented. It is also very short term, so even if the program is successful, it ends due to a lack of other available funding sources.

* **Denver:** We need to provide effective, comprehensive case management services for chronically mentally ill persons.

* **Kansas City:** There should be a significant increase in the availability of funds for substance abuse treatment (including program staff) and prevention measures.

* **Los Angeles:** We need to increase the funding for supportive services and create regional homeless service centers designed to mainstream homeless persons. These centers should provide housing, support services and training.

* **Louisville:** The federal government needs to assist in providing more flexible funding for comprehensive services. The major problem is that the services are very costly and the federal government should share in the funding of these services.

* **Minneapolis:** We need to recreate client incentive programs so that welfare is not a low income trap, but instead a conduit to self-sufficiency.

* **Nashville:** We should fund services for existing public and assisted housing to assist residents in keeping current housing. Such services include financial management, self-sufficiency counseling, assistance/treatment for alcohol and drug problems.

* **New Orleans:** We need to revamp the welfare system and have all states provide 100 percent of the national poverty level payment rate to welfare recipients.

* **New York City:** There should be increased flexibility governing the rules for funding.

* **Norfolk:** We need to provide funding for the continuum of services to the homeless from prevention to home ownership, including supportive services budgeting, household management, consumer education, household repairs, employment services, etc.

* **Philadelphia:** We need to increase support service programs to address the underlying causes of homelessness over and above housing. We should assure that there is sufficient child care to support persons who are engaged in training, seeking employment, or are employed, and assure that high quality health care is accessible and available.

* **Phoenix:** We need national medical insurance, continuation of the TEFAP program, universal breakfast and lunch programs, a national "Good Samaritan" law, and a single certification process for all programs such as AFDC, Food stamps, welfare, school feeding programs, etc.

* **Portland:** We need to make more funds available for mental health, alcohol and drug treatment, and children.

* **Saint Louis:** A coordinated managed approach is built on services. All homeless clients should receive supportive services, prepare for housing prior to placement and receive coordinated stabilization for as long as necessary after placement.

* **Saint Paul:** We need more job re-training.

* **Salt Lake City:** We need to fully fund existing federal programs aimed at eliminating hunger, poverty and homelessness.

* **San Diego:** We need to simplify access to resources.

* **Santa Monica:** The federal government should provide funding for a comprehensive rehabilitation continuum to serve homeless people suffering from alcohol, substance abuse, mental health problems and provide funding for supportive services and child care for families.

* **Seattle:** Treatment on demand should be available for all groups.

* **Trenton:** We need additional drug rehabilitation programs, educational programs and job placement programs.

Prevention

Officials in the survey cities were asked to identify the single most important action the federal government can take to prevent homelessness from occurring in the first place. Officials in 10 cities recommended actions that would create employment opportunities as well as provide additional job training. A variety of recommendations relating to housing were also made, with five cities citing the need for more housing with supportive services. Three cities cited the need for improvements in the economy. Two called for stepped up anti-drug efforts and greater availability of treatment.

Among the city officials recommendations:

* **Alexandria:** We need to provide substantial federal funding and incentives through ADC-EA or a similar mechanism to give states the option to prevent evictions and mortgage foreclosures.

* **Boston:** The federal government should provide affordable housing with support services.

* **Charleston:** It is time to refocus our battle against illegal drugs, shifting our resources to accessible, affordable treatment and education. The primary emphasis must be on long-term residential treatment that is effective, accessible and affordable for those who need it.

* **Chicago:** We need to have policies in place that allow for the free market to create employment opportunities that pay wages that are competitive and allow for persons to meet their expenses.

* **Cleveland:** We need to create jobs with adequate income and benefits.

*   **Denver:** We must continue to develop system reforms that teach self-sufficiency instead of learned dependency, and absolutely require that children stay in school.

*   **Kansas City:** We need to increase the number of job training opportunities and full time jobs that pay wages commensurate to basic living expenses and adequate benefits (i.e. health care) for employees.

*   **Los Angeles:** The federal government should convert all closing military bases into affordable housing for homeless people. Since these centers are designed to be self-sufficient communities, they could be converted into transitional housing with service and training centers at one location.

*   **Louisville:** The federal government needs to concentrate on stimulating the economy which should provide decent jobs. We need jobs that pay a decent wage with benefits. The federal government also needs to provide universal health care immediately.

*   **Miami:** The federal government should fund housing for special populations.

*   **Minneapolis:** We need to increase jobs.

*   **Nashville:** We need to focus funding on programs that address the main causes of homelessness such as unemployment, lack of job skills, etc.

*   **New Orleans:** The federal government should provide more prevention assistance to keep people in their homes. We need to equip the next generation with the skills and opportunities to be independent, through school curricula and training programs.

*   **New York City:** We need to stimulate economic activity to increase job opportunities at all levels in the private and public sectors.

*   **Norfolk:** We need to improve the economy to provide increased employment with decent wages.

*   **Philadelphia:** Housing and home ownership regulated by federal legislation will do much to prevent homelessness. We need to ensure that there are sufficient jobs in the workplace and that the educational system can train students for gainful employment. More strident action needs to be taken to deal with the drug problem within the inner-city.

*   **Phoenix:** The federal government should provide a basic minimum living allowance to all who need it and want it.

*   **Portland:** We need affordable housing and living wage jobs.

*   **Saint Louis:** The federal government should ensure that opportunities are available and reachable by all people. The atmosphere would have to be drastically altered to remove prejudice and classism and barriers to hope, achievement, and success for all people. Thereby, reducing labelling, domestic violence and hopefully, ending gangs, violence and drug use.

*　**Saint Paul:** The federal government needs to provide more Section 8 certificates and vouchers.

*　**Salt Lake City:** We need to increase employment opportunities for the poor and less educated segments of our society, and provide incentives to businesses to hire and train homeless people.

*　**Santa Monica:** We need to develop low-cost housing, employment programs and a rehabilitation service continuum.

*　**Seattle:** We need to provide safe, appropriate, affordable housing for all.

*　**Trenton:** We need to provide jobs.

TASK FORCE ON HUNGER AND HOMELESSNESS

Freeman Bosley, Jr., Sain Louis
James Scheibel, Saint Paul
Co-Chairs

Judy Abdo, Santa Monica
Jerry Abramson, Louisville
Hector Luis Acevedo, San Juan
Mason C. Andrew, MD, Norfolk
Sidney J. Barthelemy, New Orleans
Phil N. Bredesen, Nashville
Richard Riordan, Los Angeles
Vincent Cianci, Providence
Vera Katz, Portland
Emanuel Cleaver II, Kansas City
Deedee Corradini, Salt Lake City
Richard M. Daley, Chicago
David Dinkins, New York City
Thomas Menino, Boston
Donald Fraser, Minneapolis
Paul Johnson, Phoenix
Frank Jordan, San Francisco
Sharon Pratt Kelly, Washington, DC
Susan Golding, San Diego
Douglas H. Palmer, Trenton
Carrie Saxon Perry, Hartford
Edward Rendell, Philadelphia
Joseph P. Riley, Jr., Charleston
Norman Rice, Seattle
Xavier Suarez, Miami
Patricia Ticer, Alexandria
Richard Vinroot, Charlotte
Wellington Webb, Denver
Michael R. White, Cleveland
Nelson Wolff, San Antonio
Coleman A. Young, Detroit

HUNGER AND HOMELESS IN AMERICA'S CITIES
A NINE-YEAR COMPARISON OF DATA

INDICATOR	1985	1986	1987	1988	1989	1990	1991	1992	1993
HUNGER									
Increase in Demand for Emergency Food	28%	25%	18%	19%	19%	22%	26%	18%	13%
Cities in which Demand for Food Increased	96%	88%	92%	88%	96%	90%	93%	96%	83%
Increase in Demand by Families for Food Assistance	30%	24%	18%	17%	14%	20%	26%	14%	13%
Portion of Those Requesting Food Assistance who are Families with Children	NA	NA	67%	62%	61%	75%	68%	68%	67%
Demand for Emergency Food Unmet	17%	23%	18%	15%	17%	14%	17%	21%	17%
Cities in which Food Assistance Facilities must turn people away	67%	55%	67%	62%	73%	86%	79%	68%	72%
Cities which expect demand for Emergency Food to increase next year	88%	84%	84%	85%	89%	100%	100%	89%	100%
HOMELESSNESS									
Increase in Demand for Emergency Shelter	25%	20%	21%	13%	25%	24%	13%	14%	10%
Cities in which Demand increased	88%	96%	96%	93%	89%	80%	89%	88%	81%
Demand for Emergency Shelter Unmet	NA	24%	23%	19%	22%	19%	15%	23%	25%
Cities in which Shelters must turn people away	60%	72%	65%	67%	59%	70%	74%	75%	77%
Cities which expect Demand for Shelter to increase next year	88%	84%	92%	89%	93%	97%	100%	93%	88%
Composition of Homeless Population									
Single Men	60%	56%	49%	49%	46%	51%	50%	55%	43%
Families with Children	27%	28%	33%	34%	36%	34%	35%	32%	43%
Single Women	12%	15%	14%	13%	14%	12%	12%	11%	11%
Unaccompanied Youth	NA	NA	4%	5%	4%	3%	3%	2%	4%
Children	NA	NA	NA	25%	25%	23%	24%	22%	30%
Severely Mentally Ill	33%	29%	23%	25%	25%	28%	29%	28%	27%
Substance Abusers	37%	29%	35%	34%	44%	38%	40%	41%	48%
Employed	NA	19%	22%	23%	24%	24%	18%	17%	18%
Veterans	NA	NA	NA	26%	26%	26%	23%	18%	21%

POPULATION, POVERTY AND UNEMPLOYMENT DATA FOR THE TASK FORCE CITITES

CITY	1990 POPULATION ESTIMATE	1990 POVERTY RATE ESTIMATE	SEPTEMBER,1992 UNEMPLOYMENT RATE	SEPTEMBER, 1993 UNEMPLOYMENT RATE
ALEXANDRIA	111,183	7.1%	6.6%	5.3%
BOSTON	574,283	18.7%	8.3%	7.1%
CHARLESTON	80,414	21.6%	5.8%	6.3%
CHICAGO	2,783,726	21.6%	8.0%	10.3%
CLEVELAND	505,616	28.7%	12.0%	11.7%
DENVER	467,610	17.1%	6.0%	5.7%
KANSAS CITY	435,146	15.3%	6.7%	6.4%
LOS ANGELES	3,485,398	18.9%	11.7%	10.9%
LOUISVILLE	269,063	22.6%	6.8%	6.1%
MIAMI	358,548	31.2%	16.6%	10.4%
MINNEAPOLIS	368,383	18.5%	5.3%	5.1%
NASVILLE	488,374	13.4%	4.7%	3.6%
NEW ORLEANS	496,938	31.6%	7.8%	7.3%
NEW YORK CITY	7,322,564	19.3%	11.4%	8.7%
NORFOLK	261,229	19.3%	7.7%	7.5%
PHILADELPHIA	1,585,577	20.3%	8.9%	9.0%
PHOENIX	983,403	14.2%	6.5%	4.9%
PORTLAND	437,319	14.5%	7.3%	7.1%
SAINT LOUIS	396,685	24.6%	8.6%	8.3%
SAINT PAUL	272,235	16.7%	5.3%	4.7%
SALT LAKE CITY	159,936	16.4%	5.2%	3.3%
SAN ANTONIO	935,933	22.6%	7.3%	6.1%
SAN DIEGO	1,110,549	13.4%	7.8%	8.6%
SANTA MONICA	86,905	9.4%	6.9%	6.4%
SEATTLE	516,259	12.4%	7.2%	8.0%
TRENTON	88,675	18.1%	13.7%	12.6%

City_____

TASK FORCE ON HUNGER AND HOMELESSNESS
INFORMATION QUESTIONNAIRE

Please complete the following survey and return it by NOVEMBER 26, 1993 to:
Laura DeKoven Waxman
The U.S. Conference of Mayors
1620 Eye Street, N.W.
Washington, D.C. 20006
Fax (202) 293-2352

A report will be published based on the responses to this questionnaire. Experience has shown that such survey reports are effective when they include examples of individual city data. If, however, you want your city's answers to any questions held confidential, please specify those questions by number:_____
===
NOTE: The year for which information is requested is November 1, 1992 to October 31, 1993. It is referred to as "the last year" in the survey questions. Homeless persons are defined as those who reside in shelters, on the streets, in cars or in other locations not intended as residences.
===

HUNGER

1.   THE DEMAND
A)   Has the total number of requests for emergency food assistance in your city ____increased, ____decreased, or ____stayed the same during the last year?   By what percentage? _____%
If possible, please estimate the number of emergency food requests made on a typical day in November 1992 _____ and in October 1993 _____.   Please explain or expand upon your response, and include any other data which supports it.

B)   Has the number of families with children requesting emergency food assistance in your city ____increased, _____decreased, or _____stayed the same during the last year?   By what percentage? _____%
If possible, please estimate the number of emergency food requests made by families with children on a typical day in November 1992 _____ and in October 1993 _____.
Please explain or expand upon your response and include any other data which supports it.

C)   What percentage of those requesting emergency food assistance are members of families with children? _____%·

D)   What percentage of those adults requesting emergency food assistance are employed? _____%

2.   THE CAPACITY
A)   How many emergency food assistance facilities are there in your city? ____
Has that number ___ increased, ___ decreased or ___ stayed the same during the last year?

B)   Has the level of resources (e.g. funds, volunteers, food, etc.) available to emergency food assistance facilities in your city _____increased, ____decreased, or ____stayed the same during the last year? By what percentage? ____% Please explain.

C)   Are emergency food assistance facilities in your city used _____ for emergencies only, _____as a steady source of food for long periods of time, or ____both?   Please explain.

D)   For those who receive assistance, are emergency food assistance facilities able to provide an adequate quantity of food?   ____Yes   ____No Please explain.

E)   Do emergency food assistance facilities in your city have to limit the number of bags provided and/or the number of times families and/or individuals can come to get food? ____Yes ____No Please explain.

F)   Is the food provided nutritionally balanced? ____Yes ____No Please explain.

3.   CHILD NUTRITION PROGRAMS

A)   What percentage of school in your city have a School Lunch Program? ___%
What percentage have a School Breakfast Program? ___%

B)   How many children from families eligible for free and reduced price meals participate in the school lunch program? _____ In the school breakfast program? _____

C)   How many Summer Food Program sites are there in your city? _____ How many children in your city participate in the Summer Food Program? _____

4.   THE FUNDING
During the last year, has your city government spent public funds (either locally generated revenues or federal or state grants) to support local emergency food assistance efforts? ____Yes ____No If Yes, please check below the funding sources used by your city government, indicate the amount spent and whether that amount has increased, decreased or remained the same during the last year.

	Funding Source	Amount Spent	Inc.	Dec.	Same
	Locally generated revenues	$			
	State grants (not federal pass-through monies)	$			
	McKinney homeless assistance programs (please specify which ones on separate sheet)	$			
	Community Development Block Grant	$			
	Community Services Block Grant	$			
	Other federal grants (please specify):	$			
		$			
		$			
		$			

5. **THE UNMET NEEDS**

A) Do emergency food assistance facilities in your city have to turn away people in need because of lack of resources? ___Yes ___No Please explain.

B) Please estimate the percentage of the demand for emergency food assistance in your city which goes unmet. _____%
Please explain or expand upon your response, and include any data which supports it.

6. **THE CAUSES**
What are the main causes of hunger in your city?

HOMELESSNESS

7. **THE DEMAND**
A) Has the total number of people requesting emergency shelter in your city ____increased, ____decreased, or ____stayed the same during the last year? By what percentage? ____%
If possible, please estimate the number of emergency shelter requests on a typical day in November 1992 _____ and in October 1993 _____.
Please explain or expand upon your response, and include any other data which supports it.

B) Has the number of families with children requesting emergency shelter in your city ____increased, ____decreased, or ____ stayed the same during the last year. By what percentage? ____%
If possible, please estimate the number of emergency shelter requests made by families with children on a typical day in November 1992 _____ and in October 1993 _____.
Please explain or expand upon your response, and include any other data which supports it.

C) Has the length of time people in your city are homeless _____increased, _____decreased, or ____stayed the same during the last year? Please explain.

What is the average length of time that people in your city remain homeless? ____months.

8. **THE PEOPLE**
A) Please provide a brief case study (one paragraph) of an **actual** homeless individual or family in your city.

B) What percentage of the homeless families in your city are headed by single parents ____%

C) What percentage of the members of homeless families in your city are children? ____%

D)   Please describe the characteristics of your city's homeless population on the following chart:

Homeless Population	Number	Percent
Members of Families with Children		
Single Men		
Single Women		
Unaccompanied Youth (age 18 & under)		
		100%
African-American		
White		
Hispanic		
Asian		
Native American		
		100%
Mentally Ill		
Substance Abusers		
Persons with AIDS or HIV-related illness		
Veterans		

COMMENTS (please explain any significant changes which occured in the composition of your city's homeless population during the last year):

9.   **THE CAPACITY**
A)   Did the number of emergency shelter beds for homeless people in your city _____increase, _____decrease, or _____stay the same during the last year. By what percentage? _____% How many shelter beds currently exist in your city for use by homeless people? _____

B)   Did the number of emergency shelter beds specifically for homeless families in your city _____increase, _____decrease, or _____stay the same during the last year? By what percentage? _____% How many shelter beds currently exist in your city for use by homeless families? _____

C)   Did the number of transitional housing units in your city _____increase, _____decrease, or _____stay the same during the last year? By what percentage? _____% How many transitional units currently exist in your city? _____

D)   Did the number of transitional housing units specifically for homeless families in your city _____increase, _____decrease, _____ or stay the same during the last year? By what percentage? _____% How many transitional units specifically for homeless families currently exist in your city? _____

E)   Did the number of SRO units in your city ____increase, ____decrease, ____or stay the same during the last year? By what percentage? ____% How many SRO units currently exist in your city? _____

F)   Do homeless families in your city have to break up in order to be accommodated in emergency shelters?
____Yes ____No Please explain.

G)   Do homeless families have to leave the shelter in which they are staying during the day? ___Yes ___No If yes, please explain why and tell where they go during the day?

H)   Please describe the demographics of the homeless veterans' population in your city and the extent to which they are being referred to services provided by the Veterans Administration (health care, income assistance, specialized homeless assistance programs).

10.   THE FUNDING/RESOURCES
During the last year, has your city government spent public funds (either locally generated revenues or federal or state grants) to support local shelters or other services specifically for homeless people?
___Yes ___No
If yes, please check below the funding sources used by your city government and indicate the amounts spent and whether that amount has increased, decreased or stayed the same during the last year.

	Funding Source	Amount Spent	Inc.	Dec.	Same
	Locally generated revenues	$			
	State grants (not federal pass-through monies)	$			
	McKinney homeless assistance programs (please specify which ones on separate sheet)	$			
	Community Development Block Grant	$			
	Community Services Block Grant	$			
	Other federal grants (please specify):				
		$			
		$			
		$			
		$			

11.   **THE UNMET NEED**

A)   Do emergency shelters in your city have to turn away homeless families in need because of lack of resources? _____Yes ____No Please explain, including information on what happens to the homeless families that cannot be accommodated in shelters.

B)   Do emergency shelters in your city have to turn away other homeless people in need because of lack of resources? ___Yes ___No Please explain, including information on what happens to the homeless people who cannot be accommodated in shelters.

C)   Please estimate the percentage of requests by all homeless people for emergency shelter in your city which goes unmet. _____% Please explain or expand upon your response, and include any data which supports it.

D)   Please estimate the percentage of requests for emergency shelter specifically by homeless families in your city which goes unmet.____% Please explain or expand upon your response, and include any data which supports it.

E)   In order of need, select the three groups of homeless people (families with children, single men, single women, unaccompanied minors, severely mentally ill persons, substance abusers, employed persons, persons with AIDS or HIV-related illness or veterans) for whom emergency shelter or other needed services are particularly lacking in your city. For each group, identify which services are most needed but currently lacking.

Group	Services Lacking

12.   **THE CAUSES**
What are the main causes of homelessness in your city?

HOUSING

13.   **The Demand**
A)   During the last year, did requests for assisted housing by low-income families and individuals in your city ____increase ____decrease or ____stay the same during the last year? Please explain.

14.   **The Capacity**
A)   Please indicate the average wait in months in your city from the time of application for assisted housing until an applicant actual receives assistance for:
Public Housing _____ months
Section 8 Certificates _____ months
Vouchers _____ months

B)   Has your city stopped accepting applications for assisted housing programs due to the excessive length of the waiting lists? ____Yes ____No If yes, please specify the types of housing for which the waiting lists have been closed.

C)   For which categories of persons with special needs (the elderly, mentally ill persons, homelessess persons, persons with AIDS, large families, etc.) is it most difficult to find assisted housing?

D)   Please estimate the percentage of eligble low-inocme households in your city currently being served by assisted housing. ____% Please explain or expand upon your response and include any data which supports it.

THE OUTLOOK FOR THE NEXT YEAR, WHAT NEEDS TO BE DONE

15.   THE OUTLOOK
A)   Do you expect the demand for emergency food assistance in your city to _____increase, ____decrease, or ____stay the same during l994? Please explain.

B)   Do you expect requests for emergency shelter in your city to _____increase, ____decrease, or ____stay the same during l994? Please explain.

C)   Do you expect requests for emergency shelter by homeless families specifically to ____increase, ____decrease, or ____stay the same during l994?   Please explain.

16.   WHAT NEEDS TO BE DONE
A)   Many believe that if the problems of homelessness are to be solved we must address three critical issues: housing, income and services.   What is the single most important action the federal government can do to meet needs can take to meet the needs of homeless people relating to: Income?

Housing?

Services?

B)   What is the single most important action the federal government can take to prevent homelessness from occuring in the first place?

17.   Please describe the process your city uses to respond to the questions in this survey.
A)   With whom in your city do you consult?

B)   What are the sources of the data you provide?

C)   How is the data compiled?

D)   By whom is it reviewed?

Person completing form:
Name: _____
Title/Agency: _____
Address: _____
Telephone: _____

BIBLIOGRAPHY

Books

Allsop, Kenneth. *Hard Travellin': The Hobo and His History*. New York: New American Library, 1967.

Bahr, H., *Skid Row*. Oxford: Oxford University Press, 1973.

Bahr, H., and Garret, G. *Women Alone*. New York: Lexington Books, 1976.

Banks, Steven, and Hayes, Robert M. *The Rights of the Homeless*. New York: Practicing Law Institute, 1992.

Barak, Gregg. *Gimme Shelter: a Social History of Homelessness in Contempory America*. New York & London: Praeger, 1991.

Bard, Marjorie. *Organizational and Community Response to Abused and Homeless Women*. New York: Garland,1994.

Bassuk, Ellen, ed. *The Mental Health Needs of Homeless Persons*. San Francisco: Jossey-Bass, 1986.

Baum, Alice S., and Burnes, Donald W. *A Nation in Denial: The Truth About Homelessness*. Boulder, Colo.: Westview Press, 1993.

Belcher, John R., and DiBlasio, Frederick A. *Helping the Homeless: Where Do We Go From Here?* Lexington, Mass.: D. C. Health, 1992.

Beller, Janet. *Street People*. New York: Macmillan, 1980.

Berck, Judith. *No Place to Be: Voices of Homeless Children*. Boston, Houghton Mifflin, 1992.

Bingham, Richard, et al., eds. *The Homeless in Contemporary Society*. Newbury Park, Calif.: Sage Publications, 1987.

Birch, Eugenie, ed. *The Unsheltered Woman: Women and Housing in the 80s*. New Brunswick, N.J.: Transaction, 1985.

Blau, Joel. *The Visible Poor*. New York: Oxford University Press, 1992.

Bratt, R., et al. *Critical Perspectives on Housing*. Philadelphia: Temple University Press, 1986.

Brickner, Philip, et al. *Health Care of Homeless People*. New York: Springer, 1985.

Brickner, Philip et al., eds., *Under the Safety Net: The Health and Social Welfare of the Homeless in the United States*. New York: W.W. Norton and Co., 1990

Bulman, Philip Michael. *Caught in the Mix: An Oral Portrait of Homelessness*. Westport, Conn.: Auburn House, 1993.

Burt, Martha R. *Over the Edge: The Growth of Homelessness in the 1980s*. New York: Russell Sage Foundation; Washington, D.C.: Urban Institute Press, 1992.

Burt, Martha R., and Cohen, Barbara E. *America's Homeless: Numbers, Characteristics, and Programs That Serve Them*. Washington, D.C., Urban Institute Press, 1989.

Butler, Sandra S. *Middle-aged, Female and Homeless: the Stories of a Forgotten Group*. New York: Garland, 1994.

Butler, Stuart, and Kondratas, Anna. *Out of the Poverty Trap: A Conservative Strategy for Welfare Reform*. New York: The Free Press, 1987.

Caton, Carol L. M. *Homeless in America*. New York: Oxford University Press, 1990.

Coates, Robert C. *A Street is Not a Home: Solving America's Homeless Dilemma*. Buffalo, New York: Prometheus Books, 1990.

Cohen, Carl I., and Sokolovsky, Jay. *Old Men of the Bowery: Strategies for Survival Among the Homeless*. New York: The Guilford Press, 1989.

Crouse, Joan M, Trolander, Judith Ann, Altschuler, Genn C. *The Homeless Transient in the Great Depression: New York State, 1929–1941*. Albany: State University of New York Press, 1986

Dear, Michael, and Wolch, Jennifer. *Landscapes of Despair: From Deinstitutionalization to Homelessness*. Princeton, N.J.: Princeton University Press, 1987.

DeWoody, Madelyn. *Confronting Homelessness Among American Families: Federal Programs and Strategies*. Washington, D.C.: Child Welfare League of America, 1992.

Divine, Joel A., and Wright, James D. *The Greatest of Evils: Urban Poverty and the American Underclass*. Hawthorne, N.Y.: Aldine deGruyder, 1993.

Elliott, Michael. *Why the Homeless Don't Have Homes and What to Do About It*. Cleveland: Pilgrim Press, 1993.

Erickson, Jon, and Wilhelm, Charles. *Housing the Homeless*. Princeton, N.J.: Center for Urban Policy Research, 1986.

Ferrell, Frank, and Ferrell, Janet. *Trevor's Place: The Story of the Boy Who Brings Hope to the Homeless*. San Francisco: Harper & Row, 1985.

Fisher, Kevin, and Collins, John, eds. *Homelessness, Health Care, and Welfare Provision*. New York: Routledge, 1993.

Gelfand, Mark. *A Nation of Cities: The Federal Government and Urban America, 1933–1965*. Oxford: Oxford University Press, 1975.

Giamo, Benedict, and Grunberg, Jeffrey. *Beyond Homelessness: Frames of Reference*. Iowa City: University of Iowa Press, 1992.

Ginzberg, Eli, and Solow, Robert, ed. *The Great Society: Lessons for the Future*. New York: Basic Books, 1974.

Glasser, Irene. *Homelessness in Global Perspective*. Boston: G.K. Hall, 1994.

Golden, Stephanie. *The Women Outside: Meanings and Myths of Homelessness*. Berkeley: University of California Press, 1992.

Gorden, Cheryl. *Homeless: Without Addresses in America*. Tempe, Ariz.: Blue Bird Publications, 1988.

Grant, George. *The Dispossessed: Homelessness in America*. Fort Worth, Texas: Dominion Press, 1986.

Hao, Lingxin. *Kin Support, Welfare, and Out-of-Wedlock Mothers*. New York: Garland, 1994.

Hartmann, Chester, ed. *America's Housing Crisis: What Is to Be Done*. London: Routledge & Kegan Paul, 1983.

Hombs, Mary Ellen. *American Homelessness: A Reference Handbook*. Santa Barbara, California: ABC-CLIO, 1991.

Hombs, Mary, and Snyder, Mitch. *Homelessness in America: A Forced March to Nowhere*. Washington, D.C.: Community for Creative Non-Violence, 1986.

Homelessness, Health, and Human Needs. Washington, D.C.: National Academy Press, 1988.

Hooper, K., and Hamberg, J. *The Making of America's Homeless*. New York: Community Service Society, 1984.

Hope, Marjorie, and Young, James. *The Faces of Homelessness*. Lexington, Mass.: Lexington Books, 1986.

Hubbard, Jim. *American Refugees*. Minneapolis: University of Minnesota Press, 1991.

Hunter, Juanita K., ed. *Nursing and Health Care for the Homeless*. Albany: State University of New York Press, 1993.

Hurwitz, Eugene. *Working Together Against Homelessness*. 1st ed. New York: Rosen, 1994.

Huttman, Elizabeth, and Van Vliet, William, eds. *The Handbook of Housing and the Built Environment in the US*. Westport, Conn.: Greenwood Press, 1988.

Imbimbo, J., and Pfeffer, R. *The Olivieri Center: A Study of Homeless Women and Their Concept of Home*. New York: City University of New York, 1987.

Isaac, Rael Jean, and Armat, Birginia C. *Madness in the Streets: How Psychiatry and the Law Abandoned the Mentally Ill*. New York: The Free Press, 1990.

Jackson, Anthony. *A Place Called Home: A History of Low-Cost Housing in Manhattan*. Cambridge, Mass.: MIT Press, 1976.

Jencks, Christopher. *The Homeless*. Cambridge, Mass.: Harvard University Press, 1994.

Johnson, Ann Braden. *Out of Bedlam: The Truth About Deinstitutionalization*. New York: Basic Books, 1990.

Kates, Brian. *The Murder of a Shopping Bag Lady*. New York: Harcourt-Brace, 1985.

Katz, Michael B. *The Undeserving Poor: From the War on Poverty to the War on Welfare*. New York: Pantheon Books, 1989.

Katz, Steven E.; Nardacci, David; and Sabatini, Albert, eds. *Intensive Treatment of the Homeless Mentally Ill*. Washington, D.C.: American Psychiatric Press, 1993.

Kaplon, Marshall, and Cuciti, Peggy, eds. *The Great Society and Its Legacy*. Durham, N.C.: Duke University Press, 1986.

Khan, Chandra C., and Khan, Abdullah A. *Nutrition Status of Mexican American Children in the United States: Determinants and Policy Implications*. New York: Garland, 1993.

Kozol, Jonathan. *Rachel and Her Children: Homeless Families in America*. New York: Crown, 1988.

Kraljic, Matthew A., ed. *The Homeless Problem*. New York: H.W. Wilson, 1992.

Kroloff, Charles A. *54 Ways You Can Help the Homeless*. Southport, Conn.: Hugh Lauter Levin Associates; West Orange, N.J.: Behrman House: Distributed by Macmillan, 1993.

Kryder-Coe, Julee H.; Salamon, Lester M.; and Molnar, Janice M., eds. *Homeless Children and Youth: A New American Dilemma*. New Brunswick, N.J.: Transaction, 1990.

Kuhlman, Thomas L. *Psychology on the Streets: Mental Health Practice with Homeless Persons*. New York: J. Wiley & Sons, 1994.

Lang, Michael H. *Homelessness Amid Affluence: Structure and Paradox in The American Political Economy*. New York: Praeger Publications, 1989.

Leigh, Wilhemina A. *Shelter Affordability for Blacks: Crisis of Clamor?* New Brunswick, N.J.: Transaction Books, 1982.

Masten, Ann S. *Homeless Children in the United States: Development in Jeopardy*. Washington, D.C.: Federation of Behavioral, Psychological, and Cognitive Sciences, 1990.

McCauslin, Mark. *The Homeless*. 1st ed. New York: Maxwell Macmillan International, 1994.

Nardquist, Joan, ed. *The Homeless in America: A Bibliography*. Santa Cruz, Calif.: Reference and Research Services, 1988.

Newman, Sandra J., and Schnare, Ann B. *Subsidizing Shelter: The Relationship Between Welfare and Housing Assistance*. Washington, D.C.: Urban Institute Press, 1988.

Norris, Joye A., and Kennington, Paddy. *Literacy programs for Homeless Adults*. Malabar, Fla.: Krieger, 1992.

Palen, J. John, and London, Bruce, eds. *Gentrification, Displacement and Neighborhood Revitalization*. Albany: SUNY Press, 1984.

Rader, Victoria. *Signal through the Flames: Mitch Snyder and America's Homeless*. Kansas City, MO: Sheed and Ward, 1986.

Redburn, Stevens, and Buss, Terry. *Responding to America's Homeless: Public Policy Alternatives*. New York: Praeger, 1986.

Robertson, Marjorie J. and Greenblatt, Milton, eds. *Homelessness: A National Perspective*. New York: Plenum Publishing Corporation, 1992.

Rochefort, David A. *From Poorhouses to Homelessness: Policy Analysis and Mental Health Care*. Westport, Conn.: Auburn House, 1993.

Rog, Debra J., ed. *Evaluating Programs for the Homeless*. San Francisco: Jossey-Bass, 1991.

Ropers, Richard. *The Invisible Homeless: A New Urban Ecology*. New York: Human Sciences Press, 1988.

Rosen, Michael J., ed. *Home: A Collaboration of Thirty Distinguished Authors and Illustrators of Children's Books to Aid the Homeless*. 1st ed. New York: HarperCollins, 1992.

Rosenthal, Rob. *Homeless in Paradise: A Map of the Terrain*. Philadelphia: Temple University Press, 1994.

Rossi, Peter H. *Down and Out in America: The Origins of Homelessness*. Chicago: University of Chicago Press, 1989.

Rousseau, Ann Marie, and Shulman, Elix. *Shopping Bag Ladies: Homeless Women Speak about Their Lives*. New York: Pilgrim Press, 1982.

Russell, Betty G. *Silent Sisters: A Study of Homeless Women*. Washington, D.C.: Hemisphere, 1991.

Russo, Francis X. and Willis, George. *Human Services in America*. Englewood Cliffs, NJ: Prentice-Hall, 1986.

Schutt, Russell K., and Garrett, Gerald R. *Responding to the Homeless: Policy and Practice*. New York: Plenum, 1992.

Schatz, Howard, photographs by Howard Schatz. *Homeless: Portraits of Americans in Hard Times*. San Francisco: Chronicle Books, 1993.

Schwartz, David C., et al. *A New Housing Policy for America: Recapturing the American Dream*. Philadelphia: Temple University Press, 1988.

Seltser, Barry, and Miller, Donald E. *Homeless Families: The Struggle For Dignity*. Urbana: University of Illinois Press, 1993.

Smith, Neil, and Williams, Peter, eds. *Gentrification and the City*. Boston: Allen and Unwin, 1986.

Snow, David A., and Anderson, Leon. *Down on Their Luck: A Study of Homeless Street People*. Berkeley: University of California Press, 1993.

Stephens, Joyce. *Loners, Losers and Lovers*. Seattle: Washington Press, 1976.

Stronge, James H., ed. *Educating Homeless Children and Adolescents: Evaluating Policy and Practice*. Newbury Park, Calif.: Sage, 1992.

Sweeney, Richard. *Out of Place: Homelessness in America*. New York: HarperCollins, 1993.

Switzer, Ellen Eichenwald. *Anyplace but Here: Young, Alone, and Homeless: What to Do*. New York: Maxwell Macmillan International, 1992.

Timmer, Doug A.; Eitzen, D. Stanley; Talley, Kathryn D. *Paths to Homelessness: Extreme Poverty and the Urban Housing Crisis.* Boulder, CO: Westview Press, 1994.

Torrey, E. Fuller. *Nowhere to Go: The Tragic Odyssey of the Homeless Mentally Ill.* New York: Harper & Row, 1988.

Underwood, Jackson. *The Bridge People: Daily Life in a Camp of the Homeless.* Lanham, Md.: University Press of America, 1993.

Van Ry, Meredith. *Homeless Families: Causes, Effects, and Recommendations.* New York: Garland, 1993.

VanderStaay, Steven, photographs by Joseph Sorrentino. *Street Lives: An Oral History of Homeless Americans.* Philadelphia: New Society Publishers, 1992.

Wagner, David. *Checkerboard Square: Culture and Resistance in a Homeless Community.* Boulder, Colo.: Westview Press, 1993.

Watson, S., and Austerberry, H. *Housing and Homelessness.* New York: Methuen, 1986.

White, Richard W., Jr. *Rude Awakenings: What the Homeless Crisis Tells Us.* San Francisco: ICS Press, 1992.

Wolch, Jennifer R., and Dear, Michael. *Malign Neglect: Homelessness in an American City.* San Francisco: Jossey-Bass, 1993.

Wright, James D. *Address Unknown: The Homeless in America.* New York: Aldine de Gruyter, 1989.

Yeich, Susan. *The Politics of Ending Homelessness.* Lanham, Md., University Press of America, 1993.

Articles

Abbott, Ann A. "A Volunteer's Guide to Working with the Homeless," *Journal of Voluntary Action Research* 17 (1) (January–March 1988): 60–65.

Abbott, Martin L., and Blake, Gerald R. "An Intervention Model for Homeless Youth," *Clinical Sociology Review* (1988): 148–158.

Achtenberg, Emily, and Marcuse, Peter. "The Causes of the Housing Problem," in Rachel Bratt, et al., eds. *Critical Perspectives on Housing.* Philadelphia: Temple University Press, 1986.

Acker, A. "The Kid in the Cardboard Box," *Women and Environments* 10 (Fall 1987): 6–7.

Acorn, Sonia. "Emergency Shelters in Vancouver, Canada," *Journal of Community Health* 18 (October 1993): 283–91.

Adams, C. "Homelessness in the Postindustrial City: Views from London and Philadelphia," *Urban Affairs Quarterly* 21 (4) (June 1986): 527–549.

Adams, G., et al. "Homeless Adolescents: A Descriptive Study of Similarities and Differences Between Runaways and Throwaways," *Adolescence* 20 (79) (Fall 1985): 715–724.

Ah Tye, Kirk. "Voting Rights of Homeless Residents," *Clearinghouse Review* 20 (3) (July 1986): 227–235.

Alperstein, G., et al. "Health Problems of Homeless Children in New York City," *American Journal of Public Health* 78 (9) (September 1988): 1232–1233.

Anderson, Sandra. "Alcoholic Women on Skid Row," *Social Work* 32 (4) (July/August 1987): 362–365.

Anderson, Sandra; Boe, Tome; and Smith, Sharon. "Homeless Women," *Affilia* 3 (2) (1988): 62–70.

Appleby, Lawrence, and Desai, Prakash. "A Case for Asylum," *New York Law School Human Rights Annual* 4 (Fall 1986): 1–45.

———. "Documenting the Relationship between Homelessness and Psychiatric Hospitalization," *Hospital and Community Psychiatry* 36 (7) (July 1985): 732–737.

———. "Homelessness: A Case for Asylum," *Human Rights Annual* (Fall 1986): 4.

———. "Residential Instability: A Perspective on System Imbalance," *American Journal of Orthopsychiatry* 57 (4) (October 1987): 515– 524.

Appleby, L., et al. "The Urban Nomad: A Psychiatric Problem?" *Current Psychiatric Therapies* 21 (Winter 1987): 253–249.

Arce, A., and Bergare, M. "Homelessness, the Chronic Mentally Ill and Community Mental Health Centers," *Community Mental Health Journal* 23 (4) (Winter 1987): 242–249.

Athey, Jean L. "HIV Infection and Homeless Adolescents," *Child Welfare* 70 (5) (September 1991): 517–528.

Axelson, Leland J., and Dail, Paula W. "The Changing Character of Homelessness in the United States," *Family Relations* 37 (4) (1988): 463–469.

Bach, V. "The Big Chill in Federal Housing Subsidies," *City Limits* 13 (3) (March 1987).

Bacher, John C., and Hulchanski, David J. "Keeping Warm and Dry: The Policy Response to the Struggle for Shelter Among Canada's Homeless, 1900–1960," *Urban History Review* (Canada)16 (2) (1987): 147–163.

Bachrach, L. "Chronic Mentally Ill Women: Emergence and Legitimation of Program Issues," *Hospital and Community Psychiatry* 36 (10) (October 1985): 1063–1069.

———. "Deinstitutionalization and Women: Assessing the Consequences of Public Policy," *American Psychologist* 39 (October 1984): 1171–1177.

———. "The Faces of Homelessness," *Contemporary Sociology* 16 (6) (November 1987): 840–841.

———. "Homeless Women: A Context for Health Planning," *Milbank Quarterly* 65 (3) (1987): 371–396.

———. "Issues in Identifying and Treating the Homeless Mentally Ill," *New Directions in Mental Health Services* 35 Fall (1987): 43–62.

———. "Research on Services for the Homeless Mentally Ill," *Hospital and Community Psychiatry* 35 (9) (1984): 910–913.

Bachrach, L., ed al. "The Homeless Mentally Ill in Tucson: Implications of Early Findings," *American Journal of Psychiatry* 145 (1) (January 1988): 112– 113.

Balanon, Lourdes G. "Street Children: Strategies for Action," *Child Welfare* 68 (2) (March/April 1989): 159–166.

Ball, F., and Havassy, B. "A Survey of the Problems and Needs of Homeless Consumers of Acute Psychiatric Services," *Hospital and Community Psychiatry* 35 (9) (1984): 917–21.

Bard, Marjorie. "The American Dream Comes Home to Roost: One Woman's Solution to Homelessness," *Women and Environments* 10 (Fall 1987): 18–19.

Barek, Gregg, and Brohm, Robert M. "The Crimes of the Homeless or the Crime of Homelessness? On the Dialectics of Criminalization, Decriminalization, and Victimization," *Contemporary Crises* 13 (September 1989): 275–88.

Barreto, Julio. "Cisneros Outlines Plan to Shift HOME Funds Toward Homeless," *Nation's Cities Weekly* 16 (25) (June 21, 1993): 8.

Barry, A., et al. "Tuberculosis Screening in Boston's Homeless Shelter," *Public Health Reports* 101 (September/October 1986): 487–494.

Bassuk, Ellen. "The Homelessness Problem," *Scientific American* 251 (1) (Spring 1984): 40–45.

————. "Homeless Families: Single Mothers and Their Children in Boston Shelters," *New Directions in Mental Health Services* 30 (June 1986): 45–53.

————. "Homeless Women—Economic and Social Issues: Introduction," *American Journal of Orthopsychiatry* 63 (July 1993): 337–339.

————. "Social and Economic Hardships of Homeless and Other Poor Women," *American Journal of Orthopsychiatry* 63 (3) (July 1993): 340–347.

Bassuk, Ellen, and Lauriat, Alison. "Are Emergency Shelters the Solution?" *International Journal of Mental Health* 14 (4) (Winter 1985/1986): 125–136.

Bassuk, Ellen, and Rosenberg, L.; "Why Does Family Homelessness Occur? A Case-Control Study," *American Journal of Public Health* 78 (7) (July 1988): 783–788.

Bassuk, E., and Rubin, L. "Homeless Children: A Neglected Population," *American Journal of Orthopsychiatry* 57 (2) (April 1987): 279–286.

Bassuk, Ellen; Rubin, L. and Lauriat, Alison. "Is Homelessness a Mental Problem?" *The American Journal of Psychiatry* 141 (12) (1984): 1546–1550.

Bassuk, Ellen, et al. "Characteristics of Sheltered Homeless Families," *American Journal of Public Health* 76 (9) (September 1986): 1097–1101.

Bassuk, Ellen, et al. "Supplementary Statement on Health Care for Homeless People," *Humanity and Society* 12 (4) (November 1988): 313–317.

Bassuk, Ellen L., and Weinreb, Linda. "Homeless Pregnant Women. Two Generations at Risk" *American Journal of Orthopsychiatry* 63 (3) (July 1993): 348–357.

Baxter, Ellen, and Hopper, Kim. "The New Mendicancy: Homeless in New York City," *American Journal of Orthopsychiatry* 52 (3) (July 1982): 393–408.

Bean, Gerald, et al. "Mental Health and Homelessness: Issues and Findings," *Social Work* 32 (5) (September/October): 411–416.

Belcher, John. "Adult Foster Care: An Alternative to Homelessness for Some Chronically Mentally Ill Persons," *Adult Foster Care Journal* 1 (4) (Winter 1987): 212–225.

————. "Are Jails Replacing the Mental Health System for the Homeless Mentally Ill?" *Community Mental Journal* 24 (3) (1988): 185–195.

————. "Exploring the Struggles of Homeless Mentally Ill Persons: A Holistic Approach to Research," *Case Analysis* 2 (3) (1988): 220–240.

————. "Homelessness: A Cost of Capitalism," *Social Policy* 18 (4) (Spring 1988): 44–48.

————. "Rights Versus Needs of Homeless Mentally Ill Persons," *Social Work* 33 (5) (September/October 1988): 398–401.

Belcher, John, and Ephross, Paul. "Toward an Effective Practice Model for the Homeless Mentally Ill," *Social Casework* 70 (7) (September 1989): 421–427.

Belcher, John, and First, Richard. "The Homeless Mentally Ill: Barriers to Effective Service Delivery," *Journal of Applied Social Sciences* 12 (1) (Fall/Winter 1987–1988): 62–78.

Belcher, John, and Toomey, B. "Relationship between the Deinstitutionalization Model, Psychiatric Disability, and Homelessness," *Health and Social Work* 13 (2) (Spring 1988): 145–153.

Benda, Brent B. "Crime, Drug Abuse, Mental Illness, and Homelessness," *Deviant Behavior* 8 (4) (1987): 361–375.

Benedict, Annette; Shaw, Jeffrey S.; and Rivlin, Leanne G. "Attitudes Toward the Homeless in Two New York City Metropolitan Samples," *Journal of Voluntary Action Research* 17 (3–4) (July-December 1988): 90–98.

Berck, Judith. "No Place to Be: Voices of Homeless Children," *Public Welfare* 50 (2) (Spring 1992): 28–33.

Bevington, Christine. "Housing the Homeless Mother and Child," *Women and Environments* 10 (Fall 1987): 16–17.

Billig, Nancy Swire, and Levinson, Catherine. "Homelessness and Case Management in Montgomery County, Maryland: A Focus on Chronic Mental Illness," *Psychosocial Rehabilitation Journal* 11 (1) (July 1987): 59–66.

Blackwell, Barry. "Homelessness and the Mentally Ill," *American Journal of Psychiatry* 150 (June 1993): 989.

Blankertz, Laura E., et al. "Outreach Efforts with Dually Diagnosed Homeless Persons," *Families in Society: The Journal of Contemporary Human Services* 71 (7) (September 1990): 387–397.

Blau, Joel. "The Limits of the Welfare State: New York City's Response to Homelessness," *Journal of Sociology and Social Welfare* 16 (1) (March 1989): 79–91.

———. "On the Uses of Homelessness: A Literature Review," *Catalyst* (1988): 5–25.

Blodgett, N. "Americas Homeless," *ABA Journal* 73 (1987): 19–20.

Bowdler, J., and Barrell, L. "Health Needs of Homeless Persons," *Public Health Nursing* 4 (3) (September 1987): 135–140.

Bown, William. "Hidden Homeless Who Came to Stay . . ." *New Scientist* 139 (1891) (Spetember 18, 1993): 4.

Brahams, D., and Weller, M. "Crime and Homelessness among the Mentally Ill," *Medico-Legal Journal* 54 (1986): 42–53.

Breakey, William. "Treating the Homeless," *Alcohol, Health and Research World* 11 (3) (Spring 1987).

Breo, Dennis L. "Treating the American Tragedy—MDs Try to Heal the Sick Homeless," *JAMA: The Journal of the American Medical Association* 263 (23) (June 20, 1990): 3201–3203.

Breton, M. "A Drop-In Program for Transient Women: Promoting Competence through the Environment," *Social Work* 30 (November/December 1984): 543–546.

———. "The Need for Mutual-Aid Groups in a Drop-In for Homeless Women: The Sistering Case," *Social Work With Groups* 11 (4) (1988): 47–61.

Brickner, Philip. "Health Issues in the Care of the Homeless," in Brickner, Philip, et al., eds. *Health Care of Homeless People*. New York: Springer, 1985.

Browne, Angela. "Family Violence and Homelessness: The Relevance of Trauma Histories in the Lives of Homeless Women," *American Journal of Orthopsychiatry* 63 (3) (July 1993): 370–384.

Burnham, Audrey M., and Koegel, Paul. "Methodology for Obtaining a Representative Sample of Homeless Persons: The Los Angeles Skid Row Study," *Evaluation Review* 12 (2) (April 1988): 117–152.

Burns, Leland. "Hope for the Homeless in the United States: Lessons from the Third World," *Cities* 5 (February 1988): 33–40.

Busuttil, Salvino. "Houselessness and the Training Problem," *Cities* 4 (May 1987): 152–158.

Cain, Mead. "The Consequences of Reproductive Failure: Dependence, Mobility, and Mortality Among the Elderly of Rural South Asia," *Population Studies* 40 (3) (November 1986): 375–388.

Calsyn, Robert J., and Morse, Gary. "Homeless Men and Women: Commonalities and a Service Gender Gap," *American Journal of Community Psychology* 18 (4) (August 1990): 597–608.

Calsyn, Robert J.; Kohfeld, Carol W.; and Roades, Laurie. "Urban Homeless People and Welfare: Who Receives Benefits?" *American Journal of Community Psychology* 21 (1) (February 1993): 95–112.

Campbell, Richard, and Reeves, Jimmie L. "Covering the Homeless: The Joyce Brown Story," *Critical Studies in Mass Communication* 6 (1) (March 1989): 21–42.

Carew, Harold D. "A Fair Deal Wins—A Foul Dole Loses," *California History* 62 (3) (1983): 172–174.

"Caring for Homeless in Santa Barbara," *Center Magazine* 19 (6) (November/December 1986): 24–33.

Caton, C. "The Homeless Experience in Adolescent Years," *New Directions in Mental Health Services* 30 (June 1986): 63–70.

Caton, Carol L., et al. "Follow-up of Chronically Homeless Mentally Ill Men," *American Journal of Psychiatry* 150 (11) (November 1993): 1639–1642.

Chackes, K. "Sheltering the Homeless: Judicial Enforcement of Governmental Duties to the Poor," *Washington University Journal of Urban and Contemporary Law* 31 (Winter 1987): 155–99.

Chambliss, Blake. "Homeless in America: An Architect's View," *Journal of Housing* 43 (6) (November/December 1986): 238–239.

Christ, Winifred R., and Hayden, Sharon L. "Discharge Planning Strategies for Acutely Homeless Inpatients," *Social Work in Health Care* 14 (1) (1989): 33–45.

Cibulskis, Ann. "Housing the Homeless," *Housing Studies* 3 (1) (January 1988): 76–78.

Coggins, Allen. "Homelessness: Faces of the Transient are Changing: Epidemic Affects More and More People," *Tennessee Town and City* 37 (22) (December 8, 1986): 9.

Cohen, Carl, and Sokolovsky, Jay. "Social Engagement vs. Isolation: The Case of the Aged in Single Room Occupancy Hotels," *Gerontologist* 20 (1) (1980): 36–44.

———. "Toward a Concept of Homelessness Among Aged Men," *Journal of Gerontology* 38 (1) (January 1983): 81–89.

Cohen, Carl; Teresi, Jeanne; and Holmes, Douglas. "The Mental Health of Old Homeless Men," *Journal of the American Geriatrics Society* 36 (6) (June 1988): 492–501.

Cohen, Carl I., and Thompson, Kenneth S. "Homeless Mentally Ill or Mentally Ill Homeless?" *American Journal of Psychiatry* 149 (6) (June 1992): 816–823.

Cohen, N., et al. "The Mentally Ill Homeless: Isolation and Adaptation," *Hospital and Community Psychiatry* 35 (9) (1984): 922–924.

Collin, R., and Barry, D. "Homelessness: A Post-Industrial Society Faces a Legislative Dilemma," *Akron Law Review* 20 (Winter 1987): 409–431.

Colson, Paul. "The Faces of Homelessness," *Social Service Review* 61 (3) (September 1987): 541–544.

———. "Housing the Homeless," *Social Service Review* 61 (3) (September 1987): 541–544.

Conklin, John J. "Homelessness and De-Institutionalization," *Journal of Sociology and Social Welfare* 12 (1) (March 1985): 41–61.

Connell, J. "A Right to Emergency Shelter for the Homeless Under the New Jersey Constitution," *Rutgers Law Journal* 18 (Summer 1987): 765–822.

"Controversies: Money, Medicine, and Homelessness," *Society* 26 (May/June 1989): 4–23.

Corrigan, E., and Anderson, C. "Homeless Alcoholic Women on Skid Row," *American Journal of Drug and Alcohol Abuse* 10 (4) (1984): 535–549.

Coston, Charisse Tia Maria. "The Original Designer Label: Prototypes of New York City's Shopping Bag Ladies," *Deviant Behavior* 10 (2) (1989): 157–172.

Cousineau, Michael R., and Lozier, John N. "Assuring Access to Health Care for Homeless People Under National Health Care," *American Behavioral Scientist* 36 (6) (July 1993): 857–870.

Crosbie, M. "Architect Designs and Builds Prototype Homeless Shelters," *Architecture* 76 (July 1987).

Crosland, D. "Can Lawyers Really Help the Homeless?" *Human Rights* 14 (Spring 1987): 16–19.

Crystal, Stephen. "Homeless Men and Homeless Women: The Gender Gap," *Urban and Social Change Review* 17 (2) (Summer 1984): 2–6.

Crystal, Stephen, et al. "Multiple Impairment Patterns in the Mentally Ill Homeless," *International Journal of Mental Health* 14 (4) (Winter 1985/1986): 61–73.

Curriden, Mark. "Homeless Privacy Rights," *ABA Journal* 77 (July 1991): 33.

Cutler, D. "Community Residential Options for the Chronically Mentally Ill," *Community Mental Health Journal* 22 (1) (Spring 1986): 61–73.

Dadds, Mark R.; Braddock, David; and Cuers, Simone. "Personal and Family Distress in Homeless Adolescents," *Community Mental Health Journal* 29 (October 1993): 413–22.

Dakin, L. "Homelessness: The Role of the Legal Profession in Finding Solutions through Litigation," *Family Law Quarterly* 21 (Spring 1987): 93–126.

Daly, Gerald. "Homelessness and Health: A Comparison of British, Canadian and US Cities," *Cities* 6 (1) (February 1989): 22–38.

Daswani, Mona. "Shelter and Women—A Perspective," *Indian Journal of Social Work* 48 (3) (October 1987): 273–285.

Dato, C., and Rafferty, M. "The Homeless Mentally Ill," *International Nursing Review* 32 (6) (November/December 1985): 170–173.

Davis, Nancy. "Helping the Homeless," *State Legislatures* 11 (3) (March 1985): 2–23.

Davis, Nancy Harvey, and Fitzgerald, Pam. "Libraries and the Homeless," *Library Journal* 118 (4) (March 1, 1993): 27.

Dennis, Deborah L., et al. "A Decade of Research and Services for Homeless Mentally Ill Persons: Where Do We Stand?" *American Psychologist* 46 (11) (November 1991): 1129–1138.

Deutsche, R. "Krystof Wodiczko's Homeless Projection and the Site of Urban Revitalization (Union Square, New York)," *October* 38 (Fall 1986): 63–98.

DiBlasio, Frederick A., and Belcher, John R. "Social Work Outreach to Homeless People and the Need to Address Issues of Self-esteem," *Health and Social Work* 18 (November 1993): 281–287.

Dinkins, D., and Wackstein, N. "Addressing Homelessness," *Social Policy* 17 (Fall 1986): 50–51.

Doblin, Bruce H.; Gelberg, Lillian; and Freeman, Howard E. "Patient Care and Professional Staffing Patterns in McKinney Act Clinics Providing Primary CAre to the Homeless," *JAMA : The Journal of the American Medical Association* 267 (5): 698–701.

Doolin, J. "Planning for the Special Needs of the Homeless Elderly," *Gerontologist* 26 (3) (June 1986): 229–231.

Drake, Madeline. "Fifteen Years of Homelessness in the UK," *Housing Studies* 4 (2) (April 1987): 119–127.

———. "Housing and Homelessness: A Feminist Perspective," *Journal of Social Policy* 16 (2) (1987): 289–291.

Drake, Mary Anne. "The Nutritional Status and Dietary Adequacy of Single Homeless

Women and Their Children in Shelters," *Public Health Reports* 107 (3) (May 1992): 312–319.

Dreier, Peter. "Community-Based Housing: A Progressive Approach to a New Federal Policy," *Social Policy* 18 (2) (Fall 1987): 18–22.

Dreier, Peter, and Appelbaum, Richard. "The Housing Crisis Enters the '90's," *New England Journal of Public Policy*, Spring 1992, pp. 167–185.

Dumont, Matthew P. "Private Lives/Public Spaces: Homeless Adults on the Streets of New York City," *American Journal of Orthopsychiatry* 52 (2) (April 1982): 367–369.

"The Duty of California Counties to Provide Mental Health Care for the Indigent and Homeless," *San Diego Law Review* 25 (January/February 1988): 197–214.

Edelman, Marian Wright, and Mihaly, Lisa. "Homeless Families & the Housing Crisis in the United States," *Children and Youth Services Review* 11 (1) (1989): 91–108.

"The EHAP Plan (Emergency Housing Apartment Program)," *Journal of Housing* 43 (September/October 1986): 214–216.

Ehrenreich, Barbara. "Night Terrors of a Middle Class Sort: My 'Bag Lady' Problem—And Yours, " *MS.* 15 (August 1986): 34–35.

Elias, Christopher J., and Inui, Thomas S. "When a House Is Not a Home: Exploring the Meaning of Shelter Among Chronically Homeless Older Men," *The Gerontologist* 33 (June 1993): 396–402.

"Enumerating Deaths Among Homeless Persons: Comparison of Medical Examiner Data and Shelter-based Reports—Fulton County, Georgia, 1991," *Morbidity & Mortality Weekly Report* 42 (37) (September 24, 1993): 719, 725+.

Erickson, Rosemary, and Eckert, Kevin. "The Elderly Poor in Downtown San Diego Hotels," *Gerontologist* 17 (5) (1977): 440–446.

Fabricant, Michael. "Beyond Bed and Board: Teaching About Homelessness," *Journal of Teaching in Social Work* 2 (2) (1988): 113–130.

———. "Creating Survival Services," *Administration in Social Work* 10 (3) (1986): 71–84.

———. "Empowering the Homeless," *Social Policy* 18 (4) (Spring 1988): 49–55.

———. "No Haven for Homeless in a Heartless Economy," *Radical America* 20 (2/3) (March/May 1986): 23–34.

———. "Political Economy of Homelessness," *Catalyst* 6 (1) (1987): 11–28.

Fabricant, Michael, and Epstein, Irwin. "Legal and Welfare Rights Advocacy: Complementary Approaches in Organizing on Behalf of the Homeless," *Urban and Social Change Review* 17 (1) (Winter 1984): 15–19.

Fauteux, N. "Homeless Parents Fight the System," *City Limits* 13 (2) (February 1988).

Fellin, Philip, and Brown, Kaaren S. "Application of Homelessness to Teaching Social Work Foundation Content," *Journal of Teaching in Social Work* 3 (1) (1989): 17–33.

Fessler, Pamela, and Elving, Ronald. "$443 Million Homeless Aid Bill Cleared for Reagan's Signature," *Congressional Quarterly Weekly Report* 45 (July 4, 1987): 1452–1453.

"Finding a Path to Shelter," *Legal Reference Services Quarterly* 7 (Summer/Fall/Winter 1987): 5–44.

Finn, Peter. "Dealing With Street People: The Social Service System Can Help," *Police Chief* 55 (February 1988): 47.

First, Richard and Toomey, Beverly. "Homeless Men and the Work Ethic," *Social Service Review* 63 (1) (March 1989): 113–126.

First, Richard, et al. "Homelessness: Understanding the Dimensions of the Problem for Minorities," *Social Work* 33 (March/April 1988): 120–124.

Fischer, P. "Criminal Activity Among the Homeless: A Study of Arrests in Baltimore," *Hospital and Community Psychiatry* 39 (1) (January 1988): 46–51.

Fischer, Pamela, and Breakey, William. "Homelessness and Mental Health: An Overview," *International Journal of Mental Health* 14 (4) (Winter 1985/1986): 6–41.

————. "Profile of the Baltimore Homeless With Alcohol Problems," *Alcohol, Health and Research World* 11 (3) (Spring 1987).

Fischer, Pamela, et al. "Mental Health and Social Characteristics of the Homeless: A Survey of Mission Users," *American Journal of Public Health* 76 (5) (May 1986): 519–524.

Flynn, Raymond. "The Housing Crisis and Homelessness," *State Legislatures* 13 (9) (October 1987): 34.

Fopp, Rodney. "Unemployment, Youth Homelessness and the Allocation of Family Responsibility," *Australian Journal of Social Issues* 17 (4) (November 1982): 304–315.

Forrister, A. "McKenna House: In Seeking a Service, They Began to Serve Themselves," *Public Management* 69 (May 1987): 22–24.

"For the Public Good," *American Bar Association Journal* 73 (December 1987): 54–56.

Francis, M. "Long-Term Approaches to End Homelessness," *Public Health Nursing* 4 (4) (December 1987): 230–235.

Fraser, Laura. "Squatter's Rights: A Visit to Berkeley's Emphatically Unofficial Home for the Homeless," *Express* 9 (17) (February 6, 1987).

Frazier, S. "Responding to the Needs of the Homeless Mentally Ill," *Public Health Reports* 100 (5) (1985): 462–469.

Freddolino, Paul P., and Moxley, David P. "Refining an Advocacy Model for Homeless People Coping with Psychiatric Disabilities," *Community Mental Health Journal* 28 (4) (August 1992): 337–352.

Freeman, Richard, and Hall, Brian. "Permanent Homelessness in America?" *Population Research and Policy Review* 6 (1) (1987): 3–27.

French, Laurence. "Victimization of the Mentally Ill: An Unintended Consequence of Deinstitutionalization," *Social Work* 32 (6) (November/December 1987): 502–505.

Galbreath, S. "Assisting the Homeless: Policies and Resources," *Journal of Housing* 43 (September/October 1986): 211–216.

Garrett, G., and Bahr, H. "The Family Backgrounds of Skid Row Women," *Signs* 2 (2) (1976): 369–381.

————. "Women on Skid Row," *Quarterly Journal of the Studies of Alcohol* 34 (1973): 1228–1234.

Gelberg, L., and Linn, L. "Social and Physical Health of Homeless Adults Previously Treated for Mental Health Problems," *Hospital and Community Psychiatry* 39 (5) (May 1988): 510–516.

Gelberg, L., et al. "Mental Health, Alcohol and Drug Abuse, and Criminal History among Homeless Adults," *American Journal of Psychiatry* 145 (2) (Fall 1988): 191–196.

Gerwirtzman, R., and Fodor, I. "The Homeless Child at School: From Welfare Hotel to Classroom," *Child Welfare* 66 (3) (May/June): 237–245.

Gilliespie, Marcia. "And the Man Cried, 'I'm Hungry,' " *MS.* 16 (January 1988): 32–33.

Ginsberg, Leon. "Shelter Issues in the 1990's: The Potential Roles of Adult Foster Care and Community Residential Facilities," *Adult Foster Care Journal* 2 (4) (1988): 260–272.

Gittelman, Martin. "A Call to National Action for the Homeless Mentally Ill," *International Journal of Mental Health* 14 (4) (Winter 1985/1986): 137–141.

Goetz, Edward G. "Land Use and Homeless Policy in Los Angeles," *International Journal of Urban & Regional Research* 16 (4) (December 1992): 540–554.

Goldberg, Susan. "Gimme Shelter: Religious Provision of Shelter to the Homeless as a Protected Use Under Zoning Laws," *Washington University Journal of Urban and Contemporary Law* 30 (Spring 1986): 75–112.

Golden, S. "Single Women: The Forgotten Homeless," *City Limits* 13 (1) (January 1988): 12.

Goldman, H., and Morrissey, J. "The Alchemy of Mental Health Policy: Homelessness and the Fourth Cycle of Reform," *American Journal of Public Health* 75 (7) (1985): 727–731.

Gould, Martin, and Ardinger, Robert. "Self Advocacy: A Community Solution to Access Discrimination and Service Problems Encountered by the 'Homeless Disabled,' " *Journal of Voluntary Action Research* 17 (1) (January-March 1988): 46–53.

Graves, M. "Working with Homeless Women: A Transcultural Experience," *Spectrum* 7 (5) (1985): 3–6.

Greer, N. "Pilot Program in Shreveport, LA Explores Plight of Homeless," *Architecture* 76 (September 1987): 24.

———. "Working on the Local Level to Ease the Housing Problem," *Architecture* 77 (January 1988): 31.

Grinker, Mark. "The Causes of Modern Homelessness," *Food Monitor* (Winter 1988): 34–35.

Gross, T., and Rosenberg, M. "Shelters for Battered Women and Their Children: An Under-Recognized Source of Communicable Disease Transmission," *American Journal of Public Health* 77 (9) (September 1987): 1198–1201.

Hacker, Andrew. "Shopping Bag Ladies: Homeless Women Speak About Their Lives," *New York Review of Books* 29 (13) (August 1982): 15–20.

Hagen, J. "Gender and Homelessness," *Social Work* 32 (4) (July/August 1987): 312–316.

———. "The Heterogeneity of Homeless," *Social Casework* 68 (October 1987): 451–457.

———. "Participants in a Day Program for the Homeless: A Survey of Characteristics and Service Needs," *Psychosocial Rehabilitation Journal* 12 (4) (April 1989): 29–37.

Hagen, Jan L., and Hutchison, Elizabeth. "Who's Serving the Homeless?" *Social Casework* 69 (8) (October 1988): 491–497.

Hagen, Jan L., and Ivanoff, Andre M. "Homeless Women: A High-Risk Population," *Affilia* 3 (1) (1988): 19–33.

Haley, Barbara. "The Loss of Single Room Occupancy Housing in Metropolitan Areas," *Housing and Society* 16 (1989): 5–15.

Hall, H. "The Homeless: A Mental-Health Debate," *Psychology Today* 21 (February 1987): 65–66.

Hanzlick, Randy, and Parrish, R. Gibson. "Deaths Among the Homeless in Fulton County, GA, 1988–90," *Public Health Reports* 108 (July/August 1993): 488–491.

Harper, Douglas. "The Faces of Homelessness," *Qualitative Sociology* 10 (4) (1987): 404–406.

Harrington, Michael. "The Changing Faces of Poverty," *Disssent* 35 (2) (Spring 1988): 148.

Hartman, Chester. "The Housing Part of the Homelessness Problem," *New Directions in Mental Health Services* 30 (June 1986): 71–85.

Harvey, Barton F. "A New Enterprise; Allying Business, Government, and Citizens in the Fight Against Homelessness," *Humanist* 49 (3) (May/June 1989): 14.

Harvey, Brian, and Menton, Mary. "Ireland's Young Homeless," *Children and Youth Services Review,* 11 (1) (1989): 31–44.

Hausman, Bonnie, and Hammen, Constance. "Parenting in Homeless Families: The Double Crisis," *American Journal of Orthopsychiatry* 63 (3) (July 1993): 358–369.

Hersch, P. "Coming of Age on City Streets," *Psychology Today* 22 (January 1988): 28–32.

Hier, Sally J.; Korboot, Paula J.; and Schweitzer,Robert D. "Social Adjustment and

Symptomatology in Two Types of Homeless Adolescents: Runaways and Throwaways," *Adolescence* 25 (Winter 1990): 761–771.

Hill, Ronald Paul. "Homeless Children: Coping with Material Losses," *Journal of Consumer Affairs* 26 (2) (Winter 1992): 274–287.

"Homelessness in America: Involuntary Family Migration." (Part of a Symposium on: Families on the Move). *Marriage & Family Review* 19 (1–2) (1993): 55–75.

Hinzpeter, Denise Albro. "Shopping Bag Ladies: Homeless Women Speak About Their Lives," *Working Papers for a New Society* 9 (2) (March/April 1982): 58–60.

Hoch, Charles. "Homeless in the United States," *Housing Studies* 1 (4) (October 1986): 228–240.

Hombs, M. "Social Recognition of the Homeless: Policies of Indifference," *Washington University Journal of Urban and Contemporary Law* 31 (Winter 1987): 143–149.

"The Homeless," *Western City* 62 (3) (March 1986): 1–14.

"Homeless Children," *Children Today* 16 (May/June 1987): 2.

"Homeless Families: Do They Have a Right to Integrity?" *UCLA Law Review* 35 (October 1987): 159–206.

"Homeless Need More Housing: City Should Define Goal," *Northern California Real Estate Journal* 2 (33) (July 4, 1988): 14–15.

"Homelessness," *New York Law School Human Rights Annual* 3 (Spring 1986): 245–439.

"Homelessness: A Complex Problem and the Federal Response," *American Journal of Economic Sociology* 44 (October 1985): 385–389.

"Homelessness: Demographics, Causes, and Cures in a Nutshell," *Urban Land* 45 (5) (May 1986): 32–33.

"The Homelessness Exchange: A New National Clearinghouse," *Housing Law Bulletin* 17 (July/August 1987): 62.

"Homelessness in America," *Humanist* 49 (May/June 1989): 6–13.

"Homelessness: An Update," *Housing Law Bulletin* 17 (1) (January/February 1987): 5.

"Homelessness: What Can Be Done," *Housing Law Bulletin* 15 (3) (May/June 1985): 1.

"Homeless Symposium," *Washington University Journal of Urban and Contemporary Law* 31 (1987): 137–239.

"Homing in on the Problem that Won't Go Away: A Nationwide Wrapup on Efforts to Provide Affordable Housing," *Planning* 54 (Spring 1988): 11–17.

Hope, Marjorie. "Housing and Homelessness: A Feminist Perspective," *Contemporary Sociology* 17 (2) (March 1988): 253–254.

Hopper, Kim. "A Poor Apart: The Distancing of Homeless Men in New York's History," *Social Research* 58 (1) (Spring 1991): 107–132.

———. "Homelessness: Reducing the Distance," *New England Journal of Human Services* 3 (4) (1983): 30–47.

———. "More than Passing Strange: Homelessness and Mental Illness in New York City," *American Ethnologist* 15 (February 1988): 155–167.

———. "Public Shelter as 'a Hybrid Institution': Homeless Men in Historical Perspective," *Journal of Social Issues* 46 (4) (Winter 1990): 13–329.

———. "Whose Lives Are These Anyway?" *Urban and Social Change Review* 17 (2) (Summer 1984): 12–13.

Hopper, Kim, and Cox, L. "Litigation in Advocacy for the Homeless: The Case of New York City," *Development: Seeds of Change* 2 (1982): 57–62.

Hopper, K., and Hamber, Jill. "The Making of America's Homeless, From Skid Row to New Poor, 1945–1984," in Bratt, Rachel, and others, eds., *Critical Perspectives on Housing.* Philadelphia: Temple University Press, 1986.

Hopper, K., et al. "Economies of Makeshift: Deindustrialization and Homelessness in New York City," *Urban Anthropology* 14 (1–3) (Spring/Summer/Fall 1985): 183–236.

"Housing and the Homeless," *Public Interest* 85 (Fall 1986): 3–57.

"How Many Homeless People Are There?" *Editorial Research Reports* 1 (12) (March 30, 1990): 176.

Hudson, Christopher G. "The Development of Policy for the Homeless: The Role of Research," *Social Thought* 14 (1) (1988): 3–15.

Hunter, Linda B. "Sibling Play Therapy with Homeless Children: An Opportunity in the Crisis," *Child Welfare* 72 (1) (January 1993): 65–75.

Hutchison, William, et al. "Multidimensional Networking: A Response to the Needs of Homeless Families," *Social Work* 31 (6) (November/December 1986): 427–430.

Imbimbo, Josephine, and Pfeffer, Rachel. "Reflections of Home: Women in Shelters," *Women and Environments* 10 (Fall 1987): 14–15.

Jackson-Wilson, Anita G., and Borgers, Sherry B. "Disaffiliation Revisited: A Comparison of Homeless and Nonhomeless Women's Perceptions of Family of Origin and Social Supports," *Sex Roles: A Journal of Research* 28 (7–8) (April 1993): 261–377.

Jennings, W., Jr., and Forssman-Falck, R. "Virginia's Homeless: Their Health and Safety Challenge Physicians," *Virginia Medicine* 113 (1) (January 1986): 39–41.

Jonas, S. "On Homelessness and the American Way," *American Journal of Public Health* 76 (September 1986): 1084–1086.

Jones, Loring P. "Typology of Adolescent Runaways," *Child & Adolescent Social Work Journal* 5 (1) (Spring 1988): 16–29.

Kanter, S. "Homeless Mentally Ill People: No Longer Out of Sight and Out of Mind," *Human Rights Annual* 3 (Spring 1986): 331–357.

Kaplan, J. "Homeless, Hungry and Jewish," *Washington Jewish Week*, February 16, 1984.

Kasinitz, Philip. "Gentrification and Homelessness: The Single Room Occupancy and Inner City Revival," *Urban and Social Change Review* 17 (1) (1984): 9–14.

Kaufmann, Nancy. "Homelessness: A Comprehensive Policy Approach," *Urban and Social Change Reviews* 17 (1) (1984): 21–26.

Kearns, Kevin C. "The Homelessness in Dublin: An Irish Urban Disorder," *American Journal of Economics and Sociology* 43 (2) (1984): 217–233.

Keigher, Sharon M. "The Faces of Homelessness," *American Journal of Sociology* 93 (5) (March 1988): 1280–1282.

Kelly, Elinor; Mitchell, J. Clyde; and Smith, Susan J. "Factors in the Length of Stay of Homeless Families in Temporary Accommodation," *Sociological Review* 38 (4) (November 1990): 621–633.

Kerridge, Roy. "The Universal Travellers," *New Society* (1985): 427–430.

Kerson, Toba Schwaber. "Progress Notes," *Health and Social Work* 14 (2) (May 1989): 140–141.

Killeen, Damian. "The Young Runaways," *New Society* 75 (January 17, 1986): 97–98.

King, Charles E. "Homelessness in America," *The Humanist* 49 (3) (May/June 1989)

Koegel, Paul, and Burnam, M. "Traditional and Nontraditional Homeless Alcoholics," *Alcohol, Health and Research World* 11 (3) (Spring 1987): 28–35.

Koegel, Paul; Burnam, Audrey; and Farr, Rodger K. "The Prevalence of Specific Psychiatric Disorders Among Homeless Individuals in the Inner City of Los Angeles," *Archives of General Psychiatry* 45 (12) (1988.): 1085–1093.

Koegel, Paul; Burnam, M. Audrey; and Farr, Rodger K. "Subsistence Adaptation Among Homeless Adults in the Inner City of Los Angeles," *Journal* of Social Issues 46 (4) (Winter 1990): 83–107.

Korllos, Thomas S. "The Homeless in Contemporary Society," *Journal of Applied Sociology* 5 (1988): 97–99.

Kosterlitz, Julie. "They're Everywhere: Homeless," *National Journal* 19 (9) (February 28, 1987): 492–494.

Kozol, Jonathan. "Homeless Women," *MS.* 16 (April 1988): 38–43.

Krauthammer, Charles; Dear, Michael J.; and Wolchman, Jennifer R. "At Issue: Should the Homeless Mentally Ill Be Reinstitutionalized?" *CQ Researcher* 2 (29): 681.

Kufeldt, Kathleen, and Nimmo, Margaret. "Youth on the Street: Abuse and Neglect in the Eighties," *Child Abuse and Neglect: The International Journal* 11 (4) (1987): 531–543.

Kunstler, Robin. "Serving the Homeless Through Recreation Programs," *Parks & Recreaton* 28 (8) (August 1993): 16 –22 + .

Kurtz, P. David; Jarvis, Sara V.; and Kurtz, Gail L. "Problems of Homeless Youths: Empirical Findings and Human Services Issues," *Social Work* 36 (4) (July 1991): 309–314.

Kutza, Elizabeth A., and Keigher, Sharon M. "The Elderly 'New Homeless': An Emerging Population at Risk," *Social Work* 36 (4) (July 1991): 288–293.

Lally, Maureen, et al. "Older Women in Single Room Occupancy Hotels: A Seattle Profile," *Gerontologist* 19 (1) (1979): 67–73.

Lam, Julie A. "Homeless Women in America: Their Social and Health Characteristics," *Dissertation Abstracts International, The Humanities and Social Sciences* (September 1988).

Lamb, H. "Deinstitutionalization and the Homeless Mentally Ill," *Hospital and Community Psychiatry* 35 (9) (1984): 899–907.

Lamb, H., and Grant, R. "Mentally Ill Women in the County Jail," *Archives of General Psychiatry* 40 (1983): 363–368.

Langdon, James K. II, and Kass, Mark A. "Homelessness in America: Looking for the Right to Shelter," *Columbia Journal of Law and Social Problems* 19 (1985): 305–392.

Lasdon, D. "Beyond the Quagmire: The Fourth Amendment Rights of Residents of Private Shelters for the Homeless," *Human Rights Annual* 3 (Spring 1986): 245.

Laufer, William. "The Vocational Interests of Homeless, Unemployed Men," *Journal of Vocational Behavior* 18 (2) (April 1981): 196–201.

Lauriat, A. "Sheltering Homeless Families: Beyond An Emergency Response," *New Directions in Mental Health Services* 30 (June 1986): 87–94.

Lee, Alfred McClung. "Signal Through the Flames: Mitch Snyder and America's Homeless," *Humanity and Society* 11 (3) (August 1987): 409–413.

Lee, Barrett A.; Lewis, David W.; and Jones, Susan Hinze. "Are the Homeless to Blame? A Test of Two Theories," *Sociological Quarterly* 33 (4) (1992):535–552.

Lemere, Frederick. "Psychiatry and the Homeless Mentally Ill," *The American Journal of Psychiatry* 150 (July 1993): 1135.

Lempert, L. "Women's Health from a Woman's Point of View: A Review of the Literature," *Health Care for Women International* 7 (3) (1986): 255–275.

Leshner, Alan I. "A National Agenda for Helping Homeless Mentally Ill People," *Public Health Reports* 107 (3) (May 1992): 352–355.

Levine, I. "Homelessness: Its Implications for Mental Health Policy and Practice," *Psychosocial Rehabilitation Journal* 8 (1) (1984): 6–16.

———. "Service Programs for the Homeless Mentally Ill," in Lamb, H., ed., *The Homeless Mentally Ill.* Washington, D.C.: American Psychiatric Association, 1984.

Levine, I., and Kennedy, C. "The Homeless Mentally Ill: A Consultation Challenge," *Consultation: An International Journal* 4 (1984): 52–63.

Levine, I., and Stockdill, J. "Mentally Ill and Homeless: A National Problem," in Jones, B.I., ed., *Treating the Homeless: Urban Psychiatry's Challenge.* Washington, D.C.: American Psychiatric Association Press, 1986.

Levine, I., et al. "Community Support Systems for the Homeless Mentally Ill," *New Directions in Mental Health Services* 30 (June 1986): 27–42.

Levine, Irene S., and Rog, Debra J. "Mental Health Services for Homeless Mentally Ill Persons: Federal Initiatives and Current Service Trends," *American Psychologist* 45 (8) (August 1990): 963–968.

Liddiard, Mark, and Hutson, Susan. "Homeless Young People and Runaways: Agency Definitions and Processes," *Journal of Social Policy. Part 3* 20 (July 1991): 365–388.

Lieb, Kristin. "Sociologist Lives Her Research in Homeless Shelter," *Chronicle of Higher Education* 39 (4) (September 16, 1992): A5.

Linehan, Michelle Fryt. "Children Who Are Homeless: Educational Strategies for School Personnel," *Phi Delta Kappan* 74 (1) (September 1992): 61–66.

Lipton, S. "Involving the Private Sector in Housing the Homeless: Some Program Examples," *Urban Land* 45 (8) (August 1986): 6–8.

Lissner, W. "Homelessness and Poverty in Affluent America," *American Journal of Economic Sociology* 44 (October 1985): 389–390.

"Local Government Strategies," *Public Management* 69 (May 1987): 8–18.

Low, Nicholas, and Crawshaw, Bruce. "Homeless Youth: Patterns of Belief," *Australian Journal of Social Issues.* 20 (1) (February 1985): 23–34.

Luna, G. "Welcome to My Nightmare: The Graffiti of Homeless Youth," *Hospitals* 24 (6) (September/October 1987): 73–78.

Lusk, Mark W. "Street Children Programs in Latin America," *Journal of Sociology and Social Welfare* 16 (1) (March 1989): 55–77.

Mahoney, Paula. "Loving Care by Homeless Workers Helps Restore Derelict Mansion," *Western City* 62 (9) (September 1986): 12–15.

Main, Thomas. "The Homeless Families of New York," *Public Interest* 85 (Fall 1986): 3–21.

———. "The Homeless of New York," *The Public Interest* 72 (1983): 3–28.

Mair, Andrew. "The Homeless and the Post-Industrial City," *Political Geography Quarterly* 5 (October 1986): 351–368.

Mallin, Dana Stewart. "Sheltering the Homeless," *Canadian Home Economic Journal* 37 (Summer 1987): 114–116.

Mancini, Jay A., and Orghner, Dennis K. "The Contemporary Family: Consequences of Change," *Family Relations* 37 (4) (1988).

Maper, Lynda. "Faulty Food and Shelter Programs Draw Charge that Nobody's Home to Homelessness," *National Journal* 17 (9) (March 2, 1985): 474–476.

Marcos, Luis R., et al. "Psychiatry Takes to the Streets: The New York City Initiative for the Homeless Mentally Ill," *American Journal of Psychiatry* 147 (11) (November 1990): 1557–1561.

Marcuse, Peter. "Homelessness Is a Product: Government, Jobs, and the Housing System," *Christianity and Crisis* 48 (April 18, 1988): 129–134.

———. "Isolating the Homeless," *Shelterforce* 11 (1) (June/July 1988): (January 1987) 12–15.

———. "Neutralizing Homelessness," *Socialist Review* 18 (1) (January/March 1988) :69–96.

Marin, Peter. "Helping and Hating the Homeless: The Struggle at the Margins of America," *Harper's Magazine* 274 (January 1987): 39.

———. "The World of the Homeless in the City of Santa Barbara," *Center Magazine* 19 (5) (September/October 1986): 19–29.

Marotto, Robert A. "Are Those Streetpeople Part of the New Poor, Too? Toward an Applied Sociology of Social Problems," *American Sociologist* 20 (2) (Summer 1989): 111–122.

Marotto, Robert A., and Friedland, William H. "Streetpeople and Community Public Policy in Santa Cruz, California," *Journal of Applied Sociology* (1987): 71–87.

Marshall, J. P. "Rachel and Her Children: Homeless Families in America," *Social Science Journal* 26 (1) (January 1989): 111–113.

Marshall, Tony, and Fairhead, Suzan. "How to Keep Homeless Offenders Out of Prison," *New Society* 49 (885) (September 20, 1979): 616–617.

Martin, Marsha A., and Nayowith, Susan A. "Creating Community: Groupwork to Develop Social Support Networks with Homeless Mentally Ill," *Social Work with Groups* 11 (4) (1988): 79–93.

Masci, David "Limits Urged on Use of Homeless Count," *Congressional Quarterly Weekly Report* 49 (19) (May 11, 1991): 1194.

Maxwell, Bruce Edward. "Hostility, Depression, and Self-Esteem Among Troubled and Homeless Adolescents in Crisis," *Journal of Youth & Adolescence* 21 (2) (April 1992): 139–150.

McCarthy, Bill, and Hagan, John. "Mean Streets: The Theoretical Significance of Situational Delinquency Among Homeless Youths," *American Journal of Sociology* 98 (3) (November 1992): 597–627.

McCarty, Dennis, et al. "Alcoholism, Drug Abuse, and the Homeless," *American Psychologist* 46 (11) (November 1991): 1139–1148.

McCormick, B., and Newald, J. "Outreach Works in Treating Homeless Youth," *Hospitals* 60 (9) (May 5, 1986): 162.

McCormick, Erin. "Do Drop Inn: A New Solution for the Homeless," *Express* (Berkeley, California) 9(5) (September/October 1986): 19–29.

McDowell, Linda. "Housing and Homelessness: A Feminist Perspective," *International Journal of Urban and Regional Research* 12 (1) (March 1988): 166–167.

McGrath, Mike. "The Great Oakland Sleep Out: Dramatizing Homelessness in the East Bay," *Express* (Berkeley, California) 8 (21) (February 28, 1986): 3.

McKechnie, S. "Homelessness: Whose Fault?" *Contemporary Review* 248 (January 1986): 19–24.

McLarin, Kimberly J. "Giving Families a Fresh Start," *Public Welfare* 47 (3) (1989): 37–41.

Merves, Esther S. "Rachel and Her Children: Homeless Families in America," *Contemporary Sociology* 18 (2) (March 1989): 255–257.

Michael, M., and Brammer, S. "Medical Treatment of Homeless Hypertensives," *American Journal of Public Health* 78 (January 1988): 94.

Milburn, Norweeta, and Watts, Roderick. "Methodological Issues in Research on the Homeless and the Homeless Mentally Ill," *International Journal of Mental Health* 14 (4) (Winter 1985/1986): 42–60.

Miller, D., and Lin, E. "Children in Sheltered Homeless Families: Reported Health Status and use of Health Services," *Pediatrics* 81 (5) (May 1988): 668–673.

Miller, S. M. "Struggles for Relevance: The Lynd Legacy," *Journal of the History of Sociology* 2 (1) (1979–1980): 58–64.

Miner, Maureen H. "The Self-Concept of Homeless Adolescents," *Journal of Youth & Adolescence* 20 (5) (October 1991): 545–560.

Mitchell, J. Clyde. "The Components of Strong Ties Among Homeless Women," *Social Networks* 9 (1) (March 1987): 37–47.

———. "Ethnography and Networks," *Connections* 9 (1) (1986): 17–23.

Moore, C. et al. "The Politics of Homelessness," *PS* 21 (Winter 1988): 57–63.

Mossman, Douglas, and Perlin, Michael L. "Psychiatry and the Homeless Mentally Ill: A Reply to Dr. Lamb," *American Journal of Psychiatry* 149 (7) (July 1992): 951–957.

Mostoller, G. "Housing the Homeless in Central Urban Areas," *Habitat International* 10 (4) (1986): 55–62.

Mowbray, Carol T.; Bybee, Deborah; and Cohen, Evan. "Describing the Homeless Mentally Ill: Cluster Analysis Results," *American Journal of Community Psychology* 21 (1) (February 1993): 67–93.

Moxley, David P., and Freddolino, Paul P. "Needs of Homeless People Coping with Psychiatric Problems: Findings from an Innovative Advocacy Project," *Health & Social Work* 16 (1) (February 1991): 19–26.

Munro, Ingrid. "International Year of Shelter for the Homeless," *Cities* 4 (1) (February 1987): 5–12.

"New Federal Assistance for the Homeless," *Housing Law Bulletin* 17 (September/October 1987): 77–82.

Newman, S., and Schnare, A. "Housing: The Gap in the Welfare System," *Journal of State Government* 60 (May/June 1987): 117–121.

"The New Poor: Jobless and Homeless in the United States," *Futurist* 20 (March/April 1986): 44.

Nichols, J. "Is There a Right to Housing?" *Human Rights* 15 (Fall 1987): 42–45.

Nichols, J., et al. "A Proposal for Tracking Health Care for the Homeless," *Journal of Community Health* 11 (3) (Fall 1986): 204–209.

Noble, Gretel. "Housing the Homeless," *Economic Development and Law Center Report* 16 (2/3) (Summer 1988): 4–11.

"No Home? Please Hold. (Voice Mail for Homeless Helps in Getting Them Employment and Housing)" *The Economist* 329 (December 18, 1993): 29.

North, Carol S., and Smith, Elizabeth M. "A Comparison of Homeless Men and Women: Different Populations, Different Needs. (St. Louis)" *Community Mental Health Journal* 29 (October 1993): 423–431.

North, Carol S.; Smith, Elizabeth M.; and Spitznagel, Edward L. "Is Antisocial Personality a Valid Diagnosis Among the Homeless?" *American Journal of Psychiatry* 150 (4) (April 1993): 578–583.

Nyman, Thor. "Housing for the Homeless: Pandora's Box," *California Builder* 55 (3) (June/July 1987): 98.

O'Brian, Martin. "Landscapes of Despair: From Deinstitutionalization to Homelessness," *Sociology* 22 (4) (November 1988): 639–640.

O'Connor, M. "State Legislative Initiatives for the Homeless," *Human Rights Annual* 3 (Spring 1986): 245.

Osbourn, Kevin. "The Homeless, Who's to Blame?" *State Government News* 29 (7) (August 1986): 8–9.

Padgett, Deborah K., and Struening, E. L. "Victimization and Traumatic Injuries Among the Homeless: Associations with Alcohol, Drug, and Mental Problems," *American Journal of Orthopsychiatry* 62 (4) (October 1992): 525–534.

Parvey, Constance F. "Homeless Women: Priorities, Private Aid and Public Committment," *Christianity and Crisis* 47 (4) (March 1987): 94–96.

Paterson, Andrea, and Rhubright, Ellen. "Housing for the Mentally Ill: A Place Called Home," *State Legislative Report* 11 (9) (July 1986).

Paterson, Kenneth. "Shelters and Statistics: A New Face to an Old Problem," *Urban and Social Change Review* 17 (2) (Summer 1984): 14–17.

Peirce, Neal. "The City-Church Partnership in Sheltering the Homeless," *Nation's Cities Weekly* 8 (3) (January 21, 1985): 6.

———. "The Low Income Housing Crisis: Waves of Homeless Just a Start: It Can Get a Lot Worse," *Nation's Cities Weekly* 10 (17) (April 27, 1987): 1.

Peterson, Richard A., and Wiegand, Bruce. "Ordering Disorderly Work Careers on Skid Row," *Research in the Sociology of Work* (1985): 215–230.

Phillips, Jan. "Housing and Homelessness: A Feminist Perspective," *Gender & Society* 1 (1) (March 1987): 115–117.

Phillips, M., et al. "Homeless Families: Services Make A Difference," *Social Casework* 69 (January 1988): 48–53.

Pinch, Steven. "Landscapes of Despair: From Deinstitutionalization to Homelessness," *International Journal of Urban and Regional Research* 12 (3) (September 1988): 498–499.

Podschun, Gary D. "Teen Peer Outreach-Street Work Project: HIV Prevention Education for Runaway and Homeless Youth," *Public Health Reports* 108 (2) (March 1993): 150–155.

Ponessa, Jeanne. "Help for the Homeless and Hungry," *Governing* 6 (10) (July 1993): 24–25.

Potter, B. "East Orange Foregoes Traditional Models: An Emergency Program for the Homeless Has a Broad Impact," *Public Welfare* 47 (1) (1989): 13–15.

Price, Virginia Ann. "Characteristics & Needs of Boston Street Youth: One Agency's Response," *Children and Youth Services Review* 11 (1) (1989): 75–90.

Proch, D., and Taber, M. "Helping the Homeless," *Public Welfare* 45 (2) (Spring 1987): 5–9.

Putnam, Jane, et al. "Innovative Outreach Services for the Homeless Mentally Ill," *International Journal of Mental Health* 14 (4) (Winter 1985/1986): 112–124.

Rader, Victoria, and Lee, Alfred McClung. "Signal Through the Flames: Mitch Snyder and America's Homeless," *Humanity and Society* 11 (3) (August 1987): 409–413.

Rafferty, Margaret. "Standing Up for America's Homeless," *American Journal of Nursing* 89 (12) (December 1989): 1614.

Rascoe, Dale, and Dalton, Sharron. "Hungry, Homeless, and HIV: A Study of Homeless Visitors to an Outreach Meal Center for People with AIDS," *Journal of Nutrition Education* 25 (4) (July 1993): 205–207.

Rauber, Paul. "Beyond Reaganville: Berkeley Council Rejects Sweat Equity for Its Homeless," *Express* (Berkeley, California) 9 (20) (February 27, 1987): 3.

Raychaba, Brian. "Canadian Youth in Care: Leaving Care to Be on Our Own with No Direction From Home," *Children and Youth Services Review* 11 (1) (1989): 61–73.

Redburn, Steven F., and Buss, Terry F. "Beyond Shelter: The Homeless in the USA," *Cities* 4 (1) (February 1987): 63–69.

Reid, I. "Law, Politics and the Homeless," *West Virginia Law Review* 89 (Fall 1986): 115–47.

Reitzes, Dietrich C. "The Homeless Transient in the Great Depression: New York State, 1929–1941," *Contemporary Sociology* 17 (3) (May 1988): 371.

Rhodes, R., and Zelman, A. "An Ongoing Multifamily Group in a Women's Shelter," *American Journal of Orthopsychiatry* 56 (1986): 120–130.

Rife, John C., et al. "Case Management with Homeless Mentally Ill People," *Health & Social Work* 16 (1) (February 1991): 58–67.

"A Right to Shelter for the Homeless in New York State," *New York University Law Review* 61 (May 1986): 272–299.

Riordan, Teresa. "Houskeeping at HUD: Why the Homeless Problem Could Get Much, Much Worse," *Common Cause* 13 (2) (March/April 1987): 26–31.

———. "Why Homelessness Is Likely to Increase," *Utne Reader* 25 (January 1988): 38.

Ritchey, Ferris J.; La Gory, Mark; and Mullis, Jeffrey. "Gender Differences in Health Risks and Physical Symptoms Among the Homeless," *Journal of Health & Social Behavior* 32 (1) (March 1991): 33–48.

Ritchey, Ferris J., et al. "A Comparison of Homeless, Community-Wide, and Selected Distressed Samples on the CES-Depression Scale," *American Journal of Public Health* 80 (11) (November 1990): 1384–1386.

Rivlin, Leanne. "A New Look at the Homeless," *Social Policy* 16 (4) (Spring 1986): 3–10.

Roberts, Ron E., and Keefe, Thomas. "Homelessness: Residual, Institutional and Communal Solutions," *Journal of Sociology and Social Welfare* 13 (2) (June 1986): 400–417.

Robertson, J. "Homeless Adolescents: A Hidden Crisis," *Hospital and Community Psychiatry* 39 (5) (May 1988): 475.

Robertson, M. "Mental Disorder Among the Homeless Persons in the United States: An Overview of Recent Empirical Literature," *Administration in Public Health* 14 (1) (Fall 1986): 14–27.

Robertson, M., and Cousineau, M. "Health Status and Access to Health Services Among the Urban Homeless," *American Journal of Public Health* 76 (5) (May 1986): 561–563.

Robertson, Marjorie J. "Homeless Women with Children: The Role of Alcohol and Other Drug Abuse," *American Psychologist* 46 (11) (November 1991): 1198–1203.

Robson, P.W., and Watchman, P. "The Homeless Persons' Obstacle Race," *Journal of Social Welfare Law* (January 1981): 1–15.

———. "The Homeless Persons' Obstacle Race: 2," *Journal of Social Welfare Law* (March 1981): 65–82.

Rohling, H., and Moore, C. "PHAs Can Help Meet the Needs of the Homeless," *Journal of Housing* 44 (November/December 1987): 210.

Ropers, Richard. "The Rise of the New Urban Homeless," *Public Affairs Report* 26 (October/December 1985): 1–14.

Ropers, Richard, and Boyer, Richard. "Homelessness Is a Health Risk," *Alcohol, Health and Research World* 11 (3) (Spring 1987): 38.

———. "Perceived Health Status Among the New Urban Homeless," *Social Science and Medicine* 24 (8) (1987): 669–678.

Rosencrance, John. "Accommodating Negative Client Perceptions: A Process of Neutralization," *Sociological Inquiry* 58 (2) (1988): 194–205.

———. "Perceived Health Status among the New Urban Homeless," *Social Science and Medicine* 24 (8) (1987): 669–678.

Rosenheck, Robert; Gallup, Peggy; and Leda, Catherine A. "Vietnam Era and Vietnam Combat Veterans Among the Homeless," *American Journal of Public Health* 81 (5) (May 1991): 643–646.

Rosenthal, Robert. "Homeless in Paradise: A Map of the Terrain," *Dissertation Abstracts International, The Humanities and Social Sciences* (July 1988).

———. "Housing the Homeless," *Contemporary Sociology* 17 (1) (January 1988): 61–62.

Rossi, Peter, and Wright, James. "The Determinants of Homelessness," *Health Affairs* 6 (1) (Spring 1987): 19–32.

———. "The Urban Homeless: A Portrait of Urban Dislocation," *Annals of the American Academy of Political and Social Science* (January 1989): 132–142.

Rossi, P., et al. "The Urban Homeless: Estimating Composition and Size," *Science* 235 (March 1987): 1336–1341.

Roth, D., and Bean, G., Jr. "New Perspectives on Homelessness: Findings from a Statewide Epidemiological Study," *Hospital and Community Psychiatry* 37 (7) (July 1986): 712–719.

Roth, D., and Bean, J. "Alcohol Problems and Homelessness: Findings from the Ohio Study," *Alcohol, Health and Research World* 10 (2) (Winter 1985/1986): 14–15.

Roth, D., et al. "Homelessness and Mental Health Policy: Developing an Appropriate Role for the 1980's," *Community Mental Health Journal* 22 (3) (Fall 1986): 203–214.

———. "Homeless Women: Characteristics and Service Needs," *Affilia: Journal of Women and Social Work* 2 (4) (Winter 1987): 6–19.

Roth, Lisa, and Fox, Elaine R. "Children of the Homeless Families: Health Status and Access to Health Care," *Journal of Community Health* 15 (4) (1990 Aug.): 275–284.

Rothman, Robert. "Members Seek Permanent Aid for Homeless: Bills Would Provide Shelter and Services," *Congresssional Quarterly Report* 43 (March 30, 1985): 583–5.

Royce, D. "Homelessness Among Trash Pickers," *Psychological Reports* 60 (June 1987): 808–810.

"Runaway, Truant, Homeless Youth," *Friends Committee on Legislation of California Newsletter* 35 (2) (February 1986): 1.

Ryback, R., and Bassuk, E. "Homeless Battered Women and Their Shelter Network," *New Directions in Mental Health Services* 30 (June 1986): 55–61.

Sacks, Joseph M.; Phillips, John; and Cappelletty, Gordon. "Characteristics of the Homeless Mentally Disordered Population in Fresno County," *Community Mental Health Journal* 23 (2) (1987): 114–119.

Scapp, Ron. "Lack and Violence: Towards a Speculative Sociology of the Homeless," *Practice* 6 (2) (1988): 35–47.

Schide, Brad. "The Faces of Homelessness," *Catalyst* 6 (2(22)) (1988): 63–65.

Schieffelbein, C., and Snider, D. "Tuberculosis Control among Homeless Populations," *Archives of Internal Medicine* 148 (8) (August 1988): 1843–1846.

Schlosstein, Edythe; St. Clair, Patricia; and Connell, Frederick. "Referral Keeping in Homeless Women," *Journal of Community Health* 16 (6) (December 1991): 279–285.

Schmertz, M. "Housing the Homeless: A Challenge to Architects," *Architectural Record* 174 (January 1986): 15.

Schulz, Dorothy M. "Holdups, Hobos, and the Homeless: A Brief History of Railroad Police in North America," *Police Studies* 10 (2) (1987): 90–95.

Schwab, Jim. "Sheltering the Homeless," *Planning* 52 (12) (December 1986): 24–27.

Schneider, John C. "Homeless Men and Housing Policy in Urban America, 1850–1920," *Urban Studies* 26 (1) (February 1989): 90–99.

Searight, Russell H., and Searight, Priscilla R., "The Homeless Mentally Ill: Overview, Policy Implications, & Adult Foster Care as a Neglected Resource," *Adult Foster Care Journal* 2 (4) (1988): 235–259.

"Seventh Annual Review of Poverty Law," *Clearinghouse Review* 20 (9) (January 1987), special issue.

Sexton, P. "The Epidemic of Homelessness," *Dissent* 33 (1986): 137–40.

———. "The Life of the Homeless," *Dissent* 30 (1) (1983): 79–84.

Shandler, Irving, and Shipley, Thomas. "New Focus on Old Problem: Philadelphia's Response to Homelessness," *Alcohol, Health and Research World* 11 (3) (Spring 1987): 54.

Shane, Paul G. "Changing Patterns Among Homeless and Runaway Youth," *American Journal of Orthopsychiatry* 59 (2) (April 1989): 208–214.

Sheridan, Michael J.; Gowen, Nancy; and Halpin, Susan. "Developing a Practice Model for the Homeless Ill," *Families in Society: The Journal of Contemporary Human Services* 74 (7) (September 1993): 410–421.

Shinn, Marybeth; Knickman, James R.; and Weitzman, Beth C. "Social Relationships and Vulnerability to Becoming Homeless Among Poor Families," *American Psychologist* 46 (11) (November 1991): 1180–1187.

Shinn, Marybeth, et al."Alternative Models for Sheltering Homeless Families," *Journal of Social Issues* 46 (4) (Winter 1990): 175–190.

Siebert, P. "Homeless People: Establishing Rights to Shelter," *Law and Inequality* 4 (July 1986): 393–407.

Simpson, John H. "Homeless Black Youth: A Case of Persistent Unemployment," *Journal of Voluntary Action Research* 17 (1) (January-March 1988): 71–77.

Slater, Lynn. "Opportunity Center for the Homeless," *Vocational Education Journal* 68 (7) (October 1993): 63–64.

Slavinsky, Ann, and Cousins, Ann. "Homeless Women," *Nursing Outlook* 30 (6) (June 1982): 358–362.

Sloss, Michael. "The Crisis of Homelessness: Its Dimensions and Solutions," *Urban and Social Change Review* 17 (2) (Summer 1984): 18–20.

Slutkin, G. "Management of Tuberculosis in Urban Homeless Indigents," *Public Health Reports* 101 (September/October 1986): 481–485.

Smith, Nelson. "Homelessness: Not One Problem, But Many," *Institute of Socioeconomic Studies Journal* 10 (Fall 1985): 53–67.

Smith, Susan. "New Thinking About the Homeless: Prevention, Not Cure," *Governing* 1 (5) (February 1988): 24–29.

Snow, David, and Anderson, L. "Identity Work among the Homeless: The Verbal Construction and Avowal of Personal Identities," *American Journal of Sociology* 92 (May 1987): 1336–1371.

Snow, David, et al. "The Myth of Pervasive Mental Illness Among the Homeless," *Social Problems* 33 (June 1986): 407–423.

Snowman, Margaret Knight, and Crockett, Elizabeth G. "Caring for the Homeless, Hungry, and Homebound," *Journal of Nutrition Education* 24 (1) (January 1992): 78B.

Snyder, Mitch, and Hombs, Mary Ellen. "Sheltering the Homeless: An American Imperative," *Journal of State Government* 59 (4) (November/December 1986): 173–174.

"Social Isolation Defines the Homeless," *Editorial Research Reports* 1 (12) (March 30, 1990): 178–180.

Sosin, Michael R. "Homeless and Vulnerable Meal Program Users: A Comparison Study," *Social Problems* 39 (2) (May 1992): 170–188.

———. "Homelessness in Chicago: A Study Sheds New Light on an Old Problem," *Public Welfare* 47 (1) (1989): 22–28.

Stark, L. "Strangers in a Strange Land: The Chronically Mentally Ill Homeless," *International Journal of Mental Health* 14 (4) (Winter 1985/1986): 95–111.

Stefanidis, Nikolaos, et al. "Runaway and Homeless Youth: The Effects of Attachment History on Stabilization," *American Journal of Orthopsychiatry* 62 (3) (July 1992): 442–446.

Steinbach, Carol F. "Shelter-Skelter: Homeless People Are the Most Visible Sign of a Housing Crunch Affecting Millions of Americans, Including Would-Be Homebuyers:

Congress has Some Big Ideas, But Where's the Money?" *National Journal* 21 (April 8, 1989): 851–855.

Stern, Mark. "The Emergence of the Homeless as a Public Problem," *Social Service Review* 58 (2) (1984): 291–301.

Stockdill, James W. "The Homeless Mentally Ill: A Task Force Report of the American Psychiatric Association," *American Journal of Psychiatry* 143 (6) (June 1986): 790.

Stolarski, Lyn. "Right to Shelter: History of the Mobilization of the Homeless as a Model of Voluntary Action," *Journal of Voluntary Action Research* 17 (1) (January-March 1988): 36–45.

Stoner, Madeleine. "An Analysis of Public and Private Sector Provisions for Homeless People," *Urban and Social Change Review* 17 (1) (1984): 3–8.

———. "The Plight of Homeless Women," *Social Service Review* 57 (December 1983): 565–581.

———. "The Voluntary Sector Leads the Way in Delivering Health Care to the Homeless Ill," *Journal of Voluntary Action Research* 17 (1) (January-March 1988): 24–35.

Strasser, J. "Urban Transient Women," *American Journal of Nursing* 78 (1978): 2076–2079.

Stricof, Rachel L., et al. "HIV Seroprevalence in a Facility for Runaway and Homeless Adolescents," *American Journal of Public Health. Supplement* 81 (May 1991): 50–53.

Stubbs, Cherrie. "Housing and Homelessness: A Feminist Perspective," *Housing Studies* 2 (1) (January 1987): 60–61.

Sudman, Seymour; Sirken, Monroe G.; and Cowan, Charles D. "Sampling Rare and Elusive Populations," *Science* 240 (4885) (May 20, 1988): 991–996.

Sullivan, J. "Managing Homelessness in Transportation Facilities," *New England Journal of Human Services* 6 (2) (1986): 6–19.

Sumerlin, John R.; Privette, Gayle; and Bundrick, Charles M. "Black and White Homeless Men: Differences in Self-Actualization, Willingness to Use Sevices, History of Being Homeless, and Subjective Health Ratings," *Psychological Reports* 72 (June 1993): 1039–1049.

Surber, R., et al. "Medical and Psychiatric Needs of the Homeless: A Preliminary Response," *Social Work* 33 (March/April 1988): 116–119.

Susser, E., et al. "Childhood Experiences of Homeless Men," *American Journal of Psychiatry* 144 (December 1987): 1599–1601.

Sutherland, Alan R. "Health Care for the Homeless: Both for Economic and Humane Reasons, Services Must Be Expanded, Streamlined, and Integrated," *Issues in Science and Technology* 5 (Fall 1988): 79–87.

Szegedy-Maszak, Marianne. "How the Homeless Bought a Rolls for Cornelius Pitts: Getting Rich by Housing the Needy," *Washington Monthly* 19 (6/7) (July/August 1987): 11–15.

Taylor, Martha L., and Koblinsky, Sally A. "Dietary Intake and Growth Status of Young Homeless Children," *American Dietetic Association Journal* 93 (4) (April 1993): 464–466.

Teeter, Ruskin. "Coming of Age on the City Streets in 19th-Century America," *Adolescence* 23 (92) (1988): 909–912.

Thornton, Rosy. "Homelessness Through Relationship Breakdown: The Local Authorities' Response," *Journal of Social Welfare Law* (1989): 67–84.

Tiernan, Kip. "Justice, Not Charity," *Dollars and Sense* (September 1992): 12–15.

Timmer, Doug A. "Homelessness as Deviance: The Ideology of the Shelter," *Free Inquiry in Creative Sociology* 16 (2) (November 1988): 163–170.

Tomasson, Richard F. "The Homeless in Contemporary Society," *Social Science Journal* 25 (3) (June 1988): 371–373.

Torrey, E. "Finally, a Cure for the Homeless: But It Takes Some Strong Medicine," *Washington Monthly* 18 (8) (September 1986): 23–27.

"Tracking the Homeless (Minneapolis, Minnesota)," *Focus* 10 (4) (Winter 1987/1988): 20–24.

Travers, N. M. "New York Launches Two-Pronged Effort: The State Meets Emergency Needs of the Homeless While Creating Transitional Housing Models," *Public Welfare* 47 (1) (1989): 19–21.

"Tuberculosis Among Homeless Shelter Residents," *JAMA: The Journal of the American Medical Association* 267 (4): 483–484.

Tucker, William. "Homeless People, Peopleless Homes: No Vacancy in New York City," *American Spectator* 20 (February 1987): 18–21.

Turner, Suzie. "Recognition of the Voting Rights of the Homeless," *Journal of Law & Politics* 3 (1) (1986): 103–126.

Tuttle, D. "The Plight of the Homeless," *Urban Lawyer* 18 (Fall 1986): 925–933.

Van Der Ploeg, J. D. "Homelessness: A Multidimensional Problem," *Children and Youth Review* 11 (1) (1989): 45–56.

Van Vliet, Willem. "The Homeless in Contemporary Society," *Contemporary Sociology* 17 (2) (March 1988): 208–209.

Vergare, M., and Arce, A. "Homeless Adult Individuals and Their Shelter Network," *New Directions in Mental Health Services* 30 (June 1986): 15–26.

Vosburgh, William W. "Voluntary Associations, the Homeless and Hard-to-Serve Populations—Perspectives from Organizational Theory," *Journal of Voluntary Action Research* 17 (1) (January-March 1988): 10–23.

Vowels, M. "At 83: Homelessness in NYC," *Gray Panther* (Fall 1987).

Vuyst, Alex. "Self-Help for the Homeless," *The Humanist* 49 (3) (May/June 1989): 13–49.

Wagen, Jan L. "Gender and Homelessness," *Social Work* 32 (4) (July/August 1987): 312–316.

Wagner, David, and Cohen, Marcia B. "The Power of the People: Homeless Protesters in the Aftermath of Social Movement Participation," *Social Problems* 38 (4) (November 1991): 543–561.

Walker, Bruce. "Public Sector Costs of Board and Lodging Accommodation for Homeless Households in London," *Housing Studies* 2 (4) (October 1987): 261–273.

Walker, Lee. "Homelessness: A Case of Mistaken Identity," *State Government News* 31 (6) (June 1988): 26–27.

Watson, Sophie. "Definitions of Homelessness: A Feminist Perspective," *Critical Social Policy* 4 (2(11)) (1984): 60–73.

Weigard, R. "Counting the Homeless," *American Demographics* 7 (12) (December 1985): 34–37.

Weinreb, Linda, and Buckner, John C. "Homeless Families: Program Responses and Public Policies," *American Journal of Orthopsychiatry* 63 (July 1993): 400–9.

Werner, Francis, and Bryson, David. "A Guide to the Preservation and Maintenance of Single Room Occupancy Hotels," *Clearinghouse Review* 15 (April 1982): 999–1009; 16 (May 1982): 1–250.

"What Can a City Do for Its Homeless?" *Center Magazine* 19 (5) (September/October 1986): 30–35.

Wichenden, Doroth. "Abandoned Americans," *The New Republic* 192 (11) (March 18, 1985): 19–25.

Widrow, Woody. "A Shelter Is Not a Home," *Shelter Force* 8 (August 1984): 12–13.

Wiecha, Jean L.; Dwyer, Johanna T.; and Dunn-Strohecker, Martha. "Nutrition and Health Services Needs Among the Homeless," *Public Health Reports* 106 (4) (July 1991): 364–374.

Wiecha, Jean L., et al. "Nutritional and Economic Advantages for Homeless Families in Shelters Providing Kitchen Facilities and Foods," *American Dietetic Association Journal* 93 (7) (July 1993): 777–783.

Wiggans, Andy. "Critique on Homelessness: A Multidimensional Problem," *Children and Youth Services Review* 11 (1) (1989): 57–60.

———. "Youth Work & Homelessness in England," *Children and Youth Services Review* 11 (1) (1989): 5–30.

Winkleby, Marilyn A. "Comparison of Risk Factors for Ill Health in a Sample of Homeless and Nonhomeless Poor," *Public Health Reports* 105 (4) (July 1990): 404–410.

Wohl, Alexander. "Gimme Shelter: Lawyering for the Homeless," *ABA Journal* 76 (August 1990): 58–62.

Wolch, Jennifer R.; Rahimian, Afsaneh; and Koegel, Paul. "Daily and Periodic Mobility Patterns of the Urban Homeless," *Professional Geographer* 45 (2) (May 1993): 159–169.

Wolch, Jennifer, et al. "Explaining Homelessness," *American Planning Association Journal* 54 (Fall 1988): 443–453.

Wood, David, et al. "Homeless and Housed Families in Los Angeles: A Study Comparing Demographic, Economic, and Family Function Characteristics," *American Journal of Public Health* 80 (9) (September 1990): 1049–1052.

Woodhouse, Linda. "The Desperate Battle to Save Homeless: Extreme Cold Forces Cities to Take New Steps," *Nation's Cities Weekly* 8 (4) (January 28, 1985): 1.

———. "Hands Across America: $100 Million Drive for Hunger, Homeless Programs," *Nation's Cities Weekly* 9 (14) (April 7, 1986): 3.

Woodward, D. "Homelessness: A Legal Activist Analysis of Judicial and Street Strategies," *Human Rights Annual* 3 (Spring 1986): 245.

Wooster, Martin. "The Homeless Issue," *Reason* 19 (July 1987): 20–28.

Wright, James D. "Address Unknown: Homelessness in Contemporary America," *Society* 26 (September/October 1989): 45–53.

———. "The Mentally Ill Homeless: What Is Myth and What Is Fact?" *Social Problems* 35 (2) (April 1988): 182–191.

———. "The Worthy and Unworthy Homeless," *Society* 25 (July/August 1988): 64–69.

———. "Poor People, Poor Health: The Health Status of the Homeless," *Journal of Social Issues* 46 (4) (Winter 1990): 49–64.

Wright, James D., and Lam, Julie A. "Homelessness and the Low-income Housing Supply," *Social Policy* 17 (4) (1987): 48–53.

Wright, James, and Weber, Elanor. "Determinants of Benefit-Program Participation Among the Urban Homeless: Results From a 16-City Study," *Evaluation Review* 12 (4) (August 1988): 376–395.

Wright, James, et al. "Ailments and Alcohol: Health Status Among the Drinking Homeless," *Alcohol Health and Research World* 11 (3) (Spring 1987): 22.

———. "Homelessness and Health: The Effects of Life Style on Physical Well-Being Among Homeless People in New York City," in Miller, Joanne, and Lewis, Michael, eds. *Research in Social Problems and Public Policy.* Greenwich, Conn.: JAI Press, 1987.

Yacenda, James. "Providing Hope and Housing to the Homeless," *Perspectives* 4 (1) (Winter/ Spring 1988): 7.

Zevin, Rona, and Linner, John. "Liveable But Still Lacking," *Planning* 49 (2) (February 1983): 27–28.

Ziefert, Marjorie, and Brown, Kaaren Strauch. "Skill Building for Effective Intervention with Homeless Families," *Families in Society: The Journal of Contemporary Human Services* 72 (4) (April 1991): 212–219.

United States Government Documents

Bassuk, Ellen L., and Cohen, Deborah Anne. *Homeless Families with Children: Research Perspectives.* Rockville, Md.: U.S. Dept. of Health and Human Services, Public Health Service, Alcohol, Drug Abuse, and Mental Health Administration, National Institute on Alcohol Abuse and Alcoholism, 1992.

Bennett, Gerald. *Job Training and Employment Services for Homeless Persons with Alcohol and Other Drug Problems: A Technical Assistance Paper.* Rockville, Md.: U.S. Dept. of Health and Human Services, Alcohol, Drug Abuse, and Mental Health Administration, National Institute on Alcohol Abuse and Alcoholism, 1992.

O'Neill, John V., and O'Connell, Mary Ellen. *Affordable Housing for Homeless Persons in Recovery from Alcohol and Other Drug Problems: A Case Study.* Rockville, Md.: U.S. Dept. of Health and Human Services, Public Health Service, Alcohol, Drug Abuse, and Mental Health Administration, National Institute on Alcohol Abuse and Alcoholism, 1991.

United States. Alcohol, Drug Abuse, and Mental Health Administration. Task Force on Homelessness and Severe Mental Illness. *Outcasts on Main Street: Report of the Federal Task Force on Homelessness and Severe Mental Illness.* Washington, D.C.: Interagency Council on the Homeless, 1992.

United States. *Children's Nutrition Assistance Act of 1992. An Act to Amend the National School Lunch Act and the Child Nutrition Act of 1966 to Better Assist Children in Homeless Shelters, to Enhance Competition Among Infant Formula Manufacturers and to Reduce the Per Unit Costs of Infant Formula for the Special Supplemental Food Program for Women, Infants, and Children (WIC), and for Other Purposes.* Washington, D.C.: Government Printing Office, 1992.

United States. Comptroller General. *Homelessness: Implementation of Food and Shelter Programs Under the McKinney Act: Report.* Washington, D.C.: Government Printing Office, 1987.

United States. Congress. House. Committee on Agriculture, Nutrition, and Forestry. *Review of Nutrition Programs Which Assist the Homeless: Hearings, February 10, 1987 and March 6, 1987, Trenton, NJ.* Washington, D.C.: Government Printing Office, 1987.

United States. Congress. House. Committee on Banking, Finance and Urban Affairs. Subcommittee on Housing and Community Development. *Homelessness and Housing: A Human Tragedy, A Moral Challenge: Hearing, June 15, 1988.* Washington, D.C.: Government Printing Office, 1988.

United States. Congress. House. Committee on Banking, Finance, and Urban Affairs. Subcommittee on Housing and Community Development. *HUD/FEMA McKinney Act Homeless Programs:* Hearing Before the Subcommittee on Housing and Community Development of the Committee on Banking, Finance, and Urban Affairs, House of Representatives, One Hundred Second Congress, first session, October 18, 1991. Washington, D.C.: Government Printing Office, 1992.

322   **Bibliography**

United States. Congress. House. Committee on Banking, Finance and Urban Affairs. Subcommittee on Housing and Community Development. *Need for Permanent Housing for the Homeless.* Washington, D.C.: Government Printing Office, 1993.

————. *Homelessness in America, 1988: Hearing, January 26, 1988.* Washington, D.C.: Government Printing Office, 1988.

————. *Housing, Community Development, and Homelessness Prevention Act of 1987: Hearings.* Washington, D.C.: Government Printing Office, 1987.

————. *HUD Report on Homelessness, II: Hearing, December 4, 1985.* Washington, D.C.: Government Printing Office, 1986.

————. *Queens County Field Hearing on Housing for the Elderly and Homeless: Long Island City, NY, June 24, 1985.* Washington, D.C.: Government Printing Office, 1985.

————. *Urgent Relief for the Homeless Act: Hearing, February 4, 1987.* Washington, D.C.: Government Printing Office, 1987.

United States. House. Committee on Banking, Finance, and Urban Affairs. Subcommittee on Housing and Community Development. *Homelessness in America—II: Hearing, January 25, 1984.* Washington D.C.: Government Printing Office, 1984.

————. *Homelessness in America—the Need for Permanent Housing: Hearings, March 1–15, 1989.* Washington, D.C.: Government Printing Office, 1989.

————. *Housing, Community Development, and Homelessness Prevention Act of 1987: Hearings, March 11–26, 1987 on H.R. 4 and H.R. 1070.* Washington, D.C.: Government Printing Office, 1987.

United States. Congress. House. Committee on Banking, Finance and Urban Affairs. Senate. Committee on Banking, Housing and Urban Affairs. *A New National Housing Policy: Recommendations of Organizations and Individuals Concerned about Affordable Housing in America.* Washington, D.C.: Government Printing Office, 1987.

United States. Congress. House. Committee on the Budget. *Budgetary Examination of Federal Homeless and Low-Income Housing Issues: Hearing, December 17, 1987.* Washington, D.C.: Government Printing Office, 1988.

United States. Congress. House. Committee on the Budget. Ad Hoc Task Force on the Homeless and Housing. *Effect of Our Nation's Housing Policy on Homeless: Hearing, January 21, 1988.* Washington, D.C.: Government Printing Office, 1988.

————. *Effect of Our Nation's Housing Policy on Homelessness: Hearing, January 21, 1988.* Washington, D.C.: Government Printing Office, 1988.

————. *Homelessness During Winter 1988–1989: Prospects for Change: Hearing December 20, 1988.* Washington, D.C.: Government Printing Office, 1989.

United States. Congress. House. Committee on the District of Columbia. *Homeless Americans in the Nation's Capital: Oversight Hearing on Examining Government's Role in Meeting the Needs of Homeless Americans, November 7, 1985.* Washington, D.C.: Government Printing Office, 1986.

United States. Congress. House. Committee on Education and Labor. *Oversight Hearing on Runaway and Homeless Youth Program.* Washington, D.C.: Government Printing Office, 1982.

————. *Oversight Hearing on Runaway and Homeless Youth: July 25, 1985.* Washington, D.C.: Government Printing Office, 1985.

————. *Oversight Hearing on Jobs and Education for the Homeless: Joint Hearing, Los Angeles, CA, March 20, 1987.* Washington, D.C.: Government Printing Office, 1987.

United States. Congress. House. Committee on Energy and Commerce. *Health Care for *the Homeless: Hearing, December 15, 1986*. Washington, D.C.: Government Printing Office, 1987.

————. *HUD's Proposed Regulations Denying Funds to Religious Groups for Sheltering the Homeless: Hearing, April 30, 1987*. Washington, D.C.: Government Printing Office, 1987.

————. *To Transfer Jurisdiction to District of Columbia Government Property to Be Used as Shelter for the Homeless: Hearing, May 15, 1986*. Washington, D.C.: Government Printing Office, 1987.

United States. Congress. House. Committee on Government Operations. *The Federal Response to the Homeless Crisis: Hearings, October 3–December 18, 1984*. Washington, D.C.: Government Printing Office, 1985.

————. *The Federal Response to the Homeless Crisis: Third Report*. Washington, D.C.: Government Printing Ofice, 1985.

————. *Homeless Families: A Neglected Crisis, Sixty-Third Report, with Dissenting and Additional Views*. Washington, D.C.: Government Printing Office, 1986.

————. *Implementation of the McKinney Homeless Assistance Act by the Interagency Council on the Homeless: Joint Hearing, March 15, 1989, before the Government Activities and Transportation Subcommittee and the Employment and Housing Subcommittee*. Washington, D.C.: Government Printing Office, 1989.

United States. Congress. House. Committee on Government Operations. Government Activities and Transportation Subcommittee. *Providing Shelter for the Homeless on Underutilized Federal Properties Pursuant to the McKinney Homeless Assistance Act: Hearing, October 13, 1988*. Washington, D.C.: Government Printing Office, 1989.

United States. Congress. House. Committee on Government Operations. *Mismanagement in Programs for the Homeless: Washington, DC, as a Case Study: Fifth Report* Washington, D.C.: Government Printing Office, 1991.

United States. House. Committee on Post Office and Civil Service. Subcommittee on Census and Population. *Accounting for Housing and Homeless in 1990 Decennial Census: Hearing, April 11, 1986*. Washington, D.C.: Government Printing Office, 1986.

United States. Congress. House. Committee on Public Works and Transportation. *To Provide a Shelter for the Homeless at 425 Second Street, NW, in the District of Columbia: Joint Hearing, August 1, 1985*. Washington, D.C.: Government Printing Office, 1986.

United States. Congress. House. Committee on Veterans' Affairs. *Homeless and Unemployed Veterans: Hearing, September 10, 1986*. Washington, D.C.: Government Printing Office, 1986.

United States. Congress. House. Committee on Ways and Means. *Use of Emergency Assistance Funds for Acquisition of Temporary and Permanent Housing for Homeless Families: Hearing, December 12, 1986*. Washington, D.C.: Government Printing Ofice, 1987.

United States. Congress. House. *HUD Report on Homelessness: Joint Hearing, May 24, 1984, Before the Subcommittee on Housing and Community Development of the Committee on Banking, Finance and Urban Affairs and the Subcommittee on Manpower and Housing of the Committee on Government Operations*. Washington, D.C.: Government Printing Office, 1984.

United States. House. Select Committee on Aging. Subcommittee on Housing and Consumer Interests. *Homelessness in Nashville: A Briefing*. Washington, D.C.: Government Printing Office, 1984.

————. *Homeless Older Americans: Hearing, May 2, 1984*. Washington, D.C.: Government Printing Office, 1984.

United States. Congress. House. Select Committee on Children, Youth, and Families. *The Crisis in Homelessness: Effects on Children and Families: Hearing, February 24, 1987*. Washington, D.C.: Government Printing Office, 1987.

United States. Congress. House. Select Committee on Hunger. *Hunger Among the Homeless: Hearing, March 6, 1986*. Washington, D.C.: Government Printing Office, 1986.

————. *Hunger Among the Homeless: A Survey of 140 Shelters, Food Stamp Participation and Recommendations*. Washington, D.C.: Government Printing Office, March, 1987.

————. *Hunger and Homelessness: Hearing, February 25, 1987*. Washington, D.C.: Government Printing Office, 1987.

United States. Congress. House. *Stewart B. McKinney Homeless Assistance Act: Conference Report to Accompany HR558*. Washington, D.C.: Government Printing Office, 1987.

United States. Congress. Joint Committee on Banking, Finance and Urban Affairs. *Homelessness in America: Hearing*. Washington, D.C.: The Committee, 1982.

United States. Congress. Senate. Committee on Agriculture. Nutrition, and Forestry. *Nutrition for the Homeless: Hearing, April 2, 1987*. Washington, D.C.: Government Printing Office, 1987.

United States. Congress. Senate. Committee on Banking, Housing, and Urban Affairs. *Homelessness in America: Hearing, January 29, 1987, On the Emergency Needs for Thousands of Homeless Americans and [Efforts to] Provide Assistance to Help Find Employment, Permanent Housing, Education, Mental and Physical Health Care, and Other Services*. Washington, D.C.: Government Printing Office, 1987.

United States. Congress. Senate. Committee on Governmental Affairs. *Reauthorization of the Emergency Food and Shelter National Board Program and the Interagency Council on the Homeless:* Hearing Before the Committee on Governmental Affairs, United States Senate, One Hundred Second Congress, second session, on S. 2624. May 14, 1992. Washington, D.C.: Government Printing Office, 1992.

United States. Congress. Senate. Committee on Governmental Affairs. *Urgent Relief for the Homeless Act of 1987: Hearing, March 30, 1987*. Washington, D.C.: Government Printing Office, 1987.

United States. Congress. Senate. Committee on the Judiciary. *Homeless Youth: The Saga of "Pushouts" and "Throwaways" in America: Report*. Washington, D.C.: Government Printing Office, 1980.

————. *Problems of Runaway Youth: Hearing (Second Session on Problems of and Services Provided for Runaway and Homeless Youth, Focusing on Support to State and Local Governments and Nonprofit Agencies for the Development of Programs)*. Washington, D.C.: Government Printing Office, 1982.

United States. Congress. Senate. Committee on Labor and Human Resources. *Exploitation of Runaways: Hearing, October 1, 1985*. Washington, D.C.: Government Printing Office, 1986.

United States. Congress. Senate. Committee on Labor and Human Resources. *Homelessness, an American Tragedy:* Hearing before the Committee on Labor and Human Resources, United States Senate, One Hundred First Congress, first session, on examining the health and human service aspects of homelessness, September 29, 1989 and May 9, 1990. Washington, D.C.: Government Printing Office, 1990.

United States. Congress. House. Committee on Veterans' Affairs. Subcommittee on Housing and Memorial Affairs. *The DVA Loan Guaranty Program, National Cemetery System, and Programs for Homeless Veterans:* Hearing before the Subcommittee on Housing and Memorial Affairs of the Committee on Veterans' Affairs, House of Representatives, One Hundred Second Congress, second session, February 26, 1992. Washington, D.C.: Government Printing Office, 1992.

United States. Congress. Senate. Committee on Veterans' Affairs. *Services for Homeless Veterans and Housing Loans for Native American Veterans.* Washington, D.C.: Government Printing Office, 1992.

United States. Congress. Senate. Committee on Veterans' Affairs. *Veterans' Administration Fiscal Year 1988 Budget, the Vet Center Program, and Homeless Veterans Issues: Hearings, February 18 and 19, 1987.* Washington, D.C.: Government Printing Office, 1988.

United States. Congress. Senate. Special Committee on Aging. *Living Between the Cracks: America's Chronic Homeless: Hearing, December 12, 1984.* Washington, D.C.: Government Printing Office, 1985.

United States. Department of Commerce. *Census of Population and Housing (1990). Fact Sheet for 1990 Decennial Census Counts of Persons in Selected Locations Where Homeless Persons Are Found.* Washington D.C.: U.S. Dept. of Commerce, Bureau of the Census, 1992.

United States. Department of Health and Human Services. *A Factsheet for Volunteer and Nonprofit Agencies: How to Help Homeless Individuals Apply for and Receive Supplemental Security Income and/or Social Security Benefits.* Baltimore, Md.: U.S. Dept. of Health and Human Services, Social Security Administration, 1993.

United States. Department of Health and Human Services. *Helping the Homeless: A Resource Guide.* Washington, D.C.: The Department, 1984.

United States. Department of Health and Human Services. National Institute on Drug Abuse. *Prevalence of Drug Use in the Washington DC, Metropolitan Area Homeless and Transient Population, 1991.* Washington, D.C.: U.S. Dept. of Health and Human Services, 1993.

———. *Report on Federal Efforts to Respond to the Shelter and Basic Living Needs of Chronically Mentally Ill Persons.* Washington, D.C.: The Department, 1983.

United States. Department of Health and Human Services. National Institute on Alcohol Abuse and Alcoholism. *Alcohol Recovery Programs for Homeless People: A Survey of Current Programs in the United States.* Rockville, Md.: The Institute, 1988.

———. *Ethnographic Perspectives on Homeless Mentally Ill Women.* Rockville, Md.: The Institute, 1987.

———. *The Implications of NIMH-Supported Research for Homeless Mentally Ill Racial and Ethnic Minority Persons.* Rockville, Md.: The Institute, 1987.

———. *Intensive Care Management for Persons Who Are Homeless and Mentally Ill: A Review of Community Support Program and Human Resource Development Efforts.* Rockville, Md.: The Institute, 1987.

———. *Involuntary Outpatient Commitment: An Exploration of the Issues and Its Utilization in Five States.* Rockville, Md.: The Institute, 1985.

———. *NIMH-Funded Research Concerning Homeless Mentally Ill Persons: Implications for Policy and Practice.* Rockville, Md.: The Institute, 1986.

———. *NIMH-Supported Research on the Mentally Ill Who Are Homeless.* Rockville, Md.: The Institute, 1985.

———. *Outreach Services for Homeless Mentally Ill People: Report of Proceedings.* Rockville, Md.: The Institute, 1987.

————. *Report and Analytical Summary of a Meeting of DHHS-Supported Researchers Studying the Homeless Mentally Ill*. Rockville, Md.: The Institute, 1984.

————. *The Role of Nurses in Meeting the Health/Mental Health Needs of the Homeless: Proceedings of the Workshop*. Rockville, Md.: The Institute, 1986.

————. *Synopses of NIMH-Funded Research Projects on the Homeless Mentally Ill*. Rockville, Md.: The Institute, 1985.

United States. Department of Health and Human Services. Office of Human Development Services. *The Homeless: Background, Analysis, and Options*. Washington, D.C.: The Department, 1984.

————. *Runaway and Homeless Youth: Fiscal Year 1985, Annual Report*. Washington, D.C.: The Department, 1986.

United States. Department of Health and Human Services. Public Health Service. National Institute on Alcohol Abuse and Alcoholism. Interagency Council on the Homeless. *Housing Initiatives for Homeless People With Alcohol and Other Drug Problems: Proceedings of a National Conference, February 29–March 2, 1991, San Diego, California*. Washington, D.C.: U.S. Dept. of Health and Human Services, Public Health Service, 1991.

United States. Department of Housing and Urban Development. *Homeless Assistance Program*. Washington, D.C.: Government Printing Office, February 1989.

————. *HUD Announces $4.9 Million in Grants for Transitional Housing for the Homeless*. Washington, D.C.: Government Printing Office, October 6, 1987.

————. *HUD Announces $69.3 Million in Grants for the Homeless*. Washington, D.C.: The Department, 1987.

————. *HUD Announces $35 Million in Rental Assistance for Single Room Occupancy Dwellings for the Homeless*. Washington, D.C.: Government Printing Office, December 3, 1987.

————. *HUD Announces Grants for Permanent Housing for Handicapped Homeless*. Washington, D.C.: The Department, June 29, 1988.

————. *A Report to the Secretary on Homelessness in America: Hearing*. Washington, D.C.: Government Printing Office, 1984.

United States. Department of Housing and Urban Development. Office of Policy Development and Research. *Housing Special Populations: A Resource Guide*. Washington, D.C.: Government Printing Office, October 1988.

————. *A Report on the 1988 National Survey of Shelters for the Homeless*. Washington, D.C.: Government Printing Office, March 1989.

————. *SAFAH Grants: Aiding Comprehensive Strategies for the Homeless*. Washington, D.C.: Government Printing Office November 1988.

United States. Department of Labor. Employment and Training Administration. Office of Strategic Planning and Policy Development. *Job Training for the Homeless: Report on Demonstration's First Year*. Washington, D.C.: U.S. Dept. of Labor, Employment and Training Administration, Office of Strategic Planning and Policy Development, 1991.

United States. Federal Task Force on the Homeless. *Summary of Federal Programs Available to the Homeless*. Washington, D.C.: The Task Force, 1987.

United States. General Accounting Office. *Federally Supported Centers Provide Needed Services for Runaways and Homeless Youth: Report*. Washington, D.C.: The Office, 1983.

United States. General Accounting Office. *Homelessness: Action Needed to Make Federal Surplus Property Program More Effective: Report to Congressional Requesters*. Washington, D.C.: General Accounting Office, 1990.

United States. General Accounting Office. *Homelessness: A Complex Problem and the Federal Responses.* Washington, D.C.: Government Printing Office, 1985.

United States. General Accounting Office. *Homelessness: Transitional Housing Shows Initial Success But Long-term Effects Unknown: Report to the chairman, Committee on Governmental Affairs, U.S. Senate.* Washington, D.C.: General Accounting Office, 1991.

United States. General Accounting Office. *Homelessness, McKinney Act Programs and Funding Through Fiscal Year 1991.* Washington, D.C.: General Accounting Office, 1992.

United States. General Accounting Office. *Homelessness: Single Room Occupancy Program Achieves Goals, But HUD Can Increase Impact: Report to the Chairman, Committee on Governmental Affairs, U.S. Senate.* Washington, D.C.: General Accounting Office, 1992.

United States. *HUD Demonstration Act of 1993.* Washington, D.C.: Government Printing Office, 1993.

United States. Interagency Council on the Homeless. Task Force on Homelessness and Severe Mental Illness. *Outcasts on Main Street: Report of the Federal Task Force on Homelessness and Severe Mental Illness.* Washington, D.C.: U.S. Dept. of Health and Human Services: Interagency Council on the Homeless: Task Force on Homelessness and Severe Mental Illness, 1992.

United States. Library of Congress. Congressional Research Service. *The Reagan 1987 Budget and the Homeless.* Washington, D.C.: The Library, 1986.

United States. National Institute of Mental Health. *The Homeless Mentally Ill: Reports Available From the National Institute of Mental Health.* Rockville, Md.: The Institute, 1987.

Reports

Alameda County (California). Mental Health Services. The Homeless Project: Services for Homeless and at Risk of Becoming Homeless Mentally Disabled of Berkeley and Albany. Berkeley, Calif.: Berkeley Support Services, 1986.

American Nightmare: A Decade of Homelessness in the United States. New York/Washington, D.C.: National Coalition for the Homeless, December 1989.

American Psychiatric Association. Task Force on the Homeless Mentally Ill. *Treating the Homeless Mentally Ill: A Report of the Task Force on the Homeless Mentally Ill.* Washington, D.C.: American Psychiatric Association, 1992.

Anello, Rose, and Shuster, Tillie. *Community Relations Strategies: A Handbook for Sponsors of Community-Based Programs for the Homeless.* New York: Community Service Society, 1985.

————. *A Guide for Non-Profit Shelter Operators in New York City: Negotiating the Public Assistance System on Behalf of Homeless Adults.* New York: Community Service Society, 1984.

Assistance for Homeless Persons: A NAHRO Resource Book for Housing and Community Development Agencies. Washington, D.C.: National Association of Housing and Redevelopment Officials, 1988.

Avenues Out of Despair: Homelessness Programs in the San Francisco Bay Area: A Public Advocates Report. San Francisco: Public Advocates, 1987.

Bach, Victor. *Housing at Risk: Expiring Federal Subsidies. Summary Characteristics of the at-risk Inventory of HUD-Subsidized, Private Rental Projects in New York City.* New York: Community Service Society, 1988.

Bach, Victor, and Steinhagen, Renee. *Alternatives to the Welfare Hotel: Using Emergency Assistance to Provide Decent Transitional Shelter for Homeless Families.* New York: Community Service Society, 1987.

Bass, Deborah S. *Helping Vulnerable Youths: Runaway & Homeless Adolescents in the United States.* Washington, D.C.: NASW Press, 1992.

Bassuk, Ellen L. *Community Care for Homeless Families: A Program Design Manual/The Better Homes Foundation.* Washington, D.C.: Interagency Council on the Homeless, 1990.

Baumann, Donald, and Grigsby, Charles. *Understanding the Homeless: From Research to Action.* Austin: Hogg Foundation for Mental Health, University of Texas, 1988.

Baxter, Ellen. *The Heights: A Community Housing Strategy.* New York: Community Service Society, 1986.

Baxter, Ellen, and Hopper, Kim. *Private Lives/Public Spaces: Homeless Adults on the Streets of New York City.* New York: Community Service Society of New York, 1981.

Berkeley, California. Community Action Agency. *City-Wide Services for the Homeless.* Berkeley: The Agency, 1988.

Berndt, Jerry. *Missing Persons: The Homeless.* Wollaston, Mass: Many Voices Press, 1986.

Boston. Executive Office of Human Services. Policy Unit. *Comprehensive Homeless Assistance Plan Performance Report.* 1990.

Brecht, Mary-Lynn; Lindsey Ada M.; and Stuart, Irene. *Health Care Needs of the Homeless in Los Angeles.* Berkeley: California Policy Seminar, University of California, 1991.

Briefing Paper for Presidential Candidates. New York/Washington, D.C.: National Coalition for the Homeless.

Broken Lives: Denial of Education to Homeless Children. Washington, D.C.: National Coalition for the Homeless, 1987.

Brooklyn Reference Manual for Health Care Services. New York: Coalition for the Homeless, July 1988.

Burns, Leland. *Hope for the Homeless: Lessons from the Third World.* Los Angeles: School of Architecture and Urban Planning, University of California, Los Angeles, 1986.

Burt, Martha R. *Alternative Methods to Estimate the Number of Homeless Children and Youth: Final Report.* Washington, D.C.: Urban Institute, 1991.

California. Advisory Committee for the Education of Homeless Children and Youth. *Hope for the Future: The State Plan for Educating Homeless Children and Youth.* Sacramento: California State Dept. of Education, 1991.

California. Department of Housing and Community Development. *Shelter for the Homeless: Housing Element Requirements.* Sacramento: The Department, 1988.

———. *A Study of the Issues and Characteristics of the Homeless Population in California.* Sacramento: The Department, 1985.

California. Department of Mental Health. *Review of California's Program for the Homeless Mentally Disabled.* Sacramento: The Department, 1988.

California. Department of Social Services. *Report on the Provision of Emergency Assistance and Child Welfare Services to Homeless Families With Children.* Sacramento: The Department, 1987.

California. Department of Veteran Affairs. *Report to the State Legislature: Assistance to Homeless Veterans per AB 1634 (Clute) Chapter 553 of 1985.* Sacramento: The Department, 1988.

California. Department of Youth Authority. *Runaway and Homeless Youth.* Sacramento: The Department, 1985.

California. Legislature. Assembly. Committee on Human Services. *In the Matter of the Homeless.* Sacramento: Joint Publications Office, 1985.

————. *Joint Hearing in re the Homeless: Services and Senate Health and Human Services Committees: February 26, 1985.* Sacramento: Joint Publications Office, 1985.

California. Legislature. Senate. Office of Research. *Shelter and Services: Solutions to the Burgeoning Crisis of Homelessness.* Sacramento: The Office, 1985.

California. Office of Criminal Justice Planning. *A Community Response to Runaway and Homeless Youth.* Sacramento: Office of Criminal Justice Planning, 1991.

California. Office of Criminal Justice Planning. *Homeless Youth Emergency Services Program: Program Guidelines.* Sacramento: Office of Criminal Justice Planning, 1992.

Cannon, Peter. *The Homeless: A Primer.* Madison: Wisconsin Legislature, January 1987.

Causes and Recent History of Homelessness in America. New York: Coalition for the Homeless, Winter 1984.

CBC Quarterly: The Problems of the Homeless Confront the City Government. New York: Coalition for the Homeless, Spring 1982.

Center for Population Options (U.S.). National Initiative on AIDS and HIV Prevention Among Adolescents. *Out of the Shadows: Building an Agenda and Strategies for Preventing HIV Infection and AIDS Among Street and Homeless Youth.* Washington, D.C.: National Initiative on AIDS and HIV Prevention Among Adolescents of the Center for Population Options, 1990.

Condition of the Homeless of Chicago. Chicago: National Opinion Research Center, University of Chicago, 1986. (Also published by the Social and Demographic Research Institute, University of Massachusetts.)

Connecticut. Governor's Task Force on the Homeless. *An Action Plan to Address the Needs of the Homeless.* Hartford: Office of Policy and Management, 1986.

"Critter Control: Managing Lice and Scabies." Transcript of a lecture presented to the Coalition's Providers' Caucus by Dr. Richard Lauder. New York: Coalition for the Homeless, March 1983.

Crowded Out: Homelessness and the Elderly Poor in New York City. The Elderly Committee of the Coalition and Roger Sanjek for the Grey Panthers of New York. New York: Coalition for the Homeless, May 1984.

Cruel Brinkmanship: Planning for the Homeless. New York: Coalition for the Homeless, August 1983.

Cruel Brinkmanship Revisited: The Winter of 1985–1986. New York: Coalition for the Homeless, October 1985.

A Crying Shame: Officials Abuse and Neglect of Homeless Infants. New York: Coalition for the Homeless, 1985.

Daly, Gerald. *A Comparative Assessment of Programs Dealing with the Homeless Population in the United States, Canada, and Britain.* Ottawa: Canada Housing & Mortgage Corporation, n.d.

Dear, Michael J. *Community Attitudes Toward the Homeless.* Los Angeles: University of Southern California, 1990.

DeGiovanni, Frank F. *Displacement Pressures in the Lower East Side.* New York: Community Service Society, 1987.

Doing Good Well: A Report on Hands Across America Funding. Washington, D.C.: National Coalition for the Homeless, 1986.

Downward Spiral: The Homeless in New Jersey. Washington, D.C.: National Coalition for the Homeless, 1983.

Drummond, Alfred, and Shiffman, Yvette. *Saving Homes for the Poor: Low-Income Tenants Can Own Their Own Apartments (with Case Summaries).* New York: Community Service Society, 1984.

Education and Community Suppport for Homeless Children and Youth: Profiles of 15 Innovative and Promising Approaches. Washington, D.C.: U.S. Department of Education, 1990.

An Embarrassment of Riches: Homelessness in Connecticut. New York/Washington, D.C.: National Coalition for the Homeless, December 1985.

Emergency Food Box Programs. Second Harvest Foodbank Network. New York: Coalition for the Homeless, 1983.

Empty Promises/Empty Plates. New York: Coalition for the Homeless, 1983.

Ending Homelessness New York City: A Mayoral Program. New York: Coalition for the Homeless, May 1989.

Erickson, J., and Williams, C., eds. *Housing the Homeless.* New Brunswick, N.J.: Center for Urban Policy Research, 1986.

Evans, Michael, ed. *Homeless in America,* by the National Mental Health Association and Families for the Homeless. Washington, D.C.: Acropolis Books, 1988.

A False Sense: A Study of Safety and Security Issues in New York City's Municipal Shelters for Men. New York: Coalition for the Homeless, October 1989.

Federal Housing Programs and the Impact on Homelessness. New York: Coalition for the Homeless, 1982.

Financial Management System for Shelters for the Homeless, Part 1: The Bookkeeping and Financial Reporting Systems. Part 2: Financial Planning and Control Systems. New York: Community Service Society, 1985.

Forbes, Stephanie R., and Leavitt, Jacqueline. *New Solutions to Homelessness: The Effectiveness of California's Homeless Assistance Program.* Los Angeles: Graduate School of Architecture and Urban Planning, University of California, Los Angeles, 1991.

A Forced March to Nowhere: Testimony Before the House District Committee. Washington, D.C.: Community for Creative Non-Violence, September 1980.

Fordham, Dr. Robert Mayer. *Developing Shelter Models for the Homeless: Three Program Design Options.* New York: Community Service Society, 1985.

Forgotten Voices, Unforgettable Dreams: Writings and Arts by Individuals Who Are or Have Been Homeless. New York: Coalition for the Homeless.

Frazier, S. *Homelessness and Mental Health.* Address presented at Clinical Center Grand Rounds, Bethesda, Md., National Institutes of Health, October 29, 1986. Available from National Institute of Mental Health.

Fredde, Greg. *Home is Where.* Salt Lake City: Community Development Division, Department of Community and Economic Development, State of Utah, 1991.

Freeman, Richard, and Hall, Brian. *Permanent Homelessness in America?* Cambridge, Mass.: National Bureau of Economics Research, 1986.

Funderberg, Richard. *California's Homeless: Part of a Nation's Shame.* Sacramento: California State Employee's Association, 1987.

Giving to End Homelessness: A Study of the National Philanthropic Response to Homelessness. Boston: The Boston Foundation, 1992.

Hamberg, Jill. *Building and Zoning Regulations: A Guide for Sponsors of Shelters and Housing for the Homeless in New York City.* New York: Community Service Society, 1984.

Handhardt, Eva. *Collaboration or Conflict in Disposition of City-Owned Property: The Role of Community Boards and NYC Department of Housing Preservation and Development.* New York: Community Service Society, 1984.

Hayes, Robert. *The Rights of the Homeless.* New York: Practicing Law Institute, 1987.

Health Needs of the Homeless: An Overview. Transcript of a lecture presented to the Coalition's Providers' Caucus by Dr. Richard Lauder. New York: Coalition for the Homeless, February 1983.

Heflin, Juane, and Rudy, Kathryn. *Homeless and in Need of Special Education.* Exceptional Children at Risk. Reston, Va.: Council for Exceptional Children, 1991.

HomeBase (San Francisco, Calif.). *Meeting the Housing Needs of Marin's Homeless People: Evaluating Effectiveness: The Evolution of a Community-Based Service System: A Home-Base Report.* San Francisco: HomeBase, 1992.

The Homeless: A Growing National Problem. New York: Coalition for the Homeless, October 1982.

The Homeless: A Regional Crisis. New York: Public Affairs Department, Port Authority of New York and New Jersey, 1988.

The Homeless Crisis from a Rural Perspective. Washington, D.C.: Housing Assistance Council, Inc., September 1987.

The Homeless and the Economic Recovery. New York/Washington, D.C.: National Coalition for the Homeless, 1983.

The Homeless and the Economic Recovery: One Year Later. Washington, D.C.: National Coalition for the Homeless, 1984.

The Homeless Mentally Ill. Washington, D.C.: National Conference of State Legislatures, 1987.

The Homeless Persons' Survival Act of 1986. New York/Washington, D.C.: National Coalition for the Homeless, September 1986.

Homeless Youth In New York City: Nowhere to Turn. New York: Coalition for the Homeless, 1983.

Homelessness: Health and Human Needs. The Committee on the Health Care for Homeless People, Institute of Medicine. Washington, D.C.: National Academy Press, 1988.

Homelessness: The Impact on Child Welfare in the '90s: Recommendations from a Colloquium, December 1990. Washington, D.C.: Child Welfare League of America, 1991.

Homelessness in America: What the Next President Will Do—A Survey of Policies on Issues Affecting the Homeless. New York/Washington, D.C.: National Coalition for the Homeless, April 1988.

Homelessness in Philadelphia: People, Needs, Services. Philadelphia: Philadelphia Health Management Corporation, 1985.

Homelessness in the United States: Background and Federal Response—A Briefing Paper for Congressional Candidates. New York/Washington, D.C.: National Coalition for the Homeless, September 1988.

Homelessness Needs Assessment Study: Findings and Recommendations for the Massachusetts Department of Mental Health. Boston: The Human Services Research Institute, 1985.

Honig, Marjorie, and Filer, Randall K. *Causes of Intercity Variation in Homelessness.* Madison: University of Wisconsin—Madison, Institute for Research on Poverty, 1991.

Hoogterp, Bill. *Hunger and Homelessness Action.* 1st ed. St. Paul, Minn.: Campus Outreach Opportunity League, 1990.

Hopper, Kim, and Hamberg, Jill. *The Making of America's Homeless: from Skid Row to New Poor, 1945–1984.* New York: Community Service Society, 1984.

Hopper, Kim, et al. *One Year Later: The Homeless Poor in New York City, 1982.* New York: Community Service Society of New York, 1982.

Housing the Homeless in Los Angeles County: A Guide to Action. Los Angeles: School of Architecture and Urban Planning, University of California, 1985.

Housing Programs for the Homeless in Rural Areas. Washington, D.C.: Housing Assistance Council, Inc., September 1988.

How Much Is the Federal Government Spending on Programs to Help the Homeless? Fact Sheet no. 3–2. Washington, D.C.: Interagency Council on the Homeless, 1991.

Hungry Children and Mr. Cuomo. New York: Coalition for the Homeless, 1986.

Idaho Housing Agency. *Going Home: Idaho's Comprehensive Homeless Assistance Plan.* Boise, 1990.

Indefensible Failure: The Defense Department and the Emergency Shelter Program. Washington, D.C.: National Coalition for the Homeless, 1987.

The Interagency Council on the Homeless: An Assessment. New York/Washington, D.C.: National Coalition for the Homeless, March 1989.

The International Right to Shelter. New York/Washington, D.C.: National Coalition for the Homeless, July 1989.

Iowa. Office on Homelessness. *The Iowa Plan to Eliminate Homelessness.* 1991.

Johnson, Gary T., et al. *Virginia's Homeless Intervention Program: An Evaluation.* Richmond: Center for Public Affairs, School of Community and Public Affairs, Virginia Commonwealth University, 1991.

Johnson, Timothy P., and Barrett, Mark E. *Homelessness and Substance Use in Cook County: A Report Prepared for the Department of Alcoholism and Drug Abuse, State of Illinois.* Urbana, Ill.: Survey Research Laboratory, University of Illinois, 1991.

Kim, Moon Hyun. *Modelling the Geography of Children's Services in Los Angeles County.* Los Angeles: Los Angeles Homelessness Project, 1991.

LaGory, M., and Ritchey, F. *Alabama's Homeless: A Preliminary Report.* Birmingham: University of Alabama, 1987.

Lamb, R., ed. *The Homeless Mentally Ill.* Washington, D.C.: American Psychiatric Association, 1984.

Lamm, Deborah, and Reyes, Lilia. *Health Care for the Homeless: A 40-City Review.* Washington, D.C.: United States Conference of Mayors, 1985.

Lander, Richard. *Health Needs of the Homeless: An Overview.* New York: Coalition for the Homeless, 1983.

Landers, Robert K. *Low Income Housing: Problem Is Getting Worse.* Editorial Research Reports, May 8, 1987.

Laplante, Dianne. *Establishing an Emergency Shelter: A Guide Book.* Providence, R.I.: Council for Community Services, 1982.

Law, Robin M. *Homelessness and Economic Restructuring.* Los Angeles: University of Southern California, 1990.

Leonard, Paul; Cushing, Dolbeare N.; and Lazere, Edward. *A Place to Call Home: The Crisis in Housing for the Poor.* Washington, D.C.: National Low Income Housing Coalition, April 1989.

Lezak, A. *Synopses of Mental Health Community Support Program Service Demonstration Grants for Homeless Mentally Ill Persons.* Rockville, Md.: National Institute of Mental Health, 1986.

Litigation Involving the National Coalition and the Coalition for the Homeless. New York/Washington, D.C.: National Coalition for the Homeless, November 1988.

Los Angeles County (California). Commission on Human Relations. *Homeless Families and Children in Los Angeles County: Report on a Public Hearing by the Los Angeles County Commision on Human Relations.* Los Angeles: The Commission, 1991.

Los Angeles County (California). Countywide Task Force on the Homeless. *Homeless in*

Los Angeles County: Report. Los Angeles: Community and Senior Citizens Services
Department, 1985.

Los Angeles County (California). Department of Mental Health. *A Study of Homelessness and
Mental Illness in the Skid Row Area of Los Angeles.* Los Angeles: The Department, 1986.

Losing Ground, a New York State Report. New York: Coalition for the Homeless, January
1990.

Low Income Housing FY91 Budget Analysis. Washington, D.C.: Low Income Housing
Coalition, February 1990.

Maine. Interagency Task Force on Homelessness and Housing Opportunities. *By Sundown:
A Report on Homelessness in Maine.* Augusta, Maine: Maine Dept. of Economic and
Community Development, Office of Community Development, 1991.

Maine. Task Force to Study Homelessness. *To Have a Home: A Report on Maine's Homeless
and At-Risk Population.* Augusta, Maine: The Task Force, 1986.

Making a Difference: A Resource Guide on Homelessness for Students. New York/Washing-
ton, D.C.: National Coalition for the Homeless, September 1989.

Malign Neglect: The Homeless Poor of Miami. New York/Washington, D.C.: National
Coalition for the Homeless, January 1986.

Maryland. Department of Human Resources. *Interim Report on the State Homeless Program:
A Joint Report from the Department of Human Resources and the Governor's Advisory
Board on Shelter, Nutrition, and Services Program for Homeless Individuals in Maryland.*
Annapolis, Md.: The Department, 1985.

————. *Where Do You Go from Nowhere: A Study of Homelessness in Maryland.* The
Health and Welfare Council of Central Maryland. Baltimore: The Department, 1985.

Massachusetts. Department of Education. *Children Without Homes: A Report.* Quincy,
Mass.: The Department, 1990.

Massachusetts. Department of Mental Health. *Homelessness Needs Assessment Study: Findings and Recommendations for the Massachusetts Department of Mental Health.* Massachusetts: The Department, 1985.

Massachusetts. Executive Office of Human Services. *Massachusetts Homelessness Report,
1985.* Boston: The Office, 1985.

Massachusetts. General Court of Massachusetts. Legislative Bureau. *The Homeless Mentally
Ill in Massachusetts.* Boston: The Bureau, 1986.

Mayer, Robert, and Shuster, Tillie. *Developing Shelter Models for the Homeless: Three
Program Design Options.* New York: Community Service Society, 1985.

McCambridge, Ruth. *Giving to End Homelessness: A Study of the National Philanthropic
Response to Homelessness,* Boston: Boston Foundation, 1992.

McCarthy, William, ed. *Perspectives on Poverty: Issues and Options in Welfare Reform,
Health Care and Homelessness.* Washington, D.C.: National League of Cities, 1986.

McGerigle, P., and Lauriat, A. *More than Shelter: A Community Response to Homelessness.*
Boston: Massachusetts Association for Mental Health, 1983.

Meeting the Needs of Homeless Youth: A Report of the Homeless Youth Steering Committee.
New York: New York Council on Children and Families, 1984.

Merves, E. *Conversations with Homeless Women: A Sociological Examination: Summary
Reports.* Columbus: Department of Sociology, Ohio State University, 1986.

Michigan. Department of Mental Health. *Mental Health and Homelessness in Detroit: A
Research Study.* Lansing: The Department, 1986.

Michigan. Task Force on the Homeless. *Life in Transit: Homelessness in Michigan.* Lansing:
The Task Force, 1986.

Mid-America in Crisis: Homelessness in Des Moines. New York/Washington, D.C.: National Coalition for the Homeless, January 1986.

Missouri. Department of Elementary and Secondary Education. *Meeting the Educational Needs of Missouri's Homeless Children: Administrative Annual & Census Report*. Jefferson City, Mo.: The Department, 1992.

Missouri. Department of Mental Health. *Homeless People in St. Louis: A Mental Health Program Evaluation, Field Study, and Followup Investigation*. Jefferson City, Mo.: The Department, 1985.

Moving Forward: A National Agenda to Address Homelessness and Beyond, and A Status Report on Homelessness in America: A 46-City Survey, 1988–89. New York: Partnership for the Homeless, Inc., September 1989.

Multnomah County (Oregon). Department of Human Services. *Homeless Women: 1985*. Portland, Multnomah County: The Department, 1985.

National Action Plan on Housing and Homelessness. Montreal: Big City Mayors' Caucus of the Federation of Canadian Municipalities, February 1991.

National Federation of Housing Associations. *Homelessness: the Role of Housing Associations*. 1991.

National Governors' Association Center for Policy Research. *Working to End Homelessness: A Manual for States*. Washington, D.C.: Interagency Council on the Homeless,- 1991.

National Neglect/National Shame. Washington, D.C.: National Coalition for the Homeless, 1986.

Necessary Relief: The Stewart B. McKinney Homeless Assistance Act. Washington, D.C.: National Coalition for the Homeless, 1988.

A New Approach to Homelessness: A Guide for Local Governments. Washington, D.C.: ICMA, 1992.

New Jersey. Department of Human Services. Division of Youth and Family Services. *Homelessness in New Jersey: A Study of Shelters, Agencies and the Clients They Serve*. Trenton, N.J.: The Department, 1986.

New Jersey. Department of the Public Advocate. *Homelessness in New Jersey 1990–91: A Plan for Immediate Action*. Trenton: The Department, 1991.

New York. Legislature. Senate. Committee on Mental Hygiene and Addiction Control. *The Mentally Ill Homeless: Shelters Become Sanctuaries for the Victims of Neglect: A Report*. Albany: The Committee, 1985.

New York (City). Human Resources Administration. *Project Future: Focusing, Understanding, Targeting, and Utilizing Resources for the Homeless Mentally Ill, Elderly, Youth, Substance Abusers, and Employables*. New York: The Administration, 1986.

New York (City). Office of the Comptroller. *Soldiers of Misfortune: Homeless Veterans in New York City*. New York: The Office, 1982.

New York (City). President's Task Force on Housing for Homeless Families. *A Shelter Is Not a Home: Report*. New York: The Task Force, 1987.

New York State Life Management Conference. *The Challenge in Education: Meeting the Needs of the Homeless Adult Learner and New York State Life Management Conference: Conference Proceedings*. Albany: University of the State of New York, State Education Dept., Office of Continuing Education, 1991.

1933/1983—Never Again. Albany, N.Y.: Mario Cuomo for the National Governors Association, September 1981.

Oakland, California. Mayor's Task Force on Emergency Housing for the Homeless. *Report.* Oakland: The Task Force, 1985.

Oakland (California). Office of Community Development. *The Comprehensive Homeless Assistance Plan: (Title IV, Subtitle A of the Stewart B. McKinney Homeless Assistance Act).* Oakland: City of Oakland, Office of Community Development, 1990.

Off the Streets and Out of the Shelters: Homeless People Regain Housing: A Regional Roundtable, June 13, 1991, Oakland: Conference Summary. San Francisco: HomeBase, 1991.

Ohio. Department of Mental Health. *Homelessness in Ohio: A Study of People in Need.* Columbus: The Department, 1985.

One Hundred Thousand and Counting . . . Homelessness in New York State. New York: Coalition for the Homeless, February 1989.

On the Streets and in the Shelters: Legal and Policy Issues Affecting People Who Live in Public Spaces and Homeless Shelters: A HomeBase Manual. San Francisco: HomeBase, 1992.

Out in the Cold: Homelessness in Iowa. New York/Washington, D.C.: National Coalition for the Homeless, Winter 1987.

Out of Reach: Why Everyday People Can't Find Affordable Housing. Washington, D.C.: Low Income Housing Information Coalition, February 1990.

Over the Edge: Homeless Families and the Welfare System. Washington, D.C.: National Coalition for the Homeless, 1988.

Owen, Greg; Heineman, June A.; and Decker, Michelle R. *Homelessness in Minnesota. A Profile of Homeless Youth: Final Report from a Statewide Survey Conducted on October 24, 1991.* St. Paul, Minn.: Wilder Research Center, 1992.

Owen, Greg; Heineman, June A.; and Decker, Michelle R. *Homelessness in Minnesota. Homeless Adults and Their Children: Final Report from a Statewide Survey Conducted on October 24, 1991.* St. Paul, Minn.: Wilder Research Center, 1992.

Pasquarella, Robin. *Crisis on Our Streets: Plight of the Homeless Mentally Ill.* Seattle: Institute for Public Policy and Management, University of Washington, 1985.

Pennsylvania. Office of Education for Homeless Children and Youth. *Statewide Resource Directory: Services for Homeless Families, Children and Youth in Pennsylvania.* Harrisburg, Pa.: Education of Homeless Children and Youth Program. 1990.

People Experiencing an Episode of Homelessness in the Nine Counties of the Bay Area: 1990–91 Statistics. San Francisco: HomeBase, 1991.

Perchance to Sleep: Homeless Children Without Shelter in New York City. New York: Coalition for the Homeless, 1984.

Position Document on the Re-Authorization of Subtitle VII-B of the Stewart B. McKinney Homeless Assistance Act. Texas: National Association of State Coordinators for the Education of Homeless Children and Youth, January 1990.

Precious Resources: Government-Owned Housing and the Needs of the Homeless. New York/Washington, D.C.: National Coalition for the Homeless, September 1988.

A Program for Tenants in Single Room Occupancy and for Their New York City Neighbors. New York: Center for New York City Affairs, 1969.

A Progressive Housing Program for America. Washington, D.C.: Institute for Policy Studies, July 1987.

Proposal for a Model Single Family Room Occupancy Dwelling for the Homeless in Detroit. Detroit: Coalition on Temporary Shelter, 1983.

Providing Permanent Housing for Philadelphia's Homeless. Philadelphia: Pennsylvania Economy League, 1988.

Pushed Out: America's Homeless, Thanksgiving 1987. Washington, D.C.: National Coalition for the Homeless 1987.

Rafferty, Yvonne. *And Miles to Go—: Barriers to Academic Achievement and Innovative Strategies for the Delivery of Educational Services to Homeless Children.* Long Island City, N.Y.: 1991.

Reference Manual for Food, Shelter and Resources for the Homeless in New York. New York: Coalition for the Homeless, n.d.

Relos, Ruth, ed. *North Carolina's Homeless Families: Issues for the 90's: Papers from an Invitational Working Conference.* Garner, N.C.: North Carolina Conference for Social Service, 1991.

Remembrance and Poverty: The Road to Potter's Field. New York: Coalition for the Homeless, May 1986.

Report on the Status of Homelessness Within the City of Oakland. Oakland: Office of Community Development, 1990.

Response to the City's Plan for Homeless Adults. New York: Coalition for the Homeless, June 1984.

Reyes, Lilia M. *A Status Report on Hunger and Homelessness in America's Cities.* Washington, D.C.: United States Conference of Mayors, 1990.

Reyes, Lilia, and Waxman, Laura. *The Continued Growth of Hunger, Homelessness and Poverty in America's Cities, 1986: A 25-City Survey.* Washington, D.C.: United States Conference of Mayors, 1986.

———. *Continuing Growth of Hunger, Homelessness and Poverty in America's Cities, 1987: A 26-City Survey.* Washington, D.C.: United States Conference of Mayors, 1987.

———. *The Rise of the New Urban Homeless.* Berkeley: Institute of Governmental Studies, University of California, Berkeley, 1985.

Ridgeway, P., et al. *Case Management Services for Persons Who Are Homeless and Mentally Ill: Report from a NIMH Workshop.* Boston: Boston University Center for Psychiatric Rehabilitation, 1986.

The Rights of the Homeless. New York: Practicing Law Institute, 1987.

The Role of Community Foundations in Meeting the Needs of Homeless Individuals with Mental Illnesses. Alexandria, Va.: National Mental Health Association, 1986.

Rose, Laura. *Information on Homelessness in Wisconsin.* Madison: Wisconsin Legislative Council Staff, 1990.

Rossi, P., et al. *The Condition of the Homeless of Chicago.* Amherst: University of Massachusetts, 1986.

Rothman, Jack. *Status Offenders in Los Angeles County: Focus on Runaway and Homeless Youth: A Study and Policy Recommendations.* Los Angeles: Bush Program in Child and Family Policy, School of Social Welfare, University of California, Los Angeles, 1985.

Rural Emergency Shelter Need. Washington, D.C.: Housing Assistance Council, Inc., December 1983.

Rural Homeless in America: Appalachia and the South. Washington, D.C.: National Coalition for the Homeless, 1987.

Salerno, Dan; Hopper, Kim; and Baxter, Ellen. *Hardship in the Heartland: Homelessness in Eight U.S. Cities.* New York: Community Service Society, 1984.

San Diego County (California). Department of Health Services. *Women on Skid Row: San Diego's Invisible Victims, 1984.* San Diego: The Department, 1985.

Sanjek, Roger. *Crowded Out: Homelessness and the Elderly Poor in New York City*. New York: Coalition for the Homeless, 1984.

San Mateo County (California). Board of Supervisors. *Recommendations and Case Studies Regarding the Homeless and the Hungry in San Mateo County*. Redwood City: The Board, 1986.

Saving Lives: Emergency Federal Aid Reaches the Streets. Washington, D.C.: National Coalition for the Homeless, 1987.

Schwam, Keith. *Shopping Bag Ladies: Homeless Women*. New York: Manhattan Bowery Association, 1979.

Schwartz, David C.; Devance-Manzini, Donit; and Fagan, Tricia. *Preventing Homelessness: A Study of State and Local Homelessness Prevention Programs*. Orange, N.J.: National Housing Institute; New Brunswick, N.J.: American Affordable Housing Institute, 1991.

Scullion, M. *Evaluation of Women of Hope*. Philadelphia: Women of Hope, 1986.

Seldon, Paul, and Jones, Margot. *Moving On: Making Room for the Homeless. A Practical Guide to Shelter*. United Church Board for Homeland Ministries. New York: Coalition for the Homeless, December 1982.

Selling Out: Auctioned City Properties and the Warehousing of Vacant Apartments. New York: Coalition for the Homeless, June 1989.

The Shelter Worker's Handbook: A Guide for Identifying and Meeting the Health Needs of Homeless People. A Project of the Health Committee of the Coalition. New York: Coalition for the Homeless, October 1984.

Shiffman, Yvette, and Foxworthy, Nancy. *Producing Low-Income Housing in New York City*. New York: Community Service Society, 1985.

Simpson, John H.; Kilduff, Margaret; and Blewett, C. Douglas. *Struggling to Survive in a Welfare Hotel*. New York: Community Service Society, 1984.

Smith, Nancy. *Confronting Sexual Exploitation of Homeless Youth: California's Juvenile Prostitution Intervention Projects*. Sacramento: Calilfornia Office of Criminal Justice Planning, 1991.

Soldiers of Misfortune: Homeless Veterans in New York City. November 1982. City of New York, Office of the Comptroller. New York: Coalition for the Homeless, n.d.

South Carolina. Task Force on Homelessness. *The South Carolina General Assembly Task Force on Homelessness Final Report*. Columbia: The Task Force, 1992.

The Stanford Studies of Homeless Families, Children, and Youth. Stanford, Calif.: The Stanford Center for the Study of Families, Children, and Youth. 1991.

State Homeless Persons' Assistance Act Summary. New York/Washington, D.C.: National Coalition for the Homeless, January 1989.

State Mental Health Agency Role in Meeting the Problems of Homeless People. Washington, D.C.: National Association of State Mental Health Program Directors, 1985.

A State of Emergency: Hunger in the Empire State, by New York State Committee Against Hunger. Washington, D.C.: National Coalition for the Homeless, 1985.

Stemming the Tide: Housing Policies for Preventing Homelessness. New York: Coalition for the Homeless, 1986.

Suffering in the Sunbelt: Homeless in Arizona. Washington, D.C.: National Coalition for the Homeless, 1983.

Summary of the Stewart B. McKinney Homeless Assistance Act. New York/Washington, D.C.: National Coalition for the Homeless, November 1987.

The Summer Hunger Crisis. New York State Committee Against Hunger. New York: Coalition for the Homeless, July 1985.

Surplus Properties/Unmet Needs. New York/Washington, D.C.: National Coalition for the Homeless, November 1988.

Swicord, D. *Survey of Facilities for Runaway Homeless Youth, 1983–1988.* National Institute of Justice/National Criminal Justice Reference Service Microfiche Program, 1989.

Tennessee. General Assembly. Legislative Committee on the Homeless. *Report on Findings and Recommendations: Study of Tennessee's Homeless Problem.* Nashville: The Committee, 1987.

Testimony of Paul Seldon Before the Governor's Task Force on Housing the Homeless. New York: Coalition for the Homeless, April 1983.

Texas Interagency Council for Services for the Homeless. *Services for the Homeless: Moving Beyond the Gray Zone: Recommendations to the 72nd Legislature.* Austin: The Council, 1991.

Unfinished Business: The Stewart B. McKinney Homeless Assistance Act After Two Years. New York/Washington, D.C.: National Coalition for the Homeless, December 1989.

United Nations. Department of Public Information. *Building for the Homeless.* New York: The Department, 1987.

United States. Interagency Council on the Homeless. Task Force on Homelessness and Severe Mental Illness. *Outcasts on Main Street: Report of the Federal Task Force on Homelessness and Severe Mental Illness.* Washington, D.C.: Interagency Council on the Homeless, 1992.

Victims Again: Homeless Women in the New York City Shelter System. The Homeless Women's Rights Network. New York: Coalition for the Homeless, January 1989.

Walsh, B., and Davenport, D. *The Long Loneliness in Baltimore: A Study of Homeless Women.* Baltimore: Viva House, 1981.

Warehoused Apartments/Warehoused People. New York: Coalition for the Homeless, 1987.

Waxman, Laura DeKoven. *Mentally Ill and Homeless: a 22-City Survey.* Washington, D.C.: United States Conference of Mayors, 1991.

Waxman, Laura, and Reyes, Lilia. *A Status Report on Homeless Families in America's Cities: A 29-City Survey.* Washington, D.C.: United States Conference of Mayors, 1987.

Waxman, Laura DeKoven, and Reyes, Lilia M. *A Status Report on Hunger and Homelessness in America's Cities, 1990: A 30-City Survey.* Washington, D.C.: United States Conference of Mayors, 1990.

Weeden, Joel, et al. *The Homeless Mentally Ill Elderly: Problems and Issues.* San Francisco: Institute for Health and Aging, University of California, 1985.

Weitzman, Philip. *Worlds Apart: Housing, Race/Ethnicity and Income in New York City, 1978–1987.* New York: Community Service Society, 1989.

What are the Characteristics of the Homeless Population? Fact Sheet. no. 2-1. Washington, D.C.: Interagency Council on the Homeless, 1991.

To Whom Do They Belong? A Profile of America's Runaway and Homeless Youth and the Programs that Help Them. Washington, D.C.: National Network of Runaway and Youth Services, 1985.

Williams, Lydia. *Addiction on the Streets: Substance Abuse and Homelessness in America.* Washington, D.C.: National Coalition for the Homeless, 1992.

Wisconsin. Legislative Reference Bureau. *The Homeless: A Primer.* Madison: The Bureau, 1987.

Wisconsin. Office of Mental Health. *Listening to the Homeless: A Study of Homeless Mentally Ill Persons in Milwaukee.* Wisconsin: The Office, 1985.

———. *Skid Row, U.S.A.* Los Angeles: University of Southern California, 1993.

Wolch, Jennifer R. *Homelessness in America.* Los Angeles: University of Southern California, 1990.

Wright, J., et al. *The National Health Care for the Homeless Program: The First Year.* Amherst, Mass.: Social and Demographic Research Institute, University of Massachusetts, 1987.

Yates, Larry. *Low Income Housing In America: An Introduction.* Washington, D.C.: National Low Income Housing Coalition, January 1990.

Zigas, Barry. *Homelessness and the Low Income Housing Crisis.* Washington, D.C.: National Low Income Housing Coalition, 1987.

Bibliographies.

Albert, Judith. *A Precis and Related Bibliography of Selected Articles on the Condition of Homelessness.* Berkeley: Campus Planning Office, University of California, Berkeley, 1986.

————. *Selected Articles on the Subject of Homelessness, 1986–1987: A Precis.* Berkeley: Campus Planning Office, University of California, Berkeley, 1987.

Annotated Bibliography: Developing Housing for Homeless Persons with Severe Mental Illnesses. Delmar, N.Y.: Policy Research Associates, 1992.

Addendum to Annotated Bibliography: Developing Housing for Homeless Persons with Severe Mental Illnesses. Delmar, N.Y.: Policy Research Associates, 1992.

Bachrach, L. "The Homeless Mentally Ill and Mental Health Services: An Analytical Review of the Literature", in Lamb, H., ed. *The Homeless Mentally Ill.* Washington, D.C.: American Psychiatric Press, 1984.

Bahr, Howard. *Disaffiliated Man: Essays and Bibliography on Skid Row, Vagrancy and Outsiders.* Toronto: University of Toronto Press, 1973.

Buss, Terry. *Indigent Care: A Bibliography of Policies and Programs for the 1980's.* Monticello, Ill.: Vance Bibliographies, 1988.

Cibulskis, Ann, and Hoch, Charles. *Homelessness: An Annotated Bibliography.* Chicago: CPL Bibliographies, 1986.

Felsman, J. *Street Children: A Selected Bibliography.* Washington, D.C.: United States Department of Education and Welfare, National Institute of Education, 1985.

Garoogian, Andrew. *The Homeless in America.* Monticello, Ill.: Vance Bibliographies, 1984.

Henslin, James M. *Homelessness: An Annotated Bibliography.* New York: Garland, 1993.

The Homeless in America: A Bibliography. Santa Cruz, Calif.: Reference and Research Services, 1988.

Homelessness: A Selected Bibliography. New York: Coalition for the Homeless, 1982.

Homelessness and Low-Income Housing: Working Bibliography. New York: Coalition for the Homeless, July 1987.

Ince, D., and Haggard, L. *Annotated Bibliography of Literature on Women Who Are Homeless and Mentally Ill.* Rockville, Md.: National Institute of Mental Health, 1986.

Levine, Elizabeth. *Hunger and Homelessness in Urban America: A Selected Bibliography of Materials in the Chicago Municipal Reference Library.* Chicago: The Library, 1986.

Mulkern, V., and Spence, R. *Alcohol Abuse/Alcoholism Among Homeless Persons: A Review of the Literature.* Boston: Human Services Research Institute, 1984.

————. *Illicit Drug Use Among Homeless Persons: A Review of the Literature.* Boston: Human Services Research Institute, 1984.

Sexton, Patricia. *Homelessness: A Selected Bibliography.* New York: New York University, 1982.

Share, Marjorie L., and Blouin, Maryann. *Educational Resources For Homeless Health Care Providers: A Guide to Books, Manuals, Curricula, Films, Videos, and Other Resources That Address the Educational and Training Needs of Those Who Provide Health Care to the Homeless.* Washington, D.C.: National Association of Community Health Centers, Inc.'s Homeless Health Care Training and Capacity Building Project, 1990.

Teague, Edward H. *Architecture for the Homeless: A Bibliography of Recent Literature.* Monticello, Ill.: Vance Bibliographies, 1990.

United States. Department of Health and Human Services. *The Homeless Mentally Ill and Mental Health Services: An Analytical Review of the Literature.* Washington, D.C.: The Department, 1984.

United States. Department of Health and Human Services. Institute of Alcohol Abuse and Alcoholism. *Alcohol Abuse/Alcoholism Among Homeless Persons: A Review of the Literature.* Rockville, Md.: The Institute, 1984.

United States. Department of Health and Human Services. National Institute of Mental Health. *Annotated Bibliography on Case Management Services for the Seriously Mentally Ill.* Rockville, Md.: The Institute, 1986.

United States. Department of Health and Human Services. National Institute of Mental Health. Program for the Homeless Mentally Ill. *Annotated Bibliography of Literature on Homeless Women Who Are Mentally Ill and/or Have Alcohol Abuse Problems.* Rockville, Md.: The Institute, 1988.

Vance, Mary. *Low Income Housing in the United States: A Bibliography.* Monticello, Ill.: Vance Bibliographies, 1988.

———. *Runaway Children and Youth: A Bibliography.* Monticello, Ill.: Vance Bibliographies, 1988.

Van Whitlock, Rod; Lubin, Bernard; and Sailors, Jean R. *Homelessness in America, 1893–1992: An Annotated Bibliography.* Westport, Conn.: Greenwood Press, 1994.

White, Anthony. *American Homelessness in the 1980's: A Selected Bibliography.* Monticello, Ill.: Vance Bibliographies, 1987.

INDEX

Entries are filed letter-by-letter.
Boldface page numbers indicate extensive treatment of a topic.